THE BEST OF BOOKFINDER

THE BEST OF BOOKFINDER

A Guide to Children's Literature About Interests and Concerns of Youth Aged 2-18

Sharon Spredemann Dreyer, M.Ed.

American Guidance Service, Circle Pines, Minnesota 55014-1796

Anne E. Heller, Managing Editor
Helen Hlavinka and Linda Peterson, Typesetting
Matt Keller, Product Line Manager
Mary Kaye Kuzma, Production Coordinator
Theodore Remington, Assistant Editor
Maureen Wilson, Art Director

Cover design by Terry Dugan, Terry Dugan Design

Printed in the United States of America
A 0 9 8 7 6 5 4 3 2 1

Library of Congress Catalog Card Number
91-076898

ISBN: 88671-440-0 (hardcover)
ISBN: 88671-439-7 (softcover)

To Caroljean Wagner, dedicated consultant
and kindred spirit in the world of books.

CONTENTS

INTRODUCTION

ACKNOWLEDGMENTS

The *Bookfinder* represents the talents and efforts of many people. The following persons, especially, are acknowledged with gratitude:

Caroljean Wagner, former head of the Central Youth Library, Milwaukee Public Library, has been the chief consultant throughout the development of each volume of the *Bookfinder*. Her expertise and dedication to excellence are evident in every volume.

Marianna Markowetz, curriculum librarian, University of Wisconsin-Milwaukee, and Ervin S. Yanke, former director of Instructional Services, West Allis-West Milwaukee Public Schools, acted as consultants, contributing valuable suggestions and criticism as the concept of the *Bookfinder* was researched and developed.

Carl Malmquist, M.D., psychiatrist in private practice, Minneapolis, reviewed the *Bookfinder* as it was developed and offered constructive suggestions for expansion and clarification of the Subject Index.

Jane Laswell, librarian, Neenah, Wisconsin, carefully researched the great amount of recent material about bibliotherapy and the trends in reading education. She has been responsible for the arrangement and cross-referencing of the *Bookfinder* indexes and the Publishers/Producers Directory. The excellence of the *Bookfinder* indexing reflects her competence and attention to detail.

The staff at the Wisconsin Regional Library for the Blind and Physically Handicapped, Milwaukee, Wisconsin, helped identify the books available in materials for blind and physically disabled persons.

Brett Dreyer's efficiency and accuracy at the computer and in reference work has helped guarantee the accuracy and completeness of *The Best of Bookfinder*.

Many librarians made extra efforts to locate and lend the books reviewed and indexed in the *Bookfinder*. The staff at the Milwaukee Public Library was extremely helpful, as was the staff at the New Berlin Public Library, New Berlin, Wisconsin.

Children's book editors and subsidiary-rights departments of more than 75 publishing companies graciously worked to identify the publications listed in the *Bookfinder* that are also available in other printed or audiovisual media. They also supplied hundreds of books for review.

Sixteen people who participated in a field trial during the spring of 1974—teachers, librarians, counselors, and psychologists from the Milwaukee metropolitan area—provided reactions and suggestions in the initial stages of the development of the *Bookfinder*.

Professionals in 16 field-test sites in the United States and Canada contributed valuable suggestions during the spring of 1976 to help refine the publication.

More than 20 annotators read hundreds of books and prepared first drafts of the annotations that form the heart of each volume of the *Bookfinder*.

Finally, my appreciation and gratitude go to the staff at American Guidance Service. These staff members, with their consistent pursuit of quality materials to foster maximum development of human potential, their expertise, their availability, and their spirit of cooperation, are truly a joy to work with.

AN INTRODUCTION TO THE BOOKFINDER

Widely reviewed and acclaimed by professionals and laypersons who work with children, the *Bookfinder* series is a vital reference for school and public libraries, churches, synagogues, YMCAs, YWCAs, psychologists, psychiatrists, social service agencies, and other groups and individuals who work with children and young people. *Best of Bookfinder* offers annotations of the best books included in *Bookfinders 1-3*. Thus, it provides an overview of literature for children and adolescents originally published before 1983. Because many titles included in the first three volumes of *Bookfinder* have either gone out of print or are dated or stereotypical by today's standards, it is time to update the list so that the *Bookfinder* series will continue to be the most complete and accurate source of literature on the interests and concerns of children and young people.

Written words have influenced the attitudes, decisions, and behavior of humankind since the beginning of recorded history. An inscription over a library in ancient Thebes proclaimed it "the Healing Place of the Soul." The written word has also been credited with less benign effects: Abraham Lincoln once greeted Harriet Beecher Stowe, author of *Uncle Tom's Cabin*, as "the little lady who wrote the book that made this big war."

Books have an important role in everyday life. Through well-chosen books, readers may increase their self-knowledge and self-esteem, gain relief from unconscious conflicts, clarify their values, and better understand other people. By identifying with characters in books, people may come to realize that they are part of humanity, that they are not alone in their struggles with reality. Reading increases personal knowledge and invites readers to consider themselves objectively.

If children who are experiencing difficulties can read about others who have solved similar problems, they may see alternatives for themselves. By presenting possible solutions, books can help to prevent some difficult situations from becoming full-blown problems. Through encountering frustrations and anxieties, hopes and disappointments, successes and failures in fictional situations, youngsters may gain insights applicable to situations they meet in real life. All volumes of the *Bookfinder* were developed with these effects in mind.

Best of Bookfinder is a reference work that describes and categorizes 676 children's books according to more than 450 psychological, behavioral, and developmental topics of concern to children and adolescents, aged 2 and up. It is written primarily for parents, teachers, librarians, counselors, psychologists, psychiatrists, and other adults who want to identify books that may help children to cope with the challenges of life. Like the other volumes in the series, *The Best of Bookfinder* was created to fill the need for a way to match children and books.

Bibliotherapy

As people became aware that the written word could influence behavior, they began to develop ways to apply this power. During the first half of the nineteenth century, American doctors Benjamin Rush and John Minson Galt II recommended reading as part of the treatment for patients who were physically or mentally ill or both. During the early 1900s, French psychiatrist Pierre Janet believed that patients could be helped toward a better life through assigned readings. The term *bibliotherapy* was first used by Samuel McChord Crothers in a 1916 *Atlantic Monthly* article. In the 1930s, Doctors Karl and William Menninger advocated the use of literature in the treatment of their patients. Publications by the two brothers encouraged others, both professional and lay people, to use literature to help solve problems and promote coping behavior.

Bibliotherapy, the use of reading material to help solve emotional problems and to promote mental health, was used with military personnel during both world wars and with civilians in rehabilitation hospitals, tuberculosis sanatoriums, and general hospitals. Schools have used books and stories as "social helpers" for more than a century.

During the last 45 years, many theses and dissertations have been written about various aspects of bibliotherapy. One of the most significant, published by Caroline Shrodes in 1955, was especially important in establishing the background for much of the recent research into the theory and practice of bibliotherapy and the psychology of reading. Bibliotherapy continues to grow in popularity, with more research being done and more articles and papers being published. A number of colleges and universities offer class work, conduct seminars, and provide practicum experiences for people interested in learning more about the process, practice, methods, and materials of bibliotherapy.

If youngsters who are experiencing difficulties can read about children who have encountered and solved similar problems, they may see hope for themselves. For example, young children grieving the loss of a loved one may feel comforted after Margaret Stevens's *When Grandpa Died* or Trudy Madler's *Why Did Grandma Die?* is read to and discussed with them. Older children may receive comfort after reading and discussing Doris Buchanan Smith's *A Taste of Blackberries* or Peggy Mann's *There Are Two Kinds of Terrible*. Children who are upset and confused as they face their parents' divorcing may come to terms with their feelings of anger, guilt, and fear after reading Barbara Park's *Don't Make Me Smile* or Judie Angell's *What's Best for You*. Children may also become better equipped for tomorrow's challenges by meeting similar challenges in today's reading. For example, children who read about Timothy as he enters school in Rosemary Wells's *Timothy Goes to School*, or about Lloyd who is always chosen last in Doris Buchanan Smith's *Last Was Lloyd* may find their own adjustment to school much easier. Older readers may be more understanding and supportive of the sibling or classmate who is permanently disabled in an accident after reading Robin Brancato's *Winning*.

Three main steps are usually present in the process of bibliotherapy:

1. Universalization and identification. From their reading, children come to see that they are not the only persons with particular fears, frustrations, worries, or living conditions. Recognizing similarities between themselves and fictional or biographical characters, they see themselves in those characters and thus may work out their problems vicariously.

Identification is not limited to a reader's identification of self with a story character. A child may also see his or her own mother, father, or other important person in the story. As a result, the child may develop a better understanding and appreciation of the real person.

Children may identify with characters in animal stories as well as with fictional human beings when the animals have believable human characteristics. Children's reactions to James Marshall's picture books about George and Martha, two hippopotamuses, are examples. Children readily identify with these two animal friends who experience the same feelings, expectations, and companionship typical of childhood friendships.

When the parents, older siblings, and peers in a child's life are inappropriate models of behavior, characters in books may fill that child's need for an ego ideal.

2. Catharsis. A child who identifies with a fictional character lives through situations and shares feelings with that character. This vicarious experience may produce a release of tension or an imitation of the character's behavior. (When this happens, it is important that the child have someone with whom to discuss the reading, either individually or in a group.)

An advantage of reading as a therapeutic experience is that it does not force a child to participate. If the fictional situation becomes too intense, too stimulating, or too painful, the reader can back off and assume the role of observer. Control rests with the reader, not with someone else. This sort of self-direction is reassuring and can help the child learn to look at problems objectively.

3. Insight. Through reading, children may become more aware of human motivations and of rationalizations for their own behavior. They may develop a more realistic view of their abilities and self-worth.

Because the written word tends to carry a special kind of authority, children who feel doubt and suspicion toward adults and peers tend to be less doubtful and suspicious of books. Authors of fiction generally become trusted, because they rarely impose judgment explicitly.

Thus, books can become valuable companions to a developing child. Indeed, children often read beyond their tested reading levels in order to read about people faced with situations or problems similar to their own. Adults who want to help children locate the most appropriate and therapeutic books should find the *Bookfinders* and *Best of Bookfinder* valuable guides.

Using the Bookfinder

Annotations of 676 books for children and adolescents are the heart of *The Best of Bookfinder.* There are three ways to locate annotations of particular books:

1. Locate the desired subject in the Subject Index. Under the subject heading, identify the most promising books listed. Then refer to the annotations section to find summaries of those books.

2. Locate the author's name in the Author Index. Identify the desired book, and then refer to the annotations for the book summary.

3. Locate the book title in the Title Index. Identify its author, and then refer to the annotations for the book summary.

For quick and easy reference, the annotations are arranged alphabetically by author's last name; they are also numbered sequentially.

Each annotation contains the following information:

1. The *bibliographic information* includes the author's complete name. Any pseudonyms are noted. Annotations of books that have been translated into English from another language name the translator and the language of the original publication. Information about illustrations and photographs includes the name of the artist and whether the illustrations or photographs are in black and white or in color. The name of the publisher appears for each book. (All publishers' addresses* are listed in the Publishers/Producers Directory, located after *The Best of Bookfinder* indexes.) The book's copyright date is listed. In the case of a translation, the date of the original United States copyright is listed. Also indicated are the number of pages in the book. If the book's pages have not been numbered, the total number of printed pages is indicated by a number followed by the word "counted."

2. The *main subject headings*, or primary themes of the book, are listed alphabetically in uppercase letters near the top of each annotation. Significant secondary themes are listed alphabetically in uppercase and lowercase letters under the main subject headings.

---

*The directory cross-references parent publishing companies for their respective imprints.

3. The first paragraph of each annotation is a *synopsis* of the book. It introduces the main character and describes the plot and the character relationships that provide the main and secondary themes. Whenever possible, the main character's name, sex, and age or grade level are mentioned in the first sentence of the synopsis. Race, culture, religion, and social class of the characters are indicated only when they are pertinent issues in the story. Each summary is carried through to the conclusion of the story.

4. The second paragraph of each annotation is usually a *commentary* that restates the book's main message and indicates strengths or limitations in the way the message is presented. Potential uses of the book may also be suggested. Literary merit, special qualifications of the author, sequels, and the significance of illustrations or photographs may be mentioned here. Points of special concern or interest (such as premeditated violence, explicit sex, controversial language) are also mentioned.

5. A *general reading level* is indicated at or near the end of the annotation. Often, children within the stated age range will be interested in and able to read the book independently or with minimal help. All of the books listed for preschool children, and many of the books listed for primary-age children, are read-aloud volumes.

6. The final element of each annotation is information about *other forms of the publication*, such as films, filmstrips, tapes, cassettes, disks, records, paperbound editions, and materials for blind or other physically disabled people.

Application

The person who wants to use books to help children understand the challenges and problems of growing up need not be a professional counselor. Indeed, the main qualifications are an interest in and a concern for children and a willingness to become familiar with children's literature. Reading guidance can be a simple procedure. Professional therapeutic skills are necessary, however, if the child's problem is severe. In general, the *Bookfinder* can be used to good effect by nearly everyone who works with children.

Parents are in an ideal position to use the *Bookfinders* and *The Best of Bookfinder* to help their children cope with new situations. Consider the following examples: Six-year-old Timmy is scheduled to see the doctor for an examination; his symptoms indicate that surgery might be necessary. Timmy's parents tell him of the planned visit to the doctor but never mention the possibility of surgery or going to the hospital. They intend to wait until the doctor has made a definite diagnosis. When Timmy tells his playmates about his appointment with the doctor, they eagerly embellish their own experiences and what they have heard about doctors, hospitals, and surgery. A frightened little boy comes home and announces, "I may go to the doctor's office, but I'm not going to any hospital!" Acknowledging his fears, Timmy's parents refer to *The Best of Bookfinder* for stories about doctors and hospitals. At Timmy's level of understanding, they find Harlow Rockwell's *My Doctor* and Paula Hogan's *The Hospital Scares Me.* Timmy's parents read the books to him and candidly discuss the stories and illustrations. Several days later when Timmy's doctor confirms the need for surgery, Timmy confidently tells his friends, "I'm going to the hospital to have an operation."

Another family has four young teenagers—two from each of the parents' previous marriages—who are having difficulty living together as a family. Referring to *The Best of Bookfinder*, the family identifies several books about families in circumstances such as theirs. After everyone reads Joan Oppenheimer's *Gardine Vs. Hanover* and Susan Terris's *No Scarlet Ribbons*, the family spends time discussing the situations and relationships in each book. Discussing the fictional families offers some insights into this family's relationships. They recognize similarities, explore possible solutions to problems and disagreements, and are even able to laugh at incidents much like those that had led to heated arguments in the past. The reading and discussion do not solve all problems, but the foundations for meaningful communication are laid and everyone feels that the future could be compatible and satisfying and that it's worth working at.

A child can more easily understand and accept other difficult experiences—death of a loved person or pet, parental divorce, transfer to a new school, arrival of a new baby in the family—through reading about similar situations. The child's parents can use the *Bookfinder* to find an appropriate book. In sharing that book and in expressing feelings about the story, family members can increase their understanding of themselves and others. This appreciation can, in turn, lead to stronger and more trusting relationships.

School and public librarians may find the *Bookfinder* useful for helping children find books to meet their individual needs, and for helping parents, teachers, and other professionals to find materials appropriate for the particular needs of an individual or group. For example, an elementary school is about to mainstream special-needs students. To help the other students in the school understand the feelings, needs, strengths, and limitations of exceptional children, the librarian and teachers refer to the *Bookfinder* and identify appropriate books. Several of the books are read aloud and discussed in classes. Others are attractively displayed, encouraging students to do additional reading on their own. The insights the students derive from these books may increase their effectiveness in helping their new classmates feel comfortable.

Public librarians frequently have specific requests—from children, parents, teachers, and other adults who work with children—for books about particular concerns, attitudes, and developmental tasks. A librarian, sensing that some children have interests or concerns that they prefer not to talk about, puts a copy of the *Bookfinder* on top of the card catalog. A poster mounted above it invites students to peruse the index on their own to find books of personal interest.

Librarians in children's hospitals have a special role as they work with medical professionals to meet the emotional and physical needs of sick children. Hospital librarians usually seek books that promote understanding and acceptance of hospital routines and medical procedures. Lengthy and depressing hospital confinement can be made brighter and more hopeful through carefully prescribed reading.

Teachers are in a good position to match books with children's needs and concerns. A kindergarten teacher who knows that one of her or his students has had a new baby join the family may see that the child is having trouble adjusting. Consulting the *The Best of Bookfinder*, the teacher may choose Martha Alexander's *Nobody Asked Me If I Wanted a Baby Sister* or Russell Hoban's *Baby Sister for Frances* as read-aloud stories. The teacher can then invite the children to share their experiences with the class. They can compare their feelings with those of the older brother or sister in the story, and consider some of the happy aspects of having a new baby at home. After such reading and discussion, a child is likely to become more patient and less jealous of the new sibling than before.

Teachers can often promote students' understanding of themselves and others through books, by reading aloud to the class or by encouraging independent reading. Reading for this purpose is especially appealing and effective with gifted students because of their interest in books, advanced reading comprehension, and introspective nature. This reading can be enjoyable when books are chosen with reader interests and needs in mind. Then readers are likely to want to read more, and reading skills will probably improve in the process.

For example, a teacher has the class agree on one topic of interest such as aging, fear, prejudice, sibling relationships. The class locates the topic in the *Bookfinder*, and selects books to read individually. The teacher then chooses one especially pertinent book to read aloud to the class. After all the reading is completed, discussion and other activities are organized to integrate ideas from the children's varied reading experiences.

A teacher divides the class into small groups with each group first selecting a topic of interest, finding the topic in the *Bookfinder*, and then choosing a book (or books) to be read within the group. As the books are read, groups discuss them. When the reading is completed, each group prepares a culminating activity to present to the class.

Examples of thought-provoking activities that can follow the reading are: role playing, dramatization, mock interview with the book's main character, bulletin boards, recordings, films, filmstrips, supplemental reading lists, and radio and television programs related to the reading. Teachers can read open-ended stories, or they can stop reading a story just short of the conclusion and ask the class to end the story. (The teacher should then finish reading the story to the class so students can compare their conclusion with the author's.)

Teachers who read aloud to their classes have many opportunities for discussing how a character felt about something or why the character made particular decisions. Good questions and discussions can broaden students' decision-making abilities and increase their understanding of other people.

A teacher who knows that a child has a problem might introduce the child to a book about "someone who was very much like you" or "someone who also . . ." To be more subtle, teachers can introduce to the whole class that book and other books the class might enjoy. If the teacher sees the troubled child reading one of the suggested books, the teacher should show a willingness to discuss the book with the child.

The school counselor can work with the teacher and the librarian to select books for special study units—for example, on friendship, courage, fear, or other pertinent topics. Counselors working with individual children or small groups of children can choose books to suit personal needs. For example, a new student is transferring into the school. The counselor consults the *Bookfinder*, selects several appropriate titles, and suggests that the new student might like to read about others who have experienced the same kind of change. Reading about someone else in the same situation may provide some hints for making the adjustment easier.

The school counselor can use the *Bookfinder* to help students in individual or group counseling select appropriate reading to be done between counseling sessions. Such reading can extend the counseling experience and serve as a point of reference for beginning the next counseling session.

The foregoing examples are meant to show how children might face everyday concerns as well as more severe problems more confidently if they have also faced them vicariously through books. The use of books to help children can be simple or complex, depending on the children's needs and on the confidence and background of the adults who want to help. Parents, teachers, librarians, counselors, and other mental health specialists may find the *Bookfinder* useful. So may nurses, providers of child care, scout leaders, recreation leaders, camp counselors, church and synagogue youth leaders, and anyone else in a position to help youngsters expand their understanding, tolerance, and ability to cope with the challenges of life.

DEVELOPMENT OF THE BOOKFINDER

The *Bookfinder* was conceived in 1968 as a supplement to the author's thesis for the master's degree. The bibliography then included over 300 books for children aged 9 through 15. The need for easy access to children's literature about developmental problems became more apparent, and the author decided to update, expand, and reorganize the original bibliography.

Formal development of the *Bookfinder* was initiated in 1973. It began with an extensive new review of current children's literature.

Book Selection

All available bibliographies and children's book review sources were examined in the search for appropriate books. Children's book publishers submitted hundreds of books for the author to consider. Books familiar to the author, consultants, and field-trial participants were considered, as were books within the collection of the Central Youth Library in Milwaukee. More than 2,500 books were considered for each volume of the *Bookfinder.*

Book selection criteria for *The Best of Bookfinder* included the following considerations: Is the book currently in print? (A few titles included in *The Best of Bookfinder* are out of print. These titles were too outstanding to omit and should be available in many existing library collections. Also, it is always possible that an out-of-print title will be reprinted. A book currently out of print is indicated by "o.p.") Is the book still timely? Are its themes universal? Is it one of a kind—the only book on a particular topic? Does it present a topic in a particularly enduring and outstanding way?

Most of the books selected for *Bookfinder* and *The Best of Bookfinder* are hardbound. *The Best of Bookfinder* also includes books now published only in paperbound format. In addition, books selected are available through ordinary means: libraries, bookstores, book jobbers, and publishers.

Timeliness and appropriateness of content were important criteria for each volume. Timely, "here and now" books are usually more helpful to children with problems than older books are, unless the older books speak to timeless issues. The selected books are, therefore, about the modern child or are so universal in appeal that the difference in time or place is unimportant.

The book plots and themes had to be carried through to resolution or presented completely enough to provoke thoughtful consideration or discussion. The characters had to be realistic. The problems faced by the characters had to be brought out clearly and explored without moralizing.

Artistic quality was also a consideration. Literary quality, although not the prime concern, had to be acceptable to the author of the *Bookfinder.* Where many books on a particular topic were available, only the best were selected for annotation. Illustrations or photographs also had to be of acceptable quality, appropriate to the story, and supportive of its message.

Despite the author's careful concern for proper book selection criteria, the selection of each book was necessarily a subjective process. Some users of the *Bookfinder* will disagree with the inclusion of some titles or will look in vain for some of their favorites.* But every user should find many pertinent and applicable books among the 676 entries, which represent more than 350 authors and 80 imprints and publishing companies.

Many picture books are included in the *Bookfinder* series. They are not just cute stories; they have plots and characters that encourage reader identification. These books should help to prepare young children for new experiences and new stages of development and to solve current problems.

The vast majority of the indexed books—more than 90 percent—are fiction. The others are biography and a few other especially significant nonfiction publications.

Clues to meaningful book selection may come from knowledge of the child's home life, family, out-of-school activities, personal ambitions, and other interests. Important considerations are the reader's vocabulary and comprehension levels, because children should not be forced to read beyond their skills. The reading should be a voluntary and pleasant experience—not another assignment.

Annotations

The first step in writing annotations was to categorize each book according to its main theme and any relevant subthemes. For example, a subject heading of *FRIENDSHIP: Best Friend* means that the plot of the book centers around the thoughts, feelings, and activities of people who regard themselves as best friends. Much care has been taken to ensure that the subject headings accurately indicate the content of the book.

What may appear as an obvious theme to some readers may seem less so to others. A concentrated effort has been made to define themes by asking, "Does this book offer enough information about a particular situation or problem to warrant recommending it to a child who is facing that situation or problem?" Beyond that guideline, only the user can determine whether a book is suitable for a specific child with a specific need. The *Bookfinder* was not developed to prescribe books for particular children; it was developed as a reference that categorizes and describes books as objectively as possible.

**Bookfinder* users are invited to send their comments, questions, and suggestions to the publisher: American Guidance Service, 4201 Woodland Rd., Circle Pines, MN 55014-1796.

As the annotations were prepared, publishing information was carefully checked and rechecked for uniformity and accuracy. Discrepancies were found. Therefore, book titles with idiosyncratic capitalization have been given standard capitalization.

Book publishers were asked to tell which of their publications listed in *The Best of Bookfinder* are available in Braille, film, filmstrip, tape or cassette, disk, record, paperbound, or large-print editions. If a book's subsidiary rights were retained by the author or the author's agent, there is no way that the book publisher would be aware of rights sold for other formats. Some books, therefore, may be available in other media not known to either the book's publisher or the *Bookfinder's* author. It is also possible that some items may already be out of stock. Producers (addresses are included in the Publishers/Producers Directory) should be contacted directly for further information. *Paperbound Books in Print* was also used to identify books available in paperbound form. Materials available for blind and physically disabled people—tapes, cassettes, talking books, Braille editions, and large-print volumes—were identified through the indexes and catalogs of the Library of Congress, Wisconsin Regional Library for the Blind and Physically Handicapped. (Most of these materials are available only through regional branches of the Library of Congress [National Library Service for the Blind and Physically Handicapped] and can be obtained only by persons who are legally blind or physically disabled. Questions regarding materials for blind and physically disabled people should be directed to local public librarians, who can supply more information about the program and explain how to apply for service.)

Since descriptions of the plots, themes, and characters are meant to be of greatest service to the adult user, the book summaries have been written for adults. No deliberate attempt has been made to whet the reader's appetite. Nevertheless, a child with sixth-grade reading and comprehension skills could probably browse through the annotations and select books without adult assistance.

Subject Index

The Subject Index lists the primary and secondary themes of all the books in *The Best of Bookfinder.* To compile the original Subject Index, the author, publisher, and project consultants identified over 600 topics they considered important to children and adolescents. Following final book selection for *Bookfinder 1,* the number of topics decreased to about 450. In the development of later volumes, some headings were deleted because no appropriate books were found to cover those themes in a significant manner, and new headings were added.

Field Test

Field testing of the *Bookfinder* took place during the spring of 1976 in six states—Alaska, Minnesota, North Dakota, Pennsylvania, Tennessee, and Wisconsin—and in the province of Ontario. Sixteen field-test sites provided information from four types of libraries: school, general public, college and consultant, and children's public. Each site was given a field-test version of the annotated bibliography, along with limited subject, author, and title indexes and 453 rough-draft annotations. Parents, counselors, teachers, librarians, and psychologists were asked to review this material, and their comments contributed to the refinement of the *Bookfinder.* Psychiatrists and supervising librarians also suggested ways to make the *Bookfinder* more useful.

BOOK SELECTION AIDS

For more help in finding appropriate children's books, the reader may want to use the following references, many of which include titles not found in the *Bookfinder* series. *Bookfinder* titles that are included in these references are reviewed from various viewpoints or for purposes that may differ from the *Bookfinder's.*

Baskin, Barbara H. and Karen H. Harris. *More Notes from a Different Drummer: A Guide to Juvenile Fiction Portraying the Disabled.* New York: R. R. Bowker Company, 1984.

This guide to children's literature about mentally or physically disabled people or both is divided into three main sections. The first two discuss disabled people in society and literature. The third section summarizes and evaluates 348 books written between 1976 and 1981. A broad-range reading level (e.g., YC—Young Child, MC—Mature Child, MA—Mature Adolescent) is given for each entry.

Bernstein, Joanne E. and Masha K. Rudman. *Books to Help Children Cope with Separation and Loss: An Annotated Bibliography,* vol. 3. New York: R. R. Bowker Company, 1989.

The introduction to this reference describes how the bibliography was compiled, discusses separation and loss as they relate to children, and defines and explains bibliotherapy. The bibliography itself contains 606 titles published from 1983 through 1988. Most titles are fiction, although some nonfiction is included. Each entry contains bibliographic information, reading interest and reading grade levels, and a comprehensive summary of the plot. The entries are divided into subjects including death, divorce, war, living with new stepparents, and illness. The guide concludes with extensive professional bibliographies on organizations that provide services to children and adults who are facing separation and loss. Author, title, and subject indexes are included.

The Black Experience in Children's Books. New York: The New York Public Library, 1989.

This comprehensive bibliography of black literature includes books for children and books for children and adults to share. It covers "a wide range of subjects reflecting the social, political, and economic contributions Blacks are making in this country [USA] and in the developing nations in Africa." Entries are briefly annotated.

Fassler, Joan. *Helping Children Cope: Mastering Stress Through Books and Stories.* New York: The Free Press, 1978.

This resource provides access to children's books that can lead to "experiences that initiate communication, reduce anxieties, enhance development, and encourage growth." It concentrates on possible stressful situations such as: hospitalization, illness, separation experiences, financial crisis, moving, divorce, and new sibling. Each of five main sections offers professional viewpoints about the topic, followed by a description of selected children's books that might help to foster effective coping skills for a given situation. Suggested discussion questions and techniques proved successful in using literature to help children face stressful situations are included in each section of the reference, followed by appropriate children's books listed alphabetically by author.

Gagnon, Andre and Ann Gagnon, eds. *Canadian Books for Young People*, 4th ed. Toronto: University of Toronto Press, 1988.

This revised index includes Canadian children's books (preschool through age 18) written in English and French. All of these books were in print at the time the reference was printed. Each entry includes bibliographic information, an annotative sentence, and a suggested reading level. The reference is divided into two sections: the first lists books in English; the second (written in French) lists books in French. Books are organized in such categories as Picture Books, Sports and Recreation, and Fiction: Stories, Fantasy, and Historical Fiction.

Gillespie, John T. and Corinne J. Naden. *Juniorplots 3: A Book Talk Guide for Use with Readers Ages 12-16.* New York: R. R. Bowker Company, 1987.

This guide describes 80 books for children aged 11 through 16 years. Books are arranged according to eight subjects that appeal to adolescent readers. These include Teenage Life and Concerns, Adventure and Mystery Stories, Science Fiction and Fantasy, Historical Fiction, Sports Fiction, Biography and True Adventure, Guidance and Health, and The World Around Us. Each entry includes bibliographic information, plot summary, discussion of themes within the book, techniques for "book talks," suggestions for additional reading on related topics, and a bibliography of sources where the reader may find information about the author.

Lima, Carolyn W. and John A. Lima. *A to Zoo: Subject Access to Children's Picture Books.* 3d ed. New York: R. R. Bowker Company, 1989.

Over 12,000 picture books for preschool children through second grade are indexed under more than 700 categories in the guide. Picture books relating to more than one subject are listed under each relevant category. An introduction briefly tracing the evolution of the English-language picture book is followed by an alphabetical listing of subject headings and subheadings used in the guide. The subject guide lists books alphabetically by author and title only for each subject heading. Complete bibliographic information for each of the books is included in the bibliographic guide. Title and illustrator indexes are also provided.

Mills, Joyce White, ed. *The Black World in Literature: A Bibliography of Print and Non-Print Materials.* Atlanta: School of Library Service of Atlanta University, 1984.

This 66-page booklet indexes and briefly annotates children's books published in 1978 and 1979 about black people in the United States and Africa. Each book is rated Highly Recommended, Recommended, or Not Recommended. Audiovisual titles are interfiled with book titles and briefly described but not rated. The bibliography is divided into two sections: For Younger Children, ages 3-8, and For Older Children, ages 9-13. A list of adult reference sources is included.

Spirit, Diana L. *Introducing More Books: A Guide for the Middle Grades.* New York: R. R. Bowker Company, 1978.

This reference includes plot summaries of 72 books and lists additional related materials for each entry for reading, viewing, and listening. Altogether, about 500 titles are mentioned. Books are listed according to nine developmental goals for children aged 8 through 14. Among these goals are: Understanding Social Problems, Understanding Physical and Emotional Problems, Developing Values, and Making Friends. Each entry includes bibliographic information and a paragraph of thematic analysis followed by material for discussion and other related materials.

Sutherland, Zena. *The Best in Children's Books, 1979-1984.* Chicago: The University of Chicago Press, 1986.

This is a collection of 1,400 book reviews previously published in the *Bulletin of the Center for Children's Books.* Most of the books were rated as "recommended" reading. The entries are listed alphabetically by the author's name and are categorized in several indexes.

Tway, Eileen, ed. *Reading Ladders for Human Relations.* 6th ed. Washington, D C: American Council on Education, 1981.

This reference was compiled to help teachers, librarians, and other adults select appropriate reading material for children and young people. Books are briefly annotated and divided into age levels—ages 1-5, 5-8, 8-11, 11-14, and 14 and up. They are arranged in five Reading Ladders: Growing into Self, Relating to Wide Individual Differences, Interacting in Groups, Appreciating Different Cultures, and Coping in a Changing World. Each ladder has several pertinent subheadings. The introduction contains an explanation of the purpose of the reference and practical suggestions for using books with children and young people "to advance the cause of human relations."

Wilkin, Binnie Tate. *Survival Themes in Fiction for Children and Young People.* Metuchen, NJ: The Scarecrow Press, 1978.

This reference, which has comments and suggestions interspersed in the list of titles, divides entries into three main areas—The Individual, Pairings and Groupings, and Views of the World. These areas are then subdivided. The author believes "that a realistic presentation of human existence will help the children develop their own capabilities in problem solving." The books selected (some nonfiction is included) "are intended as samples that offer a certain sensitivity to some of the individual and societal issues of the day." Bibliographic information is followed by a short summary of the book. Most titles included are from the 1970s.

READINGS ON BIBLIOTHERAPY

Bauer, Carolyn K., N. Jo Campbell, and Vernon Troxel. "Altering Attitudes Toward the Mentally Handicapped Through Print and Nonprint Media." *School Media Quarterly,* Spring 1985, 110-114.

Brown, Eleanor Frances. *Bibliotherapy and Its Widening Applications.* Metuchen, NJ: The Scarecrow Press, 1975.

Carner, Charles. "Reaching Troubled Minds Through Reading." *Today's Health* 44 (1966): 32-33, 75-77.

Cianciolo, Patricia Jean. "Children's Literature Can Effect Coping Behavior." *Personnel and Guidance Journal* 43 (1965): 897-903.

Cianciolo, Patricia Jean. "Interaction Between the Personality of the Reader and Literature." *School Libraries* 17 (1968): 13-17, 19-21.

Darling, R. L. "Mental Hygiene and Books." *Wilson Library Bulletin* 32 (1957): 293-296.

Davison, Maureen McKinney. "Classroom Bibliotherapy: Why and How." *Reading World* 23 (1983): 103-107.

Edwards, Beverly Sigler. "The Therapeutic Value of Reading." *Elementary English* 49 (1972): 213-218.

Edwards, Patricia A. and Linda Simpson. "Bibliotherapy: A Strategy for Communication Between Parents and Their Children." *Journal of Reading,* November 1986.

Engelbert, Alan. "In Search of Bibliotherapy." *Show-Me Libraries* 9 (1982): 8-13.

Frasier, Mary M. and Carolyn McCannon. "Using Bibliotherapy with Gifted Children." *Gifted Children Quarterly* 25 (1981): 81-85.

Gray, Maxine. "Books—Another Use in Our Classroom." *Education* 79 (1959): 487-490.

Hartley, Helene W. "Developing Personality Through Books." *The English Journal* 40 (1951): 198-204.

Heitzmann, Kathleen E. and William Ray Heitzmann. "Science of Bibliotherapy: A Critical Review of Research Findings." *Reading Improvement* 12 (1975): 120-124.

Hoagland, Joan. "Bibliotherapy: Aiding Children in Personality Development." *Elementary English* 49 (1972): 390-394.

Jalongo, Mary Renck. "Bibliotherapy: Literature to Promote Socioemotional Growth." *Reading Teacher* 36 (1983): 796-803.

Jalongo, Mary Renck. "Using Crisis-Oriented Books with Young Children." *Young Children* 38 (1983): 29-35.

Lejeune, Archie L. "Bibliocounseling as a Guidance Technique." *Catholic Library World* 41 (1969): 156-164.

Lenkowsky, Barbara E. and Ronald S. Lenkowsky. "Bibliotherapy for the LD Adolescent." *Academic Therapy* 14 (1978): 179-185.

Lindahl, Hannah M. and Katherine Koch. "Bibliotherapy in the Middle Grades." *Elementary English* 29 (1952): 390-396.

Lunsteen, Sara W. "A Thinking Improvement Program Through Literature." *Elementary English* 49 (1972): 505-512.

McInnis, Kathleen M. "Bibliotherapy: Adjunct to Traditional Counseling with Children of Stepfamilies." *Child Welfare* 61 (1982): 153-160.

Monroe, Margaret E. *Reading Guidance and Bibliotherapy in Public, Hospital, and Institutional Libraries.* Madison: Library School of the University of Wisconsin, 1971.

Monroe, Margaret E., ed. *Seminar on Bibliotherapy.* Madison: Library School of the University of Wisconsin, 1978.

Moses, Harold A. and Joseph S. Zaccaria. "Bibliotherapy in an Educational Context: Rationale and Principles." *Advances in Librarianship*, vol. 1, edited by Melvin J. Voigt. New York: Academic Press, 1970.

Newell, Ethel. "At the North End of Pooh: A Study of Bibliotherapy." *Elementary English* 34 (1957): 22-25.

Nickerson, Eileen T. "Bibliotherapy: A Therapeutic Medium for Helping Children." *Psychotherapy: Theory, Research and Practice* 12 (1975): 258-261.

Olsen, Henry D. "Bibliotherapy to Help Children Solve Problems." *Elementary School Journal* 75 (1975): 423-429.

Rakes, Thomas A. and Annabelle Buchanan. "Using Bibliotherapy: A Synthesis of Current Practice." Memphis: Department of Curriculum and Instruction of Tennessee State University, 1980.

Rongione, Louis A. "Bibliotherapy: Its Nature and Uses." *Catholic Library World* 43 (1972): 495-500.

Rubin, Dorothy. "Bibliotherapy: Reading Towards Mental Health." *Children's House* 9 (1976): 6-9.

Rubin, Rhea Joyce. *Bibliotherapy: A Guide to Theory and Practice.* Phoenix: The Oryx Press, 1978.

Rubin, Rhea Joyce. "Uses of Bibliotherapy in Response to the 1970s." *Library Trends* 28 (1979): 239-252.

Rubin, Rhea Joyce, ed. *Bibliotherapy Sourcebook.* Phoenix: The Oryx Press, 1978.

Russell, Alma E. and William A. Russell. "Using Bibliotherapy with Emotionally Disturbed Children." *Teaching Exceptional Children* 11 (1979): 168-169.

Russell, David H. "Reading the Healthy Personality." *Elementary English* 29 (1952): 195-200.

Russell, David H. and Caroline Shrodes. "Contributions of Research in Bibliotherapy to the Language Arts Program I." *School Review* 58 (1950): 335-342.

Russell, David H. and Caroline Shrodes. "Contributions of Research in Bibliotherapy to the Language Arts Program II." *School Review* 58 (1950): 411-420.

Sanders, Jacquelyn. "Psychological Significance of Children's Literature." *Library Trends* 37 (1967): 15-22.

Schrank, Frederick A. and Dennis W. Engels. "Bibliotherapy as a Counseling Adjunct: Research Findings." *Personnel and Guidance Journal* 60 (1981): 143-147.

Schwartz, Albert V. "Books Mirror Society: A Study of Children's Materials." *Interracial Books for Children Bulletin* 11 (1980): 19-24.

Schwartz, Albert V. "Disability in Children's Books: Is Visibility Enough?" *Interracial Books for Children Bulletin* 8 (1977): 10-15.

Schwoebel, Barbara. "Bibliotherapy: A Guide to Materials." *Catholic Library World* 44 (1973): 586-592.

Sclabassi, Sharon Henderson. "Literature as a Therapeutic Tool: A Review of the Literature on Bibliotherapy." *American Journal of Psychotherapy* 27 (1973): 70-77.

Shepherd, Terry and Lynn B. Iles. "What is Bibliotherapy?" *Language Arts* 53 (1976): 569-571.

Shrodes, Caroline. "Bibliotherapy." *The Reading Teacher* 9 (1955): 24-29.

Spache, George D. *Good Reading for Poor Readers.* 9th rev. ed. Champaign, IL: Garrard Publishing, 1974. Chapter 3, "Using Books to Help Solve Children's Problems."

Stroud, Janet G. "Selecting Materials Which Promote Understanding and Acceptance of Handicapped Students." *The English Journal* 79 (1981): 49-52.

Strunk, Orlo, Jr. "Bibliotherapy Revisited." *Journal of Religion and Health* 11 (1972): 218-228.

Tartagni, Donna. "Using Bibliotherapy with Adolescents." *School Counselor* 24 (1976): 28-35.

Tews, Ruth M. "Progress in Bibliotherapy." *Advances in Librarianship*, vol. 1, edited by Melvin J. Voigt. New York: Academic Press, 1970.

Tews, Ruth M., ed. "Bibliotherapy." *Library Trends* 11, No. 2 (October 1962). Entire issue.

Tiller, Karen. "Bibliotherapy and the Treatment of Emotional Disturbances." *Catholic Library World* 45 (1974): 428-431.

Wass, Hannalore and Judith Shaak. "Helping Children Understand Death Through Literature." *Childhood Education* 53 (1976): 80-85.

Witty, Paul. "Promoting Growth and Development Through Reading." *Elementary English* 27 (1950): 493-500, 556.

Witty, Paul. "Reading to Meet Emotional Needs." *Elementary English* 29 (1952): 75-84.

Zaccaria, Joseph S. and Harold A. Moses. *Facilitating Human Development Through Reading: The Use of Bibliotherapy in Teaching and Counseling.* Champaign, IL: Stipes Publishing, 1968.

ANNOTATIONS

1

Addy, Sharon

We Didn't Mean To

Color illustrations by Jay Blair.
Raintree/Steck-Vaughan, Publishers, 1981.
(31 pages)

VANDALISM
Practical jokes/pranks
Sports/Sportsmanship

Before a track meet between the Hawks, their school's team, and the rival Rockets, Tommy and his friend Brent, both about ten, decide to spray-paint "HAWKS ARE WINNERS" on a bridge wall. While Brent works, his older sister and Tommy's older brother, both members of the Hawks, alert the boys to a Rockets slogan painted on a wall across the street. Brent goes over and changes "Best" to "Losers," and the driver of a passing car threatens to report them for vandalism. They run off but defend their actions to one another as fun, not vandalism. The night of the meet, Tommy and Brent watch from the stands, cheering the Hawks and booing the Rockets. When it becomes evident that the Rockets will win, Brent leads Tommy to what he thinks is the Rockets' locker room and suggests they throw everything out of the lockers. The boys are just starting on the second row of lockers when they hear voices and hide in a storage closet. To their chagrin, their own Hawks enter the locker room. Peeking through the door, Tommy watches his angry brother pick up his clothes and hears the coach say he will report this to the opposing team's coach. "Let this be an end to the pranks and the vandalism," he advises the Hawks. Now Brent and Tommy, further distressed when a player discovers his glasses are broken, begin to realize the consequences of their fun. The locker room grows quiet and the boys try to escape, but the coach, working in his office, hears them. He knows right away that they, not the Rockets, are the culprits. "We didn't mean to—," the boys begin, but the coach interrupts and asks if they were also responsible for the bridge painting. They confess, saying it was only a joke. "That kind of joke is called vandalism," he says. "It hurts people." He tells them to report to him in the morning with ideas on how to make up for their actions. Walking home in the rain, the boys pass their fading slogan on the bridge and speed its disappearance by rubbing out the letters themselves.

Two boys show their excessive team loyalty by acts of vandalism. When the "fun" backfires, Tommy and Brent learn the seriousness of their behavior and are eager to make amends. Very simply written with full-page illustrations, the format might deter some prospective older readers, although it enhances the book's suitability for reading with a group. The two culprits are pictured as older than the intended audience, another potential source of confusion. Still, the story encourages children "to define, analyze, and develop constructive alternatives to vandalism," and so is valuable.

Ages 8-10

Also available in:
No other form known

2

Adler, Carole Schwerdtfeger

The Cat That Was Left Behind

Houghton Mifflin Co., 1981.
(146 pages) o.p.

BELONGING
FOSTER HOME
REJECTION: Parental
Adoption: feelings about
Animals: love for
Dependence/Independence

For thirteen-year-old Chad a summer at Cape Cod with the Sorenics, his new foster family, is just another temporary situation to be endured until the time when he can live with his mother again. Although Chad has been in foster homes since he was four and his mother got sick, she has always promised that one day she would take him back. Thus, he refuses to believe she would really give him up for adoption, as she suggested in a recent letter. The first days at the Sorenics' cottage are awkward for Chad. He is afraid of the ocean, disdainful of the athletic skills of Bob, the twelve-year-old son, and wary of his foster father's gruff, commanding manner. He often withdraws to a quiet spot behind the cottage to feed and watch a stray cat he has discovered. His foster mother seems to understand his need for a retreat, as does Polly, the quiet, fourteen-year-old daughter. In time, the cat trusts Chad, approaching when he calls and sitting contentedly in the boy's lap. So too does Chad become more comfortable with his new family, and he enters willingly into their activities—swimming, jogging, household chores, repair work. The cat, his cat as he has come to think of it, leads Chad to new interests. He goes fishing with Chester, a crusty old-timer, and he works for Mrs. Saugerty, a sour old woman who chases off his cat whenever it comes around. Even so, Chad eagerly does her yard work and sends his earnings to his mother, suggesting that now is the time for them to reunite. Then concern for his cat, which Mrs. Saugerty has threatened to poison, takes his mind off his mother. The Sorenics share his concern and offer to help, but there seems no clear solution. Even locking the cat in the cottage does not work since the animal, desperate for freedom, escapes the first chance it gets. However, it remains unharmed and often returns to be with Chad. As the summer draws to a close, Chad receives the much-awaited reply from his mother: "My new husband don't want me to have nothing to do with you now and maybe it is all for the best for both of us." Chad's hurt increases as he realizes that when he leaves the Sorenics he'll have to leave the cat. He thinks, "It was a rotten thing to teach someone to love you and then to leave him." The Sorenics feel the same way. They love Chad and want to adopt him, if he is willing. It takes Chad a few days to decide to join their family, days in which they are all drawn together as they search for the cat, who has again disappeared. The cat suddenly returns when they are ready to leave and just as suddenly escapes from the car as they prepare to drive away. It is Chad who decides to leave the cat, knowing it can survive on its own and prefers to do so.

A boy adopts a stray cat that is much like him. Abandoned, it is wary of strangers and has learned to fend for itself. The main difference between the two is that the cat takes what it can get and Chad wants what he cannot have—his mother. The animal becomes a catalyst, bringing out Chad's sense of responsibility and drawing his foster family to him by their willingness to protect what is important to him. The relative ease with which Chad relinquishes his long-held dream of living with his mother and adjusts to his prospective adoption demonstrates his realization that he, unlike the cat, wants and needs someone to care for him. The story is told with sensitivity but is not sentimental.

Ages 9-12

Also available in:
No other form known

3

Adler, Carole Schwerdtfeger

In Our House Scott Is My Brother

Macmillan Publishing Company, Inc., 1980.
(139 pages)

ALCOHOLISM: of Mother
STEPBROTHER/STEPSISTER
STEPPARENT: Mother
Change: resisting
Stealing
Values/Valuing: moral/ethical

For the three years since her mother's death, thirteen-year-old Jodi and her father have been a team. Suddenly her father announces his remarriage and just as suddenly, it seems, Jodi's new stepmother, Donna, moves in with her thirteen-year-old son, Scott. Glamorous, volatile Donna, so different from Jodi's understanding, motherly mother, seems intent on redoing everything in her new home—Jodi, the house, even herself. Jodi responds with what Donna feels is cool politeness, frustrating Donna's attempts at friendship. Donna is further frustrated by the suburban housewife role she tries to play, finding it a stifling contrast to her previous life in Los Angeles. She turns to her son for support, and Scott, dropping his mask of indifference, surprises Jodi by gently bolstering his mother, becoming as protective and loving as a parent, smoothing over her irritability and dissatisfaction. When, in preparation for a dinner party, Donna orders Jodi to bathe her aging dog and keep her away from the guests, Scott both excuses his mother's abruptness and helps Jodi with the required task. Then, just when Jodi begins to like him, she learns that the street-wise Scott has stolen an African necklace from a school exhibit. Feeling that her knowledge of the theft makes her responsible for undoing it, she returns the necklace, risking being called the thief herself. She resolves to tell her father about the incident when he returns from a business trip. But before he comes home, Jodi notices Donna retreat to her room one evening with a bucket of ice. Scott tells Jodi that his mother has started drinking again and confides that he expects to watch helplessly while she destroys this marriage as she has several others. The boy asks Jodi not to tell her father, the first decent man he and his mother have known, about his theft, and Jodi agrees. Family life continues to deteriorate. Jodi's dog dies and she wrongly accuses Donna of having had her destroyed. Scott helps save Jodi's favorite retreat, a glen behind their house, from being sold to a developer. As Christmas approaches, Scott is spending more and more time shoring Donna up. Jodi wants to ask for her father's help, but Scott knows his mother will refuse it. Finally, as the boy expects, Donna abruptly gives up, buys plane tickets, and decides to exit this marriage also. Scott gives Jodi an early Christmas present—he has told her teacher the truth about the necklace, thereby removing any lingering suspicions of Jodi's complicity in the theft. Then he stuns Jodi by announcing that he and his mother are leaving the next day. Next morning, Jodi begs her father to make them stay. To her surprise, she discovers that he has tried hard to do that, even suggesting Alcoholics Anonymous, but Donna has refused all help. When Jodi returns from school that day, Scott and his mother are gone. In her room, Scott has left a framed picture resembling the glen. On it he's written, "I liked having you for a sister, even if it was only for a little while. With love, Your brother, Scott."

Because she is shown to be honest, fair, and realistic, Jodi is a dependable narrator for this story of family change. She naturally resents the intrusion of a stepmother she considers pushy and intolerant, but gradually learns that the woman is a complex person, insecure and unhappy; not a "mean stepmother," but an alcoholic who cannot be helped until she admits her problem. From her very temporary stepbrother, in some ways more mature and sensitive—certainly more worldly—than she, Jodi comes to understand a bit more about family love and survival.

Ages 10-13

Also available in:
No other form known

4

Adler, Carole Schwerdtfeger

The Silver Coach

Avon Books, 1988.
(112 pages, paperbound)

COMMUNICATION: Parent-Child
DIVORCE: of Parents
SELF, ATTITUDE TOWARD: Accepting
Grandparent: living in home of
Imagination
Maturation
Rejection: parental
Separation from loved ones

Twelve-year-old Chris, who lives with her mother and sister Jackie, seven, misses her father terribly since he moved out last year. She blames her mother for the upcoming divorce. Now, while her mother attends summer school to complete her nursing studies, Chris and Jackie will spend the summer with their father's mother. Chris feels angry and afraid at the prospect. After all, she has only met Grandmother Wallace once and that was years ago. The first night at her grandmother's remote Vermont mountain home, Chris resolves to write to her father and ask him to come get her. But the days pass quickly. Chris learns to bake bread and make preserves. Soothed by their grandmother's warm acceptance and the peaceful outdoor life, both girls thrive. Still, her father is never far from Chris's thoughts. One day Grandmother Wallace shows the girls her magic silver coach, a miniature her husband had given her when they lived in Morocco and had to make the difficult decision to send Chris's father, then seven, to boarding school in England. She had used the coach to visit her son in her imagination whenever she missed him. She tells Chris that even now, whenever she feels lonely, she uses the coach to visit friends, but that Chris must discover its secret herself. Chris soon does and imagines several perfect days with her adoring father. Then her father actually does come for a visit, an event both girls have planned for and awaited. But he arrives with a woman and her children. They are all going on vacation together and are anxious to get started. Stunned, Chris desperately asks her father for a few minutes alone with him, but he does not have time. Once she recovers a bit from the blow of discovering that her father does not love her or her family best, she begins to understand what her grandmother had told her earlier, that her father "takes care of himself first, before anybody else gets taken care of—always has, most likely always will. Your mother, on the other hand, strikes me as a lady nobody's cared about enough." One afternoon, after helping Jackie retrieve the silver coach from the pond where the younger girl accidentally dropped it, Chris invites her sister to take an imaginary ride. She imagines them visiting not their father, but their home and their mother. A few days later, their mother actually arrives to take them home. She notices approvingly how both girls have changed; they seem less self-centered, more considerate. As they leave, Grandmother Wallace offers Chris the silver coach but she refuses, realizing that her grandmother, saddened by their departure, needs it more than she.

A summer away from her mother coupled with an eye-opening visit from her father allows Chris the time and space she needs to gain a new perspective on her parents' divorce and a deeper understanding of and appreciation for her mother. Although Chris receives welcome support and advice from her grandmother, she cannot give up her romantic vision of her father until he himself callously dispels it. Both Chris and Jackie become more loving and less self-centered under the influence of the serene, realistic grandmother, who shows them how to use fantasy to heal, rather than to delude themselves. This is their father's mother but, perhaps because she knows her son's faults, she aligns herself with the mother and daughters. The changes in the two girls are made believable by strong, well-developed characterizations.

Ages 9-12

Also available in:
No other form known

A

5

Albert, Burton

Mine, Yours, Ours

Color illustrations by Lois Axeman.
Albert Whitman & Company, 1977.
(31 pages counted)

SHARING/NOT SHARING

Young children, shown in various situations, use things, parts of the body, and other people to demonstrate sharing and ownership. In one scene a boy and his mother are walking through the snow. He looks back at the footprints and says, "Mine, yours—ours." Another scene shows two children pulling on a rope, each saying "Mine." But in the next picture they are jumping rope together, illustrating *ours* and the idea of sharing. Friends, too, can be shared. A girl shares her friend with a boy and he, in turn, shares his friends with her, making all the friends "ours."

Yours, mine, and *ours* are difficult words for young children to understand. In this book, both words and pictures illustrate the concepts. The differences between individual and shared possessions are vague in some illustrations, and this might be confusing to young readers.

Ages 2-5

Also available in:
No other form known

6

Alda, Arlene

Sonya's Mommy Works

Black/white photographs by the author.
Messner (Julian), Inc., 1983.
(46 pages counted) o.p.

PARENT/PARENTS: Mother Working Outside Home
Change: accepting
Communication: parent-child

Sonya loves weekends because then she and her parents can be home together. Since her mother started to work in an office, Sonya doesn't get to see her as often as before. On Saturdays the two of them try to do some special thing together. Sonya also has time alone with her father. During the week she must be quite independent. Sometimes she wishes her mother would help her more, as she used to do. One day Sonya announces that she is going to be in a class play. Her mother promises to get time off from work to come. The day of the event, however, her parents get tied up in traffic and Sonya worries that they won't make it. But they arrive just in time and watch the performance proudly. After the play, Sonya's father goes with her class to the playground and is there to comfort Sonya when she falls off the monkey bars. She sheds some tears when she realizes her mother has gone back to work. Then one day Sonya's mother tells her she is going away on a five-day business trip. Sonya doesn't like the idea very much, but is glad that Mommy will be home before her birthday. "Would you go if it weren't for business?" asks Sonya. "No," her mother answers. "I wouldn't leave you for even one day, unless I had to." Sonya marks off the days on her calendar and looks forward to her mother's calls every night. Finally, bubbling with excitement, she goes with her father to meet her mother's plane. The next day life is back to normal, but at night the family bakes cookies together for Sonya's birthday party. All Sonya's favorite people come to help celebrate. After she has opened all her presents, she says, "It sure is a happy birthday. I like my party and, most of all, I like being six!"

Life is complicated for little Sonya when her mother begins to work away from home. However, with the loving support of both parents, she manages to accept the things she cannot change and live a normal, happy life. Realistic photographs add interest to this honest look at family feelings and adjustments.

Ages 4-7

Also available in:
No other form known

7

Alexander, Martha G.

Move Over, Twerp

Color illustrations by the author.
Dial Books for Young Readers, 1981.
(32 pages counted)

PROBLEM SOLVING
Bully: being bothered by
Resourcefulness

An excited Jeffrey, about six, is told by his mother that she soon will stop driving him to school—he is old enough now to ride the school bus. The big day arrives, and Jeffrey finds a perfect seat in the back of the bus. The bus begins to fill up and an older boy, about eight, tells Jeffrey to move, calling him a "twerp." When Jeffrey reports the incident at home that evening, his father and older sister, Katie, give him advice about being tough. The next day on the bus, Jeffrey refuses to move. The older boy again calls him "Twerp" and then picks Jeffrey up and deposits him in a different seat. Once again, Jeffrey is defeated. But that night, while reading a book about super creatures, he comes upon a solution. The next morning on the school bus when the bully calls him "Twerp" and orders him to move, Jeffrey says, "My name isn't Twerp. It's SUPERTWERP." With this, he opens his jacket to reveal a T-shirt on which he's colored a monster and the word "Supertwerp." The older boys laugh, but show a certain respect for Jeffrey's ingenuity. Jeffrey keeps his seat.

A small boy defuses a bully by using both resourcefulness and humor. Although the solution to Jeffrey's problem may seem oversimplified, it does demonstrate that children can counter superior force with ingenuity. Young readers can also discuss the power of humor to overcome obstacles. Apt illustrations are used in place of narrative occasionally to move the story along.

Ages 5-8

Also available in:
Paperbound—*Move Over, Twerp*
Dial Books for Young Readers.

8

Alexander, Martha G.

Nobody Asked Me if I Wanted a Baby Sister

Color illustrations by the author.
Dial Books for Young Readers, 1971.
(28 pages)

SIBLING: New Baby
Sibling: jealousy

Everyone admires the little boy's new baby sister, but he doesn't like her at all. He takes his sister out of her crib, places her in a wagon, and offers her for sale to people in the neighborhood. When this doesn't work, he tries to give her away to some friends, to a man who exhibits trained dogs, and to some strangers on a motor scooter. None of these people want the baby either. A newsboy passes by and says his mother likes babies, so the little boy takes his sister to the newsboy's house. He leaves her there and goes off a short distance to play. The baby sister does nothing but cry. She is not hungry, and there are no pins sticking her, so everyone wonders what could be wrong. The little boy stops playing and comes to tell his sister to stop crying. He receives quite a surprise when he discovers that only he can comfort her. Then the little boy begins to feel that his new baby sister isn't so bad after all.

Pictures contribute much to this simple story. The facial expressions of the boy portray his feelings of jealousy especially well. Young children can easily identify with his predicament.

Ages 3-6

Also available in:
Paperbound—*Nobody Asked Me if I Wanted a Baby Sister*
Dial Books for Young Readers

9

Alexander, Martha G.

When the New Baby Comes, I'm Moving Out

Color illustrations by the author.
Dial Books for Young Readers, 1979.
(32 pages counted)

SIBLING: New Baby
Communication: parent-child

When young Oliver discovers his mother painting his old high chair in preparation for the new baby, he is angry. She is giving all his old things to the baby, and he insists he still needs them: the high chair for a launching pad, the crib for his wild animals. His mother apologizes and he tearfully goes to her for comfort, but the unborn baby has taken up all the room on her lap. Now he is really angry at his mother and threatens to throw her in a garbage can, take her to the dump, and leave her. On second thought, he decides his mother can stay and he will leave and live in his tree house or his tent. He is surprised when his mother says she would miss him. She needs him to cut out the cookies and play games with her. "I guess that baby won't be much fun for you either. I better stay with you," says Oliver. When she suggests that he will get to do many special things in his new role of big brother, Oliver feels better. With hands on his mother's swollen abdomen he says, "Hurry up, baby, I have lots of plans. I can't wait to be a big brother."

Told in dialogue, this story succinctly captures the hurt and fear an only child feels at the thought of being displaced by a sibling. Oliver's mother, realizing what a threat the baby poses to her son, reacts calmly to his angry, hateful words. Simple illustrations match a concise, sympathetic text. The contrast between Oliver's idea of being a big brother (watching late-night television and eating treats) and his mother's (Oliver minding the baby while she relaxes) is perceptive and funny. This is a companion to *Nobody Asked Me If I Wanted a Baby Sister,* which continues Oliver's story after the new baby is born.

Ages 2-5

Also available in:
Paperbound—*When the New Baby Comes, I'm Moving Out*
Dial Books for Young Readers

10

Allard, Harry

Miss Nelson Is Missing!

Color illustrations by James Marshall.
Houghton Mifflin Co., 1977.
(32 pages)

SCHOOL: Behavior
SCHOOL: Pupil-Teacher Relationships

The children in Miss Nelson's class behave badly, worse than any other children in the school. Even when Miss Nelson asks them nicely to settle down during story hour, they refuse. One day Miss Nelson is gone and a substitute teacher named Miss Viola Swamp takes her place. Dressed all in black, Miss Swamp reminds the children of a witch. She tolerates no foolishness and puts the children to work. As the days go by, the children begin to long for Miss Nelson. Some of them go to the police; others go to her home, but the sight of Miss Viola Swamp walking down the street frightens them away. Just when they think Miss Nelson will never return, she appears. Everyone listens to her instructions and sits quietly during story hour. When Miss Nelson asks them why they have changed, they are secretive. But Miss Nelson has her own secret—a black dress hanging in her closet at home—and she knows why the children have changed.

Young children learn to appreciate a good-natured teacher during her seeming absence. The story, with its bid for proper classroom behavior, avoids being obviously didactic through good-natured prose and illustrations. Classes may enjoy hearing it read aloud.

Ages 5-8

Also available in:
Braille—*Miss Nelson Is Missing!*
Library of Congress (NLSBPH)

Paperbound—*Miss Nelson Is Missing!*
Houghton Mifflin Co.

11
Amoss, Berthe
Tom in the Middle
Color illustrations by the author.
HarperCollins Publishers, Inc., 1968.
(32 pages) o.p.

SIBLING: Middle

Young Tom has two brothers. Mark is much older than Tom, and John is younger. John follows Tom everywhere. He wants to ride on Tom's bike with him; he attempts to spin around as Tom does, but gets underfoot. When Tom tries to play on a swing, John stands in the way. John knocks down Tom's block houses and loses parts of Tom's games. After John tears Tom's favorite book, Tom stops playing with him and decides to play with Mark instead. Tom and Mark bathe together. They argue over the soap, so Mother chases them out of the tub. Tom plays with Mark's Monopoly game and mixes up the money. Mark shouts at him for this, so Tom decides to dress in his policeman's costume and hide from both brothers. Tom is determined to stay hidden—even if his brothers call him or look for him. When night falls, Tom quickly changes his mind and decides to come inside where it is warm and bright. He eats sugar bread with John and then makes a tent in which he and John will sleep while Mark stands watch.

This book portrays the frustration that Tom, the middle sibling, experiences when his younger brother follows him and ruins his possessions and when his older brother expresses annoyance with him. It is easy for the reader to identify with Tom and to understand his emotions. The end of the book gives the reader a sense of close friendship among the brothers.

Ages 3-7

Also available in:
No other form known

12
Andersen, Hans Christian
The Ugly Duckling
Translated from the Danish by R.P. Keigwin.
Color illustrations by Johannes Larsen.
Macmillan Publishing Company, Inc., 1987.
(54 pages)

APPEARANCE: Concern About
INFERIORITY, FEELINGS OF
Rejection

When a nest of duck eggs hatches one summer, one of the new ducklings is larger and colored differently from the rest. In the barnyard, this ugly duckling is the focal point of cruel remarks and physical abuse. Even his mother and his brothers and sisters treat him badly. Soon, the ugly duckling runs away to avoid any more abuse. As he travels around, he blames his ugliness for the various attitudes people and animals display toward him, and he spends a cold, miserable winter alone in a woodland marsh. When spring arrives, the ugly duckling sees some swans on the pond where he is swimming and he is awed by their beauty and royal bearing. Deciding to end his life, the ugly duckling swims toward the swans, hoping that they will beat him to death with their wings. When he bows his head to await their blows, he sees his own reflection in the water and is overjoyed to find that he was never really an ugly duckling: he too is a beautiful and graceful swan. The other swans accept him into their flock, and he is soon recognized as the most beautiful swan of all.

This famous children's classic, which is said to be based on the author's childhood years, first appeared as part of Hans Christian Andersen's booklet, *New Fairy Tales,* in 1845. As in the past, children will readily identify with the sad duckling's feelings of rejection and his joy when he is accepted by those he admires.

Ages 4-8

Also available in:
Braille—*The Ugly Duckling*
Library of Congress (NLSBPH)

13
Angell, Judie
In Summertime It's Tuffy
Dell Publishing Company, Inc., 1979.
(192 pages, paperbound)

CAMP EXPERIENCES
FRIENDSHIP: Meaning of
Loyalty

Eleven-year-old Elizabeth "Tuffy" Kandell is spending the summer at Camp Ma-Sha-Na. She likes the camp and her five cabin-mates; two she already knows and the others she makes friends with at once. No two are alike. Verna likes things clean and orderly; Natalie cares mostly for clothes and boys; Iris is a loner, with her nose in her books. Uncle Otto (as he is called), the camp director, wants to "run a tight ship" and the girls soon find themselves in trouble. They are late for breakfast; their cabin is a mess. When Uncle Otto fires Sheila, the girls' cabin counselor, for returning to camp long after curfew, the girls, getting the idea from one of Iris's books on magic, make a voodoo doll of Otto. Into the doll's ankle they stick a pin, and later that day Otto sprains his ankle. Fearing their own magical powers, they completely dismantle the doll. But something new and interesting is always turning up. Iris is to play her guitar in the talent show. Uncle Otto seems mellower. Tuffy turns her attention to someone very interesting indeed—a boy named Alex.

Tuffy and her cabin-mates go through some typical summer-camp experiences: minor clashes with each other and the camp director, pranks, and the dawning of warm friendships. Tuffy grows up, too, over the summer, befriending and encouraging the quiet Iris, trying to understand the director's point of view, starting to take new notice of boys.

Ages 11-13

Also available in:
Braille—*In Summertime It's Tuffy*
Library of Congress (NLSBPH)

Cassette—*In Summertime It's Tuffy*
Library of Congress (NLSBPH)

14

Angell, Judie

Ronnie and Rosey

Dell Publishing Company, Inc., 1979.
(192 pages, paperbound) o.p.

BOY-GIRL RELATIONSHIPS
DEATH: of Father
MOURNING, Stages of
Dependence/Independence
Honesty/Dishonesty
Parental: overprotection

On her first day at a new school, thirteen-year-old Ronnie Rachman is accidently knocked to the floor by Robert Rose. The two introduce themselves and find they have something in common: Ronnie, a girl, is by name often mistaken for a boy, and Robert, nicknamed Rosey, is teased about having a girlish nickname. That very same day Ronnie meets Evelyn, a friendly girl who has been Robert's best friend for years. The best friends plan a get-acquainted party for Ronnie, and there Ronnie learns that Robert is a gifted piano player, that Robert and Evelyn are rehearsing a pantomime for a local talent show, and that the two want her to join them. The three begin to hang around together, and before long Robert asks Ronnie for a date. She hangs back, afraid Evelyn's feelings will be hurt, but Evelyn assures her that she and Robert are just pals. Then, on the second night of the talent show, tragedy strikes: Ronnie's parents have an automobile accident and her father is killed. Mrs. Rachman is transformed by grief. She insists that Ronnie stay home all the time; soon she puts restrictions on all phone calls. Ronnie is not to see Robert, but the two meet secretly at Ronnie's baby-sitting jobs. They are discovered, and Ronnie is again told to drop Robert. In desperation, Ronnie declares that she wishes she had died instead of her father—and in fact she is suffering from sleeplessness and fierce headaches. Sneaking out one night to see Robert, she returns to find her mother waiting. Unable to face another quarrel, Ronnie runs away, vowing never to go home again. To Miss Fisk, her gym teacher, she sobs out the whole story. Miss Fisk notifies Mrs. Rachman of Ronnie's whereabouts, and lets her spend the night. In the morning, Mrs. Rachman comes to get Ronnie, and seems much more herself. She apologizes to her daughter and vows that the future will be better. Ronnie spends the summer with a friend in Los Angeles, and when she returns in the fall, her mother is her old self. Ronnie and Robert look forward to a good school year together.

After her father's sudden death, Ronnie has no vent for her grief, and almost completely represses all thoughts of him. It is her mother's sudden, smothering possessiveness that brings her to despair, and finally leads her to deceive her mother outright. Only then does her mother get a grip on herself, seeing that she could potentially destroy the love between herself and her daughter. Ronnie and her friends are wholly recognizable teenagers who happen to be visited by a calamity and its baffling, frightening aftermath. The story ends hopefully but not patly.

Ages 11 and up

Also available in:
No other form known

15

Angell, Judie

What's Best for You

Dell Publishing Company, Inc., 1983.
(192 pages, paperbound) o.p.

DIVORCE: of Parents
FAMILY: Relationships
Boy-girl relationships: dating
Change: accepting
Communication: parent-child
Friendship: best friend
Parental: custody

Their parents' recent divorce has Lee, Allison, and Joel in a flurry of packing, moving, and mixed emotions. Lee, fifteen, will stay with her father on Long Island for the summer; Allison, twelve, and Joel, seven, will move into New York City with their mother. Lee, who doesn't get along with her mother, is thrilled. Secretly she hopes she and her father can live together permanently. Her summer begins perfectly. She and her three best friends work part of the day for the Parks Department and spend the lazy afternoons at the beach. They call themselves the "Shuffleboard Generation," as each is shuffled between divorced parents. When Lee's mother invites her to spend the Fourth of July with her, Lee reluctantly accepts, vowing to avoid all arguments. But she quickly decides—unjustly—that her mother doesn't want any of her new friends to know Lee is her daughter. After the inevitable fight, Lee runs away, returning later to apologize. Later in July, Lee and her friends decide to have a party. They invite four boys, and Lee finds herself paired with Warren, who is new to the neighborhood. The two soon begin dating and are constantly together. Their relationship helps Lee accept her father's dating more easily. As the summer progresses, both Lee and her father realize how much they enjoy and need each other. Then Warren breaks up with Lee, and both parents try to console her. Meanwhile, Joel keeps hoping that everything will magically revert to the way it was, and, toward the end of the summer, Allison's behavior begins to worry her mother. The girl has become "mother" to Joel and spends all her time caring for him and their new apartment. The parents agree Allison will spend that weekend with her father while Lee stays with her mother. Soon after her father, Allison, and Joel leave, Lee and her mother argue. During the evening, Lee slips out of the apartment. She takes a train back to Long Beach and spends the night with a girlfriend, forgetting to call her father. When she does phone he calls her mother, calling Lee back to say her mother will come to meet with them. When Lee returns home the next morning, the entire family discusses the divorce and their living arrangements. Angrily, Lee insists, "You keep saying you want the best for us, only you're the ones who decide what's best, not us!" She declares she wants to stay with her father. Several days later her parents agree on professional counseling for Allison. They also decide that Lee can stay permanently with her father. Finally Lee has what she thinks is best, although her father helps her to keep an open mind. She and her mother may develop a less volatile relationship as time goes on.

This well-done story focuses on Lee and her family relationships, but the reader is also given candid insights into the convictions and misgivings of each family member as each struggles to adapt to the divorce. Characters emerge as many-sided human beings, and the complexities of feeling created by a family breakup are clearly and sensitively conveyed. This slice of life offers considerable insight into family dynamics during difficult times.

Ages 11-14

Also available in:
No other form known

16

Arnothy, Christine

I Am Fifteen and I Don't Want to Die

Scholastic, Inc., 1986.
(124 pages, paperbound)

DEATH: Attitude Toward
FEAR: of Death
Family: unity
War

Christine, a fifteen-year-old Hungarian, and her parents live with a group of tenants in the basement of their apartment building while war rages outside. The Nazi defense of Budapest against the Russian invasion has endangered all civilians. When the crowd in the cellar has only a single day's food left, Pista, a Hungarian soldier, arrives. During the next few days, Pista procures food and water for the group. When Christine and others from her building make a trip through the streets to the Turkish bath for the only available water in the area, she ponders the facial expressions on the corpses in the street. A few days later she confesses to a priest who has managed to come to the cellar that "she is terrified every time she goes out, because she could not help stepping on the dead as she made her way through the bodies. Their glassy eyes seem to accuse her because she is still among the living...." When the basement is flooded by the overflowing Danube River, the tenants are forced to evacuate into the street. They are confronted by two German soldiers who accuse them of stealing the soldiers' rations. The Germans hold the tenants at gunpoint, threatening to kill them if the rations are not returned. A strange soldier saves their lives when he returns the provisions, and the tenants go back to their soggy basement. When the Russians finally gain control of Budapest, Christine and her parents travel to their country home near the Austrian border. They remain there for three years until Russian suppression forces the family to cross the mined and guarded border to Austria.

This autobiographical narrative deeply involves the reader with Christine. Her fear of death, feelings of loneliness, and relationships with others are sympathetically and realistically described.

Ages 12 and up

Also available in:
Braille—*I Am Fifteen and I Don't Want to Die*
Library of Congress (NLSBPH)

17

Arnstein, Helene S.

Billy and Our New Baby

Color illustrations by M. Jane Smyth.
Human Sciences Press, 1973.
(32 pages counted)

SIBLING: New Baby
Sibling: jealousy

Four-year-old Billy has a new baby in his home. It angers him that everyone fusses over an infant that can do nothing but eat, sleep, and cry. Because Mommy is often busy caring for the baby and has no time to play with Billy, the boy is positive that his mother loves the baby more than she loves him. When Billy suggests that his parents return the baby to the hospital, his mother tells him that she understands how he feels and explains that the baby is part of the family, just as Billy is. She also tells Billy that she loves him as much as the baby. One day, Billy tries to push the baby away from his mother. Mommy gently stops him, explaining that she cannot let Billy hurt the baby, just as she would not let anyone hurt him. Billy decides that he wants to be a baby, so he begins to crawl and cry a great deal and asks to be fed from a bottle. Mommy agrees to his request but reminds him of all the things he can do that the baby can't. Billy finally decides it is better to be a big boy, and that evening he helps his mother care for the baby.

Billy attempts to draw attention from a new sibling to himself through competition and regression to an imitation of infancy. His understanding mother helps him to see his own worth and accept the new baby. This is one of several books in a series dealing with important psychological themes.

Ages 3-6

Also available in:
No other form known

18

Arrick, Fran

Chernowitz!

Bradbury Press, 1981.
(165 pages, paperbound)

HARASSMENT
PREJUDICE: Religious
Guilt, feelings of
Hatred
Hostility
Jewish
Ostracism
Revenge

Bob Cherno's troubles with Emmett Sundback started when he was fifteen and in the ninth grade. At first it was just a few remarks and some name-calling. Then Emmett began encouraging others to jeer at Bob for being Jewish. On Halloween Bob's house was defaced with eggs and a burning cross thrown on the lawn. Though filled with fear and anger, Bob threw the cross into the lake and kept his feelings to himself. Soon Bob's best friend, Brian Denny, and other boys began ignoring him and even joining in Sundback's taunts. Martha (Matty) Greeley seemed friendly and Bob asked her out. But after the movie they ran into Sundback and his crew. After that he wouldn't even look at Matty, even though she seemed ready to encourage him. Sundback's methods of terrorizing and torturing Bob were varied and numerous; Bob began to understand what mental anguish was. He couldn't understand hatred based solely on his being Jewish—his family isn't even religious. Now it's summer. Brian makes friendly overtures to him, but Bob knows it's only because Brian has nobody else to sail with. How can Brian expect him to dismiss the ugliness of the past year? Then, while substituting on a paper route, Bob has to deliver the Sundbacks' newspaper. One day when Emmett pays him, he gives Bob a "tip": a piece of paper with a swastika on it. One morning, Bob's mother's car is defaced by a huge, black swastika. Instead of washing it off immediately, she insists on calling the newspaper. Bob and his father confront the Sundbacks, but Emmett denies painting the swastika and his father defends him. On the last day of summer, Bob's mother finds their cat with a broken leg. The next day, the first day of school, Emmett sidles up to Bob and asks him how his kitty is—Bob remembers that Emmett had threatened to harm the cat in the past. Filled with rage, Bob plans his revenge. From September until December he plots and spies on Emmett and then sets in motion an elaborate scenario in which Emmett is framed as the thief of Bob's new radio. Because of Emmett's reputation, everyone supports Bob, and Emmett is suspended from school. Bob later learns that Emmett's father beat him so badly for getting in trouble that the boy spent Christmas vacation in a hospital. However, Bob can't seem to feel good about the success of his plan. Matty Greeley all but asks him out, and even that doesn't lift his spirits. Bob decides the problem is that Emmett didn't get punished for his anti-Semitism; instead, he was punished for something he didn't even do. He resolves to talk to Emmett, to confess what he's done and explain why. But the confrontation isn't at all what he expects. Emmett appears totally oblivious to the damage his bigotry is causing and has absolutely no intention of changing. Finally, Bob tells his parents the whole story. They are shocked at what he went through alone, but they agree his solution was not a good one. His mother points out that revenge never changes anyone's attitudes. Bob knows he must tell the principal too, because she was "used" in his revenge. He and his father tell her together and, though sympathetic, she says categorically that Bob was wrong to wreak revenge the way he did. They call in Emmett, but he will not respond to questions. In the end, all he wants to know is if his father will be told about him being called to the principal's office. When the principal says she won't tell him, Emmett is relieved and goes back to class. The principal promises to think of a way to handle the situation. Her solution is a special all-school assembly presenting several films showing the closing days of World War II and the Jews who were liberated from concentration camps. Everyone is appalled by the shocking images: some cry, some are sick. Afterwards, Bob's father talks to them about the dangers of allowing hatred and bigotry to exist. Bob later sees Emmett in the hall and finds him completely unaffected and unchanged by what he has seen. Shocked, Bob realizes that nothing in the world will change an Emmett Sundback. But he remembers the students who cried and were sick; he knows that people like them far outnumber the Emmetts of this world.

A teenage boy is exposed to a particularly brutal and unrelenting form of anti-Semitism, and he takes revenge upon the ringleader only to learn that revenge solves nothing. Not much attention is paid to the many followers of the chief tormentor, but thoughtful readers will recognize these students' terrible responsibility; without a crew of attendants, Sundback would not have had as much power. Bob's mother believes that people like Emmett are usually fearful, insecure, and deprived, people who can't think rationally, historically, or reasonably. Emmett's brutalization by his father seems one clue to his own brutality. Bob wants to know how such hatefulness can be stopped. This complex question has no easy answer; people like Emmett, the book concludes, cannot be changed. But there are appropriate and inappropriate ways of responding to bigotry. This is a powerful, wrenching first-person narrative. Readers will feel Bob's pain and plot his revenge with him, even though they know—as the principal clearly points out—that framing Emmett was not an acceptable action. A tense, memorable book, this should prompt considerable discussion.

Ages 12 and up

Also available in:
Paperbound—*Chernowitz!*
New American Library

19

Arrick, Fran

Steffie Can't Come Out to Play

Dell Publishing Company, Inc., (Laurel Leaf Library), 1978. (196 pages, paperbound)

PROSTITUTION
RUNNING AWAY
Dependence/Independence
Fear: of physical harm

Fourteen-year-old Stephanie Rudd, beautiful and younger than she looks, has run away from Clairton, Pennsylvania, wanting more than the drudgery of housework while her mother takes in laundry. Steffie comes to New York City to be a model. Instead, she meets a man called Favor, who promises to protect her, showers her with expensive gifts, and encourages her to stay in his luxurious apartment. Soon Steffie has come to love the man—and proves her love, as Favor has asked, by becoming a prostitute. When she begins working the street, Favor sends her to live with Brenda, another of his "wives-in-law," and here she is told that all she earns belongs to Favor and that she must do well or expect a beating. She goes along, both out of fear and to prove to Favor that she is better than his other girls and deserves his love. Arrested one evening, she makes the mistake of bragging about her pimp, and upon her release Favor makes her sorry. Another time, one of the "wives" arranges to have a customer slip Steffie a drug, to which the girl responds badly and has to be helped to Favor's car. Another "wife" picks a fight on the way and Favor, angered at the scene, slaps Steffie around. They are observed by a police officer, Cal Yarbro, who has been watching Steffie since her first day. Later, unknown to Steffie, he breaks Favor's leg and jaw, threatening more of the same if he keeps Steffie on in his stable. Favor decides that Steffie, though by now his top earner, is not worth the trouble she causes. Having nowhere to turn, Steffie takes Cal's advice and goes to a shelter for runaways. After talking with counselors there, she decides to return home.

The main character in this largely first-person narrative is a prostitute completely dependent on her pimp for love, security, and approval. He, in turn, thinks of her only as property, using her dependence to hold her. Because Steffie successfully escapes her situation, some readers may erroneously think it is easy to break away from a pimp at will. Also, early in the book, prostitution is glamorized—the new clothes, the pimp's gifts, the protection of a strong man—and this may deceptively beguile some young readers. As the story progresses, the danger and misery of prostitution become clear, without preaching. Although the book is frank, sexual encounters are not rendered explicitly. Far clearer are its treatments of the body as property, the danger from aberrant "tricks," the distrust and jealousy of other prostitutes, and the feelings of worthlessness and fear the main character suffers. Patrolman Yarbro and his partner are introduced in a third-person section in this otherwise first-person narration by Steffie.

Ages 12 and up

Also available in:
Braille—*Steffie Can't Come Out to Play*
Library of Congress (NLSBPH)

Cassette—*Steffie Can't Come Out to Play*
Library of Congress (NLSBPH)

20

Arrick, Fran

Tunnel Vision

Dell Publishing Company, Inc., (Laurel Leaf Library), 1981 (170 pages, paperbound)

MOURNING, STAGES OF
SUICIDE
Communication: lack of
Depression
Expectations
Guilt, feelings of
Reality, escaping
Sibling: relationships

Anthony Hamil, fifteen, has committed suicide, hanging himself in his room with his father's neckties. He left no note, only a theme for English class in which he equated death with peace, peace both for the dead and for the family and friends from whom a troublesome personality has been removed. One by one, those closest to Anthony learn the news and, in their shock and grief, think about him. His mother, while being questioned by the police she called when she found her son, breaks down and cannot function. Her sister, Ruth, must take over, making the funeral arrangements and calling Anthony's father, away on a business trip. In order for Anthony's younger sister, Denise, to be told, the police must pick her up; overweight, unkempt, she has skipped school as she often does and is stoned on drugs. Bitterly, she blames their perfectionist father for Anthony's death. Her brother had been popular, a top student, a superior athlete; she had envied him his success, resented the attention their parents paid him, avoided or ignored him when she could. But Anthony's success had come at a terrible price. Pushed relentlessly by his father, the boy had descended further and further into depression in recent months, staying in his room, not bathing or changing clothes, skipping school, quitting the swim team. At various times Anthony had mentioned death or suicide to his friends Carl and Ditto and to his girlfriend, Jana, but they never believed he was really contemplating such an act. Friends, family, and teachers were all concerned about him; his mother had wanted to get psychiatric help for him. But Anthony's father, denying to himself that anything was wrong with his son, refused to consider it. Jana would never let Anthony touch her but never told him the reason: she had once been raped. As the people who'd shared Anthony's life now share their guilt and sense of loss, they come to realize that no one person was responsible for this tragedy. As the police officer describes adolescents who attempt or commit suicide, "It's like each of them was caught inside a tunnel, and they couldn't see any end to it or anything at all outside."

This moving, understated exploration of teenage suicide offers no pat answers or solutions. As each character learns of Anthony's death, the reader learns of Anthony's life through their italicized flashbacks. The diversity allows a many-faceted view of the troubled boy. By confiding their grief and guilt to each other, Anthony's family and friends demonstrate how healing it can be to express painful feelings. It becomes clear that no one person was responsible for this death. The dialogue is natural, with occasional profanity.

Ages 12 and up

Also available in:
No other form known

21

Arthur, Catherine

My Sister's Silent World

Color photographs by Nathan Talbot.
Children's Press, Inc., 1979.
(31 pages)

DEAFNESS
Sibling: love for

Today is Heather's eighth birthday. As a special treat, she is allowed to choose what she, her parents, and her older sister will do to celebrate. She chooses a trip to her favorite place, the zoo. The fact that Heather is deaf doesn't prevent her from having a wonderful birthday. Heather has a hearing aid that helps her hear sounds. But she can't distinguish words or hear conversation, and she has trouble determining the direction from which a sound is coming. She is learning to talk by reading lips, by feeling the speaking person's throat and face and then imitating the sound and throat movement, and by sign language. Heather even has a private code in sign language that only she and her sister understand. At her special school she is learning to communicate more easily. Although some children are afraid of Heather or laugh at her, she is a healthy, active girl who loves to ride her bike, go to the zoo, and play. And, notes her sister, Heather especially loves her birthday!

Heather's older sister perceptively describes the vibrant world of her deaf sister. Although written about an eight-year-old and easily read independently by primary readers, the book could also be read to younger children as an introduction to deafness. The photographs of Heather and her sister at the zoo and at home are lively and unposed, giving an added dimension to Heather's story.

Ages 5-9

Also available in:
No other form known

22

Asher, Sandra Fenichel

Just Like Jenny

Delacorte Press, 1982.
(148 pages) o.p.

IDENTITY, SEARCH FOR
TALENTS
Anxiety
Boy-girl relationships
Family: relationships
Friendship: best friend
Jealousy: peer

To thirteen-year-old Stephie Nordland, pleasing Mr. Oldham and being like Jenny are two of the most important things in life. Mr. Oldham is Stephie's ballet teacher, who believes only "the gifted, gutsy few" will break into professional dancing. Jenny, fifteen, is Stephie's best friend, to Stephie one of the "gutsy few." But Stephie isn't at all sure about herself. At school Mrs. Deveraux, the music teacher, announces a talent show and asks Stephie to dance in it. Thrilled, she asks Jenny to help her choreograph a routine. That night the two create Stephie's routine and also write application letters to producers of summer stock. Jenny tells Mr. Oldham about Stephie's talent show, but after he watches her routine he merely tells Stephie she had better do well and not embarrass him. Disappointed by his lack of enthusiasm, Stephie is further upset when her mother says she could have created her routine by herself, without Jenny's help. At the school auditions, Matt Greenspan sits by Stephie and encourages her, making her feel both flattered and nervous. Then, at her ballet lesson, Mr. Oldham asks both Stephie and Jenny to audition for his special Workshop. After thinking it over Stephie declines, convinced she isn't good enough, that he only asked her because of her friendship with Jenny. When Jenny makes the Workshop, Stephie feels jealous and begins seeing less of her friend. She is edgy, tired of her constant efforts to prove herself, wondering if she should quit dancing. Even Matt is ignoring her. Her part in the talent show goes very well, but Stephie's jealousy of Jenny's success in the Workshop increases anyway. Finally, her parents take her to see Mr. Oldham, wondering if Stephie should continue dancing. When Stephie says she doesn't feel she's good enough to make it as a dancer, her teacher informs her that she is in fact very talented. But it takes more than talent to be a dancer. It takes a gutsiness that Stephie appears to have lost. Shaken, Stephie talks with Jenny and apologizes for her jealousy. Things start coming together for Stephie; even Matt renews his interest in her. Several weeks later, the two girls audition for summer stock. Stephie makes the final audition, but Jenny does not. The two decide together that, make it or not, they will always be lucky people because they'll always be dancers.

Afraid she is not one of the "gutsy few," living only to please her ballet teacher and emulate her best friend, Stephie begins to give up on herself and her talent. A successful performance, a frank discussion with her teacher, and Jenny's constant support help her regain her confidence. The book clearly conveys the dedication and hard work necessary to become a dancer, has much to say about friendship, and should have great appeal.

Ages 10-12

Also available in:
No other form known

23

Ashley, Bernard

A Kind of Wild Justice

Black/white illustrations by Charles Keeping.
S. G. Phillips, Inc., 1979.
(182 pages)

FEAR: of Physical Harm
REVENGE
Belonging
Inferiority, feelings of
Parental: negligence
School: achievement/underachievement
School: pupil-teacher relationships
Security/Insecurity
Trust/Distrust
Violence

Ronnie Webster, an English teenager, lives in fear. Four years earlier, he overheard the Bradshaw brothers, gang leaders for whom Ronnie's father, Steve, does odd jobs, threaten to break Ronnie's back if Steve ever disclosed any of their illegal activities. Since then, Ronnie's fear has become all-consuming. Any day, he feels sure, his drunkard father will betray the Bradshaws and then they will come after him. The boy makes no friends, cannot concentrate in school, and is a nonreader in a special class. He goes directly home from school each day, always watching over his shoulder for the thugs he expects to be following him. His mother, Val, cares little for anyone but herself; she offers no protection. Now the Bradshaws want Steve, a former race car driver, to drive their loot away after a robbery at the football stadium. The plan: Steve, with Ronnie in tow, will drive to the stadium in a stolen car provided by the Bradshaws. They will park under a specified window from which the money bags containing stolen entry fees will be dropped through the open top of the car. All goes well. Speeding out of the parking lot Steve follows the predetermined path, parks the car with the loot inside, and then makes a run for it with Ronnie. But as they flee Ronnie spots Manjit Mirzar, the Indian girl from his special reading class, looking right at him from a window across the way. The next day, Officer Kingsland arrests Steve: one of Ronnie's reading flash cards was found in the abandoned car. Ronnie suspects Manjit of planting the card and threatens her the next day about keeping her mouth shut, emphasizing those threats with kicks. The girl does not understand, but she is frequently mistreated by whites and has come to expect abuse. Later, Ronnie finds out from Charlie Whitelaw, the school bus driver, that his mother, who abandoned him after Steve was arrested, is now living with Bernie Bradshaw. Ronnie realizes then that his mother planted the reading card in the car to get rid of Steve. The kindly Charlie offers to help Ronnie, and the boy finally turns to the older man and his wife, finding with them a sense of security and belonging he has never had. But the security soon ends. Charlie too is being intimidated by the Bradshaws, forced to use his bus in a plan to smuggle Indians from France into England. He is to drive a group of senior citizens on a weekend tour of Paris; at a designated time during their return trip, he is to pick up the Indians and bring them along to England. Ronnie overhears the plan discussed and becomes convinced, wrongly, that Charlie is a willing participant. Having nowhere to turn, he goes to the police. Officer Kingsland urges Ronnie to return to the Whitelaws so he doesn't arouse anyone's suspicion. Upon returning, Ronnie realizes that the Whitelaws are being victimized just as he is. He also discovers that the smuggling has something to do with Manjit's family. Now Ronnie is determined to get his revenge by beating the Bradshaws at their own game. Forced to go along on Charlie's bus when the Bradshaws discover he knows of the smuggling operation (Roy Bradshaw is also along as "tour guide"), Ronnie runs from the bus during the return trip, just before they are to pick up the Indians. The passengers refuse to continue until the boy is found, the bus is delayed, and the plot is foiled. When he knows time is up, Ronnie gets the assistance of the French police, who see that the Bradshaws are turned over to the British authorities. Since the Indians were not picked up, Charlie escapes arrest, but Ronnie provides Kingsland with the evidence needed to arrest the Bradshaws: the inspector has told Ronnie that during the robbery, one of the stadium officials had managed to spray a gang member with a permanent purple dye. Ronnie noticed on the bus trip that Roy Bradshaw had purple dye on the skin under his watchband. Ronnie gets his revenge and still manages to protect his friend Charlie. His brave action wins him the respect of the neighborhood; more important, it gives him a sense of self-respect. Manjit's sadness is one discordant note: her father was to have been smuggled into the country that night. Still, as one of the officers says, "They call revenge a kind of wild justice."

A young man overcomes the paralyzing power of fear and learns to act, saving himself and other victims of terror in the process. Ronnie goes from trusting no one, least of all himself, to learning where trust can safely be placed. Suspenseful, action-packed, filled with well-drawn characters, containing some street language, this is a powerful book for the better reader. Premeditated violence runs through the plot, but it is never condoned.

Ages 12 and up

Also available in:
No other form known

24

Ashley, Bernard

Terry on the Fence

Black/white illustrations by Charles Keeping.
S. G. Phillips, Inc., 1977.
(196 pages)

DELINQUENCY, JUVENILE
STEALING
VALUES/VALUING: Moral/Ethical
Aggression: active
Gangs: being bothered by

When Terry Harmer, just eleven, stalks out of his London home, furious at his mother's and sister's unfairness, he has no idea what the next forty-eight hours will bring. Seeking shelter from a storm, Terry is accosted by a gang of boys, runs, falls, is captured and threatened with a knife by the leader, Les, fifteen, who needs a guide through Terry's school to burglarize it. At the gang's hideout, Terry, exhausted and in pain from his fall, hopelessly consents. Once inside the school, the gang is interrupted by the caretaker and leaves with only two radios. From the caretaker's description, the headmaster links Terry to the gang and tells the boy's family. Terry turns one radio over to the police, finds Les, and goes with him to a "fence" to get the other back. Found there, the two are taken to juvenile court. Les admits his guilt, despite Terry's momentary attempt to protect him, and is sent to a community home. Aware that Terry was forced into the burglary, the judge requires him to explain his protectiveness toward Les. Terry has seen the huge scar Les bears on his neck, evidence of his mother's furious temper, and sees Les himself as someone whose life has been too hard to handle properly. Though reluctant to disclose the details of Les's hardships in court, he finally explains to the judge that he had tried to protect the boy because, out of the arresting officer's sight Les had been "scratching his bad neck . . . till he made it bleed . . . he was just looking at me, asking me not to tell, and trying to smile." Hearing this, the judge discharges Terry unconditionally.

This is a frank, realistic portrayal of a boy caught in a situation he cannot cope with physically or morally. The descriptions of Les's gang terrorizing Terry and the appalling account of parental brutality and emotional aridity in Les's home are so clear they may upset some readers. Terry's family and home life are genial by comparison. Les's background is apparently responsible for his anti-social behavior, but the book does not settle this point. The British idiom and slang may make the book difficult reading here and there.

Ages 12 and up

Also available in:
No other form known

25

Bargar, Gary W.

What Happened to Mr. Forster?

Clarion Books, 1981.
(169 pages) o.p.

SCHOOL: Pupil-Teacher Relationships
Homosexuality: male
Maturation
Prejudice: sexual
School: classmate relationships
Self, attitude toward: feeling different

B

It's the fall of 1958, sixth grade is starting, and Louis Lamb vows things will be different this year. This year he'll no longer be an outsider and no one will call him "Billy Lou." The first day of school, two things happen: Louis has a new teacher, Mr. Forster, whom he quickly admires and respects, and he is befriended by a new boy, Paul Harte. Mr. Forster encourages Louis in his creative writing and even gives him a special book to use as his journal. He also coaches Louis in softball, privately, after school. Throughout the fall, Louis feels better and better about himself. His classmates seem to accept him more, even respect him, and his friendship with Paul grows. Then at the school Open House, after a man arrives to drive Mr. Forster home, Louis overhears several parents quietly talking about his teacher. When they notice several students listening, one asks if Mr. Forster is married. The last day before Christmas vacation, Louis's class puts on a play. The whole class is invited to that evening's cast party—except for Ellie Siegel, whom no one likes. Mrs. Siegel appears at the party with Ellie in tow, accusing Mr. Forster of persecuting her daughter, blaming him for Ellie's exclusion from the party. The teacher had known nothing of this slight. She also informs Mr. Forster that she knows about him and that he won't be a teacher much longer. Confused, Louis worries all through the vacation. School resumes on a Monday with mothers attending and observing. All treat Mr. Forster coolly, if not rudely. By the following Monday, Mr. Forster is gone. At recess a classmate informs everyone that their teacher was "a queer." Heartbroken, Louis leaves school and runs home. Aunt Zona, with whom he lives, tries to explain that Mr. Forster is not fit to be around young people. Not satisfied and very upset, Louis goes to Mr. Forster's house. Once there, they talk—after Mr. Forster insists on calling Aunt Zona to tell her where Louis is. She says she will come to get him immediately. Before she arrives, Mr. Forster explains to the boy that he is homosexual, that there are many ways of loving and this is his way. Louis tells Mr. Forster he needs him to be his teacher. Mr. Forster assures him he will do fine on his own with the new teacher. On Wednesday, Louis returns to class and resolves to make something out of all that has happened. With that, he opens his journal, so far untouched, and begins to write.

This sensitive story, told by Louis, revolves around the boy's changing relationships with his classmates and, particularly, with Mr. Forster. Unpopular and sheltered, Louis gains self-confidence through the gentle encouragement of his teacher. He is devastated by Mr. Forster's persecution and removal. The homosexuality issue is handled nonjudgmentally: Mr. Forster says he'll "wait and let God come to his own decision about my eternal destiny." Several other adult characters seem exaggerated, perhaps because they are viewed through a child's eyes. Overall, this is a realistic, sometimes humorous portrayal of classroom situations and classmate relationships. The issues it raises are timeless and could stimulate discussion.

Ages 10-13

Also available in:
No other form known

26

Barrett, John M.

Daniel Discovers Daniel

Color illustrations by Joe Servello.
Human Sciences Press, 1980.
(32 pages counted)

IDENTITY, SEARCH FOR
Family: relationships
Inferiority, feelings of
Jealousy: sibling
Rejection: parental
Self, attitude toward: feeling different

Nine-year-old Daniel, a reader and stamp collector, is sure that his father prefers his younger brother, Peter, to him. His mother helps him see that Peter and his father have one thing in common: they both love sports. So Daniel decides to take an interest in athletics. When he asks his father to play basketball with him, however, it becomes painfully clear that Daniel can't dribble, aim, or shoot. Later, Daniel sits close to his father during a football game on television; his father asks him to move a little so they can both see and be comfortable. Discouraged, Daniel gets on his bike and soon finds himself in front of his teacher's house. Mr. Johnson is washing his car, and he invites Daniel to help in exchange for a glass of cider. Mr. Johnson tells Daniel how proud he is of him in class. Overcome, Daniel blurts out through his tears that his father hates him. He tells his teacher how his father favors Peter. Mr. Johnson suggests he ask his father for help sometimes. Daniel replies that when he asks for help his father is always busy. He's sure his father would help him with schoolwork, but he never needs help. To cheer him up, Mr. Johnson tells Daniel that he has won the part of Captain Hook in the class play, Peter Pan. He suggests that Daniel ask his father to help him learn his part. Elated, Daniel rides home, beginning to realize that even if he "stinks" at sports he is smart and funny and a lot of people like him. Not only does his father agree to help him learn his part, he also helps plan Daniel's costume—which he'll help to make—and tells Daniel he's proud of him. When he asks Daniel to join Peter and him in a game of football, Daniel declines happily and heads for the library for books about Peter Pan. He feels just fine about himself.

Filled with doubts, his self-esteem low, Daniel longs for his father to love him as he loves Peter, his younger brother, although Daniel will never be sportsminded or athletic. A sympathetic teacher helps Daniel see what a talented, important person he is in his own right, and his new self-confidence is gladly shared by his proud father. The compassionate story is greatly enhanced by illustrations that superimpose what is actually happening in Daniel's life over sketches of what the boy imagines or hopes will happen. Readers will respond warmly to Daniel's happy discovery of his own individual worth.

Ages 7-9

Also available in:
No other form known

27

Barton, Byron

Where's Al?

Color illustrations by the author.
Houghton Mifflin Co., 1979.
(32 pages) o.p.

PETS: Responsibility for
Problem solving

Al, a puppy, chases a stick his master, a little boy, has thrown. The puppy gets lost. The young owner, upset at losing Al, cannot eat and has trouble going to sleep. The next day, the little boy posts a sign describing his lost dog. Then he begins to search for Al around a busy intersection. Concentrating on his task, the boy does not notice that Al is always "one step ahead of him."

In this short story, a young child solves an important problem through his own efforts. The book uses a minimum of words, relying heavily on pictures to tell the story.

Ages 3-7

Also available in:
No other form known

28

Bate, Lucy

Little Rabbit's Loose Tooth

Color illustrations by Diane de Groat.
Crown Publishers, Inc., 1975.
(30 pages counted)

TOOTH, LOSS OF

Little Rabbit has a loose tooth. That makes it difficult to chew hard foods, like carrots, and so she follows her mother's advice to chew hard foods with her other teeth. But while she is eating chocolate ice cream, Little Rabbit's tooth falls out. What to do with it? She could throw it away, put it in a necklace, or mount it. Instead, she puts it under her pillow for the tooth fairy, in whom she does not believe. She asks her mother to leave a present if the tooth fairy does not. In the morning, Little Rabbit wakes to find the tooth gone and a dime in its place.

Small children will recognize the inconvenience of chewing food with a loose tooth, as well as the value of the tooth—as part of the body—to the child who loses it. The existence of the tooth fairy is neither confirmed nor denied. Large, detailed pictures make this a good book to read aloud.

Ages 4-6

Also available in:
Paperbound—*Little Rabbit's Loose Tooth*
Crown Publishers, Inc.

Talking Book—*Little Rabbit's Loose Tooth*
Library of Congress (NLSBPH)

29

Bates, Betty

Picking Up the Pieces

Pocket Books, Inc., 1984.
(157 pages, paperbound) o.p.

BOY-GIRL RELATIONSHIPS
Accidents: automobile
Age: respect for
Change: accepting
Friendship: meaning of
Love, meaning of
Peer relationships: peer pressures
School: classmate relationships

Ninth-graders Nell Beaumont and Dexter Mead are old friends with a "tame boy-girl relationship." Now that they're in their final year at Troyer Junior High, things are changing. Dexter, athletic and sportsminded, is being pursued by Lacey Dunn. When Nell sees that Dexter is enjoying Lacey's attention, she gives up her relationship with him. Upset, Nell finds she can confide her feelings only to her best friend, Bonnie, and her Great-Uncle Charlie. Dexter begins associating with Lacey and four other classmates, and Nell hears about their drinking and troublemaking. Several months later, Bonnie and Nell celebrate Bonnie's birthday with a big cookout at the river. To Nell's dismay, she sees Dexter and his drunken friends in another area of the park. At the school dance the night before graduation, Dexter and Lacey are drunk and rowdy, and they and their four friends are asked to leave. Several hours later the six are involved in a serious automobile accident. At graduation, the principal announces that Dexter and one other boy are still hospitalized. Nell also hears that Dexter's leg has been permanently injured; he will limp. As the weeks go by, Nell learns that Dexter's new friends have dropped him and that he is deeply depressed. Several friends and Uncle Charlie persuade her to go see him. She is frightened, but when she notices that Dexter is surprised and happy to see her, she's glad she came. By the end of the summer Uncle Charlie, who has had a heart attack, has decided to move to Florida to live with Nell's grandparents. Dexter, on crutches, is coming home from the hospital. Nell and her friends plan a welcome-home party for Dexter, and Nell gives him Uncle Charlie's golf clubs because she knows golf is something he will be able to do. Dexter disparages his ability to play and then ignores Nell for the remainder of the party. Several days later, he calls her to apologize for his behavior, asking her to walk to school with him. So the next day they walk to high school—together again.

Nell's first-person narrative reflects many relationships in her life but focuses on the development of her love for Dexter. This special relationship survives the boy's wild phase, his accident, and his permanent injury. At the end, the reader feels that the bond between Dexter and Nell has been strengthened. Also important is Nell's love and care for her aging great-uncle. Believable character development and authentic plot details enhance the story.

Ages 10-13

Also available in:
No other form known

30

Bauer, Marion Dane

Shelter from the Wind

Clarion Books, 1979.
(108 pages)

RUNNING AWAY
Maturation

Twelve-year-old Stacy is running away—from her father's remarriage and her unsympathetic stepmother—so suddenly that she has taken nothing with her. Now, after hours in the Oklahoma sun and wind, she realizes how foolish her action has been, but is too stubborn to turn back. She wants her father to regret the remarriage and the baby that will soon be born. As night comes to the high panhandle country, Stacy—cold, hungry, and thirsty—crouches beneath a tree to sleep. When she awakens, she is befriended by a pair of white German shepherds. The dogs lead her to a small sandstone house, where Ella, a spunky old lady, gives Stacy food and water and listens to her story. Ella scolds her for being so foolish, but allows her to stay until she can make plans. During the next few days, Ella recounts to Stacy episodes from her own life. Stacy, in turn, confides in her all the anger and resentment she feels for her stepmother and the coming baby. As Stacy comes to know Ella, she begins to see her own life in the perspective of another's. When the female dog bears puppies, Stacy helps save a puppy's life, but later, to her horror, must drown it because it has a cleft palate. Meanwhile, Ella falls and badly twists her ankle, and Stacy walks to a neighbor for help. When Ella is taken to town to see a doctor, Stacy goes too, for she has decided, "I'd best go home." She will return to visit Ella, though, and pick out one of the puppies for her own.

This is a story about a girl who runs away and the wise old woman who helps her better understand herself and the "way it is." The story's ending implies that Stacy returns home with no easy answers, but that her time with Ella, both past and to come, will help her deal with the future.

Ages 10-13

Also available in:
Talking Book—*Shelter from the Wind*
Library of Congress (NLSBPH)

31

Bawden, Nina Mary Kark

Squib

Lothrop, Lee & Shepard Books, 1982.
(143 pages)

FANTASY FORMATION
Death: of father
Death: of sibling
Guilt, feelings of
Loneliness

Kate Pollack, who is nearly twelve years old, lives with her mother in a large, lonely house. Some years earlier, Kate's little brother Rupert and her father drowned. Kate's life was saved by her father, but Mr. Pollack couldn't save himself or Rupert from the outgoing tide. Kate feels guilty about surviving, and she is lonely. Kate frequents a nearby park with her friend Robin, his little brother Sammy, and his sister Prue. At the park, the four youngsters see a strange, frail, shy little boy called Squib. Several stories are told about Squib by Prue and Sammy. They claim his parents are dead and that he lives with his auntie, who is a wicked witch. She allegedly ties the boy up and does not like him to play with other children. Kate begins to fantasize about Squib. She soon convinces herself that he is her little brother who has somehow survived. Robin has his own fantasies about Squib. He thinks Squib has been kidnapped and is being held for ransom. Although these fantasies are not true, a mystery does surround Squib. The four children follow the strange boy to his home, a squalid old trailer. They discover that Squib is mistreated by his guardian. The children report this to their elders, and Squib is removed legally from the care of his guardian. Kate is forced to accept her young brother's death and the reality of Squib's identity.

The interesting mixture of mystery and suspense with fantasy develops into a sensitive account of a lonely child unable to face the reality of death. The gradual development of the plot and the eventual resolution of Kate's problems are realistic and believable.

Ages 10-13

Also available in:
Braille—*Squib*
Library of Congress (NLSBPH)

Talking Book—*Squib*
Library of Congress (NLSBPH)

32

Beckman, Gunnel

Mia Alone

Translated from the Swedish by Joan Tate.
Dell Publishing Company, Inc., 1978.
(112 pages, paperbound) o.p.

ABORTION
UNWED MOTHER
Anxiety
Decision making
Separation, marital
Sex: premarital

Seventeen-year-old Mia Jareberg fears she is pregnant. She would like to confide in someone, seek advice, but from whom? Her parents are quarreling, and Mia doesn't want to worry her boyfriend, Jan, until she knows for sure. She has tried to avoid Jan, but when he unexpectedly drops by one morning, she feels compelled to explain what is wrong. Jan is very kind and tells her he would like to marry her, but suggests they make no decision until after she knows the result of her pregnancy test. For Mia the next few days are turmoil. While she waits to know the results of the test, which has to be done twice, she tries to decide the best course if she is in fact pregnant. She spends an evening with her father, and the two share their innermost concerns. He tells her that he and her mother are going to live apart for a while; Mia will stay with him, and her sister will go with her mother. Mia confesses her suspicion of pregnancy, and he tries to help her decide for herself what is morally and psychologically best if she is proved right. Later that night, Mia gets her period. She is relieved but too exhausted to be joyful. When she tells Jan, he seems glad to have gotten off so easily. She cannot understand her own confusion and loneliness, but her father reassures her that when one has been through so difficult an experience, such a reaction is normal.

Mental anguish over her supposed pregnancy is about as far as unmarried Mia gets in trying to make the best decision for herself, her boyfriend, and the unborn child. She knows that her parents married because her mother was pregnant with *her,* and Mia does not want to marry before she is ready. Confiding in her father brings some clarity. In the end, not pregnant after all, she realizes that though she is relieved, "the relief seemed to have cost her so much." She will never again be naive. This serious, thought-provoking book is not for the reader who needs things lightened with humor; its central predicament, its characters, and its dialogue are always convincing. The author makes no judgment of Mia, and neither does her father.

Ages 12 and up

Also available in:
Cassette—*Mia Alone*
Library of Congress (NLSBPH)

33

Bennett, Jack

The Voyage of the Lucky Dragon

Prentice-Hall, Inc., 1981.
(149 pages) o.p.

COURAGE, MEANING OF
REFUGEES
Change: accepting
Family: unity
Fear: of physical harm
Freedom, meaning of
Resourcefulness
Vietnam
War

At fourteen, Quan Thi Chi and his younger sister, Ly, know only war. When the Americans withdraw from Saigon and then from all of Vietnam, Quan hopes he and his family will finally know peace. Unfortunately, North Vietnamese officials soon move into Saigon, now called Ho Chi Minh City, and soon Quan is afraid again. He and Ly are ridiculed at school for having a "capitalist" father; the man ekes out a living in a tiny store. Knowing that families are being split up and forced to move into labor camps, the children's terrified father, Phan, writes to his father in Rach Gia on the Gulf of Siam, asking to take the family there to work on the old man's boat. Then officials tell Phan that his shop is now owned by the government and the whole family will be relocated. They begin planning to leave for Rach Cia, even though Phan's father's response hasn't come. But soon the response arrives: the government has confiscated the old man's boat. Quan suggests the family go to Rach Cia anyway, steal the boat back, and escape to Malaysia. The idea terrifies Phan, but several days later the family sneaks out of Saigon in pairs. Quan leaves with Uncle Tan. The housekeeper, elderly Ah Soong, goes off with Aunt Binh, whose home has been destroyed and her husband and daughter killed. She is depressed, withdrawn, virtually unable to take care of herself. Phan, his wife, Xuyen, and Ly leave later, and all meet in Rach Cia. Phan's father has died. Quan devises a plan to get back the boat, *Lucky Dragon.* That night he and his father climb under the pier, steal the boat, and pick up the rest of the family waiting on a sandbar. The tide floats them out into the Gulf. Early the next morning, to their horror, a figure rises up out of the fish-hold: Captain Cu, who works on the boat and had slept in the hold all night. He agrees to flee with them. Several days later they reach Malaysian shores, only to be refused entry. The naval boat does give the family rice and fuel. They try again, are again refused, and then are towed to the island of Bidong where the United Nations is helping to relocate refugees. But they see that Bidong is a "seething garbage dump of unwanted people." Bitterly disappointed, they cut the towline and head out to sea. Quan suggests they go on to Australia. As the trip becomes more and more perilous, Aunt Binh reveals an almost uncanny ability to work with the others, at times as their leader. Phan, on the other hand, blaming himself for the family's plight, sinks deeper into depression. They manage to survive Thai pirates and a typhoon, but are then out of food and increasingly weakened. By now the engine pump is broken, and the family takes turns bailing water. When they finally reach Indonesia, they are again turned away. Eventually Phan is reduced to madness, and Xuyen tells Quan he must take over as head of the family. Several days after Phan dies, the exhausted, starving Ah Soong jumps overboard, after giving Quan her life savings. They spot land, and the family frantically bails as fast as possible. The *Lucky Dragon* breaks apart; the survivors cling to a makeshift raft as they swim for shore. Utterly exhausted, they crawl to the beach and sleep. The next morning Quan, his family, and Captain Cu are discovered by men in a Land Rover. Their new life in Australia begins.

Centering on the character of young Quan, who never loses hope, this is a memorable, unsentimental account of a courageous pursuit of freedom. It is also a study of various people's reactions to tremendous stress. Exciting, tense, and filled with action, the story brings to dramatic life the plight of war refugees and the strength to be found in unshakeable family loyalty.

Ages 11 and up

Also available in:
No other form known

34

Benson, Kathleen

Joseph on the Subway Trains

Black/white illustrations by Emily Arnold McCully.
Addison-Wesley Publishing Company, Inc., 1981.
(45 pages counted) o.p.

LOST, BEING

Joseph's second-grade class is taking a subway trip from Brooklyn to a museum in Manhattan, and Joseph is very excited. As the class stands on the platform with their teacher, Joseph notices a mouse between the tracks. Walking beside a waiting train to follow the mouse, Joseph is suddenly carried along with the rush of people boarding and finds himself on the subway. As the train leaves the station, he sees with dismay that his class is still on the platform and the train is moving away from them. Joseph shouts that he is not supposed to be on this train, but everyone ignores him. When the train stops, Joseph is carried by the crowd onto the platform. He asks how to get back to Brooklyn. Finally, a man tells him to get on the train to his right. Joseph obeys, but soon finds he is on a train going to Manhattan. He gets off at the next stop and wonders what to do. He has no money and no lunch. Two boys, Billy and Fatso, approach him. Joseph confesses he got the trains mixed up and wants to get back to Brooklyn. Billy says he will help, but first Joseph has to play a game. Billy and Fatso stand between two cars of a moving train, one foot on the ledge of one car, one foot on the other car. Fearfully, Joseph does the same, but he jumps off when the train stops. He finally admits to himself that he is lost and needs help. He tells a man in a token booth what has happened. The man calls the Transit Police. Soon a patrolman comes and tells Joseph that people are looking for him. Joseph and the patrolman leave the underground subway system and prepare to go back to Brooklyn.

An excited, curious little boy gets swept onto a New York subway train without the rest of his class. There's just enough suspense in this easy reader to maintain interest, and full-page illustrations help readers and listeners identify with Joseph's plight.

Ages 7-9

Also available in:
No other form known

35

Beskow, Elsa Maartman

Pelle's New Suit

Translated from the Swedish by Marion Letcher Woodburn.
Color illustrations by the author.
HarperCollins Publishers, Inc., 1929.
(15 pages counted)

COOPERATION: in Work
Resourcefulness

Pelle, a little Swedish boy, owns a lamb. As the two grow older, Pelle's suit seems to grow shorter while the lamb's coat grows longer. Pelle shears the wool from his lamb and takes it to his grandmother. She cards the wool as a favor for Pelle. In return, he pulls the weeds in her garden. He brings the carded wool to his other grandmother and tends her cows while she spins the wool into yarn. Pelle also runs an errand for a painter to earn money, cares for his baby sister while his mother weaves the cloth, and rakes hay and feeds pigs for the tailor who sews the suit. Thus, Pelle works for others while they in turn help make his new suit.

Without moralizing, this children's classic shows the value of resoucefulness and willingness to work in order to accomplish a goal.

Ages 4-7

Also available in:
Braille—*Pelle's New Suit*
Library of Congress (NLSBPH)

36

Blaine, Margery Kay

The Terrible Thing That Happened at Our House

Color illustrations by John C. Wallner.
Four Winds Press, 1980.
(40 pages)

PARENT/PARENTS: Mother Working Outside Home
Change: accepting
Communication: parent-child
Cooperation: in work
Lifestyle: change in

A young school-age girl and her little brother are happy with their mother, who is a "real" mother. She kisses them good-bye in the morning when they leave for school and fixes them toasted cheese sandwiches or tuna on a bun when they come home for lunch, and after school she listens to them talk about the day's happenings. Then she fixes them a snack and thinks up wonderful things to do. But all this changes when the mother returns to work as a science teacher. Now the children have to rush in the morning to get to school on time; they eat lunch at school; and after school their mother may be too busy with school work to talk to them. They also notice a change in their father. No longer a "real" father, now he fixes dinner and does household chores. He has no time anymore to sit and talk to the children. One night at dinner the little girl gets angry because no one is listening to her. She yells that nobody cares about anything or anyone and that since their mother has returned to work everything has changed. The whole family begins to talk about how things have changed and how to handle the changes. Soon parents and children are sharing the family workload, but are able to set aside some time every day to spend together.

The parents in this story fail to prepare their children for the changes that come about when the mother returns to work. It takes the anger and bewilderment of the young girl, who tells the story in the first person, to show the parents the difference between what they are doing and what the children have been used to. The advantages of full, frank discussion are shown. For all its humor, this book sets forth a thoroughly believable situation.

Ages 3-7

Also available in:
No other form known

37

Blume, Judy Sussman

Are You There God? It's Me, Margaret

Bradbury Press, 1970.
(149 pages)

RELIGIONS: Choice of
Decision making
Marriage: interreligious
Menstruation
School: transfer

Eleven-year-old Margaret and her parents have moved from New York City to a suburb in New Jersey to be farther away from Margaret's interfering grandmother. Margaret makes friends quickly at her new school and forms a secret club with three other girls whose main concerns are menstrual periods and boys. Although Margaret and her mixed-faith parents do not attend any church, Margaret talks to God in her own way. When Margaret needs a school project, she decides to investigate different religions. Grandma, who is Jewish, is delighted when Margaret asks to go to the Jewish temple. Margaret also attends several Christian churches with her girlfriends. She continues to talk to God about her troubles in her own way until her Christian maternal grandparents come to visit and start an argument about her religious views. This upsets Margaret, and she announces that she does not want or need either religion or God. In her school report, she concludes that she has not enjoyed her religious experiences and wants her own children to be assigned a religion from birth so that they will not have to decide for themselves. When Margaret experiences her first menstrual period, she feels so overwhelmed that she begins to talk to God again.

In this warm and sometimes humorous first-person narrative, Margaret is depicted as an intelligent and sincere individual. The four girls' concerns about their developing bodies are presented frankly and realistically.

Ages 10-13

Also available in:
Braille—*Are You There God? It's Me, Margaret*
Library of Congress (NLSBPH)

Talking Book—*Are You There God? It's Me, Margaret*
Library of Congress (NLSBPH)

38

Blume, Judy Sussman

Deenie

Bradbury Press, 1973.
(159 pages)

BRACES ON BODY/LIMBS
Appearance: concern about
Doctor, going to
Masturbation
Peer relationships

Twelve-year-old Deenie Fenner shows more interest in teen-age activities and peer relationships than in the modeling career her mother is determined she must pursue. But when Deenie's doctor explains that Deenie has a curvature of the spine and will have to wear a back brace for four years, both mother and daughter panic. The importance of beauty has always been emphasized to Deenie, and she feels uneasy around handicapped people. Often they seem repulsive to her. Deenie has a difficult time adjusting to the brace. She tries to camouflage it but does not succeed. In a fit of self-pity, she chops off her long hair. Eventually, Deenie begins to adjust. When her boyfriend urges her to remove the brace, Deenie shows acceptance of her situation by firmly replying, "No . . . I have to wear it all the time."

This first-person narrative deals candidly with friendship, jealousy, imitation, and boy-girl relationships. It convincingly details the steps preceding the actual wearing of the brace—making a plaster body cast, forming the brace from the cast, fitting the brace, and using a special body stocking to prevent irritation by the brace. This description will be of great value to anyone who faces a similar situation. A frank discussion of masturbation is also included.

Ages 10-12

Also available in:
Braille—*Deenie*
Library of Congress (NLSBPH)

Talking Book—*Deenie*
Library of Congress (NLSBPH)

39

Blume, Judy Sussman

Freckle Juice

Black/white illustrations by Sonia O. Lisker.
Four Winds Press, 1985.
(40 pages)

FRECKLES
Identification with others: peers
Imitation

Andrew, about ten years old, wants some freckles on his face like his friend Nicky. Andrew is so desperate that he spends fifty hard-earned cents to buy a secret freckle recipe from Sharon, a girl he does not like.

When he assembles the ingredients, the mixture looks and tastes horrible. Andrew's stomach soon feels horrible too. His mother gives him some medicine and has him stay home from school the next day. Still determined to have freckles, Andrew paints some on his face before he goes back to school. When the teacher sees his "freckles," she sends him to the boys' room with a secret freckle-remover formula which he is to use on his face. When Andrew returns to the classroom his "freckles" are gone. Nicky now wants to use the formula too, confessing that he hates his own freckles. The teacher points out that Nicky looks wonderful with freckles, just as Andrew does without them.

This story humorously emphasizes children's need to imitate and identify with their peers. The relationships between the students and their teacher are not developed in great depth, but the normal reactions of children are captured.

Ages 8-11

Also available in:
Braille—*Freckle Juice*
Library of Congress (NLSBPH)

Cassette—*Freckle Juice*
Library of Congress (NLSBPH)

40

Blume, Judy Sussman

Iggie's House

Bradbury Press, 1970.
(117 pages)

PREJUDICE: Ethnic/Racial
Communication: parent-child
Friendship: making friends

Winnie Barringer, who is in sixth grade, is sad because her best friend, Iggie, has moved away. But when the Garber family moves into Iggie's house, Winnie becomes excited. The Garbers are the first black family to move into the neighborhood, and Winnie is determined to make friends with them. Winnie's parents do not seem to be as interested in the new neighbors as she is; Winnie senses that her mother is rather unhappy with having "colored people on Grove street." The Garber children—Glenn, who is Winnie's age, Herbie, a year younger, and Tina, who is eight years old—seem to enjoy Winnie's company. But problems soon arise when Mrs. Landon, a neighbor who does not desire a racially integrated neighborhood, circulates a petition to inform the Garbers that they are not wanted. She also plants a sign on the Garber's lawn stating, "We don't want your kind around here." Winnie, who has been visiting with the Garber children, becomes so disconcerted that she runs home. Herbie, who is also upset, becomes ill. The next day, he expresses his bitterness by accusing Winnie of being a patronizing person. Winnie then charges Herbie with being prejudiced toward white people, and the argument is stopped only when Glenn steps in and explains Herbie's feelings of being used by whites. To further complicate matters, Mrs. Landon calls on the Barringers to tell them that her family is selling their house. She says that the Barringers would also be wise to put their house on the market while there is still time to receive a good price. Hearing this remark, Mr. Barringer explodes and shouts that no one will pressure him into selling his home. Winnie is proud of her father, but when she talks to her parents the next evening, she realizes that the real reason they are not moving is because "moving is just too much trouble," and staying (without associating with the Garbers) is "the easy way out."

This realistic story illustrates the emotions a young girl experiences when she encounters racial prejudice for the first time. To add to her confusion, her parents refuse, or are unable, to state their opinions about such prejudice. The emotional strain and bitterness such prejudice may foster is also described.

Ages 10 and up

Also available in:
Braille—*Iggie's House*
Library of Congress (NLSBPH)

Cassette—*Iggie's House*
Library of Congress (NLSBPH)

41

Blume, Judy Sussman

It's Not the End of the World

Bradbury Press, 1972.
(169 pages)

SEPARATION, MARITAL
Anxiety
Communication: parent-child
Hope
Running away

Eleven-year-old Karen feels that no one loves her. Her parents fight constantly; her fourteen-year-old brother Jeff is moody; and her six-year-old sister Amy is too young to understand Karen's feelings. When their father fails to come home one evening, the children are not told why. When their mother finally informs them that she and their father have decided to separate, Karen feels confused, frightened, and ashamed. Keeping a promise to her grandfather, she tries hard to bring her parents back together, but to no avail. Only when Jeff runs away do her parents see each other again. Even then they fight, and Karen realizes they will never be reconciled. The children begin to accept the idea that there will be even more changes in their lives: their house must be sold, their mother must find a job, and they may have to move with their mother to another part of the country.

The parents in this story do not relate well to their children, nor do they make any effort to clear up their children's confusion concerning the separation. The feelings and behavioral reactions of all three youngsters are portrayed. The open ending of the story suggests that there is hope for happier days ahead.

Ages 10-12

Also available in:
Braille—*It's Not the End of the World*
Library of Congress (NLSBPH)

Cassette—*It's Not the End of the World*
Library of Congress (NLSBPH)

42

Blume, Judy Sussman

The One in the Middle Is the Green Kangaroo

Color illustrations by Amy Aitken.
Bradbury Press, 1981.
(39 pages)

SIBLING: Middle
Identity, search for
Success

Freddy Dissel, about seven, has two problems—his older brother, Mike, and his younger sister, Ellen. "He felt like the peanut butter part of a sandwich, squeezed between Mike and Ellen," like "a great big middle nothing." One day at school, Freddy hears about a school play and decides this could be his chance to distinguish himself. His teacher tells him the play is for fifth and sixth graders, but she will see if they have a part for a second grader. They do, it seems, have a special part, and Freddy goes to audition. He is asked to jump all around. Then he's told he will play the part of the Green Kangaroo and must speak in a loud voice. At dinner, a proud Freddy announces to his family that he will be the Green Kangaroo in the school play. For two weeks he practices his part at school and at home. The day of the play Freddy nervously puts on the Green Kangaroo costume. He realizes he "wasn't in the middle. He was all by himself up on the stage." So he resolves to do a great job. The play is funny, and Freddy likes it when the audience laughs. When it's over, the director gives him a special thanks for playing the part of the Green Kangaroo. Everyone applauds. Now, at home, Freddy is not as concerned about being the middle child. "He felt just great being Freddy Dissel."

The middle child in a family finds his individuality when he plays the Green Kangaroo in a school play. Freddy's triumph should have great appeal for other "middle children," and for younger, older, and only children also. A green kangaroo highlights the illustrations in this energetic, easy-to-read, believable tale.

Ages 7-9

Also available in:
Braille—*The One in the Middle Is the Green Kangaroo*
Library of Congress (NLSBPH)

Cassette—*The One in the Middle Is the Green Kangaroo*
Library of Congress (NLSBPH)

43

Blume, Judy Sussman

Otherwise Known as Sheila the Great

Dutton Children's Books, 1972.
(118 pages)

FEAR
Boasting
Honesty/Dishonesty

Although she won't admit it, ten-year-old Sheila is afraid of dogs, water, strange noises, and imaginary creatures. Her thirteen-year-old sister Libby calls her a baby, but her parents try to understand her feelings. The family spends the summer in a small town at the home of a professor and his family who have gone to Europe for several months. Sheila is unhappy with this arrangement (she wanted to go to Disneyland) and is very upset when she discovers that a small dog lives at the house. Her parents insist that she learn to swim, and they enroll her in lessons at a pool. Sheila meets Mouse, a practical girl who is unimpressed by Sheila's constant boasting, lying, and other attempts to conceal her fears. Nevertheless, the girls become good friends, and Mouse helps Sheila see that trying to cover up her fears is ridiculous. When Sheila finally admits her fear of water, she finds it possible to learn to swim. She has started to control her fears. When it is time to return to the city, Sheila is reluctant to go. She even regrets leaving the dog.

The girl in this light, often humorous first-person narrative tries to conceal her fears by bragging and lying. She is not able to overcome her fears until she freely admits them. The parents are portrayed as understanding and helpful.

Ages 9-11

Also available in:
Braille—*Otherwise Known as Sheila the Great*
Library of Congress (NLSBPH)

Cassette—*Otherwise Known as Sheila the Great*
Library of Congress (NLSBPH)

44

Blume, Judy Sussman

Superfudge

Dutton Children's Books, 1980.
(166 pages)

FAMILY: Relationships
Change: new home
Friendship: making friends
Sibling: new baby
Sibling: relationships

Peter Hatcher, ten, feels he's adjusted very well to life with his pesky little brother, Fudge. Then his parents drop a bomb: his mother is going to have another baby. With that news Peter threatens to run away. Persuaded to stay, he agrees on the condition that he can leave if he doesn't like the baby. Five months later Tamara, called Tootsie, is born. To his surprise, Peter adjusts quite well; it's Fudge who wants to get rid of her. First he tries to sell her, then to give her away, and finally he offers to pay someone to take her. Then, once school is out, Peter must cope with more unsettling news. The family is moving from their apartment in New York City to a rented house in Princeton, New Jersey, where his father will take a year's leave to write a book. Disgusted, Peter wishes his parents would ask his opinion before making big decisions like having a baby or moving. Once in Princeton, Peter finds a friend in Alex Santo, a neighbor boy his age. Peter and Alex make extra money during the summer digging up and selling worms. When school starts, Fudge is allowed into kindergarten after being tested, although he's not yet five. The first day of school Peter is called out of class to help with Fudge, who is refusing to get off a high cabinet until his teacher calls him Fudge instead of his real name, Farley Drexel. This she refuses to do, so Fudge is transferred to the other kindergarten class, whose teacher is willing to call him Fudge. There Fudge does so well that his parents say he can have a pet. At Peter's suggestion he chooses a myna bird that he calls Uncle Feather. Fudge even makes a best friend in Princeton. At the end of the year, the family must make a choice—stay in Princeton or return to New York. They vote to return to New York. This time they've made the decision together.

Peter narrates this story of life in the Hatcher family, and all the adventures and misadventures ring true. The boy and his irrepressible little brother, Fudge, manage to adjust to a new baby and a move, but life is smoother when the whole family shares in a major decision. Written with a wonderful sense of family life and great humor, this would be especially fun to read aloud. It is a continuation of *Tales of a Fourth Grade Nothing.*

Ages 8-10

Also available in:
Braille—*Superfudge*
Library of Congress (NLSBPH)

Talking Book—*Superfudge*
Library of Congress (NLSBPH)

45

Blume, Judy Sussman

Tales of a Fourth Grade Nothing

Black/white illustrations by Roy Doty.
Dutton Children's Books, 1972.
(120 pages)

SIBLING: Oldest
SIBLING: Rivalry

At times, fourth-grader Peter Hatcher is convinced he must be a nothing because his two-and-a-half-year-old brother Fudge gets much attention while Peter hardly gets any. Peter must help with Fudge's birthday party. Fudge has a temper tantrum in the shoe store and makes a mess in the restaurant, causing everyone to notice him. When Peter's bedroom is invaded by Fudge, Peter's parents get a lock for his door. But even a lock does not stop Fudge from entering Peter's room and eating his pet turtle Dribble. The Hatchers understand how sad Peter feels about his turtle's death. They also come to realize that Peter has suffered other sadness and embarrassment because of Fudge's behavior. Peter's parents show consideration and understanding when they give him a puppy to replace Dribble.

It is easy for middle-graders to identify with Peter's difficulties with a little brother. Most incidents in the story are presented in a humorous way. Peter's parents seem overindulgent toward the younger child, yet there are moments when Peter's feelings are considered.

Ages 8-11

Also available in:
Braille—*Tales of a Fourth Grade Nothing*
Library of Congress (NLSBPH)

Talking Book—*Tales of a Fourth Grade Nothing*
Library of Congress (NLSBPH)

46

Blume, Judy Sussman

Then Again, Maybe I Won't

Bradbury Press, 1971.
(164 pages)

LIFESTYLE: Change in
MATURATION
Anxiety
Puberty
Sex: attitude toward
Wealth/Wealthy

In the summer shortly before his thirteenth birthday, Tony Miglione moves from Jersey City to Rosemont, a suburb on Long Island. Tony's father, formerly an electrician, has invented an important piece of electrical equipment and is now making a lot of money as a partner in an electrical company. In moving from Jersey City, Tony has left behind his paper route, his friends on the block, and his old lifestyle. All the kids around his plush new home are away at summer camp. When his next-door neighbor Joel returns from camp, Tony is not sure what he thinks about this new acquaintance. Tony's mother seems ready to accept everything Joel's mother does. While the two boys are in school together, Joel shows Tony pornographic books which he has carefully underlined. When Tony's friend from Jersey City comes to visit, Joel takes them both to his dad's bar, where they all get sick from drinking. Tony does not enjoy these activities. He worries about both his new lifestyle and his physical maturation. He has wet dreams and erections which he cannot control, and his anxieties result in a "nervous stomach." He likes to think about girls, and he even enjoys looking in Joel's sister's window while she is undressing. Tony is unhappy that his family's new maid has replaced Grandma in the kitchen—it had been the old woman's haven since the removal of her larynx left her speechless some time ago. Tony does not like seeing his mother hoodwinked into believing that Joel is a gentleman because he has fine manners, when all the while Tony knows that Joel is a shoplifter and does other things that upset him. Tony is also disappointed by the decision of his older brother, a teacher, to come to Rosemont to take a high-paying job with their father. His brother has been a dedicated teacher and knows nothing about electricity. With all these concerns, Tony's stomach pains grow worse and he finally ends up in the hospital. During his stay there, Tony's physician refers him to a psychiatrist who will help the boy understand, express, and cope more effectively with his thoughts and feelings.

The boy in this first-person narrative does not resolve his ambivalent feelings about urban versus suburban life, nor does he resolve his feelings about his own sexuality. But he does become more understanding of his body, his emotions, and his lifestyle. The natural dialogue adds zest to the story.

Ages 12 and up

Also available in:
Braille—*Then Again, Maybe I Won't*
Library of Congress (NLSBPH)

Talking Book—*Then Again, Maybe I Won't*
Library of Congress (NLSBPH)

47

Blume, Judy Sussman

Tiger Eyes

Bradbury Press, 1981.
(206 pages)

MOURNING, STAGES OF
Communication: parent-child
Death: of father
Friendship: meaning of
Guilt, feelings of
Maturation
Relatives: living in home of

After her father's funeral, fifteen-year-old Davey Wexler feels totally alone. She can't shake the memory of how her young father died after being shot by robbers in his Atlantic City store. Haunted, Davey begins keeping a bread knife under her pillow for protection. She gradually withdraws from other people, wishing she could stay home in bed with the blankets pulled over her head. School starts, and on the first and second days, Davey passes out. Her anxiety is causing her to hyperventilate, and her doctor advises a change for the whole family. Soon Davey, her mother, and her seven-year-old brother, Jason, go to stay with Walter and Elizabeth (Bitsy) Kronick, Davey's father's sister and her husband, in Los Alamos, New Mexico. After a week of sightseeing, Davey needs to be alone for a while. She rides a bike to a nearby canyon and decides to climb down. The beautiful landscape brings thoughts of the father she can never share it with, and she is overcome by grief. Suddenly she hears a voice and is confronted by a young hiker who calls himself Wolf. Davey tells Wolf her name is Tiger and begins to meet him daily at the same spot. Wolf asks no questions, and she appreciates that. Meanwhile, Davey's mother is put on medication for the headaches caused by her tension and depression. The medication leaves her listless and she begins delegating most of her parental responsibilities to the overprotective Kronicks, who have no children of their own. She also begins seeing a psychologist, Ms. Olnick. It is decided to enroll Davey and Jason in school in Los Alamos. Davey's anger and feelings of isolation increase with her continuing inability to talk with her mother about her father's death. When Davey volunteers as a candy striper at the hospital, she meets Willie Ortiz, who is dying of cancer. She learns that Willie is Wolf's father and that the boy has taken a semester off from college to be with the dying man. After Christmas Davey's mother improves enough to take a part-time job. But Davey's own situation worsens. Her mother begins dating a man Davey dislikes, her uncle won't let her take driver's education and the two have a running battle, Mr. Ortiz dies, and Wolf returns to college. Finally, in desperation, Davey agrees to see Ms. Olnick. Gradually able to confide in the psychologist, she tells of her fears that her mother is becoming as overprotective as her aunt and uncle. Later, she also describes the horrible night when her father died in her arms. As she leaves that memorable session, Davey realizes she had not mentioned the way her clothes had been covered with her father's blood. With sudden resolution, she hurries back to the Kronicks' house, takes a bag from her closet, and rides her bike to the canyon. There, under a pyramid of rocks, she buries the bloodstained clothes she has kept with her, resolving now to remember only the good times with her father. Two days later the mail brings Davey a tiger's-eye stone from Wolf. She and her mother go to a restaurant and finally share their grief, longing, and loss. They decide to return to Atlantic City once school is out. When they do go back home, Davey feels like a new person—not on the outside, but on the inside.

A teenage girl tells how she came to resolve her grief over her father's violent death. Details of the shocking event are revealed little by little until Davey is finally able to describe to a psychologist how she could not help her father and he died in her arms. This is a compelling, well-written story of a young girl's stages of grief and a family's efforts to cope with their sudden loss. Davey's believable narrative will capture the attention and sympathy of readers.

Ages 11 and up

Also available in:
Braille—*Tiger Eyes*
Library of Congress (NLSBPH)

Cassette—*Tiger Eyes*
Library of Congress (NLSBPH)

48

Bond, Felicia

Poinsettia & Her Family

Color illustrations by the author.
HarperCollins Publishers, Inc., 1981.
(32 pages)

FAMILY: Unity
Privacy, need for
Sibling: relationships

Poinsettia the pig, along with her parents and her six brothers and sisters, lives in a fine old house that she thinks perfect. One day she returns from the library and hurries excitedly to her favorite reading spot, the soft, red leather window seat. Unfortunately, that spot is occupied by one of her siblings, so Poinsettia hurries to the rock out front to read in peace. But she discovers piglets lying all around the rock. Next she tries the bathtub, but her sister Chick Pea is soaking. Poinsettia decides the house is not perfect after all; it is too crowded. She rebels against having no privacy, pinches and yells, and is sent to bed early for misbehaving. But the next day her father says they will all go look for a new and bigger house. Poinsettia hides and stays behind to read. She reads on the leather chair, on the rock, and in the bathtub. By nighttime it is snowing, and the family still has not returned. A lonely Poinsettia is afraid they will not come back, but just then they arrive. Now Poinsettia realizes her family is more important to her than the inconvenience of a crowded house.

In this colorfully illustrated story of a large family of pigs, Poinsettia's desire for privacy and more room is one many children share and most will sympathize with. After a day spent alone, however, Poinsettia realizes how important her family is to her. Crowded or not, the house is lonely without them.

Ages 4-7

Also available in:
Paperbound—*Poinsettia & Her Family*
HarperCollins Publishers, Inc.

49

Bond, Nancy Barbara

The Voyage Begun

Margaret K. McElderry Books, 1981.
(319 pages)

COOPERATION: in Work
MATURATION
NATURE: Living in Harmony with
Age: respect for
Change: accepting
Determination
Friendship: meaning of
Gangs: being bothered by
Helping

It is the not-too-distant future and Paul Vickers, sixteen, wanders along the coast of Cape Cod. The world is in an environmental crisis: food and energy are in very limited supply, due mainly to greed and pollution; the fishing industry has disappeared; most wildlife is gone. The abandoned summer communities on Cape Cod resemble ghost towns. Paul and his family have moved here, to the town of Warren, because his stern, unbending father has been appointed director of the local government research station. His luxury-loving mother complains continually about their hard life and deprivations. In the course of his wanderings along the shore, Paul finds an injured Canada goose in a trap. When he can't free it he goes for help to Maggie Rudd, a local conservationist. He and she slowly develop a friendship. Meanwhile, Mickey Cafferty, an eleven-year-old native of the area, spends her spare time scouting the shoreline for anything salvageable to add to her collection of bits and pieces. She meets Walter Jepson, an old man who also works at salvaging, when both find and want an old canvas raft that has washed ashore. Neither can move the raft alone and an uneasy, almost hostile relationship develops as they move the old raft to a building in the abandoned boatyard where Walter lives in a shack he's fixed up. Daily they work on the raft, and soon Mickey discovers why Walter is so secretive and suspicious. In that same building the old man is making a beautiful sailboat, an activity he has made the center of his life. Fearing people might destroy his creation, he swears Mickey to secrecy. But her brother, Shawn, suspicious about Mickey's daily disappearances, follows her to Walter's shack. Later, he and his gang, the Salvages, break into the shack while Walter is visiting a friend in a nursing home. The gang steals everything of value and sets fire to the place to cover their tracks. Mickey discovers the fire raging out of control and meets Paul as she is wandering disconsolately among the ruins. She is hostile and suspicious towards him but gradually, realizing she needs help restoring Walter's shack, comes to accept his assistance. Though they manage to make the shack livable again, Walter, now living in the nursing home himself, refuses to come back. The violence and the loss of his beloved boat have filled him with despair. Mickey, blaming herself for Walter's troubles, thinks that if she can retrieve the old man's tools and find a boat for him to restore, Walter will want to come back. So she and Paul break into the Salvages's hideout to take back Walter's tools. They are caught. Paul is beaten up and dumped on his parents' front lawn. Once he recovers, he arranges a meeting with Shawn and agrees not to press charges if Shawn will help him. Reluctantly Shawn agrees, returning the tools and soon locating an old, abandoned boat at another deserted boatyard farther along the coast. Paul, Mickey, Shawn, Maggie, and Maggie's friend Gabe, once a fisherman, now an artist, secretly work to make the sailboat seaworthy. Late one night, Gabe and Paul steal the research station's powerboat and the five manage to pull the sailboat into Warren's harbor. There they meet Paul's outraged father and many government officials. When he hears the story, Paul's father drops charges but forbids Paul to see his friends again except to say goodbye: he has requested a transfer. A month later, Paul's family is about to move and Paul returns to the boatyard. He finds Walter happily working on the sailboat, with Gabe, Maggie, and Shawn helping. Mickey, who has said her goodbyes to Paul at school, can't bring herself to speak to him. As he walks away, though, he turns to see her waving to him from Walter's little house. Paul, who at first had hated the town as much as his mother did, now leaves vowing to return someday to his friends.

Living in a bleak, exhausted landscape of the future, a group of highly individual people come together in the never-obsolete task of helping one another. Chapters are presented from either Paul's or Mickey's perspective, and the detailed plot and characterizations develop carefully and believably. This well-written story vividly conveys the isolation of these people in relation to their stricken environment and to each other. The subtle picture of what the world could become, both in human and natural terms, will be appreciated most fully by the mature reader.

Ages 12 and up

Also available in:
Cassette—*The Voyage Begun*
Library of Congress (NLSBPH)

50

Bonham, Frank

Durango Street

Dutton Children's Books, 1967.
(187 pages)

DELINQUENCY, JUVENILE
GANGS: Membership in
Crime/Criminals
Gangs: conflict between
Maturation
Parent/Parents: single

When teen-ager Rufus Henry is released from the state forestry camp where he has been serving his sentence for gang fighting and grand theft, he heads for his mother's home in the Durango Street Housing Project. His parole officer warns him that he is not to join any gang, but Rufus knows that in his section of the city he cannot be safe without gang affiliation. When the Gassers harass his little sister, Rufus seeks the Moors and joins them. The night of Rufus's induction into the gang, the police pick him up, but instead of arresting him for violating his parole, they assign Alex Robbins, a special officer, to "sponsor" Rufus and his gang. Alex is to help the boys—with their problems at home, with their jobs, with other gangs; ultimately he is to channel the gang into constructive activities. When the boys are introduced to the new program, they are suspicious. Then Rufus becomes leader of the Moors and decides to cooperate with Alex. But first he wants to take care of the Gassers. He plans a surprise attack, which all but destroys the gang. In the meantime, Alex has made arrangements with Ernie Brown, halfback for the Cleveland Corsairs, to have a day of football training for both gangs. Rufus greatly admires Ernie and has kept a scrapbook about him ever since his mother told him that Ernie was his real father. (Ernie is not Rufus's father; his mother misinformed him to stop his questions about his father's identity.) On the second day of training, the leader of the Gassers, having stolen the scrapbook from Rufus's house, brings it to the field and shows it to everyone. Rufus is furious and embarrassed. At the end of the school year, the Moors hold a community dance. When the Gassers try to ruin it, they are arrested. The dance is a success, and Rufus is proud of having instigated a worthwhile activity.

B

Durango Street describes a rough world of violence and crime. Rufus, an intelligent boy with potential for success, finds the bonds of ghetto life too tight to break without outside help. Alex Robbins provides that help, giving direction and hope to the boy. Although most of the characters, including the social worker, are Afro-American, the book is not a story of the black community. It is instead a vivid description of the elements that breed delinquency and the frustrations experienced by those who try to help delinquents.

Ages 11 and up

Also available in:
Braille—*Durango Street*
Library of Congress (NLSBPH)

51

Bonsall, Crosby Newell

The Case of the Double Cross

Color illustrations by the author.
HarperCollins Publishers, Inc., 1980.
(64 pages)

CLUBS
PREJUDICE: Sexual
Peer relationships
Problem solving

Marigold, about five, and her friends Gussie and Rosie want to belong to Wizard's private-detective club. But

Wizard and his friends Snitch, Skinny, and Tubby want nothing to do with girls—especially Marigold. In fact, the sign on the door of their clubhouse says "NO GIRLS." Marigold daydreams of situations that will make the boys beg her to join their club: she has a horse, she saves them from a flood, she runs an ice cream stand. Finally she devises a plan. Snitch receives a coded letter for the club members from a funny little man with a long beard. When the four boys cannot decipher the letter's code, they decide they have to get the little man back again. They set a trap and, after some time and confusion, catch not one little man but three. The boys soon discover they have been double-crossed: the three little men are really Marigold, Gussie, and Rosie. Just as Wizard is asking the girls to join the club so they can explain the code, Skinny figures it out. At that, the girls declare they do not want to join the boys' club; they will start their own. After much arguing, it is decided that Marigold, Gussie, and Rosie will join Wizard's club, the "NO GIRLS" sign will be taken down, and the new club will be called "Wizmars," for Wizard and Marigold.

Three little girls eager to join a boys-only club succeed by a clever trick in this delightful "I Can Read" book. Colorful illustrations capture the characters' feelings and add details not included in the text. Young children will enjoy this one.

Ages 6-8

Also available in:
Paperbound—*The Case of the Double Cross*
HarperCollins Publishers, Inc.

52

Bonsall, Crosby Newell

The Day I Had to Play with My Sister

Color illustrations by the author.
HarperCollins Publishers, Inc., 1988.
(32 pages)

SIBLING: Younger
Baby-sitting: involuntary

A young boy is trying to play hide-and-seek with his uncooperative little sister who just stands where she is as he counts, covering her eyes in the belief that this will keep her from being seen. Trying to deal with her failure to hide, the little boy shows his sister several possible hiding places. Then he covers his eyes and counts again. When he uncovers his eyes, she is gone. The boy begins to look for his sister in the hiding places he showed her, but cannot find her. When he turns around, he suddenly realizes that his sister has been following closely behind him all along. He decides to give his sister one more chance: this time he will hide, and she will look for him.

A young boy who appears to have been assigned the supervision of his sister decides to play a game with her, but he becomes irritated when she does not follow his vague instructions. The boy fails to realize that a child of his sister's age finds it difficult to understand directions. For a child who is unable to read, the illustrations alone can convey the story.

Ages 3-8

Also available in:
Paperbound—*The Day I Had to Play with My Sister*
HarperCollins Publishers, Inc.

53

Bonsall, Crosby Newell

Mine's the Best

Color illustrations by the author.
HarperCollins Publishers, Inc., 1984.
(32 pages)

BOASTING

Two little boys, each with a similar beach balloon, meet along the lake shore. An argument begins as each boy points out the special merits of his own balloon, trying to downgrade his fellow's. The dispute continues until each boy notices that the other's balloon has become "very sick." They begin to argue about who is to blame for the deflated balloons until a little girl whose balloon is intact taunts the boys. The two boys stop bickering and join forces against the girl.

The illustrations of this easy-to-read book are an integral part of the story. Each boy, feeling a great deal of personal investment in his toy, insists on the superiority of his own balloon. Excessive pride eventually destroys the possessions of both boys, as each tries to outboast the other.

Ages 3-8

Also available in:
Paperbound—*Mine's the Best*
HarperCollins Publishers, Inc.

54

Bonsall, Crosby Newell

Who's Afraid of the Dark?

Color illustrations by the author.
HarperCollins Publishers, Inc., 1980.
(32 pages)

FEAR: of Darkness

A little boy tells his friend how concerned he is about his dog, Stella, who is afraid of the dark. Stella trembles and shakes and sees frightening shapes when they go to bed. She also hears scary sounds and is not comforted when the boy assures her they are only the wind. When it rains, Stella hides and thinks the sounds on the roof are footsteps. The boy's friend, a patient listener, suggests that it is up to the boy to teach Stella not to be afraid of the dark. "Hold her and hug her," she advises. "Hang on to her in the dark. Let her know you are there. Take care of her!" The boy decides to take the advice that night. All the holding and hugging works—he and Stella are able to sleep peacefully.

A little boy describes his dog's fear of the dark, and his sympathetic friend, recognizing that it is the boy himself who is afraid, gives helpful advice. Expressive illustrations show not the boy's version of the situation, but the real one: they show him hiding, cowering, hunting for the source of the scary sounds while his dog sleeps peacefully nearby. Beginning readers will enjoy the humor in this skillful book, and read-aloud audiences will too.

Ages 3-7

Also available in:
Paperbound—*Who's Afraid of the Dark?*
HarperCollins Publishers, Inc.

55
Borack, Barbara
Grandpa

Color illustrations by Ben Shecter.
HarperCollins Publishers, Inc., 1967.
(32 pages) o.p.

GRANDPARENT: Love for
Love, meaning of

A preschooler enjoys visiting her grandpa more than anything else she can think of. She and Grandpa have great fun together because they have so much in common. They like the same foods, and they enjoy playing the same games, but most importantly, they enjoy each other. Grandpa permits her to help in his store and play in the back room. Sometimes Grandpa lets her dress up in one of his shirts. Grandpa plays with her friends and makes them laugh. She keeps Grandpa company when ladies visit Grandma. The little girl tells of a get-well letter she wrote to Grandpa once when he was in the hospital, and she also tells of his reply. When the little girl goes away, both grandparents give her a big kiss.

The grandpa in this gentle first-person narrative gives his granddaughter time, love, and interest, and the granddaughter reciprocates with adoration. Such genuine and mutual devotion makes their relationship very special indeed.

Ages 3-6

Also available in:
Talking Book—*Grandpa*
Library of Congress (NLSBPH)

56
Bottner, Barbara
Messy

Color illustrations by the author.
Delacorte Press, 1979.
(29 pages counted) o.p.

MESSINESS

Harriet, who likes to be called Harry, is six and very messy. In fact, her mother thinks Harry is the messiest child in town. Her hair is messy, her clothes are messy, and her room is messy. Harry's favorite place to play is under her bed so she will not have to clean her room. Even when Harry helps her mother in the kitchen, she is messy. At dance class all the girls look like ballerinas; Harry looks messy. But Harry is the best dancer. The teacher announces a recital for which everyone will wear a costume. Harry is chosen to be the princess and is given a beautiful white tutu with ruffles. She does not want to rumple the costume and so informs her mother that she will be neat from now on, "just like a princess." All week Harry keeps her room clean and herself neat. During the recital, she looks very neat and pretty and feels like a princess. Afterwards, her proud parents take her to a restaurant for dessert. When the food arrives, Harry twirls her napkin and spills the desserts. Messy again!

A little girl is very content to be messy until she is chosen to be the princess in a dance recital. After a week of being neat, though, Harry seems happy to be messy again. The numerous illustrations show an engaging—but messy—little girl. Children will like Harry; adults will sympathize with Harry's long-suffering mother.

Ages 4-7

Also available in:
No other form known

57
Bradford, Richard
Red Sky at Morning

HarperCollins Publishers, Inc., 1986.
(256 pages, paperbound)

MATURATION
Alcoholism: of mother
Change: accepting
Death: of father
Responsibility: accepting

In this first-person account, seventeen-year-old Joshua Arnold tells of the changes that take place in his life from 1944 to 1945. World War II is being fought, and Josh's father has enlisted in the Navy. Josh and his mother, a traditional Southern belle, move from Mobile, Alabama, to Sagredo, New Mexico. There Josh meets new friends, makes enemies, finds out about girls, and generally adjusts to a new lifestyle. But his mother, having been protected all her life, finds the change more difficult. In order to escape from making decisions and facing reality, she takes to drinking sherry. More complications arise when an old family friend, Jimbob Buel, comes for a visit and stays on. Josh suspects that Jimbob is interested in his mother. After one of her drinking bouts, his mother fires the Montoyas, old friends whom Josh's father hired to serve as caretaker and cook and who keep the household running smoothly. Josh tries to get them to come back, but they refuse to do so until someone assumes the authority his mother is not capable of holding. "I mean, goddamn, boy, are you gonna be Papacity for a while or you gonna let that . . . woman do the job?" asks Senor Montoya. Josh begins to realize that he has to take charge. His decision is reinforced by his father, who sends a document appointing Josh as head of the household in his absence. When his father is killed and his mother has a nervous breakdown, Josh continues to fill the role entrusted to him.

Both humor and pathos are present in this story of a boy growing up. The close, relaxed relationship that Josh has with his father is portrayed well. The language used in the story is extremely frank, and the profanity might offend some readers. Spanish phrases are used and can be understood within the context of the story.

Ages 13 and up

Also available in:
Braille—*Red Sky at Morning*
Library of Congress (NLSBPH)

Talking Book—*Red Sky at Morning*
Library of Congress (NLSBPH)

58

Brancato, Robin Fidler

Winning

Alfred A. Knopf, Inc., 1987.
(211 pages)

QUADRIPLEGIA
Boy-girl relationships
Courage, meaning of
Determination
Suicide: consideration of

Gary Madden, a high school senior and star football player, is strapped into a Stryker frame in his hometown hospital, unable to move. Two weeks earlier, he had fractured a vertebra during a football game and been left paralyzed. Courageously he awaits the doctor's prediction of the extent of the permanent damage. Meanwhile, friends visit; his parents spend every possible moment with him; and his girlfriend, Diane, remains loyal. The high school principal sends three of Gary's teachers to help him keep up with his lessons, one of them Ann Treer, a young woman widowed a year earlier in a car accident, who tutors him in English. Understanding of Gary's grief and shock, Ann Treer becomes his confidante. When she learns from the doctor that Gary's legs will be permanently paralyzed, she insists Gary be told. He again shows great inner strength, and spiritedly begins rehabilitation. He soon recovers limited use of his arms, and learns to use a wheelchair—but then he falls seriously ill with a bladder infection. A high fever brings delirium, and the boy becomes despondent. He thinks first that he will be a burden to others all his life, then that he is going to die, and should in fact commit suicide before he causes any more trouble. As Gary's fever breaks, he finds Ann there, and the two talk freely. Ann tells him that he is needed—by his family, by Diane, by Ann herself. She explains how he has helped her to find her own emotions again, to permit herself to feel despite her husband's death. Her encouragement helps Gary renew his own confidence.

This is the story of a young man's struggle to accept great and sudden physical limitations, and a changed appearance—diminished weight and muscle—yet a new respectable self-image. In the midst of self-doubt, he vacillates between needing and driving off friends. Ann Treer, who helps Gary believe in his capabilities, finds that her friendship with him is just the therapy she herself has needed. This honest, memorable story does not shrink from clinical detail, such as Gary's embarrassment at unwanted erections and his need for urinary catheters.

Ages 12 and up

Also available in:
Paperbound—*Winning*
Alfred A. Knopf, Inc.

59

Brandenberg, Aliki Liacouras

The Two of Them

Color illustrations by the author.
Greenwillow Books, 1979.
(29 pages counted)

DEATH: of Grandparent
GRANDPARENT: Love for
Love, meaning of

A loving grandfather makes a silver ring for his newborn granddaughter. He also makes her a bed and sings her soft lullabies. When she outgrows her bed, he makes her a bigger one and a shelf for her books. At night he tells her stories—stories that had been told to him, stories just for fun, and stories about his love for her. He takes her swimming in the ocean and walking in the woods. After school the girl helps out in her grandfather's grocery store. Sometimes she gives the wrong change but the grandfather only laughs, realizing she is just learning to count. When the grandfather retires, he and the girl spend much time in his garden where he cultivates fruit trees. In time, the silver ring fits the girl. Suddenly the grandfather becomes ill and seems old. He recovers, but is partially paralyzed and confined to a wheelchair.

Now the girl cares for him. She wheels him through the garden, sings to him at night, and tells him stories. He dies in the springtime. "She knew that one day he would die. But when he did, she was not ready, and she hurt inside and out." She cuts blossoms for him from his tree and says goodnight, but her grandfather is silent. In the fall she sits in the garden and looks at the apple tree, thinking of how it will change with the seasons. "She would be there to watch it grow, to pick the fruit, and to remember."

Illustrations and text are equally important in this sad, gentle story of love between a grandfather and his granddaughter. The soft shadings, kind faces, and warm, domestic scenes in the drawings complement the bittersweet, sometimes lyrical, text. The final picture of the girl looking at an empty chair under an apple tree skillfully captures her sense of loss and longing.

Ages 3-7

Also available in:
Paperbound—*The Two of Them*
Greenwillow Books

60

Brandenberg, Aliki Liacouras

We Are Best Friends

Color illustrations by the author.
Greenwillow Books, 1982.
(32 pages counted)

FRIENDSHIP: Best Friend
FRIENDSHIP: Making Friends
Change: accepting
Moving

When young Peter announces he is moving, Robert replies that he can't because they are best friends. They play together, fight together, and attend each other's parties. "You will miss me too much," he says. But Peter moves anyway, and Robert is lonely without him. He has nobody to play with, share with, even fight with. One day at school a new boy named Will talks to Robert, who silently looks him over. Robert decides he dislikes the boy's name, glasses, and freckles. Then Robert receives a letter from Peter telling him about the new friend he's made. Even though Robert will always be his best friend, writes Peter, he likes his new home better now that he has somebody to play with. Robert writes back, reminding Peter of all the fun things they used to do together and telling him about Will. Later, he sees Will sitting by a fence looking for a frog to replace the pet one he used to have at his other house. Robert tells Will there are frogs in his garden. "If I had a frog in my garden, I'd share it," says Will. "That's what I'm doing," replies Robert. They ride their bikes to Robert's yard, where Will catches a frog and names it after his first one. Robert tells Will how his friend Peter used to come every year to watch the tadpoles in their garden pond and how he called them "Inkywiggles." Will suggests he write and tell Peter about the new crop of "Inkywiggles." They laugh, each happy to be having fun again. Robert writes the letter and tells Peter about his new friend and their fun with the "Inkywiggles." He mails the letter and then rides his bike over to Will's.

In this story of friendship, a young boy finds that a new friend can relieve the loneliness left by his departed best friend. The new friend does not replace the old, but he makes life full and fun again. This gentle tale, with its believable dialogue and sunny, colorful illustrations, would be an excellent read-aloud story.

Ages 3-6

Also available in:
Paperbound—*We Are Best Friends*
Greenwillow Books

61

Brandenberg, Franz

I Wish I Was Sick, Too!

Color illustrations by Aliki.
Greenwillow Books, 1976.
(32 pages counted)

ILLNESSES: Being Ill
JEALOUSY: Sibling
Attention seeking

Every member of the family helps care for young Edward when he is sick, and his sister, Elizabeth, envies Edward all that attention. Besides, while he is being pampered, she must do the household chores. Elizabeth wishes she were sick, too. A few days later, she is. Now it is her turn to get all the attention, and Edward does the household tasks good-naturedly. Elizabeth wishes she were well. When she is, she and Edward do something special for each member of the family. They decide that the best part of being sick is getting well.

Elizabeth envies the attention Edward receives while he is ill, but finds little to enjoy when she falls ill herself. The illustrations in this humorous story show not a human family, but a family of kittens.

Ages 3-7

Also available in:
Paperbound—*I Wish I Was Sick, Too!*
Greenwillow Books

62

Brandenberg, Franz

Nice New Neighbors

Greenwillow Books, 1977.
(56 pages)

FRIENDSHIP: Making Friends
Change: new home

The six Fieldmouse children, Annette, Bertrand, Colette, Daniel, Esther, and Ferdinand, have just moved into a new neighborhood and want to make new friends. Father Fieldmouse points out the child next door jumping rope. The Fieldmouse children run next door to play with her. But she wants to play by herself. The children return home, and Father Fieldmouse points out the children across the street playing tag. The Fieldmouse children run across the street to play tag, too, but the Lizard children want to play by themselves. The children return, and Father tells them that the children up the street are playing ring-around-the-rosy. The Fieldmouse children run up the street to play ring-around-the-rosy with the Grasshopper children, but they too want to play by themselves. Once again the Fieldmouse children return home. This time Father Fieldmouse tells them that the children around the corner are playing hide-and-seek, and the Fieldmouse children run around the corner to join in the neighborhood children's game. But the Snail children want to play by themselves. The Fieldmouse children return home and announce that no one will let them join in their games. Mother says that the neighbor children will play with them once they get to know them better. Father suggests that they play on their own, and the children decide to perform "Three Blind Mice." Suddenly all the children in the neighborhood want parts in the Fieldmouse children's play. Parts are given to each, and the children rehearse all day; in the evening they perform for the neighborhood, to great acclaim. The next day, the Fieldmouse children jump rope and play tag, ring-around-the-rosy, and hide-and-seek with all the other children, who are happy to have made such nice new friends.

In this beginning reader, the Fieldmouse children want to make friends in their new neighborhood, but the other children are not very cordial. Newcomers often must rely on their own resources for a while. Youngsters who have encountered a new neighborhood will sympathize, and may use the Fieldmouse technique to advantage.

Ages 6-8

Also available in:
Paperbound—*Nice New Neighbors*
Greenwillow Books

63

Bridgers, Sue Ellen

All Together Now

Alfred A. Knopf, Inc., 1979.
(238 pages)

GRANDPARENT: Living in Home of
Friendship: meaning of
Love, meaning of
Maturation
Mental retardation

Casey Flanagan, twelve years old, comes to spend the summer with her father's parents. The United States is engaged in the Korean War, and Casey's father is a military pilot in Korea. Her mother is working two jobs to maintain the family's income. Casey has visited her grandparents' small-town home before, but the prospect of spending an entire summer with them is not appealing to her. Then she meets their neighbor, Dwayne Pickens, a retarded man who has "the mind of a 12-year-old." Dwayne grew up with Casey's father. The young girl and the childlike man become inseparable. Dwayne does not like girls. But he likes Casey because he assumes she is a boy, and she doesn't pursue the point. Casey is rapidly drawn into family and community life. Her Uncle Taylor, a race car driver, has a new girlfriend, Gwen. Casey watches the family's initial apprehension about this "race-track girl" change into fondness and acceptance. Taylor entertains Casey with stories of his and his brother's childhood; Casey had known very little about her father's early years. Hazard Whitaker returns to the town after many years of wandering and finally asks Pansy, his longtime love and Casey's grandmother's best friend, to marry him. Their honeymoon almost ends their marriage, however, when Hazard forgets to reserve a sleeping car for their wedding night on the train. Pansy worries that her marriage is a mistake, and Casey and Dwayne join the effort to reconcile the couple. Then Dwayne, angry and frustrated when his brother Alva's wife yells at him, takes his brother's car and drives it recklessly. Alva, who says he's concerned for Dwayne's welfare, signs a petition to have Dwayne committed to an institution. Casey and many of the townspeople, led by Uncle Taylor, gather forces to get the petition withdrawn. They are able to convince Alva that Dwayne is much loved by his friends and deserves to be happy. Towards the end of the summer, Casey contracts polio. During her convalescence, the family is drawn even closer together. Her grandparents come to regard her as the daughter they always wanted. When Dwayne finally learns that Casey is a girl, he is furious at first but then decides he loves her anyway. Casey has become an important member of her father's family and community. Now, though, the summer is over. Casey goes home to her mother, knowing that she will probably return for other summers, but none quite as special as this one.

A young girl learns much about the love of family and friends in this well-told story. Readers will easily empathize with Casey and the various people in her world, all of whom are realistically and believably drawn. The strengths and weaknesses of individuals and the complexities of relationships are nicely detailed.

Ages 11 and up

Also available in:
Cassette—*All Together Now*
Library of Congress (NLSBPH)

64

Bridgers, Sue Ellen

Home Before Dark

Alfred A. Knopf, Inc., 1988.
(176 pages) o.p.

FAMILY: Unity
IDENTITY, SEARCH FOR
LIFESTYLE: Change in
Boy-girl relationships
Death: of mother
Maturation
Migrant workers
Parent/Parents: remarriage of

James Earl Willis, his wife, and their four children have never had a place to call home. The Willises have traveled around Florida as migrant farm workers for as long as fourteen-year-old Stella can remember. But today the family is going home—to the tobacco farm in North Carolina where James Earl grew up, the farm his brother Newton now owns and operates. Stella rejoices—she longs for a home—but her mother, Mae, a faded, anxious woman, does not; Mae prefers the rootless, anonymous life of a migrant, in which she is not required to be anybody. Out of love for his brother, Newton gives the new arrivals a tenant house and furniture and provides work for James Earl. Stella works hard to make the house homey, and swears never to leave it: "What counted for her was here, inside walls that didn't move in the dark or carry her somewhere as strange and unwelcoming as the last place she'd been." Then she meets Toby Brown, a neighbor boy her age, and he falls in love with her. Stella also meets Rodney Brown, a boy from town, who has money to spend and drives a car. Stella is impressed by Rodney—he can take her places she has never been—and he, in whom no girl has ever shown an interest, is bowled over by her. Meanwhile, James Earl is beginning to feel at home on the farm, though Mae longs to be traveling again. Then one day during a thunderstorm, Mae is struck by lightning and killed instantly. Toby tries to comfort Stella, coming to see her the night of the funeral; for a long time, he holds and kisses her. Rodney sees them together, and hires two high school boys to beat up Toby. The boy is so badly hurt he must be hospitalized. He recovers, but thereafter is more cautious with his feelings for Stella. Knowing Rodney ordered Toby's beating, Stella tells him she will never see him again, and turns all her attentions to Toby. Meanwhile James Earl, struggling with his grief and loneliness, is attracted to Maggie Grover, a single woman who owns a small department store in town. Maggie, despite her money and lovely old home, is lonely too. The two begin dating and soon are married. Stella is happy for her father, but she will not leave the tenant house to live with the rest of the family at Maggie's. She stays on in the only place that has ever been home to her. Then, little by little, she comes to realize that Maggie's can be home too. Three months later, at the start of the new year, she moves in.

This novel weaves into the lives of the Willis family the stories of many friends and relations who touch them and help shape their lives. The extensive narrative is handled deftly, and characterizations remain vivid. Still, Newton's matter-of-fact description to James Earl of their terminally ill mother's violent suicide and the violence inflicted upon Toby may distress some readers.

Ages 12 and up

Also available in:
Braille—*Home Before Dark*
Library of Congress (NLSBPH)

B

65

Bridgers, Sue Ellen

Notes for Another Life

Alfred A. Knopf, Inc., 1981.
(252 pages) o.p.

CHANGE: Resisting
GRANDPARENT: Living in Home of
LOSS: Feelings of
PARENTAL: Absence
SIBLING: Relationships
Boy-girl relationships: dating
Depression
Grandparent: love for
Mental illness: of parent
Suicide: attempted
Talents: musical

For the past six years, since their father was first hospitalized for mental illness and their mother moved to nearby Atlanta to pursue a fashion career, sixteen-year-old Kevin and his thirteen-year-old sister, Wren, have lived with their grandparents, Bill and Bliss Jackson. One Saturday, after she and Bliss have made their usual hospital visit, Wren stops at her grandfather's drugstore where Kevin works to tell him that their mother is coming to see them. Wren is hopeful that this time she might stay, but Kevin discourages such optimism. Bliss is apprehensive about the visit because of Kevin's increasing moodiness, which disappears only when he is with his girlfriend, Melanie. Bliss knows how his mother's absence has hurt Kevin, understands his feeling "that she didn't need them enough, want them enough, love them enough." Their mother, Karen, arrives with the news that she has taken a new job in Chicago and that though she had always intended for Kevin and Wren to come stay with her, they won't be able to now. Wren resolves to accept her life as it is, to concentrate on her piano studies (she is talented and plans a professional career) and the family she has. Kevin, however, broods, and Wren senses and sympathizes with his disappointment. Meanwhile, Wren has captured the interest of Sam Holland, one year older and a boy she had always thought she disliked. She is warmly accepted by his large, loving family. That spring, Bliss must tell Wren and Kevin that Karen is divorcing their father. Wren simply asks if Karen will still visit. As Bliss feared, Kevin reacts by stalking silently out of the house and taking the car. Devastated, he cries for a long time. For Wren's eighth-grade graduation her grandparents take her, Sam, Kevin, and Melanie out to dinner. While dancing with Sam, Wren giddily asks him about their future. Caught up in his confidence, she believes his picture of college, marriage, and children. Another evening, alone in her house with Sam, she agrees to play the piano for him. But she finds his compliments patronizing and tersely corrects his assumption that she will one day teach piano as Bliss does; she informs him that she intends to play concert piano on stage. For Kevin, the summer begins badly. When he talks to his father about the divorce, he is shocked to learn that the man didn't know of Karen's intentions. Despite Melanie's continual efforts to buoy him up, Kevin remains depressed. Bliss asks Jack Kensley, a new minister in town, to talk with the boy. Then their father, temporarily recovered, returns home. Wren readily draws him into the family circle, but Kevin holds back. Karen comes for another visit, raising Kevin's hopes. But she soon makes it clear that she really is moving to Chicago. Later, Kevin takes out his frustration on Melanie, challenging her to prove her love for him, and she calls a halt to their relationship. The following day, Karen hesitates a bit before she agrees that Kevin could come live with her. That night, Kevin takes an overdose of sleeping pills. Bliss discovers him in time and as he recovers, she asks Mr. Kensley to begin counseling him. The minister, kind yet tough, helps Kevin think through his actions and face the truth. When Karen prepares to move and invites Kevin to come with her, he is strong enough to decline, realizing it would never work. The day she is to leave, Karen takes Wren out to celebrate her birthday. As she listens distantly to Karen's attempts to explain her past, Wren realizes her mother is trying to help her make the decisions Karen "didn't know how to make." Then, just as Kevin begins to regain confidence and emotional strength, his father's illness returns. As he feeds and cares for the listless man, Kevin realizes he will always love him. After a small family birthday celebration, Sam and Wren talk. Wren confesses that "sometimes I can't see room for anything but music." Sam recognizes the conflict, the ambition Wren shares with her mother, but thinks their relationship can weather it. That day Karen calls, and Kevin requests a real, honest talk with her when they meet again at Thanksgiving. Then it is Saturday again and Bliss prepares to return the children's father to the hospital. This time Kevin decides to accompany her and Wren.

In this complex story of loss and change, a brother and sister come to accept and understand their parents. In so doing, they learn much about themselves and their power to shape their own futures. The strong bond between the two, partially in response to their shared loss, shows up time and again in their concern for and sensitivity to one another. Though they want to help each other, in the end they each must work through their own conflicts—Kevin his depression that so resembles his father's, Wren her ambition, so like her mother's. Only when they accept themselves can they be a real support to one another.

Ages 12 and up

Also available in:
Cassette—*Notes for Another Life*
Library of Congress (NLSBPH)

66

Brink, Carol Ryrie

Caddie Woodlawn: A Frontier Story

Black/white illustrations by Kate Seredy.
Macmillan Publishing Company, Inc., 1973.
(270 pages)

MATURATION
Courage, meaning of
Family: unity
Gender role identity: female

Eleven-year-old Caddie Woodlawn is considered to be a tomboy by her family and by the residents of the 1860s Wisconsin farming community in which she lives. She enjoys doing all the things her younger and older brothers do, such as climbing trees and plowing a farm field. Even though Mrs. Woodlawn is distressed by her daughter's unladylike ways, she allows them to continue because it was this lifestyle that made Caddie strong and healthy after a serious illness. Caddie has acquired strong beliefs in freedom and justice from her father, a man of English nobility. These beliefs lead Caddie to perform an act of heroism when the community is frightened by rumors of an Indian uprising. Caddie overhears some of the men in the community plotting an attack on the Indians. Because she realizes that the Indians are peaceful, she rides to warn them and helps avoid a slaughter. Later, when a cousin arrives from Boston for a summer visit, Caddie scorns the girl's feminine ways and plays practical jokes on her cousin to make her mannerisms appear foolish. After Mrs. Woodlawn punishes Caddie for these pranks, Caddie's father suggests that Caddie has not given the womanly way a try and thus has no grounds for rejecting it. Caddie, now thirteen, takes her father's words to heart and begins to help her mother. Although she never loses the outspokenness she acquired by being with her brothers, she discovers that she enjoys being a young woman.

This children's classic describes a young girl's rejection of gender role identity, her maturation, and her eventual acceptance of this gender role. Throughout this timeless story, the reader is treated to scenes of a strongly knit family in which the Woodlawn children are guided and disciplined by loving and concerned parents. The nature of this book lends itself well to oral reading.

Ages 9-12

Also available in:
Braille—*Caddie Woodlawn: A Frontier Story*
Library of Congress (NLSBPH)

Cassette—*Caddie Woodlawn: A Frontier Story*
Library of Congress (NLSBPH)

Paperbound—*Caddie Woodlawn: A Frontier Story*
Aladdin Books

Paperbound—*Caddie Woodlawn: A Frontier Story*
Collier Books

Talking Book—*Caddie Woodlawn: A Frontier Story*
Library of Congress (NLSBPH)

67

Brown, Marc Tolan

Arthur Goes to Camp

Color illustrations by the author.
Little, Brown & Company, Inc., 1982.
(32 pages counted, paperbound)

CAMP EXPERIENCES
Homesickness
Running away
Success

Arthur's parents tell him of the fun he will have at Camp Meadowcroak, but Arthur the aardvark is determined not to go. Even though his friends get on the bus with him, Arthur is unhappy. When they pass Camp Horsewater, Meadowcroak's rival in the traditional scavenger hunt, and see all the tough-looking campers there, Arthur's distress increases. He even writes his parents a letter on the bus, telling them he is already homesick. The campers arrive and meet their counselors. Arthur finds the girls' counselor sweet and understanding, but the boys' counselor seems mean and demanding. That night the boys discover frogs in their beds and are sure the girls did it. Arthur writes home complaining about the food. In sports the girls beat the boys at everything, and as campers they are even better. Arthur continues to send home sad postcards. Then strange things begin to happen. The girls discover a smoke bomb in their tent. The boys' clothes are stolen. Everyone begins hearing strange noises at night. Arthur writes home that camp gives him the creeps. One night all the campers decide to stand watch. They soon discover that campers from Camp Horsewater are causing all the trouble. Camp Meadowcroak vows revenge. Arthur writes home vowing to run away. During the scavenger hunt he takes his backpack and a flashlight and leaves. The Meadowcroak campers scare their opponents by dressing up one of their members in a fur coat so he looks like a bear. It gets dark and all Meadowcroak needs to win is a flashlight. But there is no flashlight and no Arthur. In fact, Arthur is lost. But his friends find him—he is using the flashlight to light his way—and he helps them win the scavenger hunt. After this victory, Arthur writes home to announce, "Camp is great. I want to come back next year."

Arthur the aardvark is woefully unhappy at camp until he becomes the hero of the scavenger hunt. Then he decides camp isn't so bad after all. Bold, colorful illustrations, the amusing progression of Arthur's letters home, and the familiar camp experiences will delight the read-aloud audience. This is one of several stories about Arthur the aardvark and his animal friends.

Ages 5-8

Also available in:
No other form known

B

68

Brown, Marc Tolan

Arthur's Eyes

Color illustrations by the author.
Little, Brown & Company, Inc., 1979.
(32 pages, paperbound)

GLASSES, WEARING OF
Appearance: concern about
Name-calling
Peer relationships: peer pressures

Arthur the aardvark, a second grader, is having trouble seeing the books he reads and the blackboard at school. Sometimes he has headaches. His friends—a rabbit, a cat, a chimpanzee, a dog, and a moose—are becoming irritated because Arthur is constantly asking for help. He ruins their basketball games because he can't see the basket. Then Arthur gets glasses. Now he can see. He loves wearing his glasses until some of his schoolmates begin calling him "four eyes" and "sissy." So Arthur tries to get along without his glasses. He even tries to lose them. When he walks into the girls' lavatory at school because he can't see the sign on the door, he causes a huge screaming scene. The principal understands what Arthur is going through and reassures him about wearing glasses. Finally, Arthur learns to accept his need for glasses. He even begins to feel proud of them.

Although the text and illustrations are funny, children who are sensitive about wearing glasses will identify with Arthur the aardvark's mixed emotions. Children who don't wear glasses may begin to understand the feelings of those who do. The characters, all animals, are delightfully illustrated. This is one of several stories about Arthur and his friends.

Ages 4-7

Also available in:
No other form known

69

Brown, Marc Tolan

Arthur's Nose

Little, Brown & Company, Inc., 1976.
(32 pages counted, paperbound)

SELF, ATTITUDE TOWARD: Accepting
Self, attitude toward: body concept

School-age Arthur is an aardvark, with an aardvark's nose like the rest of his family. One day Arthur no longer likes his nose: it gets stuffed up and red when he has a cold; it gives him away in hide-and-seek; his friends seem to think it funny; and it is quite unlike any other nose in his class. Arthur feels freakish and unhappy. But his decision to have it changed takes his friends by surprise. They accompany Arthur to the rhinologist, or nose doctor, and wait outside. Inside with the doctor, Arthur models pictures of all types of noses but nothing looks right—except Arthur's own nose. When he emerges from the office with his nose intact, his friends are relieved, and he is content: Arthur likes his looks.

His unusual appearance distresses Arthur, for he wants to look like his friends. He thinks they would like him better if he did. But he finds that his nose is part of what makes him special, an individual, and he decides to keep the nose he has.

Ages 3-7

Also available in:
No other form known

70

Brown, Margaret Wise

The Dead Bird

Color illustrations by Remy Charlip.
HarperCollins Publishers, Inc., 1990.
(45 pages counted)

DEATH: Funeral Issues

Four children discover a dead bird that is still warm. Soon the bird begins to grow cold and stiff. The children regret that the bird will never fly again, but they are glad they have found it for they will be able to give it a proper burial in the place it once loved. The children carry the bird into the woods, dig a hole in the ground, and place the bird in the hole on a bed of fragrant ferns. They then cover the bird with ferns and flowers and sing it a song; they cry because the bird is dead. After covering the bird with soil and placing a stone over the grave to mark it, the children leave. Although for a time they visit the grave daily, bringing flowers and singing, they eventually forget about the bird.

The children's feelings about death seem to be detached. They are depicted as the feelings of persons observing death and mourning at a distance, rather than the intense feelings of persons experiencing the death of a loved one.

Ages 4-7

Also available in:
No other form known

71

Buck, Pearl Sydenstricker

The Big Wave

Black/white illustrations by Hiroshige and Hokusai.
HarperCollins Publishers, Inc., 1986.
(61 pages, paperbound)

MOURNING, STAGES OF
Death: attitude toward
Death: of parents
Foster home
Friendship: meaning of
Japan

Two Japanese boys, Kino and Jiya, are friends. When the volcano near their fishing village erupts, a tidal wave threatens the villagers, and Jiya's father quickly sends his boy to a farm on higher ground belonging to Kino's father. As a result, Jiya is saved, but his entire family is swept away by the tidal wave, along with the rest of the villagers. In keeping with Japanese tradition, Kino's parents take Jiya into their home and treat him as their own son. Their understanding of his loss and grief helps Jiya work through the mourning process in a manner that enhances his development.

Created by a master storyteller, this tale offers important insights into Japanese culture and attitudes toward life, love, and death. At the same time, the story poignantly illustrates the philosophy of overcoming mourning through living.

Ages 9-11

Also available in:
Braille—*The Big Wave*
Library of Congress (NLSBPH)

Cassette—*The Big Wave*
Library of Congress (NLSBPH)

72

Bulla, Clyde Robert

Daniel's Duck

Color illustrations by Joan Sandin.
HarperCollins Publishers, Inc., 1979.
(64 pages)

CREATIVITY
TALENTS: Artistic
Appalachia
Pride/False pride

It is the early 1900s. In the mountains of Tennessee, where young Daniel and his family live, wood carving is an art and Henry Pettigrew is the acclaimed master. Inspired by Mr. Pettigrew's lifelike animals, Daniel decides to carve something for the spring fair. But it isn't until late in the winter, after the rest of the family are well into their projects, that Daniel starts on his block of wood. His father makes moccasins, his mother sews a quilt, his brother carves a box, and Daniel carves a duck. He makes his duck different from most, however; his duck is looking back. His brother insists the head is backward, but his father encourages him to do it his own way. Daniel is very proud of his duck. Spring and the fair come, and the family rides the wagon to town. The father takes their handmade articles to the town hall. When the hall opens, Daniel heads for the wood carvings and joins the other onlookers in admiring a deer made by Henry Pettigrew. He is puzzled when he hears people laughing, but then realizes they are laughing at his duck. Hurt, then angry, he grabs the duck and runs down to the river. He starts to throw the duck in, but a man stops him. The man tells Daniel that the people really liked his duck; they laughed because the duck made them feel good. Daniel is not convinced. The man suggests they sit and rest. He asks Daniel if he would be willing to sell the duck, and Daniel wonders who would buy it. Some passing children greet the man and call him by name—Henry Pettigrew. Daniel looks again at his duck and now believes it must be good. Henry wants to buy the duck, but Daniel will not sell it. Instead, he shyly gives it to the master.

A little boy, proud of his first attempt at wood carving, is hurt by the reaction of others to his work. An older, more accomplished carver helps him to appreciate his work anew and understand the laughter it encourages. Appalachian life, while secondary to the story itself, is represented at its authentic best in the softly shaded illustrations touched with color. This is an "I Can Read" book, appropriate for young readers.

Ages 5-8

Also available in:
Paperbound—*Daniel's Duck*
HarperCollins Publishers, Inc.

73

Bulla, Clyde Robert

Last Look

Black/white illustrations by Emily Arnold McCully.
HarperCollins Publishers, Inc., 1979.
(81 pages) o.p.

PEER RELATIONSHIPS
Aggression
Rejection: peer
Revenge
School: transfer

Monica and her friends Fran and Audrey attend Madame Vere's summer school for girls. The three are annoyed to find a new student, Rhoda, attaching herself to their group. Monica knows that Madame Vere approves of the way they have apparently made friends with the new girl, so she rather grudgingly tolerates Rhoda. Sometimes the girls play a childhood game: last look. When two of them leave each other, one gets the other's attention and yells "last look." Then the other must try to attract the first one's glance. The object for the person who yelled "last look" is not to look. One day, Madame Vere asks for volunteers to play the roles in Beauty and the Beast, the school play. Everyone wants Monica to play Beauty, but Rhoda, daughter of an actress, insists there should be tryouts. Although Rhoda gives a better reading than Monica, the girls all insist that Monica be given the part anyway. As they walk home together, Rhoda tells the others that she never really wanted the part. As Monica turns into her yard, she yells "last look" at Rhoda. Behind her she hears Rhoda yelling for help, but she is determined not to lose the game and so doesn't turn around. The next day Rhoda's grandmother stops by Monica's house looking for Rhoda, who has not been home since the day before. She suspects that Rhoda has taken a bus to be with her mother in New York. That night, as Monica sleeps in her tent in the yard, she is awakened by a noise. She finds a note telling her that Rhoda is in danger and that she is to go alone to the deserted Fenwick house—the haunted house—at midnight on Tuesday. Monica shows her mother the note and her mother calls the sheriff. He, however, is skeptical. The next day, Rhoda is still not at school. That night at midnight, the sheriff goes by the haunted house but finds nothing. Then Monica receives another note saying she has one more chance to save her friend. Late that night, she steals out of the house and goes to the Fenwick place. Suddenly a figure tries to blindfold her, but she manages to unmask it. It's Rhoda. She explains that her disappearance started out as a response to the game, but that she really hates Monica. She tries to push Monica into a nearby well, and they both fall in. It's not very deep and the muddy bottom is soft. Rhoda apologizes. Monica tries to get out by standing on Rhoda's back, planning to push herself out and then help Rhoda escape. But Rhoda wants to stand on Monica's back instead. Once she's out, however, Rhoda replaces the well cover over Monica and shouts down, "Last look!" Much later, the sheriff and Monica's mother come to rescue her. Having found her bed empty and the note beside it, her mother had contacted the sheriff. They caught Rhoda as she was running away and made her tell them where Monica was. Later they learn that Rhoda's mother has been sent for and is to take Rhoda home with her. When Monica goes back to school, she finds another new girl. Shaken by her experience, she wonders whether the girl will turn out to be friend or foe. She is sure of one thing: she will keep an open mind until she knows.

A girl extends a reluctant hand of friendship to a newcomer and comes in for the new girl's violent attempt at revenge for the rejection she feels. Monica, unnerved by the dangerous behavior she evoked in Rhoda, resolves to be more genuinely open to new people in the future. Rhoda's extreme reaction, however, is seen to stem from deep-seated problems she brought with her; her lack of acceptance by Monica and her circle merely served as the catalyst. This is a rather suspenseful story that could stimulate discussion of how damaging peer rejection can be. Line drawings amplify the strong feelings of the characters.

Ages 8-10

Also available in:
No other form known

74

Bulla, Clyde Robert

Shoeshine Girl

HarperCollins Publishers, Inc., 1975.
(84 pages)

VALUES/VALUING: Materialistic
Dependence/Independence
Friendship: meaning of
Job
Relatives: living in home of
Responsibility: accepting

Ten-year-old Sarah Ida Becker is a handful to her parents, and so is sent to spend the summer with her Aunt Claudia when her mother falls ill. But Sarah Ida does not want to spend her summer with Aunt Claudia. Her aunt makes her help with the household chores but—on the mother's instructions—gives Sarah no allowance. Sarah Ida sees money as a means toward independence. She talks a neighbor girl into lending her money, but Aunt Claudia makes her return it. Determined to have money in her pocket, and despite her age, Sarah Ida looks for a job. She is finally hired by Al Winkler at his shoeshine stand. To Sarah Ida's surprise, Aunt Claudia does not object. Winkler teaches Sarah Ida to make shoes shine like glass and to thank a customer whether he gives a tip or not. He also tells her stories about his life. The work is hard, but Sarah Ida comes to like it and to like Al, too. One day, on an errand, Al is hit by a car. Before he is taken to the hospital, he gives Sarah Ida the key to the shoeshine stand and instructs her to lock up. Instead, Sarah Ida keeps the stand open until Al can come back. A few days after Al's recovery, Aunt Claudia receives a letter from the girl's father; his wife is going to the hospital for several months, and he badly needs his daughter at home. Although Sarah Ida does not want to leave Al and her job, she sees that her place is with her father and goes home.

This story shows how a young, unruly girl comes to respect other people and their needs through the responsibilities of a job. It also shows how her own need for independence is tempered by a friendship.

Ages 8-10

Also available in:
Braille—*Shoeshine Girl*
Library of Congress (NLSBPH)

Paperbound—*Shoeshine Girl*
Scholastic, Inc.

75

Bunin, Catherine and Sherry Bunin

Is That Your Sister? A True Story of Adoption

Black/white photographs by the authors.
Pantheon Books, 1976.
(35 pages) o.p.

ADOPTION: Explaining
ADOPTION: Interracial

Six-year-old Catherine Bunin is adopted. She is questioned a lot by other children about her family and about adoption, more than other adopted children she knows because, as she says, "my mother and I don't look anything alike. We don't have the same kind of skin or face or hair." Although the questions sometimes annoy her, she patiently answers them all. Citing the experience of her much darker-skinned four-year-old sister, Carla, she explains that children are adopted through agencies. They do not live at the agencies, but with foster parents, people who take care of them until they have permanent homes—"forever families." Catherine describes how the social worker comes and talks to all members of a family before bringing a child into their home to live. After Carla had lived with the Bunins for six months, Mr. and Mrs. Bunin had gone to court to adopt her, which simply meant they had sworn before a judge to take care of Carla. When the people ask Carla who her "real" parents are, she explains that her real parents "are the mom and dad who take care of me and love me."

Written in the first person, in Catherine's language, this book describes the feelings of an adopted child and the process of adoption. Catherine's mother, Sherry, says, "The fact that we are an interracial family presents some special situations, but it does not keep our story from being a typical account of adoption."

Ages 4-8

Also available in:
No other form known

76

Bunting, Anne Evelyn

The Big Red Barn

Black/white illustrations by Howard Knotts.
Harcourt Brace Jovanovich, Inc., 1979.
(31 pages, paperbound)

CHANGE: Accepting
Security/Insecurity
Stepparent: mother

For a young boy, the big red barn on his family's farm is a warm, friendly place filled with pleasant memories and a sense of permanence. It is where his younger sister keeps her pet goat, where the hens and pet rooster live, and where the kangaroo mice have built their nest hidden from a hungry barn owl. Despite the boy's objections, the sister shows this nest to Emma, their new stepmother. In the barn too is the hayloft, the boy's special hiding place. He remembers how he went there to cry when his mother died and how he hid there when his father brought Emma home. He wonders why they always paint the barn red and his grandfather gives him the best answer: "Red's the easiest color to see." Then one night the barn catches fire and is destroyed even before the fire engines arrive. Thinking of what he has lost, the boy begins to cry, realizing "that I had no place to go now when I needed to cry." In a few days a new, prefabricated aluminum barn is put into place. The boy hates it. So do the animals. "Change is hard. They'll take to it in time," Emma says. The boy fiercely disagrees and runs to the river, where he is soon joined by his grandfather. They talk about painting the barn red, but the boy feels it will never be the same. His grandfather agrees. "The new barn has to make its own place. It will if we give it a chance." The boy knows his grandfather is referring as much to Emma as the barn. When he realizes that he, like his grandfather, will never forget the past, he feels calmer. He shows his acceptance of the new barn when he says, "I expect silver's the next best color for a barn after red."

In this first-person story, the family barn symbolizes the permanence and security a young boy longs for after the death of his mother and the arrival of his stepmother. When the barn is destroyed, the boy feels doubly threatened. Through the help of his understanding grandfather, he comes to accept the new barn and his new stepmother. Softly defined illustrations emphasize the tender tone of this subtle beginning reader. But because of its subtlety, young readers may need help interpreting the story.

Ages 4-7

Also available in:
No other form known

77

Burch, Robert Joseph

Queenie Peavy

Black/white illustrations by Jerry Lazare.
Puffin Books, 1968.
(159 pages, paperbound)

DELINQUENCY, JUVENILE
Imprisonment
Teasing

Eighth-grade tomboy Queenie Peavy lives in the rural South during the Depression. She becomes defiant and turns to delinquency when taunted by her classmates and neighbors. Their remarks usually refer to the family's poverty and to her father, who is in prison for robbery. Queenie feels that everyone is against her. She fights and causes trouble in and out of school. One day she is responsible for a boy breaking his leg. Queenie idolizes her father and makes excuses for him. Then he is paroled, and she discovers she can no longer justify his mean, inconsiderate behavior. When he is jailed again for violating his parole, Queenie finally holds her father responsible for his own actions. She also begins to realize that her father cares very little for her or her mother. The girl starts reevaluating her own behavior. As a result of her past actions, Queenie must appear before a judge. He takes an interest in her and helps her overcome her defiant attitude and delinquent habits. When Queenie finally faces herself, she makes an effort to accept reality and correct her shortcomings.

This story realistically conveys the frustration, shame, and hostility of a young girl who believes that all her difficulties result from her father's imprisonment. Girls who rebel and become hostile in the face of unhappy, unpleasant situations might find inspiration in Queenie and her gradual change in attitude and behavior.

Ages 11-13

Also available in:
Braille—*Queenie Peavy*
Library of Congress (NLSBPH)

78

Burnett, Frances Hodgson

The Secret Garden

Color illustrations by Tasha Tudor.
HarperCollins Publishers, Inc., 1987.
(256 pages)

BELONGING
FRIENDSHIP: Meaning of
Friendship: making friends
Parental: negligence
Tantrums
Wheelchair, dependence on

After the death of her parents, who ignored her and placed her in the care of servants, ten-year-old Mary Lennox is sent to live with a reclusive uncle in England. No one has ever taken the time to love or understand her, and Mary is not aware of the spoiled, disagreeable front she displays to others. But after a number of days at her uncle's, Mary becomes less unpleasant and begins to make friends with Martha, the Yorkshire maid. Mary enjoys hearing Martha speak of her family, particularly her younger brother Dickon, who seems to be able to tame wild forest animals. Mary begins taking walks around the manor and discovers a walled-in garden. She learns that this garden has been locked since the death of her uncle's wife ten years before. On one of her daily excursions, she finds the key to the secret garden, unlocks the door hidden by ivy, and steps into a world where the untended garden has been allowed to run wild. She is thrilled to find that some early spring flowers are beginning to push through the ground. She uses a stick to cultivate the earth around them and make it easier for the flowers to grow. After leaving the garden that day, Mary resolves to ask her uncle for a small plot of gardening space. He agrees to her request just before he leaves on an extended journey. With Martha's aid, Mary orders seeds and garden tools from town. Dickon delivers the tools, and Mary instinctively knows that he will keep a secret, so she shows him the garden, which they both begin to tend. Late one night, Mary is awakened by a cry from one of the mansion's many corridors. She follows it to its source and finds her cousin Colin, a bedridden young man prone to throwing temper tantrums when his orders are not obeyed by the servants. Colin is ignored by his father because the boy looks so much like his dead mother. Mary tells Colin many stories about the garden, in which she has found so much happiness working with Dickon. Eventually, she coaxes Colin outside in his wheelchair. She and Dickon wheel him to the garden where again the garden works its magic. Colin, whose legs are only weak and not paralyzed as believed, learns to walk with the aid of his friends. The two cousins decide to save this surprise for the return of Colin's father. When Colin's father, who has realized the poor job he has done raising his son, returns, he finds two healthy children who have learned to put other concerns before their own and who have discovered, in the process of caring for the garden, the joy of friendship and belonging.

This enchanting children's classic deals with the awakening of friendship in two self-centered children who have been deprived of the experience of being loved. By first learning to value themselves and their environment, the children discover how to reach out to others, and they find that kindness is often rewarded with kindness. This book could be read to a young child.

Ages 10 and up

Also available in:
Braille—*The Secret Garden*
Library of Congress (NLSBPH)

Cassette—*The Secret Garden*
Library of Congress (NLSBPH)

Paperbound—*The Secret Garden*
HarperCollins Publishers, Inc.

Talking Book—*The Secret Garden*
Library of Congress (NLSBPH)

79

Burningham, John Mackintosh

The Baby

Color illustrations by the author.
HarperCollins Publishers, Inc., 1975.
(19 pages counted)

SIBLING: New Baby

A little boy remarks that the baby in his family makes a mess of its food. Still, he helps his mother bathe the baby and take it for carriage rides. But, the boy confides, there are times when he dislikes the baby because it cannot play with him yet; he hopes that it will soon grow up.

Colorful, simple crayon illustrations are a perfect accompaniment to the extremely simple text of this first-person narrative. These same illustrations might be used to encourage discussion. The book could prepare a very young child for the arrival of a new sibling.

Ages 2-5

Also available in:
No other form known

80

Burningham, John Mackintosh

The Blanket

Color illustrations by the author.
HarperCollins Publishers, Inc., 1975.
(19 pages counted)

TRANSITIONAL OBJECTS: Security Blanket

A young boy, who always takes a special blanket to bed, is distressed when he cannot find it. He asks his parents to help, and they search where adults would: in the bathroom, in the closet, in the car. But the boy finds it under his pillow and at once contentedly goes to sleep.

This first-person narrative makes a very small book whose size alone will attract very young children.

Ages 2-5

Also available in:
Braille—*The Blanket*
Library of Congress (NLSBPH)

81

Burningham, John Mackintosh

The Friend

Color illustrations by the author.
HarperCollins Publishers, Inc., 1975.
(19 pages counted)

FRIENDSHIP: Best Friend
Arguing

A little boy tells about his best friend, Arthur. They play in a sandbox and on a tricycle and, when it rains, play inside with toys or else watch TV. They quarrel over a teddy bear, and Arthur leaves. Dejected, the little boy admits he has other friends but says Arthur is different: he is his *best friend.*

The brief text is simple to read and ends on a happy note: the last picture shows Arthur and the boy together and smiling. The small size of this book and its amusing illustrations will appeal to very young children.

Ages 2-5

Also available in:
Braille—*The Friend*
Library of Congress (NLSBPH)

82
Burningham, John Mackintosh
The School

Color illustrations by the author.
HarperCollins Publishers, Inc., 1975.
(19 pages counted)

SCHOOL: Entering

A little boy tells us that in school he learns to read, write, and sing. He also says that at school he eats lunch, paints pictures, plays games, and makes friends. Then, after a full day, he returns home.

Colorful, simple crayon illustrations go well with this extremely simple first-person narrative. These same illustrations might be used to encourage discussion. The book could be used to help prepare a very young child for beginning school.

Ages 3-5

Also available in:
No other form known

83
Burton, Virginia Lee
Katy and the Big Snow

Color illustrations by the author.
Houghton Mifflin Co., 1973.
(40 pages counted)

RESPONSIBILITY: Accepting
Helping
Self, attitude toward: confidence
Work, attitude toward

Katy is a beautiful red crawler-tractor. She's a real tractor, not a toy. Katy has a bulldozer attached in the summer and a snowplow in the winter. She is proud of her strength. She works hard on the roads in the summer, but in the winter she stays in the garage until she is needed for a really big snowfall. Truck-type snowplows handle the ordinary snowfalls. One wintry day brings ten inches of snow. The wind blows it into drifts that reach to the second-story windows of the houses. All the truck-type snowplows get stuck. Katy is called out to assist the police, the post office, the electric company, the telephone company, and the water department. After she has cleared all of the most difficult roads for them, she is asked to plow a road to the hospital for the doctor, to make way to a fire for the fire department, and to clear the airport runways for the safe landing of an airplane. By this time Katy is tired, but she plows all the side streets so that traffic can move freely. "Then . . . and only then did Katy stop."

The "character" in this delightful children's classic is confident of her abilities and willing to give assistance whenever it is needed. She continues to help others when she has been working hard for a long time and feels very tired. Although the story concerns a tractor, children can readily identify with her feelings of responsibility and pride.

Ages 3-6

Also available in:
Braille—*Katy and the Big Snow*
Library of Congress (NLSBPH)

Paperbound—*Katy and the Big Snow*
Houghton Mifflin Co.

Talking Book—*Katy and the Big Snow*
Library of Congress (NLSBPH)

84
Burton, Virginia Lee
Mike Mulligan and His Steam Shovel

Color illustrations by the author.
Houghton Mifflin Co., 1939.
(46 pages)

FRIENDSHIP: Meaning of
Loyalty

Mike Mulligan is the proud owner of a steam shovel named Mary Anne. After many years of digging roads, canals, airports, and basements for skyscrapers, Mary Anne is still in excellent condition because Mike has taken good care of her. But since she is not diesel-powered, she is considered obsolete and is not hired for any new digging jobs. Mike refuses to abandon Mary Anne. He knows she is just as good as ever, and he takes her to Popperville to prove her worth. He tells the town selectman, Henry B. Swap, that he will be able to dig the cellar for the new town hall in one day. Henry doubts him but decides to give him a chance. The only condition is that if the cellar is not dug in one day, the city will not have to pay for it. As the day passes, Mike and Mary Anne dig faster and faster. When the dust settles, the basement is finished, but Mike has forgotten to leave a way for Mary Anne to get out. The selectman decides that since Mary Anne is still in the hole, the basement is incomplete and Mike will not be paid. Suddenly, a little boy suggests that Mary Anne become the new furnace in the town hall and Mike be the janitor. The townspeople agree, so Mike and Mary Anne are not only paid for their work but also have a permanent home.

This charming children's classic portrays a friendship between Mike Mulligan and his steam shovel. Mike maintains his faith in Mary Anne's ability to perform her duties, and he proves his loyalty to her. The reader is drawn completely into the story and rooting for Mike and Mary Anne to succeed in digging the basement.

Ages 4-8

Also available in:
Braille—*Mike Mulligan and His Steam Shovel*
Library of Congress (NLSBPH)

Cassette—*Mike Mulligan and His Steam Shovel*
Library of Congress (NLSBPH)

Paperbound—*Mike Mulligan and His Steam Shovel*
Houghton Mifflin Co.

Talking Book—*Mike Mulligan and His Steam Shovel*
Library of Congress (NLSBPH)

85

Butler, Beverly Kathleen

Light a Single Candle

Putnam Berkley Group Inc., 1962.
(242 pages) o.p.

BLINDNESS
Education: special
Peer relationships
Pets: guide dog

It stuns fourteen-year-old Cathy Wheeler to learn that she is losing her sight from glaucoma. An unsuccessful operation is performed, leaving Cathy blind. Suddenly, people begin to treat her as if she were helpless, insensitive, and simple-minded. Their attitudes, as well as rejection by her best friend Pete Sheridan, lead Cathy to enroll in the Burton School for the Blind. However, teachers at the school also treat blind persons as if they are incapable of studying anything complex or learning anything other than simple vocations. After one frustrating semester with the teachers and students at Burton, Cathy returns home. She receives help in training a guide dog and enrolls in her hometown high school. There, Cathy is expected to perform as the other students do—to move about without help, to take notes, to study, and to make friends. She meets the challenge.

The difficulties of accepting blindness, training a guide dog, and moving through a sighted world are described with insight and sympathy. Author Beverly Butler brings a special knowledge to the book, since she herself is blind. The sequel, *Gift of Gold,* describes Cathy's experiences as a college student in the field of speech therapy.

Ages 10 and up

Also available in:
Braille—*Light a Single Candle*
Library of Congress (NLSBPH)

Cassette—*Light a Single Candle*
Library of Congress (NLSBPH)

86

Butterworth, William Edmund

LeRoy and the Old Man

Four Winds Press, 1980.
(154 pages) o.p.

DECISION MAKING
VALUES/VALUING: Moral/Ethical
African-American
Crime/Criminals
Fear: of physical harm
Gangs: being bothered by
Grandparent: living in home of
Grandparent: respect for
Lifestyle: change in
Responsibility: accepting

Eighteen-year-old LeRoy Chambers sees three members of the Wolves gang mug and stab an old woman in his Chicago housing project. When questioned by police, he denies having seen anything, fearing reprisals, but the victim has told police LeRoy was a witness. Threatened by the gang, his family's apartment vandalized, LeRoy takes a bus to New Orleans. There his father's father meets him and takes him to his home in Pass Christian, Mississippi, where he'll stay until the trial is over. His grandfather refuses to mention LeRoy's father's name; he deserted LeRoy and his mother six years ago. When LeRoy explains why he needs to stay far away from Chicago, his grandfather says the place for people who knife old women is behind bars, and he suggests that LeRoy ought to help put them there. The old man is a fisherman and LeRoy, though he feels superior toward his grandfather at first, is soon working six days a week hauling in nets and then delivering the shrimp and crabs to restaurants and stores in New Orleans. To help him make these deliveries, his grandfather teaches him to drive. They also begin to rebuild the old man's house, which was destroyed by a hurricane. (He now lives in a shack.) They decide to go into business for themselves, buying catches each day and then marketing them. When his grandfather comes home with a panel truck that says, "A. Chambers & Grandson," LeRoy's eyes fill with tears. The day the roof on the house is finished they drink champagne together. Then police officers from Chicago come to get LeRoy's statement about the crime. He is reluctant to get involved, insisting that the Wolves will cut him to pieces if he testifies. He does give his statement, but before he signs it the officers admit that the victim has died, and they are now dealing with a murder charge. LeRoy's grandfather promises the officers that LeRoy will testify and he tells the boy he'll protect him, which strikes LeRoy as a bit ludicrous. A few weeks later the local sheriff receives orders to place LeRoy in custody as a material witness. This usually involves jail unless bond is paid. Because the sheriff is a good friend of LeRoy's grandfather, he asks LeRoy for just ten dollars bail, but warns him not to go anywhere. Then one night LeRoy finds his long-missing father waiting for him at one of the restaurants where he delivers shrimp. LeRoy meets him later at his hotel. His father wants him to jump bail and hide out in New York with him and his lady friend. He can't ask for a divorce from LeRoy's mother because she'll want six years' child support if she finds out where he is. LeRoy notes with disgust his father's diamond ring and gold watch. He and his mother have had to scrape by for so long. He excuses himself to use the restroom and ducks out. But his father catches up with him another night, claiming to have inside information that the Wolves don't intend to let LeRoy live long enough to reach the witness stand. Again he urges the boy to come to New York with him. He runs his own little numbers racket, and LeRoy could make some easy money. Knowing that LeRoy disapproves of him, he remarks, "I may not be the father you want, but I'm doing the best I know how." When the call comes for LeRoy to testify before the grand jury, his grandfather buys himself and LeRoy new suits. Now LeRoy has a choice: he can use the money his father gave him and go to New York, or he can return to Chicago and testify. But he realizes that he fears one thing even more than he fears the Wolves: the loss of his grandfather's affection and respect. When the old man takes LeRoy to the airport, he mentions that there will probably be a plane for New York at the St. Louis stop. LeRoy realizes that his grandfather has known all along about his father's visit. The two embrace and weep. LeRoy assures the old man that he'll never go the way of his father.

In this outstanding, memorable story, an inner-city teenager learns that the harsh rules and twisted values he picked up in Chicago don't apply in rural Mississippi. LeRoy arrives at his grandfather's shack a cynical, suspicious product of the ghetto, only to hear the old man insist that there are more good people in the world than the other kind. His grandfather's respectful, deep friendships with black and white people surprise and impress LeRoy, giving him a powerful counterweight to his father's seductive promises of easy money in New York. Both LeRoy and his grandfather come vividly alive for the reader in language that is delightfully immediate and colorful. The subtle wit and teasing interplay between the two contribute to the lively, realistic tone of this richly rewarding book.

Ages 12 and up

Also available in:
No other form known

87

Byars, Betsy Cromer

The Animal, the Vegetable, and John D Jones

Black/white illustrations by Ruth Sanderson.
Dell Publishing Company, Inc. (Yearling Books), 1983.
(160 pages, paperbound)

MATURATION
Arguing
Change: accepting
Jealousy: sibling
Parent/Parents: single
Peer relationships

Sisters Clara and Deanie are looking forward to their vacation alone with their divorced father. When he informs the girls that a widowed friend of his, Delores Jones, and her son, John D, will be sharing the beach house, both are very upset. Meanwhile, John D is totally opposed to a vacation with anyone but his mother. She warns him that he'd better be nice. He will go because he has to, replies John D, and he will "do nothing crude. I will cause you no embarrassment. My perfect behavior will quite possibly make Sam's daughters look like the Wicked Stepsisters." The meeting of the two families is extremely uncomfortable. As Delores and John D approach the beach house they overhear Clara and Deanie sniping at each other but uniting in their derogatory remarks about the two of them. But John D, master of the verbal putdown, feels far superior to the girls, labeling Clara "animal" and Deanie "vegetable." For their part, the sisters vow to make weird John D miserable. He silently vows the same thing but, although he normally enjoys being alone and special, can't help feeling lonely here and out of place. Several days of strain and even open hostility pass. One day the two adults go into town, Clara and Deanie go to the beach, and John D stays on the porch. Clara takes a rubber raft and floats around on the waves near the shore. Feeling at peace for the first time since her vacation started, she falls asleep. Several hours later, John D suddenly notices that Clara is not in sight. He recalls the warning he heard about the dangerous ocean currents in the area and runs to tell Deanie, blaming her for the disaster since she should have been watching her younger sister. The two hitchhike into town and find their parents. Soon the four are at the Coast Guard station awaiting word on Clara's rescue. They get discouraging reports at first and are especially frightened when Clara's empty raft is found. Meanwhile, Clara wakes up to realize she has been swept out to sea. Cold and terrified, she drifts for several more hours, steadily losing hope. Finally she is found by a fishing boat with no radio and returned to her father. Everyone is emotionally drained, and the two girls are told they can go home if they want. Deanie wants to leave, but Clara decides to stay. If she left now, it would be like running away and she would always recall "The Terrible Thing That Broke Up the Vacation." "But," she tells Deanie, "it won't be as terrible if I stay." John D seems happy at her announcement, but be's also confused. He knows that for the first time he has allowed himself to care about other people.

In this perceptive, deftly written story, three children from two different families are forced together on a two-week vacation. Two perspectives, the girls' and John D's, help to define the characters. Witty and believable, the story leaves the reader feeling optimistic about the future of all concerned. Several well-placed illustrations capture the mood.

Ages 10-12

Also available in:
Braille—*The Animal, the Vegetable, and John D Jones*
Library of Congress (NLSBPH)

Cassette—*The Animal, the Vegetable, and John D Jones*
Library of Congress (NLSBPH)

88

Byars, Betsy Cromer

The Cartoonist

Black/white illustrations by Richard Cuffari.
Dell Publishing Company, Inc., 1981.
(119 pages, paperbound) o.p.

INFERIORITY, FEELINGS OF
Creativity
Deprivation, emotional
Jealousy: sibling
Loneliness
Privacy, need for

The single thing that lonely, pigeon-toed twelve-year-old Alfie likes about his dreary, untidy home is the attic, where he retreats to draw cartoons. He hopes to become a famous cartoonist some day, but right now he cannot even interest his family in what he draws. His mother is addicted to TV and garrulous reminiscences of no-good Bubba, the older son she idolizes; his grandfather endlessly complains about government; and his older sister, Alma, resenting her mother, is aloof toward them all. At school, Alfie's fascination with cartooning receives no more encouragement than at home. His best friend, Tree, thinks drawing pictures a huge waste of time, and the mathematics teacher, not amused at all when she finds him drawing instead of figuring, tells Alfie he is flunking math. Hurrying home from school to the seclusion of the attic, Alfie meets Alma and gets unwelcome news: Bubba has lost his job, and he and his wife are coming to live in the attic. Unwilling to lose his refuge, Alfie locks himself in. Neither the family nor Tree can coax him down, and Alfie, silent and numb, listening to the talk below, remains overnight in the attic with his cartoons. Next day, Bubba's plan changes: they will go to live with his wife's parents. Weary, aware that he has won nothing by his stand, Alfie rolls up his cartoons and carries them downstairs, knowing that, for better or for worse, that is where he belongs.

Here is the spare, haunting story of a boy whose talent goes unrecognized however much he seeks the approval of others, and who then retreats to a private place of his own. What he fails to recognize is how much he relies for inspiration on his sometimes comic, always lively family. The ending suggests (but does not insist) that he will henceforth pursue his ambition, neither dodging nor deferring to the unheeding life around him.

Ages 8-12

Also available in:
Cassette for the Blind—*The Cartoonist*
Library of Congress (NLSBPH)

89

Byars, Betsy Cromer

Go and Hush the Baby

Color illustrations by Emily A. McCully
Viking Penguin, 1971.
(31 pages counted)

BABY-SITTING: Voluntary
Creativity
Sibling: middle

Mother, busy painting pictures, cooking, and doing other household chores, often sends young Will off to "hush the baby." Will is very resourceful in his attempts to amuse the young child. He sings songs, does magic tricks, and makes up interesting stories that succeed in entertaining both of them. When Mother gives Baby his next bottle, Will is released from his happy duty and goes off to play baseball.

Children who are often charged with minding younger siblings might be interested in both the willing cooperation and the creative methods of this little boy. The simple pictures capture the humor of the story, which has little plot but a great deal of action.

Ages 3-6

Also available in:
Paperbound—*Go and Hush the Baby*
Puffin Books

Talking Book—*Go and Hush the Baby*
Library of Congress (NLSBPH)

90

Byars, Betsy Cromer

Goodbye, Chicken Little

HarperCollins Publishers, Inc., 1979.
(103 pages)

DEATH: of Relative
GUILT, FEELINGS OF
Anxiety
Family: relationships
Fear: of death
Friendship: best friend
Mourning, stages of

It is four days before Christmas when Jimmie Little, about ten, is summoned by his best friend, Conrad, to the banks of the Monday River. There Jimmie finds that his Uncle Pete has accepted a dare to walk across the ice. Though Jimmie, once again embarrassed by the foolhardy actions of his family, asks him to give up the idea, Uncle Pete forges ahead, entertaining a small crowd with his antics. Halfway across, he falls through the ice and drowns. When Jimmie returns home to tell his mother, she accuses him of encouraging Pete to attempt the crossing. Jimmie is overcome by guilt. His mother later apologizes, saying Jimmie was in no way responsible for Uncle Pete's death and that she tends to say things she doesn't mean when she is distraught. But Jimmie is not comforted. When his father died in a coal mine accident years earlier, the boy had started to call himself Chicken Little. He had been overwhelmed with nameless fears then, and the feelings have returned now, with Uncle Pete's death. He is unable to put the drowning out of his mind and neglects the loyal Conrad. Conrad is hurt, Jimmie thinks him uncaring, and the two fight. In an attempt to overcome her own grief, Mrs. Little decides to throw a party for the remaining family members in Pete's honor, even fetching ninety-two-year-old Uncle C.C. from the nursing home. Watching his colorful family enjoy themselves recalling Uncle Pete's pranks, what fun he was and how he had enjoyed life, Jimmie sees that people can express and cope with grief in different ways. Comforted, he feels proud to be a Little. When he notices Conrad peeking in a window, watching the festivities enviously, Jimmie invites him in.

In this fast-moving story, a quiet, cautious boy comes to grips with several disturbing events and emotions: grief and guilt over the accidental deaths of close family members; confusion about a friendship; and anxiety about his place in an outgoing, often unpredictable family. Jimmie's growth in understanding and insight is realistically developed and the story told with warmth and humor.

Ages 9-11

Also available in:
Paperbound—*Goodbye, Chicken Little*
HarperCollins Publishers, Inc.

91

Byars, Betsy Cromer

The House of Wings

Black/white illustrations by Daniel Schwartz.
Viking Penguin, 1972.
(142 pages)

ABANDONMENT
Grandparent: living in home of
Nature: respect for

Ten-year-old Sammy and all of the household belongings have been loaded in the back of the truck. The family is going to Detroit where Dad hopes to get a job. Sammy is excited about going to live in a big city. Late one night, the family stops at Grandfather's home in Ohio. Sammy is so tired that he barely hears Mom's comments about how run-down the place looks. He hardly notices that he has to walk around several geese in the hallway of the house. Late the next morning, Sammy realizes that his parents have left for Detroit without him. His grandfather explains that Sammy's parents have left him only temporarily, and when they are settled in Detroit, they will send for him. Sammy doesn't believe him and shouts "Liar!" Angry and frightened, Sammy runs away. He hates the run-down dwelling, the owl and geese around the house, and most of all, he hates his grandfather. When Grandfather finds Sammy later in the morning, Sammy refuses to be comforted until he is intrigued by his grandfather's command, "Boy, quick! Come here if you want to see something." Sammy approaches his grandfather and discovers a beautiful crane. The big bird is battered and injured. Sammy and Grandfather work together to make the bird well. When Sammy tempts the crane with a frog and the crane eats it, Sammy and his grandfather know that it will live. Drawn close to his grandfather by their efforts to save the crane, Sammy realizes that he loves the old man: "He didn't know how it was possible to hate a person in the middle of one morning, and then to find in the middle of the next morning that you loved this same person."

Unable to accept the fact that his parents would abandon him, Sammy is left with only his distracted old grandfather to serve as a target for his aggressive feelings. Grandfather, who admittedly is more interested in birds than in people, expresses a genuine reverence for life. This gentle, poignant story takes place within a twenty-four-hour time period. Sammy's acceptance of his love for his grandfather and his ability to adjust to life without his parents result naturally from the incidents portrayed.

Ages 9-12

Also available in:
Paperbound—*The House of Wings*
Puffin Books

Talking Book—*The House of Wings*
Library of Congress (NLSBPH)

92

Byars, Betsy Cromer

The Night Swimmers

Black/white illustrations by Troy Howell.
Dell Publishing Company, Inc. (Yearling Books), 1980.
(131 pages, paperbound)

PARENT/PARENTS: Single
RESPONSIBILITY: Accepting
Baby-sitting
Change: accepting
Loneliness
Sibling: oldest

Eleven-year-old Retta (for Loretta Lynn) and her two younger brothers are night swimmers. Although they're always fearful of being discovered, they sneak into Colonel Roberts's pool at night after he and his wife go to bed. This is one of many diversions Retta has found for nine-year-old Johnny (for Johnny Cash) and little Roy (for Roy Acuff). The children's mother died two years ago and their father, Shorty, works nights as a country-western singer and sleeps during the day. So Retta is in charge of the boys day and night. The neighbors disapprove of the lack of adult supervision, but the girl cooks, cleans, shops, and tries to make a home for her brothers. She picks up homemaking tips from television and from observation, but sometimes feels no one appreciates her. Shorty loves his children but, in his drive to become a star, doesn't have much time for them. However, his girlfriend, Brendelle, is sympathetic to Retta's position and feelings. Johnny has made friends with Arthur, a boy his age, and Retta fears she is losing control over him. She also feels a bit resentful that Johnny has turned to someone other than her. One night Johnny slips out when the children are supposed to be sleeping. Retta hears him leave and follows him, discovering Johnny and Arthur at a park launching a small hot-air balloon. Meanwhile, Roy awakes, discovers both Retta and Johnny gone, and decides they have gone swimming at the Colonel's without him. He sneaks over to surprise them, runs up on the diving board, and dives in—even though he can't swim. Retta and Johnny return home from the park to discover Colonel Roberts, who has saved Roy from drowning. Shorty is called home. Retta feels everything has been her fault, but as the adults and children talk she realizes that she must give the boys more room to grow as individuals. Perhaps she has needed them more than they needed her. This becomes clear to her later, when she and Brendelle discuss the evening's events. Sadder but wiser, Retta is somewhat comforted by the hope that Shorty and Brendelle will marry.

Although their life is lonely and largely unsupervised, three siblings stick together, trying to make the most of each day. This is a touching, understated story of a young girl who takes seriously the adult responsibilities thrust upon her, though her family fails to realize she is too young for such demands. Well-done illustrations give an added dimension to the characters and situations. The lack of a standard happy ending seems appropriate to a story that is believable throughout.

Ages 10-12

Also available in:
Cassette—*The Night Swimmers*
Library of Congress (NLSBPH)

93

Byars, Betsy Cromer

The Pinballs

HarperCollins Publishers, Inc., 1977.
(136 pages)

FOSTER HOME
FRIENDSHIP: Meaning of
Security/Insecurity

One summer three unrelated foster children come to live with the Masons. Thirteen-year-old Harvey's legs have been accidently run over by his drunken father. Thomas J. has been a foundling in the home of elderly twin sisters since he was two. Now, six years later, both sisters are hospitalized. Carlie, in her early teens, does not get along with her second stepfather, and when he knocks her unconscious during a fight, she is taken to the Masons. Each child reacts differently in the new household. Harvey, his legs in casts, is quiet and discouraged; he tells the others he broke his legs playing football. Thomas J. is lonesome for the elderly sisters; any reminder of them makes him sad. Carlie is bossy, stubborn, and insulting, but also fiercely loyal to anyone she likes. She grows to like Harvey and Thomas J. Mr. and Mrs. Mason offer encouragement to each child, and little by little this uneasy grouping becomes a family. Mr. Mason takes Thomas J. to the hospital to see the sisters, and by reminiscing about his own feelings as a boy, helps the boy express himself. Mrs. Mason teaches Carlie to sew, and explains that it is because she cannot bear children of her own that she and her husband have opened their home to foster children. One day Harvey's father comes to visit him. Harvey accuses him of confiscating all the letters his mother ever sent him, but his father insists that the mother—who had left home years earlier—has never written to him. When his father leaves, Harvey feels hollow. Withdrawn, he refuses to eat or talk. Worse, a serious infection develops in one of his legs and he must be hospitalized. Carlie is determined to "save" him. She plans a celebration for his birthday, and she and Thomas J. get him a puppy for a gift. The puppy brings Harvey tears of joy, and from then on his health improves steadily. Meanwhile, the elderly twin sisters have died, and little Thomas J. attends their funerals. By now a real bond has developed among the three children. Carlie sums up one result of this solidarity in announcing that she wants to live a purposeful life.

Life at the Masons' contrasts sharply with the pathetic home life each child has left. Carlie's enthusiasm, backed up by the loving guidance of the Masons, cheers all three children. Carlie herself, who has felt like a "pinball"—an object having no control over itself—learns that she can, with effort, lead a life that makes things better. Humor keeps this satisfying story from becoming sugary.

Ages 10-13

Also available in:
Cassette—*The Pinballs*
Library of Congress (NLSBPH)

Paperbound—*The Pinballs*
HarperCollins Publishers, Inc.

94

Byars, Betsy Cromer

The TV Kid

Black/white illustrations by Richard Cuffari.
Viking Penguin, 1976.
(123 pages)

REALITY, ESCAPING
Imagination
Parent/Parents: single
School: achievement/underachievement

Lennie, about eleven, not only watches TV constantly, he also turns his experiences and daydreams into TV characters and plots. Apart from TV, Lennie is friendless, for he and his mother have picked up and moved far too often to have put down roots in a community. Now they have a home, a motel inherited by his mother, but TV still dominates Lennie's life. His mother has to forbid his watching it until his grades improve. Even so, he fails a test but persuades his mother that it was far from a total loss. Thinking TV, though not watching it, he wanders off to a nearby lake, where he enjoys entering and playing in vacant summer homes. A police car on patrol sends him underneath a house to hide, and, after the car has passed, as he is crawling out, Lennie is bitten by a rattlesnake. Lennie desperately attempts to seek help, but he's slowly overtaken by the effects of the venom. He treats the wound as he has seen it done on TV—cutting into it, sucking out the blood and venom, and applying a tourniquet—and hopes someone comes. The policemen return (they have heard of a "prowler" there), and rush Lennie to a hospital. His friendship with the policeman who found him helps lighten his hospital stay, but Lennie's real joy comes when his mother rents a TV set for his hospital room. Yet with the first commercial Lennie realizes TV is not life. "It was close enough to fool you . . . if you weren't careful, and yet those TV characters were as different as a wax figure is from a real person." Equally sudden is his determination to work on a report for school about rattlesnakes to make up for his failing grades.

For Lennie, watching TV is more than a simple diversion; it is an alternative to a life the boy has not done well at. But his "coming up against life hard" discredits TV and its pat formulas in Lennie's eyes. The boy chooses real life, and his eagerness to write about something that concerns him illustrates the change. Although Lennie's mother is obviously struggling alone to run the motel and raise her son, no explanation is given for his father's absence.

Ages 9-12

Also available in:
Paperbound—*The TV Kid*
Puffin Books

95

Caines, Jeannette Franklin

Abby

Black/white illustrations by Steven Kellogg.
HarperCollins Publishers, Inc., 1973.
(32 pages)

ADOPTION: Explaining
Sibling: younger

C

Abby, who is about three or four years old, knows she is adopted. While looking at her baby book, she questions her adoptive mother about where she was born. She also wants to know how old she was and what she was wearing when her adoptive parents brought her home. She asks big brother Kevin to read a book to her, but he refuses, saying he does not have time. Abby asks him if he likes girls, and he emphatically replies, "No!" With that, Abby bursts into tears. Ma explains Abby's reaction to Kevin, telling him that Abby loves him and wants him to like her. Kevin, sorry for hurting Abby's feelings, tries to make up for what he has done by reading to her. He asks their mother if he can take Abby to school for show-and-tell time and explain to the class that she is adopted. Later, Abby asks whether Kevin also is adopted. When Ma explains that he is not, Abby asks if they can adopt a boy for Kevin to play with. Ma promises she will discuss it with Daddy.

This brief story depicts a loving and sensitive relationship between a mother and her two children, one of whom is adopted. The children are aware of the difference in their origins and accept that difference.

Ages 3-7

Also available in:
Paperbound—*Abby*
HarperCollins Publishers, Inc.

96

Caines, Jeannette Franklin

Daddy

Black/white illustrations by Ronald Himler.
HarperCollins Publishers, Inc., 1977.
(32 pages) o.p.

DIVORCE: of Parents

Every Saturday, Windy's father takes her to spend the day with him and Paula. Young Windy loves these Saturdays, when Daddy plays hide-and-seek with her, takes her to the supermarket, and makes chocolate pudding with her. Paula makes dinner, and dresses Windy in old curtains to play bride. When they are apart, Windy worries about her daddy. When they are together, she is joyful.

A little girl enjoys spending Saturdays with her father, who always makes their day a special occasion. Although it is never stated, the reader is led to believe that Windy's parents are divorced. Whether Daddy is now married to Paula is not clear. But being with an absent father regularly is shown to be sheer happiness. This could distress children whose parents don't visit regularly.

Ages 4-8

Also available in:
No other form known

97

Caines, Jeannette Franklin

Window Wishing

Black/white illustrations by Kevin Brooks.
HarperCollins Publishers, Inc., 1980.
(20 pages)

GRANDPARENT: Love for
Visiting

Summer vacation for Bootsie, about four, and his sister, about seven, is spent with Grandma Mag. The children think Grandma Mag is special, and they love visiting her. She wears sneakers all the time, raises worms for fishing, and likes picnicking in the cemetery because it is a peaceful place. She makes special lemonade, lets them set the table with different-colored dishes, and always gives them gingersnaps and cheese with sassafras tea for dessert. They especially enjoy their bike trips downtown to "window wish." Every week each child has two special evenings for looking in store windows and wishing for toys and books. One summer day is particularly special for Bootsie—it's his birthday and he can wish all day long.

Bootsie's sister tells of the joys of visiting Grandma Mag, who enjoys sharing herself with her visiting grandchildren. The story has no problem to solve or situation to resolve; it simply describes the special love between a grandmother and her two beautiful grandchildren. The book is enhanced by softly shaded pictures that help convey the mood of the visits.

Ages 4-7

Also available in:
No other form known

98

Calhoun, Mary Huiskamp

Katie John and Heathcliff

HarperCollins Publishers, Inc., 1980.
(154 pages)

BOY-GIRL RELATIONSHIPS
Maturation
School: classmate relationships

The summer before seventh grade, Katie John Tucker reads and rereads *Wuthering Heights,* mooning over the book's dark, mysterious hero, Heathcliff. When she starts junior high that fall, she begins looking at all the boys as potential Heathcliffs. This is a radical switch for the girl who, the year before, started a boy-haters' club. Now she thinks of little else—as she says, it's a case of "here a boy, there a boy, everywhere a boy-boy!" Romance colors all her activities; even the elderly, unmarried woman whose room she helps clean becomes an aged Cinderella whose prince has never come. Katie has had a satisfying, long-standing friendship with Edwin, a fellow adventurer who lives in the cemetery where his father is caretaker. But the boy she feels could be Heathcliff is shaggy-haired, pale-eyed Jason, an eighth grader in her cooking class. As she tries to interest Jason in a "relationship," Katie becomes involved in school activities and in new and continuing friendships. She tries out for the cheerleading squad but loses the spot to Trish, a more sophisticated classmate. Instead, Katie ends up in a comic five-girl kazoo band that becomes a real crowd pleaser at football games. Always trying to be more "romantical," she has her ears pierced. Some of her friends pair off with boys, but Katie has mixed feelings when the K. C. (Kissed Club) is formed. She is sorry not to be a member, yet secretly glad she has so far escaped being kissed. Having attended her first boy-girl party, Katie decides at Halloween to have her own and to invite Jason. At the party she sees Jason in his true colors: rather cynical and bored, interested only in his date with Trish afterwards, no romantic hero at all. When Edwin invites her to his house "to see what a cemetery is like on Halloween," Katie realizes that this is the boy she really admires. She gladly accepts the invitation.

Although there is little real conflict in this light, humorous treatment of a girl's awakening to boys, readers enjoy Katie John (this is the fourth novel about her) and will find this book appealing, despite its predictable ending. Certain expressions and phrases have become dated, however, and may strike some readers as corny.

Ages 9-11

Also available in:
Cassette—*Katie John and Heathcliff*
Library of Congress (NLSBPH)

Paperbound—*Katie John and Heathcliff*
HarperCollins Publishers, Inc.

99

Cameron, Ann

The Stories Julian Tells

Black/white illustrations by Ann Strugnell.
Pantheon Books, 1981.
(71 pages)

FAMILY: Relationships
IMAGINATION
Friendship: making friends
Sibling: relationships
Tooth, loss of

When Julian, about seven, and his younger brother, Huey, disobey orders and eat most of the lemon pudding their father has painstakingly made for their mother, their father threatens a beating and a whipping. The boys' fear turns to surprise when they discover they are to beat and whip another pudding for their mother! Then the family decides to plant a garden, and the father sends for a seed catalog. When Huey asks what a catalog is, Julian tells him that a catalog has cats in it, that "cats help with the garden." When the catalog arrives and the father discovers why Huey is so disappointed (no cats), he saves the day by telling the boys that catalog cats are so fast that most people never see them. They can't be ordered; they just help in gardens whenever they please, making the work go faster. Since Huey expects the garden to grow especially fast with the help of the catalog cats, Julian spends an evening outside once everything is planted, whispering encouragement to the seeds. Julian receives a fig tree for his birthday. His father tells him the tree will grow as fast as he does. So Julian, who notices that the tree is growing more than he is, secretly eats each new leaf to speed up his own growth. When the tree hasn't grown at all in a year, his father threatens to dig it up and replace it. Only then does Julian decide to leave it alone and let it grow. This same tactic makes Julian change his mind about having his tooth pulled. When he asks his father to pull his baby tooth because the permanent tooth has come in, his father suggests using a pliers and other unacceptable methods. His mother mentions that a cave boy would have been grateful for that extra tooth when eating tough mastodon meat, and Julian takes to this idea immediately. But just as he is thoroughly enjoying his "cave-boy tooth," it comes out when he eats an apple. A new girl, Gloria, moves into the neighborhood, and she and Julian get along famously from the start. She shows him how to make a kite and tie little slips of paper to the tail with secret wishes on them. "When the wind takes all your wishes, that's when you know it's going to work," says Gloria. When they draw the kite in, all the wishes are gone. Julian guesses that one of Gloria's wishes is the same as his—that they will be best friends for a long time.

Julian tells the stories in this easy reader, and he is a curious child eager to learn about and master his world. His parents, especially his father, firmly yet kindly guide him toward acceptable outlets for his energy and creativity. Warm family relationships are emphasized in these chapters, each of which can be read independently as a short story. The illustrations are especially lively, with Julian's alert look as constant as his wild-haired father's calm, steady expression.

Ages 7-9

Also available in:
Braille—*The Stories Julian Tells*
Library of Congress (NLSBPH)

Cassette—*The Stories Julian Tells*
Library of Congress (NLSBPH)

Paperbound—*The Stories Julian Tells*
Alfred A. Knopf, Inc.

100

Carle, Eric

The Grouchy Ladybug

Color illustrations by the author.
HarperCollins Publishers, Inc., 1977.
(40 pages counted)

AGGRESSION
SHARING/NOT SHARING

At five o'clock one morning, two ladybugs, one friendly and one grouchy, land on the same leaf, both eager to breakfast upon the juicy aphids they find there. The friendly ladybug offers to share them, but the grouchy one offers to fight, winner take all. Then, when the challenge is accepted, the grouchy one backs down, saying, "Oh, you're not big enough for me to fight," and flies off. Hour by hour thereafter, the grouchy ladybug challenges ever-larger creatures: at six o'clock, a yellow jacket, at seven a beetle, at ten a lobster, at noon a snake, and at four an elephant, all of whom, although reluctant to fight, accept the challenge. But to even the puzzled elephant, the ladybug replies, "Oh, you're not big enough," and flies off. At five o'clock, the bug encounters a whale. It hurls its challenge but gets no answer. It challenges just the whale's fin: no reply. Finally it challenges the whale's tail—and is slapped clear across the sea, back to the land and the very leaf it had left at five o'clock that morning. The friendly ladybug, still feasting on aphids aplenty, offers to share some of its dinner. The grouchy ladybug says, "Thank you." The friendly ladybug says, "You're welcome."

This story of a disgruntled bug who learns the advantages of getting along with others is told on pages that become wider as the creatures whom the bug challenges get bigger. The page showing the yellow jacket is less than two inches wide; the lobster's page is four inches; the whale's (and binding of the book) is eight and a half inches. A clock pictured at the top of each page shows the hour of each encounter. The illustrations are large and brightly colored; they and the format will appeal to very young readers.

Ages 3-7

Also available in:
Paperbound—*The Grouchy Ladybug*
HarperCollins Publishers, Inc.

101

Carle, Eric

The Mixed-Up Chameleon

Color illustrations by the author.
HarperCollins Publishers, Inc., 1984.
(31 pages counted)

SELF, ATTITUDE TOWARD: Accepting

A small chameleon is quite content with its uneventful life of color changes and fly-catching until it views the splendid animals in a zoo. It is only then that it thinks itself little and weak, and wishes it were more like the animals it sees. As the chameleon speaks its wish, it begins to imagine itself growing parts of the animals it admires. This is lovely—until the chameleon discovers that it is so confused by its new appendages that it cannot catch a fly when it is hungry. Its heartfelt wish to return to its former state is granted, and that state is the loveliest of all.

In this colorfully illustrated story of self-acceptance, the chameleon's desire to be more impressive is one any small child can share. Though the text is brief, the lesson is clear. Vivid illustrations show all the imagined changes the chameleon undergoes.

Ages 4-8

Also available in:
Paperbound—*The Mixed-Up Chameleon*
Library of Congress (NLSBPH)

102

Carrick, Carol

The Accident

Color illustrations by Donald Carrick.
Clarion Books, 1981.
(30 pages counted)

DEATH: of Pet

Young Christopher and his parents are vacationing at their summer cottage. One evening Mother and Father go canoeing, leaving Chris at the cottage watching television with his dog, Bodger. Soon Chris decides to walk to the lake with Bodger to meet his parents on their return. Traffic on the road is heavy, and when a pickup truck suddenly rounds a bend, Christopher calls Bodger a split-second too late from the other side of the road. Bodger runs right in front of the truck and is killed. The driver stops, examines the dog, and sadly explains to the stunned little boy that the dog is dead. Just then Christopher's parents appear, and the boy is sure they can make everything all right. They cannot, and his father just nods while the driver explains what happened. Christopher is angry and hurt. That night all he can think about is how he could have avoided the accident, and how much the dog's death was his fault. Next morning, his father tells him he has buried Bodger by the brook, and Christopher runs angrily into the woods. But he returns, and his father suggests they take the canoe and hunt for a stone to mark Bodger's grave. Christopher becomes absorbed in finding the perfect stone and finally chooses one with markings that remind him of the birch tree by the brook. As they put the stone on the grave, his father recalls how the dog used to try without success to catch trout in the brook. Christopher starts to laugh, then cries, and feels better when his father comforts him.

This quiet story with its subdued illustrations sensitively and honestly expresses a young boy's feelings of anger, guilt, and grief at the death of his pet. With his parents' support and understanding, Christopher is able to accept the death.

Ages 4-8

Also available in:
Cassette—*The Accident*
Brilliance Corp./Houghton Mifflin Co.

Paperbound—*The Accident*
Clarion Books

Talking Book—*The Accident*
Library of Congress (NLSBPH)

103

Carrick, Carol

The Foundling

Color illustrations by Donald Carrick.
Clarion Books, 1979.
(30 pages counted)

PETS: Love for
Decision making

Weeks afterward, young Christopher still mourns the loss of his dog, who was run over by a truck. Though he plays with a puppy from next door, he cannot imagine any dog taking the place of Bodger. His father, thinking the boy needs a dog of his own, takes him to an animal shelter. Shown several dogs, one of which he likes a lot, Chris maintains he wants no pet. He does not know why, he just feels that way. On the return drive, he tells his father that taking another dog would be unfaithful to Bodger. Without pressing the point, his father explains that rescuing an abandoned dog would in fact show love for Bodger. Confused, Chris wanders to the docks—and finds the puppy from next door. But when he brings it back to its owner, she disclaims it, grumbling that the summer tourists must have left it. Chris names the puppy Ben and tells his parents that Ben is now his.

Children often think that acquiring a new pet means disloyalty to a lost or dead one. Chris never actively decides to take the puppy he has found: it is there; no one claims it; and he finally understands that caring for a needy pet is no betrayal of a dead one. This warm story is a sequel to *The Accident,* and is one in a series of books featuring Chris.

Ages 5-8

Also available in:
Paperbound—*The Foundling*
Clarion Books

Talking Book—*The Foundling*
Library of Congress (NLSBPH)

104

Carrick, Carol

Some Friend!

Black/white illustrations by Donald Carrick.
Houghton Mifflin Co., 1979.
(111 pages) o.p.

FRIENDSHIP: Best Friend
FRIENDSHIP: Meaning of
Loyalty
Self, attitude toward: respect

Mike and Rob, each about ten, have been friends since kindergarten but have had their share of quarrels, mostly over Rob's insistence on having everything his way. For Mike, however, there is no one else he would rather be with. That is why he usually gives in to Rob and why he is now selling greeting cards door-to-door with him. After Rob makes a particularly good sale, he spots his mother driving by and abruptly goes off with her, leaving Mike standing there holding the cards. The next morning Rob calls Mike all excited about plans for a club; Mike, remembering how Rob's many other clubs have fizzled, is less enthusiastic. The first meeting at Rob's house includes the usual group and one extra—Kenny, the class oddball, there because Mike felt sorry for him. Through a fluke, Kenny is elected president. Rob promptly disbands the club, using his mother and her supposed disapproval as an excuse. Mike knows he is just being a poor loser and angrily starts to leave. Then Kenny, playing the clown, accidentally bumps Mike into Rob's bicycle, knocking it into the street. Rob orders Mike to pick it up, but he refuses and goes home. That night, after waiting in vain for Rob, Mike hurries alone to the movie at the Boy's Club. He grabs the last empty seat, which turns out to be right in front of Rob and his friend Bubba. At intermission, as Mike stands by himself drinking a can of pop, Rob deliberately bumps him. While Mike is brushing himself off, Bubba steals his treasured baseball cap, given to him by a Red Sox coach. Rob and Bubba and several others toss the hat back and forth, ignoring Mike's pleas to give it back. Finally, Rob heads downstairs with the hat and throws it over the railing when Mike grabs him. For the first time in the history of their friendship Mike attacks Rob in earnest and ends up shoving him down the stairs. He is immediately regretful, but simply retrieves his cap and leaves. At home, Mike decides to call Rob and apologize, only to find that Rob has gone to spend the night at Bubba's. At baseball practice the following morning, Mike tries to ignore Rob. But when he and Rob make a double play on their opponents, Rob smiles at him and Mike is encouraged to approach him after practice. He apologizes for Rob's black eye, anticipating an apology in return, but Rob just shrugs. Mike suggests they take the greeting cards around, but they quarrel again when Rob tells him of his new plan to buy a BB gun with both their profits. At home, Mike tells his mother how angry he is at Rob. "He is the way he is," observes Mike's mother. "You have to decide whether his friendship is worth it." Soon Rob shows up with a bag from a sporting goods store. But instead of a new cap for Mike, he pulls out a new baseball glove for himself. Mike realizes then that to Rob, everything, even friendship, can be replaced. Still, they have a good time together. Mike concludes, "I knew it wasn't going to last—Rob would still make me mad sometimes. But I wasn't going to expect him to be someone he wasn't. It was enough that we were still friends."

C

In this first-person story of friendship, Mike learns as much about his own personal limits and principles as he does about Rob's weaknesses and lack of loyalty. After a serious quarrel he must face what he has sensed for some time: he cares more about their friendship than Rob does. In the end, though wiser, he renews the friendship anyway. This well-told account describes believable, everyday events and relationships. Interesting illustrations that extend the text give the book special appeal for the reluctant reader.

Ages 9-12

Also available in:
Braille—*Some Friend!*
Library of Congress (NLSBPH)

Cassette—*Some Friend!*
Library of Congress (NLSBPH)

105

Caudill, Rebecca

A Certain Small Shepherd

Color illustrations by William Pène Du Bois.
Holt (Henry) and Company, Inc., 1965.
(48 pages)

MUTENESS
Giving, meaning of

Jamie's mother died the day he was born. As Jamie grows up, it becomes apparent that he cannot talk, and there seems to be little hope that this will change. When he is unable to communicate his thoughts to people, Jamie gets frustrated and kicks and screams. His father tries to give extra time to Jamie to make the boy feel needed. When Jamie's father sends him to school, the people of Jamie's small town say that it is a waste of time trying to educate a "no-account boy." But Jamie learns to read, write, and spell. At Christmastime, the whole school plans to put on a play at the little white church not far from Jamie's house. At first, the teacher wants Jamie to pretend to sing carols, but the boy becomes so disruptive that she gives him the part of a shepherd. Jamie throws himself into the role. However, a blizzard forces the cancellation of the play. During the blizzard, a man and a woman come looking for a place to stay. They have already been refused shelter at three other houses by people who told them there was no room. Jamie's father, after first putting them in his stable, worries that it is too cold for them, so he takes them to the church, where there is a stove. During the night, the woman has a baby. In the morning, Jamie puts on his shepherd's robes. The boy gives his own Christmas gifts to the mother and child, and he speaks his first words.

This is a captivating book that is more than just a Christmas story. Although the characterizations are not developed in depth, they nevertheless clearly convey the feelings of love and support between family members. The heartwarming Christmas present of speech for Jamie will capture the sympathy and evoke the emotions of the reader.

Ages 8 and up

Also available in:
Braille—*A Certain Small Shepherd*
Library of Congress (NLSBPH)

Cassette—*A Certain Small Shepherd*
Library of Congress (NLSBPH)

Paperbound—*A Certain Small Shepherd*
Dell Publishing Company, Inc.

Talking Book—*A Certain Small Shepherd*
Library of Congress (NLSBPH)

106

Chalmers, Mary Eileen

Come to the Doctor, Harry

Color illustrations by the author.
HarperCollins Publishers, Inc., 1981.
(32 pages) o.p.

DOCTOR, GOING TO

When young Harry's tail is accidentally slammed in the door, his mother, Mrs. Cat, tells him she must take him to the doctor. But Harry says he doesn't like doctors. "Why?" wonders his mother. Harry replies, "Because." Telling him that's not a good enough reason, the mother cat hurries her kitten off to the doctor's office. There Harry meets a variety of interesting patients: a large dog with a cast on his leg, a small dog with a bandage on his ear, a rooster with a sore throat. The friendly doctor puts some powder and a bandage on Harry's injured tail and tells Mrs. Cat that Harry will be better tomorrow. As he's leaving, Harry comforts three kittens in the waiting room, telling them not to be afraid because "there's nothing to it!" Mother and son head home, with Harry showing off his bandage and relating to everyone he meets the story of how brave he was at the doctor's office.

Simple illustrations and language, humorously combined, make this little book a charming read-aloud. The story offers a completely reassuring view of what goes on at a medical clinic, and so may not prepare children for what might actually be in store for them on their own visit to the doctor. But the animal characters and the warm, friendly experience depicted will appeal to very young children. This book is one in a series about Harry.

Ages 2-5

Also available in:
No other form known

107

Chapman, Carol

Herbie's Troubles

Color illustrations by Kelly Oechsli.
Dutton Children's Books, 1981.
(32 pages counted)

BULLY: Being Bothered by
PROBLEM SOLVING
School: classmate relationships

Herbie, six-and-a-half, likes school until he meets Jimmy John. Jimmy John wrecks the tunnel Herbie makes in the sandbox. He splashes paint on Herbie's picture. He smashes Herbie's granola bar. He ties knots in Herbie's jacket sleeves. The last day of this miserable week, Jimmy John holds the bathroom door shut so Herbie cannot get out. The torment continues until finally, Herbie decides not to go to school anymore. One Monday morning, he resolves to stay home. Sophie, from down the block, suggests that Herbie go to school and be assertive. So Herbie goes to school and tries to stand up to Jimmy John; Jimmy John pulls a button off Herbie's sweater. The next day Herbie decides he really will not go to school. Mary Ellen, from across the street, advises Herbie to share a treat with Jimmy John. So Herbie goes to school and, at lunchtime, tries to share his cake with Jimmy John. Jimmy John smears it all over Herbie's shirt. The next day Herbie vows to stay home. Jake, from around the corner, tells him to punch Jimmy John in the nose. So Herbie goes to school and punches Jimmy John in the nose. Jimmy John punches Herbie in the stomach. They both get sent to the office. The next day Herbie vows he will never go to school again. No one's advice has worked. Then Herbie has an idea of his own and he goes to school. When Jimmy John splashes paint, Herbie ignores him. When he wrecks Herbie's tunnel in the sandbox, Herbie ignores him. Jimmy John swipes his granola bar; Herbie ignores him. Finally

Jimmy John declares that Herbie is no fun anymore. And Herbie once again likes school.

After trying the advice of each of his friends on how to deal with a bully, Herbie solves his problem himself—he cuts off the bully's fun by simply ignoring him. No adults ever get involved. The listening and reading audience should derive great satisfaction from this cleverly illustrated tale about a triumph over adversity.

Ages 5-7

Also available in:
No other form known

108

Childress, Alice

A Hero Ain't Nothin' but a Sandwich

Avon Books, 1977.
(126 pages, paperbound)

DRUGS: Dependence on
Abandonment
Stealing
Stepparent: father

Thirteen-year-old Benjie Johnson is an African-American heroin addict who denies his drug dependence. He claims that he can quit taking heroin any time he wishes, but says that he just does not want to stop right now. Benjie lives with his mother, his grandmother, and his "stepfather," who is not married to his mother. After two teachers turn Benjie in for drug use, he is sent first to a "rehab center" and then home on the condition that he return to see his social worker. He is also to stay away from drugs, but he starts using heroin again anyway. Butler Craig, his "stepfather," tries to help Benjie by accompanying him to ball games, trying to talk with him, and taking him to see the social worker. But when Benjie steals Butler's suit to buy heroin, Butler decides that he has had enough and walks out on Benjie and his mother. When Benjie later tries to steal a toaster from Butler's apartment, Butler chases him. Benjie slips on the edge of a roof, and Butler saves his life. Butler now realizes that he cannot desert Benjie, and the boy, feeling wanted for the first time in years, appears to wish to go straight.

The book is written as a series of first-person narratives: Benjie's mother, his grandmother, his teachers, his pusher, his "stepfather," his principal, and one of his friends each tell Benjie's story from their own point of view. Some of the dialogue is written in Black English. The profanity in some of the dialogue could be offensive to some readers. Throughout the book, Benjie insists that he is not "hooked" on heroin. He blames his teachers, his home situation, a friend, and society in general for his drug problem. The book's open ending might be used to begin a discussion.

Ages 12 and up

Also available in:
Braille—*A Hero Ain't Nothin' but a Sandwich*
Library of Congress (NLSBPH)

Talking Book—*A Hero Ain't Nothin' but a Sandwich*
Library of Congress (NLSBPH)

109

Childress, Alice

Rainbow Jordan

Coward–McCann, 1990.
(142 pages)

AFRICAN-AMERICAN
FOSTER HOME
PARENTAL: Negligence
PARENTAL: Unreliability
SELF, ATTITUDE TOWARD: Accepting
Fear
Honesty/Dishonesty
Love, meaning of
Sex: attitude toward

At fourteen, Rainbow Jordan is used to being left alone. But this time her young mother, Kathie, is stranded at a resort with her latest boyfriend, waiting for a go-go dancing job, and Rainbow is faced with an eviction notice on their apartment door. So the social worker takes her to an interim foster home again, to Miss Josie. Not wanting anyone to know about her mother's absence, Rainbow tells her boyfriend, Elijay, and her best friend, Beryl, that Miss Josie is her aunt. When Rainbow arrives, Miss Josie says that her husband, Hal, is out of town on business. Aware that the first days for her "repeat" children, particularly Rainbow, are often difficult, Miss Josie tries to ease the tension by keeping the girl busy. She's a seamstress and has Rainbow help with the sewing. She takes Rainbow to a fitting, plans outings to museums, and teaches the girl to prepare meals and set an attractive table. On one of her previous visits Rainbow started her first menstrual period. Miss Josie had gently talked with her about sex, a subject Kathie evades; Kathie also refuses to give Rainbow permission for sex education classes at school. Miss Josie's advice is to use self-control. "Don't let mother nature decide your future too soon. She'll take over and run you ragged." Rainbow appreciates Miss Josie, even if she is "square," but her mother is rarely out of her mind. She worries about her safety and when she'll return. At school Rainbow is studying death. "But how bout the loss of a loved one who still livin?" she wonders, thinking of the times her mother is away, or Elijay stops speaking to her because she won't "go all the way," or Beryl and she start drifting apart. Besides these troubles with her friends, Rainbow is under pressure from her teachers. One needs her mother to come in for a conference by Tuesday at the latest. Rainbow has run out of excuses, and by Monday Kathie has not returned. She has telephoned, however, promised to be back for the conference, and had her ex-husband send a check for the rent. The longer she stays with Miss Josie, the more Rainbow notices that the woman, usually patient and polite, seems short-tempered and snappish, particularly when questioned about her husband. Then Miss Josie, realizing she has been overly strict with Rainbow, grants her permission to go to the teen center after school. Instead, Rainbow takes the key to her mother's apartment, which Miss Josie has denied her time and again, and plans a rendezvous there with Elijay. Although she is terrified of getting pregnant, she has decided to give in to him because she fears losing him to another girl. Elijay finally arrives—with his new girlfriend. Rainbow is at first polite, but eventually orders them out. Miss Josie arrives soon after that and, though relieved to learn that nothing happened, lectures Rainbow all the way back to her house. Once there, Miss Josie must leave again on a quick errand and Rainbow waits for her on the front steps. She learns from a nosy neighbor the truth about Miss Josie's husband: he has run off with another woman. At this, Rainbow rushes into Miss Josie's apartment and finds her secret papers strewn all over, including her passport listing her age as fifty-seven, not fifty as she tells everyone. When Miss Josie returns, Rainbow demands to know why she lied about her age, why she's been pretending. This time it is Rainbow giving advice about facing up to things, Rainbow who reads the letter Miss Josie has received from Hal asking for a divorce. The next morning at breakfast, conference day, Miss Josie must tell Rainbow that Kathie called late last night and cannot get back. "Miss Josie," Rainbow says, "my mother doesn't love me as much as I love her." Then she asks if Miss Josie loves her. Miss Josie assures Rainbow that she cares about her deeply and will go to school with her. Furthermore, she suggests that Rainbow stay on with her for six months or so, and Rainbow agrees. On the way to school, Miss Josie volunteers to tell the teachers she is Rainbow's aunt, but Rainbow says no. She recognizes that the lie Miss Josie tells about her age is a little one, not one that hurts anyone. She decides to stop her own big lies about her mother.

This story of emotional growth is written from three viewpoints—Rainbow's, Kathie's, and Miss Josie's—but it is focused on Rainbow. It is she who comes to realize that her mother will not change and so she herself must stop pretending and start living. For all her years Rainbow has lived in fear—fear that Kathie will hurt her, fear that she will do something Kathie disapproves of, fear that Kathie will not return, fear that Kathie does not love her. The quiet support she receives from Miss Josie and the way Miss Josie faces her own lie and fear of abandonment encourage and strengthen Rainbow, enabling her to admit her fears. In the end, she reveals a budding inner strength. By presenting the viewpoints of all three characters and thus gaining sympathy or understanding for each, the author demonstrates the complexity of their situations. Use of black dialect strengthens, rather than obscures, this memorable story, which includes several candid discussions about sex and some profanity.

Ages 12 and up

Also available in:
Braille—*Rainbow Jordan*
Library of Congress (NLSBPH)

Cassette—*Rainbow Jordan*
Library of Congress (NLSBPH)

Paperbound—*Rainbow Jordan*
Avon Books

110

Christopher, Matthew F.

Johnny Long Legs

Black/white illustrations by Harvey Kidder.
Little, Brown & Company, Inc., 1988.
(144 pages, paperbound)

SPORTS/SPORTSMANSHIP
Expectations
Friendship: making friends
Height: tall
Name-calling

Twelve-year-old Johnny Reese is looking foward to life with his new stepfather and younger stepbrother Toby. He finds the small town of Lansburg different from the New York neighborhood where he used to live. Johnny is a couple of inches taller than the rest of the boys his age, and having played some scrub basketball, he becomes the center on Toby's team. Although everyone expects him to be outstanding, Johnny knows that being tall does not necessarily make him a good basketball player; his height impedes his coordination. It is discouraging to find that shorter boys can outplay him. Soon the fans are calling him names—"leadfoot," and, worst of all, "Johnny Long Legs." He must also contend with tough Jim Sain, a star player on another team, whose practical jokes almost cost Johnny his life. Instead of seeking revenge, Johnny approaches Jim's coach, who has suspended the prankster, and asks that Jim be given another chance. The two players become friends. After much practice with Toby, Johnny learns to take advantage of his height. As his play improves, he gains self-confidence. The name-calling ceases to bother him; he even takes Johnny Long Legs as his nickname.

This basketball story concentrates on Johnny and his teammates. The boy's adjustment to his mother's remarriage is secondary. Although the relationships between the characters are not developed in depth and the solution to Johnny's problem seems especially easy, readers can readily identify with his frustration and anger when he cannot measure up to the expectations of others.

Ages 9-11

Also available in:
No other form known

111

Cleary, Beverly Bunn

Beezus and Ramona

Black/white illustrations by Louis Darling.
William Morrow & Company, Inc., 1955.
(159 pages)

SIBLING: Younger
Parental: overpermissiveness
Tantrums

Beatrice Quimby (nicknamed Beezus) is a nine-year-old with a big problem: her four-year-old sister, Ramona. Ramona uses every means at her disposal to get what she wants. She frequently throws tantrums or threatens to get what she wants. She is a pest. Mother laughingly says, "I'm afraid all we can do is wait for her to grow up." While Beezus is working on a gift for Aunt Beatrice, Ramona pesters her until Beezus agrees to reread Ramona's favorite book again and again. Tired of reading the same book, Beezus takes her sister to the library to borrow a different one. When Ramona "writes her name" in purple crayon on each page of the library book, Mother gives the girls money to pay for replacing it. Ramona is disappointed when the librarian gives Beezus the book, which has to be discarded because of the damage. Ramona had hoped to be the owner of her new favorite book. One afternoon, Ramona decides she wants a party. She invites the neighborhood children without telling her mother about it. Unprepared, Mother and Beezus must work very hard to entertain all the guests until their mothers come for them. On Beezus's birthday, Ramona ruins the first two cakes Mother tries to bake. After Ramona has been sent to her room because she made a mess of her food and talked back to her parents at dinner, Beezus blurts out that she does not love Ramona. Mother and Aunt Beatrice calmly tell Beezus stories of their childhood when they were anything but happy with each other, and Beezus can see that the two sisters are good friends now.

The adults in this sometimes humorous book are sympathetic to Beezus's problems, but they appear to assume that Ramona will outgrow her tantrums and willfulness with very little discipline. Although she suffers abuse from her sister, Beezus feels guilty when she realizes she does not always love Ramona. Through the understanding of her elders, she learns that such feelings are natural and acceptable.

Ages 8-10

Also available in:
Braille—*Beezus and Ramona*
Library of Congress (NLSBPH)

Talking Book—*Beezus and Ramona*
Library of Congress (NLSBPH)

112

Cleary, Beverly Bunn

Henry and the Clubhouse

Black/white illustrations by Louis Darling.
William Morrow & Company, Inc., 1962.
(192 pages)

RESPONSIBILITY: Accepting
Problem solving

Young Henry Huggins confronts numerous obstacles when he tries to deliver newspapers and obtain new customers for his route. Conscientious, if not always prompt, Henry carries his papers past mean dogs and through uncomfortable weather—despite constant pestering from Ramona, his young neighbor. Henry also finds time to build a clubhouse with other boys in the neighborhood. Ramona, who is always playing pranks on Henry, deliberately locks him in the clubhouse. Henry tries everything he can think of to get out without revealing the secret hiding place of the padlock key for the clubhouse door. Soon, he realizes that he cannot get out by himself, and he must be free by six o'clock to deliver his papers. He finally sends Ramona to get her sister, Beezus, who releases him only after he teaches her the club's secret entry words. Ramona continues to pester. One day she insists on helping Henry deliver papers in snowy weather, but she soon becomes too tired to walk. Henry feels sorry for her and says, "Get on the sled, and I'll pull you home." Soon a "Dear Editor" letter appears in the newspaper, commending Henry's fine work on his route and his kindness in helping little Ramona. Henry, although proud of himself, realizes that if it had not been for Ramona, the letter would not have been written. He cannot help thinking, "Good old Ramona."

Henry learns several lessons about responsibility in this amusing book. He faces each new challenge with boyish guile and readiness. The believable characters and delightful humor will endear *Henry and the Clubhouse* to young readers. There are numerous other books about the characters in this story, including *Henry and the Paper Route.*

Ages 8-10

Also available in:
Braille—*Henry and the Clubhouse*
Library of Congress (NLSBPH)

Cassette—*Henry and the Clubhouse*
Library of Congress (NLSBPH)

113

Cleary, Beverly Bunn

Henry and the Paper Route

Black/white illustrations by Louis Darling.
William Morrow & Company, Inc., 1957.
(192 pages)

RESPONSIBILITY: Accepting
Friendship: making friends
Job
Peer relationships
Problem solving

The world of ten-year-old Henry Huggins is a neighborhood of front porches, girlfriends with pesky kid sisters like Ramona, and dogs like Ribsy at his heels. One day when he is looking for something interesting to do, Henry decides to apply to Mr. Capper for a newspaper route. Henry's friend Scooter, who is a newsboy, frankly doubts that Henry can handle such an important job, since Henry is not quite eleven, the proper age for a newspaper carrier. But Henry believes he can do the work. To prove it, he goes to the district manager himself and asks for a route. Unfortunately, Henry has four kittens stuffed inside his jacket at the time, and because they cause such a funny commotion, he does not appear very mature. Mr. Capper concludes that Henry is not quite ready to become a carrier. During the following weeks, Henry tries to demonstrate his responsibility. He substitutes on Scooter's route, and as his eleventh birthday nears, he thinks he has a good chance of getting the route. His hopes are temporarily dashed when an older boy who is new to the neighborhood gets the route. But before long, the new boy regrets having taken the route that Henry wanted, and he cannot cope with the troublesome Ramona; so he gives it up. Henry becomes the new paperboy and invents a game that keeps Ramona from picking up the papers along the route.

Warm humor and skillful storytelling shine through in this story. Henry's acceptance of responsibility and use of creativity in solving problems are woven into the text in a nonmoralizing way.

Ages 7-10

Also available in:
Braille—*Henry and the Paper Route*
Library of Congress (NLSBPH)

Talking Book—*Henry and the Paper Route*
Library of Congress (NLSBPH)

114

Cleary, Beverly Bunn

Mitch and Amy

Black/white illustrations by George Potter.
William Morrow & Company, Inc., 1967.
(232 pages)

TWINS: Fraternal
Bully: fear of
School: achievement/underachievement

Nine-year-old twins Mitch and Amy fight each other, but they also show mutual love and concern. Each twin has a particular difficulty in school. Mitch struggles with reading while arithmetic troubles Amy. Their mother tries to help them both, but the twins rarely offer to help each other. Yet it is Amy who finds the book which captures Mitch's interest and starts him reading. When each is confronted by Alan, a bully, the brother and sister show a united front. During the course of their year in fourth grade, the twins learn to deal with their academic difficulties. Near the end of the year, the problem with the bully is also finally solved. Alan makes the mistake of losing his temper and saying angrily, "I'll wreck your whole box. H-O-W-L. Whole box!" The resulting laughter shames him so much that it is unlikely he will ever bully anyone again. Amy realizes that Alan has the same trouble with words that Mitch had.

This vivid, realistic presentation of the problems and the joys of being fraternal twins is lightened with humor. The mother in this story is present when her children need her. However, the father's involvement is limited to repetitions of his two standard lectures to the children.

Ages 9-11

Also available in:
Braille—*Mitch and Amy*
Library of Congress (NLSBPH)

115

Cleary, Beverly Bunn

Otis Spofford

Black/white illustrations by Louis Darling.
William Morrow & Company, Inc., 1953.
(191 pages)

PRACTICAL JOKES/PRANKS
School: behavior

Otis Spofford, about ten, greatly enjoys "stirring up a little excitement." He accomplishes this by playing practical jokes on his classmates in Room Eleven at Rosemont School. He particularly likes to trick a girl named Ellen Tebbits because she is so neat and well behaved. He knows he can always make her angry. "Someday," his teacher promises, "you will get your comeuppance." After each prank he plays, Otis asks his teacher if he has gotten his comeuppance yet. Finally, he does an unforgiveable thing. For months, Ellen has been trying to grow her hair long enough to make pigtails. Otis, pretending to be an Indian, cuts off her locks. Nobody laughs, and Otis knows he has gone too far. The next day, when Otis goes skating, the boys ignore him, and Ellen takes his special shoes with glowing green and pink shoelaces home with her. Otis must chase her all the way home on his skates in order to retrieve his shoes. In the process he ruins his skates, get blisters, and meets his mother. Although she usually says nothing about Otis's pranks, this time she soundly scolds him for chasing Ellen. Otis has finally received his comeuppance.

The reader is left with the impression that Otis will revert to playing more practical jokes but will probably become more considerate of others' feelings. Each chapter of this book contains a complete, humorous episode, making it good read-aloud material for older children. Otis and Ellen have appeared in another book by the author entitled *Ellen Tebbits.*

Ages 8-10

Also available in:
Braille—*Otis Spofford*
Library of Congress (NLSBPH)

116

Cleary, Beverly Bunn

Ramona and Her Father

Black/white illustrations by Alan Tiegreen.
William Morrow & Company, Inc., 1975.
(187 pages)

FAMILY: Relationships
Parent/Parents: mother working outside home
Smoking

Seven-year-old Ramona is alarmed to learn that her father has lost his job. Hoping to make money herself, she starts acting out television commercials in private, but when one day a homemade crown for a margarine ad gets so entangled in her hair that her father has to cut it out, her show-business career is nipped in the bud. Home life turns grim. Mom is working full time, and her father becomes bored with housekeeping. Ramona and her sister, Beezus, launch a campaign to get him to quit smoking—but when he tries, he becomes even more irritable. Soon both parents are down on Ramona for having volunteered to play a sheep in the approaching church Christmas pageant on the understanding that her hard-pressed mother will make her costume. Home life improves when her father gets a job, but when the night of the pageant arrives and Mom has only managed to convert a pair of pajamas into a "sheep suit," Ramona balks at wearing it. Then some older girls call her "cute" and blacken her nose with mascara. She thinks herself a fine sheep after all. Seeing her parents in the audience, she feels proud of them. Seeing her father wink at her, she knows they are proud of her, too.

A period of family ups and downs teaches Ramona new things about her family, and her father's anxious irritability ends by only drawing her closer to him. Both text and illustrations are brisk and delightful. This is one in a series of books about Ramona and her family and friends.

Ages 7-10

Also available in:
Braille—*Ramona and Her Father*
Library of Congress (NLSBPH)

Cassette—*Ramona and Her Father*
Library of Congress (NLSBPH)

117

Cleary, Beverly Bunn

Ramona and Her Mother

Black/white illustrations by Alan Tiegreen.
William Morrow & Company, Inc., 1979.
(208 pages)

C

CHANGE: Accepting
FAMILY, Relationships
Parent/Parents: mother working outside home
School: pupil-teacher relationships
Sibling: rivalry
Sibling: younger

Howie Kemp is Ramona Quimby's best friend, but Willa Jean is his little sister—and a pest. When Ramona, seven-and-a-half, overhears neighbors say that little Willa Jean reminds them of her when she was younger, the girl is highly insulted. She thinks Willa Jean is spoiled and a show-off, not at all like her. But when she asks her mother about it later, her mother tells her that she was indeed a lively little girl with a lot of imagination. This information upsets Ramona, as do other events in the Quimby household. Ramona's father, after being out of work for quite a while, at last has a job, as cashier at the Shop-Rite Market. But he hates it and sometimes comes home grouchy. Ramona is sure her mother will now quit her full-time job and once again become a full-time mother; she misses their times together. However, to her disappointment, she learns that her mother plans to continue working. This means Ramona has to go to the Kemps' house after school. She worries that she and her mother have grown apart since her mother started working. She also feels that Beezus, her seventh-grade sister, gets more of their mother's attention. When her mother and Beezus quarrel over Beezus's hairdo, Ramona is glad to see they aren't getting along. Yet she worries a little because she wants the family to be happy. Several weeks later, Ramona is given a new pair of flannel pajamas. She loves them so much she decides to wear them to school under her clothes. Her teacher, Mrs. Rucker, notices how hot Ramona looks, and finally Ramona tells her about the pajamas. To the girl's surprise, Mrs. Rucker does not laugh at her, and Ramona feels they share a special secret. That Saturday she overhears her mother talking to Mrs. Rucker on the phone. Sure that her teacher is telling her mother their secret about the pajamas, Ramona screams that she hates Mrs. Rucker. She also screams that nobody likes her, not even her own mother and father, and that Beezus gets all the attention. Beezus, in turn, argues that Ramona gets more attention and has fewer chores than she does. Ramona then declares she is running away. Her mother helps her pack, all the while explaining how to pack a suitcase properly. When Romana finds that the suitcase is so full she can't lift it, she knows her mother didn't mean to let her go. She also learns that Mrs. Rucker's call was about Ramona's nose twitching. She was wondering if Ramona was nervous about something. Ramona explains that she was pretending to be a rabbit. Assured of her family's love and Mrs. Rucker's concern, Ramona goes happily off to roller skate.

This funny and touching story shows the struggles of a little girl trying to cope with changes in her family's lifestyle resulting from hard economic times. Ramona comes to realize that these changes, while upsetting, do not affect her parents' love for her. This is one in a series of books about Ramona and her family and friends, and it makes appealing, satisfying reading. Each episode is appropriately illustrated and exceptionally true to life.

Ages 7-10

Also available in:
Braille—*Ramona and Her Mother*
Library of Congress (NLSBPH)

Cassette—*Ramona and Her Mother*
Library of Congress (NLSBPH)

118

Cleary, Beverly Bunn

Ramona Quimby, Age 8

Black/white illustrations by Alan Tiegreen.
William Morrow & Company, Inc., 1981.
(190 pages)

FAMILY: Relationships
Money: management
School: classmate relationships
School: pupil-teacher relationships

It's the first day of school and things are a bit different in the Quimby family. Ramona will be riding the bus for the first time and, because of changes in the system, she and the other third graders will be the oldest kids at school. Beatrice (called Beezus) is starting junior high. Their mother has taken a job, and their father is returning to school to become a teacher. Ramona still has to go to Howie Kemp's grandmother's house after school, where Howie's little sister, Willa Jean, still drives her crazy. One week, all the kids bring hard-boiled eggs for lunch. A clowning Ramona becomes an angry and embarrassed Ramona when she cracks her egg open on her head and discovers her mother hasn't boiled it. While the principal helps her wash the egg out, she overhears some teachers talking and is devastated when her teacher, Mrs. Whaley, refers to her as a show-off and a nuisance. From then on, Ramona tries anxiously to avoid being a nuisance. One day she ruins everything by throwing up in the classroom. Sick as she is, she must wait in the office for some time before her mother can leave work and come for her. Then she finds that the car has broken down and they must take a taxi. In other circumstances, Ramona would have loved the excitement of her first taxi ride. But now she's too distressed and ill. She can't bear to tell her mother that she didn't let Mrs. Whaley know she felt sick because she was trying hard not to be a nuisance. But her mother stays home from work to take care of her and doesn't seem to mind. The family continues to have its ups and downs. The car needs a new transmission, which they can't afford; Beezus is worried about a party she's invited to; and Ramona is worried about a book report she has to give. Searching for inspiration, she decides to give the report as if it were a cat-food commercial. She even wears a cat mask. From behind it, she feels brave enough to tell Mrs. Whaley about her fears of being a nuisance. The teacher explains that Ramona misunderstood; Mrs. Whaley meant that washing egg out of hair was a nuisance, not that Ramona was a nuisance. Restored to good spirits at school, Ramona worries anew about her family. Her parents, she knows, fret about the future. Ramona herself worries about her father getting locked in the frozen-food warehouse where he now works part-time. One rainy Sunday when the Quimby house seems particularly small and its inhabitants especially grouchy, Mr. Quimby suggests they all go to a fast-food restaurant and never mind the cost. A stranger, an older gentleman, pays for their dinner because, he tells the waitress, they look like such a nice family. On the way home, Mrs. Quimby says she thinks the man was right—they are a nice family. Not all the time, maintains Ramona. But her father says nobody is nice all the time unless they're very boring. Ramona decides in the end that "she was a member of a nice sticking-together family."

Well known to most young readers, Ramona Quimby stars in another story of everyday life in the Quimby family home and at school. This time the Quimbys must cope with the changes that attend the father's decision to return to school. Plucky Ramona must also learn to adjust to a new teacher she's sure dislikes her. But all is either resolved or accepted in this realistic, appealing, and funny story with its whimsical illustrations. Old and new fans of Ramona Quimby will be thoroughly pleased.

Ages 8-10

Also available in:
Braille—*Ramona Quimby, Age 8*
Library of Congress (NLSBPH)

Cassette—*Ramona Quimby, Age 8*
Library of Congress (NLSBPH)

119

Cleary, Beverly Bunn

Ramona the Brave

Black/white illustrations by Alan Tiegreen.
William Morrow & Company, Inc., 1975.
(190 pages)

FAMILY: Relationships
SCHOOL: Pupil-Teacher Relationships
SIBLING: Relationships
Fear: of darkness

Six-year-old Ramona Quimby is bursting with anticipation: In September she will begin first grade, and soon after she will have a bedroom all to herself. She and her older sister, Beezus, have been sharing a room, but now, thanks to her mother's new part-time job, the family can afford to have a new room built on to the house. But Ramona's first-grade teacher turns out to be stiff, strict, and unresponsive, and Ramona decides Mrs. Griggs dislikes her. Moved into the new bedroom, Ramona finds she is afraid of the dark and misses talking and giggling with Beezus. Trying to be brave, she tells none of this to her parents, and her life becomes routinely miserable day and night. When Mrs. Griggs includes two complaints in the girl's favorable school progress report, Ramona is furious. Worse, she thinks her parents side with the teacher; she bursts into tears, crying that everyone is against her. At last, she and her parents talk everything over, and she begins to feel better. "Show us your spunk," says her father, and Ramona finds the courage to start over both with Mrs. Griggs and the new bedroom.

This is an amusing and touching story of a little girl who tries to keep all her woes to herself. When, inevitably, the adults in her life seem insensitive, she learns the value of opening up. The illustrations are also amusing. This book is one in a series about Ramona and her family and friends.

Ages 7-10

Also available in:
Braille—*Ramona the Brave*
Library of Congress (NLSBPH)

Talking Book—*Ramona the Brave*
Library of Congress (NLSBPH)

120

Cleary, Beverly Bunn

Ramona the Pest

Black/white illustrations by Louis Darling.
William Morrow & Company, Inc., 1968.
(192 pages)

SCHOOL: Classmate Relationships
SCHOOL: Entering
SCHOOL: Pupil-Teacher Relationships
Identity, search for

Five-year-old Ramona is glad she is beginning kindergarten because now she will be like her older sister. When she enters the classroom, her teacher, Miss Binney, guides her to a small chair and tells her to "sit here for the present." A present! Ramona is overjoyed. Ramona sits through a talk on class rules, the assignment of cupboards, and a new song about the "dawnzer lee light." Finally, when the class goes outside to play a game and Ramona still does not budge, Miss Binney asks the girl why she will not leave her seat. Ramona calmly informs Miss Binney that she is waiting for her present. To Ramona's disappointment, Miss Binney tells her that "for the present" means "for now." Ramona decides to play with her class but ends up being reprimanded because she cannot resist pulling Susan's sausage-shaped curls to see if they go "boing." When Halloween arrives, Ramona wears a witch costume and a scary mask for the school parade. At school, she discovers that no one recognizes her, and she finds it unsettling to be unknown. She takes off her mask, but Miss Binney tells her she must wear it. She decides to make a sign with her name on it and solve her "identity crisis" by wearing the sign. On another day, things go terribly wrong in school. After "boinging" one of Susan's curls, Ramona receives an ultimatum: she must stop pulling Susan's hair or remain home until she is able to stop. Ramona, who is irresistibly drawn to those curls, says "no" to Miss Binney. So Miss Binney sends Ramona home explaining that she can return when she is able to leave Susan's hair alone. After refusing to attend school for about a week, Ramona receives a note from Miss Binney requesting her return. This makes Ramona feel much better.

This book, although written for an older child, describes a five-year-old's first few months at kindergarten. It is easy for readers to sympathize with Ramona, having probably once had similar feelings themselves. The relationships in the story are quite credible, although the adults never seem to lose their tempers or to have much insight into the world of children.

Ages 8-10

Also available in:
Braille—*Ramona the Pest*
Library of Congress (NLSBPH)

Cassette—*Ramona the Pest*
Library of Congress (NLSBPH)

Talking Book—*Ramona the Pest*
Library of Congress (NLSBPH)

121

Cleary, Beverly Bunn

The Real Hole

Color illustrations by Mary Stevens.
William Morrow & Company, Inc., 1986.
(32 pages counted)

TWINS: Fraternal
Imagination

Jimmy and Janet are four-year-old twins. Although they have the same parents and the same birthday, they do not always like the same things. Janet likes to pretend with her toys. Jimmy prefers real things. One day Jimmy attempts to dig a hole with his toy shovel, but the handle breaks off. He tries using his father's shovel, but it is too big. Father gives Jimmy a trench shovel, which is just the right size, and Jimmy works until lunch time while Janet swings. After lunch, he continues working on his excavation while Janet rides her hobby horse. By nap time, Jimmy has dug a big hole. He digs again after his nap. Janet suggests uses for the hole: a fishing pond, a rabbit hole, or a bird nest. Jimmy, however, wants to leave the hole as it is. Father says he has an idea and drives away in the car. When he returns with a small spruce tree, they plant the tree in the hole and water it. Next Christmas the family will have two trees—one inside and one outside.

The parents in this book recognize that the twins have very different personalities, and they treat the children accordingly. The children get along in spite of their differences.

Ages 3-6

Also available in:
Braille—*The Real Hole*
Library of Congress (NLSBPH)

Cassette—*The Real Hole*
Library of Congress (NLSBPH)

122

Cleaver, Vera and Bill Cleaver

Grover

Black/white illustrations by Frederic Marvin.
HarperCollins Publishers, Inc., 1987.
(125 pages)

SUICIDE: of Parent
Communication: parent-child
Illnesses: of parent
Mourning, stages of

Eleven-year-old Grover is looking forward to another long, hot, lazy summer in the little town of Thicket, Florida. Although he has never been told of it, his mother has been ill for some time and needs surgery. Grover's father, uncle, and aunt seem to know something they are not telling him. He worries about the possibility that his mother will die, but he refuses to talk about it. When Mother returns home from the hospital and seems to feel quite well, Grover's fears decrease. But he notices that Mother wants to talk to him a great deal. Her condition worsens, and one day while Grover is outside playing, she shoots herself. At this difficult time, Grover has no one to confide in. His father becomes withdrawn, and although Grover likes and respects him, he has never been able to think of his father as someone with whom he could talk. They go to church, and after a talk with the minister, Grover feels a little better about his mother's death and his father's withdrawal. Visiting his mother's grave with Father, Grover comes to understand that life must go on. His father begins to realize this too.

This book tells of the confusion experienced by a child who must face the illness and suicide of a parent without the support of family members. The portrayal of the father's grief and its effect on the child will evoke the sympathy and understanding of the reader.

Ages 9-12

Also available in:
No other form known

123

Cleaver, Vera and Bill Cleaver

Me Too

HarperCollins Publishers, Inc., 1973.
(158 pages) o.p.

EGOCENTRISM
Mental retardation
Separation, marital
Twins: fraternal

Lydia, an intelligent twelve-year-old, assumes that her happy life with her parents and her retarded twin sister Lorna will continue indefinitely. She is shocked when she sees Father leaving with a suitcase one night. Actually, this is the third time that her father has left the family because of his shame over Lorna's retardation. These feelings also resulted in his overcompensating for Lorna's deficiency by pushing Lydia to excel. Without the financial support of her husband, Muzz cannot keep her daughter Lorna in the special school she attends and must bring her home for the summer. Lydia sees this as an opportunity to help Lorna become as smart as she is, despite the fact that no one has been able to raise Lorna's achievement level above that of a five-year-old. Lydia believes that she can reach Lorna through her love, so she sets up a "schoolroom" and devotes herself to teaching Lorna to the exclusion of all her other interests. Lydia believes that Father will return by the end of the summer and is determined to teach Lorna before he comes back. She refuses to accept the fact that Lorna cannot learn, until a freak act of nature changes her mind. A sinkhole opens in the earth and almost swallows Lydia. Lorna is unable to help her sister because she cannot even recognize that Lydia is in danger. Lydia eventually manages to struggle free without help. After this experience, Lydia finally accepts the fact that Lorna will go back to school in the same condition in which she left, and she realizes that their father will not return.

This book portrays a girl who is selfish, despite her professed concern for her sister. Instead of considering Lorna's needs, Lydia tries to make Lorna a duplicate of herself. The acceptance of the fact that her twin never will be as capable as she is brings Lydia to a deeper sense of understanding and a first tentative step toward maturation.

Ages 9-11

Also available in:
Talking Book—*Me Too*
Library of Congress (NLSBPH)

124

Cleaver, Vera and Bill Cleaver

Queen of Hearts

HarperCollins Publishers, Inc., 1987.
(158 pages)

GRANDPARENT: Living in Home of
RESPONSIBILITY: Accepting
Age: respect for
Dependence/Independence
Sibling: older

Twelve-year-old Wilma, who is "not a great thinker or a great anything," has many friends, all imaginary. But they suddenly desert her when she moves in to care for her seventy-nine-year-old grandmother, Josie, who has suffered a mild stroke. Granny seems bent on regaining her independence by driving out Wilma and her six-year-old brother, humiliating the girl and accusing the boy of stealing. But Wilma stays, knowing "Granny was afraid. Of someone who might come in the night to rob and harm her, of people in the street, of living, of dying, of herself, of having now to depend on others to tell her what to do, of trying to make some sense out of a world she could not flee until that too was decided for her, Granny was afraid." As the girl watches Granny and a neighboring old widower struggle, sometimes foolishly, to maintain their independence, Wilma begins to see that the way people treat old people makes growing old an awful business. Yet her sympathies for old people do not change the dreary reality of caring for Granny, and the girl leaves happily when a couple move in to take over. Still, she cannot regain her imaginary friends—and soon is unwillingly back with Granny, who has driven out the too-watchful couple. Seeing that Granny needs to be needed, Wilma talks her into baking bread for sale. The scheme works well, but again Wilma welcomes release when an aunt comes to take charge. Soon the aunt is sent packing, and this time Wilma comes back willingly—though not eagerly—aware that she, not Granny, calls the shots.

Although there is no love lost here between grandmother and granddaughter, either in the beginning or the end, along the way the two come to respect each other as the girl cajoles, lures, and sometimes physically maneuvers her grandmother to a practical point between dependence and independence. Wilma's candid views of adults, her parents included, as well as the horrors inflicted on old people, cut through personal and social appearances without being cynical. The ending offers no happy resolution; rather, the reader is left feeling that the girl and her grandmother will go on together indefinitely.

Ages 10-13

Also available in:
Cassette—*Queen of Hearts*
Library of Congress (NLSBPH)

Paperbound—*Queen of Hearts*
HarperCollins Publishers, Inc.

C

125

Cleaver, Vera and Bill Cleaver

Trial Valley

HarperCollins Publishers, Inc., 1987.
(158 pages)

RESPONSIBILITY: Accepting
Appalachia
Boy-girl relationships
Family: unity
Orphan

Sixteen-year-old Mary Call Luther, her parents dead, lives with her younger brother and sister in a small house in the Blue Ridge country of North Carolina. An older sister, Devola, and her husband, Kiser Pease, are their legal guardians and want to take them in. But Mary Call resists, wanting to raise the two children herself. And while they complain she is a hard taskmaster, the children do love her dearly. One day they find a five-year-old boy in a wooden cage nailed to a tree. He tells them his name is Jack Parsons, that he was left in the cage by the "Widder Man," and knows nothing about his mother or where he came from. Kiser and Devola wish to adopt the child, but Jack wants to stay with Mary Call. Despite her reluctance to take on another child, she is drawn to the boy and takes him home. Meanwhile, Mary Call muses on two young men who want to marry her: an honest, hardworking neighbor; and a well-to-do social worker from Virginia. But she has her hands full. The authorities, unable to find out anything about the boy, place him with the Peases as a ward. During his first night with them, Jack runs away. Both the family and the townspeople search the mountains but cannot find him. Mary Call then remembers the wooden cage. The searchers find the boy there, but as he rushes to meet them, he falls into a rain-swollen creek. Mary Call dives in to save him. Both her suitors are there: the neighbor rescues the boy; the social worker rescues

Mary Call. The episode enables her to make two decisions: that raising Jack is a responsibility she wants; and that, though she doesn't yet plan to marry, she favors the neighbor over the social worker, because he saved Jack.

Mary Call is an avid reader; she pursues knowledge and wants her younger brother and sister to do the same. She also impresses upon them the importance of self-respect, honesty, loyalty, and kindness. She herself tells the story, a sequel to *Where the Lilies Bloom.*

Ages 12 and up

Also available in:
Cassette—*Trial Valley*
Library of Congress (NLSBPH)

Paperbound—*Trial Valley*
HarperCollins Publishers, Inc.

126

Cleaver, Vera and Bill Cleaver

Where the Lilies Bloom

Black/white illustrations by Jim Spanfeller.
HarperCollins Publishers, Inc., 1969.
(174 pages)

RESPONSIBILITY: Accepting
Appalachia
Death: of father
Family: unity
Promise, keeping
Resourcefulness

Mary Call Luther, age fourteen, lives in the mountains of North Carolina with her father, a sharecropper named Roy Luther; her eighteen-year-old "cloudy headed" sister, Devola; her ten-year-old brother, Romey; and her five-year-old sister, Ima Dean. Roy Luther knows he is dying. He pleads with Mary Call to promise she will bury him secretly, keep the family together, never accept charity, and never let their landlord, Kiser Pease, marry Devola. When Roy Luther dies, Mary Call and Romey bury him secretly as promised, concealing his death to prevent the welfare department from sending them all to the County Home. The family turns to "wildcrafting"—picking and digging medicinal plants to sell to a drug company—so they can buy food. After a bitter winter in a drafty cabin, Mary Call prepares to move the family to the shelter of a large cave so she can stand by her promises to her father. Devola resolves the family's survival problems and preserves Mary Call's sense of responsibility by announcing her decision to marry Kiser Pease. In turn, Kiser Pease helps the family.

This moving first-person narrative presents a picture of a girl's strength of character in the face of severe adversity. The portrayal of low-income Appalachian life is realistic. The descriptions of family relationships and the children's desperation and resourcefulness are filled with compassion and sympathetic humor.

Ages 11 and up

Also available in:
Cassette—*Where the Lilies Bloom*
Library of Congress (NLSBPH)

Paperbound—*Where the Lilies Bloom*
HarperCollins Publishers, Inc.

Talking Book—*Where the Lilies Bloom*
Library of Congress (NLSBPH)

127

Clifford, Ethel Rosenberg

The Rocking Chair Rebellion

Houghton Mifflin Co., 1978.
(147 pages)

AGE: Aging
NURSING HOME, LIVING IN
Careers: planning
Helping
Problem solving

Fourteen-year-old Penelope "Opie" Cross does not foresee that when she promises to visit her elderly neighbor and friend, Mr. Pepper, at the Maple Ridge Home for the Aged, she will soon be working there as a volunteer. By summer, Opie is working at Maple Ridge four days a week. One of the residents Opie likes best is Mrs. Sherman, who has purchased a headstone for her cemetery plot, finds that the company has gone out of business, and cannot afford to buy another stone. Opie enlists her father's aid, and the two of them hit on a solution to which Mrs. Sherman agrees: she crochets a bedspread, raffles it off to women in the neighborhood, and thereby earns enough to buy another headstone. Meanwhile another Maple Ridge resident, Mrs. Longwood, confides to Opie that she is having trouble getting spending money from her guardian. Opie again turns to her father, a lawyer, asking him to advise Mrs. Longwood. She also persuades the Maple Ridge Home's administration to change the site of its annual Family Fair to the public street, so that the neighbors and residents can mingle. Both clearly enjoy the event, and it is because of the party that old Mr. Pepper and some of the home's active residents see and purchase a house for sale on the same street. There they plan to live, share chores, and be far more independent than they have been in Maple Ridge. But some neighbors who want no communal living on the block try to prevent the move by taking Mr. Pepper to court. Mr. Cross defends him and wins the case. Soon, the newly self-sufficient senior citizens are settled and valued in the neighborhood.

Opie's first-person narrative illuminates some of the troubles that can beset elderly people living in nursing homes. Throughout her story, two views of the elderly are expressed: first, that they "are in the way, especially if they're any kind of physical or financial problem" to their relatives; second, that the elderly may be capable people preferring to lead independent and productive lives. A second theme finds Opie's career plans at odds with those her parents have for her, although all the arguing that arises on the subject seems premature in the life of a fourteen-year-old.

Ages 11-13

Also available in:
Cassette—*The Rocking Chair Rebellion*
Library of Congress (NLSBPH)

128

Clifton, Lucille

Everett Anderson's Nine Month Long

Black/white illustrations by Ann Grifalconi.
Holt (Henry) and Company, Inc., 1978.
(31 pages counted)

SIBLING: New Baby
STEPPARENT: Father
African-American
Family: unity
Love, meaning of

Everett Anderson, a young black boy, decides that even though his mother has become Mrs. Tom Perry, he will keep the name he has. Nobody minds. Mr. Perry says that whatever their names are, the three of them have a lot of love—enough, Everett decides when he learns his mother is pregnant, to share with the new arrival. But Mama seems tired and does not play with him as much as she did before. To Everett, it seems as if this is Mr. Perry's fault. He and his stepfather have a serious conversation, and Mr. Perry explains that, though Mama may seem different, she is still the same person who has always loved her firstborn. Thus Everett Anderson soon announces with great pleasure indeed the arrival of little Evelyn Perry.

It is sometimes difficult for a child to share a parent with a new stepparent or new sibling. This story, with its warm illustrations and gentle verse text, reassures the reader that a child can be loved as much after a parent's remarriage or the arrival of a new sibling as he or she was before. There are a number of other stories about Everett Anderson.

Ages 4-7

Also available in:
Paperbound—*Everett Anderson's Nine Month Long*
Trumpet Book Club

129

Clymer, Eleanor Lowenton

My Brother Stevie

Dell Publishing Company, Inc. (Yearling Books), 1989.
(76 pages, paperbound)

GRANDPARENT: Living in Home of
Parental: absence
Responsibility: accepting
School: pupil-teacher relationships

Twelve-year-old Annie and eight-year-old Stevie have lived with their grandmother since their mother left home a few years ago. Their father is dead. Just before departing, Mother told Annie to "take care of Stevie," a responsibility Annie has accepted but resents. Grandma does not understand Stevie. The boy has always been mischievous and recently has begun playing with older boys. Both children feel unwanted and unloved. Annie learns that Stevie is getting into trouble, but she does not tell Grandma, nor does she know what to do about it. But when she remembers that Stevie likes his new teacher, Miss Stover, Annie goes to her for aid. Miss Stover helps Stevie until she is unexpectedly called home. Annie secretly takes Stevie and follows Miss Stover by train. When they arrive at their destination, they discover she is helping her sick foster mother care for foster children. The weekend the children spend with Miss Stover's family has a sobering and maturing effect on Stevie. As a result, his relationship with Grandma improves, and Annie feels less imposed upon.

The burden of too much responsibility can lead a child to feel confused and resentful. This candid first-person narrative shows the beneficial influence an adult—in this case a teacher—can have on a child who needs and is searching for understanding.

Ages 8-11

Also available in:
Braille—*My Brother Stevie*
Library of Congress (NLSBPH)

130

Coerr, Eleanor

Sadako and the Thousand Paper Cranes

Black/white illustrations by Ronald Himler.
Putnam Berkley Group, Inc., 1977.
(64 pages)

ILLNESSES: Terminal
Courage, meaning of
Death: attitude toward
Japan
Leukemia

Eleven-year-old Sadako is a runner, and dreams of being the best runner in her school in Hiroshima, Japan. One day, following a race, a strange dizziness comes over her. After that, and not only when she runs, the dizzy spells recur, and she decides not to tell anyone. But one day in the schoolyard, the dizziness consumes her and she collapses. At the hospital, her illness is diagnosed as leukemia—the result of radiation poisoning from the atomic bomb dropped on her city some years before. The family is grief-stricken, but Sadako vows to get well. In the hospital, her best friend brings her a gift, a crane made of folded gold paper. The friend teaches Sadako how to fold paper cranes and tells her a legend: if she folds a thousand paper cranes, the gods will make her healthy. Sadako begins, and each day her brother hangs from the ceiling the day's new cranes. For a time her health seems to improve, but when the sickness drains her energy and causes her great pain, she knows she will not recover. Yet she continues to make paper cranes. One night she makes number 644. It is her last. She dies, a heroine to her family and friends. Her classmates continue making cranes until all one thousand are folded; they are buried with her.

According to the prologue, the story of Sadako is "based on the life of a real little girl who lived in Japan from 1943 to 1955. She was in Hiroshima when the United States Air Force dropped an atom bomb on that city. . . . Ten years later she died as a result of radiation from the bomb. Her courage made Sadako a heroine to children in Japan." A monument has been erected in the Hiroshima Peace Park in Sadako's memory. This book is a memorable, poignant but not sentimental account, carefully researched.

Ages 11 and up

Also available in:
No other form known

131

Cohen, Barbara Nash

The Innkeeper's Daughter

Greenwillow Books, 1990.
(159 pages, paperbound)

INFERIORITY, FEELINGS OF
Boy-girl relationships
Family: unity
Lifestyle
Parent/Parents: single
Weight control: overweight

Sixteen, overweight, and self-conscious, Rachel Gold spends her time reading and studying, rather than socializing. She wishes she could live like "ordinary people." Instead, she lives with her mother and younger brother and sister in the Waterbridge Inn in New Jersey. Her attractive, self-assured mother owns the Inn and has successfully run it alone since Rachel's father died seven years earlier, in 1941. Rachel's mother loves antiques and one Saturday morning returns with a huge painting, a portrait of an eighteenth- or early nineteenth-century Scottish laird, which she hangs in the Inn's entry. Rachel hates it. Even when an antique dealer says it may be worth one thousand dollars, Rachel is unimpressed. She hates the Inn and now she hates the painting. She also dislikes Ted Jensen, a divorced businessman who frequently stays at the Inn, because she suspects that he and her mother are having an affair. This is later confirmed when, late one night, she hears them together in her mother's bedroom. Ted introduces the Golds to Jeff Dulac, his special accountant, and Jeff temporarily moves in while working on the Jensen account. Rachel and Jeff, eleven years her senior, find they share an interest in books. At the Inn's Christmas party, the two spend the evening dancing and Jeff even kisses Rachel. But he also tells her he has completed his job with Jensen and is leaving the Inn. Despite herself, Rachel is heartbroken. Her mother, while noting that Jeff is too old for her, comforts the girl by suggesting that his attentions should prove to her that she really is attractive after all. Then disaster strikes. As the Golds prepare for their New Year's Eve party, an electrical fire starting in the attic forces them to vacate the Inn. Before the fire can be contained, the place is destroyed. The firefighters do save one thing—the antique painting. After the Golds settle in a small apartment and Mrs. Gold announces her plans to marry Ted Jensen, Rachel decides to find out more about the painting she hates. Researching at the library, she discovers they are owners of a very valuable painting worth thousands of dollars. She and her brother and sister happily approve of their mother's marriage plans, but they insist that the Inn be rebuilt, wedding or not. Rachel has found a new satisfaction in being an innkeeper's daughter.

A girl's fears about her own unattractiveness are remedied by the attentions of an admirer and by an improved relationship with her attractive mother in this entertaining first-person narrative. The story and characters are interesting and believable, never dated, although the events take place in the 1940s. The reader shares Rachel's trials and triumphs as the girl grows in self-awareness.

Ages 11-14

Also available in:
No other form known

132

Cohen, Barbara Nash

Thank You, Jackie Robinson

Black/white illustrations by by Richard Cuffari.
Lothrop, Lee & Shepard Books, 1988.
(125 pages)

PARENT/PARENTS: Substitute
Death: of friend
Friendship: meaning of
Shyness
Sports/Sportsmanship

Sam Greene often describes himself as a "scrungy, freckle-faced little Jewish kid." He befriends Davy, the sixty-year-old Afro-American cook at the inn run by Sam's widowed mother. Davy usually avoids any contact with strangers, but the two are drawn together by their love of the Brooklyn Dodgers. After spending many afternoons discussing the team, Davy takes Sam to his first Dodgers game. As the next two seasons pass, they attend many more games together. When Davy is hospitalized with a severe heart attack, the boy decides that a baseball autographed by all the Dodgers will make him well. Sam buys a ball and a ticket to the Dodgers game. Despite his shyness, he attracts the attention of Jackie Robinson during batting practice, telling him the story of Davy's illness. After the game, the great second baseman presents Sam with a ball signed by the entire team. Davy's daughter and son-in-law sneak Sam into the hospital to see Davy and give him the prize. But the gift fails to prevent Davy's death. For a long time Sam does not want to do anything. He does not even listen to his beloved Dodgers games. But eventually he turns on the radio to listen to a game, begging Jackie to "hit one for Davy"—and Robinson does.

This is a sensitive story of an unusual friendship between a boy and an old man who are brought together during the years 1947-1949 by a love of baseball. Sam gains the adult male companionship he lacks and begins to overcome his shyness. The reader will respond to his joy as well as to his grief.

Ages 10-13

Also available in:
Braille—*Thank You, Jackie Robinson*
Library of Congress (NLSBPH)

Talking Book—*Thank You, Jackie Robinson*
Library of Congress (NLSBPH)

133

Cohen, Miriam

"Bee My Valentine!"

Color illustrations by Lillian Aberman Hoban.
Greenwillow Books, 1978.
(32 pages counted) o.p.

SCHOOL: Classmate Relationships
Consideration, meaning of

Jim, in first grade, excitedly awaits Valentine's Day. Louie, who is new to the class, asks, "What is Valentine's?" Anna Marie and Willy explain that it is a holiday on which everyone tries "to get the most cards." But the teacher emphasizes that "everybody must send a card to everybody else in first grade. Then nobody will be sad." But the children ignore their teacher's admonition, and when valentines are distributed at the class party, George, having received the fewest, hides in the coatroom. Worried that George may even be crying, the students play musical instruments and dance to entice him back. When George reappears, Willy places a paper crown on his head and Sammy gives George a favorite instrument. Soon George is playing along with the others and enjoying the party.

In this engaging story of a richly mixed grade-school class, the students see their responsibility for heedlessly causing one boy's feelings to be hurt. The feelings expressed by the children, and the hubbub created by a class party, are effectively portrayed. The book is one in a series about Jim and his classmates.

Ages 5-7

Also available in:
No other form known

134

Cohen, Miriam

Best Friends

Color illustrations by Lillian Aberman Hoban.
Macmillan Publishing Company, Inc., 1971.
(32 pages counted)

FRIENDSHIP: Best Friend
School: classmate relationships

Jim feels betrayed when Paul, his best friend, rushes into school one morning without even saying "hello." Paul is hurrying because he wants to watch the eggs in the class incubator hatch. Nothing goes right for Jim all day. Paul plays with another friend, Danny. When Jim tries to draw a picture of himself, it does not turn out right. Anna Marie asks Jim who his best friend is, and before Jim can reply, Sammy, who has just broken up with his best buddy, announces that he is Jim's best friend. Anna Marie also wants to be Jim's best friend. Then Paul becomes angry with Jim and refuses to sit next to him for milk and cookies because, he says, "Everybody is your best friend except me!" At recess, the teacher forgets the balls and sends Jim and Paul to get them. They notice that the light in the incubator is out. They know if they do not act quickly, the chicks will die. So while Jim tries to keep the eggs warm, Paul hastens to get the janitor to replace the light bulb. The chickens are saved, and Paul and Jim know that they are best friends again.

The colored drawings reflect the humor of the story. This book is excellent both for reading aloud and stimulating discussion with younger children.

Ages 5-7

Also available in:
Paperbound—*Best Friends*
Aladdin Books

135

Cohen, Miriam

First Grade Takes a Test

Color illustrations by Lillian Aberman Hoban.
Dell Publishing Company, Inc. (Young Yearling Books), 1983.
(32 pages counted, paperbound)

SCHOOL: Classmate Relationships
Education: special
School: pupil-teacher relationships

A woman from the principal's office gives the first grade a standardized multiple-choice test. All but Anna Maria have some trouble with the test. She is the only one to finish and declares it easy. Sometime later the woman returns and takes Anna Maria to a special class because she did so well on the test. The remaining children begin to call each other "dummy" because they weren't selected for the special class. Their teacher reassures them that a test cannot measure important things like drawing pictures, building things, reading books, or being kind to friends. Then she gives them cookies, and the children feel better. Despite her transfer, Anna Maria stops by her old classroom each morning. She worries that the plants may not get watered and that George isn't getting enough help with his arithmetic. At the end of the week she returns to her old class to stay. When the other children ask why, Anna Maria says, "I told them I had to come back. I told them first grade needs me." The teacher remarks that it's good to be all together again.

A standardized test that results in a bright classmate's temporary placement in a special class causes some unhappiness for a group of first graders. But the teacher discounts the test's ability to measure "important things" about a person, and soon Anna Maria returns happily to her old class. The damage to children's self-esteem that can result from school placement based on test scores is worth considering, and the book provides an amusing look at the ways children react to standardized test items. Sammy, for example, when asked what firemen do, thinks of his uncle being helped by firemen when he got his head stuck in a pipe. But an anti-intellectual bias is present here, and the idea that a child could leave a special class after one week because her friends need her is farfetched indeed. This cleverly illustrated story is one in a series.

Ages 5-7

Also available in:
No other form known

136

Cohen, Miriam

No Good in Art

Color illustrations by Lillian Aberman Hoban.
Greenwillow Books, 1980.
(32 pages counted)

Talents: Artistic
School: classmate relationships
School: negative experiences
School: pupil-teacher relationships

When Jim was in kindergarten, his art teacher criticized his drawing, saying the man in the picture had no neck and the grass should be drawn with thin lines. She even painted over the boy's work. Now Jim is in first grade. His new art teacher asks the children to paint a picture about what they want to be when they grow up. Jim's classmates begin eagerly and the teacher praises everyone's picture, even though some do not meet the assignment. But Jim doesn't even attempt a picture. He's "no good in art," he says, and doesn't know what he wants to be. So the teacher tells him to paint a picture of what he likes to do. Reluctantly Jim begins, and as he continues to paint he thinks of many ways to make his picture beautiful. When the teacher asks the class to put their names on their pictures and turn them in, only Jim hides his picture under his desk. But classmates Willy and Sammy take Jim's picture and hand it in. The teacher hangs up all the pictures and everyone admires Jim's wondering whose it is. Willy and Sammy identify the artist by pulling Jim to the front of the room. His classmates ask what the picture shows. He tells them, "Its me eating pizza." Then Sara another classmate, asks Jim what he is going to be when he grows up. Willy and Sammy suggest that Jim might be an artist. The art teacher agrees. Another classmate, Paul, tells Jim, "You're good." Finally Jim is convinced he has actually drawn a beautiful picture.

With encouragement from his new art teacher and his classmates, a talented little boy overcomes the insecurity and fear of drawing planted in him by a former teacher. Young readers will sympathize with Jim's feelings, and adults may be helped to remember how powerful their influence on children can be. This colorfully illustrated book is one in a series about Jim and his classmates.

Ages 5-7

Also available in:
No other form known

137

Cohen, Miriam

When Will I Read?

Color illustrations by Lillian Aberman Hoban.
Greenwillow Books, 1977.
(32 pages counted)

EDUCATION: Value of
Goals
School: classmate relationships

Jim wants terribly to be able to read. It is not enough that he recognizes signs and his own name, for "that's not really reading." Jim's friend George claims to be reading when he recites the words of his favorite story but another student insists that George is reciting from memory. Even when Jim and the other students have dictated an experience to the teacher and Jim is "reading" his aloud, he feels thwarted. It is just after he has decided to stop "worrying about reading" that he notices that the sign on the hamster cage reads, "Do let the hamsters out," instead of "Don't let the hamsters out." He hurriedly informs his teacher. She congratulates him: he has "really read the sign." Jim is thrilled because, as he says, "I waited all my life" to read.

In this honest picture of classroom life, the reader meets a boy with a yearning to be able to read. The illustrations no less than the text catch both his impatience and his delight amid the bustle of the classroom. This book is one in a series about Jim and his classmates.

Ages 4-6

Also available in:
Cassette—*When Will I Read?*
Library of Congress (NLSBPH)

138

Cohen, Miriam

Will I Have a Friend?

Color illustrations by Lillian Aberman Hoban.
Macmillan Publishing Company, Inc., 1967.
(30 pages counted)

FRIENDSHIP: Making Friends
School: entering

It is Jim's first day in kindergarten, and he worries that he will not have a friend. On his way to school, he asks his dad if he will find a friend, and his dad replies that he thinks Jim will. All morning, Jim looks at the children, wondering who will be his special friend. He makes a clay man but has no one to whom he can show it. He finally thinks of something to say to someone, but the boy he speaks to is munching a mouthful of cookies and cannot answer him. As the day progresses, Jim becomes more at ease. At nap time, Jim finds his friend, a boy named Paul who is lying next to him.

The colorful pastel illustrations depict Jim's anxiety and uncertainty before finally finding a friend. This book could be read aloud to young children.

Ages 4-6

Also available in:
Paperbound—*Will I Have a Friend?*
Aladdin Books

139

Colman, Hila Crayder

Diary of a Frantic Kid Sister

Pocket Books, 1985.
(119 pages, paperbound)

SIBLING: Jealousy
SIBLING: Rivalry
Ambivalence, feelings of
Maturation

Eleven-year-old Sarah Grinnell dislikes her sixteen-year-old sister Didi. She believes that if she writes her feelings down in her new diary, they will go away. But as the year progresses, Sarah finds that her feelings of anger and jealousy remain just as intense. Her older sister continues to irritate her: Didi borrows Sarah's clothes, belittles Sarah's birthday celebration (a movie followed by dinner at home), and insists on and receives a dinner party at a restaurant and an evening at the theater with her girlfriends and their dates. To add to Sarah's frustration, she is continually compared to Didi in the private school they both attend. Sarah can't understand why she must like and do well at the same things as her sister. Sarah envies the close relationship that her mother and Didi appear to have: Didi and her mother both like music and share confidences. Later that year, Sarah's mother, a former concert pianist, becomes depressed because she is no longer performing. She finds psychiatric help. After attending a family counseling session, Sarah begins to understand her feelings about herself, her mother, and Didi. When Didi breaks up with her boyfriend and prepares to leave for a vacation in Europe, Sarah realizes that she does not dislike her sister. She also discovers that she and Didi are different people who enjoy different things and have their own individual talents.

This open-ended, realistic first-person narrative shows the jealousy a younger sister may feel toward an older sister who is given more freedom than she is. Although there is intense rivalry between these sisters, Sarah finds that she both likes and dislikes Didi.

Ages 10-13

Also available in:
Talking Book—*Diary of a Frantic Kid Sister*
Library of Congress (NLSBPH)

140

Conford, Ellen

Anything for a Friend

Little, Brown & Company, Inc., 1979.
(180 pages)

CHANGE: New Home
FRIENDSHIP: Lack of
FRIENDSHIP: Making Friends
Change: resisting
Moving
Name, dissatisfaction with

Eleven-year-old Wallis Greene is sure that her new home near New York City will be just like her past new homes: she will hate the place and make no friends. Her mother and grandmother urge Wallis to change her attitudes, to be a friend in order to make friends. Unconvinced, Wallis replies that her father's frequent career-related moves are selfish and have forced her into a friendless life. Furthermore, her parents' naming her after the Duchess of Windsor has compelled her to spell and explain her first name constantly. Now she has one more cross to bear: her embarrassment over the fact that the former owner of their new house was murdered by his wife. Still, Wallis does consider changing her attitudes and lets a boy her age, Stuffy (for Stafford W. Sternwood), walk her to school the first day. Once there, Wallis immediately spots "The Girl Nobody Likes," Ruth, and shuns her. She tries to cultivate "The Important Girls," but feels thwarted when Ruth seeks her out. Annoyed by Ruth's attention, Wallis goes along with Stuffy's scheme to write a phony love letter from their teacher, Mr. Ryan, to Ruth, who has a crush on him. After they give Ruth the letter, Stuffy enjoys watching the girl moon over Mr. Ryan, but Wallis wishes she had never gotten involved in the distasteful scheme. Again at Stuffy's urging she writes another letter, but so dislikes watching Ruth make a fool of herself that she tells Stuffy she is through. When Ruth asks her for help in writing a letter to Mr. Ryan that will end their "affair," Wallis writes one for her, promises to mail it, and then secretly tears it up, concluding the deception. Then word gets out that Wallis lives in a house where a murder took place. She fears the news will end her chances for friendship, but of course it makes her the center of interest. Wallis takes advantage of the interest and makes two friends. Meanwhile, the resourceful Stuffy decides to capitalize on the interest in the murder and talks Wallis into holding a seance-party to contact the dead man. Wallis, lured by the prospect of making more friends, agrees. Stuffy insists that he will handle everything. The seance goes well until Wallis learns that Stuffy has charged admission. Outraged, she forces him to repay her guests. In the following months, Wallis makes friends and begins to feel she belongs. Then a position in her father's company opens up on the West Coast. Wallis despairs, but her mother and grandmother reason with her. If she has made friends here, why not in California? With help and encouragement from her friends and family, Wallis soon accepts the argument: she made friends here, and now she expects to make friends in her new home.

A young girl, forced to make frequent moves as her father's career advances, refuses even to try making friends. But she gradually comes to see that she can have friends, and that she really won't do "anything for a friend" if it means compromising her self-respect and hurting others. Stuffy, the young con man, adds interest and humor to this first-person account.

Ages 9-11

Also available in:
No other form known

141

Conford, Ellen

Felicia the Critic

Black/white illustrations by Arvis Stewart.
Little, Brown & Company, Inc., 1973.
(145 pages)

FRIENDSHIP: Making Friends
Loneliness
Reputation

Felicia Kershinbaum, a fourth grader, constantly annoys people by criticizing them. Her mother suggests that she try constructive criticism instead, and Felicia agrees to experiment with it. She composes a list of ways the school crossing guard can improve the traffic flow around school. But when she gives her list to the guard, he pays attention to it instead of his duties, causing a large traffic jam. When Felicia tries to return a fatty roast to the market and is treated rudely, she uses her mother's stationery to write a letter to the store manager. Felicia's mother is happily surprised to receive a four-dollar refund for the roast. As winter approaches, Felicia is asked by four of the girls in her class to join their club—on the condition that she not criticize ideas that come up during club meetings. Felicia agrees to this, although she is unhappy about the stipulation. When the girls decide to hold a carnival to raise money for the club, Felicia believes it is a poor idea: no one, she thinks, holds an outdoor carnival in winter. But she abides by her promise and does not criticize the plan. As she feared, wind-blown snow and a temperature of nineteen degrees ruin the carnival. Now the other girls accuse Felicia of remaining silent when she foresaw the problems. But Felicia's best friend, Cheryl, reminds them that they did not allow Felicia to criticize their plans. If they had listened, they might have avoided disaster.

In a humorous manner, this book points out that although people do not like to hear constant criticism, constructive criticism does have its place. Felicia's reputation as a critic precedes her; thus she finds it difficult to make friends. The relationships described between family members and between classmates are realistic, and the dialogue is natural. This story has enough variety to hold the reader's interest, despite the narrow focus of the plot.

Ages 9-11

Also available in:
Braille—*Felicia the Critic*
Library of Congress (NLSBPH)

Cassette—*Felicia the Critic*
Library of Congress (NLSBPH)

142

Conford, Ellen

The Revenge of the Incredible Dr. Rancid and His Youthful Assistant, Jeffrey

Little, Brown & Company, Inc., 1980.
(119 pages)

SELF, ATTITUDE TOWARD: Feeling Different
Bully: being bothered by
Courage, meaning of
Friendship: meaning of
Imagination
Reality, escaping
School: classmate relationships

Jeffrey Childs hates it when bully Dewey Belasco calls him "chicken," "coward," and "childish." Although he's in sixth grade, Jeffrey considers his best friend to be Bix, a neighbor three years younger. Since Dewey came into his life a year ago, Jeffrey's main form of enjoyment and escape from his problems has been secretly writing a book called "The Revenge of the Incredible Dr. Rancid and His Youthful Assistant, Jeffrey." At school Jeffrey's seat partner is Coco Siegelman, whom he likes very much. One day he sees Coco with a "slam" book. He grabs the book and reads what the girls in his class have written about him. Always sure no one likes him, Jeffrey finds his suspicions confirmed. In the most recent chapter of his book, Jeffrey writes of rescuing Coco from Dewey with his stun gun. His writing is interrupted by a telephone call and he ends up baby-sitting for a neighbor. While he's there, the youngest boy cuts his lip and Jeffrey rushes him to the doctor. He's hailed for his quick thinking and begins to feel a bit heroic for a change. At school the next day, Dewey makes fun of Coco. Jeffrey makes a weak attempt to step in, only to have Coco herself hit Dewey. Humiliated at being unable to defend Coco, let alone himself, Jeffrey pretends to have a virus the next day and is allowed to stay home from school. He longs to tell his parents about Dewey, but is afraid they will also think him a coward. Jeffrey returns to school with a new determination to stand up to Dewey. He's tired of feeling bad about himself and pretending everything is fine. When Dewey taunts him in class, Jeffrey tells Dewey he has incurable stupidity. At lunch Dewey challenges him, Bix steps in, and a fight ensues. Jeffrey holds his own. The fight is stopped by a teacher, and the two are required to shake hands and apologize. When he realizes the class is on his side, Jeffrey feels great. "I'd stood up to the guy who'd been terrorizing me for months, and I'd lived to tell the tale." A proud Jeffrey tells his parents what has happened. That weekend several school friends stop by, and even Coco visits. Jeffrey realizes his classmates do like him, and he writes the final chapter in his book: Dewey is dead from a pulverizer gun and Jeffrey is Coco's hero.

A shy young boy feels himself a coward for not standing up to a bully, relieving his feelings by writing a book about his own imagined heroic deeds. Finally determined not to back down anymore, Jeffrey stands up to the bully and not only wins the self-respect he needs, but also the admiration of his classmates. This first-person narrative describes with humor and insight the feelings and fears of a likeable, imaginative boy.

Ages 10-12

Also available in:
Cassette—*The Revenge of the Incredible Dr. Rancid and His Youthful Assistant, Jeffrey*
Library of Congress (NLSBPH)

143

Corcoran, Barbara

Child of the Morning

American Printing House for the Blind, 1982.
(112 pages, large print) o.p.

EPILEPSY
SELF, ATTITUDE TOWARD: Accepting
Fear: of the unknown
Friendship: making friends
Talents

Susan Bishop has had "little spells" for almost a year. They started after she suffered a concussion playing volleyball. The family's doctor, Dr. Blake, is not overly concerned about the injury, so the family tries to ignore Susan's occasional spells and blackouts. When school lets out for the summer between her sophomore and junior years, Susan begins looking for a job. But the people in her small Maine town are afraid to hire her: local gossip about her blackouts has spread. At a church supper, Susan meets several people from New York City who are in Maine to start a summer theater. The next day she rides her bike to this theater and gets a job distributing posters advertising the weekly productions. She is thrilled when Steve, the young man who hired her, tells her she can also watch rehearsals. Soon she is coming to the theater daily, helping Steve. Since she loves to dance, she begins watching the dance class, memorizing the steps and practicing them when she's alone. Mr. Ross, the producer, is so impressed with her skills at helping Steve that he hires her as a full-time summer member of the company. Although elated, Susan fears she will have a spell and be fired. Usually she can feel a spell coming—a headache comes first—and can sit down and breathe deeply until it passes. But the episodes are beginning to occur more frequently. When she suffers a blackout in Steve's presence, he encourages her to see a neurologist. Instead, Susan returns to Dr. Blake, who gives her headache pills. He also mentions he is retiring and a Dr. Magone will take over his practice. Back at the theater Susan is asked to do three short dance numbers for the upcoming show. She reluctantly agrees, terrified she will have a spell. The week of performances goes well. Then, during the last scene of the second-last performance, Susan blacks out. She awakens to find Dr. Magone helping her. He asks how long she has had epilepsy, and Susan is dumbfounded. Dr. Magone takes her to a neurologist in Boston. He explains epilepsy to her and the drugs used to control it. For three months, Susan's doctors try various drugs, many with bad side effects, to control her seizures. Finally a medicine without side effects is found to help her. For the first time in over a year, Susan feels well enough to be truly hopeful about her future.

A teenage girl who has "little spells" that her family doctor discounts is finally diagnosed as having epilepsy and can be treated and helped to live a normal life. Susan manages to break free of the scary state of not knowing what's wrong with her and of denying that anything is wrong. Although shallow in characterization, the book does offer insight into the symptoms, effects, and treatment for epilepsy. Also clear is the need for intelligent, specialized medical care. Susan's experiences with the theater group will add appeal for some readers.

Ages 10 and up

Also available in:
No other form known

144

Corey, Dorothy

Everybody Takes Turns

Color illustrations by Lois Axeman.
Albert Whitman & Company, 1980.
(32 pages counted)

SHARING/NOT SHARING
Patience/Impatience

"I take a turn. You take a turn." Some people get the first turn. Other people get the second turn. When one person's turn is up, it's somebody else's turn. Small children, big children, and adults all take turns sometimes. Even pedestrians and drivers take turns. "It's fun to have your turn!"

By alternating simple, colorfully illustrated examples of "my turn, your turn," this little book presents sharing and taking turns as facts of life. One short sentence accompanies each illustration; young children will enjoy the repetition of "my turn, your turn." This is a useful, if not exciting, single-concept book, which could be elaborated upon in discussion.

Ages 2-6

Also available in:
No other form known

145

Corey, Dorothy

We All Share

Color illustrations by Rondi Collette.
Albert Whitman & Company, 1980.
(32 pages counted) o.p.

SHARING/NOT SHARING

A young boy shares his puppy, and his friend shares his kitten. When a third boy joins with a rabbit, they all share their pets. The boys also share popcorn and a sandwich. Later, the narrator's friend shares some paper, the narrator shares his paints, and they both share their paintings with his mother. A tent, a swimming pool, bubbles, cars, and a fire truck are all shared. So is a baby brother. The narrator and his friends share drums, Halloween candy, mittens, and a sled. "We all share!"

Alternating brightly colored, appealing illustrations with black-and-white ones, this simple, engaging book shows children sharing their pets, toys, and favorite things. The young narrator presents sharing as fun and rewarding.

Ages 2-6

Also available in:
No other form known

146

Corey, Dorothy

You Go Away

Color illustrations by Lois Axeman.
Albert Whitman & Company, 1976.
(31 pages counted)

SEPARATION ANXIETY

Parents go away and come back, and so do children. There are brief separations: a mother hides behind a blanket for a moment and then reappears; a child runs across the room and back; a child disappears under a bed and pops back out again. Some separations last longer: two children lose sight of their mother in a supermarket; a group of children stay with a baby-sitter while their mothers shop; a little girl goes to kindergarten. Sometimes parents go on a trip, with suitcases, leaving the children with Grandmother. When the parents return, everyone is delighted.

This simple picture book with a brief text is not intended to overcome a child's deep-seated fear of being separated from parents. But it provides an opportunity to talk with very young children about separation, and about being with people besides one's parents.

Ages 2-5

Also available in:
No other form known

147

Coutant, Helen

First Snow

Black/white illustrations by Vo-Dinh.
Alfred A. Knopf, Inc., 1974.
(33 pages) o.p.

DEATH: Attitude Toward
DEATH: of Grandparent
Buddhist
Grandparent: love for

It is the second week of December, and Lien, about six, is anxiously waiting for snow to cover the hills around the small New England town in which she lives. Because her family has recently come from Vietnam, Lien has never seen snow, and she spends afternoons showing her sick grandmother pictures of it. On a "gray and heavy morning," the doctor, who has just examined Grandmother, observes that snow will surely fall before night. He then tells the family that Lien's grandmother is dying. Since Lien is Buddhist, she asks her mother if she may light incense for Grandmother. She then questions her parents about what dying means, but since neither offers her an explanation, she decides to ask Grandmother. Grandmother tells her to go out into the garden, hold her hand up to heaven, and be patient about discovering what dying means. In the bitter cold, Lien gazes at the dark clouds and sees the first tiny snowflakes fall. A beautiful and delicate flake balances itself on her outstretched hand. When the sun breaks through the clouds, the flake catches the sunlight and seems to burst into sparkling beauty. As she is thinking, the snowflake melts, falls to the ground as a drop of water, and is gone. Lien, dropping to her knees and searching for the droplet, discovers a small seedling that it has watered. Lien then understands what dying means: things are not really gone; they only change.

This poignant story dealing with the Buddhist belief that "life and death are but two parts of the same thing" imparts a feeling of warmth and security in its gentle approach to death.

Ages 7-9

Also available in:
Cassette—*First Snow*
Library of Congress (NLSBPH)

148

Crowe, Robert L.

Clyde Monster

Color illustrations by Kay Chorao.
Dutton Children's Books, 1976.
(29 pages counted, paperbound)

FEAR: of Darkness
Bedtime

Clyde is a young monster who lives in the forest with his monster parents. He is growing up well for a monster: he lives in a cave, is becoming uglier every day, and knows how to breathe fire on the lake to make steam rise. Clyde also loves to play and turn somersaults. But Clyde is afraid of the dark and refuses to sleep in his cave. When his parents ask him what he is afraid of, he responds, "People. I'm afraid there are people in there who will get me." Even though Clyde's father breathes fire into the cave to light it up and show him there are no people hiding there, Clyde fears that some will jump out from under rocks and get him once he is asleep. His mother asks him, "Would you ever hide in the dark under a bed or in a closet to scare a human boy or girl?" Clyde answers, "Of course not!" Then his father explains that people would not do that either since a long time ago people and monsters made a pact not to scare each other. Clyde is somewhat reassured and goes into his cave to sleep, asking only that they "leave the rock open just a little."

Although Clyde is reassured enough by his parents to try sleeping in his cave, his fears do not disappear all at once. Talking about a child's fear of darkness from a monster's point of view can be an amusing and reassuring experience for a child. The color illustrations of engaging, not frightening, monsters enhance the story.

Ages 3-6

Also available in:
No other form known

149

Cuyler, Margery S.

The Trouble with Soap

Dutton Children's Books, 1982.
(104 pages)

FRIENDSHIP: Best Friend
Friendship: making friends
Peer relationships: peer pressures
School: behavior
Schools, private: girls'

Thirteen-year-old Laurie Endersby's best friend and partner in crime is Lucinda Sokoloff, otherwise known as Soap. When the two put Saran Wrap over the toilet bowls in the boys' restroom at school, they are suspended for two weeks. Soap's mother decides to send Soap to Miss Pringle's school, an elite private girls' academy. Soap pressures Laurie into applying there too, and so the girls change schools together. Laurie wants to make new friends at Miss Pringle's, but Soap snubs everyone and sticks to Laurie. A classmate, Hilary, invites Laurie to spend the night with her. Against her better judgment but believing Hilary to be more sophisticated than she, Laurie allows Hilary to cut her hair. Then, feeling guilty, Laurie goes to see Soap—but Soap only wants to make trick phone calls. Laurie thinks the activity very immature, but allows herself to be persuaded. However, when Soap picks up the phone she overhears her father telling some woman that he can hardly wait to see her. Soon after, Soap writes a derogatory limerick on the board. Although everyone knows she did it, she declines to confess and the whole class is punished. Laurie wonders why Soap is so negative, so eager to make enemies. Feeling torn between Hilary and Soap, she decides that Soap will just have to make it on her own; Laurie really wants Hilary's friendship. Then Soap finds out that her father is meeting his woman friend at noon in the park. She talks Laurie into coming with her to spy on them. It turns out that Mr. Sokoloff's friend is none other than Miss Helms, the girls' English teacher. Soap feels betrayed and demoralized. They arrive back at school late and get in trouble with Miss Pringle. Hilary begs Laurie to tell her where they were, but loyal Laurie won't. Next evening Laurie, nervous and excited, goes to Hilary's party. One boy upsets her; another, Oliver, is comfortable to be with. After the party, Laurie and two other girls sleep over. The others pressure Laurie to tell what she and Soap were doing when they skipped school. Enjoying being the center of attention, Laurie tells them all about Soap's father and Miss Helms. The next week, Soap discovers what Laurie's done. She doesn't return to school for two days. Hilary fixes Laurie up with a blind date, Anthony, and the four get stoned on marijuana. Laurie gets up and leaves in the middle of the movie when Anthony persists in his advances. She calls her older brother to pick her up, telling him all her troubles. When she asks him why it's so hard for her to say no, he says all people want to be liked. Laurie apologizes to Soap for what she's done and Soap forgives her, although she notes that she wouldn't have betrayed Laurie. In any case, her father has told her mother about Miss Helms, so it's public knowledge. Laurie feels somehow comforted, realizing that Hilary isn't as perfect as she thought and that Soap is changing and maturing. She suspects she has a lot to look forward to—maybe even Oliver.

A young girl is torn between loyalty to an old friend who often gets her into trouble and new friends who seem more sophisticated and mature. Laurie is easily manipulated; even when she's talked into doing something fairly innocent, she often goes against her own feelings. But she recognizes this tendency and by book's end is beginning to remedy it. She also comes to a more realistic view both of the flighty but endearing Soap and of the attractions of her new friends. A delightful—in some spots, very funny—book, this first-person story is a quick, entertaining read that touches on some very real problems of early adolescence.

Ages 10-13

Also available in:
No other form known

150

Dacquino, Vincent T.

Kiss the Candy Days Good-Bye

Delacorte Press, 1982.
(129 pages) o.p.

DIABETES
Boy-girl relationships: dating
Change: accepting
Communication: importance of
Family: relationships
Hospital, going to
School: classmate relationships

Seventh-grader Jimmy Jones loves wrestling and is excited about being workout partner with Butch Farelli, the team's captain. But Jimmy has a secret worry. Although he's eating more—trying to equal Butch's weight—he is losing weight. He'd like to talk to his girlfriend, Margaret, but she hasn't been to school for the past few days. Afraid to confide in his parents or younger brother, Jimmy worries silently, not only about his weight loss but also his temper flare-ups, continual hunger, frequent urination, and great thirst. He's afraid something serious is happening to him. Determined to talk to Margaret, he goes to her neighborhood one day after school and learns from a neighbor that she has moved. Confused and distressed, Jimmy walks home feeling very weak and dizzy. When he reaches his apartment building, he passes out. An ambulance takes Jimmy and his mother to the hospital. The results of Jimmy's blood and urine tests lead the doctors to suspect diabetes mellitus. Jimmy, feeling like part of a horror movie, spends the next seven days in the hospital. He undergoes more tests and starts a series of insulin shots to control his sugar level. Along the way, Jimmy learns about diabetes and struggles to accept everything that is happening to him, unjust as it seems. He is relieved when his doctor tells him he can still wrestle. When Margaret, now living with relatives, visits Jimmy in the hospital, she brings her cousin Santiago with her. Santiago will be attending their school, and Margaret asks Jimmy to help him adjust. Finally, Jimmy is released from the hospital. He and his parents now know how to give him insulin injections, rotate the site of the shots, check his urine, and watch his diet. The family plans to spend the weekend in their cabin in the mountains, and Jimmy asks Margaret to come too. She accepts, but only if Santiago comes along. Jealous, Jimmy reluctantly agrees. Soon, though, they're all enjoying the hiking, fishing, and swimming. But all this vigorous exercise lowers Jimmy's blood-sugar level, and he has an insulin reaction during one of their outings. He feels sweaty and clammy and his arms and legs tingle. Recovering by eating the candy he carries for emergencies, he laughs off the episode. Later he feels miserable, not about the reaction but "that I wasn't man enough to admit what was happening." He must agree when his brother confronts him about the incident: if he lies about a reaction, no one will ever know when he needs help. Jimmy returns to school with his new friend Santiago and everything returns to normal—except the candy days are over.

A young teenager is found to be diabetic and must learn to accept the new conditions of his life. Although somewhat didactic, the story gives an excellent description of the early struggles and necessary education of a newly diagnosed diabetic boy and, secondarily, his family and friends. It emphasizes that although diabetes can't be cured, it can be controlled, and that diabetic people are not abnormal but different, with certain special needs. Jimmy's story encourages openness with others to increase understanding of diabetes. Young diabetic readers may find the book useful and comforting; others will increase their awareness and understanding. Although the book is detailed, home blood-testing isn't mentioned.

Ages 10-14

Also available in:
No other form known

151

Danziger, Paula

Can You Sue Your Parents for Malpractice?

Delacorte Press, 1979.
(152 pages)

AUTONOMY
Boy-girl relationships: dating
Family: relationships
Peer relationships: peer pressures
School: classmate relationships

Lauren Allen finds it disgusting to be fourteen and have no rights. She is looking forward to a special elective class at school called "Law for Children and Young People." Lauren wants eventually to be a lawyer so she can help kids get an even break, something she never gets. Her entire family is a trial to her. Melissa, her older sister, goes to college and never seems to be home, although she still lives there. Lauren has to share a bedroom with her younger sister, Linda, who tells jokes incessantly. Her mother is forever writing to quiz shows asking to be a contestant, and her father, an insurance salesman, complains constantly about the family's finances. To make matters worse, Lauren's boyfriend just broke up with her to date another girl. The Saturday before the special class starts, Lauren and her best friend go to the shopping mall and have their ears pierced, against Lauren's parents' wishes. At the mall she meets Zack Davids, an eighth grader whose family recently moved to the neighborhood. Lauren is attracted to Zack but can't understand why, since he is a year younger than she is. When she returns home, her father is furious about her pierced ears. She yells that she will sue him for malpractice for being a lousy father. On Monday, Lauren discovers Zack is also in the special class. The group is assigned to do a paper on laws affecting children and young people, and Zack asks Lauren to be his partner. Hesitant because of what classmates might say about the age difference, Lauren finally agrees. But if her social life is improving, her home life is exploding. Melissa has moved in with her boyfriend, and her father is not speaking to her. He is also furious at her mother for returning to substitute teaching. Lauren's life has become a soap opera, she feels. At school, her fellow ninth graders begin teasing her about Zack, saying she is robbing the cradle. Confused and hurt, Lauren is soon angry at everyone. She visits Melissa, hoping for help in understanding her mixed-up feelings about Zack, her friends, and her father. Zack and Lauren continue working on their law project together, and Lauren decides she really cares for him despite the kidding. When her former boyfriend comes back, expecting her to go steady with him, Lauren finds she prefers Zack, even if he is younger and can't drive a car. As she contemplates her family, her friends, her class, and her relationship with Zack, Lauren realizes she is beginning to cope better with each upsetting situation in her life. "Maybe suing my parents for malpractice isn't as important as making sure that I don't do malpractice on myself."

A feisty teenage girl struggles for her own individuality against family and peer pressures. Told by Lauren, the story is well paced with believable characters. It is written with a delightful sense of humor and with considerable insight into young adolescents—their special code of living, their pains and joys.

Ages 10-14

Also available in:
Braille—*Can You Sue Your Parents for Malpractice?*
Library of Congress (NLSBPH)

Cassette—*Can You Sue Your Parents for Malpractice?*
Library of Congress (NLSBPH)

Paperbound—*Can You Sue Your Parents for Malpractice?*
Dell Publishing Company, Inc. (Laural Leaf Library)

152

Danziger, Paula

The Cat Ate My Gymsuit

Dell Publishing Company, Inc. (Yearling Books), 1974.
(147 pages, paperbound)

INFERIORITY, FEELINGS OF
SELF, ATTITUDE TOWARD: Body Concept
SELF, ATTITUDE TOWARD: Feeling Different
Parent/Parents: fighting between
Parent/Parents: punitive
Values/Valuing: moral/ethical
Weight control: overweight

Thirteen-year-old Marcy Lewis thinks that she looks like a mousey, brown-haired blimp wearing wire-frame glasses. She dislikes her father, who constantly shouts at her, accusing her of being a failure and causing family arguments. When a replacement English teacher, Ms. Finney, takes over Marcy's English class, Marcy begins to gain confidence in herself. Ms. Finney encourages the students in her class to express their feelings to others and holds after-school group sessions to help students learn more about themselves. Because of her experiences in her English class, Marcy begins to verbalize her opinions at home and in school. She even begins influencing her mother's attitudes and lifestyle, encouraging her to be more independent. This angers Marcy's father, who feels that his wife and daughter should simply mirror his opinions and see to his creature comforts since he is the breadwinner of the family. When Ms. Finney is dismissed for her unconventional teaching methods and her refusal to recite the Pledge of Allegiance, Marcy and some of the other students from the English class form a committee to protest the dismissal. Marcy's group is soon joined by her mother and other parents who recognize the positive effect of Ms. Finney's teaching methods. At a school board meeting which is attended by many of the townspeople, Ms. Finney is reinstated. She resigns in front of the group, however, stating that the controversy would inhibit her ability to teach her students properly. When she departs, Ms. Finney leaves behind seeds of change: Marcy is dieting and seeing a psychologist, and Mrs. Lewis is attending night school.

The heroine of this first-person narrative expresses many of the views and worries of adolescents: the need to express opinions, lack of popularity, boredom with school, and concern about appearance. Through the efforts of an understanding and accessible teacher, the girl gains self-confidence and begins to communicate openly with her mother. Characterizations—including that of the father, who appears as a "male chauvinist"—are well drawn.

Ages 11 and up

Also available in:
Paperbound—*The Cat Ate My Gymsuit*
Dell Publishing Company, Inc. (Laurel Leaf Library)

Talking Book—*The Cat Ate My Gymsuit*
Library of Congress (NLSBPH)

153

Danziger, Paula

The Divorce Express

Delacorte Press, 1982.
(148 pages)

DIVORCE: of Parents
Boy-girl relationships
Change: accepting
Change: new home
Communication: parent-child
Friendship: best friend
Parent/Parents: remarriage of
School: behavior

Fourteen-year-old Phoebe's divorced parents have joint custody of her, which means she lives half the week with one parent, half with the other. She needs a calendar to avoid becoming hopelessly confused, as she was the weekend each parent thought she was staying with the other and she had no place to go. When she gets in trouble at school, her parents decide she'll live with her father in Woodstock all week and spend the weekends with her mother in New York City, "riding the Divorce Express," a bus filled with kids whose divorced parents have made similar living arrangements for them. Phoebe is sure the transportation industry would go bankrupt without divorce; she wonders if it will ever stop hurting to think about her family's breakup. Her best friend, Katie, and her boyfriend, Andy, live in New York, and Phoebe is lonely in Woodstock until she befriends Rosie, the half-black, half-white daughter of divorced parents. She's doubly glad to have Rosie when she learns that Katie and Andy have started dating each other in her absence. When Rosie stays overnight with Phoebe at Phoebe's mother's New York apartment, the girls overhear a comment that suggests Rosie's mother and Phoebe's father are interested in each other. Phoebe wonders how Rosie can take this news so calmly. Phoebe doesn't take it calmly at all when she learns that her mother is planning to marry Duane, a man Phoebe positively detests. Duane likes hunting, thinks children should be seen and not heard, and doesn't like emotional displays. Phoebe tries to tell her mother how she feels, but they don't really listen to each other. Phoebe rides the Divorce Express back to Woodstock very upset. Waiting for her and Rosie at the bus depot are Rosie's mother and Phoebe's father. They all go home and talk about her mother's remarriage until Phoebe feels somewhat better about the situation. Then Rosie interrogates her mother and Phoebe's father about their own relationship, which turns out to be fairly serious. They hadn't wanted to tell the girls, for fear of interfering with their friendship. But both say they don't mind at all. Phoebe even decides to attend her mother's wedding. She's not feeling so trapped anymore: "I'm learning to have my own place in the world."

A teenage girl manages to survive a number of changes in her life and recovers her balance with more self-confidence and self-knowledge than she had before. Readers will feel for Phoebe as she struggles to accept her parents' divorce, their new partners, her own loss of friends, her new school, and, ultimately, her need to find a sense of self independent of either parent. This is a perceptive, humorous first-person narrative that should have great appeal.

Ages 11-14

Also available in:
Braille—*The Divorce Express*
Library of Congress (NLSBPH)

Cassette—*The Divorce Express*
Library of Congress (NLSBPH)

Paperbound—*The Divorce Express*
Dell Publishing Company, Inc. (Laurel Leaf Library)

154

Danziger, Paula

The Pistachio Prescription: A Novel

Dell Publishing Company, Inc. (Laurel Leaf Library), 1978.
(154 pages, paperbound)

INFERIORITY, FEELINGS OF
Appearance: concern about
Asthma
Boy-girl relationships
Parent/Parents: fighting between
Sibling: rivalry

Unlike her Greek namesake, thirteen-year-old Cassandra Stephens does not make dire predictions; her life is bad enough as it is. Every time her parents quarrel—and they often do—Cassie suffers an asthma attack. Teasing by her older sister, Stephanie, or by her mother—almost anything at all—can likewise plunge Cassie into such attacks, or into an array of imagined illnesses for which her accustomed "cure" is pistachio nuts. Only Andrew, her younger brother, and Vicki, her best friend, can be depended on not to distress her. Such is Vicki's faith in her that she urges Cassie to lead a slate of candidates against a clique running for "freshperson" (ninth-grade) offices at school. Through real fears and imagined illnesses, Cassie campaigns well until she suffers a self-inflicted disaster: trying to look better for Bernie, a boy she has met and is attracted to while campaigning, Cassie tweezes out her eyebrows and must resort to sunglasses. In the dark himself about the glasses, Bernie sticks by her anyway. She fears others will laugh at her "plucked chicken" appearance if she doffs the glasses before the eyebrows have grown back. In fact, it is after she stands up to a strict, often unjust, and unpopular teacher, who orders her to remove the glasses, that she gains enough recognition and popularity to win a narrow victory as class president. But instead of celebrating, Cassie has a severe asthma attack that night—when her parents announce their plans to divorce. But that is when Stephanie and Cassie, seeing that their age-old rivalry stems from uneasiness in the family, come together and make plans to try to reconcile their parents. Soon, though, both girls know and accept that their parents never will live together again.

The girl narrating this story in the first person starts out vacillating between love and hate for her family members, and ends by understanding and accepting them. Of particular note in Cassie's personal growth is her friendship with Bernie, for it is here that she discards a morbid concentration on her health and appearance and learns to be considerate of Bernie's needs and vulnerabilities. These contemporary teenagers are portrayed with humor, understanding, and some playful exaggeration, the last to ease young readers into a little self-appraisal themselves.

Ages 11-13

Also available in:
Braille—*The Pistachio Prescription: A Novel*
Library of Congress (NLSBPH)

Cassette—*The Pistachio Prescription: A Novel*
Library of Congress (NLSBPH)

155

Danziger, Paula

There's a Bat in Bunk Five

Dell Publishing Company, Inc. (Yearling Books), 1982.
(150 pages, paperbound)

CAMP EXPERIENCES
MATURATION
Boy-girl relationships
Responsibility: accepting

Marcy, almost fifteen, is excited about her upcoming job as a counselor-in-training at a creative arts camp. She is a last-minute replacement, picked by a favorite former teacher. Marcy decides that at camp she will concentrate on developing her character and growing up. In short order she meets Ted, a counselor and high school senior; Corrine, the head counselor in her bunkhouse; and the ten girls she is to work with. All the girls seem pleasant except ten-year-old Ginger, who was nasty last year and is ornery and unkind still. Marcy soon enjoys camp life and falls hard for Ted. Corrine, regarding Marcy as a little sister, helps her with the girls and encourages her, suggesting she not expect too much from herself or others. Ted and Marcy get a day off together and spend it in nearby Woodstock, shopping and walking around—Marcy is sure she's in love. They return to pandemonium in Marcy's bunk number five, caused by a bat that Ted kills with a broom. The girls conduct a short funeral service for it. When Corrine goes into the infirmary with poison ivy—caused by Ginger who rubbed wet poison ivy over her sheets—Marcy is left in charge of the girls. They trick her into believing there's another bat in the bunk, but this time it's only a baseball bat. Then Ginger runs away and Marcy blames herself for not giving her more attention. When the girl is found in Woodstock, Marcy realizes how troubled Ginger is. She also sees that she herself has been focusing too much on her own feelings and problems, not enough on the lives of others. This insight makes it hard for Marcy to face the end of her stay at camp, yet intensifies her desire to go home and get on with her life. "It's all kind of funny and sad and joyful and exciting at the same time."

This humorous first-person narrative follows the adventures and maturation of a young camp counselor. All the people Marcy works with, staff members and campers alike, help her lose some of her self-absorption and begin to look around her. This sequel to *The Cat Ate My Gymsuit* is easy to read and should appeal to reluctant readers.

Ages 10-14

Also available in:
Paperbound—*There's a Bat in Bunk Five*
Dell Publishing Company, Inc. (Laurel Leaf Library)

Talking Book—*There's a Bat in Bunk Five*
Library of Congress (NLSBPH)

156

De Paola, Thomas Anthony

Andy (That's My Name)

Color illustrations by the author.
Prentice-Hall, Inc., 1973.
(32 pages counted)

SELF, ATTITUDE TOWARD: Confidence
SELF, ATTITUDE TOWARD: Respect
Courage, meaning of

Andy is pulling a wagon that has standing in it the large letters A-N-D-Y. He comes upon a group of older children who are looking for something to do. Noticing the letters in the wagon, the older children take them and make words with them. Andy makes several attempts, first to be included in their word games, then to get his letters back. But the older children put him off by saying, "You're too little!" Within a short time, Andy asserts himself, retrieves his letters, and goes off remarking, "I may be little but . . . I'm very important!"

In this picture book, older children take advantage of a much younger child. The small child shows exceptionally good judgment in coping with a threatening situation. Excellent illustrations are an integral part of the story.

Ages 3-5

Also available in:
Paperbound—*Andy (That's My Name)*
Prentice-Hall, Inc.

157

De Paola, Thomas Anthony

Nana Upstairs and Nana Downstairs

Color illustrations by the author.
Putnam Berkley Group, Inc., 1973.
(31 pages counted)

GRANDPARENT: Love for
GREAT-GRANDPARENT
DEATH: of Grandparent
DEATH: of Great-grandparent

Tommy, about four years old, has a grandmother and a great-grandmother whom he dearly loves. He has given his grandmother the name Nana Downstairs, since he usually finds her at the kitchen stove when he and his family come to visit each Sunday. Tommy has named his great-grandmother Nana Upstairs because at the age of ninety-four, she is bedridden and can always be found in her room upstairs. Tommy and Nana Upstairs do many things together: they share stories and mints and take naps at the same time. One morning, Tommy's mother informs him that Nana Upstairs has died and "won't be here anymore." Tommy refuses to believe his mother until he sees the empty bed in Nana's room. Then he sits on the floor and cries until his mother tells him that he can bring Nana Upstairs back in his memory by thinking about her. One night, Tommy sees a falling star, and his mother says, "Perhaps that was a kiss from Nana Upstairs." When Tommy is grown up, Nana Downstairs dies too. As he looks up at the starry sky, he thinks, "Now you are both Nana Upstairs."

This simple and touching story shows a close, loving relationship between a child and his great-grandmother. Tommy's grief over the death of his great-grandmother and his mother's words of comfort are sensitively presented in this short text.

Ages 3-8

Also available in:
No other form known

158

De Paola, Thomas Anthony

Now One Foot, Now the Other

Color illustrations by the author.
Putnam Berkley Group, Inc., 1981.
(45 pages counted)

GRANDPARENT: Love for
ILLNESSES: of Grandparent
Helping

Bobby was named after his grandfather, Bob. Bob has often told Bobby how he taught him to walk, holding his hands and saying, "Now one foot, now the other." The two like to play with wooden blocks, stacking them into a tall tower. When the last block—the elephant block—is put on top, Bob pretends to sneeze and the tower comes tumbling down. One day, not long after Bobby's fifth birthday, Bob has a stroke and is hospitalized. Bobby misses his grandfather terribly, but it is many months before Bob comes home again. When he does he can't walk or talk, and he doesn't seem to know any of the family. He frightens the little boy now, especially one day when he makes a strange noise. His mother tells Bobby that Bob can't help himself. When the boy returns to his grandfather, he seems to see a tear rolling down Bob's face. Bobby begins to talk to him and is convinced Bob knows him, although his mother thinks it's Bobby's imagination. When Bobby builds a tower of blocks and places the elephant block on top, Bob makes a noise like a sneeze. "Bobby laughed and laughed. Now he knew that Bob would get better." Bob slowly begins to talk a little, to move his fingers and hands, and to attempt feeding himself. Bobby helps him. Bob requests stories, so Bobby tells him some. Then Bob rests his hands on Bobby's shoulders and learns to walk as Bobby tells him, "Now one foot. . . . Now the other foot." On Bobby's sixth birthday, he builds the block tower and Bob sneezes as the last block goes on. Bobby asks Bob to tell him some stories, and Bob does. Then Bobby tells the story of how he helped his grandfather learn to walk again.

A little boy and his grandfather exchange roles when, after a stroke, the grandfather is helped to walk by the child he taught to walk years earlier. Bobby helps the man who once helped him, telling him stories, playing their special game with blocks, helping his grandfather feed himself. It is Bobby who first realizes that Bob does recognize and understand people, even though he cannot speak or move. Beautifully and simply illustrated in soft colors, this warm story is about intergenerational love and respect. Young children will easily understand the text and may learn something of what a stroke is and means. Although all stroke victims do not have the rapid recovery shown here, the book suggests the value to them of a caring, supportive relationship. This is a companion volume to *Nana Upstairs and Nana Downstairs.*

Ages 4-7

Also available in:
Paperbound—*Now One Foot, Now the Other*
Putnam Berkley Group, Inc.

159

De Paola, Thomas Anthony

Oliver Button Is a Sissy

Color illustrations by the author.
Harcourt Brace Jovanovich, Inc., 1979.
(46 pages counted, paperbound)

GENDER ROLE IDENTITY: Male
Name-calling
Success
Teasing

There is one little boy in the neighborhood who doesn't like to play ball. His name is Oliver Button. He doesn't like to do the other things boys are supposed to do either. Instead, he enjoys reading books, drawing pictures, jumping rope, and playing dress-up. Since he also likes to dance, his parents decide to send him to Ms. Leah's Dancing School. His father, who is uncomfortable with his son's interests, rationalizes that the dancing is "especially for the exercise." When Oliver takes his shiny new tap shoes to school, the boys tease him and write on the wall that "Oliver Button is a Sissy." But in spite of the continued teasing, Oliver keeps working on his dancing. When Ms. Leah asks him to be in a talent show, Oliver joyfully accepts the challenge. He gets a new costume and practices his routine tirelessly. On the Friday before his performance, his teacher at school announces the time and place of the show and encourages the other children to go and cheer for their classmate. On Sunday afternoon Oliver performs before a packed theater. The audience claps and claps. But when the prizes are announced, Oliver is left out. He is very disappointed and afraid of what people will think of him now. Ms. Leah and his parents, however, greet him with big hugs. His father rewards his "great dancer" by taking him out for a "great pizza." Nevertheless, the next day Oliver doesn't want to go to school and face the other children. But he does go, and as he walks by the wall where the cruel message about him is written, he is surprised to see that the word "Sissy" has been crossed out. The message now reads, "Oliver Button is a Star."

This is a book about the pain of being different, especially of varying from the accepted activities and interests of one's sex. It illustrates the struggle the nonconforming child may have in winning acceptance. Oliver does not fight back; he just endures and continues to find his happiness in doing his special things. The talent competition gives him his chance to prove to himself and others that what he does is worthwhile. Although things do not turn out as he had hoped, he does win the admiration of his family and classmates—the most important prize of all. Expressive illustrations help to emphasize the uniqueness of the main character and of his way of experiencing life.

Ages 4-7

Also available in:
No other form known

160

DeClements, Barthe

Nothing's Fair in Fifth Grade

Viking Penguin, 1981.
(137 pages)

REJECTION: Peer
Differences, human
Friendship: making friends
Friendship: meaning of
Parental: negligence
Rejection: parental
School: transfer
Weight control: overweight

The new girl in Jenifer's fifth-grade class, Elsie Edwards, is grossly overweight and fast becomes the "classroom reject." When money begins disappearing from the classroom, Jenifer suspects Elsie; she's seen her buying licorice and knows Elsie's harsh mother, who demands that the girl lose weight, doesn't give her money for food. Elsie is caught and has to spend recess in the principal's office. Jenifer and her best friends, Diane and Sharon, are as scornful of Elsie as everyone is until the day Elsie's skirt falls off in class; she's been losing weight, but her mother hasn't bought her any new clothes or altered her old ones. The teacher asks Jenifer to help Elsie. Elsie tells Jenifer her father was the only person who ever loved her—before he left home about five years ago and her parents divorced. Jenifer offers to be friends, although Elsie doesn't respond, and she defends Elsie to her classmates. When Jenifer comes home with a low grade in math, her parents suggest a tutor. Since Elsie is excellent at math, Jenifer's parents pay her fifty cents an hour to tutor Jenifer; with the money, Elsie can repay what she took from classmates. Elsie is a natural teacher, and Jenifer does much better on her next math test. One day Jenifer visits Elsie's house and is appalled at Elsie's mother's hostility toward her daughter. At Diane's slumber party, Elsie tells the others that her weight problems began with her parents' marital troubles and got worse after her father left home. She's only seen her father once since the divorce and then, when he talked about seeing her again, the woman with him signaled no. Diane's mother sews Elsie's slacks, which have gotten so big for her that she has them all pinned together. Later, Elsie's mother calls and screams at Diane's mother for touching her daughter's clothes. Diane's mother retorts, "It's about time you paid attention to her!" On Monday, Elsie is wearing a new jumper and shoes. One Saturday the four girls, along with Jenifer's and Elsie's younger siblings, decide to attend a carnival. Diane flags a truck driver and, against Elsie's opposition, they all climb on. The truck driver drives for a long time, and the girls notice they're in the country. They manage to jump off, but the truck drives away with Robyn, Elsie's little sister, still aboard. They call the police. When Elsie's mother arrives at the police station, she blames Elsie for the crisis and tells her she'll soon be sent away to a boarding school. After Robyn is found unharmed, apparently only the victim of an innocent mix-up, Jenifer's mother tries to dissuade Mrs. Edwards. But the woman seems determined to get rid of Elsie. Then their teacher tells Mrs. Edwards that Elsie has improved more than any other student in their class. She would never steal money again, she helps others with their schoolwork, and she is successfully losing weight. Elsie's mother and the principal agree to give Elsie another chance. She'll return to school in the fall, to the delight of all the girls—especially Elsie.

Jenifer tells this episodic but compelling story of pathetic, overweight Elsie, class outcast until the other students learn to see beyond her physical appearance to the suffering human being inside. Jenifer is appalled by Elsie's hostile, unloving, neglectful mother, and she and her friends unite to defend and protect Elsie. Readers will see how family turmoil—in this case, a divorce with custody going to a parent with little affection for her child—can cause a person to become an overweight outcast. Friendship redeems Elsie, and the relationships among the girls are well drawn.

Ages 8-11

Also available in:
Braille—*Nothing's Fair in Fifth Grade*
Library of Congress (NLSBPH)

Cassette—*Nothing's Fair in Fifth Grade*
Library of Congress (NLSBPH)

Paperbound—*Nothing's Fair in Fifth Grade*
Puffin Books

161

Delton, Judy

I Never Win!

Color illustrations by Cathy Gilchrist.
Carolrhoda Books, Inc., 1981.
(32 pages)

SELF, ATTITUDE TOWARD: Accepting
Identity, search for
Inferiority, feelings of
Success
Talents: musical

Charlie, about six, never wins at anything. He comes in second in a sack race at school. In Monopoly he lands on Boardwalk and must pay a lot of money. In Little League he strikes out. At a friend's birthday party, he loses at all the games. Other kids win prizes, but not Charlie. Terribly upset, he goes home and practices the piano, playing very rapidly because he's so angry. When his grandfather comes to visit on Monday, Charlie loses four games of checkers to him. Wednesday at a potluck dinner with his family everyone wins at Bingo except him. Charlie is so upset he screams at his mother when she tries to reassure him.

At home again he plays the piano, practicing "The Flight of the Bumblebee" until he can play it perfectly. On Friday Charlie goes to the State Fair with his friend Tim and Tim's father. Tim and his father win at games; Charlie does not. Frustrated beyond endurance, he returns home and works some more on "The Flight of the Bumblebee." The next morning Mrs. Teasley, his piano teacher, calls and invites Charlie to her house that evening. He is to play the piano for "some important people." He plays "The Flight of the Bumblebee" and then three other songs on request. Mrs. Teasley calls Charlie her very best student. At last Charlie feels like a winner! "I guess not every prize is one you can see."

A little boy's frustration at always losing translates into great success at the piano, since whenever Charlie loses at something he practices the piano furiously. Thus his playing becomes more than just a way of releasing his anger. It becomes his means of discovering his own worth. Children will appreciate Charlie's unexpected triumph in this beginning reader, also a good read-aloud selection. Simple illustrations accented with red help convey Charlie's feelings.

Ages 4-7

Also available in:
No other form known

162

Delton, Judy

It Happened on Thursday

Color illustrations by June Goldsborough.
Albert Whitman & Company, 1978.
(30 pages counted)

SUPERSTITION
Illnesses: of parent

Jamie believes that Thursday is his lucky day. His Cub Scout den meets then; he once had a perfect spelling paper on that day; his birthday once fell on a Thursday; and on a Thursday he once received a baseball autographed by Hank Aaron. That is why, when Jamie's mother falls ill and is hospitalized, he counts on things to improve on Thursday. But by Thursday his mother is in the hospital and her condition appears to have grown worse. Not until Friday, when the family receives word that tests have come out favorably and Mother will be home Sunday, do things brighten. And by Sunday, Jamie realizes that, though one can look for good things to happen on Thursdays, they may happen all week long.

Children reading this story may begin to see that good fortune does not necessarily obey the calendar or any other automatic summons. Secondarily, they may be interested in how a family feels and acts about the illness of one of its members.

Ages 5-8

Also available in:
No other form known

163

Delton, Judy

My Mom Hates Me in January

Color illustrations by John Faulkner.
Albert Whitman & Company, 1977.
(32 pages counted)

COMMUNICATION: Parent-Child
PATIENCE/IMPATIENCE

Because young Lee Henry's mother is sick and tired of winter—it is January—she finds nearly everything he does or wants to do too messy, too noisy, or taking too much of her time. Finally, in exasperation, she sends him outside with instructions to keep dry, have a good time, not slide into a tree or lose his mittens, and not to get snow in his boots. Outside, Lee Henry slides on his saucer and just misses a tree, makes angels in the snow and gets all wet, and loses a mitten. When he returns, his mom is unhappy to see him back so soon. He sneezes and she sends him to take a warm bath, then complains because he splashes on the floor. At dinner she tells him not to tip his chair. By now, Lee Henry wants winter to go away, too. Next morning his mom sees a robin outside, and her mood brightens at the prospect of spring. Now she feels like doing the things Lee Henry wants to do. They make popcorn balls and make monsters out of clay, and she reads him his favorite book. They talk about how much fun he will have when it gets warm, and then they go into the kitchen to share a popcorn ball and a milkshake. Lee Henry says, "My mom hates me in January (unless she just hates *January*). But she'll love me again in May."

Parents are human, and their feelings about outside events often influence the way they treat their children. The mother in this first-person narrative is impatient with her son because she dislikes the weather, but he shows how children can both understand mood changes in their parents and see that bad moods are only temporary.

Ages 3-6

Also available in:
Cassette—*My Mom Hates Me in January*
Educational Enrichment Materials

Filmstrip—*My Mom Hates Me in January*
Educational Enrichment Materials

164

Delton, Judy

My Mother Lost Her Job Today

Color illustrations by Irene Trivas.
Albert Whitman & Company, 1980.
(32 pages counted)

PARENT/PARENTS: Unemployed
Anxiety
Communication: parent-child
Imagination
Security/Insecurity

Barbara Anne, about six, worries that things will never be the same now that her mother has lost her job. Her fears grow as she watches her mother work around the house with tears in her eyes, bang silverware, slam the door, and fail to notice the dandelion bouquet Barbara Anne picks. That evening, Barbara Anne puts herself to bed, dirty knees and all, imagining the worst: no more birthday parties, no more Christmas, no more visits to the zoo. When her mother comes in to say goodnight, Barbara Anne offers to help out by baby-sitting, shoveling snow, and cutting grass. Realizing how upset the child is, her mother assures her that she won't need to get a job. As mother and daughter snuggle together, the mother explains that right now she feels "sad and mad and all mixed up," but that things will eventually work out for them. She'll get another job, maybe a better job than she had. Comforted, Barbara Anne goes to sleep.

Small children will readily understand the plight of a little girl frightened by the signs of distress in her newly unemployed mother and needing to be reassured that life will eventually return to normal. Text and illustrations complement each other especially well in this first-person narrative. Pictures of Barbara Anne's fearful imaginings are distinct enough from those of real occurrences to be easily distinguished by young children.

Ages 3-7

Also available in:
No other form known

165

Delton, Judy

The New Girl at School

Color illustrations by Lillian Aberman Hoban.
Dutton Children's Books, 1979.
(30 pages counted)

SCHOOL: Transfer
Change: accepting
Fear: of school

Marcia, about six, is the new girl at school. The first day, the other children stare at her and do not even notice she has on her new dress with the octopus. Marcia feels out of place, doesn't know where things are, and doesn't understand subtraction. That night when she tells her mother she does not like her new school, her mother tells her it will be better tomorrow. But Tuesday Marcia still feels out of place and tells her mother so. Marcia's mother encourages her to "give it time." Wednesday Marcia cries and doesn't want to get on the bus, but her mother insists. At recess that day Marcia plays Captain-May-I with the other girls and even makes it to second base when they all play baseball. That night when her mother asks about school, Marcia says, "Give it time." On Thursday her teacher displays Marcia's paper airplane, and a boy notices the octopus on the dress she has worn again. A new friend even invites Marcia to her birthday party. On Friday, when Marcia's mother suggests that perhaps Marcia can stay with her grandmother and go back to her old school, Marcia replies that she is used to this new school now. Besides, there was a new girl at school today and she doesn't understand subtraction either.

Nervous about going to a new school, a little girl finds the adjustment difficult at first. But before too long she begins to make friends and feel at home—and soon there's a newer student than she. Children will find it easy to sympathize with and discuss Marcia and the feelings of new students. Turquoise-tinted illustrations add a light touch.

Ages 4-7

Also available in:
No other form known

166

Dixon, Paige, pseud.

May I Cross Your Golden River?

Atheneum Publishers, 1975.
(262 pages) o.p.

DEATH: Attitude toward
Amyotrophic lateral sclerosis
Courage, meaning of
Family: unity
Sibling: relationships

Eighteen-year-old Jordan's life has been happy and commonplace. He is part of a close-knit, if fatherless, family, where mother and youngster are mutually respectful. He plays tennis, has a girlfriend, and thinks he may one day become a lawyer. The sudden weakness in his knees is at first dismissed as "tennis knee." Later, when he loses the use of one leg and cannot raise his arm, he decides to see his family doctor, who recommends tests at the Mayo Clinic. The finding is amyotrophic lateral sclerosis, Lou Gehrig's disease, progressive, incurable, and fatal. At first he is furious at the doctor for being unable to cure him. Then he fastens his hopes on the chance of a wrong diagnosis, or, failing that, the possibility that the disease will arrest itself. But his brother warns: "Be ready. Don't tell yourself fancy stories and have to be jolted out of them later on." Coming home, Jordan looks around the house with aching nostalgia.

His emotions surprise him: the sudden fighting of tears at being given a puppy, nearly unbearable gratitude for the kindness and concern of his family, and his anger that the family doctor cannot stop the disease either. Slowly Jordan admits to himself the truth of the disease and his own limits. "Discipline" and "Carpe Diem"—seize the day—become his words. He considers suicide once, but decides against it. Illness or not, life goes on, as his family prepares for a wedding and a birth. As the disease progresses, Jordan makes known his preferences for a memorial service and arranges to donate his body to science. Two goals he must achieve before he is bedridden: to be best man at his brother's wedding and to take part in the christening of his sister's baby. A few weeks after the christening, Jordan collapses and is carried to bed. As the book ends, he is still alive but too weak now to talk.

Though Jordan's death is finally imminent, the reader is left not with the grievousness of his dying, but with the value of his life. Throughout his illness, he, his family, and his friends clear-sightedly struggle to transform their fear and grief into words and deeds that allow Jordan the dignity of dying in his own way. His mother resists over-protecting her son; his brother listens steadily through all of Jordan's changing moods; and his best friend simply treats the boy with respect. Jordan's realistic struggle is not melodrama but a moving affirmation of life.

Ages 12 and up

Also available in:
Cassette—*May I Cross Your Golden River?*
Library of Congress (NLSBPH)

167

Donnelly, Elfie

So Long, Grandpa

Translated from the German by Anthea Bell.
Crown Publishers, Inc., 1981.
(92 pages)

DEATH: Attitude Toward
GRANDPARENT: Love for
Cancer
Death: of grandparent
Family: relationships
Grandparent: living in child's home
Illnesses: terminal

Micky Nidetzky holds strong opinions for a boy of ten. For example, his mother is not to enter his room without knocking. But she does, and this, along with her strictness, her close supervision, and especially her criticism of his beloved grandfather, drives him wild. He's also at his wit's end about his older sister, Linda, who takes after their mother in all things and never fails to tattle on Micky. Dad is all right but it is Grandpa Nidetzky, who lives with the family, that Micky especially loves. Still, the boy doesn't seem particularly concerned when his father tells him that Grandpa has cancer. To Micky, cancer is just another illness, like flu. When Dad announces that he has bought a vacation home in the Canary Islands and that the family will go there next week, Micky becomes engrossed in vacation plans. There is a brief flare-up when Micky, assuming Grandpa will accompany them, talks with him about the trip before his parents have decided if the old man's health will permit him to go. But then his parents decide Grandpa should come along and they fly from their home in Austria to their vacation place adjoining a beach. At first, Micky loves his vacation. But then he sees Grandpa's condition worsen so dramatically that Micky asks his parents if Grandpa will die. Shocked, his mother replies, "People don't talk about that kind of thing!" After Grandpa suffers a sharp attack of pain, Mrs. Nidetzky asks angrily why they brought along such a "sick old man." Grandpa overhears and the two have a long argument. Next morning, Grandpa is gone. Mrs. Nidetzky blames herself. Later in the day, Micky finds Grandpa calmly working crossword puzzles in an empty fisherman's hut. He wanted some peace and quiet and soon announces his intention to stay on the island until he dies. But the family persuades him to return with them. From then on, Grandpa rapidly loses weight and has increased pain and fatigue. Micky tries to grasp the fact that Grandpa will never recover. When he and Grandpa talk, Grandpa admits he doesn't believe in God. After Micky accompanies Grandpa to the funeral of an old friend, the two talk about people's odd ceremonies of burial, their use of phrases like "passing on" to conceal the fact of death. Although Grandpa's health steadily deteriorates, he remains cheerful and refuses to be morbid. Micky profits from Grandpa's straightforward attitude and is able to ask the doctor how long Grandpa has left, a question his father is unable to complete. About two to four weeks, the doctor replies. Soon Grandpa is dead, dying in his sleep. Seeing the body in bed, Micky suddenly feels cheerful: "Grandpa's alright now!" But when the time comes to throw earth on the coffin, a ritual he and Grandpa had smiled about, Micky faints and is confined to bed. His father comforts him by showing him a letter Grandpa had written asking Micky to take care of all his little "treasures." Micky is not to be sorry about Grandpa's death, the old man wrote. He hopes Micky's life will be as happy as his own has been. Himself again, Micky tells his mother to stop crying. Grandpa lives as long as someone thinks of him, and Micky always will.

A young boy whose beloved grandfather is dying of cancer learns to disentangle death from its social trappings and see it clearly in this thoughtful first-person narrative. Micky's is an honest account of death, dying, and mourning, one that could comfort children in similar situations. Though not at all anti-religious, the book does present a humanistic approach to death in its criticism of the various social and religious rituals that surround human mortality, and so calls for a discerning reader or an adult's explanation. Family relationships, strained by terminal illness, are realistically presented.

Ages 9-11

Also available in:
No other form known

168

Due, Linnea A.

High and Outside

Spinsters Aunt Lute, 1980.
(195 pages, paperbound)

ALCOHOLISM: Adolescent
Friendship: best friend
Loneliness
Suicide: attempted

Niki Etchen seems to have everything going for her. A junior at Lincoln High, Niki is the champion pitcher on the girls' softball team, an honors student, and an editor on the school paper. But Niki is also an alcoholic. Three years ago her parents allowed her to start drinking wine, and she has gradually worked her way to gin-and-tonic cocktails, wine at dinner, and beer after dinner. Her parents don't see the problem. Her best friend, Martha, tries hard to cover up for Niki's erratic behavior and changing moods. When Niki's drinking begins noticeably affecting her pitching game, her coach, Scotty, offers to talk with her about her drinking and then gives her an ultimatum: no more hangovers at practices or games or Niki will be off the team. After she skips practice the following day because of a hangover, Scotty tells Niki that she will either join Alcoholics Anonymous or leave the team. In a rage, Niki quits the team. Another teammate, Teri, who goes to Al Anon because her father is an alcoholic, encourages Niki to go to AA. But Niki keeps denying she is an alcoholic, although she has blackouts almost every time she drinks. Finally, after a dramatic confrontation with Martha, Niki tries AA. But she finds that sobriety leaves her angry and irritable, and she rationalizes that she is probably not an alcoholic. Niki starts drinking again, but feels depressed and resentful toward herself and others. After school ends for the summer, her drinking gets worse. Then Martha, who has been attending Al Anon with Teri, confronts Niki, saying she no longer wants the pressure of Niki's drinking and never wants to see her again. Niki continues drinking heavily and one day attempts to slash her wrists. But even alcohol doesn't allow her to cut deeply enough. In despair, Niki decides on her own to concentrate on the AA slogans, "first things first" and "one day at a time." After six weeks of lonely sobriety, she decides to attend an AA and then an Al Anon meeting. At the Al Anon meeting she sees Martha, and they have an emotional reunion. Niki is finally able to acknowledge that she has to conquer her drinking problem one day at a time.

A teenage alcoholic graphically describes her blackouts, loneliness, and suicidal feelings. Though her parents give her little support when she confronts them with her alcoholism, Niki finds her friends and coach very supportive, even when she is not willing to accept their concern and advice. The characteristics of teenage alcoholism and its effects on the young victim and her friends are handled realistically. Much less convincing is the shallow characterization of Niki's parents, whose obtuseness seems highly unlikely. The dialogue is generally believable and includes some profanity.

Ages 13 and up

Also available in:
No other form known

169

Duvoisin, Roger Antoine

Petunia

Color illustrations by the author.
Alfred A. Knopf, Inc., 1962.
(30 pages counted)

PRIDE/FALSE PRIDE

All the barnyard animals think that Petunia is a silly goose. One day, Petunia discovers a book lying in the meadow. She tucks it under her wing, recalling that Mr. Pumpkin once said, "He who owns books and loves them is wise." The closed book never leaves her side, and Petunia becomes very proud knowing she is so wise. With her newly discovered wisdom, she advises the animals when they have problems and answers questions for them. She tells the rooster King that his comb is red plastic and will fall off if he shakes it. King never shakes his majestic comb again. Petunia helps Ida the hen count her chicks. Ida ends up with six chicks instead of nine, but Petunia assures her that six is much more than nine. Petunia also helps Noisy the dog free himself from a hole in the ground, helps Straw the horse "get rid of" a toothache, and rescues Cotton the kitten from a tree. The animals discover a box marked "DANGER FIRE-CRACKERS," and they ask Petunia to read the label. She tells them it says "candies." Seven greedy mouths tear open the box. A loud explosion follows. Petunia's book is blown open by the blast, and she sees its pages for the first time. She thinks about the words and finally begins to understand that it is not enough to carry wisdom under her wing: she must put it in her mind and heart.

Barnyard animals are amusingly used to illustrate the theme of false pride. The reader is also shown that owning a book is only the beginning: one must read it and learn from it as well.

Ages 4-8

Also available in:
Braille—*Petunia*
Library of Congress (NLSBPH)

Cassette—*Petunia*
Library of Congress (NLSBPH)

Paperbound—*Petunia*
Alfred A. Knopf, Inc.

170

Duvoisin, Roger Antoine

Petunia, I Love You

Color illustrations by the author.
Alfred A. Knopf, Inc., 1965.
(35 pages counted)

GREED
Gratitude
Honesty/Dishonesty

Raccoon has thought about feasting on Petunia the goose for a long time. He decides not to waste any more time hunting other animals, turning all of his attention instead to Petunia. Raccoon resorts to trickery, since Petunia is stronger than he. He tells Petunia that he loves her and wants to take her to visit his aunt who lives in the woods. This attempt fails. Raccoon thinks of several other ways to snare Petunia, but each time, he succeeds only in getting caught in his own trap. He falls into the river, gets stung by bees, and is knocked down by a rock. Raccoon becomes so hungry that he goes after the bait in a farmer's trap and is caught. Petunia releases the trap, and Raccoon escapes just before the farmer reaches him. Raccoon is so grateful to Petunia that he tells her he will always be her friend.

The results of greed and lying are clearly shown in this story: the raccoon has many accidents while the trusting goose remains unharmed. The raccoon's gratitude at the end of the book appears genuine.

Ages 3-7

Also available in:
No other form known

171

Duvoisin, Roger Antoine

Veronica

Color illustrations by the author.
Alfred A. Knopf, Inc., 1961.
(34 pages counted)

ATTENTION SEEKING
Self, attitude toward: accepting

Veronica, a young hippopotamus, lives on a river bank with her parents, brothers, sisters, and numerous other relatives. She is unhappy because she feels ordinary and inconspicuous. Aspiring to be famous, Veronica leaves home and after several days arrives at a city. When she lumbers down the sidewalk, she bumps into people. When she walks in the street, cars bump into her. Everyone notices her. A policeman shows her a parking lot where she can sleep for the night. The next morning, Veronica takes a bath in a fountain and eats fruit and vegetables from a vendor's cart. She is arrested and taken to jail. A nice old lady hears of Veronica's plight, arranges her release from jail, and sends her home to the river bank in a moving van. Now Veronica is famous. All of her relatives gather to hear her tales of city life.

The hippopotamus in this delightful story discovers that although it is nice to be noticed, it is possible to become too conspicuous and too well known. She is glad to return to her familiar environment.

Ages 4-7

Also available in:
Braille—*Veronica*
Library of Congress (NLSBPH)

172

Dyer, Thomas A.

The Whipman Is Watching

Houghton Mifflin Co., 1979.
(177 pages)

GRANDPARENT: Living in Home of
NATIVE AMERICAN
Ambivalence, feelings of
Discipline, meaning of
Identity, search for
Rebellion
School: negative experiences

Thirteen-year-old Angie lives on an Indian reservation in Oregon with her grandmother, called Katla, her younger sister, Carysa, and her older cousins, Cultus and Marta. Katla is very mindful of Indian traditions, clinging tenaciously to the old ways, and Marta follows her example. Angie is somewhat impatient with the discipline of Indian life. But Cultus is more than impatient—he is a troublemaker, the kind that gives Indians a bad name, according to Katla. Angie can't understand Cultus's bull-headedness when it is so much easier "just to get along." The reservation is forty-nine miles from the school, so the children take the bus there and back every day. Although many of them behave badly, Cultus is the worst, fighting and instigating fights whenever he can. One day the bus driver tells Katla that Cultus will not be allowed to ride the bus for a week. The grandmother says it's up to the driver to make the children behave. In the old days, she remembers, Indian children behaved because they got whipped regularly by the Whipman, a tribe member responsible for discipline. Cultus has no other way to get to school, but the bus driver refuses to relent. That night Cultus doesn't come home. He returns the next day accompanied by his Uncle Dan, who agrees with the boy that he shouldn't have to attend the white people's school. Although it is Saturday, Katla insists that Dan drive her to the principal's home so she can talk to him about Cultus. Angie, horribly embarrassed, must accompany her, but to her relief the principal isn't home. On Monday the bus driver refuses to take Cultus, so Katla gets on instead and rides to school to see the principal. Again she makes Angie, deeply mortified at being singled out, come with her. Distressed by the wild, destructive behavior of all the children on the bus, Katla tells the principal that someone must make them behave. But he says discipline is up to the parents. Katla spends the school day with Angie, since she must wait for the bus to get home. Angie's best friend, Lois, with whom she's quarreled, makes fun of Katla and is sent out of the classroom. As they wait for the bus, Katla sees Lois write a dirty word in a white girl's textbook. When Katla slaps her Lois fights back, pushing the old woman down and fracturing her arm. While Katla is in the hospital, things fall apart at home and Angie's desperation mounts. Carysa won't wash in cold water in the traditional Indian way, and Cultus won't ride the bus even with permission. Angie's friendship with Lois continues to deteriorate. When Katla comes home, there are only two days left before Powwow, a time of dancing and feasting, and Angie stays home from school to help with the preparations. Despite her gloom, she and Lois make up their quarrel, and after Powwow the family goes home and falls asleep by the fire while Katla tells a story about the old days. When Angie returns to school on Monday, her health teacher refuses to let her make up the test she missed and gives her an F: "we just can't let our students miss school for every little thing." That afternoon, Cultus pushes Lois down while they're waiting for the bus, and when the driver tries to discipline him Cultus runs off. He is brought home later that day by Jobie Sohappy, a sympathetic young reservation policeman who is the current Whipman. Cultus has stolen and wrecked a pickup truck and will have to stay in Group Home until a court hearing decides what should be done about him. When the case comes up, the judge orders the whole family into her chambers for a discussion. There Katla speaks eloquently about the struggles Indian children have at the white school where there is little understanding of their culture. The judge invites Katla to address the school board and puts Cultus on two years' probation under Jobie's supervision. When Cultus returns home after his stay in Group Home, his attitude toward his culture has changed. He has been strengthened by Katla's words and Jobie's support. "I'm going to show them I ain't afraid to be Indian." Angie, who has recognized some of Cultus's doubts within herself, begins to rethink her own attitudes about being Indian. Feeling that their life may now begin to right itself, Angie looks to the future with some hope.

The struggles of young Native Americans to find a place in white society without surrendering their traditional culture are believably described in this tightly written story. Angie and Cultus both find that even the smallest rebellion is, in effect, a denial of part of themselves. Their grandmother, strong in her tradition but confused and frustrated by the turmoil of the young people, finally succeeds by sheer eloquence and determination in strengthening her grandchildren's sense of identity. This is a sympathetic portrayal of characters and situations, enriched by details of traditional Indian culture.

Ages 10-14

Also available in:
No other form known

173

Dygard, Thomas J.

Winning Kicker

Puffin Books, 1990.
(199 pages, paperbound)

WOMEN'S RIGHTS
Leader/Leadership
Prejudice: sexual
Sports/Sportsmanship

In his thirty-seventh and final year coaching football at Higgins High School, tough, blunt, decisive John Earlingham looks forward to a great season—until seventeen-year-old Kathy Denver, a senior, tries out for place-kicker. Nothing he can do will dissuade her from trying out. As for his hopes she will fail, Kathy proves to be his best place-kicker. And as for his fear her presence will disrupt the team, it soon comes true. During practice the players watch the crowds and reporters out to watch Kathy. Opposed by a weak team in its opening game, Higgins plays so badly that Earlingham blames his team for making a circus of practice. Though Kathy kicks the crucial point that wins the game, 7-6, she later quits because she feels that her presence is a detriment to the team's performance. By now, Earlingham knows the team can solve its problems only if she remains, but he does not try to change her mind; he just silently approves when she gives in to the players' persuasion and rejoins the team. This time, the players concentrate on football. Then the coach of the team Higgins is to face that week questions Kathy's eligibility and calls her very presence on the field unfair because no player will be rough with a girl. These questions go unresolved and Higgins, aided by Kathy's field goal, wins again. Before the next game, against the powerhouse of the conference, the State High School Athletic Association urges the coach to withhold her from play "in the interests of fairness to all concerned," but Earlingham refuses. Kathy is ruled eligible. But early in the game, a player is blocked into her and she falls, breaking an ankle. Nonetheless, Higgins sweeps to a 47-0 victory. The next day Coach Earlingham, who has given special athletic letters to only two players, gives a special letter to Kathy for leadership.

Told from a coach's viewpoint, this story is only secondarily about a girl who plays on a football team and primarily about a coach who sees his job as making men out of boys—and his perplexity when one of the boys is a girl. His solution to the different courses of action urged on him by feminists and traditionalists is to treat Kathy as he would any male player—on her merits.

Ages 11-14

Also available in:
Cassette—*Winning Kicker*
Library of Congress (NLSBPH)

174

Ernst, Kathryn

Danny and His Thumb

Color illustrations by Thomas Anthony De Paola.
Prentice-Hall, Inc., 1975.
(32 pages) o.p.

THUMB SUCKING

Danny, about six, has sucked his thumb for a long time. He likes the way his thumb tastes, and he feels comfortable and happy sucking it. He sucks his thumb when he goes to the movies with his sister, when he waits for his mother, when he rides in the car, when he gets a haircut, and even when he thinks. But Danny's favorite thumb-sucking time is at night, when he is falling asleep. One September day, Danny decides that he does not like sucking his thumb as much as he used to. He is tired of listening to his mother's remarks about thumb sucking and wants to get rid of the "bump" (callus) he has on his thumb. Danny also notices that his friends do not suck their thumbs. Soon Danny finds that he is too busy to suck his thumb. He cannot suck his thumb while feeding his fish, learning to read, riding his bike, carrying out the garbage, working in the garden, talking on the telephone, eating his dinner, or holding hands with the boys and girls in his class. He soon goes to sleep without sucking his thumb, and his callus disappears.

A young boy gains security in stressful situations by sucking his thumb. Peer and maternal pressure cause him to dislike his thumb sucking but not to discard it. When the child begins to succeed at more adult tasks and gains confidence in himself, his thumb sucking no longer is a necessary source of security.

Ages 3-7

Also available in:
No other form known

175

Evans, Mari

JD

Black/white illustrations by Jerry Pinkney.
Avon Books, 1982.
o.p.

POVERTY
African-American
Bully: being bothered by
Drugs: abuse of
Embarrassment
Wishes

JD is a young African-American who lives in a housing project with his mother. In the first of four short stories, JD finds an old metal box in a vacant lot where he plays, and he tries without success to open it. He hopes and dreams that the box contains a million dollars, and he imagines the good and beautiful things he can get for his mother with all that money. He also dreams of the dog he will buy for himself. In the second story, JD feels unnoticed until a pretty woman says hello to him. In his elation, he intervenes in a fight between a bully and a little boy; the little boy then becomes JD's friend. The third story tells of JD's not wanting to go to school because Mama does not have the money for his book rental fee. Knowing that his teacher will embarrass him in front of the entire class if he cannot pay the fee, he decides to help Mama by earning money selling greeting cards. In the fourth story, JD sees his hero—Papa Go, the best athlete in the neighborhood—"shooting up" with drugs. JD is stunned. As he starts to walk away, he is caught and beaten by Coolaid, a bully.

This is a group of four short stories sympathetically written by a "black poet about a black child." Each story has an open ending that can provide an excellent invitation to group discussion.

Ages 9-12

Also available in:
No other form known

176

Fassler, Joan

The Boy with a Problem

Color illustrations by Stuart Kranz.
Human Sciences Press, 1971.
(31 pages)

ANXIETY
Communication: lack of
Friendship: meaning of
Problem solving

Johnny has a problem that bothers him so much that he is unable to eat, sleep well, or concentrate sufficiently on his schoolwork. Because his problem makes the whole world seem gloomy to him, Johnny begins to walk with his head bowed and almost never smiles. Sometimes Johnny's problem makes him feel like throwing up, and most days he does not feel like playing with his friends. Johnny's mother takes him to a doctor, who gives Johnny medicine for his upset stomach and vitamins to boost his energy. But this doesn't help because the problem still remains. When Johnny tries to tell his mother about his problem, she merely pats his head and tells him that if he forgets about it, everything will be fine. This does not help either, so Johnny decides to talk to his teacher. She interrupts him and instructs him to follow her advice, which she proceeds to give. Johnny tries to follow her counsel but still is plagued by his problem. The next day, Johnny's friend Peter asks him to go for a walk. During the walk, Peter listens "in a very serious, special way" as Johnny pours out his troubles. Not once does Peter offer advice or interrupt his friend. After the walk Johnny goes home, eats a large dinner, sleeps well, and feels better. He smiles again, begins to concentrate on his schoolwork, and starts to play with his friends.

This book is one of a series which, according to the publisher, provides a "sound psychological basis for helping young children cope with behavioral problems." The fact that the specific nature of Johnny's problem is not mentioned aids the reader in identifying with the boy.

Ages 4-8

Also available in:
No other form known

177

Fassler, Joan

Don't Worry Dear

Color illustrations by Stuart Kranz.
Human Sciences Press, 1971.
(29 pages)

ANXIETY
Enuresis
Speech problems: stuttering
Thumb sucking

Jenny is little. She is only as tall as Daddy's knee—unable to reach the doorbell, but able to walk under the dining-room table without bumping her head. Jenny still wets the bed at night, stutters, and sucks her thumb, especially when she is tired. But Mother assures her that she will outgrow these things in time. Three of Jenny's aunts suggest that Mother put bad-tasting medicine on Jenny's thumb so that she will stop sucking it. But Mother tells them that one day Jenny will no longer want to suck her thumb and therefore does not need medicine. Because she is young, Jenny believes that her toy animals are real—especially Barky. She feeds Barky, talks to him every night, patches him when he is torn, and gives him medicine when he is sick. Mother pretends with her. One morning, when Jenny is a little older and wakes up with a dry bed, Mother reminds her that she is growing up. One day Jenny speaks without stuttering. Jenny's brother peeks in on her one evening, and he sees that she is no longer sucking her thumb. But even though Jenny is growing up, she still likes to pretend that Barky is real—and Mother pretends right along with her.

This book is one of a series which, according to the publisher, provides a "sound psychological basis for helping young children cope with behavioral problems." In a pleasant manner, this book emphasizes that Jenny's understanding, supportive parents give her the freedom to outgrow her thumb sucking, bedwetting, and stuttering at her own rate.

Ages 4-6

Also available in:
No other form known

178

Fassler, Joan

Howie Helps Himself

Color illustrations by Joe Lasker.
Albert Whitman & Company, 1975.
(32 pages counted)

CEREBRAL PALSY
Perseverance
Wheelchair, dependence on

Howie is a happy little boy who likes things other boys like: eating chocolate ice cream, watching the snow fall, riding in his father's car. But because Howie has cerebral palsy and needs a wheelchair, there are some things he cannot do—run, jump, hold a pencil, play with blocks. His parents help him do things he cannot do himself. Sometimes his sister finds time to play ball with him or draw him funny pictures. When his grandmother visits, she takes him to the park. Howie likes his family, and school too. He goes every day in a special bus to a special class. The bus has an elevator that lifts him and his wheelchair aboard. At school Howie learns the alphabet, learns to pronounce words, learns to count. He also does exercises to strengthen his arms and legs. But what he wants to learn more than anything else is to move his wheelchair all by himself as his classmates do. His teachers show him the way, but Howie cannot do it. He works at it but sometimes gives up in tears. One day as Howie's father arrives to take him home, Howie looks at him standing in the doorway across the room, takes a deep breath, and turns the wheelchair around by himself. Then he pushes the wheels as far and as hard as he can. When he looks up, he is right in front of his father. He and his father hug and drive home.

Handicapped children may have to acquire special skills and strengths in using special equipment. This same specialness in the way they do things can cause embarrassment or fear in other children, feelings this book seeks to allay. Handicapped children will identify with Howie, but almost any child will recognize Howie's will to get about on his own steam.

Ages 5-8

Also available in:
Cassette—*Howie Helps Himself*
Educational Enrichment Materials

Cassette—*Howie Helps Himself*
Library of Congress (NLSBPH)

Filmstrip—*Howie Helps Himself*
Educational Enrichment Materials

179

Fassler, Joan

My Grandpa Died Today

Color illustrations by Stuart Kranz.
Human Sciences Press, 1983.
(31 pages)

DEATH: of Grandparent
MOURNING, STAGES OF

David's grandpa teaches him to play checkers. He also reads stories to him, shows him how to hit a baseball, and always roots for David's team. One day while David and Grandpa are taking a long walk, Grandpa tells the boy that he is getting old and will not live forever. With his arm around David's shoulder, Grandpa explains that he is not afraid to die because he knows that David is not afraid to live. Two days later, as he rocks in his chair, Grandpa dies. David's parents cry, and so do the many visitors to the house. Grandpa is taken away and buried. The shades in David's house are drawn; the mirrors are covered; and David, feeling as though the whole house is crying, cries also. Then, because he does not feel like sitting with the "gloomy grownups," he goes to his room and plays quietly. The next day, David's parents let him play baseball, and when it is David's turn at bat, he tries to forget his sadness. Planting his feet on the ground, he hits a grand-slam home run. As he imagines Grandpa's happy smile, the boy's grief disappears. It is then that David understands what Grandpa meant when he said, "I am not afraid to die because I know you are not afraid to live."

This book is one of a series which, according to the publisher, provides a "sound psychological basis for helping young children cope with behavioral problems." The vividness of the love David and Grandpa share, and the boy's sadness after his grandfather's death, enable the reader to sympathize easily with the child. The book makes it clear that it is acceptable for a young child to play while the rest of his family is mourning.

Ages 4-8

Also available in:
Paperbound—*My Grandpa Died Today*
Human Sciences Press

180

Fassler, Joan

One Little Girl

Color illustrations by M. Jane Smyth.
Human Sciences Press, 1969.
(22 pages counted)

MENTAL RETARDATION

Laurie is a pretty girl about ten years old. Although she does many things well, adults call Laurie a "slow child," and this makes her very unhappy. It is true that Laurie is slow at school, particularly in reading, writing, and arithmetic. It often takes her a long time to understand what the teacher is telling the class, and sometimes she does not understand at all. Laurie's mother takes her to "a special kind of doctor" who tests her and talks with her. A few days later, her parents receive a letter from the doctor stating that Laurie has difficulty with some tasks but is adept at others, and that her most important asset is her good self-image. Soon Laurie notices that instead of noticing the things she cannot do, adults pay more attention to what she does well. They also stop calling her a "slow child." This helps Laurie feel pride in herself, and she loses the unhappy feelings she had about being a "slow child."

Laurie feels guilty and upset because she cannot perform some of the tasks expected of her. The purpose of this book, according to the publisher, is to provide mentally retarded children with "an understanding of themselves and how they can relate positively to their environment." At the same time, the book will inform more typical children about the problems and special talents of their peers. This is one of several books in a series about exceptional children.

Ages 5-8

Also available in:
No other form known

181

Fitzgerald, John Dennis

The Great Brain Reforms

Dial Books for Young Readers, 1973.
(165 pages)

HONESTY/DISHONESTY
Friendship: keeping friends
Justice/Injustice
Sibling: relationships

Tom Fitzgerald, known at the "Great Brain," is a self-centered twelve year old who enjoys manipulating other people. In the summer of 1898, he comes home from boarding school to his small Utah village. He plays capricious and sometimes dangerous stunts on neighborhood boys, including his little brother John. When Tom tries to hypnotize, blackmail, and cheat his gullible brother and neighborhood friends, John decides that he must bring about his older brother's reform. While the little boy is wondering how to do this, Tom builds a wooden raft and charges his peers for rides down the river. One rainy afternoon, Tom and two other boys almost drown because the rushing water has risen to flood stage. After the trio recovers from the mishap, John and the neighborhood boys decide to try Tom in a mock trial. They present all the evidence against the "Great Brain's" cruel and less-than-honest deeds. The trial by his peers convinces Tom of his guilt more effectively than any other method could, and he decides he must reform himself.

In this humorous but thought-provoking first-person narrative, John describes Tom's "con jobs" as only a victimized younger brother could. The story's presentations of sibling competition, parental discipline, and personal thoughts of a little brother are lightened by humor. Because it is written from a youngster's point of view, this book would appeal to the energetic boy or girl who seems to get into trouble without trying.

Ages 10-13

Also available in:
Braille—*The Great Brain Reforms*
Library of Congress (NLSBPH)

Cassette—*The Great Brain Reforms*
Library of Congress (NLSBPH)

182

Fitzgerald, John Dennis

Me and My Little Brain

Black/white illustrations by Mercer Mayer.
Dial Books for Young Readers, 1971.
(137 pages) o.p.

IDENTITY, SEARCH FOR
IMITATION
Adoption: explaining
Death: of parents
Death: of sibling
Orphan
Problem solving

J.D., aged ten, plans to take over as the "great brain" of the family when his older brother Tom goes away to school. However, J.D. fails miserably in his first attempt. Although he hires two friends to do his chores, he ends up spreading manure on the vegetable garden because his mother feels he has enough spare time for the task. He then tries his hand at "trading up," starting with an old Indian costume and bartering up to a piglet, which he has to return because his mother will not allow a pig in her yard. To add to J.D.'s frustration, four-year-old Frankie Penworth comes to stay with the family. Frankie witnessed the recent deaths of his parents and brother, buried in a mud slide, and since this he has been mute. Frankie develops feelings of hostility toward J.D. and his parents because they remind him that he once had a family of his own. Frankie kicks shins, throws food and rocks, and manages to hurt everyone within reach. After several days of this, J.D. loses his temper and spanks Frankie soundly. After the shock of the painful spanking, Frankie begins to speak freely and tells of his ordeal. His feelings of hostility diminish. J.D.'s parents adopt the boy, and Frankie is happy to become a member of their family. J.D., who is loved and respected by his new brother, uses quick thinking to rescue Frankie from a robber one day. J.D. realizes that although he is not the shrewd conniver his older brother was, he can be satisfied with his own "little brain."

This first-person narrative humorously and somewhat fancifully depicts a boy's acceptance of his newly adopted brother and an orphan's adjustment to the death of his parents and brother. The four-year-old's anguish after witnessing the death of his family is vividly portrayed, making it easy for the reader to sympathize with him.

Ages 9-12

Also available in:
Braille—*Me and My Little Brain*
Library of Congress (NLSBPH)

Cassette—*Me and My Little Brain*
Library of Congress (NLSBPH)

183

Fitzhugh, Louise

Harriet the Spy

Black/white illustrations by the author.
HarperCollins Publishers, Inc., 1964.
(298 pages)

MATURATION
Friendship: keeping friends
Peer relationships: avoiding others
Separation anxiety

Eleven-year-old Harriet Welch wants to be a writer. To "train her powers of observation," she keeps a notebook in which she writes down her thoughts about people she knows. Ole Golly, Harriet's governess, encourages Harriet to write but, oddly enough, never reads the girl's notebook. Harriet is devoted to Ole Golly and feels that no one understands her as well as her governess does. She hopes Ole Golly will never leave. But Ole Golly departs to get married. Shortly after her governess "deserts her," Harriet's classmates find the notebook and read what Harriet wrote about them. The notebook contains many frank and unkind observations, for Harriet seems to have observed and described her peers at their most unflattering moments. Her classmates retaliate by refusing to speak to her and by playing cruel tricks on her. Harriet tries to stay home to avoid her "friends." Mr. and Mrs. Welch force her to attend school, but she misbehaves and runs back home. Her parents now see that they really do not know their daughter and have no idea how to help her, so they take her to a psychiatrist and ask her teachers to help change her attitude.

The psychiatrist suggests that Harriet's parents write to Ole Golly and ask her to correspond with Harriet. Before receiving a letter from Ole Golly, Harriet is kept out of school for six days. When she receives the letter, it instructs her to begin writing something besides notes in her notebook, to apologize to her friends, and to be more kind in her observations of others, even if that requires her to tell small lies. After this letter, and after she is appointed editor of the sixth-grade page in the school newspaper, Harriet regains friends and comes to be at peace with herself.

Harriet's blunt manner of writing hurts others' feelings, and they react by rejecting her friendship and badgering her. Harriet tries to escape the situation instead of face it. She feigns illness so that she will not have to go to school. When this does not work, she fights and runs away. The book explains that her bad behavior results from her governess's departure. Harriet again appears in Louise Fitzhugh's *The Long Secret.*

Ages 10-12

Also available in:
Braille—*Harriet the Spy*
Library of Congress (NLSBPH)

Cassette—*Harriet the Spy*
Library of Congress (NLSBPH)

Paperbound—*Harriet the Spy*
HarperCollins Publishers, Inc.

Talking Book—*Harriet the Spy*
Library of Congress (NLSBPH)

184

Fitzhugh, Louise

The Long Secret

Black/white illustrations by the author.
HarperCollins Publishers, Inc., 1965.
(275 pages, paperbound)

BELONGING
Anger
Friendship: meaning of
Grandparent: living in home of
Inferiority, feelings of
Menstruation
Parental: absence
Parental: rejection
Shyness

Shy, twelve-year-old Beth Ellen lives with her grandmother. Although she knows she is welcome there, Beth Ellen feels that the arrangement is temporary and that she really doesn't belong. She and her friend Harriet Welsch decide to solve a local mystery: someone who seems to know quite a bit about people's personal lives is leaving poison-pen notes to be found by various residents of the town. In an attempt to discover the identity of the mysterious note writer, Beth Ellen and Harriet sneak behind hedges and under windows, listening to conversations and watching what people do. One rainy afternoon, Grandmother tells Beth Ellen that her mother is returning after an absence of several years. Beth Ellen feels strangely empty; it is difficult for her to have feelings for a mother she has not seen since she was five. After her mother, Zeeney, arrives with Beth Ellen's stepfather, the girl discovers she does not like either one of them. Zeeney takes Beth Ellen with her wherever she goes, but ignores her in favor of adult friends. She has Beth Ellen's hair temporarily straightened and shortens the girl's name to Beth, feeling that the longer name is unfashionable. When Zeeney decides that Beth Ellen will travel with her rather than stay with Grandmother, Beth Ellen runs screaming to her room and begins throwing everything in sight. She locks herself in the bathroom and soaks in the shower. It is only after the chauffeur breaks down the bathroom door and the maids dry her and put her to bed that Beth Ellen calms down. Beth Ellen and Grandmother have a talk the next day, and it is decided that Beth Ellen will remain with her grandmother. Overjoyed at finally belonging somewhere, Beth Ellen calls Harriet and asks her to spend the night at her house. That night Harriet too has an announcement: she has discovered that Beth Ellen is the mysterious note writer. Beth Ellen confesses, adding that she no longer has to do such a thing.

F

Beth Ellen feels she does not belong anywhere. Her shyness masks the anger she feels about her rejection, and the anger manifests itself in the anonymous condemning notes she writes. When she realizes that she really does have a special place in someone's life, Beth Ellen begins to overcome her shyness and ceases to write the notes. This book deals candidly with religion and with menstruation and its myths. Beth Ellen and Harriet first appear in Louise Fitzhugh's *Harriet the Spy.*

Ages 9-12

Also available in:
Talking Book—*The Long Secret*
Library of Congress (NLSBPH)

185

Foley, June

It's No Crush, I'm in Love!

Delacorte Press, 1982.
(215 pages) o.p.

IDENTITY, SEARCH FOR
SCHOOL: Pupil-Teacher Relationships
Boy-girl relationships
Death: of father
Family: relationships
Friendship: best friend
Identification with others: story characters
Parent/Parents: single
Roman Catholic

At fourteen, Annie Cassidy wants to be exactly like her favorite heroine, Elizabeth Bennet of *Pride and Prejudice.* There are already similarities: Annie too has three sisters, her mother isn't a very "scintillating" person, and she obviously takes after her father.

He, however, died in an automobile accident nearly two years ago. Now Annie plans to find a perfect man with whom she can lead a perfect life teaching in a university and writing scholarly books about the novels of Jane Austen. On her first day at Sacred Heart High School, she meets the man she has been looking for: David Angelucci, her dignified and handsome English teacher. Annie's best friend, Susanna Siegelbaum, well acquainted with Annie's idealism but the practical type herself, asks immediately what Annie is "going to do about it." Annie responds that she's going to think about David a lot. She also, of course, studies harder for English than for any other subject and looks for chances to impress her teacher. After a couple of months of this, however, Annie grows impatient. When Mr. Angelucci asks for help with the school newspaper he advises, she quickly volunteers. Instead of being with him, though, she finds herself frequently in the company of the newspaper's editor, Robby Pols. Robby is the exact "opposite of Mr. Angelucci. Not brilliant. Not handsome. Not charming. Not mature. Not very pleasant, even." But because her mother has gotten a job and Annie has to care for her sisters after school, Robby must come to her house to work on the paper and before long is practically one of the family. Annie tolerates him, but dreams about David Angelucci. With Susanna for company, she starts to spend Saturdays secretly observing David in his "natural habitat," the public library. When Robby agrees to let her interview David for the paper, she learns that he is doing research for his doctoral dissertation and needs a research assistant. She volunteers. In the meantime, though, another relationship has started to demand some of her attention: her mother is dating a man in her office and seems "looser" and more carefree than usual. She confides to Annie that, as the oldest of eight children, she never before had time to play. As Annie's attitude toward her mother softens, she also starts to appreciate Robby and accepts when he invites her to Saturday's Winter Dance. Then, unexpectedly, David calls and asks her to work late Saturday night and to share a surprise with him afterwards. Sure he will now admit his love for her, Annie cancels her date for the dance. She is a bit disturbed when Robby invites Susanna to go in her place. At the library on Saturday, she watches David intently for some sign of affection. She notices nothing but a few flaws in his appearance she hadn't seen before. Finally, at ten o'clock that evening, he announces that he has to pick up his date who will help him chaperone the Winter Dance. When Annie reminds him of the surprise, he shows her a rough draft of his dissertation. Devastated, she runs all the way home. Later, as she talks to her mother, Annie is comforted by the rare closeness she and her mother share. She also cheers up when Susanna reports that she spent most of the evening listening to Robby talk about Annie. Annie decides that most people don't care if she never becomes perfect like Elizabeth Bennet—it's all right for her just to be Annie Cassidy.

Though Annie imagines she is nothing like her mother, both seek perfection: Annie models herself after a Jane Austen heroine and her widowed mother has tried hard to be the ideal homemaker, mother, and Catholic layperson. Both become more realistic as they learn more about life and other people, and in so doing they grow closer to each other. The realism of Annie's crush on her English teacher is marred somewhat by the reader's early recognition that Mr. Angelucci is callous, uncaring, and dislikes teaching teenagers, a task he'll soon be free of. However, readers will cheer Annie's realization that "ordinary" people like Robby and her mother are special after all, and they'll like the delicious humor throughout the story. Especially funny are Susanna's loyal attempts to trail Mr. Angelucci for Annie. Each time, her prey turns out to be someone else—a priest, a janitor.

Ages 11-13

Also available in:
No other form known

186

Forbes, Esther

Johnny Tremain

Black/white illustrations by Lynd Ward.
Houghton Mifflin Co., 1943.
(256 pages)

DEFORMITIES
IDENTITY, SEARCH FOR
Courage, meaning of
Orphan
Self-improvement

Johnny Tremain, who is fourteen years old in 1773, lives in Boston. Recently orphaned, he is apprenticed to an old silversmith, Mr. Lapham. Already Johnny is a skilled craftsman, and he arrogantly bosses the other apprentices. One day a crucible of molten silver breaks, burning Johnny's right hand so badly that he can no longer use it for delicate work. He is forced to leave the Lapham shop. In desperation he seeks help from wealthy Merchant Lyte, who his mother had told him was a relative. Johnny owns a silver cup that bears the Lyte insignia. The cup was given to him by his mother. He shows it to Mr. Lyte, who accuses him of stealing it and takes Johnny to court. Meanwhile, Rab, a young printer for the *Observer,* has befriended the boy. Rab gets Josiah Quincy to defend Johnny, and they win the case. Johnny next takes a job delivering papers for the *Observer* and becomes involved with several Boston patriots who meet secretly in the attic of the newspaper office. He assists in the Boston Tea Party. After his friend Cill Lapham goes to work at the Lyte mansion, Johnny is able to learn the facts of his relationship to the wealthy family: he is a grand-nephew to Merchant Lyte. By now, British troops are stationed in Boston, and the Minutemen are organized and training. Boston remains peaceful for a while, but one day Johnny, who is spying among the British troops, senses a change in the atmosphere. He learns that an expedition to Lexington will begin that night. The British campaign is unsuccessful; the

Minutemen are victorious. Two days later, Johnny travels to Lexington and finds that Rab, wounded in battle, is dying. After the death of his friend, Johnny talks with Dr. Warren, who tells him that his maimed hand can be restored. In spite of the somber situation around him, Johnny feels new courage and new hope.

This classic novel takes place during a crucial time in our country's history. Esther Forbes gives a fascinating interpretation of several heroes: Paul Revere, John Hancock, Dr. Warren, Rab, and Johnny Tremain himself. More than an historical account, this is the story of a youth growing up, accepting responsibility, acquiring poise and tact, and accepting and overcoming a physical handicap.

Ages 10 and up

Also available in:
Braille—*Johnny Tremain*
Library of Congress (NLSBPH)

Cassette—*Johnny Tremain*
Library of Congress (NLSBPH)

Talking Book—*Johnny Tremain*
Library of Congress (NLSBPH)

187

Fox, Paula

Blowfish Live in the Sea

Peter Smith Publishing, Inc., 1970.
(116 pages)

MATURATION
Reality, escaping
Alcoholism: of father
Communication: parent-child
Sibling: half brother/half sister

Twelve-year-old Carrie lives in New York with her parents and her eighteen-year-old half brother, Ben. Ben's father left him and his mother when the boy was very young. About a year ago, Ben began acting strangely. Now he has quit school and refuses to look for work. He does not seem interested in anyone or anything. Father and Mother do not know how to cope with his changed behavior. When Ben receives an unexpected message to meet his father in Boston, he asks Carrie to go along, and their parents agree. Ben's father does not show up at the scheduled place, and Ben, although disillusioned, remains determined to find the man. Both young people are shocked by the alcoholic person they finally meet. Carrie is appalled by the man's appearance and his tall tales about successful adventures and business deals, but Ben seems to like him. In making the decision to stay with his father and try to help him, the boy feels that he has found a purpose in life.

This first-person account shows a preteen's love and concern for her older brother. She does not understand him any better than their parents do. Nevertheless, she tries to help him. The sensitive characterizations—especially that of the lonely drifter who proves to be Ben's father—make this a memorable story.

Ages 11 and up

Also available in:
Braille—*Blowfish Live in the Sea*
Library of Congress (NLSBPH)

Paperbound—*Blowfish Live in the Sea*
Macmillan Publishing Company, Inc.

188

Fox, Paula

A Place Apart

Farrar, Straus & Giroux, Inc., 1980.
(184 pages)

FRIENDSHIP: Meaning of
Change: resisting
Cruelty
Death: of father
Parent/Parents: remarriage of
School: classmate relationships

After the sudden death of her father, thirteen-year-old Victoria Finch finds her life completely changed. Their income reduced, she and her mother must move from Boston to a small, ramshackle house in the town of New Oxford. There Victoria meets and is captivated by wealthy, sixteen-year-old Hugh Todd, who seems impressed by a dramatic scene she has written for English class. Full of self-importance, Hugh urges her to expand the scene into a play so he can direct its performance—as he has other school plays—the next year when he'll be a senior. Victoria isn't interested in writing a play, but has neither the strength nor the desire to oppose Hugh's wishes. Her best friend, Elizabeth, considers Hugh a high-handed egotist whose humor is most often at the expense of others. Victoria realizes Hugh's shortcomings, but for her they enhance his attractiveness. When the school year ends, Hugh, about to leave for Italy with his parents, tells Victoria to spend her vacation getting her play in shape. She tries, but hers is a difficult summer. Still grieving for her father, Victoria is hurt when her mother begins dating Lawrence Grady. When school resumes, Victoria discovers that Hugh is not interested in her, only in enhancing his reputation by directing her play. She refuses to continue with it, and so Hugh finds someone else to manipulate: Tom Kyle. When Elizabeth finds a boyfriend and her mother announces plans to remarry, Victoria's loneliness intensifies. She tries to maintain her relationship with Elizabeth by agreeing to join her and her boyfriend on a dangerous drive up to Mt. Crystal. By chance, Tom Kyle is invited along. The mountain road is slick with ice and they almost crash. In his fear Tom wets his pants and he is humiliated before the entire school when the incident is made known, probably by Hugh. To prove himself, Tom repeats the treacherous trip up the mountain and has a near-fatal accident. Disgusted by the cruelty and callousness of people, Victoria is almost glad her mother is marrying

Lawrence Grady and they are moving back to Boston. After her hurt and anger have subsided, however, she comes to appreciate all she has learned during her year in New Oxford.

This moving story, told by Victoria herself, recounts a year's worth of emotional upheavals in the life of a young girl. The death of a beloved parent is wrenching; learning the difference between true and false friends brings both suffering and joy; the spite of her peers fills her with disgust. Sorting out these experiences leads to maturity. The book is realistic and well written, with believable dialogue and relationships.

Ages 12 and up

Also available in:
Braille—*A Place Apart*
Library of Congress (NLSBPH)

Cassette—*A Place Apart*
Library of Congress (NLSBPH)

189

Fox, Paula

Portrait of Ivan

Black/white illustrations by Saul Lambert.
Bradbury Press, 1969.
(131 pages)

FRIENDSHIP: Making Friends
IDENTITY, SEARCH FOR
Communication: parent-child
Loneliness
Parental: absence

Eleven-year-old Ivan has his portrait painted by Matt Mustazza. The artist hires an elderly spinster, Miss Manderby, to read to Ivan so that the boy will not fidget during the sittings. Ivan discovers it is easy to talk with Matt and Miss Manderby, and he tells them about his life. Ivan sees very little of his father, who usually is away on business, and he knows very little about his deceased mother, a Russian refugee. After Ivan describes how his mother, her brother, and his grandmother escaped from Russia by sledge during the winter, Matt sketches a sledge so Ivan will know what one looks like. Matt takes Ivan and Miss Manderby to an opening exhibition of work by a friend who is a sculptor. One Saturday, Matt announces that the next few sittings will have to be postponed because he has been commissioned to make sketches and paintings of a Florida plantation house that will soon be torn down. Because of the disappointment he sees in Ivan's face, Matt invites the boy along, and Miss Manderby as well. Shortly before they depart, Matt adds a driver, who resembles the sculptor, to his drawing of the sledge. In Florida, Ivan meets Geneva, a girl his age who befriends him during his stay. Before Ivan leaves for home, Matt adds to his drawing of the sledge two people who look like Miss Manderby and Matt. After returning home, Ivan questions his father about the photographs of his mother and is shown the only picture of her that his father has saved. From his Uncle Gilbert, Ivan learns the facts surrounding his mother's death. At his next sitting, Ivan learns that Miss Manderby is remaining in Florida and that Matt will be moving to San Francisco. A few days later, Ivan's father brings home the boy's portrait and the sketch of the sledge—which is now complete with Ivan's mother, who looks like Geneva.

Characters in this low-key story ring true; they are not sentimentally portrayed. The reader watches Ivan's self-image develop along with the sketch of the sledge. The open-ended conclusion leaves the reader with the impression that Ivan's new confidence in people will help him bridge the gap between himself and his father.

Ages 11 and up

Also available in:
Cassette—*Portrait of Ivan*
Library of Congress (NLSBPH)

Paperbound—*Portrait of Ivan*
Aladdin Books

Talking Book—*Portrait of Ivan*
Library of Congress (NLSBPH)

190

Fox, Paula

The Stone-Faced Boy

Black/white illustrations by Donald A. Mackay.
Bradbury Press, 1968.
(106 pages)

FEAR
Inferiority, feelings of
Sibling: middle

Fifth-grader Gus Oliver never allows his face to express emotion. He first used his stone-face to cover his embarrassment at school when students laughed at a question he asked. Having protected himself in this deadpan style for several years, he fears that he is no longer able to show any facial expression. Great-Aunt Harriet unexpectedly visits the Oliver family, and Gus must give her his bedroom and sleep in an attic room. Gus is very afraid of the attic because it is ugly, blue, and empty with cracks on the walls and ceiling. As he spends the night there, Serena, his younger sister, hears her dog howling pathetically in the winter night. She goes to Gus and pleads with him to search for her pet. Gus, though frightened, goes out in the cold, dark night and faces some of the other things which make him fearful—an old well about which he once had a nightmare, an old deserted shed, and the dog itself. Somewhat braver and more confident, Gus returns home at dawn with the dog.

This is a touching story that presents a problem but offers no pat solutions. The reader is left with the feeling that Gus, as a result of his night's adventure, has overcome some of his fears, and that he will be more self-confident in the future. Feeling trapped as the middle child in the family, Gus is unable to verbalize his fears, and his parents seem unaware of their son's anxieties and his defensive behavior. Because of its many unanswered questions, this story could provide a good basis for discussion. The boy's character, though, is not developed in detail, and the relationship between the parents and the children is not adequately described.

Ages 10-12

Also available in:
Braille—*The Stone-Faced Boy*
Library of Congress (NLSBPH)

Paperbound—*The Stone-Faced Boy*
Aladdin Books

191

Frank, Anne

Anne Frank: The Diary of a Young Girl

Translated from the Dutch by B. M. Mooyaart-Doubleday.
Doubleday, 1967.
(258 pages) o.p.

PREJUDICE: Religious
Boy-girl relationships
Communication: parent-child
Jew
Maturation
War

In 1942, Anne Frank receives a diary for her thirteenth birthday. Anne, her older sister Margot, and their parents are Jews living in Holland and suffering under the German occupation. The Frank family lives as normal a life as possible, adjusting to the changing rules of the authorities. But when Margot receives a "call-up" notice to go to a concentration camp, they all move into hiding in a warehouse attic that has been prepared in case of need. They are aided by Dutch business associates of Anne's father. Soon the Franks are joined by Mr. Dussel, Mr. and Mrs. Van Daan, and the Van Daan's son, Peter. As the threat of discovery increases, everyone experiences the tensions of having to be quiet all day and never being able to go outside. Anne especially feels the strain of missing her friends and worrying about their fate as the German oppression worsens. Anne needs to talk about her feelings; and since she does not believe she can talk with her mother, who she feels is unsympathetic and unloving, she confides in her diary. Gradually Anne changes from a talkative, mischievous girl to a calm, thoughtful young woman. After a year and a half in hiding, she becomes aware of Peter's charms. She describes her emotions as her affection for Peter grows. The girl discusses proper courtship behavior with her parents, and then records her own thoughts on the matter. Anne feels more conflict with her mother than with her father, and finally she declares her independence from her mother. Group tensions increase as the people in the hiding place hear of friends discovered by the enemy. In the last entry, Anne writes about her maturing feelings.

This famous diary graphically shows the emotions of an introspective young girl as she matures over a two-year period. Anne writes of her relationship with her parents, her changing body, and her first love. She tries to perceive her situation with good humor and never loses hope. Although the circumstances described are unusual, the emotions portrayed are universal. Anne's story is concluded in an afterword that describes the fate of Anne, her family, and her friends.

Ages 11 and up

Also available in:
Braille—*Anne Frank: The Diary of a Young Girl*
Library of Congress (NLSBPH)

Cassette—*Anne Frank: The Diary of a Young Girl*
Library of Congress (NLSBPH)

Talking Book—*Anne Frank: The Diary of a Young Girl*
Library of Congress (NLSBPH)

192

Freeman, Don

Corduroy

Color illustrations by the author.
Viking Penguin, 1968.
(32 pages)

BELONGING
Friendship: meaning of

Corduroy is a teddy bear who lives in the toy department of a large store. He is waiting for someone to come and take him to a real home, but no one seems to want to buy a small bear in green overalls. One day a little girl named Lisa buys Corduroy with her own money. When she takes him to her house and shows him her room, he realizes that he finally has found a real home. Corduroy also discovers what it is like to be taken care of and to have a friend.

This touching story about the need to belong and to feel wanted should appeal to any young child.

Ages 3-8

Also available in:
Paperbound—*Corduroy*
Puffin Books

Talking Book—*Corduroy*
Library of Congress (NLSBPH)

193

Freeman, Don

Dandelion

Color illustrations by the author.
Viking Penguin, 1982.
(48 pages)

SELF, ATTITUDE TOWARD: Accepting
Imitation

Dandelion the lion has received an invitation to a tea-and-taffy party at the home of Jennifer Giraffe. He decides to spruce himself up at the barber shop by getting a haircut, a shampoo, and a manicure. When the barber is finished with the cut, Dandelion's mane is "frizzy and fuzzy and completely unrulish." The barber then shows Dandelion how the well-dressed lion styles his mane and the sort of clothes he wears. So Dandelion curls his mane and buys a plaid jacket, a cap, and a walking stick. When he rings the bell at Jennifer's house, he feels quite pleased with his new appearance. The door is opened and then slammed in his face because Jennifer does not recognize him. After a storm blows Dandelion's cap away, washes the curl out of his mane, and soaks his jacket, he decides to ring Jennifer's bell again, looking just as he did before he went to the barber shop. This time, Jennifer is happy to see him.

After changing his appearance to fit the suggested norm, Dandelion discovers that he is unrecognized and rejected by his friends. Those who know him have accepted him as he is and do not want him to alter his appearance or personality. This book might be helpful for children who want to change themselves just to please people who refuse to accept them as a friend. The illustrations are integral to the limited text.

Ages 3-8

Also available in:
Paperbound—*Dandelion*
Puffin Books

194

Gackenbach, Dick

Do You Love Me?

Color illustrations by the author.
Clarion Books, 1979.
(46 pages counted)

FREEDOM, MEANING OF
Loneliness
Nature: respect for
Pets: love for

Lonely Walter Becker, about six, lives on a farm with no playmates, only his parents and his older sister, Boots. One summer day, Walter spies a strange little bird darting back and forth by the mailbox and making a humming sound. Walter is so interested that be wants to catch the bird and keep it for a pet. When it darts into the mailbox, Walter slams the door—and accidentally kills the bird. Frightened and sad, the boy carries the limp body to his sister. Boots gently explains that she cannot make the bird well, and furthermore that some animals are not meant to be handled or held captive. Walter buries the bird. Pondering this idea of a need to be free, Walter frees his bug collection and the turtle he has kept in a shoe box. "Do you love me," he wonders as they depart. That afternoon Boots surprises Walter with a puppy. The boy is apprehensive at first, thinking he may hurt the puppy by fondling it. But the puppy snuggles up to him and licks his face. The two play together all afternoon and Walter is no longer lonesome.

The accidental death of a bird helps a young boy to understand that different creatures have different needs. The puppy's warm response to Walter is the perfect antidote for his sorrow over killing the bird. This gentle little story is one that children may want to discuss.

Ages 5-8

Also available in:
Cassette—*Do You Love Me?*
Library of Congress (NLSBPH)

Record—*Do You Love Me?*
American Printing House for the Blind

195

Gallico, Paul

The Snow Goose

Alfred A. Knopf, Inc., 1940.
(58 pages) o.p.

DEFORMITIES
LOVE, MEANING OF
Loneliness
Nature: appreciation of

Philip is an artist who lives alone in an abandoned lighthouse on the wild, swampy Essex coast. He avoids people because of his hunchback and his crippled arm—deformities which have repelled most of the people he has met during his twenty-seven years. Philip loves nature and enjoys sailing his boat. He has established a bird sanctuary around his lighthouse and often treats injured birds. One day, a timid twelve-year-old girl named Frith brings him an injured Canadian snow goose, despite her fear of this strange-looking man. Philip tells her a story about the bird's origin and migratory habits, putting her at ease. The girl begins to visit the bird regularly. But when the snow goose migrates north with the other geese, Philip is sure that he will never see the bird or Frith again. In the fall, however, the goose returns, and when Frith learns of this, she resumes her visits. A warm friendship develops between Philip and the girl over a period of several years. Philip is shocked one fall day when he realizes that Frith is no longer a child. But he cannot overcome his fear of rejection and is unable to express his affection for her. Frith regards Philip as a dear friend, but she does not understand her deep love for him until just before the Battle of Dunkirk. When Philip hears a radio request for boats to rescue the trapped soldiers at Dunkirk, he immediately prepares his sailboat to aid in the mission. Frith begs him not to go, but she still does not express her love for him. With the snow goose flying above his boat, Philip saves many men before he is finally killed. Then the goose returns one more time to the lighthouse where Frith is waiting before flying away forever.

The quiet, sensitive girl in this well-known story sees beyond the grotesque body of this deformed man to the gentle, talented person within. Philip is unable to express his love for the girl because he fears rejection, but a strong bond exists between the two. While he is risking his life to save others, Philip feels truly needed and accepted for the first time in his life. This touching story is told with an understanding sensitivity that does not moralize.

Ages 12 and up

Also available in:
Braille—*The Snow Goose*
Library of Congress (NLSBPH)

Cassette—*The Snow Goose*
Library of Congress (NLSBPH)

196

Garden, Nancy

Annie on My Mind

Farrar, Straus & Giroux, Inc., 1982.
(234 pages)

HOMOSEXUALITY: Female
Guilt, feelings of
Harassment
Justice/Injustice
Love, meaning of
School: negative experiences

Liza Winthrop, a freshman at MIT, tries to write a letter to Annie. To organize her thoughts, she thinks back over the past year. It's the previous November and Liza is president of the student council at coed Foster Academy. At a museum she meets Annie Kenyon, who attends a public high school, and they exchange a look like nothing Liza's ever experienced. The meeting leaves her so off-balance that she fails to report her friend Sally for piercing students' ears in the basement, and she and Sally are suspended for a week. Ms. Baxter, assistant to Mrs. Poindexter, the director, points out that Foster Academy is in danger of closing because of lack of funds, and that the current fund-raising drive will be hurt by any adverse publicity. During Liza's week of suspension, she spends every possible moment with Annie. "Just sitting there in the growing darkness with Annie was so special and so unlike anything that had ever happened to me before that magical seemed like a good word for it and for her." That Sunday as they sit on the Coney Island beach watching the sun go down, they suddenly begin hugging and kissing. After the first startling moments, Annie admits that she's always wondered if she were gay. Later, Liza remembers her own feelings of being different, isolated, of preferring to be with girls rather than boys, of imagining her future with another woman instead of a man. That winter the two see each other often, and Liza daydreams constantly about Annie. Her younger brother, Chad, teases her about being in love, but thinks it's with a boy. Liza admits to herself and to Annie that she really is in love. For Christmas they give each other rings. Liza feels that Annie is her other half. They talk about the physical part of their love, but have no place to be alone. Then Liza offers to feed the cats of two teachers during their absence over the two-week spring vacation: Ms. Widmer, who teaches English, and Ms. Stevenson, the art teacher. Liza and Annie meet daily at the teachers' house and gradually become lovers. To their surprise, they discover that Ms. Widmer and Ms. Stevenson share the large double bed and that the bookcases upstairs are full of books about homosexual love. On Sunday, the day the teachers are expected home, Annie and Liza decide to make love in the big double bed. They are discovered by Ms. Baxter and Sally, who have come to find out why Liza skipped the fund-raising meeting that morning. The girls are barely dressed, and Ms. Baxter storms upstairs to find that the bed has been used. She talks about sin and ugliness. Just then the two teachers arrive home. They try talking to Liza and Annie, but all are too upset to make any decisions. The first thing Monday morning, Mrs. Poindexter tells Liza she's suspended pending an expulsion hearing. She must go before the Board of Trustees, and her parents must be notified. Liza's mother is supportive, remembering that when she was young, she and a friend had experimented in a giggly way with hugging and kissing each other. Seeing the fear, pain, and love in her mother's eyes, Liza lies and says she and Annie never went further than that. But when her father comes home, he admits to having recognized the intense nature of Liza's relationship with Annie. He used to think he was open-minded about homosexuality, but now that it involves Liza he's frightened and unhappy. Chad, after being questioned privately by Mrs. Poindexter, cries himself to sleep. The Board of Trustees hearing is unbearable for Liza, but they decide that her actions don't involve the school or other students and so are not in their province. However, they hold a hearing for Ms. Widmer and Ms. Stevenson during which Sally testifies that their lesbian relationship influenced Liza, who admired them very much. The two teachers are fired. In reality, Liza never even knew they were gay. At school, Chad is teased but sticks up for Liza. Liza too has her tormentors. She and Annie visit Ms. Stevenson and Ms. Widmer, who have each taught for twenty years. They are making the best of their forced retirements and advise the girls not to punish themselves for something that really isn't their fault. Losing a job is a small matter, as long as nobody separates them. After reflecting on all the happiness and sadness of the past year, Liza decides not to write the letter to Annie. Instead, she telephones and tells Annie she loves her. They make plans to meet during the Christmas vacation.

A high school senior discovers her love for another young woman and tries to cope with the effects the relationship has on her family, school, and friends. On one level, this is a simple love story: recognition, attraction, growing love, delight in the other person, physical expression of the love, and a feeling of wholeness when together. Because it is a love not generally approved and encouraged by society, there are other levels to the story. Written largely in the first person (transition passages of Liza at college are third person), the book doesn't answer the many questions it raises. It comes closest to offering a message when

G

Ms. Stevenson says that "what matters is the truth of loving, of two people finding each other." Annie and Liza's lovemaking is not described in detail, and the physical side of their love is not emphasized except insofar as it intensifies all their feelings. Not all young people who may feel homosexual actually are; Liza's mother points out that it is normal for adolescents to be confused about their sexual feelings and even to experiment. But Liza's feelings about Annie are quite well delineated, and Liza herself is sure she loves Annie. This is a strong, convincing, affecting story.

Ages 13 and up

Also available in:
Cassette—*Annie on My Mind*
Library of Congress (NLSBPH)

Paperbound—*Annie on My Mind*
Farrar, Straus & Giroux, Inc., (Sunburst Books)

197

Gardiner, John Reynolds

Stone Fox

Black/white illustrations by Marcia Sewall.
HarperCollins Publishers, Inc., 1980.
(81 pages)

DETERMINATION
Grandparent: living in home of
Grandparent: love for
Illnesses: of grandparent
Pets: love for
Resourcefulness

Ten-year-old Willy, his grandfather, and Willy's big dog, Searchlight, live together on a potato farm outside Jackson, Wyoming. When Grandfather becomes ill, Willy goes for Doc Smith. Doc says Grandfather is not really sick; he simply does not want to live anymore. But neither of them knows why. Willy is determined to make Grandfather want to live again and feels the problem will be solved if he harvests the potato crop. By hooking Searchlight to the plow, Willy harvests the potatoes and then sells them. He prepares for winter by stacking wood and stocking up on food, but Grandfather does not improve. Willy goes to school that fall with Searchlight pulling him over the snow on his sled five miles each way. One day when Willy returns home, a state official awaits him. He has come to collect five hundred dollars in back taxes. Without it, the state will take the farm. Willy tries to borrow money, but without success. Then he sees a poster at the general store in Jackson announcing the National Dogsled Race in February—a race ten miles long over snow-covered countryside. The prize is five hundred dollars. Willy withdraws his college savings of fifty dollars to enter the race. Also entered is Stone Fox, a giant of an Indian who has never lost a dogsled race. By the day of the race, the odds are heavily in favor of Stone Fox. At the sound of the gun, Willy and Searchlight jump out to a huge lead. As they race past their farm, Willy is encouraged to go even faster when he sees Grandfather sitting by the window. Close to the finish, Stone Fox and his five Samoyeds are neck and neck with Willy and Searchlight. One hundred feet from the finish line, old Searchlight's heart bursts and she dies instantly. Stone Fox, who knows Willy's story, stops and fires his rifle, signaling the other approaching racers to stop. He motions to Willy, who carries Searchlight across the finish line.

Based on a legend from the Rocky Mountains, this story of a boy's devotion to his grandfather and to his faithful dog is believed to be true. The dog seems almost human, able to understand her master's needs and struggling to help him all she can. The setting is of an earlier era, and the pencil illustrations add to that feeling. Although this is written for an older child, younger children would enjoy having it read aloud.

Ages 8-10

Also available in:
Braille—*Stone Fox*
Library of Congress (NLSBPH)

Paperbound—*Stone Fox*
HarperCollins Publishers, Inc.

198

Garrigue, Sheila

Between Friends

Scholastic, Inc., 1986.
(160 pages) o.p.

DOWN SYNDROME
Change: new home
Friendship: meaning of
Prejudice: toward handicapped persons
Sibling: new baby

Jill Harvey, a sixth grader who has recently moved from California to Massachusetts, discovers that all the girls who might be her friends are away on vacation. As one way to occupy her time, she fakes a job walking Mrs. Lacey's dog. On these strolls, Jill often passes the home of Dede Atkins, an eighteen-year-old girl with Down Syndrome. They talk, and a friendship develops. When the other neighborhood girls return, Jill finds that they want nothing to do with Dede. When Dede comes over, Jill's own mother avoids her. Jill is puzzled. She knows Dede to be a sensitive friend and an excellent listener. Still, when school begins, Jill sees less of her friend, who attends a special school. But when she invites Dede to a party, one mystery is cleared up: Mrs. Harvey confesses beforehand to having once borne a severely deformed baby who lived only a few hours, and to finding Dede a constant reminder that the baby she now expects may also be born handicapped. Having faced her fear, Jill's mother now tries to be nice to Dede. It is at Christmastime that Jill's friendship is sorely tested. Dede invites the younger girl to her school Christmas party. Unsure how she will feel about the students who attend Dede's school, Jill hedges. But a discussion of her fears with her father and Dede's mother leads her to accept. Then she is offered a weekend in Boston with school friends and cancels the acceptance. Plagued by guilt, she can hardly plan the Boston trip. Finally she cancels that, even in the face of hurt feelings, and goes to Dede's party instead. She enjoys herself, finding no reason to fear the special people she meets. A few months later, Dede moves to Arizona. Jill realizes that she will miss this girl who, of all her acquaintances, "knows more about being a friend than anyone else."

This sensitive story explores the fears and prejudice that often surround mentally handicapped people. It demonstrates that retarded people can possess special talents, unseen because of their handicap. But Jill's life is touched by more than Dede. The sudden death of Mrs. Lacey, and the girl's feelings about that; adjustments to a new home; other new friends—all these, too, are important to Jill. Although this book is written for the intermediate reader, its appeal extends to the adolescent and would encourage discussion in groups.

Ages 9-12

Also available in:
No other form known

199

George, Jean Craighead

My Side of the Mountain

Black/white illustrations by the author.
Dutton Children's Books, 1988.
(178 pages, paperbound)

NATURE: Appreciation of
NATURE: Living in Harmony with
RESOURCEFULNESS
Autonomy
Running away

Young Sam Grebley, about thirteen, runs away from his New York City home to some family-owned land in the Catskills. Sam arrives there in May with little more than the clothes on his back, only a slight knowledge of the woods, and a few pieces of flint and steel to start a fire. As the summer progresses, he adds to his wood lore by frequenting a library in a nearby town. He supplies himself with meat from traps he has built; he fishes with a hook fashioned from carved and lashed pieces of wood; and as time passes, he picks roots and berries to supplement his diet. A large hemlock tree, which he hollows out, keeps him hidden from anyone who might enter the woods and provides him with a dry and sturdy shelter. From a nest on a rocky ledge, Sam steals a young falcon and he trains the bird to help him hunt. The falcon, which he names Frightful, becomes his companion and a confidante. Summer passes and Sam begins to prepare for the approaching winter. He begins collecting and preserving food, and tanning hides to supplement his meager wardrobe. When a poacher kills a deer, Sam hides the dead animal and takes the deerskin for clothing, the venison for food, and the sinews for thread in sewing his hides. One day Sam meets a man be calls Bando, who stays with him for a few weeks. Bando teaches him how to make pottery for storing food and helps him preserve some stores for the winter. Bando promises that he will not reveal Sam's whereabouts, but when Sam travels to town, the rumor begins to spread that there is a wild boy living in the mountains. The story reaches the newspapers, and a reporter eventually finds Sam and interviews him. Soon Sam's family joins him and they begin a new life on the mountain . . . in a house.

This first-person narrative details the knowledge and experience Sam gains by living in the wilderness. It also emphasizes the boy's resourcefulness and how he learns to live in harmony with nature, taking only what he needs. Although most readers would never encounter this type of experience, it is easy to identify with Sam, empathize with his feelings, and appreciate the manner in which he handles situations he encounters.

Ages 11-14

Also available in:
Braille—*My Side of the Mountain*
Library of Congress (NLSBPH)

Cassette—*My Side of the Mountain*
Library of Congress (NLSBPH)

200

Giff, Patricia Reilly

Fourth Grade Celebrity

Black/white illustrations by Leslie Morrill.
Dell Publishing Company, Inc. (Yearling Books), 1984.
(117 pages, paperbound)

RESOURCEFULNESS
SELF, ATTITUDE TOWARD: Accepting
Attention seeking
Friendship: best friend
Imagination
Inferiority, feelings of
Jealousy: sibling
School: classmate relationships

Casey Valentine, nine, wants to be popular like her pretty older sister, Van. "I have no zip. No style. I'm a lump of vanilla pudding." Determined to become a celebrity, Casey decides to be president of the fourth-grade class. Walter Mole, her best friend, agrees to nominate her on one condition: Casey must take Walter's place as pen pal to Tracy Matson. The Moles and Matsons met on vacation, and Walter's mother has been forcing this correspondence. Casey does become class president, although not by a popularity vote. Her name is drawn out of a box in which every fourth grader's name has been placed after all the other contenders drop out of the race. Undaunted by how she was "elected," a thrilled Casey promptly starts a school newspaper, with the approval of her teacher, Mrs. Petty. Casey picks a committee of three others, names herself editor, and the work begins. To help promote the paper, the four decide to sell raffle tickets for a mystery prize. Casey is determined to sell the most tickets. She and Walter sneak into school on a Saturday to steal Van's class list of the sixth grade so Casey can get a head start over the weekend. While in the building, Casey also uses the school ditto machine to run off a newsletter to Tracy in which she tells an imaginary story of how she has received a medal for saving her school from a fire. The following Monday, Casey and her news reporters try to run off copies of the newspaper, only to have the school secretary, Mrs. Crump, scoot them out of the ditto room. But Mrs. Crump promises to run off and staple the papers for them. At lunchtime, as they're selling the newspapers, Casey notices there is one more page than she expected. To her horror, she realizes she left the ditto master for Tracy's letter at school on Saturday and Mrs. Crump has mistakenly run it off too. A mortified Casey runs home after school to hide. There Van tells her the letter was terrific and reports that Mrs. Petty called Casey creative. Casey is a celebrity after all.

A young girl living in the shadow of an older sister tries to get out in various elaborate, sometimes underhanded ways. She finally becomes a "celebrity"—but legitimately, because of her writing ability. This funny story captures the whirlwind life of a messy, active, imaginative fourth grader. Portions of Casey's story are told in letters to her pen pal, Tracy. Pencil drawings enhance the story, a companion volume to *The Girl Who Knew It All.*

Ages 8-10

Also available in:
No other form known

201

Giff, Patricia Reilly

The Gift of the Pirate Queen

Black/white illustrations by Jenny Rutherford.
Dell Publishing Company, Inc. (Yearling Books), 1982.
(164 pages, paperbound)

COURAGE, MEANING OF
Death: of mother
Diabetes
Family: relationships
Relatives: living in child's home
School: classmate relationships

Since her mother's death the year before, eleven-year-old Grace O'Malley has tried to take care of her father and her younger sister, Amy, who has diabetes and worries Grace by ignoring her special diet. Grace is apprehensive when her father says his cousin, Fiona, is coming from Ireland to visit them. Just before Fiona's arrival, Grace accidentally breaks her teacher's prized glass Christmas bell. All the sixth graders fear and dislike Mrs. Raphael, and Grace knows she can never confess what she's done. Fiona arrives bearing little gifts and immediately tells Grace that she reminds her of the other Grace O'Malley, the brave and bold pirate queen. Fiona's love for Katie, Grace's mother, inspires her father to explain the circumstances of Katie's accidental death for the first time. Meanwhile, Grace worries about Mrs. Raphael's broken bell. Lisa, a new girl in school, always unkempt and the butt of her classmates' jokes, mentions that she saw a bell just like it in a shopping mall thirty miles away. Grace's father is too busy to take her there, so Fiona does. After buying the bell, Grace feels less relieved than she'd expected to; something is still nagging at her. Fiona tells Grace that this is her happiest Christmas: after years of living alone, working in the parish rectory in Ireland, she finally has a family to love. When Grace slips the new bell under the classroom Christmas tree, she decides to improve Lisa's standing with Mrs. Raphael by writing that the bell is from Lisa. But her plan backfires when Mrs. Raphael suspects Lisa of replacing the bell because she broke it. That afternoon Amy gets sick and must go to the hospital. Grace handles the emergency with Fiona's help. Later, Amy jokes about Grace bringing her a box of candy, and Grace bursts out that she hates Amy for frightening her all the time and for not doing what she ought to do. The next day Grace's father brings her a message from Amy: she loves Grace and wants Grace to know that it's very hard to stay on her diet, that sometimes she just wants to pretend she doesn't have diabetes at all. Grace's father admits he's guilty of the same thing. If he just didn't talk about Katie's death, he'd thought, he could pretend she was around somewhere. Now he and Grace need to help Amy stop running away from her diabetes and become "everyday brave." Remembering her own words to Amy about doing what she ought to do, Grace tells Mrs. Raphael the truth about the bell. The teacher is surprised to learn the children fear her, saying she must think about that and how she has changed over the years. She and Grace both apologize to Lisa. After school, Grace can't find Fiona at first and realizes how much she needs and loves her. When Fiona comes in, Grace begs her to stay with them permanently. Fiona had told Grace's father she would only stay if she were asked, and only until they didn't need her anymore. She talks about courage. When Grace tells her about the bell, adding that she is not bold and brave like the pirate queen, Fiona says courage is a gift that we don't always have with us. For Christmas, Fiona gives Grace an old photograph of her mother and Fiona herself, taken long ago in Ireland. For Grace, who has no pictures of her mother and has begun to forget what she looked like, it is a gift almost as precious as the gift of courage.

A young girl discovers there are many kinds of courage and that all the important people in her life struggle with fears just as she does. In this beautifully illustrated, well-written, and touching story, various examples of courage are presented in terms easy to understand and apply to readers' own lives. The stages of mourning and the trials of diabetes are skillfully woven through the plot, as are details of Irish customs and folklore.

Ages 9-12

Also available in:
No other form known.

202

Giff, Patricia Reilly

The Girl Who Knew It All

Black/white illustrations by Leslie Morrill.
Dell Publishing Company, Inc. (Yearling Books), 1984.
(118 pages, paperbound)

FRIENDSHIP: Meaning of
SCHOOL: Achievement/Underachievement
Inferiority, feelings of
Responsibility: avoiding
Self-discipline
Teasing

Tracy Matson, about nine, has just started summer vacation, and she wants Leroy Wilson to be her summertime best friend. Unfortunately, Leroy wants to play with his friend Richard, and both boys love to tease Tracy for being a slow reader. Tracy likes to ignore her reading problems by showing off and acting like a know-it-all. Her father has asked her to read fifteen minutes every day during the summer. Instead of the daily readings, she keeps track of the minutes she owes and always writes an IOU. Tracy does try to be helpful, but something always seems to go wrong. As a surprise, she decides to touch up a newly painted shutter on the house of Mrs. Bemus, the new school principal. Reaching for a can of turpentine, she misreads the label and uses Turkey Red paint. To cover up her mistake, Tracy paints a red rose on the shutter. When she hears voices, she hides and then sneaks away. Vacation begins to improve when Casey Valentine, Tracy's pen pal, comes to town with her parents for the summer. Tracy and Casey quickly become the best of friends. They decide they need to earn money for the County Fair, so they get a joint baby-sitting job. When this doesn't bring in the revenue they need, they enlist Leroy, Richard, and two other children from town to plan a play they can present and charge admission for. As usual, Leroy and Richard tease Tracy about her poor reading ability. This surprises Casey because Tracy told her that she loves to read. Casey offers to help Tracy with her reading. Embarrassed, Tracy screams for everyone to leave. She then runs into her house, discovering that her dog, Rebel, is sick. Both parents are working and no one else is available, so when Tracy spots Mrs. Bemus outside her house, she asks the principal to drive her to the veterinarian's. On the way home, overcome with guilt, Tracy blurts out that it was she who painted the shutter because she misread the label on the can. Mrs. Bemus invites Tracy into her house to talk. She encourages the girl to let Casey help her with her reading. She also offers to help the group earn money for the fair by having them paint her garage. A grateful Tracy apologizes to Leroy and Richard for her outburst and tells them about the garage. She then offers to teach Casey to paint a garage if Casey will help teach her to read.

A girl covers up her reading deficiencies by showing off and playing tricks. When a friend discovers her secret and a sympathetic principal takes an interest in her, Tracy can finally admit to herself that she needs help. Though her problem is not solved, Tracy becomes determined to improve her reading. This is an enjoyable story, filled with humor and true-to-life characters. Lively pencil drawings enhance this companion volume to *Fourth Grade Celebrity.*

Ages 8-10

Also available in:
Cassette—*The Girl Who Knew It All*
Library of Congress (NLSBPH)

203

Giff, Patricia Reilly

Today Was a Terrible Day

Color illustrations by Susanna Natti.
Viking Penguin, 1980.
(26 pages)

SCHOOL: Achievement/Underachievement
Inferiority, feelings of
Success

Ronald Morgan, in second grade, is having a terrible day at school. When he crawls under his desk to retrieve his pencil, his classmates call him Snakey. Then, because his mother forgot to sign his homework, he signs her name. Not only does Miss Tyler, his teacher, tell him that forgery is a crime; she informs him that he spelled his mother's name incorrectly. The children all laugh. During reading time Ronald, hungry, sneaks to the closet and eats a sandwich—from Jimmy's lunch bag. Then Ronald, who knows he is in the "dumb group" in reading, has to ask how to do a workbook page. He feels even dumber when Rosemary, also in his group, asks, "Don't you even know how to do that?" In line to get a drink of water, Ronald holds his finger on the water and splashes a girl's dress. A third-grade teacher marches him back to his class, warning him that if he doesn't learn to behave he will never get into third grade. A classmate says Ronald may not get to third grade anyway because he can't read. At recess, Ronald misses a fly ball and loses his ice cream money. That afternoon he makes mistakes while reading aloud for his teacher. Just before it is finally time to go home, Ronald is reminded that it is his turn to water the plants. While watering, he knocks a pot off the windowsill. As he leaves for the day, Miss Tyler hands him a note and tells him to read it himself, with help from his mother if necessary. Ronald surprises himself by reading the whole note without help. It says that Miss Tyler is sorry for his bad day and hopes tomorrow will be better. Ronald can read after all! Elated, he runs home to tell his best friend. He also decides to take Miss Tyler a new plant tomorrow for her birthday.

A day of assorted mishaps and failures ends triumphantly for a little boy when he is able to read his teacher's encouraging note all by himself. Ronald, in the "dumb" reading group, tells his own story, and his feelings of inferiority and incompetence, changing to happiness and pride, come through clearly. Colorfully illustrated, this beginning reader tells a lighthearted but sympathetic story.

Ages 6-7

Also available in:
Paperbound—*Today Was a Terrible Day*
Puffin Books

204

Giff, Patricia Reilly

The Winter Worm Business

Black/white illustrations by Leslie Morrill.
Dell Publishing Company, Inc. (Yearling Books), 1981.
(132 pages, paperbound)

FRIENDSHIP: Making Friends
REJECTION: Peer
Change: new home
Family: relationships

LeRoy Wilson is less than thrilled when his cousin Mitchell, also ten, moves to town with his mother and younger sister after his father leaves the family. Winter is just beginning, and LeRoy and his friend Tracy expect their worm business to pick up smartly when the ice-fishing season gets underway. Mitchell wants painfully to be part of LeRoy's life, but he does one thing after another that LeRoy considers intrusive, obnoxious, or embarrassing. Furthermore, LeRoy's mother signs LeRoy up as Aunt Louise's first piano student, over his strenuous objections. Mitchell tags along when LeRoy goes to visit his bachelor friend, Gideon Cole, who lives in a mountain cabin by himself during the winter and goes deep-sea fishing in the Atlantic during the summer. To keep Mitchell away from Gideon's mountain, LeRoy tells him about the fearsome mountain monkeys, which resemble Abominable Snowmen. Gideon, however, praises LeRoy for helping Mitchell; it must be hard to move to a new place, he remarks, and he's sure LeRoy is introducing Mitchell around and helping him get settled. LeRoy thinks to himself that Mitchell has no trouble at all—he just moves in and takes over. On the first snowy morning, Mitchell gets up early and contracts with just about everyone in town to shovel their walks. LeRoy, beaten to this job opportunity, is incensed to the point of tears. As it turns out, though, Mitchell intends for both of them to do the walks and split the money. Then, at his first piano recital, LeRoy can't remember how his piece ends so he just keeps repeating it—whereupon Mitchell pretends to faint, releasing LeRoy from his endless loop. The next day the ice fishermen arrive. Tracy, LeRoy, and Mitchell take the worms out onto the ice to sell. But Mitchell's sister bumps into him as he's holding the worms and almost all of them fall in an ice hole. Even Tracy gets mad at Mitchell then. When Mitchell leaves, his sister reports his intention of saving LeRoy; LeRoy realizes that his cousin has gone to protect him from the mountain monkeys (they eat anyone who warns another person against them). Tracy says Mitchell really needs a friend. He tries so hard to help other people. LeRoy reluctantly agrees and decides to go after him. When he finds Mitchell, he tells him that the mountain monkey story is a hoax told to all new kids. Mitchell is glad to know he's not a new kid anymore.

LeRoy realizes that nobody is perfect and that his cousin's good points far outweigh his bad ones. This is not a profound tale, but readers may see past Mitchell's apparently abundant self-confidence to the trials of the new kid on the block trying to fit in. Attractive, lively illustrations perk up this story of cousins' rivalry.

Ages 8-10

Also available in:
No other form known

205

Gilson, Jamie

Do Bananas Chew Gum?

Lothrop, Lee & Shepard Company, 1980.
(158 pages)

LEARNING DISABILITIES
Baby-sitting
Education: special
Inferiority, feelings of
School: achievement/underachievement
School: classmate relationships
Self, attitude toward: feeling different

Sam Mott is twelve and in the sixth grade, but he reads on a second-grade level. His parents believe his reading difficulties stem from the family's frequent moves. Sam believes he can't read because he's dumb. When they lived in California, Sam was tested and said to have "learning disabilities." But now, in Illinois, Sam has been placed in a regular sixth-grade class and doesn't want to take any more tests. He overhears his parents discussing him, his mother worrying that he might be retarded. Sam knows he is just dumb. Then Sam is hired to baby-sit for two little boys after school. The first afternoon, he can't read the note from their mother and so does not let the dog out or give one of the boys his medicine. The mother, Mrs. Glass, is angry, and Sam promises to do better. She then asks Sam to write down his orthodontist's name; Sam is sure he'll now be fired for stupidity because he can't spell and his writing is illegible. The next day Mrs. Glass asks Sam to read to her boys, but he cannot. At school Alicia, the smartest student in class but highly disliked because of her boasting and superior attitude, asks Sam if he can read; she has seen through his bluffing and joking. He ignores her. The next day, while he's baby-sitting, Alicia comes by and offers to help him with his spelling. Angry that now Alicia,

Mrs. Glass, and his teacher know he can't read, Sam refuses when his parents tell him he is to be tested again. Then Mrs. Glass confronts Sam about not being able to read. She tells him he is not stupid—he has proved that by being such a good baby-sitter—but he needs help. So Sam agrees to be tested by Ms. Huggins, the special education teacher whom Sam, unaware of her position, has seen and admired before. When Sam tells her he is dumb she replies, "You're not allowed in my door unless you're smart." Ms. Huggins says this because a different teacher works with students who have lower ability. Ms. Huggins finds that Sam is excellent in math, but that he learns better by hearing than by reading. She shows him some easier ways to read and encourages him to use a tape recorder, reading into it so he can hear himself and taking notes with it. These are just the first of the things she'll work through with him, she promises. After the testing, Sam talks with Alicia. He tells her he feels better about himself and is determined not to feel dumb anymore. They agree that, just as Sam has told Alicia not to keep telling people she's smart, Sam will stop telling people he is dumb.

Feeling dumb and different, a young boy with a learning disability stumbles through school until he agrees to be retested and is given the special help he needs. This isn't an in-depth account, but it does offer a sympathetic and hopeful look at someone living with a learning disability. Humor lightens the mood, but the painful feelings that can result from repeated school failures are clearly drawn. Also effectively done is Sam's friendship with Alicia, who lacks friends because she thinks too much of herself, rather than too little. Oddly, the story is written in the first person (quite a feat for someone who can't read or write), but most readers will not notice this discrepancy.

Ages 9-11

Also available in:
Cassette—*Do Bananas Chew Gum?*
Library of Congress (NLSBPH)

206

Ginsburg, Mirra

Two Greedy Bears

Color illustrations by Jose Aruego and Ariane Dewey.
Macmillan Publishing Company, Inc., 1976.
(32 pages counted)

GREED

Two bear cubs set out to explore the world—two very competitive bear cubs. If one is thirsty, the other is thirstier. If one drinks his fill, the other drinks more. If one has a stomachache, the other's is worse. And when they come across a big, round cheese, of course they fall to quarreling over how to divide it. And while they argue, a sly fox approaches and offers to settle the matter. She breaks the cheese in two, making sure one piece is bigger than the other. Of course the bears object, and so the fox takes a bite from the bigger piece. Again the bears complain that the pieces are unequal. Begging their patience, the fox continues to reduce the two pieces by turns until only two scraps remain. Having eaten her fill, the fox flicks her tail and walks off leaving two tiny crumbs of cheese, exactly equal.

This story, adapted from a Hungarian folk tale, wittily shows how greed can turn gain into loss.

Ages 3-8

Also available in:
Paperbound—*Two Greedy Bears*
Aladdin Books

207

Girion, Barbara

A Handful of Stars

Dell Publishing Company, Inc., 1986.
(179 pages) o.p.

G

EPILEPSY
Boy-girl relationships: dating
Family: relationships
Maturation
School: classmate relationships
School: pupil-teacher relationships

Julie Meyers, in cap and gown waiting for high school graduation ceremonies to begin, reminisces about a time early in her sophomore year. It is during a party at Elyssa Winston's house that Julie suddenly begins walking in circles, talking about algebra and then pounding on the door. Afterwards, she has no recollection of anything. One day she finds herself in the gym holding a notebook she doesn't recognize. After several more episodes, Julie begins to wonder if she's going crazy. But how could she be, she, Julie Meyers, member of the "in" crowd, one of the stars of the first school play, the object of Steve Marks's attentions! At the tryouts for *Guys and Dolls,* the spring play for which parts usually go to juniors and seniors, Julie gets an enthusiastic response to her audition. The next day, increasingly worried about her health, she sees Dr. Carlson, a neurologist, who administers a number of tests. Dr. Carlson explains to Julie and her parents that Julie has epilepsy. "The word epilepsy dropped into that room like a punch in the stomach." Dr. Carlson gives her medication and the family is relieved to think the pills will stop her spells. Several days later, Julie is delighted to learn she got a part in *Guys and Dolls.* But that evening she has another seizure, this time right in front of a horrified Steve. When she recovers he is polite but distant. Julie remembers her extreme sense of isolation: "As if I was struggling alone in some deep dark tunnel." Every time she has a seizure Dr. Carlson readjusts her medication. After a basketball game, the kids try to coax her into having some beer. Knowing that alcohol could be very dangerous combined with her medications, Julie pretends to drink some and spills the rest. Her parents and grandmother watch her constantly and the household revolves around Julie and her spells, to her older sister Nancy's growing resentment. Then Julie has a particularly public seizure, in the school cafeteria. She hears the kids talking about her, calling her names. Ms. Barish, the drama teacher and Julie's idol, finds her crying behind the stage. When Julie confides in her, the woman "relieves" her of her part in the play—she will not risk a seizure in the middle of a production. Her cowardice is hard for the girl to accept. Little by little, Julie's life begins to shred "the way a tissue will when it's held under a water faucet." Classmates are nice enough in school, but Julie is no longer included in parties and extracurricular activities. The night *Guys and Dolls* opens, Julie feels her heart is truly breaking. Several weeks later, Elyssa invites Julie to a slumber party. But that Friday Julie has a seizure in school, and Elyssa's mother calls Julie's mother to say it would probably be better if Julie didn't sleep overnight. Julie locks herself in her bedroom all weekend and meticulously cuts up her new pajamas. She also dumps all her pills in the wastebasket, though later she retrieves a few. She withdraws even more from those around her. During her junior year, Julie's parents send her to visit Nancy, now a freshman at Duke University. With Nancy and her friends, who don't seem to care about her epilepsy or her pills, Julie feels more like her old self. At a fraternity party, she meets freshman David Seegar, who takes her announcement about her epilepsy very calmly. They dance and talk and plan to keep in touch, possibly to see each other during Christmas vacation. That visit doesn't materialize, but David does manage to come at the end of Julie's junior year and Julie falls in love with him. During her senior year, Julie is accepted at three universities, including Duke. Duke seems such a safe choice: Nancy and David are there to smooth her way. But Julie decides that a safe choice isn't necessarily a good one; she will attend Colgate instead. Her parents are upset, but her grandmother, who has so often come to her rescue, insists that Julie must be allowed to make her own decisions. David attends her graduation ceremony, and Julie looks forward with confidence to whatever the future brings.

When a teenage girl learns she has epilepsy, she must cope not only with unexpected seizures and continual medication, but with the ignorance and small cruelties of classmates and adults. Julie tells her own story in flashbacks and, although in her case it's epilepsy that sets her apart, it is the story of any teenager ostracized by peers. Well-written and perceptive, the book presents an accurate picture of epilepsy, its symptoms, treatment, and social implications, without obscuring a compelling story about growing up. It is dedicated to the author's son Eric, "who faced it all with courage and grace."

Ages 12 and up

Also available in:
Cassette—*A Handful of Stars*
Library of Congress (NLSBPH)

208

Girion, Barbara

A Tangle of Roots

Putnum Berkley Group, Inc., 1985.
(154 pages) o.p.

DEATH: of Mother
MOURNING, STAGES OF
Boy-girl relationships: dating
Family: unity
Friendship: best friend
Jewish
Maturation

When sixteen-year-old Beth Frankle is called out of class by the principal and told her mother is dead, she is sure there must be some mistake. But there is no mistake; Beth's young mother has died instantly from a cerebral hemorrhage. Beth and her father, grandmother, and Aunt Nina somehow manage to stumble through the funeral and the week of Shiva, the traditional Jewish period of mourning. When Beth returns to school, Joyce, her best friend, and Kenny, her boyfriend, try to help her adjust to her mother's death. But Beth cannot. She misses her mother terribly, she hates seeing her father so sad and lonely, and she resents her grandmother's attempts to take over their household. Then Beth's father, trying to recover, invites her to go with him into New York City from their home in New Jersey for an evening of fun. Beth would rather go out with Kenny, but feels she must accompany her father. Although she has a good time, she realizes again how lonely her father is. Her emotions receive another jolt when she hears from Joyce that Kenny was with someone else that night. At Thanksgiving her father invites her to go with him on a business-vacation trip to Miami. This time too Beth would rather stay home with Kenny but, although she feels torn, she chooses to go with her father. In Miami she is disturbed when Stacy Arnold, a business associate, seems to be interested in her father. Beth accepts a date with a tennis pro, but ends it early and abruptly when he tries to seduce her. She begins to see that she is angry at her mother for dying and causing her this emotional upheaval. Back home, Beth learns that Kenny has begun dating another girl. As the weeks pass, Beth sees her father looking happier and going out more. She is glad, yet fears that he is already forgetting her mother. Beth is also afraid that her father's increasingly independent life will leave her all alone. Over Christmas vacation, her father goes on a ski trip to Vermont with Stacy and some other couples. On New Year's Eve day, Beth is filled with loneliness as she remembers how her father always gave her mother a dozen yellow roses on this day. Terribly sad, she asks Aunt Nina to drive her to the cemetery. Alone at her mother's grave, she discovers a dozen yellow roses under the newly fallen snow. She sees that, although his life has to go on, her father still loves and misses her mother. Relieved and somehow comforted, Beth leaves the cemetery.

A girl shares her feelings of grief, anger, guilt, and loneliness following the sudden death of her mother. Stricken anew by the breakup with her boyfriend, Beth at first resists her father's efforts to recover from his grief and go on living. But time and a moving visit to her mother's grave help her come to some acceptance of what has happened. Beth is a compassionate, believable narrator, and her story is enriched by details of Jewish family life.

Ages 12-16

Also available in:
No other form known

209

Goff, Beth

Where Is Daddy? The Story of a Divorce

Black/white illustrations by Susan Perl.
Beacon Press, 1969.
(27 pages)

DIVORCE
Anger
Guilt, feelings of
Magical thinking

Janey, who is three or maybe four, lives with her parents and her dog, Funny. At least she does until she wakes up one morning and finds Daddy is gone. Upset, she thinks Daddy has left because she begged him to play with her. Daddy returns and takes Janey to the beach, where they have fun until Daddy explains that he and Mommy are planning to be divorced. Mommy and Daddy argue later at home, and Janey feels "a pain inside her" as she senses their bad feelings toward each other. After Mommy, Janey, and Funny go to live with Grandma, Mommy gets a job and begins to stay away all day. Grandma is impatient with Janey and scolds her. Janey, worrying that her mother will leave her as her father did, believes that her own angry feelings are causing these hurtful things to happen, and so she becomes very quiet. She decides she must never say anything angry again. One day when Funny doesn't come home until Janey has called seven times, she hits the dog repeatedly. When Mommy sees her striking Funny and questions her, Janey explains that she is angry because Funny "went away like you and Daddy and I hate him!" Mommy understands. The next day, she takes Janey to see the place where she works and reassures her daughter that Janey is not the reason for the divorce. Grandma tries to be more patient and understanding; Daddy comes to visit again; and Janey begins to feel better.

The Director of Inpatient Service at Children's Psychiatric Hospital at the University of Michigan comments at the end of the book, "This touching story is psychologically sound." He suggests ways in which the book might be used with preschoolers who are feeling the "grief, confusion and loneliness" that follow divorce.

Ages 4-8

Also available in:
Paperbound—*Where Is Daddy? The Story of a Divorce*
Beacon Press

210

Gold, Phyllis

Please Don't Say Hello

Black/white photographs by Carl Baker.
Human Sciences Press, 1975.
(47 pages)

AUTISM
Education: special
Friendship: meaning of

When Paul Mason and his family move into their new home, Billy, Alan, Jimmy, and Charlie—all neighborhood boys—introduce themselves to Paul. They also meet his younger brother, nine-year-old Eddie, and ask why he seems to ignore them. Paul explains that Eddie is afraid—of the new house and all the new neighbors, and "sometimes Eddie is just afraid." Dropping over to Paul's during the summer, they find that Eddie avoids them, does not talk the way most boys do, and often runs away when they talk to him. Finally Billy's parents forbid him to associate with Paul, and Mrs. Mason and Paul's older sister, Lizbeth, sit down to explain Eddie's handicap to the boys. Eddie, and children like him, are autistic—"have trouble getting outside of themselves enough to get along with other people in what would be considered the normal way." The boys point out that while Eddie has trouble doing some simple things, he can do other very difficult things easily; Lizbeth explains, "I think for all of us some things are easier and some things are harder to do. For Eddie it's even more that way." Mrs. Mason adds that, though no cure is known for autism, Eddie attends a special boarding school where "they understand his special problems and know ways to help him." When school begins, the boys lose track of Eddie, but in the spring, Mrs. Mason asks them to join the family when they pick him up for summer vacation. At the school, the boys observe the special help being given to autistic students. And later, at home, they notice that Eddie has changed in some ways. He now seems more interested in watching children and calls himself "I" instead of "you."

This simple portrayal of autism describes some of its symptoms and tries to show the reader that understanding and acceptance can do much to help the autistic child get along in the world. In addition, the book explains the educational instruction available to autistic children and touches briefly on some of the behavior modification that helps counter the autistic child's isolation. The author, herself the mother of an autistic child, explores the mystifying condition with compassion and intelligence. Here is a well-presented message for children and adults too, about a complicated, misunderstood, and still not wholly explained phenomenon.

Ages 7 and up

Also available in:
Paperbound—*Please Don't Say Hello*
Human Sciences Press

211

Golding, William

Lord of the Flies

Coward–McCann, 1962.
(187 pages)

VALUES/VALUING: Moral/Ethical
Cruelty
Problem solving

Jack, Ralph, Simon, and Piggy, all close to twelve years old, are among a planeload of boys stranded on a desert island during a war. Their plane has crashed, killing every adult on board. The youngsters begin their struggle for survival by attempting to create a society with patterns and rules to follow. The intentions of the majority to create an orderly and rational society soon deteriorate. The physically stronger leaders use human fear of the unknown, symbolized by an evil "beasty," to expand and maintain their influence. The struggle between rationality and savagery begins with arguments about priorities and leads to the killing of some group members. Finally, only Ralph is left to encourage intelligent, rational behavior in dealing with the boys' situation. The "tribe" begins to hunt him down. In the process, they set the island afire. At this point, a naval officer who has spotted the fire arrives to rescue them.

The emotions of fear, hatred, and distrust are explored in this story. When authority is removed, most of the characters' actions degenerate to a level of primitive brutality. The author implies that human beings are innately savage and that intelligence and rationality generally fall victim to irrationality and physical force. The book's symbolism, intricate style, and scenes of violence make it appropriate only for mature readers.

Ages 13 and up

Also available in:
Braille—*Lord of the Flies*
Library of Congress (NLSBPH)

Cassette—*Lord of the Flies*
Library of Congress (NLSBPH)

Paperbound—*Lord of the Flies*
Wideview/Perigee

212

Goldman, Susan

Grandma Is Somebody Special

Color illustrations by the author.
Albert Whitman & Company, 1976.
(32 pages counted)

GRANDPARENT: Love for
Visiting

When a little girl visits her grandmother in the city, they make up the cot, look at photo albums, and watch fire engines and buses from the balcony of the tall apartment building where the grandmother lives. They fix the dinner that the girl likes best; then she draws her grandmother a picture, which "she hangs right up on the kitchen door." They play cards, read stories, look at Grandma's jewelry, and thoroughly enjoy each other.

A little girl tells this story of her visits to Grandma, visits she enjoys because her grandmother lives an exciting life, working and going to school in the big city. The visits matter greatly to the girl because her grandmother pays so much attention to her: listening to her read, helping her bathe, brushing her hair. This is a loving account of the special love a grandparent can give a child, a love especially welcome when a new baby has arrived in the family.

Ages 4-7

Also available in:
No other form known

213

Graeber, Charlotte Towner

Mustard

Black/white illustrations by Donna Diamond.
Macmillan Publishing Company, Inc., 1982.
(42 pages)

DEATH: of Pet
Communication: parent-child
Loss: feelings of

Eight-year-old Alex insists that his family's cat, Mustard, is not really getting old. He accuses his younger sister, Annie, of bothering the cat. But when Mustard is taken for a check-up, the veterinarian says his heart is not as strong as it used to be; Mustard must take medicine and shouldn't be subjected to any stress. Unfortunately, a few days later, the big dog belonging to the newspaper boy corners Mustard and frightens him so badly he suffers a heart attack. That night Alex has Mustard sleep next to him. The boy is awakened in the middle of the night by strange noises. He finds Mustard walking back and forth in the closet, making awful crying noises and bumping into the walls. He can't seem to see or to walk straight. For the rest of that night, Alex's parents keep Mustard in their room.

The next morning Mustard looks worse, but Alex must go to school while his father takes Mustard to the vet. His parents warn Alex that Mustard will probably not get better and that the best the vet can do is make his death painless. Alex comes home from school to see his father standing in the backyard with a small box and a shovel. Alex looks at Mustard one last time, and then they bury him. Alex keeps Mustard's collar and Annie, his catnip mouse. Alex and his father take the rest of Mustard's things to the animal shelter. When the woman there hears about the loss of their pet, she asks if they'd like a kitten. Alex and his father agree they aren't yet ready for another cat. Maybe next year.

Fine pencil drawings distinguish this story of how a boy and his family cope with the illness and death of a much-loved pet. Alex is supported by parents who share his grief, show their own, and are honest about what is happening to Mustard. The book could be helpful to children whose pet has died or is old and ill.

Ages 4-10

Also available in:
Cassette—*Mustard*
Library of Congress (NLSBPH)

214

Gramatky, Hardie

Little Toot

Color illustrations by the author.
Putnam Berkley Group, Inc., 1939.
(91 pages counted, paperbound)

RESPONSIBILITY: Accepting
Loneliness

Although Little Toot is a very small tugboat and cannot make loud noises with his whistle, he can create a great deal of smoke. His ability to create smoke makes him feel important, but actually he is quite useless and frivolous. In fact, his antics are so silly that the other tugs are annoyed by him. They make fun of him, and this hurts his feelings. Little Toot is lonesome because when the tugs are not making fun of him, they ignore him. Feeling sorry for himself, Little Toot floats downstream to the ocean. Meanwhile, a storm develops, and by the time Little Toot reaches the open water, the storm has wedged a big ocean liner between huge rocks. Little Toot has a marvelous idea: he decides to puff an SOS signal from his smokestack and alert all the other tugs. But when the other tugs see the signal and try to come to the rescue, they cannot make any headway against the rough sea. Little Toot, frightened as can be, skims across the top of the waves and reaches the ocean liner. Little Toot guides the large ship into the harbor and is treated like a hero by his fellow tugs.

This classic story portrays the loneliness often felt by someone who is different. It also illustrates how one can accept responsibility and be successful when a real effort is made.

Ages 3-7

Also available in:
Braille—*Little Toot*
Library of Congress (NLSBPH)

Talking Book—*Little Toot*
Library of Congress (NLSBPH)

215

Grant, Eva

I Hate My Name

Color illustrations by Gretchen Mayo.
Raintree/Steck-Vaughan Publishers, 1980.
(31 pages)

NAME, DISSATISFACTION WITH
Teasing

When Demelza Smith starts school she begins hating her name. Her classmates laugh when her name is called. Demelza's parents explain that she was named after her great-grandmother, a beauty and an accomplished pianist. Demelza admires her great-grandmother's pictures in the old photo album, but she still hates her name. The teasing at school continues and is more and more hurtful. Finally, Demelza's parents explain that when they named her, they gave her the middle initial "J." They tell Demelza to pick out any "J" name she likes and they will call her by it. Excitedly, Demelza tries on various names but finds something wrong with each of them. "They all sounded so . . . boring." Demelza decides that her own name is the most interesting. From then on, when she's teased, she stands up for herself. One day she overhears two girls talking. One insists she sees nothing wrong with the name Demelza. Demelza breaks in emphatically. "It may not be the most beautiful name in the world, but I think it's the most interesting!" She is surprised when some of her classmates cheer.

This spirited first-person narrative considers the problems an unusual name can cause a child. Helped by her supportive parents, Demelza learns to take pride in her name. Although the resolution is oversimplified, the book would be appropriate for discussions about how teasing hurts. Colorful illustrations help sustain interest.

Ages 5-8

Also available in:
No other form known

216

Grant, Eva

Will I Ever Be Older?

Color illustrations by Susan Lexa.
Raintree/Steck-Vaughan Publishers, 1981.
(31 pages)

SIBLING: Rivalry
Sibling: love for
Sibling: younger

David is seven and fears he will "never catch up" with his ten-year-old brother, Steven. David gets Steven's hand-me-downs, and the jeans often have patches. He gets Steven's old soccer shoes, his old roller skates, even his former teachers, who compare the younger boy unfavorably with his brother. Sometimes his grandmother forgets and calls him Steven. David wishes that Steven didn't exist. One day, when David and his mother go to pick Steven up after soccer practice, Steven isn't there. His mother is worried but David is delighted: maybe they'll never find Steven and then he, David, will get to be the oldest. He asks his mother if it's possible for him ever to be older than Steven. She tells him it's not, but that perhaps being the oldest isn't always best. She explains that she and the boys' father had practiced child rearing on Steven because he was first. When Steven was David's age, he had to go to bed much earlier than David does now. As David starts to look for Steven, the older boy runs out, eager to tell his mother that he's been selected to attend a soccer clinic that weekend. On Saturday, David finds there's nobody to kick the soccer ball around with. Steven's not there to fix his roller skates or to watch a favorite show with him. When his brother finally comes home, David admits, "I was surprised at how nice it felt to have Steven back." After they're in bed for the night, David tells Steven how he feels about the hand-me-downs and about Grandma forgetting his name. Half asleep, Steven confesses that sometimes Grandma forgets and calls him David!

This gentle, low-key account of sibling rivalry is narrated by the younger brother and provides a simple example of what can become a more serious problem. David begins by detailing his complaints about being number two in the family, but ends by showing that he does love and appreciate his brother. An introductory page for parents and teachers suggests that the story "will stimulate many discussions, as it provides a useful reminder to both parent and child of the universal nature of the sibling experience." The illustrations are outstanding: charming, detailed, appealing.

Ages 5-8

Also available in:
No other form known

217

Greenberg, Jan

The Iceberg and Its Shadow

Farrar, Straus & Giroux, Inc., 1980.
(119 pages)

FRIENDSHIP: Best Friend
FRIENDSHIP: Meaning of
Family: relationships
Ostracism
Peer relationships: peer pressures
School: classmate relationships

Anabeth, a sixth grader at Skokie Elementary School, is one of the most popular girls at school. She is student council president, loves her teacher, Mrs. Thilling, and is best friends with Rachel. Although Anabeth is outgoing and Rachel quiet and withdrawn, they have been best friends since kindergarten. Then one day everything changes. Mindy—loud, aggressive, and bossy—moves to Skokie and joins their class. Anabeth finds her exciting. Before long Mindy is the unofficial class leader, disturbing others and demanding her own way. Soon Anabeth, Mindy, Carolyn, and Tracy dub themselves the "Fabulous Foursome," excluding Rachel because she has told Mrs. Thilling that Mindy copied her work. Anabeth feels guilty about ignoring Rachel and not defending her, but seems compelled to follow Mindy; she is half-afraid not to. "I felt like a rubber ball bouncing back and forth between them, but I didn't want to land on either side." Finally, Anabeth confronts Mindy about her bossiness and accuses her of being mean. At a class party later that day, Mindy, Carolyn, and Tracy ignore Anabeth and later harass her. They rename themselves the "Three Musketeers" and soon get others to shun Anabeth. Anabeth now realizes what Rachel must be feeling, but she is too embarrassed to apologize. Finally she breaks down and tells her parents the whole story. They've suspected that something was amiss and react with concern and support, helping Anabeth realize that as a leader in the class, she could have and should have stuck up for Rachel. By the end of the school year, Anabeth has managed to regain the respect of her classmates. Feeling confident at last, she calls Rachel to apologize and they agree to meet. Anabeth hopes to show Rachel she really cares.

Anabeth finds that the excitement of being notorious is less satisfying than a real friendship. When she herself is ostracized, she understands how unfair she has been toward her best friend. Told by Anabeth, this well-paced story is filled with humor, interesting characters, and satisfying family relationships. It describes problems of peer pressure common to this age group.

Ages 10-12

Also available in:
Paperbound—*The Iceberg and Its Shadow*
Farrar, Straus & Giroux, Inc., (Sunburst Books)

218

Greenberg, Jan

The Pig-Out Blues

Farrar, Straus & Giroux, Inc., 1982.
(121 pages)

WEIGHT CONTROL: Overweight
Autonomy
Boy-girl relationships
Communication: parent-child
Expectations
Parent/Parents: power struggle with
Parental: control
Self-esteem

At fifteen, Jodie Firestone is overweight, broke, and bored. She lives in Connecticut with a beautiful mother, Vanessa, who despises anything fat. Until Jodie was thirteen she was a stringbean, but then as she stopped growing taller she began to grow wider. Her mother nags her constantly about being a walrus, which makes Jodie run for the refrigerator. The girl's favorite activity is the school drama group, and when they decide to present *Romeo and Juliet,* Jodie decides to lose weight so she can be Juliet. Her mother puts her on a strict diet; the only restaurant in town she's allowed to patronize is Mr. Wheatley's Health Food Store. She jogs with her mother and takes a laxative every night before bed. She loses twenty pounds. But the tryouts for the play are a disaster. The role of Juliet goes to Maude St. James, a newcomer from England—partly because while Jodie is reading the part of Juliet she faints, and the director says she needs to build herself back up before she can handle a heavy role. David Simms, older brother of Jodie's best friend, Heather, gets the part of Romeo. Though Jodie would love to play Juliet to his Romeo, on or off stage, she is given the role of the old nurse. When she gets home, her mother screams at her as if she lost the role deliberately. The girl goes into hiding after that. She skips school, forging a note of excuse, and spends her days eating great quantities of food. The sympathetic Mr. Wheatley offers her a part-time job, and she accepts it gratefully. But Vanessa doesn't want Jodie working anywhere near food and considers waitressing a low-status job. The two scream at each other and end up physically fighting. After that, Vanessa leaves Jodie alone. The girl returns to school and works at her job, but the silent battle with her mother goes on. "With every bite of food I took, I knew I was the loser, but I couldn't stop. Why should I starve myself for her?" Rehearsals are going very badly; Maude St. James is a poor actress, unable to learn her lines or respond to direction. When Jodie tries to help, Maude has a tantrum. Then life gets a little easier for Jodie. Wanda Sue, a likeable and popular classmate who is even heavier than Jodie, helps Jodie see that she can be loved despite her size. Vanessa and Jodie hug each other for the first time in years. When Vanessa and her friend decide to spend two weeks in the Caribbean, Jodie stays with the Simms, who give her a hearty welcome and seem to love her for herself. After ten days of the family's normal, healthy meals, Mr. Wheatley's sprout sandwiches, and no Vanessa to nag her, Jodie is considerably thinner. "There were moments when I was tempted to take a second helping or sneak into the icebox, but no one cared whether I did or not, so I didn't." One night when she goes to the refrigerator for comfort after a stressful dream, she says no to herself and wakes up the next morning feeling strong and renewed. Vanessa writes a letter admitting she's made mistakes and offering a truce. The troubled production of *Romeo and Juliet* is cancelled, and David, dogged by a sense of failure, disappears. Jodie has heard him speak of spending days in the Metropolitan Museum of Art in New York, two hours away, and after he's been gone two days she goes there and finds him. They talk and then take the train home. Vanessa has returned. Jodie hates the thought of going back home to their dingy apartment where everything will be the same. But then she realizes that if she can change, situations can too. Maybe even Vanessa can change. Her mother has brought her a yellow bedspread, the first time she's ever given Jodie anything that wasn't a reward for losing weight or getting good grades. She suggests that if she were Jodie, she'd redo her bedroom in bright colors. Jodie says quietly that she loves the spread and will use it. However, she will consider the color scheme more carefully before deciding. She is not, after all, her mother.

An overweight teenager learns that she, not her fierce mother, is in control of her body. Along the way she learns that it's also up to her to choose her own values and friends. Jodie's is a compelling first-person narrative with well-drawn characters, especially that of Vanessa, who, though she's rather likeable, is actually a verbally and psychologically abusive parent from whom Jodie must free herself. Jodie's success with her weight is entirely realistic as presented, although readers with more serious weight problems may find her victory superficial and unlikely. However, Jodie's weight problem is secondary to her struggle for autonomy, and her efforts to define herself in the face of parental controls will speak to many readers.

Ages 12 and up

Also available in:
Paperbound—*The Pig-Out Blues*
Farrar, Straus & Giroux, Inc., (Sunburst Books)

219

Greenberg, Jan

A Season In-Between

Farrar, Straus & Giroux, Inc., 1979.
(150 pages)

ILLNESSES: Terminal
MATURATION
Anxiety
Death: of father
Family: unity
School: classmate relationships
Self, attitude toward: accepting
Self, attitude toward: feeling different

For as long as she can remember, thirteen-year-old Carrie Singer has been awkward, too tall, and teased by other kids. In fourth grade, Carrie decided to protect herself by adopting an indifferent attitude. By now she and Fran Steiner, the other Jewish student at Miss Elliot's Academy, stand leagued against the school and the middle-class values it epitomizes. Yet Carrie's moods continually shift. One moment she is withering in her criticism of Courtney Allen, a "golden girl"; the next, she considers Courtney to be perfection. Never before interested in boys, Carrie still convinces herself to avoid them. Secretly, though, she hopes Dewy Daumatt, an athletic neighbor, will ask her out. Easily hurt, Carrie just as quickly conceals the hurt with a wisecrack or an indifferent shrug. Her isolation deepens when her father, a warm and friendly man, must go away for cancer surgery, and Carrie's mother accompanies him. Carrie becomes increasingly troubled. She feuds constantly with Sonny, her eight-year-old brother; their live-in maid, Dorothy, is sorely tried to keep the peace. Carrie also does badly at school, and her parents' return does not lift her anxiety. The already strained relationship with her mother, to Carrie a cool perfectionist, deteriorates. Though her father steadily weakens, Carrie cannot break through her shell to tell him of her love and anxiety. One night she hears him coughing and buries her head under her pillow. Gradually, though, Carrie lets her feelings show. She tearfully tells Dewy her worries; she takes a night walk with her father and talks to him. He tells her that he too is frightened, but is grateful for his family's support. It is only after her father dies, however, that Carrie's anxiety dissolves under the pressure of her grief. She comes to see that behind her mother's cool exterior is a great need for her daughter. Carrie also understands Sonny's bewilderment at their father's death and comforts him. She helps as her mother takes over the father's business, and she and Dewy begin dating. More and more, Carrie learns to accept people for what they are—including herself.

A lonely, troubled young girl endures the illness and death of her father, pulling out of her grief and self-absorption as she gains insight into herself and the people around her. Carrie tells her own story with a serious, but not morbid, tone. Her maturation and the closer relationship developing with her mother provide an encouraging conclusion.

Ages 11-13

Also available in:
No other form known

220

Greene, Bette

Get On Out of Here, Philip Hall

Dial Books for Young Readers, 1981.
(150 pages)

BOASTING
LEADER/LEADERSHIP
Boy-girl relationships
Clubs
Peer relationships
Self, attitude toward: confidence
Success

As teenager Beth Lambert practices her acceptance speech for the Brady leadership award to be given that evening at the Old Rugged Cross Church in Pocahontas, Arkansas, her mother comes in and advises her not to count her Bradys before they hatch. Later, at the awards ceremony, when Rev. Ross begins to describe the winner—someone who uses leadership ability quietly and humbly—Beth stands up and waits for her name. Instead, the award goes to Philip Hall, and Beth is ridiculed and laughed at for her presumption. She runs out of the tent and hides in the woods all night. When she finally goes home, she tells her mother that she's planning something so important people will remember it for years. She calls an emergency meeting of the Pretty Pennies Girls Club and, as its president, announces that they will challenge the boys' club, the Tiger Hunters, to a relay race on the town's Dollar Day. She herself will coach the team. A big, excited crowd assembles on the great day, and the mayor publicly praises Beth for her involvement, inspiration, and hard work. The relay begins with Philip Hall and Beth. She runs as fast as she's ever run in her life, but Philip is faster. In desperation, she throws the red handkerchief to the second runner, Bonnie, instead of handing it over as she's supposed to. As a penalty, the sheriff makes Beth do the handoff again, losing them valuable time. Bonnie takes off and runs as hard as she can, but the race is already lost— "a race that I had lost singlehandedly, without a bit of help from anybody." Afterwards, Beth tries to disappear but is confronted by angry members of the Pretty Pennies. She knows that "even a hundred years won't be nearly time enough for me to forgive myself for what I had done here today." A week later, Philip Hall, who's still her friend, tells her the Pennies are having a meeting without her and that Bonnie hopes to take over the presidency. Beth, outside the window, listens to their meeting, and when she hears that they plan to boot her out, she rushes in to protest and apologize. But when the vote is in, Bonnie is elected the new president. Overwhelmed by her failures,

Beth tells her mother she wants to move to a different town, a different county, where nobody will know her. Her sympathetic parents agree to her moving to Walnut Ridge to live with her grandmother. Once there, she promptly organizes a girls' club, but declines the presidency when they offer it to her; she's come to Walnut Ridge to be a follower, not a leader. But she can't help whispering suggestions to B.J., the new president, although she berates herself later. The club is sponsoring the town's New Year's Day party, and B.J. admits she has no idea how to plan a party for two thousand people. So Beth offers to do it. On Christmas Day her family all comes to Grandma's house. Her parents ask Beth when she's coming home. She tells them she can't until she gets through the New Year's Day party. To Beth's relief, the party is a great success, not only for Walnut Ridge but for the many Pocahontas people who attend. Philip Hall is one of them, and he urges Beth to come home again. She sees what a true friend Philip has been and tells him he deserved the Brady leadership award. Three of the Pretty Pennies ask Beth to return and be their president again, since Bonnie hasn't done anything. As long as there aren't any more secret meetings, Beth replies, because they hurt people. For the first time, Beth can laugh about her mistake in the relay race. She tells her parents she's ready to go home.

Beth Lambert is an energetic, idea-filled girl who's gotten a bit big for her britches since readers last met her in *Philip Hall Likes Me. I Reckon Maybe.* Through several humbling experiences and a few successes, she learns not to be so full of her own importance and to appreciate the true nature of her leadership abilities. This fast-moving, entertaining book asks, "How can others toot your horn when you're so busy doing it yourself?" Beth changes believably from cocky to quietly competent. The black dialect in her first-person narrative adds authenticity and doesn't obstruct the story line.

Ages 9-12

Also available in:
Cassette—*Get On Out of Here, Philip Hall*
Library of Congress (NLSBPH)

221

Greene, Bette

Philip Hall Likes Me. I Reckon Maybe

Black/white illustrations by Charles Lilly.
Dial Books for Young Readers, 1974.
(135 pages) o.p.

GENDER ROLE IDENTITY: Female
Allergies
Friendship: meaning of
Self, attitude toward: confidence

Twelve-year-old Beth Lambert is a rural Arkansan. She excels at almost everything she does. Only Philip Hall, a neighbor and classmate, surpasses her, partly because Beth usually allows Philip to be first or best in schoolwork and other areas in which they compete. Although Beth is anxious that Philip like her and includes Philip in her vegetable-selling project, Philip only has time for her if his male friends are not around. One day Beth rescues Philip when he foolishly wanders into a heavily wooded area and hurts his foot. But she is constantly aware of Philip's disdain for girls and his belief that he can do things better than she can simply because he is a boy. Beth finally reasons, "Where in the Good Book is it written that a girl's calf can't be in the same contest with a boy's calf? Well, Mr. Philip Hall, for too long I've been worried that you wouldn't like me if I became the number-one best student, ran faster in the relay race, or took the blue ribbon for calf-raising." Beth does win the calf-raising contest, and the friendship of the two survives with Philip's ego slightly hurt but still intact.

This timeless story of the friendship and competiton between a boy and a girl is made particularly engaging by the author's honest and direct approach. Beth believes in herself and succeeds because of this self-confidence. A minor but important theme in the book is that of Beth's allergic reactions to dogs. Beth desperately wants a dog and her parents make every effort to find one to which she is not allergic. But when she reacts to even the usually nonallergenic poodle, Beth unhappily concedes that a dog is one pet she will have to do without.

Ages 10-13

Also available in:
Cassette—*Philip Hall Likes Me. I Reckon Maybe*
Library of Congress (NLSBPH)

222

Greene, Constance Clarke

Al(exandra) the Great

Viking Penguin, 1982.
(133 pages)

FRIENDSHIP: Best Friend
Decision making
Illnesses: of parent
Maturation
Parent/Parents: single

At twelve, the narrator is a year younger than her best friend, Al, short for Alexandra. Now that school is out for the summer, Al is looking forward to leaving New York City and visiting her father and his new family on their farm in Ohio. However, Al, who "suffers a lot from role reversal," worries that her mother works too hard and coughs too much. She insists that her mother go to the doctor, who discovers she has pneumonia and immediately puts her in a hospital. The narrator's father has Al stay with them in her mother's absence. That evening he even takes his daughter and Al to a fancy restaurant—secretly upsetting the narrator, who would prefer to be alone with her father. Al visits her mother daily and envies her best friend's stable family. For her part, the friend envies Al going to Ohio and the farm. But Al finally decides she cannot leave her mother. Reluctantly she telephones her father and explains the situation. Al's mother is proud of her daughter's decision, and she cheers Al up by promising her a vacation in a beach cottage on the Jersey shore. Several days later Al receives a package from Ohio, a T-shirt saying "AL(exandra) THE GREAT." An enclosed note from her father praises her for her devotion. Al hugs her best friend and her new shirt.

Excited about spending three weeks with her father and his new family, Al's dream is dashed when her mother becomes ill. But as the narrator—Al's best friend—notes, Al's decision to stay with her mother was the right one. This warm, humorous book shows two best friends learning a lot about responsibility. The story is a sequel to three previous books about Al, her best friend, their families, and their other friends.

Also available in:
Braille—*Al(exandra) the Great*
Library of Congress (NLSBPH)

Cassette—*Al(exandra) the Great*
Library of Congress (NLSBPH)

Paperbound—*Al(exandra) the Great*
Puffin Books

223

Greene, Constance Clarke

Beat the Turtle Drum

Black/white illustrations by Donna Diamond.
Viking Penguin, 1976.
(119 pages)

DEATH: of Sibling
SIBLING: Love for
Mourning, stages of

Kate tells how her younger sister, Joss, almost eleven, is saving money to rent a riding horse. She loves horses, and would own one if she could. Mr. Essig rents horses for thirty dollars a week, and Joss is sure she will have that much when she gets her birthday money. Kate, at twelve, is Joss's best friend, and though she does not share Joss's fervent love for horses, she does help her clean the garage for the horse to sleep in. On her birthday, as anticipated, Joss receives money in the mail from Grandma, and so is able to take the required thirty dollars to Mr. Essig. When the horse is delivered later that day, Joss is ecstatic, pampers him thoroughly, and gives rides to the neighborhood children. Some days later, the sisters take Prince and go for a picnic. They climb an apple tree to eat their lunch, and Joss climbs higher to look down at Prince. Suddenly the branch breaks, and Joss is hurled to the ground. Kate, terrified by Joss's silence, runs for help. But Joss is dead. Kate's world is turned upside down, and in the days and weeks that follow she tries to understand what has happened. Only after time does she see that someday the pain of her loss will be lessened. Right now, the hurt remains.

Kate narrates the story of her last, and special, summer with her sister. The days immediately following Joss's death—the funeral and the parents' grief—are handled sensitively but without sentimentality.

Ages 10-13

Also available in:
Cassette—*Beat the Turtle Drum*
Library of Congress (NLSBPH)

224

Greene, Constance Clarke

Double-Dare O'Toole

Puffin Books, 1990.
(158 pages, paperbound)

RISK, TAKING OF
Death: of friend
Friendship: meaning of
School: classmate relationships
Sibling: relationships

When Francis Xavier O'Toole, known as Fex, was five, his older brother, Pete, dared him to walk on his hands up the center aisle of a store. The applause of Fex's first audience hooked him into taking all dares offered him. Now Fex is almost twelve and, though he knows that accepting dares always gets him into trouble, he continues to succumb to every challenge. He is frequently victimized by a classmate, Barney Barnes, who exploits Fex's weakness by daring him into escapades that Barney himself would never attempt. Barney's latest dare, to put "Palinkas is a pig," complete with illustration, on the desk of Mr. Palinkas, the principal, has cost Fex a week of mandatory after-school chores. Mr. Palinkas, however, is sympathetic to Fex and encourages him to resist his compulsion to take dares. As Fex knows, "There's nothing worse than knowing you've been a fool and have no one to blame but yourself." Pete is now a good-looking, athletic, fifteen-year-old sophisticate who offers Fex instructions about "making out" with girls. The inexperienced Fex, taking the instructions for a dare, attempts to try them out on his childhood friend, Audrey. But Audrey calls him "cuckoo" and runs into the kitchen. Barney gives a boy-girl party at which he dares Fex to "make a move" on an older girl when the lights are turned off. The lights come back on to reveal Fex being dumped on the floor by the indignant girl. Everyone but Audrey laughs at him. Several days later, Fex takes his young baby-sitting charge, Charlie, to the fishing pond. Barney and his gang appear and dare Fex to jump in the water. Fex is determined to avoid dares and does not oblige. But when the gang dares Charlie, the little boy plunges into the water and is swept away by the current. Fex manages to save the child, with the aid of two men, and becomes a local hero, complete with picture and story in the newspaper. Slowly, with his parents' and younger brother Jerry's support and sympathy, the new "hero" begins to gain the self-confidence he needs to withstand Pete's teasing and Barney's bullying. He has been helped all along by the good advice of his main confidante, Angie, a sixtyish storekeeper. Shortly after the rescue of Charlie, Angie dies suddenly. Audrey and Fex go together to the wake, where Fex faints from the pressure of his emotions. When he revives, he and Audrey walk home hand in hand.

A boy begins to overcome his weakness for accepting dares in this sympathetic, entertaining account. Supported by understanding family members and friends, Fex gains the self-confidence he needs. The relationships between Fex and the other characters, especially Audrey and Angie, are well drawn and the dialogue is natural, although the plot itself is a bit thin.

Ages 9-11

Also available in:
Braille—*Double-Dare O'Toole*
Library of Congress (NLSBPH)

225

Greene, Constance Clarke

A Girl Called Al

Black/white illustrations by Byron Barton.
Viking Penguin, 1969.
(127 pages)

SELF-IMPROVEMENT
Death: of friend
Divorce
Parental: rejection
Weight control: overweight

Al (short for Alexandra) is an overweight nonconformist who still wears braids in the seventh grade. Al and her girlfriend often talk with Mr. Richards, the assistant superintendant of their apartment building. The girls consider him their best listener and favorite person. Al's parents are divorced. She lives with her mother, whom she says she "likes but does not love." Al receives letters from her father, as well as money which she spends on candy. Two incidents suggest new directions for Al's life. After an especially enjoyable evening out with her mother and her mother's boyfriend, Al decides to improve her appearance by losing weight and buying clothes, instead of candy, with her father's money. When Mr. Richards dies unexpectedly, Al is grief-stricken. Al's mother, seeing her daughter's grief, begins to realize that Al needs more love and attention than she has been getting.

This is a first-person narrative written by Al's friend. Al is ignored by both of her parents. She tries to overcome her feeling of rejection by treating herself to sweets and assuming an "I don't care" attitude. The story ends with the implication that the mother-daughter relationship and Al's self-concept are beginning to improve.

Ages 11 and up

Also available in:
Braille—*A Girl Called Al*
Library of Congress (NLSBPH)

Cassette—*A Girl Called Al*
Library of Congress (NLSBPH)

Paperbound—*A Girl Called Al*
Puffin Books

226

Greene, Constance Clarke

I and Sproggy

Black/white illustrations by Emily McCully.
Dell Publishing Company, Inc., 1981.
(155 pages) o.p.

JEALOUSY
STEPBROTHER/STEPSISTER
Change: resisting
Parent/Parents: remarriage of

Ten-year-old Adam lives in a New York City apartment with his mother, but his divorced father, who has remarried in England, is coming with his new wife and daughter to live in Adam's neighborhood. The boy is overjoyed at having his father so near, but he loathes the idea of sharing him with an English stepsister. Sproggy (as for some reason she is called), also ten, seems "taller, stronger, smarter, able to handle herself better than he." Adam behaves rudely to her from the very start. When his best friends, Kenny and Steve, make her a member of their hitherto all-male club, he is furious. Adam's good friend Charlie, the apartment handyman, tells him not to be so nasty; Sproggy needs friends in her new country. For their part, Charlie and his wife, having enrolled in night classes at a city university, are honored by the governor during Continuing Education Week with an invitation to a lawn party at his mansion. Adam has always longed to get inside the nearby mansion and is overjoyed for Charlie. But more surprises await Adam. The day before the party, he comes across a group of neighborhood girls teasing Sproggy. She slips and falls in the street, and he helps her up and treats her to a Coke. Sproggy is all gratitude and Adam quite puffed with pride. The next day, Charlie wheels his invalid wife to the mansion, with numerous neighborhood children tagging along. Adam and Sproggy peer through the fence and then Sproggy spies her uncle among the other party guests. Uncle Dick invites the two to come in, and Adam feels his kindness to Sproggy more than rewarded.

A boy who often daydreams of being a hero is surprised first by his own surliness toward his stepsister, then by her regarding him as a hero and how good that makes him feel—about both of them. An invitation to the governor's party suggests that it even pays to be her friend. This is a perceptive, often amusing book, peopled with vivid, lively characters whose dialogue seems exactly right.

Ages 9-11

Also available in:
No other form known

227

Greene, Constance Clarke

I Know You, Al

Black/white illustrations by Byron Barton.
Viking Penguin, 1975.
(126 pages)

FRIENDSHIP: Best Friend
PARENTAL: Absence
Maturation
Menstruation
Parent/Parents: remarriage of
Parent/Parents: single
Puberty

At twelve-and-a-half, the narrator is a year younger than her best friend, Al, short for Alexandra. Al is the only girl in her own class who has not had her menstrual period, but she takes this casually, saying that she may never have it. Al's more immediate concern is her divorced mother's boyfriend. She hopes her mother will not remarry; Al already has a father—one she has not seen in six years. Soon the long-absent father comes to town, calls her up, and asks her out to dinner. Al is angry that he can suddenly appear after such a long absence and smugly expect to see her. But her friend, the narrator, says, "I know you, Al. . . . You'll go—anything for a free meal." The next day Al, very excited, says her father wants her to attend his wedding. Al is unsure about going, and again her friend tries to calm her: "Al, I know you. You will do the right thing and go." By now, Al's feelings have put a strain on both girls, but during preparations for the trip, the two make up. After the wedding, Al calls her friend long-distance and tells her all went well: she likes her father's new family and they like her; she has had her first period; and she has met an interesting boy. Back at home, Al tells her friend she understands her father better and will try to forgive his earlier neglect. "The older I get, the more I know that not only is almost nothing perfect, but almost nobody, no person, is either."

In this story the narrator's level-headedness and common sense help her friend Al through some trying events. The author shows a keen ear for adolescent dialogue. With all its humor and informality, the story rings true. This book will appeal more to girls than boys, and is a sequel to *A Girl Called Al* but stands on its own.

Ages 11 and up

Also available in:
Braille—*I Know You, Al*
Library of Congress (NLSBPH)

Cassette—*I Know You, Al*
Library of Congress (NLSBPH)

Paperbound—*I Know You, Al*
Puffin Books

228

Greene, Constance C.

The Unmaking of Rabbit

Viking Penguin, 1980.
(125 pages) o.p.

BELONGING
Appearance: concern about
Friendship: meaning of
Grandparent: living in home of
Parental: absence
Parental: rejection
Peer relationships: rejection
Self, attitude toward: accepting

Paul, eleven, has lived unhappily with his grandmother for nine years, ever since his father disappeared. Paul's mother promises him that he can come to live with her when she finds a larger apartment or marries a man who wants Paul too. The boy has no friends at school. The other children put pencil shavings in his lunch box, call him Rabbit because his ears stick out, and mock him because he stutters. Paul tells himself that their teasing does not matter because he will soon be leaving to join his mother. On his next visit with her, however, he realizes that they probably never will be reunited. He also discovers, after placing himself in danger in a desperate attempt to win the acceptance of his classmates, that he does not want their type of friendship after all. Some time later, he finally experiences true friendship with the son of one of Gran's acquaintances.

At the beginning of the story, Paul waits for his mother to want him and for the boys at school to accept him. He constantly tries to please his mother, but since she never seems to appreciate him and seldom even pays attention to him, he finally realizes that she is concerned only with herself and decides that living with Gran is better after all. As the story progresses, Paul develops a more positive sense of self-worth which enables him to reach out for genuine friendship.

Ages 10-13

Also available in:
Braille—*The Unmaking of Rabbit*
Library of Congress (NLSBPH)

229

Greene, Constance Clarke

Your Old Pal, Al

Viking Penguin, 1979.
(149 pages)

FRIENDSHIP: Best Friend
Anger
Expectations
Jealousy: peer

Thirteen-year-old Al's best friend tries to encourage her as she waits expectantly for promised letters from her father and his new wife and from a boy named Brian whom she met at her father's wedding. But despite her friend's efforts, Al's moods swing uncontrollably from eager anticipation to crushing disappointment. After meticulously composing a letter to Brian, Al reads it to her friend. The friend advises Al never to mail such a self-deprecating letter; it's "bad," she tells her, "it stinks," "it's a bummer." As Al vacillates between sending and not sending it, her friend accepts an invitation for a two-week stay with Polly, whose parents are going on safari in Africa. This latest desertion is the last straw, and Al's emotional turmoil erupts in anger. She insults her friend and impulsively mails the letter. Meanwhile, Al's friend, angry also, picks a fight with Polly, and a temperamental triangle results. Tension grows until at last, ashamed of themselves, the girls apologize to each other and become friends again. Al has received her long-awaited invitation for a month's stay with her father and new stepfamily. Then, soon after the friends' reconciliation, an excited Al gets a postcard from Brian. In the same mail, her ill-considered letter is returned because of insufficient postage. On friendly terms once more with her friends and the world, Al decides "If only I could figure some way to get mad and not say anything mean until I got over being mad. It's the things people say to each other when they're mad that cause the trouble."

As three volatile young teenagers work through their jealousy and anger, they learn the hurting power of thoughtless words, They also make some discoveries about apologizing and forgiving. As told by Al's unnamed best friend, this perceptive and funny story will strike responsive chords in anyone who has ever been estranged from a best friend. This is the third book about Al and her best friend.

Ages 9-13

Also available in:
Braille—*Your Old Pal, Al*
Library of Congress (NLSBPH)

Cassette—*Your Old Pal, Al*
Library of Congress (NLSBPH)

230

Greene, Sheppard M.

The Boy Who Drank Too Much

Dell Publishing Company, Inc., 1980.
(149 pages) o.p.

ALCOHOLISM: Adolescent
ALCOHOLISM: of Father
Boy-girl relationships
Child abuse
Deprivation, emotional
Friendship: best friend
Parent/Parents: single
Sports/Sportsmanship

The fifteen-year-old narrator (whose name is never given) is intrigued by Buff Saunders, a fellow player on the school hockey team. But the narrator's best friend, Art, warns that Buff is nothing but a troublemaker, a liar, a wise guy. In spite of the warning, the narrator accompanies Buff to the hospital the day he is hit in the face by a hockey puck during a game and loses four teeth. Afterwards, he takes Buff home to a "dump" of an apartment in an old house and shares a can of stew with him and his father. Buff's father, who begins drinking as soon as he walks in the door, is a former hockey player who takes great pride in Buff's game. He is delighted by the missing teeth, gleefully predicting that Buff, like him, won't have a tooth left by the age of eighteen. Buff says he'd like to quit hockey, but his father won't hear of it. The argument ends when the drunken father slaps his son in the face, right on the twelve stitches he's just had. The narrator later describes the evening to Ruth Benedict, a recovered alcoholic for whom he does odd jobs. They talk about why people drink. Ruth tells him it's a way, a bad way, of coping with problems. The narrator is first exposed to Buff's own drinking at a party given by Tina, Art's girlfriend. There the narrator meets a girl named Julie. When Buff arrives with a case of beer, three cans missing, he says he needed to "limber up" before the party. Tension grows during the evening because of Buff's attentions to Tina, and he and Art end up fighting. Art nearly severs a tendon when he steps on a broken bottle during the fight, and he must give up hockey for the rest of the year. He demands that the narrator end his friendship with Buff, but the narrator feels grateful to Buff for his help with hockey and sorry for his troubles. One day he learns that Buff keeps miniature bottles of liquor in his pocket "for emergency use only"—whenever he gets tensed up at practice. The narrator gives up his first date with Julie to keep Buff from drinking after a disappointing performance in a hockey game. But Buff doesn't show up that night and is missing for the next several days. Then Julie calls the narrator out of class to say that she's found Buff, dead drunk, behind the school. They call Ruth, who comes at once and takes Buff home with her. Julie and the narrator then go to Buff's father in an attempt to enlist his help and support for Buff. But the drunken Mr. Saunders roughs up the narrator trying to find out where Buff

G

is. When they get back to Ruth's, Buff tells them how he tried to run away, but began drinking instead. Then his father, having discovered where Buff is, arrives at Ruth's, violently drunk. When they won't let him in, the man throws a barbecue grill through Ruth's window. Buff calls the police and finally strikes his father after Saunders taunts and ridicules him. Then Buff runs off, and the narrator follows him to a garage, hoping to comfort him. He finds Buff sitting in a 1960 T-bird that his father completely rebuilt. It is the car his mother was killed in, his drunken father at the wheel. Buff believes his father loves the car far more than he loves him. He then announces his plans to take the car and head for Canada, where he was born. He challenges the narrator to go with him. His friend pledges his loyalty, promising to stick with Buff. Finally convinced that this friendship is real, Buff tells the narrator that if he will help him get through a rehabilitation program Ruth has mentioned, he will postpone going to Canada. In a playoff game at the end of the season, the narrator and Buff, now living at Ruth's house, both play well. Afterwards, Buff tells his friend that he now realizes he doesn't have to be exactly like his father. He is his own person. Buff receives the Most Improved Player trophy, but still hasn't made up his mind whether or not he will play hockey next season.

As he wrestles with his own drinking problem as well as his father's, a boy finds support in the friendship of several peers and of an older, recovered alcoholic. Buff desperately wants his father's love and approval, but comes to realize he probably won't ever have it and can live without it if he must. The sympathetic narrator must cope with troubles of his own, as he is torn between his old and new friend and enters his first boy-girl relationship. He also has to come to terms with the violence and abuse he sees between Buff and his father. The story is believable, and readers are left feeling that Buff has his drinking problem under control.

Ages 12 and up

Also available in:
No other form known

231

Greenfield, Eloise

Africa Dream

Black/white illustrations by Carole Byard.
HarperCollins Publishers, Inc., 1989.
(29 pages counted)

AFRICA
AFRICAN-AMERICAN

A girl dreams one night that she journeys to the Africa of long ago, the Africa of her ancestors. And there, in that time, she wanders through its markets, and reads and understands its ancient books. Then she dreams herself in the village of her "long-ago granddaddy with my daddy's face"; joyously welcomed there, she dances and sings a song of greeting. Tired after wandering all over Africa, she dreams that her long-ago grandma rocks her to sleep.

In this first-person narrative, a young black girl tells of the long-ago Africa of her dreams. Simple verse and attractive illustrations convey the pride, warmth, and familiarity of the Africa she imagines.

Ages 3-6

Also available in:
Paperbound—*Africa Dream*
HarperCollins Publishers, Inc.

232

Greenfield, Eloise

Grandmama's Joy

Color illustrations by Carole Byard.
Putnam Berkley Group, Inc., 1980.
(32 pages counted)

GRANDPARENT: Love for
Change: accepting
Empathy
Grandparent: living in home of
Moving

Grandmama is sad and little Rhondy doesn't know why. To cheer her, Rhondy has Grandmama stop taking old clothes out of the closet and stuffing them in a box; she must watch Rhondy put on one of her singing shows. But the show doesn't make Grandmama smile as it usually does. So Rhondy goes to visit Mrs. Bennett and suggests that Mrs. Bennett give Grandmama a call to make her feel better. But Grandmama doesn't answer the phone. Then Rhondy finds a pretty, speckled rock in the yard and gives it to Grandmama, explaining that there are lots of pretty things in their yard. Grandmama starts crying. She says they have to move because the rent is too high. Rhondy thinks about missing her friends, her school, and her neighbors, but she doesn't dwell on that now. Instead, she asks Grandmama to tell her the story once again of how the two of them came to live together. Grandmama recalls that after an accident that took Rhondy's parents' lives, she picked up the infant Rhondy from the hospital and declared that Rhondy would always be her joy. As long as she had her joy, she always thought, she'd be all right. Rhondy wants to know if she is still Grandmama's joy. Will she be Grandmama's joy when they move? Grandmama, "smiling a real smile," says yes and hugs Rhondy. The little girl "felt so happy in her grandmama's arms because as much as she was Grandmama's joy, Grandmama was her joy, too."

When her grandmother is unhappy and discouraged about being forced to move from her house, little Rhondy reminds her of the really important things in life: the love and concern the two have for each other. This beautiful portrayal of the affection between a child and an aging adult features outstanding illustrations and a simple, tender text. The younger audience might need adult guidance in fully appreciating the love, concern, and care that remain for Rhondy and Grandmama despite difficult times.

Ages 4-8

Also available in:
No other form known

233

Greenfield, Eloise

Me and Neesie

Color illustrations by Moneta Barnett.
HarperCollins Publishers, Inc., 1975.
(36 pages counted)

IMAGINARY FRIEND
School: entering

Young Janell enjoys playing with her imaginary friend, Neesie, though Janell's mother does not quite understand it. Getting ready for a visit from Aunt Bea, the mother says: "I guess I can stand you making up a friend, but Aunt Bea's old and nervous, and I don't want you upsetting her." Later, when Aunt Bea starts to sit down on the couch, Janell cries out, "Don't sit on Neesie!"—and Aunt Bea beats on the sofa with her cane to get rid of "the ghost." The next day is Janell's first day of school. Neesie is sad and stays in bed, but the excited Janell goes off to school and has a wonderful time. When she returns, she cannot find Neesie—her best friend, her only playmate until now. Then Janell thinks about school and her new friends there. She decides not to tell them about Neesie because she is "just mine." Then Janell puts her head in her mother's lap and listens to her read.

This first-person narrative describes a young girl with no playmates who fills her need for them with an imaginary friend. Although her parents don't encourage this friendship, they are tolerant and understanding. The abrupt disappearance of the imaginary friend after the child's first day at school may seem contrived.

Ages 4-7

Also available in:
Paperbound—*Me and Nessie*
HarperCollins Publishers, Inc.

234

Greenfield, Eloise

She Come Bringing Me That Little Baby Girl

Color illustrations by John Steptoe.
HarperCollins Publishers, Inc., 1974.
(31 pages)

SIBLING: New Baby
Sibling: jealousy

A five- or six-year-old boy wants a baby brother, but when his mother comes home from the hospital, she brings a girl instead. The boy hugs his mother, although she hugs back with only one arm because she is holding the baby in the other. The boy is very disappointed that the baby is a girl. He can't understand why his parents look at the baby as if she were "the only baby in the world" even though she cries loudly and is ugly and wrinkled. The boy's aunts and uncles bring gifts for the baby, and he feels ignored. He pulls a chair over to the window and stares out at a squirrel. When Mama puts the baby in his lap, he says he doesn't want to be a big brother to a girl. Mama replies that the baby needs his help, and that she was once a baby girl and her big brother took care of her. When the boy tries to picture his mother as a baby and his uncle as a young boy, he bursts out laughing. Then the boy brings in his friends to show them the baby. He decides his sister can have one of Mama's arms "as long as she knows the other one is mine."

G

The boy in this first-person narrative is jealous of a new sibling. He wants to ignore and reject her, but when his parents and relatives pay attention to him and explain that his parents and the baby need his help, he suddenly realizes that he is proud of the baby and is willing to share his mother's love with her.

Ages 3-7

Also available in:
Talking Book—*She Come Bringing Me That Little Baby Girl*
Library of Congress (NLSBPH)

235

Greenfield, Eloise

Sister

Black/white illustrations by Moneta Barnett.
HarperCollins Publishers, Inc., 1974.
(83 pages)

IDENTITY, SEARCH FOR
Death: of father
Sibling: relationships

As Doretha Raymond, whom everyone calls Sister, rereads her "memory book," it all comes back—those wonderful days that ended three years ago with her father's fatal heart attack. For the thirteen-year-old and her once-happy family, things are different now.

Mother comes home every night tired from working in a towel laundry and argues with Alberta, Doretha's older sister. Alberta, whose best friend has just moved away, has become sullen and withdrawn. She often leaves home, not returning for several days and never saying where she has been. Alberta tries not to care about anyone but herself for fear that she will be left again. As Sister rereads her diary's account of the family's pain and joy, she discovers she can laugh at some of the bad times. This new perspective gives her the strength to cope with her sorrow. She resolves not to become hardened like her sister Alberta, whose "eyes . . . cry no tears."

Sister's brief, anecdotal sketches of the past four years reveal the warm, strong family ties that existed before her father's death. The feelings of loss, confusion, and dissension that follow are not developed in great depth but do call forth the reader's sympathy. The book's large print and short chapter lengths will appeal to poor readers.

Ages 10-12

Also available in:
Braille—*Sister*
Library of Congress (NLSBPH)

Paperbound—*Sister*
HarperCollins Publishers, Inc.

Talking Book—*Sister*
Library of Congress (NLSBPH)

236

Greenfield, Eloise

Talk About a Family

Black/white illustrations by James Calvin.
HarperCollins Publishers, Inc., 1978.
(60 pages)

FAMILY: Relationships
SEPARATION, MARITAL
SIBLING: Relationships

Genny, about eleven, eagerly awaits the arrival of her oldest brother, Larry, who is coming home from the Army. Her friend Mr. Parker agrees to let Genny's family and friends hold a homecoming party in his backyard, and Genny's happiness is complete except when her parents argue, which is often. When Larry does arrive, all disputes are temporarily set aside, and the family enjoys an evening at home together. But in the morning, while Larry is out seeing friends, the parents fight again. Genny's younger sister, Kim, is so distressed that she locks herself in her room. Genny and her parents pull themselves together and go to Mr. Parker's to prepare the party for Larry. When they return, they find that Kim has posted signs all over the house, saying, "UGLY." Larry comes home and demands an explanation. Getting it, he characteristically talks everyone into high good humor, and they go to the party and stay that way. Next morning at breakfast, however, Father announces that he is moving out of the house. Kim, thinking she is at fault, begins to cry. Genny gets angry—at her parents first, then at Larry, because for the first time she can ever remember, he cannot set things right. She seeks out Mr. Parker for comfort, and he explains that people and families are always changing. When she joins her brothers and sister at the park, she knows they will talk and face the situation together. The family will be different, but they will get used to it.

Young Genny is angry and confused, because her parents cannot work out their differences and keep the family together. Disappointed in her adored older brother, who has always been able to "fix things," she must finally accept the fact that he cannot glue together a broken marriage. There is no pat resolution here. The pain of a sundering family is not denied, but neither is the strength of enduring love.

Ages 8-10

Also available in:
No other form known

237

Greenfield, Eloise and Alesia Revis

Alesia

Black/white illustrations by George Ford.
Black/white photographs by Sandra Turner Bond.
Philomel Books, 1981.
(61 pages) o.p.

HANDICAPS: Multiple
Determination
Wheelchair, dependence on

Alesia was nine years old when she was hit by a car and almost completely disabled. Now she is seventeen and a junior in high school. Although usually confined to a wheelchair she has, after many years of hard work, regained some movement in her body. One of her best friends is Lisa Hall, a girl she met at a summer camp for disabled children. One Saturday in March Alesia attends a party at Lisa's house and enjoys dancing. She loves parties, even though she has to lean against the wall or put her weight on the boy in order to dance. Some boys just say "never mind" when she has to lean on them, but she doesn't waste her time with people like that. Besides parties and dancing, Alesia enjoys most things other teenage girls do: going to movies, attending basketball games, shopping for clothes. When Alesia goes out in public she doesn't like adults to stare at her, although she doesn't mind answering children's questions. Some people move away when they see her wheelchair, as if she has some kind of disease. When this happens, she thinks to herself, "They have disabilities, too—faults and things like that, everybody has them. Mine is just more noticeable." Some people try too hard to help her, and she doesn't like that either. She wants to do as many things as she can by herself. If anyone were to ask her what she wants "most in the whole world," she'd say, "To be able to walk again." She recalls her accident. After coming out of a five-week coma, she had first to learn to crawl. Years of physical therapy followed. Gradually she tried to take steps, first with help and then by herself, wearing leg braces. Now she can go for walks outdoors, always holding onto and supported by friends. At the Interstate Commerce Commission, where she works for the summer, she often gets around by holding onto her wheelchair and pushing it in front of her. When school starts in September, Alesia has just about decided to go to college. She wants to live on campus and be on her own. Alesia feels she would be letting down all the people who are pulling for her if she doesn't keep trying to do more things. When she worries about her future, she remembers how the doctors told her parents at the time of the accident that she would probably be a "vegetable" the rest of her life. Knowing that didn't come true gives her faith and courage. One goal dominates her thoughts about graduation. She wants to walk across the stage all by herself to get her diploma. She practices faithfully and dreams of the day when this will be possible.

This book consists of the entries in Alesia Revis's diary between March 19 and October 24, 1980. The reader gets a very personal look at the daily life of a disabled teenage girl determined to overcome her physical limitations. As we follow her thoughts and observe the accompanying photographs and illustrations, it is impossible not to admire Alesia's courage and buoyant spirit. The diary format does make for somewhat disjointed reading, but the story is an inspiring one.

Ages 10-14

Also available in:
Cassette—*Alesia*
Library of Congress (NLSBPH)

238

Grimes, Nikki

Something on My Mind

Black/white illustrations by Tom Feelings.
Dial Books for Young Readers, 1986.
(31 pages counted, paperbound)

EMOTIONS: Identifying
African-American

In short stanzas of free verse, children examine their feelings. Some black children wish they could move to a country where there is no prejudice. A little girl on her way to church with her mother wonders why they could not invite the Lord over to their house. Another little girl hopes soon to be playing with some children on the other side of a gate, and yet another tells of feeling happy and safe when she is with her older sister. While one child longs for school to begin, another ponders what to write for school composition. Other children voice bewilderment over a mother who refuses to communicate, speculate about how school can change the way people live, and muse on the death of a grandparent.

Each verse in this short anthology expresses an emotion or thought common to children, sometimes in language common to black people. The children in the illustrations are black; the thoughts expressed are universal to children. This book can stimulate group discussions of children's feelings.

Ages 5-9

Also available in:
No other form known

239

Gross, Alan

The I Don't Want to Go to School Book

Color illustrations by Mike Venezia.
Children's Press, Inc., 1982.
(31 pages)

FEAR: of School
Decision making
Imagination

G

A young boy isn't sure he's well enough to go to school. He's certainly not well enough to face such things as forgetting his bus money, getting all sweated up in gym, or perhaps having to wrestle with Big Bruce Novak again. He could catch a bad cold from the chilly shower after gym and an older boy might snap him with a towel. What if he forgets his locker combination again or can't tell which boots are his? What if his zipper breaks! Somebody might throw up in school, or he could be reported by the crossing guards for something he didn't do. He might get caught passing a note and have to read it aloud, or the kids could make fun of his lunch, or he might have to raise his hand to go to the bathroom and everybody would know why his hand was up. Of course, on the other hand, if he stays home he won't get to see his friends or play with them after school. There's nothing on daytime television and nobody will feed the homeroom fish if he's not there to do it. Sometimes his teacher is funny and shows them interesting things; sometimes they work with clay. He'll fall behind in his work if he misses a day. So maybe he'd better go to school. "But if school doesn't work out today, I'm going to stay home tomorrow."

This humorous look at a boy trying to evaluate the pros and cons of going to school will appeal to any reader who's ever had a bad day at school. The realistic ending keeps the door open for the boy to reconsider his decision tomorrow. Some of the school incidents seem more appropriate for older readers, although the reading level and format of the book seem geared for younger students. Still, this will be great fun for the read-aloud audience. Large, bold illustrations enhance the text.

Ages 5-9

Also available in:
Paperbound—*The I Don't Want to Go to School Book*
Children's Press, Inc.

240

Gross, Alan

What if the Teacher Calls On Me?

Color illustrations by Mike Venezia.
Children's Press, Inc., 1980.
(31 pages)

SCHOOL: Pupil-Teacher Relationships
Self, attitude toward: confidence

A little boy worries about being called on in class. Even when he knows the answer, he gets "mixed up" with everyone looking at him and the teacher waiting. She tries to help by rephrasing the question and asking if he understands, but still he sits tongue-tied. Certain that his classmates think him stupid, he tells himself that he knows the answers but just cannot say them. He's noticed that he's usually called on when he's not paying attention—when he's daydreaming or making paper airplanes. So he decides his teacher will not call on him if he pretends to know the answer and is eager to volunteer it. But he has outfoxed himself: "Oh, no. Me? Um . . . ah, repeat the question, please?"

This first-person story presents a familiar classroom dilemma and should be a good discussion starter. Cartoonlike illustrations add humor, but the situation remains real. Readers will notice that the narrator ponders his dilemma instead of paying attention in class and so is caught answerless once again.

Ages 5-7

Also available in:
Paperbound—*What if the Teacher Calls On Me?*
Children's Press, Inc.

241

Guest, Elissa Haden

The Handsome Man

Macmillan Publishing Company, Inc., 1989.
(192 pages, paperbound)

AMBIVALENCE, FEELINGS OF
LOVE, MEANING OF
Boy-girl relationships
Family: relationships
Friendship: best friend
Friendship: meaning of
Separation, marital

Fourteen-year-old Alexandra Barnes lives in Greenwich Village, attends a private, progressive school, worries a lot, and wears a black-and-white-checked newsboy cap everywhere she goes. When she notices a handsome man in the neighborhood, she and her best friend, Angela Sinclair, decide to follow and find out about him. They record everything they discover in their notebooks. Alex daydreams about meeting H.M., their code name for Handsome Man. One day Alex and Angie spot H.M. sitting at a cafe by himself. They take the next table. He notices Alex's cap, tells her he's a photographer, and invites her to his apartment some Saturday so he can take her picture. Alex can't go the next weekend because the headmaster from her brother Nigel's school calls with the news that Nigel and a girl have been found together in bed smoking pot. Alex's parents leave for Nigel's school, putting her in charge of her little sister, Eloise. When her parents return they report that Nigel is on probation, but Alex senses that something even more serious is wrong although her parents deny it. Upset about the missed meeting with H.M., Alex sees him later and he says she can come by on Friday. Friday arrives and Alex, who has invented a school activity to explain her absence, goes to H.M.'s apartment—although she's filled with last-minute fears about the wisdom of what she's doing. H.M., actually Terry Gray, takes many pictures of Alex in her newsboy cap, telling her she reminds him of turn-of-the-century New York. Afterwards, he takes one last picture: Alex holding Tallahassee, the neighborhood cat. As she runs home she thinks, "I love him so much it feels like I'm dying." A week later, Terry tells Alex that the picture of her and Tallahassee made a big hit at an ad agency he contacted. They want to use it for a cat-food advertisement. Her parents need to sign a release, and then Alex will earn three hundred fifty dollars for modeling. But Alex is afraid to tell her parents because she's sure they'll disapprove of how she met Terry. Angie accuses Alex of neglecting her, of being totally wrapped up in H.M. Alex reassures her, but she herself is anything but reassured when she overhears her mother crying to her father that she knows all about "her." A few days later, she and her mother have a celebration dinner for her mother's good grades—she is working for a master's degree. But Alex senses undercurrents. "Something is happening at home and I think maybe if I stay away long enough it will disappear." She does tell her father, who tells her mother, about the cat-food advertisement, and her father signs the release. Terry calls and invites her over, and Alex is cheered at the thought of seeing him again. But that evening her mother announces that she, Alex, and Eloise will be spending the summer at the Cape. Her father will stay in New York. Alex objects and pleads and argues, but her mother is adamant. It is "best" this way. When her father comes home, Alex fearfully asks him if he and her mother are getting a divorce, but he says it's just a "breather." Alex storms out of the house and runs to Terry Gray's apartment. The visit ends with Alex crying on his shoulder, telling him about her family's troubles. He comforts and kisses her, saying she's a lovely girl and he'll miss her. She leaves and goes down by the dock, knowing she'll never see Handsome Man again, that all her daydreams of him are over. But the kiss is real and hers forever. She tosses her cap into the river where it sinks out of sight.

This first-person novel is a warm and humorous portrayal of the crush of a teenage girl on an older man. Terry, unaware of Alex's feelings, is merely kind, interested only in photographing her. Many readers will identify with Alex's conflicts, her ambivalent feelings toward her parents, the Handsome Man, even her best friend. Her parents' impending separation is not dealt with in depth; it provides part of the uneasy background against which Alex tries to make sense of her changing emotions and attitudes.

Ages 12 and up

Also available in:
No other form known

242

Guest, Judith

Ordinary People

Puffin Books, 1976.
(263 pages, paperbound)

DEPRESSION
GUILT, FEELINGS OF
Communication: parent-child
Mental illness: of adolescent

Seventeen-year-old Conrad Jarrett has recently returned home after eight months in a mental hospital. He had almost managed to commit suicide by cutting his wrists with a razor blade. Now he is back at school, trying to adjust to life on the "outside." Twice a week he visits Dr. Berger, a psychiatrist, who tries to help him understand the events of the last year and a half. The trouble had begun with the death of Conrad's adored roistering older brother, Buck, who had drowned two summers earlier in a sailing accident. After that, Con had become more and more remote. His good grades had dropped, and he had lapsed into severe depressions. Then he had cut himself, and confinement had followed. Now he must learn again to care about school assignments, to get along with his parents (who he thinks mistrust his sanity), and to get close to his friends. Dr. Berger does help him to see how all this can be done, and life looks brighter. Con begins dating Jeannine; his school work goes well. One day, talking to Dr. Berger, he is struck by a sudden new thought: ever since the accident, he has felt his mother blames him for Buck's accident—and he has blamed himself, for hanging on to the overturned boat while Buck had let go and drowned. Meanwhile, Con's parents are gripped by the death and its aftermath in deeper and deeper ways. Cal Jarrett accuses his wife of being uncaring, too involved with herself. Beth Jarrett finds Cal unduly anxious and over-protective of Con. Both parents have changed in their grief. The two drift apart, and finally, at Beth's request, separate. Con, however, has understood a good deal. He has forgiven his mother for what he had thought was her blame of him. And he has stopped blaming himself. He has accepted his father's wisdom: there are some things in life that cannot be explained—only endured.

We meet Con on his return to school; all prior events are revealed through dialogue and flashbacks. Alternating chapters are told from Con's point of view and his father's. This intensely dramatic story presents three distinctive personalities, each attempting to surmount inadequacy in the grip of grief and self-doubt.

Ages 13 and up

Also available in:
Braille—*Ordinary People*
Library of Congress (NLSBPH)

Cassette—*Ordinary People*
Library of Congress (NLSBPH)

243

Guy, Rosa Cuthbert

The Disappearance

Dell Publishing Company, Inc. (Laurel Leaf Library), 1979.
(246 pages, paperbound)

PREJUDICE: Ethnic/Racial
Alcoholism: of mother
Appearance: concern about
Crime/Criminals
Death: murder
Foster home
Friendship: meaning of
Justice/Injustice
Reputation
Trust/Distrust

When sixteen-year-old Imamu is falsely accused of murder, his mother is noticeably absent from the court hearing. But Ann Aimsley sits in on all the proceedings and her calm, cool presence helps the boy through. Ann has escaped the ghetto's poverty and when, after Imamu's case is dismissed, she offers him her help and her home, he gladly, if apprehensively, accepts. Packing his meager belongings, Imamu moves from his filthy, cockroach-ridden apartment in Harlem to Ann's middle-class home in Brooklyn. As he leaves he remembers that before his father was killed in Vietnam he had a mother who loved and cared for him. He feels a deep sense of responsibility toward the woman she was, rather than the helpless alcoholic she has become. Originally named John Jones, Imamu became a Muslim to keep himself from alcohol and drugs, which are forbidden by Islam. Besides Ann, whom he adores, his new family includes her husband, Peter, strong-willed with set ideas; Gail, seventeen and a bright college freshman who feels a secret affinity for Imamu; and little Perk, full of laughter and mischief. Close to the family is Perk's godmother and Ann's best friend, Dora Belle, whose whole life revolves around her appearance—especially her long, black hair—her home, and her two rental properties. Imamu is surprised when the beautiful, sultry West Indian woman seems interested in him, a Harlem street kid. On Imamu's second day in Brooklyn, Perk disappears. Blood from a cut on his hand and a yellow ribbon belonging to Perk that is found in his room seem to incriminate Imamu. He is terribly hurt when Ann looks accusingly at him, and his tenuous relationship with Peter is destroyed. Hauled down to police headquarters, Imamu is wrapped in cold towels and beaten

G

with rubber hoses. Gail is furious at her mother for her hasty judgment. She finds evidence to prove Imamu had cut himself on a broken glass and, despite her parents' protests, she goes to the police in his defense. The next day Imamu is released for lack of evidence, and although Gail pleads with him to return to her home, he picks up his drunken mother from the police bench and takes her back to Harlem. Determined to solve the mystery and to clear himself, he does return to Brooklyn that night, but intends to stay only until he and Gail have found Perk. Responding to Dora Belle's flirtations, Imamu goes to her house one evening and surprises her getting out of the shower. Shocked by the sight of her bald head dotted with tufts of gray hair, Imamu is unprepared for her violent, furious attack. He escapes, but suddenly remembers several other odd incidents that now convince him of what has happened to Perk. Stealthily, by flashlight, he climbs in the cellar window of one of Dora Belle's rental properties and begins hacking with a pick in a patch of new cement. Someone tells Dora Belle of an intruder on her property, and she and the Aimsleys find him there. When he explains his purpose, Dora Belle goes berserk and reveals her terrible crime. The day Perk disappeared, the girl had gone to her godmother's house to have her hair combed specially for a school party. She also had intruded upon Dora Belle without her wig. In a murderous rage Dora Belle had shaken her goddaughter and then let her go suddenly, causing Perk to fall and fatally hit her head. Some years earlier, the Aimsleys learn from a mutual friend, Dora Belle had suffered a tropical fever that destroyed her hair and affected her mind. The grief-stricken Aimsleys again offer their home to Imamu, this time with sincerity, but his conscience forces him back to Harlem to care for his mother. He does accept a job from Peter Aimsley, however, for he has begun to see his way out of Harlem, perhaps with Gail.

A Harlem teenager struggles to rise above the violence all around him in this harsh, powerful novel. Tied to his nightmare existence by his sense of responsibility for his alcoholic mother, Imamu strives to be neither victim nor criminal. Finding violence and murder even in the comfortable surroundings of his foster family, he resolves to find his way out of poverty without abandoning his mother. Vivid characterizations make this suspense-filled story memorable; West Indian dialect lends it authenticity.

Ages 12 and up

Also available in:
Cassette—*The Disappearance*
Library of Congress (NLSBPH)

244

Guy, Rosa Cuthbert

The Friends

Holt (Henry) and Company, Inc., 1973.
(203 pages)

FRIENDSHIP: Meaning of
PRIDE/FALSE PRIDE
Change: new home
Child abuse
Death: of mother
Guilt, feelings of
Peer relationships: isolation
Self, attitude toward: feeling different
West Indian-American

Fourteen-year-old Phyllisia and her older sister, Ruby, have come to New York from the West Indies to join their parents. Their father owns a small restaurant. He is a proud man and rules his children like a tyrant. To him, the most important thing in life is to become "one of the richest men in Harlem." Although Ruby finds it easy to adjust to life there, Phyllisia's problems seem overwhelming. Her classmates persecute her because of her fine clothes and her strange accent, and because she gives correct answers in school. Only one classmate—Edith Jackson—likes Phyllisia. Edith always comes late to school with her clothes unpressed and her stockings full of holes, but Phyllisia accepts the girl's overtures of friendship because Phyllisia feels the need for protection. At first resentful and ashamed of Edith, Phyllisia begins to like her and enjoy her company. Her father's pride is offended, however, when he discovers that Phyllisia has become friendly with "one of those ragamuffins," and he forbids his daughter ever to see Edith again. Without telling her father, Phyllisia continues to associate with her friend until Edith is forced to drop out of school to take care of her brother and sisters. When Phyllisia discovers that her beloved mother is dying from cancer, she needs a friend more than ever—someone who can understand what she is going through and who will help her bear the anguish of her mother's pain. Phyllisia reestablishes her friendship with Edith and invites her home to visit her mother. But the good intentions are ruined. Upset by her mother's stories of their own earlier poverty, Phyllisia makes sarcastic comments that drive Edith out of the house. After her mother's death, Phyllisia becomes ill. Ashamed of how cruel she has been to Edith, she cannot force herself to seek out Edith and make amends. It is only when her father, who has become unreasonably strict with his daughters, decides to send them back to the West Indies that Phyllisia goes to see Edith once more. After their reunion, Phyllisia begs her father to change his mind and let her stay where she is.

This powerful story depicts intense feelings of false pride, friendship, love, and hate. The conflicts and the complex relationships among the characters are vividly portrayed.

Ages 12 and up

Also available in:
Cassette—*The Friends*
Library of Congress (NLSBPH)

Paperbound—*The Friends*
Bantam Books

Paperbound—*The Friends*
Dell Publishing Company, Inc.

245

Hall, Lynn

Danza!

Charles Scribner's Sons, 1981.
(186 pages)

ANIMALS: Love for
Family: relationships
Grandparent: respect for
Identification with others: adults
Responsibility: accepting

Eleven-year-old Paulo is with the Paso Fino mare named Twenty the day she gives birth to a stud colt they call Danza. Paulo thinks Twenty is the best of all his grandfather's horses even if she is only a mare. His grandfather has nothing but contempt for the mares and for a boy who prefers riding a mare to riding a stallion. Paulo feels himself an outcast in the family. He is uncomfortable with his father, dislikes his older brother, and sees the younger children get love and hugs aplenty while he gets none. One day when Paulo is home alone, an American, Major Kessler, comes to inquire about buying some Paso Fino horses to take back to the States with him. The boy meets Kessler several months later at a horse show in which Danza places second in the weanling class. Paulo's grandfather refuses to discuss selling any of his horses to an American. Major Kessler confides his frustration to Paulo, who is flattered by the man's attention. Major Kessler doesn't treat him like a "no-account little kid." Three years later, when Danza has developed into a magnificent stallion and Paulo is fourteen, Major Kessler returns to Puerto Rico, still trying to buy a Paso Fino stallion. After a horse show, while the Major and his grandfather are discussing business, Paulo puts Danza in his stall but fails to shut the gate properly. Thirsty, Danza gets out of his stall, drinks the water left in the trough, and then knocks over an ice chest and finishes off the ice and ice cream he finds there. The next morning the horse is seriously ill; for many days he lies near death. Guilt-ridden, Paulo believes he's killed "the only thing in the world that loves me"; his grandfather has been right to distrust him. Just after his grandfather decides Danza will have to be shot, Major Kessler proposes taking the horse to the States where he's sure the university veterinarians can save him. There's one condition: Danza will then be his. The grandfather consents to send Danza to the States, but insists the Major must return him. He does agree that the Major can breed Danza. Paulo volunteers to go along to do round-the-clock nursing, and they soon leave for Louisiana. From the start Danza makes progress, and Paulo enjoys being useful and independent. He basks in the Major's praise and approval, which "came down on him like winter sunshine." When spring comes and Danza is well enough to be ridden and to breed, the Major tells Paulo about his plan to show Danza in a couple of months. The boy is a little confused. Will the Major be pocketing stud fees and prize money that ought to go to his grandfather? Shouldn't he and Danza return home? At Danza's first show, the pressure is on. If Danza doesn't win under Paulo, he is to be turned over to a professional trainer. Paulo knows that Danza's legs aren't back to normal yet. Danza places third; another horse fancier remarks that the judges won't take seriously a horse that can be managed by a youngster. So the Major brings in Jordan Welch to train and ride Danza. Danza promptly takes two firsts, including a championship. The Major is elated, but Paulo has noticed that Danza moves as if in pain. He overhears some talk about how Welch was once blacklisted because of his illegal methods, particularly his use of "soring," putting something painful on the horses' feet to make them lift their feet snappily. Welch will not allow Paulo near Danza to verify his suspicions, but the next morning Paulo forces a confrontation before witnesses with the Major and Welch. A show official says Welch has acted illegally and that Paulo may take Danza home with him. Paulo writes to his grandfather for the money to return home. Instead, his grandfather comes to Louisiana. Since the National is only a few days away, they decide to stay for it. In a superb performance Danza wins the stallion class, but immediately afterwards he begins limping and can't go on to compete in the Championship class. Paulo and his grandfather talk, and the old man confesses his fear of losing Paulo as he lost all his sons except Paulo's father—all went to the States. They return to Puerto Rico with a new sympathy for each other.

A boy's love for a horse takes him far from his home in Puerto Rico and helps him mature and grow closer to his family. In some ways a typical horse story, this has added interest because of its Puerto Rican hero and his difficult family relationships, the details about an unusual breed of horse, and a secondary plot about admiring the wrong sort of person. Readers will find the book involving.

Ages 9-12

Also available in:
Cassette—*Danza!*
Library of Congress (NLSBPH)

Paperbound—*Danza!*
Aladdin Books

246

Hall, Lynn

The Leaving

Charles Scribner's Sons, 1980.
(116 pages)

IDENTITY, SEARCH FOR
Communication: lack of
Communication: parent-child
Decision making
Family: relationships

Roxanne Armstrong, eighteen, is moving to Des Moines to find a job, leaving behind her parents and the family's small farm in northern Iowa. She'll miss the security of the farm but feels she must prove her worth—not only to herself, but to her parents. Roxanne's mother, Thora, is quiet, withdrawn, seemingly without affection for her daughter or her husband, Clete. Clete takes no obvious interest in either wife or daughter, apparently preferring the company of his drinking buddies. Roxanne's leaving is painful and awkward for all three. Clete hopes Roxanne will hug him, but she does not, and he feels a stranger to his only child. In his mind he reviews his plan for escape from the farm and Thora: he has sold Roxanne's horse and will use the money to return to the city of Waterloo, to his former job and his friends. Thora longs to tell Roxanne how much she loves her, but she can't find the words. As the two drive to Des Moines that Thanksgiving weekend, Thora tells her daughter not to compromise, not to settle for anything less than the best for her life. Slowly Roxanne realizes that her mother's life has been nothing but compromises. "She felt suddenly as though she were a repeat of her mother, starting over again with a new life, and it was crucial that she know what mistakes to avoid." During the car ride, Thora also manages to convey her love to Roxanne, something Roxanne has never felt. Between Thanksgiving and Christmas, Roxanne finds a room and a job in Des Moines, Clete leaves Thora and the farm (he is gone when Thora returns from Des Moines), and Thora finds the first real peace she's known in thirty years. Roxanne comes home for Christmas, and she and her mother celebrate the best Christmas she can remember. That spring two friends invite Roxanne to share an apartment with them. Now the girl must decide: should she stay in Des Moines or should she return home? Roxanne decides to go home—to the farm, to the life she loves, to the mother she has come to understand only by leaving.

A girl's bid for independence provides the occasion for a shake-up of her unhappy family that leaves each member changed. Moving from the present to the past, the narrative brings the reader close to all three characters, detailing the nature of each person's dissatisfaction and search for release. Roxanne, the main character, discovers her mother's love for her and her own love for their farm life, bringing her search full circle. This is a thoughtful story of the unexpressed pain some families endure and of the inner resources people discover to lessen that pain.

Ages 12 and up

Also available in:
Paperbound—*The Leaving*
Collier Books

247

Hallman, Ruth

Breakaway

The Westminster/John Knox Press, 1981.
(92 pages, paperbound)

DEAFNESS
RUNNING AWAY
Boy-girl relationships
Love, meaning of
Maturation
Parental: overprotection
Self, attitude toward: accepting
Success
Talents: athletic

A diving accident has left seventeen-year-old Rob Cory, a talented athlete, almost totally deaf. His return to normal life is hampered by his mother, who seems unable to cope with her son's impairment and won't let him out of her sight. Rob's girlfriend, Kate, cannot bear seeing him shut out of life and insists on visiting him every day. When an angry Mrs. Cory forbids Kate to come back, Kate persuades Rob to run away with her. After she tells her parents that she's off to spend the rest of the summer with a friend, as in other years, she and Rob take a bus to a large city in another state. There they rent a room in a seedy boardinghouse in a rough neighborhood. The owner, a feisty old woman named Hattie Gogan who also runs the grocery store next door, doesn't really believe the two are brother and sister, as they claim, but she takes them in anyway after insisting there be no "hanky-panky." That first night, Hattie has a stroke and must be hospitalized. She asks Rob and Kate to look after the house during her absence, in exchange for their room and board. Besides taking on the cleaning and cooking, the two devise a course of study for Rob; he learns lipreading and some sign language. When Hattie returns, she demands to know their real story and Kate confesses all, sure now that the woman enjoys helping people in trouble. Sure enough, Hattie encourages Rob in his efforts to accept and adjust to his deafness. She even manages to get him a dog trained to assist the deaf. One day Rob comes home covered with mud. He's been plastered by some neighborhood kids after he failed to answer their calls. Spurred on by Kate, Rob goes back out and finds the boys, angrily explaining that he is deaf. In time, he begins coaching them in football and basketball, and they become special to each other. Their mutual admiration proves unexpectedly valuable when Rob and the boys subdue two robbers who hold up Hattie's grocery store and are about to take Kate hostage. As a grateful Hattie and Kate prepare a surprise dinner for the boys, Kate hears a familiar voice at the door. Rob's mother has arrived with a policeman and a judge—unknown to her, both friends of Hattie's. Rob is not yet home, and after the two law officers persuade Hattie to let Mrs. Cory in, his mother is told all about his rehabilitation. When Rob and the boys enter the yard, Mrs. Cory watches through the window as her son communicates successfully with his friends. Convinced and grateful, Mrs. Cory begins to thank Hattie, but Hattie insists she is not the one to be thanked. So Mrs. Cory thanks Kate.

An overprotective mother, both domineering and dependent, keeps a teenage boy from accepting his hearing loss and getting on with his life. The boy's determined girlfriend, a sympathetic landlady, and Rob's own will to recover help him learn the skills he needs to cope successfully with his disability. No judgment is made on Rob and Kate's decision to run away, but the successful outcome could be read as an endorsement. This story is very simply written, perhaps a bit contrived, but should be appealing to young people with limited reading skills. Especially worth notice are the descriptions of Rob as he learns to live with his deafness.

Ages 12 and up

Also available in:
No other form known

248

Hamilton, Virginia

M. C. Higgins, the Great

Macmillan Publishing Company, Inc., 1974.
(278 pages)

FRIENDSHIP: Meaning of
Anxiety
Boy-girl relationships
Hope

Thirteen-year-old Mayo Cornelius Higgins, known as M.C., lives with his family on Sarah's Mountain. He does most of his serious thinking atop a forty-foot metal pole he has erected in the backyard. His father, Jones Higgins, is unemployed, and although M.C.'s mother, Banina, works in the nearby village, food and money are scarce in their family. Jones is a superstitious man who has strong ties to Sarah's Mountain. His family has owned the mountain for four generations, and all his ancestors are buried there. The Killburn family lives on a neighboring mountain. Because the Killburns are rumored to have supernatural healing powers, and because each one of them has six fingers and toes on each hand and foot, the neighboring mountain people will not associate with them. However, M.C. has befriended young Ben Killburn, and the two boys secretly play and hunt together. This summer M.C. is worried, and he feels his family should leave the mountain. Up the slope lies a great spoil heap—a monstrous pile of trees and dirt plowed up during coal strip mining. M.C. fears that the spoil heap will wash down the mountain and destroy their home. Meanwhile, a man named James K. Lewis has come to the mountain, bringing the Higginses hope of escaping the dangerous spoil heap. He wants to record Banina's beautiful singing. M.C. is convinced that his mother will become a star and that the family will then be able to move to the city. Another visitor to Sarah's Mountain is Lurhetta Outlaw, a girl slightly older than M.C. who is spending her summer sightseeing. M.C. becomes infatuated with Lurhetta, only to be disappointed by her sudden departure. Reality strikes another blow when M.C. learns that Mr. Lewis has recorded his mother's singing only for his own enjoyment. When M.C. realizes that his family must remain on Sarah's Mountain, he starts constructing a wall to protect them from the spoil heap. For M.C., the best event of the summer is a confrontation with his father concerning the friendship with Ben Killburn. After the confrontation, the two boys are able to meet openly.

This story is set in a haunting and beautiful world of mysterious hidden paths, veiling mists, and talk of "witchies." The past has a strange hold on the mountain people, and M.C. must learn for himself how to live with superstition and his backwood heritage while coping with realities of the outside world.

Ages 12 and up

Also available in:
Braille—*M.C. Higgins, the Great*
Library of Congress (NLSBPH)

Paperbound—*M.C. Higgins, the Great*
Collier Books

Talking Book—*M.C. Higgins, the Great*
Library of Congress (NLSBPH)

249

Hamilton, Virginia

Zeely

Black/white illustrations by Symeon Shimin.
Macmillan Publishing Company, Inc., 1967.
(122 pages)

SELF, ATTITUDE TOWARD: Accepting
African-American
Ego ideal

Eleven-year-old black Elizabeth Perry and her younger brother John are spending the summer with Uncle Ross on his farm in the southern United States. During the train ride to Uncle Ross's, Elizabeth decides that this summer is going to be different from any other. To help make it different, she quickly thinks of new names for herself and John. She will be "Geeder," and John will be "Toeboy." One night while sleeping outside, Geeder sees Zeely Tayber, a very tall, beautiful black woman wearing a long white smock. Uncle Ross tells Geeder that Zeely and her father own the house near him and that they use part of his land to raise their hogs. Geeder is fascinated by the distinguished-looking woman. While tying up old magazines for Uncle Ross, Geeder finds a picture of a Watutsi queen who resembles Zeely. She tells some other children in the village that Zeely is a queen and fantasizes about her. When Zeely and her father take their prize hogs to market, they have to march them through town. Geeder is watching and rushes out to help Zeely when one of the hogs stumbles in the road. Later, Zeely thanks Geeder, and finally Geeder has a chance to talk with her idol. She learns that Zeely really is a descendant of the Watutsi and that she wears long smocks because of her height. As grand as her background is, she and her father must raise hogs for their living. Zeely tells Geeder that the most important thing that anyone can do is to accept oneself.

Elizabeth is a dreamer who is brought back to reality by Zeely, whom she respects and admires. This engrossing story includes many interesting details of black history, and the illustrations are effective.

Ages 10-12

Also available in:
Braille—*Zeely*
Library of Congress (NLSBPH)

Paperbound—*Zeely*
Aladdin Books

Talking Book—*Zeely*
Library of Congress (NLSBPH)

250

Hansen, Joyce

The Gift-Giver

Houghton Mifflin Co., 1980.
(118 pages) o.p.

AUTONOMY
FRIENDSHIP: Meaning of
African-American
Boy-girl relationships
Change: accepting
Foster home
Maturation
Parent/Parents: unemployed
Responsibility: accepting

Doris and her friends Sherman, Russell, Yellow Bird, Dotty, and Mickey are in the same fifth-grade class. They also all live on 163rd Street in The Bronx. But Doris feels less fortunate than her friends because her parents want her to avoid the playground. They're afraid of the gangs and the drug dealing. Since Doris wants to play with her friends, she occasionally gets grounded for defying her parents and going to the playground. One day in April, Amir joins their class. He is quiet and solitary, more content to observe than to take part in games. Doris is drawn to the boy and his quiet spirit, and soon a friendship develops. When Sherman runs away from the foster home he has just been placed in, Amir persuades him to return and make the best of it. Doris then discovers that not only is Amir himself now in a foster home, but that he has been in many such homes. He has also run away repeatedly, for which he spent time in reform school. After school is out for the summer, Doris, more and more curious about Amir, finally asks him how he managed to adjust to all the homes and changes he has known. Amir tells her of an old man he befriended in one home. "He said kindness always comes back to you. He told me I'd been a blessing to him. He called me the little gift-giver." Shortly thereafter, Doris's father is laid off. Her parents discuss sending Doris and her baby brother to live with separate relatives so both parents can work. Terrified at the prospect of the family breaking up, Doris begs them to give her a chance to watch Gerald and take care of the apartment. Reluctantly, her parents agree. To everyone's surprise, Doris proves to be a capable baby-sitter and a responsible housekeeper. Although in two weeks Doris's father returns to his old job and the house returns to normal, the girl feels she has proven her worth. Just before school starts in the fall, Doris learns that Amir's foster family is moving to California, and so he must go upstate to a group home. Doris will lose a good friend, but he has been a gift-giver. He has helped her understand herself and others a bit better.

A young girl growing up in a tough urban ghetto tells a poignant story of survival and friendship. The author understands her characters and their milieu and makes events come alive for the reader. The dialect adds to the story's authenticity and should present no difficulties in comprehension.

Ages 9-12

Also available in:
Cassette—The Gift-Giver
Library of Congress (NLSBPH)

251

Harris, Audrey

Why Did He Die?

Color illustrations by Susan Sallade Dalke.
Lerner Publications Co., 1965.
(28 pages) o.p.

DEATH: Attitude Toward

Scott, around six years old, wants to play with his friend Jim, but Jim cannot come out because "his Granddad passed away." When Scott asks his mother why Jim's grandfather died, she explains that he was very old and sick and could not live any longer. She also tells Scott that everything must die or cease to function someday, reminding Scott of the leaves that withered in the fall, their dog who died, and the motor that failed in Father's old car. Then Scott tells his mother of a little girl who died; she did not die because she was old. Mother explains that occasionally a child is not strong enough to live and must also die, but she assures Scott that he is strong. When Scott asks if Jim's grandfather will ever come back, Mother tells him that the man's body is dead but that the children's memories of him are still alive. Then Scott asks about burial, and mother tells him that the body is in a box in a cemetery "with plants and trees and flowers—with God."

The story, written in verse, provides answers to questions children ask when faced with death. The poetic explanations are simple, direct, and satisfying for children.

Ages 4-7

Also available in:
No other form known

252

Harris, Robie H.

I Hate Kisses

Color illustrations by Diane Paterson.
Alfred A. Knopf, Inc., 1981.
(31 pages counted) o.p.

MATURATION
Transitional objects: toys

Some sudden changes have taken place in little Peter. He decides he is now too grown up for some of the things he liked a short time ago. For one thing, he now hates kisses. He doesn't want his stuffed dinosaur, Nellie, anymore and gives her to his father, along with her baseball cap, quilt, and sweater. He'd rather play with his new robot. At dinner Peter wants to eat string beans, something he's never liked before, so his muscles will grow big. After dinner, however, Peter falls on top of his robot and hurts his knee. "Where's my Nellie?" Peter sobs. That night the dinosaur stays on Peter's pillow, and there is a goodnight hug for both his parents. Still no kisses, but Peter decides, "Maybe I'll have some . . . in the morning."

This is a charming, reassuring book for children who are trying to grow up but still need kisses and a favorite toy now and then. When Peter falls and hurts himself, he forgets for a time how big and strong he's become. Bright illustrations add to the warmth and humor of the story.

Ages 2-5

Also available in:
No other form known

253

Hartling, Peter

Oma

Translated from the German by Anthea Bell.
Black/white illustrations by Jutta Ash.
The Overlook Press, 1990.
(95 pages) o.p.

GRANDPARENT: Living in Home of
GRANDPARENT: Love for
Maturation
Orphan
Parent/Parents: substitute

Kalle, five, is orphaned by a car accident and goes to live with Oma, his 65-year-old grandmother in Munich. The first few months he stays home from school, getting to know Oma, making her rounds with her—to market, to visit friends, to the Welfare Office, where she demands the support money due her. The boy often winces at her brusque, sometimes insulting manner, but he likes her keen humor and the fact that she takes him seriously. It is mutual. Once in school, where he makes friends quickly, he must rebuke her interference in a fight, and Oma learns to let him choose both his friends and his fights. Kalle, in turn, learns to listen patiently to her oft-repeated stories, one of her favorites deriving from their vacation honoring Kalle's eighth birthday. Out walking with him, Oma had fallen into a turnip pit. Sputtering mad, she had dragged herself out, but afterward, retelling the story, she makes her escape sound more colorful than it had been, and Kalle rebukes her for lying. Oma only laughs: "When you've had a dull life as I have, you have to invent some excitement. . . . During Kalle's third year in school he gets into trouble for unfinished homework, but when the volatile Oma comes to talk with his teacher, Kalle offers deep thanks for her unexpected tact. Still, the trouble at school brings the social worker. Her questions about Oma's health and provision for the boy frighten him—and anger the grandmother. "I won't be sick!" she vows. But shortly before Kalle's tenth birthday she does fall ill and must stay in the hospital for two weeks. For her return, Kalle puts out a "Welcome" sign and hugs her for the first time, as she has always hugged him. Kalle is deeply relieved and feels his life is back to normal—but Oma reminds him, "You must learn to do without me, you know." After his birthday party, she talks frankly with him about his future and how long she expects and hopes to be a part of it. "I've made up my mind to live as long as I can," she says. "But making up your mind isn't enough, though it helps."

Orphaned at the age of five, a boy begins a new life with his loving, outspoken grandmother. She knows she does much that seems strange to the boy, but she does not attempt to stand in for his parents; instead, she makes time for them to get used to each other. They learn from each other, and grow to love and need each other. As the boy grows older and more independent they can at last discuss her inevitable death and his future. The short, diary-like comments by the grandmother following each chapter offer frank, sometimes poignant, insights into an older woman who is coping with increasing age and her grandson's strengthening youth.

Ages 8-11

Also available in:
No other form known

254

Hassler, Jon Francis

Four Miles to Pinecone

Fawcett, 1989.
(117 pages, paperbound)

CRIME/CRIMINALS
VALUES/VALUING: Moral/Ethical
Guilt, feelings of
Loyalty
Peer relationships

Tom Barry, a high school boy from St. Paul, begins his story with the words "Summer is over"; this book is the story of that astonishing summer. Tom first recalls the end of the school year, when his report card reported an F for English. He goes to see the English teacher to request a change of grade, pointing out that he has gotten all As and Bs on the tests. Mr. Singleton points out the forty-seven Fs earned on the assignments Tom has never turned in. The teacher offers one avenue to a passing grade: Tom must write a story forty-seven pages long. The drama of that summer commences the very next day, when the grocery store where Tom is working is held up, and the owner badly beaten. Tom has recognized one of the robbers as his school friend Mouse Brown. But he cannot bring himself to tell Mr. Afton, the police detective—out of loyalty to his friend and the knowledge, too, that Mouse is supporting an unemployed, suicidal father, a neurotic mother, and two little brothers. For the rest of the summer, Tom struggles with the guilt of thus protecting Mouse. He is still struggling when, over the Labor Day weekend, he journeys to the wilds near Pinecone, Minnesota, to watch his aunt and uncle's resort while they are away. Someone has been stealing boat motors from residents in the area. At the resort, Tom goes out fishing with an elderly recluse named Lester Flett, and they talk about loyalty in friendship. That night Tom sees a motor being stolen from his uncle's boat, and when he runs to get Lester he finds him storing the stolen motor in a shed full of motors. Suddenly a van drives out of nowhere and nearly runs Tom down. Hiding, he hears Lester and the driver of the van, Bruno Rock, making plans to drive all the stolen motors to Canada and sell them. Bruno wants to find Tom and kill him, but Lester says no. Heading for town to get the sheriff, Tom is overtaken by the van, and Lester and Bruno leap out. Eluding them and circling back, Tom is himself just pulling away in the van when Bruno leaps onto its roof. With Bruno stuck there, Tom drives the four miles to Pinecone and turns the case over to the sheriff. Convinced now that crime cannot be looked away from, Tom returns to St. Paul and tells Mr. Afton everything he knows about Mouse Brown. At the library, he writes the whole story for Mr. Singleton, not in forty-seven pages but in the 117 we have just finished reading.

This exciting novel captures urban life in St. Paul and life in the wilds of northern Minnesota in the words of a high school junior. But the English teacher, the grocer, Mouse Brown, Lester Flett, and Tom's father are portrayed no less warmly and memorably for that. The story stresses the working-class values of working hard, telling the truth, and getting through school. Crime—and laziness—do not pay. When, at the end, Tom explains to Mouse why he has turned him in, and Mouse spits in his face, Tom knows both that he has betrayed a friend and that he was right to do so.

Ages 10-14

Also available in:
No other form known

255

Hassler, Jon Francis

Jemmy

Fawcett, 1988.
(175 pages, paperbound)

IDENTITY, SEARCH FOR
Alcoholism: of father
Deformities
Dropout, school
Friendship: meaning of
Native American
Prejudice: ethnic/racial
Sibling: relationships
Talents: artistic

In October of Jemmy Stott's senior year, her father tells her to quit school. A house painter turned alcoholic, he wants Jemmy to keep up the house and take care of her eleven-year-old brother, Marty, and her six-year-old sister, Candy. Jemmy accepts the news calmly; most Indians in northern Minnesota don't finish high school anyway. Actually, Jemmy is a "half-breed." Her mother, dead for almost six years, was a Chippewa, and her father is white. The girl has never felt herself a full member of either race. The next day Jemmy drives to school and withdraws herself. For a change, she decides to go home by way of the forest road. A blizzard begins to rage and Jemmy's car runs out of gas. She stumbles along the road on foot until she finds a barn. Once inside she collapses from exhaustion and cold. There she is discovered by Otis Chapman. He and his wife, Ann, feed Jemmy and give her warm clothes and shelter for the night. Jemmy learns that Otis is a famous artist commissioned to paint a large mural for a building in Minneapolis. The painting is to commemorate Minnesota's Indian heritage, and Otis is in the area researching the lore about the Maiden of Eagle Rock. Studying Jemmy's features, Otis asks if he can use her as his model. Jemmy readily agrees, happy for the first time in years to be an Indian. Otis and Ann discover Jemmy's interest in sketching and buy her a sketchbook. Soon the Chapmans get to know Jemmy's family. Marty and Candy quickly adore them, but Mr. Stott avoids them, obscurely resentful of their generosity to his children. Otis and Ann give Jemmy a paint box and easel, and Otis begins teaching her to paint. When Christmas comes Mr. Stott refuses the Chapmans' invitation, preferring to take Marty into town to celebrate. When his father gets drunk, the mortified boy runs to hide in the schoolhouse. He is accidentally trapped in the unheated building and is found unconscious with frostbitten hands. Two fingers must be amputated and Marty, fearing ridicule, refuses to return to school. With the Chapmans' help, Jemmy persuades him to go back. Meanwhile, Jemmy learns from Ann that Otis himself used to be an alcoholic. Before one of his frequent trips to Minneapolis to work on his mural, Otis suggests that Jemmy's father paint his dilapidated barn. When he returns and finds that Mr. Stott has barely touched the barn, he shocks the man by calling him a no-good drunken bum. Otis finally finishes his mural and Jemmy, knowing the couple will now move from the area, can't bring herself to attend the dedication. But to her surprise she realizes that her father has become kinder towards his children, that he isn't drinking as much. He even begins scraping their house in preparation for painting. Otis Chapman's rebuke has changed him. Several days after the Minneapolis dedication, Jemmy drives in to see the mural. She is astonished at the painting's beauty and at the likeness of herself. When she recognizes the Indian brave in the mural's background as Otis, both loss and joy wash over her. She realizes that in the six months she has known the Chapmans, they have made a painter out of her and a new man out of her father. She is grateful.

Half Indian and half white, a demoralized girl is helped by generous, loving friends to discover her artistic talents, her identity as a Native American, and her individual worth. In the process she witnesses the start of a recovery for her alcoholic father and a drawing together of her family. This low-key, well-written story is distinguished by vivid descriptions of the natural and human scene and by strong characterizations.

Ages 11 and up

Also available in:
No other form known

256

Hautzig, Deborah

Second Star to the Right

Alfred A. Knopf, Inc., 1988.
(151 pages, paperbound)

ANOREXIA NERVOSA
GUILT, FEELINGS OF
SELF, ATTITUDE TOWARD: Body Concept
Family: relationships
Friendship: best friend
Hospital, going to

At fourteen, Leslie Hiller tries to feel happy about her family, her good friend Cavett French, and the girls' school she and Cavett attend. Yet deep inside she is dissatisfied, unable to resolve her guilt over her stormy relationship with her mother. She decides that if she lost ten pounds she would like herself more: "If I were thin, my life would be perfect." During Christmas vacation Leslie gets the flu and loses a few pounds. She decides that now is the time to diet and begins counting calories and doing sit-ups. Soon she is losing weight rapidly. She begins to enjoy feeling hungry. She also feels the presence inside her of a "dictator" who forbids her to eat. Her parents, afraid she is losing too much weight, insist that she eat. So Leslie does—and then induces herself to vomit. She reaches her goal of one hundred and five pounds, a loss of twenty pounds. But Leslie can't understand why she still doesn't feel thin. She decides her goal will be ninety-nine pounds. By early spring Leslie is no longer menstruating, her fingernails are blue, and she is always tired. She insists on eating dinner in her room, but instead of eating she throws the food out the window. Her parents, Cavett, and her teachers are distraught over Leslie's appearance. Existing on three curds of cottage cheese a day, she is constantly nauseated, cold, and weak. Her lips are cracked and will not heal, and her hair is falling out. Yet Leslie feels fat and unhappy. In desperation her mother takes her to a doctor who weighs her at eighty-six pounds. He tells her to eat and come back in two weeks. After a week Leslie is too weak to go to school. She returns to the doctor weighing seventy-six pounds and is placed in the hospital. There a psychologist tells Leslie she has anorexia nervosa, Latin for "nervous loss of appetite," but does little to help her. Her parents find two specialists at a different hospital, and there Leslie is befriended by two other girls with the same condition. Discovering she is not the only person in the world with the problem relieves her somewhat. She's not forced to eat, but must drink five glasses of caloric liquids a day. She also begins sessions with Dr. Wilcox, a psychiatrist, who tells her that starving will not make her unhappiness go away. With his help and the encouragement of other anorexia nervosa patients at the hospital, Leslie begins to maintain her weight and feel a little better about herself. Although her problems are not solved, she gains some insight into herself and her relationship with her mother and slowly starts coming around.

Confused about her feelings toward herself and her mother, Leslie decides her happiness will begin when she is thin. Her first-person narrative leads the reader through her long and torturous journey of near-starvation. Though her problems are left unresolved, it appears that Leslie will eventually recover from anorexia nervosa with psychiatric help. It may seem a bit unlikely that Leslie's first doctor and psychologist fail to diagnose or treat her true condition, but there is value here for siblings and peers of those with anorexia and for those curious about the illness. Written with compassion, this book deals honestly with the emotional upheaval suffered by a girl who wants to please and be good and in striving to improve almost kills herself.

Ages 12 and up

Also available in:
Braille—*Second Star to the Right*
Library of Congress (NLSBPH)

Cassette—*Second Star to the Right*
Library of Congess (NLSBPH)

257

Hautzig, Esther Rudomin

A Gift for Mama

Black/white illustrations by Donna Diamond.
Puffin Books, 1987.
(64 pages, paperbound)

GIVING, MEANING OF
Family: relationships
Love, meaning of
Resourcefulness

Sara Domin, about ten, has always followed the "family tradition" of making gifts for birthdays, Hanukkah, and other special occasions. Her artistic mother believes that the best presents are handmade. Sara, however, does not agree. With Mother's Day coming soon, she is determined to give Mama a pair of black satin slippers to wear with her new black satin robe. Since Sara does not get an allowance, she must find a way of raising the nine zlotys she needs. She decides to discuss the matter with her Aunt Margola, her mother's younger sister, a student at the university near their home in Vilna, Poland. Margola always comes to Sara's house the day after Sara's parents have given a party. She brings her friends to help eat the delicious leftovers. Since there was a party on Sunday, Margola and her friends come as expected, after classes on Monday. As Sara watches the students eat, she notices that much of their clothing needs repair. She asks Margola to find out if her friends would be willing to pay her for mending their clothes. Margola comes back a few days later with the good news that the students agree to let Sara be their "clothes doctor." For the next two weeks Sara goes straight from school to Grandmother Hanna's house to work on her secret project. As she mends, darns, and turns worn collars, she and Grandmother talk together. She learns about her mother as a child. Although Sara is not overly fond of making things, Mama always loved to paint and draw and make objects out of clay. Sara earns her money just in time to buy the slippers for Mother's Day. She is very pleased with herself as she presents the shoe box to her mother on Sunday morning. But, much to her sorrow, Mama is not very enthusiastic about her "store-bought" gift. Later in the day, however, Margola brings her friends by in their newly mended clothing. Each one shows Mama the bit of work that Sara did for them to earn money for the gift. Mama is deeply touched. She leaves the room and returns in her black satin robe and matching slippers. Sara watches happily as her mother, looking "just like a movie star," serves her guests around their dining room table.

In this gentle story of family love and understanding, a young girl comes to recognize that her mother's insistence on handmade presents stems mainly from her own artistic yearnings. Only when Mama learns that Sara earned the money for her "store-bought" slippers by mending clothing does she accept and appreciate her daughter's gift. Expressive illustrations contribute greatly to the old-country atmosphere of the book, which takes place in pre-World War II Poland.

Ages 8-12

Also available in:
No other form known

258

Hazen, Barbara Shook

Even If I Did Something Awful

Color illustrations by Nancy Kincade.
Atheneum Publishers, 1981.
(30 pages counted)

GUILT, FEELINGS OF
LOVE, MEANING OF
Discipline, meaning of

A little girl breaks the special vase that Daddy gave to Mommy for her birthday. What will Mommy do? The child asks, "Would you love me no matter what I did?" When the mother assures her that she would, the little girl persists. "Even if I did something awful?" "Like what kind of awful?" asks Mommy. The little girl imagines many things she might have done. What if she had gotten orange crayon on the carpet? Her mother answers, "I'd love you even if you crayoned the whole house. But I'd make you clean it up." "Would you love me if Mouser and I were playing rough and we pulled down the dining room curtains?" asks the girl. Says Mommy, "I'd love you even if you played so rough you pulled down the Empire State Building. But I'd make you pick it up." The game goes on with the same kind of questions and the same kind of answers until the little girl finds the courage to mention the real incident. If she broke the vase while playing ball in the living room after being told not to, would her mother still love her? Mommy, realizing that the pretending is over, still answers yes. She goes on to say that she "might be mad and yell things like 'I told you a thousand times!' and 'This is the last straw!' and 'I've had it with your disobeying!'" She might also send the little girl to her room without dessert. But then, after tears on both sides, Mommy says, "I'd still love you no matter what, no matter how mad, no matter how awful. And I always will."

A little girl who needs to confess that she has disobeyed her mother and broken a vase bolsters her courage by proposing imaginary misdeeds and asking, "Would you still love me?" Her mother counters with imaginative responses that emphasize both love and discipline. The little girl learns that even though she may make her mother unhappy or angry, and even though she may be punished, she cannot destroy the love that Mommy has for her. This message will be reassuring to young children. The illustrations enhance the fanciful quality of the dialogue.

Ages 3-6

Also available in:
No other form known

259

Hazen, Barbara Shook

If It Weren't for Benjamin (I'd Always Get to Lick the Icing Spoon)

Color illustrations by Laura Hartman.
Human Sciences Press, 1979.
(30 pages counted)

SIBLING: Rivalry
Sibling: relationships

A little boy maintains that if it weren't for Benjamin, his older brother, he'd get to lick the icing spoon, receive all the Christmas gifts, and never have to share. He wants to be bigger than Benjamin, but he never is, and Benjamin gets to do things he can't do. He realizes that Benjamin sometimes wishes he were the younger brother so he could be babied, and although the younger brother never quite catches up with Benjamin, he can do a few things Benjamin can't, such as whistle, wiggle his ears, and make up songs. Still, after thinking about what life would be like "if it weren't for Benjamin," he tells his mother it's not fair. She says it's not possible to be absolutely fair. The little boy feels slighted when his grandmother makes a fuss over Benjamin's drawing, but she explains that both boys are special to her and each is good at different things. She then asks him to make up a song for her. When his father takes Benjamin to a double-header, the smaller boy decides his father must love Benjamin more. But his father points out that he gets to go to shows and to the zoo. He asks his mother whom she loves better. She says she loves them both very much, each one for what he is. He tells his mother that he wishes sometimes for Benjamin to disappear. His mother explains that parents' love for their children is different from siblings' love for each other and that it's okay to feel the way he does, as long as there's no hitting or hurting. That night, he begins to think of all that he'd be missing "if it weren't for Benjamin": the jokes, the helping hand, the encouragement. "Funny," he muses, "how you can hate someone sometimes and other times be glad he's your brother."

A younger brother gives a first-person account of life with an older sibling: the advantages and disadvantages as well as the vain search for absolute equality and justice. The book touches on many of the feelings children have about their siblings, but it does not convey (perhaps intentionally) the clenched-teeth, urge-to-kill emotions often found in real life. The low-key, slightly pedantic tone reassures children that their feelings of doubt, resentment, even hate, are normal. The book could be used to initiate a helpful discussion on sibling rivalry. The illustrations clearly depict the emotions and activities described.

Ages 3-7

Also available in:
Paperbound—*If It Weren't for Benjamin (I'd Always Get to Lick the Icing Spoon)*
Human Sciences Press

260

Hazen, Barbara Shook

Tight Times

Black/white illustrations by Trina Schart Hyman.
Viking Penguin, 1979.
(32 pages counted)

PARENT/PARENTS: Mother Working Outside Home
PARENT/PARENTS: Unemployed

A little boy wants a dog. His working mother brushes aside the request. His father says no also because of "tight times," claiming the child is too little to understand. But after his mother goes to work, his father explains over breakfast that tight times are "the times when everything keeps going up." Tight times are the reason the family eats Mr. Bulk instead of cereal in little boxes, and why they went not to the lake but "to the sprinkler" last summer. Tight times are also why they eat soupy things with lima beans instead of roast beef on Sundays, and why a baby-sitter, rather than his mother, picks the boy up from school. One afternoon the father comes home looking angry and dismisses the sitter. He makes "special drinks" and explains to the boy that he has lost his job—it seems to the child as if something were lost behind a radiator. When his mother returns from work, she gives the child a candy bar and says she wants to talk to Daddy alone. Outside, the boy hears crying coming from a trash can. A passerby rescues a bedraggled kitten from the can. The kitten seems hungry but refuses a part of the child's candy bar, and the passerby says it wants milk. The boy takes the kitten into the kitchen and tries to give it a dish of milk, but instead spills the container. As the kitten rushes to the milk, the parents run into the kitchen. The child explains that a nice lady said he could keep the kitten. Suddenly both parents begin to cry. They make "a sandwich hug with me in the middle." Then the boy starts to cry and his father says the kitten can stay, so long as there is no more talk about wanting a dog. After dinner, while the father reads the want ads and the child rests on his thigh, kitten on chest, the father asks the kitten's name. "Dog," the child replies. He plays with the "great cat," gets tickled by chin whiskers, and hopes Dog likes lima beans.

The everyday meaning of economic hard times, parental love, and the company of pets is made clear in this compact work. The little boy who tells the story sees his parents harried and depressed, and his father explains "tight times" in comprehensible terms. The parents affirm their enduring love in a tearful hug, and the kitten—even if it isn't a dog—quickly wins the child's heart. Detailed illustrations supplement the slender but effective text.

Ages 5-7

Also available in:
Paperbound—*Tight Times*
Puffin Books

261

Hazen, Barbara Shook

Two Homes to Live In: A Child's-Eye View of Divorce

Color illustrations by Peggy Luks.
Human Sciences Press, 1978.
(40 pages counted)

DIVORCE: of Parents

Before Niki's parents' divorce, the boy had overheard their quarrels, which had frightened him. After one particularly bitter one, Niki's father had left home, but not before assuring him that the divorce would not be Niki's fault, that "grown-up problems" were the cause of his departure, that he loved Niki very much and would always be his father. Niki's mother had also assured her son that, though parents may "fall out of love," they never stop loving their children. In Niki's words, "They are divorced from each other. But not from me." Despite his anger over the divorce, Niki endeavors to accept both his homes. But he confesses to wishing that his parents would remarry. Both tell him firmly that his wish is impossible. It is then that Niki begins to dwell less on the divorce and more on the good things he does with each parent. In fact, he recognizes that he is happy and loved in both homes.

In this first-person narrative about his parents' divorce, a child struggles against taking sides, feeling walked out on, grief, and anger. The child's own language is persuasive, as is the continuing love his parents show for him and his growing sense that they are three different but connected people. Though written for young children, this book could prove useful to the older children of divorcing parents. The illustrations show an appealing, tousled child in jeans who could be a boy or girl, thus allowing easier identification by all children.

Ages 5-8

Also available in:
Paperbound—*Two Homes to Live In: A Child's-Eye View of Divorce*
Human Sciences Press

262

Head, Ann

Mr. and Mrs. Bo Jo Jones

New American Library, 1968.
(253 pages) o.p.

MARRIAGE: Teen-age
Abortion
Death: of infant
Maturation
Parental: interference
Pregnancy

Sixteen-year-old July Greher and seventeen-year-old Bo Jo Jones have eloped because July is pregnant. Both families are shocked and want the marriage annulled, but July and Bo Jo reject the suggestion. The newlyweds begin housekeeping in a garage apartment. Bo Jo does computer programming at the bank where July's father is president, while July struggles with her feelings of boredom and emptiness as a homemaker. One day, shopping for groceries, July meets eighteen-year-old Lou Consuela. They become friends. Lou, who hates children, becomes pregnant, has an abortion, and leaves her husband. In contrast, July and Bo Jo, who are not in love, try to make their marriage work because of the respect they feel for each other. Their marriage is threatened by their own doubts and by their parents when their baby, born two months prematurely, dies. Despite their parents' contention that the marriage should be dissolved now that there is no baby to consider, both July and Bo Jo are determined to make their marriage work.

July's first-person narrative illustrates that pride and respect help to build and strengthen a marriage. The problems and emotions of two young people who find themselves in a marriage they are not ready for are vividly and honestly portrayed. The couple achieve a new level of maturation which gives them the courage to accept the lasting quality of marriage.

Ages 13 and up

Also available in:
Braille—*Mr. and Mrs. Bo Jo Jones*
Library of Congress (NLSBPH)

Cassette—*Mr. and Mrs. Bo Jo Jones*
Library of Congress (NLSBPH)

263

Helmering, Doris Wild

I Have Two Families

Color illustrations by Heidi Palmer.
Abingdon Press, 1981.
(46 pages counted) o.p.

DIVORCE: of Parents
Anxiety

Eight-year-old Patty and her younger brother, Michael, have two homes. One is with their mother and a cat named Harry at 22C Park Street. The other is with their father and a dog, Pancake, at 1622A Skinker Avenue. When Patty first learned that her parents were getting a divorce, she worried about what would happen to her. Maybe she would be separated from Michael. If her mother and father could fall out of love with each other, maybe they could also stop loving her. Perhaps neither one would want her anymore. Then one day the uncertainty ended. Mom and Dad called a conference to discuss the family's future. They announced that since Dad had a job with regular hours, both children would live mainly with him. Since Mom worked for an airline and had irregular hours, they would stay with her when she was home. Now Patty and Michael have a happy life again. At their Skinker Avenue apartment they share the chores and follow a now-familiar routine. Michael goes to day care, and Patty goes to her friend Jane's house after school. As they ride home in their father's car, they play a game Patty loves called "catch-up." Each person has to tell at least two things that happened during the day. When they get home, Patty feeds the dog and sets the table while Dad makes dinner. Sometimes Michael helps by getting out the napkins. In the evening the children watch television, read books, or play Chinese Checkers. They go to bed at 8:30. Wednesdays, however, are different. Mom picks Michael up from day care and Patty from school. She takes them to their home at 22C Park. There, life is not quite the same because "every family is different, you know." At this home Patty empties the dishwasher and helps get dinner, while Michael feeds the cat and sets the table. After dinner they play cards or watch television. Sometimes Mom reads to them. As always, they go to bed at 8:30. On Thursday morning Patty gets her hair braided. If Mom doesn't have to work, she keeps Michael with her all day, making Patty a little jealous. Thursday night, the children go back to Skinker Avenue. Saturday morning, Dad takes them grocery shopping. In the afternoon they go roller skating or to a movie. On Saturday night Dad usually goes out on a date. Michael and Patty don't like this very much, but they understand that they must be "pleasant" to the person Dad is dating. Sundays are always spent with Mom. After Sunday school, they go to a movie, go bowling, or visit relatives. If Mom's schedule permits, they get to stay overnight. Life is quite agreeable for Patty and Michael. The only difference between them and most of their friends is that they are part of two families—one on Park Street and one on Skinker Avenue.

This timely first-person narrative, told by Patty, shows that children can live a normal, stable life after their parents' divorce. Patty and Michael experience all the fears and uncertainties that most children of divorce feel. Yet, because their parents are supportive and cooperative, they are able to adjust and make a new life much like the old one. The book may be reassuring for children in a similar situation, enlightening for those who need to understand what divorce means. The illustrations complement the text, which is optimistic without being sugar-coated.

Ages 6-8

Also available in:
No other form known

264

Henriod, Lorraine

Grandma's Wheelchair

Color illustrations by Christa Chevalier.
Albert Whitman & Company, 1982.
(32 pages counted)

GRANDPARENT: Love for
WHEELCHAIR, DEPENDENCE ON
Helping

Four-year-old Thomas gets dressed in the morning just as his older brother does, but when Nate goes off to kindergarten, Thomas runs down the street to Grandma's house. As soon as Thomas arrives, he and Grandma telephone to let his mother know he arrived safely. Thomas thinks his mother probably lies down for a while after she hangs up the phone; she's been getting a lot of rest lately while waiting for the new baby. His mother doesn't have much of a lap anymore for Thomas to sit in, but Grandma always has a lap because she is always sitting in a chair—a wheelchair. After Grandma reads Thomas some stories, they do her work together. He helps her make applesauce, fold the clothes, and dust. When his stuffed hippopotamus falls and spills a lot of sawdust out of a hole in its head, he gets the vacuum. It's heavy, but he and Grandma pull it into the living room. "We are strong, Grandma and me, together." Then, when they go outside to wait for Nate to come home at lunchtime, Grandma's wheelchair tire has a blowout. Thomas tries to push her, but the chair is too heavy. Grandma remembers an old wheelchair in the garage. Thomas digs it out and watches as Grandma uses her "slippery board" to change from one wheelchair to the other. When Nate comes to Grandma's house after school and tells Thomas that he has his own special seat in kindergarten and that you need to be five years old to attend, Thomas replies that he doesn't care. At Grandma's house, there's always a special seat for a four-year-old whenever he needs it.

A preschooler spends his mornings helping his wheelchair-bound grandmother in this realistic, sometimes amusing first-person account. Chores that might be too much for either one are easily done when they work together. Having a special function in Grandma's life gives Thomas a sense of pride and accomplishment that young children will find especially satisfying. Even his older brother's glowing descriptions of kindergarten do not lessen Thomas's pleasure. The warm, domestic tone is accented by drawings of homely, but appealing, characters.

Ages 3-7

Also available in:
No other form known

265

Hentoff, Nat

Does This School Have Capital Punishment?

Dell Publishing Company, Inc. (Laurel Leaf Library), 1983. (160 pages, paperbound)

SCHOOL: Classmate Relationships
VALUES/VALUING: Moral/Ethical
Age: aging
Communication: parent-child
Justice/Injustice
Marijuana
Schools, private: boys'

Sam Davidson is beginning the ninth grade as a new student at Burr Academy, one of New York's most prestigious private schools. On his first day he meets Rob Holmes, with whom he has much in common. Both boys have "inflammable" tempers and reputations for being quick with their fists. When they meet, Sam is waiting to see Mr. Monk, the headmaster. Rob rushes into the office. He has promised Mr. Monk that whenever he is "seized with an overwhelming urge to strike someone," he will come to see him first. The person he wants to hit is Jeremiah Saddlefield, a very unpopular student who has destroyed a rare book of American Indian history given to Rob by his father. But Jeremiah has his defenders on the faculty. Mrs. Wolf, who has a "thing about misfits," spends a lot of time with Jeremiah and other "castoffs" who need help. As a teacher, Mrs. Wolf has a reputation for being tough. She gives her students difficult assignments, like the one in Oral History to interview and write a report about the life and times of some person over sixty—not a relative. At his father's suggestion, Sam decides to study Major Kelley, a renowned jazz trumpeter. Sam, who plays the trumpet himself, begins to attend Kelley's performances and is able to "open himself to the music." Appreciating this, Major Kelley allows Sam an inside look at his world. He teaches him about jazz and shares his personal philosophy of life. Meanwhile, Rob's troubles with Jeremiah intensify when Jeremiah frames both Sam and Rob for possessing marijuana. He throws one of his own butts on the floor, the two boys pick it up to throw it away, and they are intercepted by Mr. Levine-Griffin, director of the high school, who won't believe their explanation. When Sam tells Major Kelley of the frame-up and the possibility of their expulsion, Kelley goes to a friend who works for Jeremiah's father and finds out that Jeremiah has had emotional problems requiring psychiatric counseling. With this information Major Kelley decides that the best way to help Sam and Rob is to help Jeremiah. So when he comes to Mrs. Wolf's class with Sam, he pays special attention to Jeremiah, inviting him to his performances. Sam feels betrayed and angry, but Kelley wants to help Jeremiah take that "terrible weight off his soul" and confess. Jeremiah does come and hear the jazz musicians play, and their music seems to awaken something in him "from a long, long sleep." But when they stop, he feels alone again. He manages to tell Major Kelley about the frame-up, but explains that if his father finds out he will cut him out of his life. Mr. Saddlefield, a powerful newspaperman with a reputation for ruthlessness, has many enemies and would never allow Jeremiah's pranks to fuel their fires. Major Kelley suggests that if his father is really that bad, Jeremiah needn't care what he thinks. So Jeremiah tells his father—who respects his son for having the backbone to confess. When he tells the truth to Mr. Monk, the headmaster decides to be lenient. He suspends Jeremiah for the rest of the year, but will allow him to make a "new beginning" in the fall. Jeremiah also volunteers and is required to apologize publicly to Rob and Sam. A grateful Sam realizes that somehow his "fairy godfather" has set him, as well as Jeremiah, free.

Boys at a private school are changed for the better by a famous jazz trumpeter, a man as "sharp and clean" as his music. A delightful sequel to an earlier story about Sam Davidson, *This School Is Driving Me Crazy,* the story beautifully captures both life in the world of professional jazz and life in a boys' private academy. The development of the relationship between Sam and the elderly Major Kelley adds humor and poignancy. Readers will revel in the story and emerge with food for thought.

Ages 11 and up

Also available in:
No other form known

266

Hentoff, Nat

This School Is Driving Me Crazy

Dell Publishing Company, Inc. (Laurel Leaf Library), 1978. (154 pages, paperbound)

COMMUNICATION: Parent-Child
Discipline, meaning of
Promise, keeping
School: negative experiences
Schools, private: boys'

Twelve-year-old Sam Davidson goes to Bronson Alcott School, where his father is headmaster. Sam wants his father to treat him like a son, but Mr. Davidson, busy and professional, treats Sam like any other student. The boy wants to transfer to another school, where he could be just that, but his father won't let him. At Alcott, Sam's pranks and jokes earn him a reputation as a troublemaker. His mother thinks he is trying to attract his father's attention, but Mr. Davidson thinks Sam likes to make trouble. That reputation makes Sam a suspect when thefts break out at school. Tim Rawlins, a classmate, confesses to Sam that he is forced to steal by three bullying tenth graders. Fearing he will be beaten up if this gets out, Tim makes Sam promise not to tell. When Tim is then caught stealing, the tenth graders force him to tell Mr. Davidson that Sam is behind the thefts. His father confronts Sam with the accusation, but he denies it and refuses to explain: "I made a promise not to tell *anybody.*" They argue and Sam runs from the office. He convinces Tim to come with him the following morning to tell the headmaster the truth. While the boys are talking to Mr. Davidson, two of Sam's friends find another student who was forced to steal and bring him to the meeting. The older boys are expelled. Later, Mr. Davidson assures Sam that he has faith in him and never believed the accusation.

Sam is a bright, energetic, and rebellious boy. He yearns to be closer to his father, but Mr. Davidson gives little time to him outside of school and little attention inside. After the run of thefts, Mr. Davidson begins to treat Sam as a son, not simply another student. The dialogue includes profanity.

Ages 11-15

Also available in:
No other form known

267

Herman, Charlotte

Our Snowman Had Olive Eyes

Puffin Books, 1989.
(103 pages, paperbound)

AGE: Aging
GRANDPARENT: Living in Child's Home
GRANDPARENT: Love for
Maturation

Ten-year-old Sheila has misgivings about her elderly grandmother, Bubbie, moving into their apartment. She likes Bubbie and has enjoyed many overnight visits at Bubbie's apartment—but giving up half of her room, even for someone she loves, is another matter. Besides, her best friend, Rita, warns that even the most loving grandmothers, once moved in, turn into witches. Happily, Bubbie proves a pleasure to have around: she bakes wonderful cookies and shows Sheila how to take cuttings from plants. She likes Bach, Sheila's favorite composer, and they share secrets—including Sheila's peeking at her sister's private journal. No, it is the grandmother who is dissatisfied—bored with only sleeping, eating, and being scolded hy her daughter for overdoing. One night Sheila hears her crying. She tells her mother, who then invites Rita's grandmother, Mrs. Plumb, for lunch—company Bubbie's own age. Bubbie dislikes Mrs. Plumb but takes to pretending to go to lunch with her every day just to get out of the house. She really visits an elderly antique-shop owner for long talks and the exquisite lunches he cooks. When Sheila follows Bubbie one day and discovers her secret, it becomes one more the two can share. Sheila's mother, in her turn, finds out, and is so delighted at Bubbie's new friendship that she invites Julius to dinner. But her nerves over cooking for a gourmet prompt Sheila to call on him and ask what he likes. For good measure, she assures Julius that, married to Bubbie, he need not worry about money: their family will gladly help out. That evening the eagerly awaited Julius never comes. Bubbie goes to see what has happened and returns, shocked at his believing that she wants to get married. Sheila is crushed. But Bubbie says Julius was no great friend if he would not even bother to ask if what Sheila had said was true. Deprived of her daily outing and hopelessly bored, Bubbie decides to go live with her son. Sheila considers running off too, but realizes that Bubbie has to live her own life. To expect her to stay forever would be selfish. Before Bubbie leaves, she gives Sheila a new diary for her very own—and shows her a hiding place for it.

Sheila and her grandmother understand each other. Unlike her mother, the girl has no preconceptions about aging and thinks of Bubbie as a friend, not an old person who must be coddled. But as a friend herself, Sheila has to understand that what is fine for her is not necessarily adequate for Bubbie. Sheila tells this story.

Ages 9-11

Also available in:
No other form known

268

Hermes, Patricia

Nobody's Fault

Dell Publishing Company, Inc., 1983.
(107 pages) o.p.

DEATH: of Sibling
GUILT, FEELINGS OF
Reality, escaping

Emily Taylor doesn't like her older brother's teasing, especially when he makes fun of her ability to play baseball. Emily dreams about being the first woman in the major leagues, but Matthew (Emily calls him Monse, short for Monster) knows she is afraid of the ball and insists she will never make it. He also deliberately causes trouble between her and her best friend, Mary Elizabeth, and Emily decides she must get even. Knowing he is afraid of snakes, she decides to find a dead one and put it in his bed. While she is busily carrying out her plan, Monse is cutting the grass in the backyard with the riding mower—despite Emily's reminding him of their father's rule that neither child may use the mower unless an adult is around. On this morning both parents have gone to work and Millie, the housekeeper, has not yet arrived. But Monse is anxious to finish his job so he can go to baseball practice. When Emily returns to the kitchen, she notices that the mower sounds a bit strange. Then she sees it, riderless, pushing against the stone wall in the back field. She runs outside and finds her brother lying in the grass with blood all over him. Frantically she tries to get him up, but can't. She runs inside and calls the emergency number, bringing the police and ambulance. Monse is rushed away and it is only later that her parents tell Emily what they think happened. Monse apparently had hit a wasps' nest and had fallen or jumped off the mower to escape the attacking insects. The mower ran over him, and he has bled to death. Emily's responsibility for this tragedy comes over her in a flash; if she hadn't been hiding the snake in Monse's bed, she would have heard his cries and been able to save him. The enormity of her guilt overwhelms the girl and her mind begins to shut out reality. She writes in her diary that Monse is hurt and will be in the hospital for a while. She becomes physically ill and can't even leave her bed to attend the funeral. She stops eating and spends most of her time sleeping. When the family doctor comes to see Emily, she suggests that the girl is "coping with something she hasn't told anyone about" and should get psychiatric help. Emily then begins to see Dr. Weintraub, an older man with a small, friendly voice and penetrating eyes. One day Emily hears the sound of air drills on the street below his office and is reminded of the noise the mower made. Frightened, she begins to confide in the doctor but then stops. He gently explains that she can't run away from her thoughts indefinitely. Even sleeping can't keep the pain away forever. Realizing he is right, Emily tells the doctor what has been tormenting her. Dr. Weintraub asks her to consider what might have happened if her father had not told Monse to cut the grass before going to practice that day, or if her mother had stayed home until the housekeeper came. Perhaps Millie could have skipped her hair appointment that morning and not been late. Emily finds herself responding automatically, "It's nobody's fault! . . . Accidents happen." Surprised by her own words, she quickly realizes that they apply to her as well. Finally able to acknowledge Monse's death and to face her grief, she visits the cemetery to say goodbye. Then, wearing her brother's baseball hat, she is ready to play baseball again, to talk to Mary Elizabeth again, to get on with her life.

Like most siblings, Emily and Monse have a complicated relationship—part love, part rivalry. After Monse's death, Emily poignantly describes her emotional journey from guilt and denial to acceptance and honest grief. Neither gory nor maudlin, the story has a realism that will attract readers who have struggled with their own feelings of guilt or who have observed others in mourning.

Ages 10-12

Also available in:
No other form known

269

Hermes, Patricia

What If They Knew?

Dell Publishing Company, Inc. (Yearling Books), 1981. (128 pages, paperbound)

EPILEPSY
FRIENDSHIP: Meaning of
Grandparent: living in home of
School: transfer
Secret, keeping
Self, attitude toward: feeling different

Jeremy Marin, age ten, is enjoying her summer in Brooklyn with her grandparents until she learns she will be attending school there while her parents remain in England on business. She is very much afraid that everyone will discover her well-kept secret: Jeremy has epilepsy. Before getting the news about school, she had been having a better summer than she ever anticipated and has also made some good friends—notably, twins Mimi and Libby. Then there is Carrie, another classmate, small in size but an awfully big pain to Jeremy. The girls' summer adventures have included exploring a sewer filled with rats and playing tricks on Carrie. Before school starts, Mimi shows Jeremy a notebook in which she has written characteristics or peculiarities of all the kids in the class. Jeremy does not want her friends and classmates to think her odd because of her epilepsy. Her grandparents find it difficult to discuss her condition, but Jeremy decides to talk over her fears with Grandpa and feels much better afterwards. He reassures her; she hasn't had a seizure all summer, which shows that her daily medication is effective. Grandpa also tells her that if she should have a seizure, "you'll cope just fine." School begins well for Jeremy. After several weeks, the girls in the class get together to plan their revenge on Carrie for all the nasty things she's done recently. One of Carrie's misdeeds involved Jeremy. After finding one of Jeremy's anti-seizure pills, Carrie has started the rumor that Jeremy is on drugs. In revenge, the girls decide to put dead mice in Carrie's desk and in the folder containing her speech for Parents' Night. Two days before Parents' Night, Jeremy has several spells of not feeling well, and later that day she has a seizure at school. She has been careless about taking her medicine. Mimi and Libby are concerned and very supportive, but Carrie decides everyone should know about Jeremy's "fit" and proceeds to spread the word. The day of Parents' Night, Carrie finds the mice and runs screaming from the building, yelling that she will not give her speech to the parents that evening as planned. Miss Tuller, the principal, asks Jeremy to give the address about friendship instead. Overcoming her nervousness, Jeremy speaks very personally: "A friend doesn't really care if you're—different in some ways." Seeing Carrie in the audience, Jeremy finds herself including something she had not planned: "And a friend can be—a friend can even be—somebody who's mean to you sometimes."

A young girl with epilepsy hates to be different from her classmates and so tries to keep her condition a secret. But in the process, as Jeremy's first-person narrative describes humorously and believably, she learns quite a bit about the highs and lows of friendship. Finding friends who are supportive and accepting of her epilepsy leads Jeremy to be more tolerant and forgiving herself. The author has epilepsy, and the book provides insight into this often-misunderstood condition.

Ages 9-11

Also available in:
No other form known

270

Hermes, Patricia

You Shouldn't Have to Say Good-bye

Harcourt Brace Jovanovich, Inc., 1982.
(117 pages)

DEATH: of Mother
ILLNESSES: Terminal
Cancer
Death: attitude toward
Family: unity
Fear: of open or public places
Loss: feelings of

When thirteen-year-old Sarah Morrow learns early in the school year that her mother is dying of melanoma, a particularly virulent form of cancer, Sarah's first reaction is anger; her mother had postponed seeing a doctor, although she hadn't felt well. When her mother gets home from the hospital, she teaches Sarah how to do the laundry, explaining that she'd been thinking of all the things Sarah needs to know how to do for herself from now on. Sarah tries to ignore what her mother is saying, although her mother pleads with her to face the truth. When she talks about all the good books she wanted to give Sarah and now won't be able to, Sarah finds herself hating her mother for dying. She finally cries, with her mother holding her. They go to a bookstore where her mother buys several books for Sarah to read in the future. Sarah tells herself she'll never read these "getting-ready-to-die books" and hides them in the back of her bookcase. The Saturday before Christmas, Sarah and her parents have a Christmas party for all their friends. Sarah's mother is very happy. But the next day her arms and legs hurt, and her skin has a yellowish tinge. When Sarah comes home from school Monday, nobody is there. She calls her father's office and suspects from his colleague's evasive answers that her mother has been rushed to the hospital. Trying to avoid thinking, she returns to school. But the building is locked, so Sarah goes over to her friend Robin's house, although nobody ever visits Robin at home. Sarah always knew Robin's mother was somehow different, but Robin never talked about it. Today, however, when Sarah asks why her mother looks frightened, Robin explains that her mother has agoraphobia. She appears to be getting a little better, and Robin hopes she will attend their big gymnastics show that evening. Robin, who often does daredevil stunts, is toying with the idea of adding a forbidden, dangerous move to her routine. Before the show, Sarah thinks that since her parents probably won't be there, she could jump off the high bar onto the trampoline, something she's never done and her coach certainly wouldn't allow. But once the girls start their performance, they see their parents in the audience and abandon the dangerous stunts. Sarah's mother is weak, she needs help to get in the house, but she is home. The next day, Christmas Eve morning, she asks Sarah what she was planning to do during her gymnastics act; she had noticed her hesitation at the end. After Sarah tells her, her mother says people often do dangerous things to avoid facing threats from inside. She asks Sarah not to take that way out. Christmas at the Morrow house has its old and loved rituals. So Sarah is very upset when her parents want to open gifts on Christmas Eve afternoon instead of on Christmas morning as they've always done. Her mother is sitting rigidly, seeming to hold tightly onto something. Sarah shouts that they never do things this way and she doesn't like it. But with encouragement she agrees and goes to get her presents for her parents. Before they can be opened, Sarah's mother holds out her hands to Sarah, her eyes pleading, and dies. Sarah screams and screams; then she runs to her room where she is still crying when her father comes to find her. She asks him what her mother wanted from her at the end. He says she just wanted to live, to see Sarah grow up, but of course no one could give her that. Sarah goes to say goodbye to her mother before her body is taken away. Her mother has left Sarah a book. She wrote in it constantly after she learned she was dying, all the things she wanted to tell Sarah. Sarah reads this frequently in the months following her mother's death. Part of it makes her happy; some of it makes her sad. The most comforting lines are the very last ones her mother wrote to her: "Don't let anybody tell you differently. What we're going through stinks. It just plain stinks."

In this moving, first-person story of death and loss, a young girl experiences anger, denial, avoidance, and other wrenching emotions as she does her best to come to terms with her mother's dying. Although few people will be able to read the book with dry eyes, the story is not maudlin or melodramatic. The characters and their emotions seem authentic, and there is a strong emphasis on people's strength and ability to survive even the cruelest of blows. Sarah's father is willing to assume a larger role in her life and is able to share her grief. Also distinctive is the close relationship between mother and daughter and the ways the parents themselves deal with terminal illness and impending death. Readers will remember this sad but basically hopeful book for a long time.

Ages 10-13

Also available in:
No other form known

271

Hill, Elizabeth Starr

Evan's Corner

Color illustrations by Nancy Grossman.
Viking Penguin, 1990.
(46 pages counted)

PRIVACY, NEED FOR
Resourcefulness

Young Evan longs for a place of his own, but since he lives with his parents, three sisters, and two brothers in a two-room apartment, privacy is a luxury. Evan's mother, however, believes she has the perfect solution: she gives each person in the family a corner. Evan gets first choice and selects the corner with a small window and a bit of polished floor. Evan eats in his corner and draws a picture to hang on the wall. He even makes furniture for his place. He earns money by offering to carry heavy grocery bags for shoppers, and with his earnings he buys a pet turtle for his private spot. He places a plant in his window, and it thrives and grows tall. But even though he can do whatever he likes there, Evan sometimes gets lonely in his corner. He still is not happy. Evan asks his brothers and sisters what else he needs in his corner, but they do not know. When his mother comes home from work, she has the answer: she tells Evan that he needs to get out of his corner and help somebody else. With that advice in mind, Evan finds happiness by helping his younger brother Adam decorate his corner. Evan makes Adam happy too.

This story, set in Harlem, features a warm and loving black family. The little boy's desire for privacy and his mother's sympathetic understanding are portrayed well. Although there is a father in the home, his role in the story is minor.

Ages 6-9

Also available in:
Talking Book—*Evan's Corner*
Library of Congress (NLSBPH)

272

Hill, Margaret

Turn the Page, Wendy

Abingdon Press, 1981.
(176 pages) o.p.

ABANDONMENT
RUNNING AWAY
Belonging
Child abuse
Children's home, living in
Emotions: accepting
Foster home
Guilt, feelings of
School: truancy

At sixteen, after a year in a mental health center and six years at a children's home, Wendy Carmichael has been living in Virginia Hall for two years. Dr. Elizabeth Blair, Virginia Hall's superintendent, tells Wendy a foster family wants her and she will spend the weekend with them. The Abbenoth family is kind to her, but Wendy doesn't just want a family: she wants her family. In fact, she hates all families because they're not hers. She also hates the father who never claimed her and the mother who gave her away "to the nightmare couple" who called themselves her foster parents. She thinks about baby Joel who died. Son of her foster parents, he was always hungry and feeble. She used to scavenge food for him. One day, during a school trip to a writing workshop at the high school in Tyler, a nearby college town, Wendy sees a woman who greatly resembles her. Telling her bus driver that she'll return home on the other bus, Wendy slips away to find the woman she thinks may be her mother. She eventually loses sight of her and spends the night in an unlocked car. The next day she finds an old, abandoned boarding school and moves in. Afraid that Virginia Hall will set the police on her trail, Wendy goes to the local high school to lose herself among other teenagers. She remembers that when she was sent to the office to get some papers for the workshop, she overheard discussion about a file on Kim Coverly, a girl who was to attend the school but never showed up. On an impulse, Wendy presents herself as Kim Coverly. She's given the file and told to go to the guidance counselor's office. On the way, Wendy reads the file and learns that Kim is an excellent student who wants to be a clinical psychologist. The counselor, Mr. Platner, looks at her suspiciously, but does not challenge her. He invites her to be part of a special group of students who are working with children having difficulty adjusting to school. He thinks that "Kim," with her interest in psychology, will enjoy the group. When she meets with this special group, Mr. Platner tells Wendy that "her" child is an eight-year-old named Jane who won't speak to anyone. The next day, he lends her a copy of *Throwaway Children,* a book about abused children, and the last period of that day she meets Jane. That night she reads the book and realizes she and Joel were not the only children in the world subject to abuse and neglect. She barely gets through the next school day; both her math and physics teachers are surprised when she fails fairly simple tests. So Wendy decides to leave the school the next day, telling the office that her family is moving. Then she calls Virginia Hall to tell them she's coming back and is surprised when they don't seem either worried about her or particularly glad that she's returning. It seems the Tyler police called them at the beginning of the week. Wendy was "allowed" to stay there while the police and some school staff kept an eye on her. When she gets back to Virginia Hall, she has a rude awakening. She's told they may not be able to keep her because of her truancy, lying (to the bus driver), and lack of any respect or concern for those who care about her. Although she protests she didn't really run away, Dr. Blair condemns her for her years of self-pity, excuses, and impulsive behavior. Wendy tries to explain her actions, but Dr. Blair points out that good intentions are not sufficient. When Wendy mentions Joel, as she so often does, Dr. Blair insists that she finally bring that whole story into the daylight where it can't continue to haunt her. Wendy confesses that she had found a carton of milk the day Joel died. On her way to take it to him, she had drunk it all herself. Ever since, she has been obsessed by guilt, sure Joel would have lived had he gotten that milk. Dr. Blair has Wendy read a poem that the girl herself wrote about Joel; she realizes from her own words that Joel would have died anyway. As they talk, Wendy notes how seldom she has recognized or shared her emotions. The Abbenoth family wants to talk to Wendy again, even though they are disappointed in her. After she explains some of her feelings and actions, they decide having Wendy in their family would be good for all of them.

Abandoned by her parents, left with abusive foster parents, Wendy is a girl of impulsive actions and repressed emotions. A fruitless search for her birth mother leads to her discovery that she has herself abandoned people who care about her. Wendy learns that she need not always be rootless; she can make her own roots. This is a poignant, realistic story about the universal need to belong to someone. The session with the perceptive Dr. Blair is especially well done.

Ages 10-14

Also available in:
No other form known

273

Hinton, Susan E.

The Outsiders

Viking Penguin, 1967.
(188 pages)

DELINQUENCY, JUVENILE
IDENTIFICATION WITH OTHERS: Peers
Aggression: active
Death: of friend
Death: murder
Gangs: conflict between
Prejudice: social class
Sibling: love for

Ponyboy, fourteen, Sodapop, seventeen, and Darry, twenty, are brothers living alone, with court permission, after the death of their parents. They and their friends Johnny, Dallas, Two-Bit, and Steve are known as "greasers" who live in the poor section of town. They are in constant conflict with a group of wealthy teen-agers called Socs (short for Socials). Late one evening, after Ponyboy has an argument with Darry about discipline, he and Johnny go for a walk in the park. They are jumped by five Socs, who hold Ponyboy's head underwater, almost drowning him. Johnny, frightened beyond reason, draws a recently purchased knife and kills one of the attackers. Afraid of being arrested, the two boys get help and money from Dallas, who tells them to hop a freight train to a small town and hide in a deserted church there. After the boys have hidden in the church for five days, Dallas comes to check on them and takes them to lunch. Johnny decides to turn himself in, and they return to the church to pick up their belongings. Arriving at the church, they see a group of picnickers huddled around the burning building and are told that five children are trapped inside. Ponyboy and Johnny, thinking one of their cigarettes may have started the fire, rush in and save the children by passing them through a window. Ponyboy scrambles out the window with his jacket in flames and then faints. While climbing out the window, Johnny is struck on the back by a falling beam. Dallas pulls him to safety, but Johnny's back is broken and he has been seriously burned. Back in town, events move rapidly for Ponyboy. A court hearing is scheduled to investigate the death in the park, and Johnny dies of the injuries received in the fire. Dallas, grief-stricken by Johnny's death and wanting to die himself, robs a store, threatens the police with an unloaded gun, and is killed while his friends watch in stunned silence. At the hearing, it is determined that Ponyboy killed his attacker in self-defense. Things return to normal, but Ponyboy realizes that he, like his brothers, wants to better his life.

Detailed characterizations add to this starkly realistic, first-person narrative. Envy and hate on the part of the poor teens are manifested in active aggression, and grief over the death of a friend also spawns violence. The reader easily senses the closeness and companionship between the youths and recognizes that the tough exterior they display is a front to hide other feelings.

Ages 12 and up

Also available in:
Braille—*The Outsiders*
Library of Congress (NLSBPH)

Cassette—*The Outsiders*
Library of Congress (NLSBPH)

Paperbound—*The Outsiders*
Bantam Books

Paperbound—*The Outsiders*
Dell Publishing Company, Inc. (Laurel Leaf Library)

Paperbound—*The Outsiders*
Doubleday

Talking Book—*The Outsiders*
Library of Congress (NLSBPH)

274

Hinton, Susan E.

Rumble Fish

Delacorte Press, 1975.
(122 pages)

IMITATION
Alcoholism: of father
Deprivation, emotional
Gangs: membership in
Loneliness
Sibling: younger

Rusty-James, a young adolescent, wants to be exactly like his older brother, Motorcycle Boy, leader of a street gang before the gangs were wiped out by narcotics. The toughest "cat" in the neighborhood, Motorcycle Boy is a combination of "Robin Hood, Jesse James, and the Pied Piper," feared or admired by everyone. But the younger brother never uses his head, and is always in trouble for stealing or drinking or fighting. True, he resembles his brother physically, but there is something more than thinking things through that sets the older boy apart. "People looked at him," Rusty-James tells us, "and stopped and looked again. He looked like a panther or something. Me, I just looked like a tough kid, too big for my age." The boys' alcoholic father, a one-time lawyer, talks to the older boy in sober moments—long discussions that Rusty-James cannot follow. He wishes they would "talk normal." About the gang days which Rusty-James yearns for, Motorcycle Boy says things like: "Apparently it is essential to some people to belong—anywhere." He understands that people will follow him. What bothers him is that he cannot think of anywhere to go. Rusty-James knows what he wants, but it does him no good. When a sly former friend steals Rusty-James's girlfriend, it looks as if the younger boy has lost what little respect he has ever had. He can think of nothing to do but continue to follow Motorcycle Boy around, hoping the secret of his success will rub off. One night the two break into a pet shop, but to Rusty-James's amazement, instead of rifling the cash register, his brother turns all the animals loose. Motorcycle Boy is trying to reach the river to liberate a bowl full of Siamese fighting fish when he is shot dead by a police officer. Rusty-James spends five years in a reformatory.

This story is told in flashback in Rusty-James's first person, after the boy has left the reformatory. It is a realistic but depressing story of two young losers, whose lives, if stark, bleak, and often violent, are memorable, and provide many openings for discussion.

Ages 12 and up

Also available in:
Braille—*Rumble Fish*
Library of Congress (NLSBPH)

Paperbound—*Rumble Fish*
Dell Publishing Company, Inc. (Laurel Leaf Library)

Talking Book—*Rumble Fish*
Library of Congress (NLSBPH)

275

Hinton, Susan E.

That Was Then, This Is Now

Viking Penguin, 1971.
(159 pages)

FRIENDSHIP: Best Friend
Boy-girl relationships: dating
Delinquency, juvenile
Drugs
Ghetto
Maturation
Orphan

Sixteen-year-old Mark has lived with Bryon and his mom in the inner city ever since Mark's parents shot each other to death during a quarrel. The two boys are like brothers: they have grown up learning to smoke together, play pool together, and street fight together. Although Mark still hot-wires cars and sets up pool games so that Bryon can hustle a little money in Charlie's bar, things are beginning to change for Bryon. His interest in Cathy is different from his interest in the other girls he's dated; he no longer likes to beat up guys just for fun; and he even gets a job in a supermarket. But more than that, he's beginning to think responsibly about his actions. When Charlie the bartender is shot and killed defending the two boys in an alley fight, Mark shrugs the incident off and calls it fate, but Bryon is shaken. The boys gradually spend less time together, and Bryon begins to see more of Cathy. He is concerned about "M & M," Cathy's thirteen-year-old brother who has run away to live with a group of hippies. He and Cathy search for the youngster. The night they finally find him, he is hallucinating on a bad LSD trip. The two become very upset seeing the thirteen-year-old in such a state. When Bryon goes home that night, he finds a container of drugs under Mark's mattress and realizes immediately the source of Mark's recent increase in income—Mark is a pusher. Shocked by this discovery, Bryon calls the police. Mark is arrested, tried, and sentenced to five years in prison. When Bryon is finally able to see him, Mark tells Bryon he hates him.

Told from Bryon's viewpoint, this contemporary first-person narrative captures the atmosphere of violence and the general sense of justice in a society that demands retribution at any cost. The scenes portrayed are often harsh and ugly. Although the conclusion of the story offers no solution to the problem of delinquency, the book as a whole treats this problem honestly. Most teen-agers will readily identify with the people portrayed. The author has included the background and some of the characters from her first book, *The Outsiders.*

Ages 12 and up

Also available in:
Cassette—*That Was Then, This Is Now*
Library of Congress (NLSBPH)

Paperbound—*That Was Then, This Is Now*
Bantam Books

Paperbound—*That Was Then, This Is Now*
Dell Publishing Company, Inc. (Laurel Leaf Library)

Paperbound—*That Was Then, This Is Now*
Doubleday

Talking Book—*That Was Then, This Is Now*
Library of Congress (NLSBPH)

276

Hoban, Lillian Aberman

Arthur's Funny Money

Color illustrations by the author.
HarperCollins Publishers, Inc., 1981.
(64 pages)

MONEY: Earning
PERSEVERANCE
Cooperation: in work
Goals
Resourcefulness
Sibling: relationships

Arthur, a young chimp, needs five dollars so he can buy a special cap and a T-shirt with the name of his team, "Far Out Frisbees," printed on it. He and his younger sister, Violet, decide to have a bike wash so that Arthur can earn the money. They buy soap and scouring pads and set up shop, with Violet, who needs to practice her arithmetic, keeping track of all expenditures and earnings. Things do not go as planned, however. Arthur is charging twenty-five cents per bike, but Norman and his brother want him to wash both a bike and a trike for forty-two cents. Wilma, Peter, and John need a wagon, a scooter, and a skateboard washed, and Arthur is willing to do the jobs until it becomes clear that they expect to receive his services free of charge. Disgusted, Arthur announces that he'll wash bikes only and for exactly twenty-five cents apiece. Then he and Violet run out of soap. They return to the store, only to find that the price has gone up since they were there in the morning. So they decide to look elsewhere for soap. Passing the general store, Violet notices a sign advertising the window-sample "Far Out Frisbees" shirt and cap at a special price. The saleswoman adds the figures on Violet's piece of paper and tells Arthur that he has more than enough to buy the items at the reduced price of $4.25. With the eighteen cents change, sister and brother buy licorice, dividing the five pieces of candy evenly.

This story shows the value of cooperation and the ins and outs of earning and saving money—humorously and not didactically. Arthur, who "knows numbers," discovers the many complicated and frustrating aspects of running a business. His sister proves an alert and able assistant, and she gets some needed practice with her arithmetic. This "I Can Read" book with its colorful illustrations will challenge young readers to solve some of Arthur's and Violet's arithmetic problems on their own.

Ages 6-8

Also available in:
Cassette—*Arthur's Funny Money*
Library of Congress (NLSBPH)

Paperbound—*Arthur's Funny Money*
HarperCollins Publishers, Inc.

277

Hoban, Lillian Aberman

Arthur's Pen Pal

Color illustrations by the author.
HarperCollins Publishers, Inc., 1976.
(64 pages)

SIBLING: Older
Prejudice: sexual

Instead of having the younger sister he has, Arthur, a chimpanzee, would prefer a younger brother—in particular, Sandy, his pen pal. Arthur does not like his sister Violet's complaining and the fact that she is able to best him at jumping rope. He is sure that Sandy, who is learning karate and plays the drums, would be much more chipper and fun. But when Sandy sends him a photograph showing that she is a girl, Arthur decides that Violet is a more suitable sister. After all, Violet cannot beat Arthur at wrestling as Sandy can her brother.

This book, written for the beginning reader, makes no bones about the dissatisfaction a brother can feel with a younger sister. Though it is not emphasized, sexual prejudice is evident in Arthur's assuming that only boys learn karate and play drums.

Ages 4-7

Also available in:
Braille—*Arthur's Pen Pal*
Library of Congress (NLSBPH)

Cassette—*Arthur's Pen Pal*
Library of Congress (NLSBPH)

Paperbound—*Arthur's Pen Pal*
HarperCollins Publishers, Inc.

278

Hoban, Russell Conwell

A Baby Sister for Frances

Color pictures by Lillian Aberman Hoban.
HarperCollins Publishers, Inc., 1964.
(31 pages counted)

SIBLING: New Baby
Running away
Sibling: jealousy

Frances is a little badger who feels slighted because she thinks her new baby sister Gloria is getting more than her fair share of attention. So Frances packs her knapsack and runs away, hiding under the dining-room table. When she overhears her parents talk about how much they miss her and how Frances and her baby sister are both important, each in her own special way, the runaway returns.

This entertaining story offers a rather shallow solution to a familiar problem. Since it portrays a mild case of jealousy within a loving and understanding family, the story would be appropriate for situations not involving intense sibling rivalry.

Ages 3-7

Also available in:
Paperbound—*A Baby Sister for Frances*
HarperCollins Publishers, Inc.

Talking Book—*A Baby Sister for Frances*
Library of Congress (NLSBPH)

279

Hoban, Russell Conwell

Bedtime for Frances

Black/white illustrations by Garth Williams.
HarperCollins Publishers, Inc., 1960.
(28 pages)

BEDTIME
Fear: of darkness
Imagination

It is bedtime for Frances, a little badger. She tries to postpone it with a glass of milk, a piggyback ride, more good night kisses, extra toys in bed, and by opening the closed bedroom door, but she is not successful. Because she can't sleep, Frances's imagination begins to create fearful images. She sees a tiger in the corner, but her father says he is friendly, and she must go back to bed. Frances sees a giant, a dangerous crack in the ceiling, and something moving the curtains. Many explanations from her sleepy father and a visit from a moth help allay her fears and put Frances to sleep.

A child's mind can play tricks when the child must go to bed in a dark room. Many children will empathize with Frances and her fears of the dark.

Ages 3-7

Also available in:
Paperbound—*Bedtime for Frances*
HarperCollins Publishers, Inc.

Talking Book—*Bedtime for Frances*
Library of Congress (NLSBPH)

280

Hoban, Russell Conwell

Best Friends for Frances

Color illustrations by Lillian Aberman Hoban.
HarperCollins Publishers, Inc., 1969.
(31 pages)

FRIENDSHIP: Meaning of
Prejudice: sexual
Rejection
Sibling: relationships

Frances, a young badger, picks up her bat, her ball, and some chocolate sandwich cookies and goes to play with Albert. Her little sister Gloria asks Frances to play with her instead, but Frances says no. When Frances reaches Albert's house, he says he can't play ball with her because he is "going wandering." He also informs Frances that she may not come along. She goes home and plays with Gloria. The next day Albert won't let Frances play baseball because it is a "no-girls game." Again she goes home and plays ball with Gloria. Frances decides she will no longer be Albert's friend. When Gloria shows Frances a clever way to catch frogs, Frances decides to be Gloria's friend. She and Gloria go on a picnic carrying a sign which reads, "BEST FRIENDS OUTING. NO BOYS." Later, Frances's difficulties with Albert are at least temporarily resolved when Frances and her sister agree to be friends with him.

Snubbed twice by a friend because she is a girl, Frances turns for companionship to her younger sister, whom she had previously rejected. To her surprise, she discovers that her little sister is someone she can enjoy playing with. This is a simple story of friendship told with a light, humorous touch.

Ages 4-7

Also available in:
Cassette—*Best Friends for Frances*
Library of Congress (NLSBPH)

Paperbound—*Best Friends for Frances*
HarperCollins Publishers, Inc.

Talking Book—*Best Friends for Frances*
Library of Congress (NLSBPH)

281

Hoban, Russell Conwell

Dinner at Alberta's

Black/white illustrations by James Marshall.
HarperCollins Publishers, Inc., 1976.
(39 pages counted)

ETIQUETTE

Arthur Crocodile has terrible table manners. His mother says he eats "like a regular little beast." Faced with family complaints, Arthur goes to his room and plays his electric guitar loudly. One day his sister, Emma, brings home her friend Alberta Saurian; Arthur, impressed by Alberta's beauty, plays for her as never before. Alberta stays for dinner, but Arthur can hardly eat for trying to imitate her perfect manners. After Alberta goes home, Arthur makes up a song in her honor. When Alberta invites Emma and Arthur to dinner at her house, Arthur practices good table manners for a week, learning to chew with his mouth closed, hold his fork properly, and use his napkin. The evening at the Saurians is a success; Arthur's manners are flawless. Resentful of the attention Arthur is getting, Alberta's brother, Sidney, watches him all evening, trying to copy his good manners. Arthur's after-dinner guitar-playing delights everyone but Sidney, who coaxes Arthur outside to see his treehouse. When the two return, Sidney's clothes are dirty and he has a puffed-up lip. Arthur has momentarily set aside his new manners to try to teach Sidney to improve his own. Arthur and Emma return home in a good mood.

Arthur, pictured as a thoroughgoing crocodile, declines to improve his table manners until he sees a good reason for doing so—his infatuation for Alberta. Witty illustrations assist this humorous, painless lesson for the very young.

Ages 5-7

Also available in:
Talking Book—*Dinner at Alberta's*
Library of Congress (NLSBPH)

282

Hobby, Janice Hale
with Gabrielle Rubin and Daniel Rubin

Staying Back

Black/white illustrations by Carol Richardson.
Triad Publishing Company, Inc., 1982.
(93 pages, paperbound)

SCHOOL: Achievement/Underachievement
SCHOOL: Retention
School: negative experiences
Self, attitude toward: accepting
Success

When Billy hears he has to repeat first grade, he feels terrible. He's hated school, never did his work, and was one of the smallest children in class. But now he finds he likes being one of the older and bigger kids in his class. Lyndon has sickle-cell anemia and is usually too tired to keep up with his class. After he misses fifty-three days of second grade, his teacher and parents decide he'll be better off if he repeats the year. Now everything is a little easier and Lyndon knows his subjects better. Lilly, who is deaf, transfers in third grade from a special school to a regular school. Everything goes well at first, but then Lilly's classmates and teacher (who wears a mustache that hinders Lilly's lipreading) grow careless about facing Lilly when they talk. If the teacher asks her if she understands the assignments, she says yes because she's too embarrassed to say no. As a result her schoolwork suffers, even though she's a bright girl. When her parents tell her she must repeat third grade, Lilly gets very upset. Her parents insist she is not a failure, that she is doing very well. After thinking about it, Lilly looks forward to the next school year and is delighted to find that her teacher, who shaved off his mustache, is also looking forward to a good year with her. Fourth grade is the worst year of Jennifer's life. After much arguing and unhappiness her father moves out, her parents get divorced, and she "flunks" fourth grade. The next year, things are better at home and Jennifer's teacher helps her with her schoolwork and tells her she is smart. Jennifer is thrilled, since she is used to thinking of herself as stupid. Chip's teacher thinks he is lazy and fooling around when he can't read simple sentences, so Chip finally stops trying altogether. He begins to feel like the dumbest kid who ever lived. When the school psychologist diagnoses a learning disability, Chip is relieved that someone finally understands. She says he's as smart as anyone else, and he is enrolled in a special school instead of having to repeat fifth grade. There he is happy and successful. When Ryan's family moves to Florida, he finds his new school unfriendly and strict and the schoolwork more advanced than what he is used to. After a difficult year, Ryan is asked to repeat fifth grade. He is comforted when he learns that one of the most popular boys in his class was in his second year of fifth grade. Ryan's own father admits he had to repeat a grade. Ronnie's parents appear to have his whole life planned out for him. They want him to be the best, and by sixth grade he's tired of the pressure. The more they push, the more he resists. When he fails sixth grade his parents enroll him in summer school, but he does no better there. In his second year of sixth grade, his parents leave him strictly alone—Ronnie doesn't know if they were told to or if they just gave up. But he finds he likes discovering his own talents and working for himself. Matthew is one of the smallest and youngest members of the third grade, and he never gets his seatwork done. At first he feels sad when he is told he must repeat third grade. Later he's glad because he feels more competent now academically, socially, and physically.

Seven children relate their experiences of repeating a grade. The reasons for the retentions are familiar but vary widely, from illness to learning disability to parental pressure; none is completely remedied by the repeated year, but each is shown to be improving. Illustrations showing students of various races and ethnic backgrounds accompany the children's reflections on their feelings, fears, and reactions. At the back, a "Message to Parents" and "Let's Talk about Staying Back" provide step-by-step suggestions for parents: how to help the child accept and discuss his or her feelings, how to help other family members express their feelings about the matter, how to help the child view this experience as an opportunity to be successful, how to establish future guidelines and limits, and how to emphasize those things the child does well. Also included are discussion questions based on each child's story.

Ages 6-12

Also available in:
No other form known

283

Hogan, Paula Z.

I Hate Boys I Hate Girls

Color illustrations by Dennis Hockerman.
Raintree/Steck-Vaughan Publishers, 1980.
(31 pages)

BOY-GIRL RELATIONSHIPS
FRIENDSHIP: Meaning of
Clubs
Peer relationships: peer pressures
Teasing

Peter's long, lonely summer improves rapidly when a girl his own age, about eight, moves next door. He and Dawn spend nearly every day together until school starts. Then Peter, to avoid being teased by his male friends for having a girlfriend, joins the "I Hate Girls Club." In retaliation, Dawn forms her own "I Hate Boys Club." At the boys' first meeting, the leader proposes a mean trick on the girls. Peter silently disapproves but feels pressured to participate. They sneak to the girls' playhouse, and Peter overhears Dawn's comment on boys: "First they're your friends. The next day they're not." He knows she means him. Then the attack begins. The boys throw a pail of dusty dirt inside the playhouse windows while Peter holds the door shut so the girls can't escape. Later, at home, he talks with his father about the club and how the other boys made fun of him for his friendship with Dawn. His father asks, "You mean you just lost a good friend because of what other people were saying about you?" Peter does not answer. The next morning he grabs his squirt gun and goes to visit Dawn. He apologizes for the dirt, but she wants to know why he has the squirt gun. He suggests a squirt gun fight, and she grabs his gun and tries to squirt him with it. Then they laugh and forget about their clubs, friends once again.

A young boy denies his friendship with a girl in order to avoid harassment and teasing from his male friends. His father helps him realize that a true friendship is something to be cherished, not to be subjected to approval by others. Readers of this age group will sympathize with Peter's and Dawn's feelings and may gain a stronger appreciation of their own friendships with the opposite sex. Illustrations show a lively group of ethnically varied boys and girls.

Ages 5-8

Also available in:
No other form known

284

Hogan, Paula Z.

Sometimes I Don't Like School

Color illustrations by Pam Ford.
Raintree/Steck-Vaughan Publishers, 1980.
(31 pages)

FEAR: of School
Perseverance
Problem solving
School: achievement/underachievement
Success

George, about eight, has come to dread school. On this Monday morning he pretends to be ill, but his mother mentions calling the doctor and George suddenly recovers. "He was too miserable to tell his parents the real reason he didn't want to go to school." Every morning his class plays an arithmetic game. George is always the first one out, the first to sit down, because he never knows the answer to the addition problem on the card his teacher holds up. This morning is no exception, even though George has tried to stop the game by letting the classroom hamsters loose. Not only does his teacher wrongly blame another student for the incident, but once the hamsters are retrieved she proceeds with the game. George hears the now-familiar giggles of his classmates when he gives the wrong answer. "I don't like this game!" he thinks. "And sometimes I don't like school, either!" On the way to school the following morning, George passes the muddy baseball field and jumps into the mud, slipping again and again. When thoroughly dirty, he returns home to change and misses the arithmetic game. The next day his mother sees that George is at school early. When his turn comes to solve the addition problem, George stalls. His teacher asks if he's having trouble seeing the card. Seizing this new excuse, George claims he can't see it. But while talking with his teacher after school, he confesses that he really can see, that it was he who let the hamsters out, and that his unhappiness with school is due to the game. "It's hard to do it while everyone's watching," he says. His teacher understands and gives George an extra set of cards to practice with at home, promising not to tell his classmates. The next morning, after one night's practice with his patient, supportive father, George answers his first problem correctly and then is downed, smiling, on his second problem. Some days later, after much practice and with a newfound enjoyment of arithmetic, George is one of two players left in the game. Although he does not win, he receives a cheer from his classmates for his great improvement. His teacher tells him, "You've worked hard. We're glad you're in this class." "So am I!" thinks George.

Embarrassment about his poor performance in arithmetic clouds a young boy's feelings about school. Rather than confide in his parents or seek help, he desperately tries to avoid the situation entirely. However, his understanding teacher recognizes his need for help and extra practice. Once George admits his problem, he can and does take the necessary steps to solve it. The text is complemented and extended by colorful illustrations.

Ages 6-9

Also available in:
No other form known

285

Hogan, Paula Z.

Sometimes I Get So Mad

Color illustrations by Karen Shapiro.
Raintree/Steck-Vaughan Publishers, 1980.
(31 pages)

ANGER
Emotions: accepting
Friendship: meaning of
Problem solving
Self-discipline
Sibling: older

Karen, about eight, has been invited to go swimming with Janet, an older neighborhood girl, and is searching for her beach bag when her mother reminds her that she is responsible for her younger sister, Rosie, that afternoon. Karen grudgingly takes Rosie along, leaving her to trail behind as soon as Janet joins them. At the beach, Rosie plays on shore while Karen and Janet swim. Karen doesn't want to swim past the marker as Janet does and suggests instead that they go back to shore for some cookies. But Janet spots a friend and the two leave Karen and go back in, swimming out past the marker. Karen helps Rosie with her sand castle, now glad for the little girl's company and secretly proud of her efforts. Janet returns from her swim only to tell Karen that she is going home with her friend. Fighting tears, Karen takes out her hurt and anger on Rosie and kicks over her sand castle. A few days later, Karen is surprised and delighted when Janet invites her to go to a movie. She promptly leaves a note for her mother and meets Janet at the theater. When Janet seems to be taking an awfully long time to get popcorn, Karen goes to find her. Janet is not at the refreshment stand so Karen walks back down the aisle with the drinks she has bought. Then she spots Janet sitting with her classmates. When Karen starts to sit next to her, a boy blocks her way, saying those seats are only for fourth graders. Janet joins in the laughter. Speechless with anger, Karen pours her grape drink on Janet's head. That night, after her mother gets a call from Janet's mother, Karen tearfully tells her story and Rosie joins in, mentioning the day at the beach and the sand castle Karen ruined. "Sometimes I get so mad that I just have to do something!" Karen explains. Her mother suggests that the best thing to do is to let people know when and why they make her angry. So next morning, after apologizing to Janet for pouring the drink on her, Karen explains why she was so angry. Janet agrees that she behaved badly and she invites Karen to play. But Karen turns her down—she has promised to help Rosie build a playhouse. "Even though she's just a little kid, she likes me a lot and we have fun together." The two agree to get together another day, and Karen feels so happy she begins to skip.

Angered by the rejection of an older girl she admires, Karen reacts by striking back, first at her sister, then at the older girl. Guided by her mother's advice, she learns to accept her anger and to express it verbally and forthrightly. Then she's ready to express other emotions honestly, such as her affection for her sister. Expressive illustrations extend the text, which, if a bit simplistic, may be useful in discussions of ways to express feelings constructively.

Ages 5-8

Also available in:
No other form known

286

Hogan, Paula Z.

Will Dad Ever Move Back Home?

Color illustrations by Dora Leder.
Raintree/Steck-Vaughan Publishers, 1980.
(31 pages)

COMMUNICATION: Parent-Child
DIVORCE: of Parents
Change: resisting
Running away

Laura, about nine, is unhappy because her parents don't live together anymore. She hates the too-quiet house when she comes home from school and her mother's irritability when she gets home from work. While Laura sets the table she thinks about her parents but says nothing, aware that her mother dislikes discussions about her father. After dinner she wanders into her brother John's bedroom. Every Saturday they take turns visiting their father. "Do you think Dad will ever move back home?" she wonders. No, says John, not even if they are good, because the problem does not have to do with them. Saturday comes and Laura waits for her father, but her mother disappoints her by leaving before he arrives. She had hoped her parents would talk together, but her mother says there is no point. Things will get better, she tells Laura. But the girl lashes out. "I just wanted us to be a real family again, and you won't even try!" Then Laura has such a good time with her father that she forgets all about the fight with her mother. When they stop for lunch, Laura asks if she can move in with him. He is so much more fun than her mother. But her father says they need to give this arrangement a fair trial. Besides, he tells her, if she lived with him she would see how busy and tired he is most of the time. Laura accuses him of not wanting her. The next morning she gets up early and sneaks out of the house. She will run away, since her parents hate her. On the way she passes two of her friends, and they suggest she go to the deserted house on Elm Street. She stands hesitating in front of the rundown house with the Keep Out sign, now frightened, but finally finds an open basement window and jumps in, a very long jump. Once inside, she can't get back out. Then she hears noises on the other side of the locked basement door, coming closer and closer. Panicked, she runs, trips, and screams when the door opens. But it's her parents, and she rushes to them. As the three walk back home together, her father tells her that they have decided he will spend more time with her and her brother, time just to be together. When they reach the house, he leaves and Laura goes inside with her mother. They sit and talk, her mother assuring her that both parents still love her even though other things have changed. Laura volunteers to help with some housework, but her mother just wants to sit and talk. Laura hugs her.

The effects of divorce on children are clearly described in this story of Laura's struggle to understand and adapt to the changes in her life. She tries to talk about her feelings with her parents, but they are not always ready to listen; some feelings she keeps to herself. When she runs away, her parents realize the depth of her unhappiness and resolve to be more available to her, reassuring her of their love. The resolution demonstrates how divorced parents can and do unite in caring for their children. This expressively illustrated book may be helpful to some families as they work to establish or maintain communication.

Ages 7-10

Also available in:
No other form known

287

Hogan, Paula Z. and Kirk Hogan

The Hospital Scares Me

Color illustrations by Mary Thelen.
Raintree/Steck-Vaughan Publishers, 1980.
(31 pages)

HOSPITAL, GOING TO
Fear: of the unknown
Surgery

Young Dan Martin's fall from the monkey bars results in a dreaded trip to the hospital to have his injured ankle mended. His mother's presence and reassurance are not enough to calm the little boy's fears. At the hospital Dan is helped onto a cart and is greeted by people in "funny clothes" under bright lights. A sympathetic nurse explains that she is putting a temporary bandage on his ankle. Then, after examining Dan's ankle, Dr. Waters tells him about the X rays that need to be taken to determine the extent of the injury. While the Martins wait for Dr. Chun, the bone specialist, to arrive, the nurse gives Dan an injection for his pain. Dan hates shots, but this one is not bad enough to make him cry. Dr. Chun explains to the Martins that Dan's ankle is indeed broken and it cannot heal unless he operates on it right away. He gets a room for Dan on the children's floor and reassures him by admitting that "this is all very strange to you, Dan, but there is nothing to be afraid of." But Dan is still afraid. Once upstairs, he is told why he must wear a hospital gown and he meets Dr. Hood, his anesthesiologist, who tells Dan what she'll do during his operation. "I will help you fall into a special sleep . . . so it won't hurt while Dr. Chun is fixing your ankle." Dan continues to learn more about hospital procedures even in the operating room—about the uniforms, lights, and machines—before he falls into a deep sleep. When Dan opens his eyes, he is back in his room with his family. The operation is over. Dan's parents explain to him why his leg is in a cast and how the strange bottle of medicine and the tube attached to his arm will help prevent infection. The next day, Dan worries about missing so much school. His mother tells him about a special worker at the hospital who will help him with his schoolwork. As the days pass, Dan feels better and better. Dr. Chun puts a walking cast on his leg and helps him walk with crutches. Finally, Dan is able to go home and back to school. His teacher encourages him to tell the class about his hospital visit. Then everyone takes a turn signing Dan's cast.

This reassuring, simple, but informative account of a little boy's surgery and hospital stay could help prepare children for a hospital visit. It might also be useful for describing the hospital experience to a patient's siblings and peers. Dan is very clear about his feelings and observations, making him an engaging character. Large, colorful illustrations add to the appeal.

Ages 3-8

Also available in:
No other form known

288

Holland, Isabelle

Dinah and the Green Fat Kingdom

HarperCollins Publishers, Inc., 1978.
(189 pages, paperbound)

FAMILY: Unity
WEIGHT CONTROL: Overweight
Harassment
Imagination
Pets: substitute for human relationship
Security/Insecurity
Self-Improvement

Dinah Randall, twelve, often retreats to her Green Kingdom, a great oak tree, to daydream and write about a world where fat people are liked. At home, Mother nags her to lose weight, and Dad agrees with Mother; Dinah's teenage brother, Tony, teases her; and her ten-year-old cousin, Brenda, who shares her room, is an unfailing model of neatness and thin perfection. Brother Jack, nine, is sympathetic to Dinah, and an ungainly puppy she buys for 23¢ loves her outright. Dinah also meets acceptance at the Van Hocht house, where three nicely fat adult sisters live in contentment. One of the sisters has a son about Dinah's age, Sebastian, who stammers and limps from cerebral palsy. Dinah feels uncomfortable talking to him. As for the puppy, to keep him Dinah agrees to meet conditions her mother sets down: eat no snacks, return directly home after school, and attend a nutrition class. Wary of the class, Dinah relaxes when her teacher points out that no one can or will bully her into losing weight; she can only do it for something she wants. In a week, she loses five pounds. Expecting to be praised, she is only teased again by Tony (her dress is too tight, still) and criticized by Mother. A quarrel ensues, and Dinah cries out that they are "a rotten family" and runs into the rainy night. With her puppy she comes to the oak tree. Unable to recapture the Green Fat Kingdom, Dinah writes stories about other things; then, fearing she has forfeited the puppy, she takes it to Sebastian for safekeeping. For the first time she can talk to the boy about his handicap. The Van Hochts call the Randalls to tell them she is there. On the way home, Dad comforts her and says that she and her mother must come to terms; he cannot mediate between them. Mother then admits she has mistreated Dinah, and promises to stop it. She even has praise for Dinah's stories and encourages her to keep on writing.

In this first-person narrative, we get the viewpoint of a girl who feels that other people make her fatness a problem: a perfectionist mother, a teasing brother. In the end she comes to distinguish what her father calls the "mechanics" of losing weight from her reactions to unflattering comments. The discussions here of the psychology and physiology of fatness in America, though preachy at times, provide sound information and portray a variety of attitudes toward it.

Ages 10-13

Also available in:
No other form known

289

Holland, Isabelle

Heads You Win, Tails I Lose

Fawcett, 1988.
(159 pages, paperbound)

WEIGHT CONTROL: Overweight
Alcoholism: of mother
Drugs: abuse of
Parent/Parents: fighting between
Separation, marital

Fifteen-year-old Melissa feels caught in the middle of her parents' constant battles. When they're not fighting with each other, they nag Mel about her weight. She would like to lose weight but doesn't want to follow a diet. When Mel wins a role in the school play, the drama coach, Miss Ainsley, begins taking an interest in her. Unfortunately, her situation at home worsens. Mel feels anger and resentment when her father moves out of the house. She steals diet and sleeping pills from her mother to lose weight. Because Mother has begun drinking heavily, she doesn't notice the missing pills. Mel and Vic, a boy in the play, become good friends. One afternoon, Mel experiences a "bad trip," and Vic discovers her pills. They are "speed." Mel promises Miss Ainsley and Vic that she will tell her mother, stop taking the pills, and see her doctor. At her doctor's suggestion, Mel tells her father about her mother's drinking. She finds she doesn't hate her father as she had thought and that he loves her. Father decides to go home temporarily to help Mother.

This first-person account deals with many contemporary problems. A sympathetic teacher and a boy who shares several of Melissa's difficulties contribute to the successful solution of Mel's problems with her weight and her parents.

Ages 12 and up

Also available in:
Braille—*Heads You Win, Tails I Lose*
Library of Congress (NLSBPH)

H

290

Holland, Isabelle

The Man Without a Face

HarperCollins Publishers, Inc., 1988.
(159 pages)

IDENTITY, SEARCH FOR
LOVE, MEANING OF
Divorce
Homosexuality: male

Fourteen-year-old Charles Norstadt has had little experience with love and responsibility. His mother is about to marry her fifth husband. Charles, her middle child, is the only offspring of her second husband. When faced with the prospect of spending the winter with his mother and two sisters, Charles decides to try to pass the St. Matthew's boarding school entrance exam, which he once failed because he was careless. He is totally unprepared to pass the exam, so he decides to find a tutor to help him. The only prospective tutor at his family's summer beach colony is a grim man named Mr. McLeod. Because McLeod's face is scarred from burns, he is known as "the man without a face." Apprehensively, Charles asks him to be his tutor, and Mr. McLeod agrees. Mr. McLeod demands absolute discipline and intellectual integrity from Charles. A close relationship develops between the two people who regard themselves as misfits. The boy studies, swims, and discusses ideas with Mr. McLeod. For the first time in his life, Charles experiences discipline and understanding. Sometimes when he is with McLeod, the boy is overwhelmed by mental blackouts resulting from memories of his father. Charles doesn't know how to cope with his emotions, and when he reaches out for physical reassurance, McLeod gently rebuffs his advances. In a moment of crisis, when Charles learns that his father has died from alcoholism, the boy runs to McLeod's bedroom and sleeps with him. Although McLeod assures Charles that the homosexual experience that night resulted from stress and has no further meaning, the boy worries about it and wants to end their relationship. When he leaves his summer home, Charles passes his entrance exam and goes to St. Matthew's. Later, he runs away from school to find McLeod and tell him that he still values their friendship. Charles learns that McLeod has died, but he is also told that Mr. McLeod considered Charles to be his friend. Just before his death he wrote his will, leaving his home to Charles.

In this first-person narrative, an insecure teen-ager learns the meaning of love and responsibility through the affection and discipline of an older man. This engaging fourteen-year-old is funny, thoughtful, undisciplined, and lovable. The boy's character represents a verbally sophisticated but emotionally immature contemporary teen-ager. The homosexual incident is subtly handled.

Ages 13 and up

Also available in:
Talking Book—*The Man Without a Face*
Library of Congress (NLSBPH)

291

Holland, Isabelle

Now Is Not Too Late

Lothrop, Lee & Shepard Books, 1980.
(159 pages)

MATURATION
Alcoholism: of mother
Change: accepting
Grandparent: living in home of
Love, meaning of
Nightmares
Stepbrother/Stepsister

Eleven-year-old Cathy Barrett loves spending the summer with her paternal grandmother on an island off the coast of Maine, although she wishes her stepbrother, Andy, could come too. She regards Andy more as a brother than a stepbrother. In his absence, Cathy spends time with Marianne, her summer best friend. Marianne warns Cathy about the Wicked Witch, an odd woman who lives alone in a cottage up a steep hill and has lots of animals. Her curiosity piqued, Cathy asks her grandmother about the woman. Her name is Elizabeth, the grandmother replies; she's known her for thirteen years. She then changes the subject. Still curious, Cathy decides to go see Elizabeth, this Wicked Witch. She is surprised to meet a woman of about forty, beautiful but sad. Elizabeth paints and does illustrations for children's books, and she asks Cathy to model for her. They dicker about payment, and Cathy agrees to sit two hours a day for twenty-five days. She plans to use the money for the bicycle she wants. As she leaves Elizabeth's cottage, she decides to tell neither Marianne nor her grandmother about the arrangement. That night Cathy has a terrifying nightmare, like the ones she often had as a child. The modeling begins, and Cathy tells Elizabeth that her mother died when she was five. Elizabeth tells Cathy that she had a daughter once, but scared her badly when she was little. Then Andy arrives at Cathy's grandmother's house, coming early from camp. With him is his friend Don, whom Cathy soon resents because of the attention Andy gives him. One day Cathy asks her grandmother about her mother. She was sick in mind as well as body, her grandmother replies, but she encourages Cathy not to judge her mother. While she's with Elizabeth, Cathy begins to draw, and their two hours each day become very important to her. When Andy, Don, Marianne, and Cathy go to the mainland for a movie, they see Elizabeth and follow her into a church. There they overhear her testimony to an Alcoholics Anonymous meeting. She confesses to screaming at and verbally abusing her little daughter. Old memories flood Cathy's mind and her nightmare becomes a reality. She runs away, back to the island, and hides on a cliff over the ocean. Confused and terrified, she nearly falls over but is rescued by an old man and his dog and taken to her grandmother's house. Cathy asks if Elizabeth is her mother. Yes, her grandmother admits; Cathy has been lied to. When she's able to face Elizabeth again, Cathy goes and talks with her. Elizabeth gives the girl a check for her bike. Maybe they can see each other in New York someday. Back at her grandmother's, Cathy has a sense of how much this summer has meant to her.

Cathy's island summer turns dramatic when she learns that Elizabeth, the "Wicked Witch," is the source of her nightmares—the alcoholic mother she'd thought dead. Although the reader realizes this considerably earlier, Cathy's first-person narrative is so compelling that interest never flags. The relationship between the girl and her grandmother is especially well drawn.

Ages 10-13

Also available in:
No other form known

292

Holman, Felice

Slake's Limbo

Charles Scribner's Sons, 1974.
(117 pages)

RUNNING AWAY
Deprivation, emotional
Fear
Loneliness
Orphan
Reality, escaping
Resourcefulness

Aremis Slake is a thirteen-year-old orphan. His aunt permits him to sleep on a cot in the kitchen of her run-down apartment, but she treats him cruelly and he never has enough to eat. To his teachers and classmates he is a worthless lump, and boys on the street tease and beat him. His refuge is the New York subway system, where he rides the cars for hours. One day, he escapes a gang of pursuing boys by running into a subway tunnel. There he accidently discovers a small concrete room built into the side of the tunnel. He claims this room for his own and for the next four months lives in it, hidden away from all who mistreat him. Each morning he comes into the terminal where he sells old newspapers to make money. He cleans the floor of a coffee shop to earn a meal every day. Slake finds a kind of security in his new lifestyle, until the day a portion of the tunnel caves in. When Slake learns that the tunnel will soon be repaired, he is sure that his home will be discovered. Frightened and hopeless, he goes to his hideout and waits. Since he has neither food nor water, he soon is starving and feverish. In a state of shock, he finally wanders out onto the tracks where Willis Joe, a subway motorman, finds him. He is taken to the hospital and given food and care; he slowly recovers. Encouraged by a card and flowers sent by Willis Joe, he decides he can make it on his own again. Instead of waiting for the social worker to place him in a family, he leaves the hospital. "Slake did not know exactly where he was going, but the general direction was up."

Interspersed with the open-ended story of Aremis Slake are glimpses into the life of motorman Willis Joe. The kindness of a few people who touch Slake's life provides him with just enough encouragement to keep going. At the end of this poignant story, he truly has hope for a better life—even the imaginary bird that has been pecking at his insides when he is hungry or frightened finally flies away.

Ages 12 and up

Also available in:
Paperbound—*Slake's Limbo*
Aladdin Books

Talking Book—*Slake's Limbo*
Library of Congress (NLSBPH)

293

Holmes, Efner Tudor

Amy's Goose

Color illustrations by Tasha Tudor.
HarperCollins Publishers, Inc., 1977.
(27 pages counted, paperbound)

LONELINESS
ONLY CHILD
Animals: responsibility for
Freedom: meaning of
Nature: respect for

Young Amy lives on a farm with her mother and father. One day while they are hard at the harvest, preparing for winter, Amy hears the sound she has been waiting for all fall: the cry of the wild geese who stop at the nearby lake every year on their journey south. Their work done and supper eaten, Amy and her father head down to the lake with a sack of corn. But a marauding fox gets there first and injures one goose. Amy and her father carry the goose back to the barn and nurse it back to health. Amy longs to keep it for a pet, but the flock remains at the lake, unwilling to leave without their companion. One gander circles over the barn every night, calling to his mate. Then one day the flock rises up into the sky, its unison farewell cry filling the air. Amy knows that her cherished goose is well enough to join them. A lone bird drops out of the immense V-formation and circles back, as if searching—and Amy rushes to the barn, embraces the goose, then sets her freely soaring. Amy is left alone, thinking of spring, when the flock will come again.

In this moving story a lonely only child on a farm longs for a close friend to care for and love. She thinks she has found this friend in a wild goose, but in the end recognizes the need for it to join its mate. The deep respect for nature and wild creatures, out of which this story rises, is beautifully conveyed in full-color illustrations depicting the loneliness of the child no less vividly than the exaltation of the flight of the geese.

Ages 8-11

Also available in:
No other form known

294

Hopkins, Lee Bennett

I Loved Rose Ann

Black/white illustrations by Ingrid Fetz.
Alfred A. Knopf, Inc., 1976.
(39 pages counted) o.p.

COMMUNICATION: Misunderstandings
Boy-Girl relationships
Friendship: keeping friends

Harry Hooper loves Rose Ann enough to send her two valentines. But in return, he receives one he does not like—a letdown. Then Rose Ann goes to a Little League baseball game with Larry Lyon and insults Harry's ability after he has asked to walk home with her—betrayal! But Harry chooses to forgive Rose Ann and offers her one more chance to respond to his affection by printing "Harry Loves Rose Ann" on the sidewalk. Next day, he finds his name changed to Larry's and accuses Rose Ann of making the change—clearly this girl is no longer worth serious attention! Poor Harry, little does he know that Rose Ann had given him what she thought was her best valentine. He would also be surprised to learn that she went to the baseball game with Larry and his sister and his mother, just because Rose Ann's mother arranged it. And she regrets her remark about Harry's baseball prowess. Most of all, Harry would be surprised to learn that Rose Ann, having never liked Larry, was not the one who changed Harry's inscription on the sidewalk. Too bad, Rose Ann now prefers to spend time with her best friend, Vera. "Having one friend like Vera is better than loving Harry or Larry, who both act stupid!"

This two-part first-person narrative enacts a pre-adolescent crush in two stories, the same incidents being told from Harry's and Rose Ann's points of view. What is shown is that neither knows or tells the whole story, and neither asks the other what happened. Here is amusing and thought-provoking material for discussion.

Ages 6-9

Also available in:
No other form known

295

Houston, James A.

Frozen Fire: A Tale of Courage

Black/white illustrations by the author.
Margaret K. McElderry Books, 1977.
(160 pages)

COURAGE, MEANING OF
FRIENDSHIP: Meaning of
Eskimo
Parent/Parents: single
Resourcefulness
Values/Valuing: moral/ethical

During his thirteen years, Matt Morgan has lived many places. After his mother dies, Matt accompanies his father, a geologist, to Frobisher Bay in the Canadian Arctic, where Mr. Morgan hopes to find copper. But he must find it before other prospectors do and busies himself planning a helicopter search while Matt attends school and makes friends with an Eskimo boy his age named Kayak. When Mr. Morgan's helicopter goes down in a storm and an ice fog grounds air searchers, Matt and Kayak set off on a snowmobile to search. (Matt is the only person to whom his father confided his true flight plan.) But the boys are forced to abandon the snowmobile and a blizzard sweeps down on them, forcing them to rely on survival techniques taught Kayak by his grandfather. Lost and with slim chances to survive, they stumble on the dwelling of a wild man, a former Frobisher Bay resident, who gives them a night's lodging before telling them to leave. On the journey out, Matt finds gold nuggets, which he stuffs into his pack. Later, just as Kayak had foreseen, Matt discards the gold as too heavy to carry. The next day they set out across the frozen Frobisher Bay for home, only to be swept out to sea as the ice begins to break up. They face certain death—until Matt signals a plane with a mirror, and the ring of seal's blood Kayak has spread attracts a rescue helicopter. Hospitalized back at the settlement, Matt is reunited with his father, who has walked away from the crash, and has decided to take a job as teacher at the local school.

This fine adventure story tells of two youths, one an Eskimo, combining talents in order to survive. At times their disparate values work against them—Matt's acquisitiveness and Kayak's moments of fatalism, for example. But the boys prevail, and Matt comes to recognize the wisdom of Eskimo customs, however odd they seem to him. The Eskimos themselves, and the Arctic locale, are vividly described.

Ages 10-13

Also available in:
Paperbound—*Frozen Fire: A Tale of Courage*
Aladdin Books

296

Hughes, Dean

Switching Tracks

Atheneum Publishers, 1982.
(166 pages) o.p.

GUILT, FEELINGS OF
Age: aging
Ambivalence, feelings of
Depression
Friendship: making friends
School: classmate relationships
Suicide: of parent

Mark Austin's father has died, he and his mother and younger brother have moved to another house, and Mark is attending a new junior high. An elderly neighbor, Willard, offers to pay Mark to help him put together the model railroad set he has in his basement. Mark refuses at first, but later accepts when he needs money to play the video games at the arcade. Since his father's death, Mark doesn't do schoolwork, he won't make friends, he screams at his brother—all he seems to want to do is play video games. To his concerned mother, Mark says he hated his father and doesn't care that he's dead. But secretly he must spend most of his energy trying to suppress the unidentifiable voices that return to haunt him. The tension builds in the boy: he's failing in school, his mother begins dating a man named Don, some boys on the bus tease him about Willard. The voices in his head try harder to break through, especially when his mother asks how he would feel if she and Don married. Mark continues saying anything he can to hurt his mother, denying that he used to love his father, admitting no good in him. His mother tries to present his father as a man riddled with problems that could explain, if not excuse, his physical abuse and drinking. Only Mark and his mother know that Mark's father's death was not an accident, but she insists they had no choice that last day when he begged his family to take him back—they had to send him away. Willard tries to get through to Mark, accusing him of having chosen hatred as a way of life. But Mark cannot forget the last words he said to his father. Then Willard tells Mark he's dying of cancer and wants to leave Mark his house and his train set. Furious that Willard has kept his illness a secret, feeling cheated and somehow betrayed, Mark spends the following day in such a daze that one teacher asks him if he's on drugs. He can't remember any of the afternoon and, after a hazy incident on the bus, wakes up in a hospital a day later. Mark realizes he has to tell someone all that's burdening him. He asks for Willard, who has also been hospitalized for some tests. He tells Willard the whole story: how his father threatened to kill himself if his family didn't take him back, how he described the exact suicide he planned (which he later carried out). Mark had gone out to talk to him and found him crying by his car. When his father again repeated his intention of killing himself, Mark had told him he didn't have the guts to do it. Those were the last words he ever spoke to his father. Mark believes his father must have hated him to leave him with this legacy of guilt. Gently, Willard points out that Mark both hated and loved his father. The weeping boy admits he misses his father terribly. Willard helps Mark see that while the family gave his father many second chances, Mark was given no second chance to apologize or undo his hasty words. He persuades the boy to talk further with some of the hospital staff. Earlier, when Willard offered him the train set, Mark angrily turned it down. Now he tells Willard he'd like to accept the gift.

In this painful and gripping novel, a boy is driven by guilt to the brink of mental illness when he suppresses his memories of the day his father killed himself. When he finally sees the necessity of unburdening himself, he chooses the elderly man who has befriended him and is himself dying. Mark and Willard take courage from each other: one learns to live and the other to die. Tense and fast-moving, not depressing, the book focuses on the close relationship that develops between the boy and the old man.

Ages 10-14

Also available in:
No other form known

297

Hughes, Shirley

Alfie Gets In First

Color illustrations by the author.
Lothrop, Lee & Shepard Books, 1981.
(32 pages counted)

RESOURCEFULNESS
Problem solving
Success

Alfie, his mother, and his little sister, Annie Rose, return from a shopping trip. Mom unlocks the door, sets the basket of groceries and her keys inside, and then walks back down the apartment steps to get Annie Rose out of her stroller. Alfie, pretending to be racing with his mother, runs inside ahead of her shouting, "I've won, I've won!" and slams the door, leaving himself and the keys on the inside, Mom and Annie Rose on the outside. Even with his mother's encouragement he can't reach the door catch, and he's too short to shove the keys through the mail slot. Mrs. MacNally from across the street comes to see what the commotion is about and is soon joined by her daughter, Maureen. Mom suggests Alfie get his little chair from the living room to stand on so he can push the keys through the mail slot. But he is busy crying, Annie Rose is crying, and Mrs. MacNally, Maureen, and Alfie's mother try to think of a way to get inside. The milkman and a window cleaner contribute a ladder and the suggestion that they climb in the bathroom window. But when the window cleaner is halfway up the ladder, the front door suddenly opens.

H

Alfie has used his little chair to climb up and has managed to release the door catch. "He was very pleased with himself." Everyone comes in and they all have tea together.

A little boy who accidentally locks his mother and baby sister outside their apartment overcomes his feelings of helplessness and gets the door open. The delightful illustrations play an integral part in the story. While the text concentrates on the activities of the adults, the reader sees Alfie going for his chair, standing on it, and unlatching the door. The sudden opening of the door surprises Alfie's mother and the neighbors, but the reader has seen it coming. Children will love this satisfying tale.

Ages 3-5

Also available in:
Braille—*Alfie Gets In First*
Library of Congress (NLSBPH)

Talking Book—*Alfie Gets In First*
Library of Congress (NLSBPH)

298

Hughes, Shirley

David and Dog

Color illustrations by tbe autbor.
Prentice-Hall, Inc., 1981.
(32 pages counted) o.p.

TRANSITIONAL OBJECTS: Toys
Giving, meaning of
Loss: of possessions
Sibling: love for

His older sister, Bella, has seven teddy bears, all of which she takes to bed, and his baby brother likes hard, biteable toys; but David, about three, has only one soft toy, named Dog, which he takes everywhere. Thus Dog comes along to school when David goes with his mother to pick up Bella. Waiting, David holds Dog up to view preparations for the school fair, and then Bella comes amid a flurry and bustle, and David forgets about Dog. At bedtime, after being unnaturally quiet, David says, "I want Dog." But a search turns up nothing, and David spends a restless night missing Dog sorely. At the fair the next day, Bella asks David if he wants to race. No, he does not feel like racing. And he becomes, if anything, sadder when Bella wins a huge teddy bear. Wandering off to look at the goods for sale, David spots Dog in a used-toy stall. Not having enough money to buy him back, he races to find his parents but only finds Bella. Together they rush back—only to meet a little girl carrying Dog away. She refuses Bella's offer to buy him. But Bella, seeing the girl admire the newly won teddy bear, arranges a trade: bear for Dog. David first hugs Dog, then Bella.

A boy's complete attachment to a toy changes to complete misery when he loses it. Pleasant illustrations vividly convey a range of emotions—including Bella's mixed feelings about the trade. All the same, Bella comforts David by saying she did not much like the teddy bear; besides, there would be no room in her bed for it.

Ages 4-7

Also available in:
Talking Book—*David and Dog*
Library of Congress (NLSBPH)

299

Hughes, Shirley

Moving Molly

Color illustrations by the author.
Lothrop, Lee & Shepard Books, 1988.
(32 pages counted)

CHANGE: New Home
MOVING
Loneliness

Little Molly and her family move from their basement apartment in an English city to a house in the country. Her mother and father are soon busy fixing up the house and yard. Molly's brother and sister go to school every day, and when they're home Patrick rides his bike and Joanie cares for her guinea pigs. Everybody has something to do but Molly. In the city she'd never been at a loss for friends. She finds a hole in their fence and begins spending her days in the neglected yard next door. It's become a jungle for cats, so she plays with them. She tends some abandoned plants and keeps herself amused. Then one day she sees a moving van pull up next door. Twins Kevin and Kathy, her new neighbors, peek at her through the hole in the fence. They like to do the same things she does, so now Molly is as busy as the rest of her family.

A child adjusts to the move her family makes, once she finds some friends next door. Accompanying the simple, appealing text are lively, old-fashioned illustrations that realistically depict the English setting. Readers will want to linger over some of them.

Ages 3-5

Also available in:
Talking Book—*Moving Molly*
Library of Congress (NLSBPH)

300

Hunt, Irene

The Lottery Rose

Putnam Berkley Group, 1987.
(100 pages, paperbound)

CHILD ABUSE
FEAR: of Physical Harm
HATRED
LOVE, MEANING OF
Children's home, living in
Death: of friend
Deprivation, emotional
Giving, meaning of
Mental retardation
Trust/Distrust

Frequent physical abuse at the hands of his mother and her boyfriend, Steve, has left seven-and-a-half-year-old Georgie fearful and sullen. His only interest and delight is a school library book about flowers and gardens. Suddenly, in a neighborhood lottery, he wins "best prize in the world"—his very own rosebush. But where to plant it? Then Georgie is hospitalized after a brutal beating by Steve and later sent to a boy's school in the country, still brooding on the welfare of his rosebush. When Georgie meets the school director, Sister Mary Angela, she kindly suggests several locations on the school grounds for his rosebush, but Georgie has seen a beautiful garden: the perfect setting. But no, the woman who lives there, with her five-year-old mentally retarded son, Robin, and his grandfather, allows no one to tamper with her garden, a memorial to her husband, recently killed in a car accident along with her older son. Georgie plants his rosebush in Molly Harper's garden anyway, only to find it lying on the school grounds next morning. He immediately goes to replant it, but Molly appears and threatens to burn it. Overcome by fear, anger, and illness, Georgie collapses at her feet and his shirt slips off his back, revealing the scars of many beatings. Molly dissolves at the signs of such suffering and carries the unconscious boy back to school. While recuperating, Georgie learns that his rosebush flourishes in Molly's garden. Now he refuses to believe in her change of heart; someone must have forced her to do what she has done. That summer, Georgie makes good friendships with Robin (whom he plays with patiently for hours) and with Robin's grandfather (who teaches him to read). But his hatred for Molly remains unchanged, though many try to change it. Still he is curious about her, curious about her dead son. He declines to study dramatics because Molly, a former actress, will be teaching the class, but he does watch the rehearsals, learning everybody's lines. Then a player has to be let go—and Georgie is delighted to step in and perform his part. Afterwards, he retreats to his rosebush. One morning, little Robin, left unattended, slips out of the yard and drowns in the nearby lake. The death of his young friend is almost more than Georgie can bear. After the funeral, he digs up his rosebush and, placing it in a wheelbarrow, walks the three miles in the dark to the cemetery. Molly drives up just as Georgie starts to dig a hole by Robin's grave. Together they plant Georgie's gift to Robin. When they are finished, Georgie is finally able to ask Molly the question that has been on his mind for so long: "Did you born me a long time ago and I forgot?" She replies, "I didn't 'born' you, but you're mine—no matter where I go or what I do—you're mine. . . .

When a young boy who has been physically and emotionally abused is rebuffed by a stranger, he withdraws. When he receives love and affection he slowly learns how to love in return. Fear, distrust, and hatred are emotions Georgie has known for so long that they seem safe and right. Fortunately, he is not pressed to change, but rather given plenty of time to test the people in his new surroundings and develop a feeling of safety. Readers will strongly sympathize with Georgie and applaud his strong will. Though the passages on physical abuse are short and not too graphic, this melodramatic story is painful to read. Children who have been abused may also find Georgie's eventual good treatment too good to be true.

Ages 11 and up

Also available in:
No other form known

301

Hunt, Irene

Up a Road Slowly

Putnam Berkley Group, 1987.
(192 pages, paperbound)

MATURATION
Alcoholism: adult
Family: extended
Jealousy
Love, meaning of
Parent/Parents: substitute
Relatives: living in home of
Stepparent: mother

After the death of their mother, sever-year-old Julie Trelling and her nine-year-old brother, Christopher, are sent to live with their maiden Aunt Cordelia. Their father feels that he cannot cope with two small children. Only Laura, their seventeen-year-old sister who has been quite close to Julie, remains at home with their father. Having been pampered at home, Julie is unaccustomed to Aunt Cordelia's strict discipline. This, along with the feeling that Aunt Cordelia favors Christopher, keeps Julie from warming up to her aunt. Julie often visits her father and sister since they live only five miles from town. By the time Julie is ten, Christopher has gone to boarding school and Laura has married. A year after Laura marries, she invites Julie to visit her. Julie assumes that their relationship is the same as before, but she soon discovers that her pregnant sister is more concerned with her own home than with Julie's troubles. The sisters argue, and Julie leaves for home feeling very guilty for having hurt her sister. The train conductor senses her misery and makes Julie realize that she must think of making others happy before she can be happy herself. In the spring before Julie enters high school, her father remarries. Julie is quite fond of her new stepmother and considers moving back with them, but a weekend visit leaves her feeling uncomfortable and out of place. She realizes that she loves Aunt Cordelia, and on her return from town she tells her aunt she would like to remain with her during her high-school years. In high school, Julie becomes interested in writing as a career and begins to write stories in her spare time. She maintains a grade point average high enough to become valedictorian of her graduating class. Julie falls in love with Danny Trevort, a childhood friend, and after graduation it is decided that Julie will attend State University. She and Danny plan to marry after college.

This first-person narrative deals with a young girl's maturation from seven to seventeen. The reader will easily identify with the characters—especially Julie—and will respond to the warm account of her growing love for her aunt. Her experiences ring true as Julie argues with family members, displays her self-will, and makes errors in judgment. The book also vividly describes her grief over her mother's death and her influence on an alcoholic uncle.

Ages 12 and up

Also available in:
Braille—*Up a Road Slowly*
Library of Congress (NLSBPH)

Cassette—*Up a Road Slowly*
Library of Congress (NLSBPH)

Talking Book—*Up a Road Slowly*
Library of Congress (NLSBPH)

302

Hunt, Irene

William: A Novel

Charles Scribner's Sons, 1977.
(188 pages)

FAMILY: Unity
Change: accepting
Cooperation: in work
Death: of mother
Determination
Responsibility: accepting

Their father is dead, their mother dying, and the Saunders children—Amy, thirteen; William, eight; and nearly blind Carla, four—fear being separated. Seeking help to ensure that they remain together, Mrs. Saunders turns to Sarah West, a pregnant, unwed sixteen-year-old girl who has moved onto their Florida street. Sarah turns out to be resourceful and just as determined as Mama Saunders to keep the family together. She even increases it, being quite as determined to keep her own baby, Elisabeth, after the child is born during a hurricane. Their home destroyed by the storm, the Saunders move in with Sarah. Three years after Mama has died, the family, aided by friends and neighbors, remains intact. William works at gardening and Sarah, besides working in town, sells her paintings and manages the household. But increasingly, Amy bridles at family responsibilities. William worries that the constant quarrels between Sarah and Amy will break the household. They do. Amy, brought home drunk from a wild party, bitterly accuses Sarah of trying to run her life and goes to live with a neighbor. Only after Carla undergoes surgery that gives her sight are Amy and Sarah reconciled. Amy settles down and marries. But a new threat arises: friends urge Sarah to attend art school. Promising to return, she reluctantly accepts a scholarship to a school far away, while her cousin moves in to take her place at home. But William knows that things will never again be the same.

This chronicle of how a family of three black children and a white girl and her baby stay together for four years is told from William's viewpoint. Readers will sympathize with his desire to keep a young, loving family together, but they will also see the impossibility of his hopes. "Nothing abides," Sarah tells him consolingly as they part; he must face things as they are, not see them as he wants them to be.

Ages 12 and up

Also available in:
Cassette—*William: A Novel*
Library of Congress (NLSBPH)

303

Hunter, Evan

Me and Mr. Stenner

Dell Publishing Company, Inc., 1978.
(157 pages) o.p.

DIVORCE: of Parents
STEPPARENT: Father
Parent/Parents: remarriage of

Eleven-year-old Abby O'Neill does not want her mother to divorce her father. Neither does she want Mr. Stenner to divorce his wife and marry her mother. Loyal to her father, Abby refuses to like Mr. Stenner at all. She likes the new house she and her mother have moved to, but resents Mr. Stenner's moving in and playing father to her before either divorce is settled. Yet little by little, likable traits in Mr. Stenner impress her. Still, she is embarrassed that he and her mother cannot yet marry. Eventually, both divorces are final, and Mr. Stenner and her mother are married. They plan a leisurely honeymoon in Italy—and they take Abby with them. Happy to be included, enchanted with the trip, she comes to feel a genuine warmth toward her stepfather. Yet no matter how many good times they enjoy, loving two fathers continues to seem wrong. All the same, just before the three are to go home, Abby does admit to herself that she loves Mr. Stenner and tells him so. He says he loves her too.

This frank, first-person narrative dramatizes some of the dilemmas divorce can cause. Abby will no longer live with her father, yet feels uneasy accepting a stepfather. She does not finally settle on one or the other, but sees that her love and respect for her stepfather in no way diminishes what she has always felt for her father. Touches of humor throughout the book prevent it from becoming depressing or discouraging.

Ages 10-13

Also available in:
No other form known

304

Hunter, Mollie, pseud.

A Sound of Chariots

HarperCollins Publishers, Inc., 1972.
(242 pages)

MOURNING, STAGES OF
Death: of father
Fear: of death
Giftedness
Loneliness
Maturation
Nightmares

The mother of nine-year-old Bridie McShane returns from the hospital to inform her children that their father, who had been sick for some time, has just died. Stunned, Bridie and her sister Aileen automatically go about delivering Sunday papers. Then, as Bridie rides along on her bike, the reality of her father's death hits her and she howls with grief. She remembers all she can about her father: his dancing eyes, the white flash of his smile; his love for poetry; the Irish songs he taught her; his socialistic philosophy; his concern for improving the conditions of the common man. She recalls the closeness she shared with him because she was his favorite child and even looked like him. As she pedals through the small Scottish village where she lives, she is devastated by grief. Nightmares of death haunt the girl—those of her father's death, her mother's, and even her own. Since her mother is too overwhelmed by her loss to be able to console her daughter, Bridie struggles along alone, trying to come to grips with Time and Death. After a while, her grief abates into loneliness. She stops pitying her mother and finds a deeper relationship with her. By her twelfth summer, she has gained a new maturity and begins to see her mother as an individual; their relationship improves. Yet she feels pursued by the passage of time carrying her on toward death. By the age of fifteen, she is disappointed, for she had hoped that time would soften the pain caused by her father's absence and it has not. Two years later, at the close of her formal schooling, she talks with her teacher, Mr. McIntyre. He tells her that she cannot overcome her father's death by continuing to question and grieve. She can only do it by living her own life to the fullest. She must live for her father.

This intense and moving drama of a young girl growing up is told in two parts: Part I, a flashback of Bridie's childhood with her father; and Part II, her struggle to accept his death. Bridie is a sensitive girl, mature beyond her years even in early childhood. She has a special kind of perceptivity and love for language.

Ages 12 and up

Also available in:
Paperbound—*A Sound of Chariots*
HarperCollins Publishers, Inc.

Talking Book—*A Sound of Chariots*
Library of Congress

305

Hurwitz, Johanna

Aldo Applesauce

Black/white illustrations by John Wallner.
William Morrow & Company, Inc., 1979.
(127 pages)

CHANGE: New Home
NAME, DISSATISFACTION WITH
Friendship: making friends
Moving
School: classmate relationships
School: transfer
Teasing

It is January and fourth-grader Aldo Sossi wakes up in his new house, filled with apprehension about entering his new school. For a time, all his fears seem justified. He is assigned a seat next to DeDe, a girl who wears a false mustache. He says the teacher's name wrong. At lunch, when he smells DeDe's tuna sandwich, Aldo explains that he is a vegetarian and wants to become a vet. He likes birds too much to eat them, he tells her, and cannot eat tuna since he read that dolphins are often killed in tuna nets. Then DeDe slips, knocking his applesauce to the floor, and Aldo acquires the embarrassing nickname "Applesauce." Some boys steal his hard-boiled egg and play catch with it. DeDe tells him to bring another the next day, but it too is stolen and tossed around. The third day DeDe herself brings an egg, this one raw. Snatched and tossed, it breaks messily, and a smiling aide tells Aldo and DeDe that she thinks the tricks are over. At home, Aldo pursues his usual animal-loving routine. He saves his toast crusts for the birds and scatters leftover spaghetti and wheat germ. After two months at his new school, Aldo still has only one friend, DeDe, and still suffers the burden of his nickname, Applesauce. He constantly wonders why DeDe wears the mustache, but doesn't ask. Curious about why he has been invited to a classmate's birthday party when the boy has never said a word to him, Aldo learns that all the boys from class were invited. "The more kids, the more presents," says the birthday boy. Since hot dogs and hamburgers are on the birthday menu, Aldo eats only potato chips, a pickle, and orange soda. By the time the cake is served, his stomach is so jumpy

H

he can only eat a little bit. He is despondent on the way home and his father, aware of Aldo's painful nickname, explains his own brother's monicker—Tomato Sauce for Thomas Sossi. At school DeDe is glum, so Aldo invites her to his house. While they wait for Aldo's sister's applesauce cake to bake, DeDe tells him not to be offended by his nickname: "Everybody in the school knows you better if you have a nickname." After lunch at DeDe's the next Saturday, Aldo is finally emboldened enough to ask his friend why she wears a fake mustache. She tells him that she wants to look like her father, divorced from her mother and painfully missed. She has always been told she resembles her father, so now that he's grown a mustache she is wearing one too to maintain the similarity. If her father goes bald, Aldo asks her, will she shave her head? He assures her that her father will remain her father no matter where he is or how much they differ in appearance. Both friends are comforted.

This second of several books about Aldo shows the boy quietly struggling to fit in at his new school without violating his strongly held principles or being something he's not. He befriends another lonely, nonconforming child, and the two comfort and sustain each other. Aldo is gentle and likeable and his story is told with a light, humorous touch that remains true to the concerns and feelings of sensitive, individual children. Amusing illustrations capture the tone.

Ages 7-9

Also available in:
Braille—*Aldo Applesauce*
Library of Congress (NLSBPH)

Cassette—*Aldo Applesauce*
Library of Congress (NLSBPH)

306

Hurwitz, Johanna

The Law of Gravity

Black/white illustrations by Ingrid Fetz.
William Morrow & Company, Inc. 1978.
(192 pages)

DIFFERENCES, HUMAN
Communication: parent-child
Friendship: making friends
Weight control: overweight

Margot Green is stumped. Her teacher tells the graduating fifth graders to undertake projects over the summer. But what, Margot asks herself, can she learn during the long, hot summer in New York City? Her father, a concert musician, will be on tour; her mother is no help; and the few friends Margot has are leaving town. Suddenly she hits on the ideal project: getting her mother to come down from their apartment. Not once in nine years has she descended to the street, her only explanation: "What is there to go downstairs for?" Margot searches the library for clues to her mother's behavior, and Bernie, a sixth grader from her school, offers to help. Soon Bernie is helping her on the project and taking Margot to places she has never heard of. One day he suggests that Mrs. Green is embarrassed to come down because she is so fat; Margot tries to interest her mother in a diet. But nothing works. Finally Bernie asks why bringing her downstairs is so important to her. Margot ignores the question and decides to frighten her mother into going out by hiding overnight in the public library. it works. When Bernie takes he home, they meet Mrs. Green on the street talking to a policeman. Rather than rejoice, Margot goes upstairs and cries. Her mother, crying herself, confesses that however much she tries to go downstairs, she cannot force herself to. Margot drops the project, calling in "rotten." Less harsh, her father reminds her that we can only change ourselves; no one should try to manipulate someone else.

In this first-person narrative a girl comes to appreciate the attractions of the city where she lives and the importance of accepting people as they are, not as she would have them to be. Her father's advice to love and accept her mother helps her to answer Bernie's question about why changing her mother is so important to her: she had wished her mother to be like other mothers.

Ages 10-13

Also available in:
Cassette—*The Law of Gravity*
Library of Congress (NLSBPH)

307

Hurwitz, Johanna

Superduper Teddy

Black/white illustrations by Susan Jeschke.
William Morrow & Company, Inc., 1990.
(80 pages)

SELF, ATTITUDE TOWARD: Confidence
Money: earning
Pets
Separation anxiety
Shyness
Sibling: relationships

In "An Invitation for Teddy," the five-year-old boy, who is much shyer than his older sister, Nora, and who wears a superman cape when he needs to feel brave, is invited to a birthday party but doesn't want to go. His mother leads him there step by step, but when he is confronted with the big, noisy crowd, Teddy insists he doesn't know a soul and won't go in. The gathering turns out to be the wrong party; he is later very happy to spend the afternoon at the real party, which consists only of him and his best friend. In "Grandpa Tells a Story," Teddy and Nora, uneasy and bored when their parents go out of town and leave them with their grandparents, listen to Grandpa's modern version of the Cinderella story. In "Teddy Gets a Job," the little boy cares for a neighbor's cat and earns his first salary, something even Nora has never done. "Squabbling" is what Teddy and Nora do a great deal of, but they end up playing Little Red Riding Hood together and all ends well. Teddy finds "A

Superduper Pet," solving a longtime family problem. He and Nora have always wanted a pet, but their mother is allergic to anything with fur and objects to anything that's too big, too noisy, or too expensive. Mr. Hush is a tortoise who meets all the requirements. Then in "Teddy Entertains," the shy little boy surprises his mother by bringing his entire kindergarten class to his apartment for cookies and milk on their way home from a class walk through the neighborhood. While they are there, he even donates his superman cape to the kindergarten costume box because he is now too big for it. "Teddy was feeling super."

Six anecdotal chapters show little Teddy growing in self-confidence as he fights shyness, assumes some independence, solves problems, and proudly relinquishes his superman cape. Children will find much that is familiar here, and they will enjoy the lively illustrations of gnomelike characters. Several other books about Nora and Teddy feature Nora as the main character.

Ages 4-7

Also available in:
No other form known

308

Hurwitz, Johanna

Tough-Luck Karen

Black/white illustrations by Diane de Groat.
William Morrow & Company, Inc., 1982.
(157 pages)

SCHOOL: Achievement/Underachievement
Change: new home
Family: relationships
Friendship: making friends
Self-improvement
Success

Thirteen-year-old Karen Sossi hasn't made any friends since her family moved from New York City to New Jersey, and she blames her "rotten luck" for the trouble she's been having with schoolwork. Schoolwork just isn't important to her, especially compared with her two great loves, cooking and her new baby-sitting job. Her mother, concerned about her lack of friends, gets Karen to attend a Halloween party given by the math teacher. There Karen becomes friendly with Annette and even talks to Roy, a boy she's admired from a distance. But when Annette comes over to spend Saturday afternoon, Karen blames her "bad luck" when Annette is allergic to Karen's two cats and has to leave. Karen continues to do poorly in all her school subjects, and her mother goes with her to talk to the English teacher. Her mother shows the teacher a letter that Karen has written to one of her many pen pals, and the teacher is impressed with Karen's writing. She suggests that Karen write future assignments on stationery, since she seems to have no trouble writing that way. Then Karen must complete a science project and is forbidden to baby-sit and later to use the kitchen for her baking and cooking until the assignment is done. Everyone in the family offers suggestions, but the deadline approaches and Karen still has no ideas for the project. Her mother allows her to bake bread one day and Karen gets a brainstorm: she'll demonstrate how yeast works to make bread rise. The project is a success, especially since Karen brings along some freshly made bread to share with classmates. Usually silent in class, she now finds she's actually enjoying leading a discussion. Later she realizes that her classmates accept her and that her bad luck this fall has been entirely the result of her own laziness and carelessness. "Good luck was like making bread. It took time and effort."

A young teenager in a new school makes friends and learns to take responsibility for the "bad luck" that dogs her schoolwork. Readers equally disenchanted with school will empathize with Karen and may get some ideas from her use of a favorite activity—baking bread—for a school project. Luck has little to do with Karen's problems and even the encouragement of her family cannot really help her; she must help herself. Expressive illustrations and humorous touches enhance the book. The Sossi family will be known to readers of the books that feature Karen's brother, Aldo.

Ages 10-13

Also available in:
Cassette—*Tough-Luck Karen*
Library of Congress (NLSBPH)

Paperbound—*Tough-Luck Karen*
William Morrow & Company, Inc.

309

Hutchins, Patricia

Happy Birthday, Sam

Color illustrations by the author.
Greenwillow Books, 1978.
(30 pages counted)

DEPENDENCE/INDEPENDENCE
Height: short
Resourcefulness

Young Sam wakes on his birthday, delighted to be "a whole year older." He stretches to reach the light switch in his room, but still cannot; it is the same for the hanger for his clothes and the faucets on the sink. Unable to reach the doorknob, he must wait for his mother to let in the postman, who brings a birthday package. The gift, from Sam's grandfather, is a small chair. Standing on it, Sam switches on the light, takes his clothes from the hanger, and does everything he has always been too short to do.

A child finds that a birthday, though marking an advance in years, by itself brings no sudden increase in physical capacity. But the intelligent use of a birthday gift does help him to do things he could not do before. Children will readily identify with the importance Sam gives to doing things "all by himself."

Ages 5-7

Also available in:
Paperbound—*Happy Birthday, Sam*
Greenwillow Books

310

Irwin, Hadley, pseud.

The Lilith Summer

The Feminist Press at The City University of New York, 1979.
(109 pages, paperbound)

AGE: Respect for
Love, meaning of

Ellen's mother has persuaded her that being a summer companion to elderly Lilith Adams will earn her the money for the bike she wants. At twelve, Ellen considers herself too old to require a baby-sitter, but she needs something to do this summer since her mother is going back to school. Lilith had been her Grandma Pearl's best friend. Ellen's mother and Lilith's daughter have made the arrangements for Ellen's job. Unfortunately, however, Ellen quickly decides that both Lilith and her house are depressingly old. Furthermore, Lilith gives a lot of orders and acts more like a baby-sitter than a helpless old woman who needs a companion. Then one day Ellen sees a check written to Lilith by her mother. She suddenly realizes that Lilith is her baby-sitter! They are being paid to look after each other. When she tells Lilith about the deception, the old woman, although upset, tries to convince Ellen that daughter and mother are acting out of love and concern. Still, they both feel humiliated and angry—but they need the money. They agree, therefore, to call a "truce" and make the best of the situation. As the mark of their agreement, they set aside one hour of the day, between four and five, to do quiet things together. During this time they read aloud, write poems, draw, and make up a private language called Lilellenish. A sympathy begins to grow between the two. Ellen notes Lilith's kindness toward her aging friends, her tolerance as she explains their oddities. During the course of the summer, Ellen herself has many chances to experience Lilith's love and understanding. When she impulsively steals a pearl ring from a store, Lilith helps her return it with an apology. But then she gives Ellen the money to buy it back. When the girl is frightened by a bad storm, Lilith consoles her by talking about her own fears. Even now, confides Lilith, she has lots of fears. Her daughter and niece want her to give up her house and move to a nursing home. But she is afraid of "not being needed. Only needing. . . . Of being outdated. Of not being old enough to be a genuine antique. Just old enough to be junk." By the end of the summer, Ellen is able to tell Lilith, "I think when I grow old . . . I want to be just like you, Lilith. I think you're very brave and I don't think you're so old . . . or useless . . . or junky." Then she learns, to her sadness, that her family will soon be moving to Minneapolis. Eight years later, Ellen stands at her college dormitory window remembering a song that Lilith used to sing. In her hand she holds a newspaper clipping: "LILITH E. ADAMS, 85, PASSED AWAY YESTERDAY AT HER HOME AT 212 LAKE STREET." Ellen fondly remembers "that summer. The Lilith Summer."

Despite their initial resentment, a young girl and an old woman left to care for each other one summer develop an abiding affection and respect. Ellen and the reader discover the truth of Lilith's conviction that "all of us are many people: the people we once were, the people who have loved us, even the people who have hurt us." Well-drawn characters distinguish this insightful story about the treasures that the old can offer the young.

Ages 9-13

Also available in:
No other form known

311

Irwin, Hadley, pseud.

Moon and Me

Margaret K. McElderry Books, 1981.
(150 pages)

BOY-GIRL RELATIONSHIPS
FRIENDSHIP: Meaning of
MATURATION
Grandparent: living in home of
Parental: absence
Perseverance
Resourcefulness

E.J. is fourteen and has recently moved to Bluff Farm, Iowa, to live with her grandparents for six months while her mother accompanies her father on a business trip out of the country. E.J. herself has traveled all over the world; prior to coming to Iowa, she lived in France for two years. Now she chafes at the rural, unsophisticated, dull life in Bluff Farm. At the close of the school year, E.J. meets Harmon Wells, known as Moon. He is brilliant and a very mature twelve, but E.J. finds him too young and too short to be interesting. In fact, he irritates her. The only farm activity E.J. likes is riding her horse, Lady Gray. One day during her ride, she meets Moon. He suggests that E.J. enter a one-hundred-mile endurance ride to be held in midsummer—with him as her trainer. Appalled by the boy's persistence, E.J. rides away from him. But the next morning when she gets up, she finds Moon already in the kitchen talking with her grandparents. The three are engrossed in plans for the endurance ride, an event her grandparents used to participate in. Miffed that no one has even consulted her, E.J. reluctantly agrees to enter. The last day of school Moon reminds her that they have exactly fifty-seven days to train for the ride. He has their entire regimen plotted: obstacle courses for the horse, a special diet for E.J., a daily schedule including physical exercises, even a reading program about horses. In spite of her objections, E.J. finds she cannot argue with Moon, so well researched and logical. Besides, both her grandparents support him enthusiastically. So E.J. complies with Moon's rigorous training program. The last few days before the ride, Moon gives E.J. a rest while he rides his bike over the trail so he can make a precise map for her. Then the ride begins. Moon has plotted the course with his usual accuracy; he meets E.J. at every rest point with information and encouragement. All the training pays off: E.J. completes the rugged trip in the allotted three days' time. When she checks in at the finish, Moon is nowhere around. Despite herself, E.J. misses him. When the awards are given out, Moon appears with a big camera to take E.J.'s picture. He is truly proud of her; in fact, a mutual friend, Angie, tells E.J. that Moon loves her. But E.J. wants a romance and not with Moon. Now that the endurance ride is over, Moon decides to enter a bike marathon across Iowa, and E.J. goes with Angie and her mother to their lake cabin. Moon rides eighty-three miles in one day, joining the girls for supper at the lake. The three talk together; E.J. mentions her desire for a real relationship with a boy. Moon is quiet, but after that night E.J. doesn't see him for the rest of the summer. When school starts, she seeks him out. He tells her he is researching meaningful relationships and has planned the strategy for E.J. to get a date with Rick Adams, the tall, handsome senior she has dreamed of dating. Pleased, E.J. follows Moon's directions and, according to schedule, Rick asks her to the homecoming dance. The date, however, is less than exciting. Rick, a true Iowa pig farmer, can only think of his favorite boar who had unexpectedly died that day. His dancing is terrible, he's shy and speaks in monosyllables, and when he suggests she go with him to see a new hog he wants to buy, E.J. excuses herself and says she'll catch a ride home. She starts to walk and along comes Moon. E.J. is happy to see him. Somehow it seems appropriate that he walk her home from her first date. She notices that Moon is now almost as tall as she. When she tells him she will be leaving Bluff Farm the following week, E.J. knows she will truly miss him. Quietly they tell one another how much their friendship means. Both seem to realize that someday it may develop into something more.

An offbeat friendship develops between a sophisticated teenage girl and a younger but unusually bright and mature boy in this enjoyable, often humorous study of relationships and maturation. E.J. ponders the distinction between friendship and romance, discovering that the boundary can change in surprising ways. The riding competition adds interest to this well-written story.

Ages 11-14

Also available in:
No other form known

312

Isadora, Rachel

Max

Color illustrations by the author.
Macmillan Publishing Company, Inc., 1976.
(30 pages counted)

GENDER ROLE IDENTITY: Male
Play

Young Max plays a good game of baseball. On Saturdays, he walks with his sister Lisa to her dancing school, then on to the park for his weekly baseball game. One Saturday, with lots of time before his game, he goes into Lisa's class and watches. Soon he is stretching at the *barre,* trying to do splits, joining in at the *pas de chat,* and trying leaps with the other students. Max has fun in ballet class. Later, when he is up to bat, he hits a home run. Max has discovered a new way to warm up for baseball: Lisa's dancing class.

Young Max is portrayed as an energetic youngster, who discovers that ballet is not only fun, but an excellent way to warm up for baseball. He includes it in his regular baseball training. The all-girl dancing class accepts Max; no sex discrimination is shown by Max or the class.

Ages 4-7

Also available in:
Paperbound—*Max*
Aladdin Books

J

313

Jacobs, Dee

Laura's Gift

Black/white illustrations by Kris Karlsson.
Oriel Press, 1980.
(58 pages)

MATURATION
MUSCULAR DYSTROPHY
Death: attitude toward
Family: relationships
Fear: of death
School: behavior
Twins: identical
Wheelchair, dependence on

They are twins, best friends, and eighth graders at St. Hilda's School for Girls, but that's about all Catherine and Laura Devon have in common. Catherine is opinionated, outspoken, and impatient; Laura is quiet, patient, and confined to a wheelchair by muscular dystrophy. Catherine hates Miss Vertue, school principal and English teacher, and is forever receiving demerits. Laura likes her and is always trying to smooth things out between the two. One Saturday afternoon the twins make their weekly trip to the library. Catherine is silly and makes Laura laugh.

Eventually Catherine wanders off, intending to look up a word she saw on her mother's desk: "pseudohypertrophic." Her good humor turns to fear for her sister when she discovers the term has to do with respiratory weakness and paralysis ending in death. At home Laura promises Catherine candy if she'll practice her piano scales, and Catherine is warmed by her sister's ability to make life's drudgeries a bit more pleasant. Then both girls have fevers and are taken to the hospital. Laura is hospitalized as a precaution; Catherine goes home. After a week Catherine is fine, but Laura has pneumonia, and Catherine convinces herself that her sister is dying. She becomes obsessed with getting Laura back home and stops practicing the piano and doing her homework. Their mother asks Catherine to help her redecorate the twins' room as a surprise for Laura, but Catherine adamantly opposes the change and refuses to help. She is sure her parents are redecorating because Laura is dying. That Saturday Catherine sits on the front steps alone. Miss Vertue joins her and encourages her to be optimistic. Both girls have given gifts to each other, she says: Laura has given Catherine the gift of discipline, and Catherine has given Laura the gift of laughter. Catherine mustn't throw away these gifts, Miss Vertue urges. Catherine's terror resumes when her parents are called to the hospital. But late that evening she learns that Laura's fever has broken and she will be fine. The next morning, Catherine talks with her father, confessing how afraid she was that Laura would die. Her father encourages her to talk to Laura about death, since Laura herself has accepted her condition and her uncertain future. Feeling somehow comforted, Catherine looks forward to Laura's return.

When Catherine believes her beloved sister is dying, she gives up on everything—including herself. Her understanding school principal helps her see that she and Laura have each given the other a special gift. Her father urges her to let Laura's acceptance of her uncertain future guide Catherine's own feelings, and Catherine's deepened understanding is the only resolution to this memorable character study. Not explained is the parents' failure to discuss muscular dystrophy and its dangers with both girls more thoroughly. With its dark, haunting illustrations and probing text, this is a book for mature readers.

Ages 10-13

Also available in:
Paperbound—*Laura's Gift*
Oriel Press

314

Jarrell, Mary

The Knee-Baby

Color illustrations by Symeon Shimin.
Farrar, Straus & Giroux, Inc., 1973.
(30 pages counted)

SIBLING: New Baby
Sharing/Not sharing

Alan, who is about two or three, does not want to sit on his chair. He wants to sit on his mother's lap as he used to before his little sister was born. His baby sister, Little Bee, is sitting on his mother's lap; his father is at work; and his grandmother lives far away. Alan sits on the floor at his mother's knee, and she plays a game with him, having him imagine what his grandmother might be doing. Alan sits and thinks about the good times he has had at his grandmother's house. Then his mother bathes Little Bee. Alan waits for them to finish, but there is "always one more one-minute-thing to do for Little Bee." He still does not get to sit in his mother's lap, but must take his nap. After the children awaken, Alan plays with Little Bee, pretending to be a baby himself. Mother teases him about being a baby and starts the game about Grandma again. Suddenly, Alan finds it is his turn to have his mother's lap "all to himself."

This is a charming story of the relationship between a loving mother and a small child who feels left out because of a new baby. The illustrations contribute to the effectiveness of the book.

Ages 3-6

Also available in:
Paperbound—*The Knee-Baby*
Farrar, Straus & Giroux, Inc. (Sunburst Books)

315

Jeffries, Roderic

Trapped

HarperCollins Publishers, Inc., 1972.
(150 pages, paperbound)

PEER RELATIONSHIPS: Peer Pressures
Leader/Leadership
Risk, taking of

Fourteen-year-old Gerry and his mother have moved to a small town on the southeast coast of England after Gerry's father's death. The boy has entered his new school in the middle of a term and has been trying to make a place for himself there. He especially wants to come to terms with Bert, the self-appointed class leader, who has been rather provocative. One cold day, on his way to visit his grandparents, Gerry meets Bert, who mockingly suggests that Gerry go hunting with him during low tide. Gerry senses a new test but agrees. Bert "borrows" a boat and the two boys go far downstream to a vast mud flat, where they beach the boat and look for ducks. When it suddenly starts snowing, the two boys stop hunting for the boat. It has disappeared. Gerry and Bert must leave quickly because high tide will soon cover the flat, but visibility has become very poor. Gerry realizes that Bert cannot take the lead. He pushes, prods, and forces Bert to keep moving even after darkness falls and they really have no hope of being saved. He still is trying to keep Bert on his feet when help finally arrives.

Trapped is a fast-paced suspense story in which all the action is concentrated into less than a single day. During their nightmarish experience, the boys discover each other's strengths and weaknesses. Their harrowing adventure overcomes the boys' strained relationship, and grudging respect develops into friendship. The suspenseful action in the book almost completely overshadows the development of the relationship between the boys.

Ages 11-13

Also available in:
No other form known

316

Johnson, Annabel Jones and Edgar Raymond Johnson

The Grizzly

Black/white illustrations by Gilbert Riswold.
HarperCollins Publishers, Inc., 1964.
(160 pages, paperbound)

COURAGE, MEANING OF
Communication: parent-child
Fear: of physical harm
Parental: overprotection
Separation, marital

Eleven-year-old David leads a sheltered life in the city with his mother. His father left them several years before to take a job in Africa. David is afraid of seeing his father again; he often has nightmares in which his father makes him do something dangerous and Mother always screams at Father to stop. Father returns and takes David fishing high in the mountains of Montana. David fears that the trip is a test; perhaps his father will desert him, make him swim, or even shoot him. When their food at the campsite is ruined, Father realizes there are bears in the area. A mother grizzly bear attacks, chasing David up a tree and wounding Father, who refuses to shoot her because she has cubs. The bear damages the truck, and Father cannot fix it quickly. David does not panic, but discovers he almost enjoys his newfound ability to cope with trouble. He cares for Father's wound, tries catching fish for them to eat, and helps repair the truck. He even decides that he likes his father and begins plotting to reunite his parents.

This is a fast-moving, exciting story of an overprotected youngster who is suddenly removed from his sheltered life and placed in real danger. His newly discovered courage helps him understand his parents and their concern for him. As he gets to know his father, David realizes the man loves him and wants him to become a capable, confident person instead of a fearful, helpless one.

Ages 10-13

Also available in:
Braille—*The Grizzly*
Library of Congress (NLSBPH)

Talking Book—*The Grizzly*
Library of Congress (NLSBPH)

317

Jones, Rebecca Castalldi

Angie and Me

Macmillan Publishing Company, Inc., 1981.
(113 pages) o.p.

ARTHRITIS, JUVENILE RHEUMATOID
DEATH: of Friend
Change: accepting
Dependence/Independence
Hospital, going to
Illnesses: terminal
Maturation

When eleven-year-old Jenna sees a doctor about her hot, swollen, painful knees, she is told she has juvenile rheumatoid arthritis and must spend several weeks in a children's hospital in Columbus—a place too far from her home for her parents to visit except on weekends. She doesn't understand how a child can have arthritis, why she can't just take aspirin, or why she must go into the hospital. She's upset when her younger sister refers to her "crippled" legs. Her father helps her see that she has a choice: to stay as she is (she has pain and can barely walk) or get some help. Jenna's hospital roommate is twelve-year-old Angie Salvador, who has some sort of blood ailment. Jenna also meets Bill, whose leg problems eventually lead to an amputation; Sam, who undergoes brain surgery; and Wendy, an accident victim who protects herself from pity by her haughty manner. Wendy announces that the whole hospital is full of losers. Angie replies that Wendy only feels sorry for herself. She, on the other hand, hasn't time for self-pity. One day Angie, who faints frequently, takes a long time to recover from one of her spells. After that she seems weaker and more listless. Her mother takes a room across from the hospital. Angie complains that everyone is too nice to her. As for Jenna, after several weeks of whirlpool baths, physical and occupational therapy, cortisone injections that make her puffy, and a lot of enforced rest, she is told she's making progress and can soon go home. Her parents have kept from her the possibility of surgery if she had not responded to treatment. Now that it's been ruled out, they tell her, and Jenna is angry about being denied information. She pushes them for facts about her future, and they agree she has a right to know. Her future is somewhat uncertain, they tell her. Meanwhile, Angie explains to Jenna that blood is leaking from the capillaries in her brain into her spinal fluid, but her doctor is unable to find which capillaries are involved. The head nurse says Angie must move to a private room. Jenna, Bill, Sam, and Wendy make up a Sunshine Box for Angie, but they aren't allowed to see her for several days. Jenna's legs are getting better, and when she thinks about returning to school she realizes she's changed. She understands Angie's insistence on being independent: "She wanted me to be Jenna Matthews. Not the crippled kid." She wants Angie to tell her how she can keep from being a crippled kid when her legs don't work right. But when she gets to Angie's room, it's empty and the bed is neatly made up. Angie has died. Jenna screams and screams. She feels that Angie abandoned her just when she needed her most. Angie's mother has left Jenna the kite she had given Angie, sure that Angie would want her to have it back. As Jenna goes home with her family, she refuses her sister's offer to fly the kite for her. She knows that Angie would approve of her decision to fly the kite herself, in whatever way she can manage it.

A girl comes to terms with her rheumatoid arthritis and, with the help of a terminally ill roommate, rejects seeing herself as a person defined solely by her illness. This affecting, often humorous first-person account realistically shows Jenna's growth as she learns about and copes with an illness that can create permanent disability. The story line and the medical information are smoothly integrated, although character development, aside from Jenna and Angie, is minimal.

Ages 9-11

Also available in:
No other form known

318

Jones, Ron

The Acorn People

Black/white illustrations by Tom Parker.
Bantam Books, 1977.
(76 pages, paperbound)

COURAGE, MEANING OF
HANDICAPS
Camp experiences

At first the sheer unanimity of disease and disfigurement at the summer camp for severely handicapped children stuns the new counselor. He has signed on for what he supposed was a comfortable summer job helping children, not for being a round-the-clock nurse. Yet every movement of the five children he and his co-counselor Dominic care for requires the young men's assistance. Convinced the job is hopeless, the narrator strings together a nut necklace from acorns—a nutty symbol for the craziness he feels. Soon everyone in the cabin makes necklaces. They become known as the Acorn People: Benny B., the wheelchair rocket; Spider, the limbless talker; Thomas, victim of muscular sclerosis who nonetheless endures; Martin, wise in his blindness; and Aaron, confined to a wheelchair and unable to eliminate his wastes normally. But their building solidarity and venturesomeness is bound to collide with the strict schedule set down by the camp director. So they ignore it. They swim when the girls do; they climb a mountain, discovering as much about themselves as about the land. Catching the mood, the camp nurse, Mrs. Nelson, teaches the girls to apply makeup. But the director, alarmed by these departures, orders a return to the schedule. Led by Mrs. Nelson, the camp resists and on the final day stages a Water Extravaganza that caps an unruly and joyous stay.

The author of this true, first-person narrative cannot initially see beyond these children's obvious pain, afflictions, and limitations, and his zeal to help them cannot stay the distance. But as his charges reveal themselves to him, he finds he can back up their own spirit and confirm their own insights. They cannot conquer their handicaps—an epilogue notes that the five boys were dead by the time of publication. But they temporarily conquer the social pressures that would confine them with labels "blind child," "cripple," and so on. Readers of this memorable book may well forget the handicaps but not the courage of these children.

Ages 10 and up

Also available in:
Braille—*The Acorn People*
Library of Congress (NLSBPH)

Cassette—*The Acorn People*
Library of Congress (NLSBPH)

319

Jones, Toeckey

Go Well, Stay Well

HarperCollins Publishers, Inc., 1979.
(202 pages) o.p.

APARTHEID
FRIENDSHIP: Meaning of
Dependence/Independence
Education: value of
Maturation
Prejudice: ethnic/racial
Values/Valuing: moral/ethical

When Candy, a white girl born and raised in South Africa, sprains her ankle, she is helped by Becky, a Zulu girl. A friendship develops between the two fifteen-year-olds. Becky tells an amazed Candy of the prejudice and poverty that her people have endured. South African whites attend school free, but Zulus must pay for their education. An embittered Becky explains that Zulus "mustn't be encouraged to become too educated. . . . Too much education would make us too clever and 'cheeky.'" The girls want to remain friends, but social mores forbid friendships between blacks and whites. To justify their meeting, they decide that Becky will give Candy weekly lessons in the Zulu language. Candy must then persuade her initially resistant parents to allow these lessons. Her bigoted older brother is especially insulting and hostile. But Candy prevails, and Sunday after Sunday the girls sit and talk in her room. They can't go swimming or play tennis together, but their desire to overcome their own prejudices—Becky's bitterness, Candy's unexamined assumptions about the races—bonds their friendship. One Sunday, Becky doesn't come for their usual meeting. There is rioting in Soweto, the black township where she lives. Candy tries desperately to find out what has happened to her friend. Finally Becky comes to Candy's house in urgent need of money. Her family must bribe the officials for a permit to stay in their house. Tension is high between the girls, Candy sensing how deeply Becky's pride must be suffering. She attempts to comfort her, but Becky backs away. She trusts no one; her only goals are survival and education. As the violence in Soweto settles down, Becky resumes her visits. Meanwhile, Candy meets and begins dating Dirk, an Afrikaner. She worries about Dirk's reaction to her friendship with Becky, since the Afrikaner government is largely responsible for the history of black suppression in South Africa. She is surprised and gratified to discover that Dirk has no prejudices against blacks. Determined to widen her awareness and overcome her remaining inner prejudices, Candy proposes to go with Becky to Swaziland to visit Becky's relatives. Candy's parents are shocked at the prospect and deeply opposed, but Candy resolves to defy them and go anyway. Her Uncle Jack comes to the rescue; he and his wife will take the girls to Becky's relatives' home and then vacation nearby. Although this appeases Candy's mother, her father doesn't give his blessing until the girls are about to leave. When he does, Candy can embark on this adventure with happiness.

This thought-provoking, well-written book provides a revealing, candid look at South Africa and apartheid. Varied perspectives of South African life are given through the eyes of Candy, her parents and brother, an old, black family employee, her Afrikaner boyfriend, and Becky. Characterizations and relationships have depth and complexity, and the story treats apartheid, a subject rarely found in children's literature, with exceptional clarity.

Ages 12 and up

Also available in:
No other form known

320

Jordan, Hope Dahle

Haunted Summer

Lothrop, Lee & Shepard Books, 1967.
(158 pages)

ACCIDENTS: Automobile
GUILT, FEELINGS OF
Conscience
Friendship: meaning of
Responsibility: avoiding

While driving a floral delivery van to earn money for college, high-school senior Rilla Marston accidentally hits paperboy Lyle Abbot and leaves the scene without identifying herself. A witness's description of her short hair and casual dress leads the police to search for a male hit-and-run driver. The accident shatters Rilla's summer plans of earning college tuition and concentrating on her golf game in preparation for competition. She spends an anxious summer worrying that she might make a mistake that will lead to her arrest. She is haunted by guilt. To ease her conscience, Rilla sends part of her earnings to Lyle, then lies to her family about her lack of funds. Rilla's fear of discovery increases when the hit-and-run story appears in local and state newspapers and in a national magazine. At one point she admits her guilt to a close friend, Seth Cone, but when he does not readily believe her, she laughs off her story as a joke. Later, Seth realizes the truth of Rilla's statement and comes home from college to help her. Rilla finally decides to confess her act publicly. With the support of her family and Seth, Rilla goes to the police station.

This first-person narrative deals with the feelings of guilt, fear, and anguish experienced by a hit-and-run driver. Even though the main character faces an uncertain future at the close of the story, she expresses relief for having accepted responsibility for her actions.

Ages 11 and up

Also available in:
No other form known

321

Kantrowitz, Mildred

Maxie

Color illustrations by Emily A. McCully.
Four Winds Press, 1980.
(33 pages counted)

LONELINESS

Maxie, a little, white-haired elderly lady, lives in a three-room apartment with her cat and canary. Every day Maxie follows the same routine: she gets up at seven; uncovers, feeds, and places her bird in the window; and puts her teakettle on to boil at 8:45. One day, Maxie feels desolate and depressed, so she goes to bed and does not get up the next morning. The doctor is called, and he says that Maxie is not sick, but lonely because she feels that nobody needs her. Many of Maxie's neighbors crowd into her small room to tell her how they rely on the sounds she makes in the morning to start their days: Mrs. Trueheart hears Maxie's bird and knows it is time to wake her husband for work; Susie hears Maxie's teakettle and knows it is time for her to catch the school bus; and others depend on her, too. After Maxie hears how important she is to the people in her building, she gets up and makes tea for everyone.

This story is a poignant statement about the effects of loneliness. It stresses the necessity of telling friends and loved one that they are needed.

Ages 5-8

Also available in:
No other form known

322

Kantrowitz, Mildred

Willy Bear

Color illustrations by Nancy Winslow Parker.
Four Winds Press, 1989.
(31 pages counted)

FEAR: of School
TRANSITIONAL OBJECTS: Toys
School: entering

The night before his first day at school, a little boy is talking to his toy bear, Willy, about what the next day will bring. The boy is nervous and cannot sleep. Pretending that it is Willy who is sleepless, the boy turns on a light, gets the bear a glass of water, and finally takes him into bed to snuggle. When morning comes, the boy rushes around, brushing his teeth, washing his face, getting dressed, and eating breakfast. Willy remains in the bedroom and is not ready. The little boy leaves without him, promising to tell him all about school when he returns.

This funny monologue, a boy's talk with his toy bear, expresses many children's nighttime worries, in particular those that arise the night before the first day of school. The boy's nervousness is alleviated by caring for his "friend" the bear. Preschool and kindergarten children may well enjoy it read aloud.

Ages 4-6

Also available in:
Paperbound—*Willy Bear*
Aladdin Books

323

Keats, Ezra Jack

Peter's Chair

Color illustrations by the author.
HarperCollins Publishers, Inc., 1967.
(32 pages counted)

SIBLING: New Baby
Running away
Sibling: jealousy

Little Peter has been told to play quietly because there is a new baby in the house. His baby cradle and crib have been painted pink, and now his high chair is being painted too. Jealous of the infant and angry at being displaced, Peter decides to run away. He takes his little blue chair (which has not been painted yet), and his toy crocodile, and his baby picture, setting up housekeeping on the sidewalk in front of his house. When he tries to sit in his blue chair, however, he finds it is too small. When his mother asks him to return home, Peter agrees. He then helps his daddy paint the little chair for his sister, who is small.

This simple, charming story describes the importance a little boy feels when he suddenly realizes he is a *big* brother.

Ages 3-7

Also available in:
Braille—*Peter's Chair*
Library of Congress (NLSBPH)

Cassette—*Peter's Chair*
Library of Congress (NLSBPH)

Paperbound—*Peter's Chair*
HarperCollins Publishers, Inc.

324

Keller, Helen Adams

The Story of My Life

Black/white photographs.
Doubleday, 1954.
(374 pages)o.p.

BLINDNESS
DEAFNESS
MUTENESS
Education: value of
Perseverance

Helen Keller, left blind and deaf by a childhood illness, has almost no communication with the world around her. Then, when she is six years old, Anne Sullivan becomes her teacher. Miss Sullivan helps Helen understand language and thus opens to her the windows of understanding. A sparkling, determined little girl, Helen wins the admiration of many well-known people who provide her with numerous opportunities to broaden her scope of learning. She attends the Perkins Institute for the Blind, then the Wright-Humason School for the Deaf, and later the

Cambridge School for Young Ladies, where she prepares for entrance to Radcliffe College. It is during her sophomore year at Radcliffe that she is encouraged by Charles Copeland, her English teacher, to write her autobiography. Helen Keller closes her story with a tribute to the many friends who enriched her life by introducing her to literature, the world of nature, outdoor sports, and a host of wonderful people.

The Story of My Life is composed of three sections. Part One is Helen's own recollection of her early life and education. Part Two is a collection of her letters written to friends and acquaintances between the years 1887 and 1901, from the first letter she ever wrote through those she wrote during her first year at Radcliffe. The letters enrich her story and reveal "her growth in thought and expression." Part Three, edited by John Albert Macy, gives a further account of Helen's character and achievements. The material for this section is drawn mainly from information, records, and letters provided by Helen's beloved teacher, Anne Sullivan Macy.

Ages 11 and up

Also available in:
Braille—*The Story of My Life*
Library of Congress (NLSBPH)

Cassette—*The Story of My Life*
Library of Congress (NLSBPH)

Talking Book—*The Story of My Life*
Library of Congress (NLSBPH)

325

Keller, Holly

Cromwell's Glasses

Color illustrations by the author.
Greenwillow Books, 1982.
(32 pages counted)

GLASSES, WEARING OF
Sibling: relationships
Teasing

Cromwell looks like all the other little rabbits, but in one way he's very different. As the doctor explains to Mama, "He's terribly nearsighted." Before long, Cromwell knows what the doctor means. He gets lost so many times when he's out playing with his sisters and brother that Mama finally has to tell him he can't go along anymore. He stumbles over things and his sister Lydia calls him "a pain." He tries to be helpful, but something always goes wrong. When Martin gets his kite stuck in a tree and Cromwell thinks it's a bird, Cynthia laughs at him, and a frustrated Cromwell kicks her foot as hard as he can. That night, as Mama tucks him in, she tells him to be patient because soon he'll be old enough to wear eyeglasses. When the day of his appointment with the eye doctor finally arrives, his mother gives him a new doll to help him feel brave. The examination takes a long time, but in a few days Cromwell's glasses are ready. Now he sees so much better that he can help Mama in the supermarket. His sisters and brother, however, make fun of the way he looks, and for a while Cromwell hates his new glasses even more than he hates not being able to see. But when Mama sends the children to the park and someone else makes fun of Cromwell's glasses, Cynthia becomes angry and shouts, "You can't talk about my brother like that!" She then plays with Cromwell on the jungle gym and applauds when he misses only one rung. Martin lets him play marbles, and he hits a shiny red one on the second try. He doesn't miss the ball when he plays catch and gets all the way to four on hopscotch. Cynthia tells him when it's time to leave that she thinks his "glasses are going to be okay," and he agrees. Exhausted, Cromwell sleeps all the way home.

Cromwell is teased when he can't see and teased when he wears glasses. This no-win situation ends when his siblings finally stick up for him. The book will be helpful both to children wearing glasses and to those who should be supportive of them. Softly colored illustrations of the rabbit family add appeal.

Ages 3-6

Also available in:
Cassette—*Cromwell's Glasses*
Library of Congress (NLSBPH)

326

Kellogg, Steven

Much Bigger Than Martin

Color illustrations by the author.
Dial Books for Young Readers, 1976.
(30 pages counted)

SIBLING: Youngest
Resourcefulness

Sometimes Henry finds it fun being Martin's little brother. But lately Henry is tired of being the smallest. When he and Martin play together, Martin always runs things. He also gets the biggest piece of cake and is allowed to swim out to the raft. Henry wishes he could grow even taller than Martin. He tries stretching himself, watering himself, and eating lots of apples but he does not grow an inch. He only gets a stomachache from eating too many apples. Henry imagines growing big as a giant, but soon realizes he would be too big to fit in the house or play with the other children. When Henry finally finds out that Martin was little once too, he is much happier. Martin himself tries to make Henry feel better about being the littlest. And Henry tries to help himself by making a pair of stilts.

This good-humored first-person narrative faces squarely the annoyance of being littler than others. Henry finds that his imagined ways of becoming bigger than Martin are simply impractical while the stilts he makes are a temporary help. The detailed, cleverly drawn illustrations will interest young children.

Ages 4-7

Also available in:
Paperbound—*Much Bigger Than Martin*
Dial Books for Young Readers

327

Kenny, Kevin and Helen Krull

Sometimes My Mom Drinks Too Much

Color illustrations by Helen Cogancherry.
Raintree/Steck-Vaughan Publishers, 1980.
(31 pages)

ALCOHOLISM: of Mother
Communication: parent-child

Maureen, about eight, is unhappy because her mother drinks too much. When she does she behaves strangely, upsetting their once-stable family. Sometimes Maureen is afraid of her mother. One day when her mother yells at her about not doing her homework and says she won't get any dinner until the homework is done, Maureen is too frightened to tell her she doesn't have any homework. Later, her mother apologizes and takes her out to eat, confusing Maureen even more. On the day of Maureen's school orchestra concert, which her father is conducting, her mother arrives late and must be helped to her seat. Maureen is embarrassed, especially when her mother claps too long afterwards and Maureen's friend Yoshi asks if her mother is drunk. The mornings when her mother is too sick from drinking to go to work and her father calls her company to say she has the flu, Maureen feels sorry for both of them. The mother is often unpredictable: she arrives late for a special dinner Maureen and her father have prepared and then is not interested in eating. At Maureen's birthday party her mother again disappoints and frightens her when she falls, drops the cake, and then lies on the floor laughing. Neither Maureen nor Yoshi think anything is funny. In fact, Maureen gets angry and wonders why her mother is so mean to her. "Why does Mom hate me?" she asks her father. He explains that her mother has a sickness called alcoholism that makes her drink too much and behave strangely. Her mother's illness, he assures the girl, has nothing to do with Maureen. Still, the mother's behavior affects them all. Sometimes when her father is especially upset with her mother, he yells at Maureen. Maureen is happiest when she is with her friends, and she gets support from her sympathetic teacher. One day, after her mother has been staying home from work more than usual, Maureen comes home from school and finds no one there. A note from her father says he will be home for dinner and not to worry, but Maureen worries anyway. When her father gets home, he tells Maureen her mother will be in a special hospital for a few weeks; she and her boss felt it could help her. Maureen wonders if her mother will be well when she returns; her father tells her that "no one knows for sure." The mother will still need help from them and from other people. "But you and I always have to remember that she has a sickness that's not our fault. We can help her get well, but she has to help herself too." Maureen wants to help right away by setting the table, but her father suggests she call Yoshi instead and invite her to go out with them for hamburgers.

A young girl struggles to understand and cope with her mother's alcoholism. Her father tries to help by providing information, explaining that her mother's behavior is caused by a sickness called alcoholism, not by anything Maureen has done. Readers experiencing similar emotional turmoil may be helped to understand alcoholism as a disease. The prospects for the woman's recovery are simply and honestly discussed. Of special note is the employer's supportive role in securing treatment for her. Expressive illustrations show an attractive woman trying and failing to maintain even the appearance of normality due to alcohol abuse.

Ages 5-8

Also available in:
No other form known

328

Kent, Deborah

Belonging: A Novel

Putnam Berkley Group, Inc., 1979.
(200 pages) o.p.

BLINDNESS
Belonging
Friendship: making friends
Identity, search for
Maturation
School: pupil-teacher relationships

Wanting to feel just like everyone else her age, Meg chooses to attend public high school instead of the Institute for the Blind. On the first day, the crush of students nearly overwhelms her, but she is no less happy to be one of the crowd at last. She finds her classes easily, and though annoyed by well-meaning but over-solicitous fellow students, maintains her composure. What troubles her more is the welter of school regulations. Happily, her English teacher, Frances Kellogg, turns out to be not one to go by the book; when Ms. Kellogg mentions that she needs students to work on the school literary magazine, Meg jumps at the chance to work with congenial people. At magazine staff meetings she meets Lindy and Keith, two outright misfits who prefer their individuality to being popular. Lindy does a lot of unpopular things: among them riding a bicycle to school, running a paper route, and hiking to picturesque spots. Meg likes Lindy, but this new friend's delight in doing only what she likes—when Meg wants so desperately to be just like everyone else—makes Meg hold back. Keith, on the other hand, is apt to burst into Wagnerian arias at the top of his voice at inopportune times. Uneasy over this, Meg prefers not to be seen with him. In the way of "normal" friends, Meg gets to know Jeff, a football player, and his girlfriend, Karen. Soon she has a crush on him and is jealous of Karen—not only because of Jeff but also because Karen has so many friends and gives so many parties. Though Meg has nothing in common with Karen, she feels complimented when Karen asks her to help with English homework. In return for that help, Karen invites her to a party. Meg is so transported by the prospect of an evening with the "right" crowd that she forgets she had promised to go with Ms. Kellogg, Keith, and Lindy to see "La Traviata" the same night. She lies to get out of that. But the party, to her dismay, is a disaster. It is all drinking, smoking pot, and playing kissing games. When Jeff makes deprecating remarks about Ms. Kellogg, the last of Meg's desire to belong to Karen's circle disappears. Afraid her defection may have cost her a real friendship, she apologizes to Lindy and explains her feelings. Having herself had the feelings once, Lindy understands. More pressing is the suddenly looming possibility that Ms. Kellogg will be fired because she is thought to be emotionally unstable. Meg herself has noticed oddities in her teacher's behavior, but nothing serious enough to be fired for, as Lindy and Keith agree. All the same, Ms. Kellogg is forced to resign—and the three friends publish an editorial in her defense. The principal is appalled, accuses them of not knowing all the facts, and considers suspending Keith and Lindy. Although the editorial had been her idea, he offers to excuse Meg because of her blindness. The girl flatly insists on equal treatment. Fortunately for the three, their parents understand, and Meg, Keith, and Lindy spend part of their three-day suspension attending a Broadway musical. Meg knows now what is worth "belonging" to.

In this sensitive first-person narrative, Meg discovers that it is not her blindness that sets her apart from her contemporaries but her individualism. She realizes she belongs with those who appreciate her talents and share her interests. Blind students may be inspired by this story and sighted students instructed how the blind feel.

Ages 11-14

Also available in:
No other form known

329

Kerr, Judith

When Hitler Stole Pink Rabbit

Black/white illustrations by the author.
Coward–McCann, 1972.
(191 pages)

REFUGEES
Change: accepting
Change: new home
Change: resisting
Jew
Ostracism
Prejudice: religious

In 1933, nine-year-old Anna must leave her settled life in Berlin, Germany, because her father, a well-to-do anti-Nazi writer, is afraid that the Nazis may gain power in the upcoming election. He leaves for Switzerland. Anna, her mother, and her brother, Max, follow two weeks later with a few meager possessions. At the inn where they are staying in Switzerland, they hear that Hitler has indeed been elected and that the police have confiscated all the belongings the family left behind. Although Father does not make much money now and they have few possessions, they are glad that they are at least safe. In an incident at the inn, German guests stop their children from playing with Anna and Max because they are Jewish. Soon afterward, Father decides to move the family to France. They settle in Paris. Anna feels sure she will never learn to speak the language fluently or have any friends. When she enrolls in a school where no one speaks German, she is forced to use her limited French. Despite the language barrier, she is accepted by the girls at school and soon becomes part of a group. Because of the friendships she makes and her daily use of French, Anna comes to feel quite at home in Paris and grows proficient in her adopted language. After two years in Paris, Anna's family moves again, this time to England. But Anna is not apprehensive because she realizes that she will be able to adjust to England just as she adapted to France.

Although Anna accepts one sudden move, she cannot accept being uprooted again to a place where she must confront not only religious prejudice, but also a language barrier. The danger of the prewar period is portrayed not only by the experiences of this family, but also by the experiences of a friend who remains in Berlin and suffers persecution and, finally, death. This moving novel is based on the author's own childhood experiences. Its realism is enhanced by the inclusion of homey details of family life.

Ages 10-12

Also available in:
Braille—*When Hitler Stole Pink Rabbit*
Library of Congress (NLSBPH)

Paperbound—*When Hitler Stole Pink Rabbit*
Dell Publishing Company, Inc. (Yearling Books)

Talking Book—*When Hitler Stole Pink Rabbit*
Library of Congress (NLSBPH)

330

Kerr, M. E., pseud.

I'll Love You When You're More Like Me

HarperCollins Publishers, Inc., 1977.
(183 pages)

BOY-GIRL RELATIONSHIPS
IDENTITY, SEARCH FOR
Expectations

Wally Witherspoon, almost a high school senior, is the son of a funeral director in a New York City suburb. Wally's father, a conservative, stuffy man, expects him to enter the family business after graduating and to marry Harriet Hren, a willful, prudish girl who tells Wally what to do. One day at the beach, Wally meets Sabra St. Amour, teenage star of a popular daytime television serial. He meets her again later that week when he, Harriet, and his friend Charlie, who claims to be a homosexual, are spending an evening at the local dance club. The two boys invite Sabra to join them after the dance, and jealous Harriet walks out. Wally, Charlie, and Sabra go for a stroll on the beach anyway, and find they like one another. The three continue to see each other and finally Harriet writes Wally that he and she are finished. More relieved than sorry, he continues seeing Sabra. One day, talking with his father yet again about the family business, Wally announces that he will not become a mortician but he is going to college to pursue a career in linguistics. Meanwhile, Sabra has been trying to decide whether or not to stay with her television show or go to college herself. One night, Wally takes her to a party. Sabra, never at ease with people her own age, can only play out her television personality. Embarrassed and unhappy, she gladly leaves with Wally, and the two drive into New York City, where she tells Wally she cannot leave show business after all. She also says good-bye. Back at home, Wally does not see her again. But he does look forward to his senior year, while Charlie takes a job at the funeral home.

Wally talks about his father's business wittily, but the prospect of being forced to become a funeral director is finally too much for him to take. Like Wally's father, Sabra's mother has tried to keep her locked into a prearranged future, and for Sabra independence may prove more difficult. This story is told alternately by Sabra and Wally, and its characterizations, dialogue, and relationships are convincing.

Ages 12 and up

Also available in:
Braille—*I'll Love You When You're More Like Me*
Library of Congress (NLSBPH)

Cassette—*I'll Love You When You're More Like Me*
Library of Congress (NLSBPH)

Paperbound—*I'll Love You When You're More Like Me*
HarperCollins Publishers, Inc.

331

Kerr, M. E., pseud.

Little Little

HarperCollins Publishers, Inc., 1981.
(183 pages)

BOY-GIRL RELATIONSHIPS
DWARFISM
Autonomy
Orphan
Parental: overprotection

Sydney Cinnamon, a seventeen-year-old dwarf with a humped back, was abandoned by his mother at birth to an orphanage for malformed children. When he was fifteen he designed a "roach costume" for himself and became the mascot for his school's football team. Mr. Palmer, owner of a local pest control company, hired "The Roach," as Sydney came to be called, and the boy became a local hero through public appearances and television advertisements. Bella La Belle, known as Little Little, is the daughter of a prominent businessman in the town of La Belle. She too is a dwarf, though perfectly formed, pretty, and overprotected by her parents. The weekend of her eighteenth birthday an organization called "Tadpoles," a club for dwarfs, is holding a convention in La Belle. Included in the weekend festivities is a huge birthday party for Little Little. By coincidence, as a favor for a business associate, Mr. Palmer has arranged to have "The Roach" make a guest appearance at the party. Sydney comes to town early and, by chance, meets Little Little at an amusement park. The two are attracted to one another. Sydney performs as "The Roach" at an afternoon football game attended by Little Little and her snobbish parents, who tell Little Little that they hope she would never associate with that particular dwarf. They dislike the "offensive, vulgar, show-biz aspects of this fellow." In defiance, Little Little goes to a movie with Sydney that night. Her angry father comes to the theater and carries his daughter out. Meanwhile, another well-known dwarf is coming to La Belle for the weekend: Knox Lionel, a sharply dressed, smooth-talking evangelist and con man, known to all as Little Lion. Little Lion has been writing love notes to Little Little since last year's Tadpole convention, and this year, convinced she would be an added attraction at his evangelical meetings, he proposes to her. He preaches a Sunday morning church service and gives an altar call especially directed to Little Little. But by now she has decided she is quite uninterested in him, his preaching, and his proposal, and she ignores him. So when another girl, just as pretty, answers his altar call, Lion starts a new romance. The finale of the weekend, Little Little's birthday party, ends in chaos when Lion and his new girlfriend dump Little Little's birthday cake onto her lap. Soon after the party, Sydney moves to La Belle and he and Little Little, to the annoyance of her parents, become close friends. However, when their English teacher prefers Sydney's composition to

Little Little's, the competitive girl's interest in Sydney seems to cool.

Growing up as a dwarf can be complicated and frustrating, but it need not be defeating. Despite his size, appearance, and bizarre upbringing, Sydney has become highly motivated and self-educated. Similarly, Little Little's difficulty is not her size but her domineering parents. This unusual and well-written story is told in alternating chapters, first from Sydney's perspective, then from Little Little's. Strong characterizations and believable, often humorous dialogue overcome the strange details and settings.

Ages 11 and up

Also available in:
Paperbound—*Little Little*
HarperCollins Publishers, Inc.

332

Kerr, M. E., pseud.

Love Is a Missing Person

HarperCollins Publishers, Inc., 1975.
(164 pages)

MATURATION
Boy-girl relationships: dating
Jealousy: sibling
Parent/Parents: remarriage of
Prejudice: ethnic/racial
Values/Valuing: materialistic

Suzy Slade, fifteen years old and with wealthy, divorced parents, is in ninth grade at a high school in a fashionable Long Island community. She says of herself, "I am . . . the Slade daughter the father chose *not* to take to New York to live with him." Suzy works as a volunteer at the local public library and feels close to two people on the staff: Nan Richmond, a junior in high school and the first black ever employed at the library; and Gwendolyn Spring, middle-aged and still missing a lover of thirty-five years before. Suzy spares little thought for her family and resents her older sister, a radical named Chicago, who is the Slade daughter who does live in New York City with their father. Suddenly, Chicago returns, announcing that she is disillusioned with her father and his wealth. When Mr. Slade invites Suzy to New York, hoping that she will now live with him, she finds that he has married a nineteen-year-old working girl who memorizes famous quotations to impress her. Feeling sorry for her father, Suzy departs, only to find worse disarray on Long Island: Chicago has fallen in love with Nan Richmond's boyfriend, Roger Cole III, an all-star black athlete and valedictorian of the class. Gwendolyn Spring's wartime lover has returned, not to marry her, as she hoped (he has married someone else), but to borrow money from her. And a valuable painting is missing from the library's erotica collection, one which Nan had taken to show Roger, not knowing of his new love, and which Chicago and Roger now plan to keep until the library agrees to certain demands: abolition of fees for library cards, acquiring a bookmobile, enlarging the collection of black literature, and opening the erotica collection to the public. Suzy discovers the painting in Chicago's knapsack and tells Miss Spring, who calls the police. Chicago and Roger are arrested but released on bail put up by Mr. Slade. They jump bail and disappear.

Suzy Slade tells this story of her family and friends, of loving and losing. She is perceptive about people's strengths and weaknesses and no less so about the contradictions in society, seeing the irony of her sister's becoming a revolutionary who daydreams on her silk monogrammed sheets of "leveling" social differences, and treats her black lover to a ride in her new motorboat. Yet this book takes economic inequality and racism seriously, along with divorce and remarriage and interracial dating. Suzy ponders the power of love to create missing persons out of old friends. This is a richly plotted story whose dialogue crackles.

Ages 12 and up

Also available in:
Paperbound—*Love Is a Missing Person*
HarperCollins Publishers, Inc.

Talking Book—*Love Is a Missing Person*
Library of Congress (NLSBPH)

333

Kherdian, David

The Road from Home: The Story of an Armenian Girl

Greenwillow Books, 1979.
(238 pages)

COURAGE, MEANING OF
WAR
Family: relationships
Refugees

Veron Dumehjian's earliest memories, from 1907, are of her family's white stucco house in the Armenian quarter of Azizya in Turkey. This home was surrounded by beautiful poppy fields belonging to her father, who was a wealthy merchant of the poppy gum used in making opium. Her father's family was large and wealthy, and Veron was surrounded by many relatives. She had an especially loving relationship with her grandmother, her Aunt Lousapere, and her cousin Hrpsime, who was her own age. When she was eight, Veron's idyllic childhood came to an abrupt end. World War I was raging and the Turkish government, allied with Germany, decided to eliminate the Armenians living in their country. Since two uncles were serving in the Turkish army, their wives, children, and mother, Veron's grandmother, were allowed to stay in Azizya. Aunt Lousapere and Hrpsime were also among those permitted to stay. The rest of the family, including Veron, were given three days to pack their wagon and prepare themselves for deportation. Veron, a happy and optimistic child, was determined that someday she would return to Azizya and the loved ones left behind. On the journey across Turkey, the people suffered from exhaustion and lack of food. Old people who fell along the way were killed by the gendarmes who controlled the procession. The Dumehjians were able to keep going because of their wealth: Papa could bribe the soldiers. After entering Syria, however, many of the deportees contracted cholera. The three younger Dumehjian children died. Veron, however, survived, and in spite of all the sadness still had a strong will to live. But her gentle mother could not bear the loss of her children and soon died also. Knowing now that they were nearing the end of their journey and that death was imminent for all of them, Papa bribed one of the gendarmes to let them escape back into Turkey, which was free again. After arriving in Biriji, Papa was called away with his wagon to serve the Turkish government. He died while on this assignment and Veron was left in the care of her "aunties," solitary Armenian women who had survived the march. Eventually she came to live in an orphanage for Armenian refugee children in Syria. Then, when she was nearly twelve, she was reunited with her grandmother. She found, however, that everything had changed in Azizya. Aunt Lousapere, having lost her husband, had taken Hrpsime to live in Smyrna. The other members of the family did not "know how to be of comfort to one another." Then more fighting broke out. The Greeks, Christians like the Armenians, began to fight the Turks for the control of Smyrna. Azizya was bombed and Veron, severely wounded in the leg, was sent to a hospital in nearby Afyon. A Greek general who came regularly to the hospital met her and, several weeks later, asked to adopt her. He wished to protect her, to take her to his sister's home in Smyrna and later to Athens. Fearing that she would be killed if the Turks defeated the Greeks in Afyon and again turned against the Armenians, Veron consented. The home in Smyrna was very beautiful, but the girl could not be happy. She started to think about her parents, sister, and brothers: "I felt that if I went to Athens with the general and became Greek, I would not only lose my church and my nation and my grandmother, but in a sense I would lose all of those who had died, as well. I had to remain an Armenian, a Dumehjian, the girl my parents and grandmother had reared." She ran away and, after another hospitalization for her injured leg, was found by her Aunt Lousapere and reunited with Hrpsime. After much more travail, at the age of sixteen, Veron left for America to become the bride of an Armenian refugee who had asked for an Armenian wife. His parents and Veron's aunt had arranged the marriage, and Veron was satisfied with the prospect.

In this wartime biography of his mother, writing in his mother's voice, David Kherdian has described an amazingly resilient young girl's struggle to survive terrible persecution without giving up her "hope and belief in life" or her "faith in God." Veron always knew that she was not made for sadness and it was this natural optimism, along with a desire to bring joy to others, that helped her go on when others could not. The view of the persecution itself, as seen through the eyes of this loving child, is extremely penetrating but not gory, explicit, or melodramatic. The book gives insight into a period of history not commonly known and is eloquent testimony to the grief and futility of war.

Ages 12 and up

Also available in:
Cassette—*The Road from Home: The Story of an Armenian Girl*
Library of Congress (NLSBPH)

334

Kingman, Lee

Break a Leg, Betsy Maybe!

Dell Publishing Company, Inc., 1979.
(245 pages) o.p.

BOY-GIRL RELATIONSHIPS
IDENTITY, SEARCH FOR
Loneliness
Maturation
Peer relationships
Talents: artistic

Seventeen-year-old Elizabeth Cythera Wilkersen Maybe bears a weight in life more substantial than her name. Her parents and her stepfather, too, are dead. Therapy undergone earlier has defined her condition—a double identity crisis and shock over three deaths—without improving it. Now Betsy lives with her aunt and uncle and attends a public high school. Both withdrawn and bored, her chief interest is in Nick Gretschkin, a classmate, but he is virtually engaged to Francena "Stackie" Delahey. An acquaintance urges her to try out for the school's drama club, and since Nick is a member, she does, and wins a role in a play. Stackie and Nick, as usual, earn leading roles. But Betsy finds in theater the direction and involvement she needs. At the cast party, Betsy and Nick are suddenly alone together, talk companionably and, just as Nick kisses Betsy, Stackie walks in. That ends that: Nick remains with Stackie, and Stackie ignores Betsy. As winter passes, everyone except Betsy makes plans for college. She, on the other hand, inquires about a drama school in England. That spring all her efforts are directed at winning the leading female role in *Our Town* but it goes to Stackie. Suddenly Nick quits the play and he and Stackie are no longer together. Betsy learns from Stackie that Nick may have cancer. Betsy talks to Nick and finds him relieved: tests have confirmed he has Hodgkins Disease, but his chances of recovery are excellent. When she is accepted by the English drama school, Betsy almost declines to go so as to remain with Nick, for they have grown closer and closer. But he persuades her to go after all. By now, Betsy knows she is reconciled to life: "Who wants to run away from any of it, anywhere? No matter what comes next, I'm ready for it."

This first-person narrative, written partly in the style of a play and partly as a diary, discovers Betsy's pleasure in acting and her difficulty in winning a boy from a talented, popular, pretty girl. Through both she comes to find herself. Their story also involves many subplots about members of the drama club. Over all, the pace is leisurely but plot and characters are realistic. Readers interested in theater will find pleasure in the theater lore and practice woven through this book.

Ages 12 and up

Also available in:
No other form known

335

Kingman, Lee

Head Over Wheels

Dell Publishing Company, Inc., 1981.
(186 pages) o.p.

QUADRIPLEGIA
TWINS: Identical
Accidents: automobile
Anger
Family: unity
Guilt, feelings of
Nightmares
Self, attitude toward: feeling different
Wheelchair, dependence on

Kerry and Terry Tredinnick are identical seventeen-year-old twins—until an automobile accident leaves Terry with a shattered jaw, a broken leg and ankle, and a broken neck. Kerry escapes the same accident (which kills the driver) with only slight injuries. During his first weeks in the hospital, Terry is placed in a Stryker frame, which holds him immobile until surgery fuses his crushed vertebrae. The family is told by the doctors that, though Terry's arms can move a little, he is considered quadriplegic, having no feeling from the shoulders down, and will never walk again. This news and Terry's helplessness make Kerry feel guilty: he is walking and Terry never will. To lighten his burden of guilt and to support his twin however he can, Kerry visits Terry as much as possible. But other thoughts plague Kerry during these visits: why is Terry so withdrawn? And does he, against the doctors' firm diagnosis, really believe he will walk again? Terry's girlfriend is far more troubled, refusing at first to see him; then, when she does, recoiling physically and emotionally, although Terry does not at first notice. She finds herself powerfully drawn to Kerry instead. Kerry's girlfriend is far steadier, more natural, and more encouraging with Terry, while remaining loyal to his brother. As Terry's condition improves, he is taken off the Stryker frame and moved to the rehabilitation center. While he is there, he and Kerry both go through periods of depression, withdrawal, and anger. Meanwhile, their parents and younger brother and sister adjust to Terry's condition and try to meet the mounting hospital bills. Terry also endures therapy sessions which will help him utilize those muscles he can control. The sessions are no less demoralizing than helpful. As a quadriplegic, Terry cannot sense his body; he becomes nauseated when he sits up, cannot cough, sneeze, or belch, and must haul his useless legs wherever he goes. At long last, he is able to go home, to live in the basement apartment that has been adapted to his needs. There he takes care of his personal needs and begins to see friends. But he has so little to do with his family that Kerry senses he is building a wall between them and himself. And it is not until Terry suddenly wants to share a confidence with Kerry, and torturously hoists and drags himself up most of the two flights of stairs, that the twins come to see that, although they will never be identical again and must lead their own lives, they will always be close.

In this tense, candid story the reader is taken through the accident, injury, and slow rehabilitation of an adolescent boy. Events are viewed from both Terry's and Kerry's perspectives—giving the reader an understanding of both the victim and one who escaped. The abilities and limitations of quadriplegics, depending upon the degree and location of spinal damage, are explained in detail. So too the monetary hardship the extended hospital stay places on the family, how each family member adjusts to the situation, how the quadriplegic views himself and the way others view him. Withal, this is a serious story without being depressing or melodramatic.

Ages 12 and up

Also available in:
Cassette—*Head Over Wheels*
Library of Congress (NLSBPH)

336

Klein, Norma

Confessions of an Only Child

Black/white illustrations by Richard Cuffari.
Pantheon Books, 1974.
(93 pages)

ONLY CHILD
Death: of infant
Sibling: new baby

Toe, short for Antonia, is an only child who is nearly nine years old. Soon there will be a new baby in the family, and Toe is not sure she wants that. Her friend Libby has a little sister—and she often smells bad. Toe's father begins fixing up a room for Toe to move into when the baby comes. Her parents try to convince her that a baby in the family will not be so horrible. One Saturday morning, Toe learns that her parents have gone to the hospital. When Dad comes home, he tells her that the baby boy is not breathing properly. The next day, he reports sadly that the baby has died. Toe is glad she is still an only child, but sad that the baby died. She tries to cheer her mother. Toe is angry with her friend Libby when Libby does not even say she is sorry about the baby's death. Although Mom is very unhappy, she says that she plans to "start another one" soon. When Mom becomes pregnant again, Toe is sure that the dead baby has come back, but later she realizes that this will be a different baby. When the baby is born, Toe is genuinely happy to have a little brother.

The girl in this first-person narrative feels ambivalent about being an only child. After the first baby dies, she realizes that she actually had been looking forward to the baby's arrival and that she is ready to accept a newcomer.

Ages 9-11

Also available in:
Braille—*Confessions of an Only Child*
Library of Congress (NLSBPH)

Paperbound—*Confessions of an Only Child*
Alfred A. Knopf, Inc.

337

Knox-Wagner, Elaine

My Grandpa Retired Today

Color illustrations by Charles Robinson.
Albert Whitman & Company, 1982.
(30 pages counted)

GRANDPARENT: Love for
RETIREMENT
Empathy
Lifestyle: change in
Loss: feelings of

The day her grandfather retires from his barbershop, young Margey is the only child at his party. She eats large quantities of chocolate cake and tidies up the shop, asking her grandfather if she should wash the combs. He tells her to throw out the old newspapers instead and they salute one another in a familiar little ritual. Then comes the big surprise. Grandpa is presented with his own barber chair, now decorated with ribbon and unbolted from the floor. "Since no one can take your place, Al, we decided you should take it with you, Grandpa's partner says. The friends clap, the guest of honor stares, and Margey runs to the bathroom to be sick. When she returns she tells her concerned grandfather that she just had too much cake, and together they clean the shop for the last time. When it is time to leave, she refuses his offer to lock the door, telling him he should do it this time. They walk home slowly. Grandpa suggests activities they could do together during the summer, but Margey only says, "I like barbershops." He tells her he will miss the shop too. That night Margey finds her grandfather sitting in his barber chair, looking lonesome and sad. She jumps on his lap and tells him, "There is more to life than working in a barbershop." He laughs and sends her to bed with a promise of things they will do in the morning. In bed, Margey thinks about those things—the sticky drawers they will fix and the dresser they will paint, the backgammon game her grandfather and his friend will teach her and her friend, and the barbershop they may visit. "But not to stay," she says. "Because, today, my grandpa retired."

This warm story about the feelings of loss that retirement can bring, as seen through the eyes of a little girl, is simple but expressive. Margey shares her grandfather's elation at the party, his emptiness at its end, and his sadness upon leaving his barbershop for the last time. When she begins to see the positive aspects of the change—more time to be together—she cheers her grandfather by telling him what she's discovered. This story, with its detailed illustrations, may help children understand what retirement means.

Ages 4-7

Also available in:
No other form known

338

Knudson, R. Rozanne

Rinehart Lifts

Farrar, Straus & Giroux, Inc., 1980.
(88 pages)

DETERMINATION
FRIENDSHIP: Best Friend
Friendship: meaning of
School: classmate relationships
Sports/Sportsmanship

Arthur Rinehart is the fifth grade's Mr. Nice Guy. He is smart, gets A's on tests, and reads aloud to the class. He also loves plants and has all kinds growing in his room at home. But Rinehart, as his best friend, Suzanne "Zan" Hagen, calls him, is not athletic. "Rinehart couldn't roll or toss or pitch or fling or bowl. He was uncoordinated as maple syrup. He was the slowest runner in the fifth grade. Face it. Rinehart was a sports slouch." Zan wants Rinehart to excel in at least one sport. She is tired of Randy, Fritz, Eugene, and Dum-Dum, the "Mighty Four," paying him a quarter not to play with them. Rinehart is satisfied being a sports slouch, but Zan threatens to end their friendship if he can't perform in the next sport she sees on TV. That Saturday, Zan watches weight lifting on TV and decides this is one sport in which Rinehart can be successful. He wants her friendship and agrees to try. The two buy a book about weight lifting and a one-hundred-pound starter set with two dumbbells and one barbell. Zan sets up a gym in Rinehart's garage. He works out each day while Zan encourages him. Zan even decorates the garage with a rug and Rinehart's plants. By December Rinehart has begun to love lifting and has advanced from beginner to intermediate. In January Zan challenges the Mighty Four to a lifting match with Rinehart. They laugh and ignore her, not knowing what she means by "lifting." In February Zan tries them again. Instead, the four boys sneak into Rinehart's garage and destroy the plants and pots. Zan wants revenge; Rinehart wants a contest. In April he is in the advanced weight-lifting program and Zan once again challenges the Mighty Four to a "Lifting Spectacular." Having no idea what they are getting into, they accept. Each wants to win the "Mr. Arlington" contest that Zan has set up. The day of the contest, the four boys arrive confident of victory, only to discover none can lift the one-hundred-pound barbell over his head. Confidently Rinehart poses, flexing his muscles, and then lifts the weights—to the amazement of the Mighty Four and his own and Zan's satisfaction.

Two friends with opposite personalities defeat a band of local "jocks" in this easy-to-read story. Rinehart is indifferent to sports; Zan is athletic, knowledgeable, and competitive. Together they succeed in making Rinehart excel at something besides his schoolwork and his horticulture. In three companion books featuring Zan, *Zanballer, Zanboomer,* and *Zanbanger,* Rinehart is Zan's coach. In this book they exchange roles. The ending shows Rinehart a victor at last, but leaves hanging his future relationship with the Mighty Four.

Ages 10-12

Also available in:
Paperbound—*Rinehart Lifts*
Farrar, Straus & Giroux, Inc. (Sunburst Books)

339

Knudson, R. Rozanne

Zanbanger

HarperCollins Publishers, Inc., 1977.
(162 pages) o.p.

GENDER ROLE IDENTITY: Female
PREJUDICE: Sexual
SPORTS/SPORTSMANSHIP
Competition
Cooperation: in play
Justice/Injustice
Problem solving

With the new gym floor installed, Suzanne "Zan" Hagen can hardly wait to begin girls' basketball practice. Her best friend and private coach, Arthur Rinehart, has helped Zan greatly with her shooting, and she is optimistic about her team's chances for the coming season. But she has not reckoned on her coach's zeal for femininity. Mrs. Butor disapproves of Zan's aggressive play, preferring instead decorum at all times. Zan feels helpless. As usual, Arthur comes up with a plan; he flatters Mrs. Butor outrageously and gains her assent. He coaches Zan and E. J., the two best players on the girls' team, for eight days, then matches them against the rest of Mrs. Butor's girls. Zan and E. J. easily outscore the others, after which the boys' team—the Generals—takes over the gym, and Coach O'Hara invites Zan to scrimmage with them. All but one of the boys give her a hard time, but Zan holds her own, as Arthur takes notes from the sidelines. But that Monday Zan finds she has been cut from the girls' team. Faithful Arthur then goes to Coach O'Hara and asks that Zan be allowed to play on his team; but O'Hara says the principal and school board would never allow it. Arthur decides to take her case to court, where he himself pleads for her right to play with the Generals. On the second day of the hearing Coach O'Hara surprises everyone by testifying for Zan himself. "I want her on my team . . . because she plays well," he says, adding, "Hagen's a winner, make no mistake." The judge rules in Zan's favor and orders immediate tryouts with the Generals for all eligible girls. Zan makes it as a substitute, and E. J. is added later in the season to replace an injured player. But now Zan is resented by both her own teammates and opposing teams, some of which simply refuse to play against a girl, and forfeit their games. But as the season progresses, the Generals are playing team ball more and winning more. The Generals—all but the team captain and his friend—are accepting Zan, realizing she is not just a determined player but a good one. Then, near the end of the season, a crucial loss shows the team's problem. The two holdouts begin to cooperate and the Generals win their final game, the league championship, and the tournament. "We had won," says Zan. "We had won each other."

K

In this timely story of sexual discrimination in school athletics, a teenage girl wins the legal right to play on the team of her choice, then earns the right with her playing skill. Interestingly, it is her male friend who comes to her rescue time and again, and he is the one who brings her case to court. Away from the basketball court, Zan seems helpless, unable to defend herself. Basketball lingo abounds in this book and will itself attract some readers. Although a first-person narrative, the story quotes other viewpoints to summarize some events. *Zanballer* precedes this book and *Zanboomer* follows it, both of them dealing with Suzanne Hagen and sports.

Ages 10-13

Also available in:
Cassette—*Zanbanger*
Library of Congress (NLSBPH)

340

Knudson, R. Rozanne

Zanboomer

HarperCollins Publishers, Inc., 1978.
(183 pages) o.p.

DETERMINATION
SPORTS/SPORTSMANSHIP
Friendship: meaning of
Loyalty

Suzanne "Zan" Hagen, an ardent high school athlete, has been playing baseball since she was a child. This is an exciting spring for her: she has qualified to play shortstop for the high school baseball team. Her best friend, Arthur Rinehart, acts as Zan's personal coach, filming her, analyzing her strengths and weaknesses, showing her how to improve. Zan becomes the team's power hitter and earns the nickname "Zanboomer," taking the team through the exhibition season undefeated. But the first conference game, however, brings disaster. In the seventh inning, Zan whacks the ball into outfield, but as she slides into home plate, she collides with both pitcher and catcher. She goes to the hospital with a concussion and torn shoulder ligaments. Her baseball season is over. To keep her spirits up while her shoulder is healing, Rinehart persuades her to run every day and helps her improve her stride and speed. He reads books on running and turns his basement into a training room. Zan herself hopes to get back to baseball for the championship round of the state tournament, but her team is eliminated in the playoffs. School closes for the summer, and Zan is overwhelmed with the feeling that she failed her team by not rejoining them soon enough. She refuses to get out of bed. Rinehart is not heard from for several days, and when he reappears it is with yet another scheme: Zan will begin training now for cross-country running in the fall. At first she refuses, seeing no point in playing a non-team sport, but Rinehart brings her around. Zan cooperates enthusiastically. After rigorous training all summer Zan competes in her first race and wins the trophy.

This first-person narrative, told by Zan but interrupted briefly by Rinehart, is the story of two powerhouses: Zan, who loves to compete and achieve, and Rinehart, a brilliant coach and organizer. Rinehart's loyalty is extraordinary and his tact is no less so; he helps Zan without using her. But his scientific mind does meditate on possible reasons for her competitiveness. The long, detailed descriptions of training and competition here will appeal to girls who love sports. Hardly a model of graceful prose, this book could encourage girls to overcome obstacles on the way to all sorts of goals. It is preceded by two other books about Suzanne Hagen and sports, *Zanballer* and *Zanbanger.*

Ages 10-13

Also available in:
Cassette—*Zanboomer*
Library of Congress (NLSBPH)

341

Konigsburg, Elaine Lobl

About the B'nai Bagels

Black/white illustrations by the author.
Atheneum Publishers, 1969.
(172 pages)

MATURATION
Friendship: keeping friends
Friendship: making friends
Jew
Little League
Parent/Parents: respect for/lack of respect for
Prejudice: ethnic/racial
Responsibility: accepting

A twelve-year-old Jewish boy, Mark Setzer, is upset because his friend Hersch Miller has moved to a wealthier neighborhood and things have changed between them. To add to his worries, he is now on the Little League baseball team his mother has volunteered to manage and his twenty-one-year-old brother is coaching. At first the boys on the team object to having a woman manager, but eventually they grow to respect her. Hersch is also on the team. Mark tries to renew their friendship, but he soon realizes that Hersch prefers the friendship of Barry Jacob, a sophisticated youth from his new neighborhood. Unhappy, Mark begins practicing on Saturday afternoons with other team members. When one of the boys makes anti-Semitic remarks about him, Mark is tempted to tell his mother so that the boy will be removed from the team, but he decides to keep the information to himself so that he will not appear to be taking advantage of his mother's position. Mark still tries to rekindle his old, close friendship with Hersch; but it is not until late in the season, when Barry irritates them both by boasting about how well he played, that Mark and Hersch team up again. Mark soon realizes, however, that their friendship cannot be the same because Hersch is still friends with Barry. Accepting this, Mark concentrates on the last game. His team wins, but Mark is aware that the game has been won because two team members, identical twins, have exchanged positions. At first he suspects that his mother is behind the ruse, but after confiding in his father, he feels assured that his mother would not cheat to win. Dreading censure by his teammates, he tells his mother the truth about the win. Mrs. Setzer forfeits the game, and Mark is not blamed for the forfeit.

In spite of the seriousness of its themes, this first-person narrative has a generally humorous tone. In it, a preteenager learns to accept responsibility and solve his own problems. The reader is able to recognize the close-knit relationships in the boy's family and to empathize with his feelings about prejudice, friendship, his brother, and the actions and attitudes of his parents.

Ages 10-13

Also available in:
Braille—*About the B'nai Bagels*
Library of Congress (NLSBPH)

Talking Book—*About the B'nai Bagels*
Library of Congress (NLSBPH)

342

Konigsburg, Elaine Lobl

Altogether, One at a Time

Black/white illustrations by Gail E. Haley, Mercer Mayer, Gary Parker, and Laurel Schindelman.
Atheneum Publishers, 1971.
(79 pages)

AGE: Respect for
ETIQUETTE
LEARNING DISABILITIES
PREJUDICE: Ethnic/Racial
WEIGHT CONTROL: Overweight

"Inviting Jason," the first narrative in this collection of four short stories, introduces Stanley, whose mother tells him he must invite Jason to his birthday party. Stanley fears that the learning-disabled Jason will ruin the games he had planned. A guest with some influence improves everybody's understanding and tolerance of dyslexia. In the second story, "The Night of the Leonids," Lewis and his grandmother go to Central Park to view a Leonid meteor shower, but it is clouded out. To find out how old Grandmother would be the next time she had such an opportunity, she tells Lewis to "add it up." Sixty-three (Grandmother's present age) plus thirty-three (the number of years until next predicted star shower) is ninety-six. Lewis realizes that Grandmother's disappointment is even greater than his own, for she will never have another chance to see a Leonid meteor shower. In the third story, "Camp Fat," Clara attends a camp for people who want to lose weight. She does not want to be there and does not want to lose weight. The mysterious Miss Natasha helps Clara view the camp and herself differently. The last story, "Momma at the Pearly Gates," is about a young black girl who travels across town alone on the bus to an all-white school. Since she travels so far, she must stay for lunch. Alone during the lunch hour, she amuses herself by drawing pictures on the chalkboard. She meets a white girl who also stays for lunch. The girls demean each other's skin color.

All four short stories show that even a good situation may have its bad aspects, and that good can come from bad situations. Each story conveys, with humor and honesty, a child's perception of human relationships and situations.

Ages 9-11

Also available in:
Paperbound—*Altogether, One at a Time*
Aladdin Books

343

Konigsburg, Elaine Lobl

From the Mixed-Up Files of Mrs. Basil E. Frankweiler

Black/white illustrations by the author.
Atheneum Publishers, 1969.
(162 pages)

RUNNING AWAY
Maturation
Sibling: loyalty
Sibling: respect for

Eleven-year-old Claudia feels put upon because her parents give her more chores than they give her younger brothers. Also dissatisfied with herself, and wanting to feel "different" about her attributes, she decides to run away and live in the Metropolitan Museum of Art. She asks her nine-year-old brother, Jamie, to join her because he has more than twenty-four dollars to add to her five. Together the children leave home. They choose a place to live in the museum and develop a method of eluding the guards and museum workers. During a walk through the museum one day, Claudia comes upon a "mystery statue" so beautiful that she feels compelled to find out the sculptor's identity. To do this, she and Jamie go to the library and then to visit the statue's previous owner, Mrs. Basil E. Frankweiler. Claudia believes that the sculptor must have been Michelangelo. Mrs. Frankweiler makes a deal with the children: She will reveal the sculptor's identity if they will agree to return home after telling her their story of running away. Both Claudia and Jamie agree. Mrs. Frankweiler shows them an old letter and a sketch by Michelangelo, proving to Claudia's satisfaction that he was, indeed, the sculptor.

In this first-person narrative told by Mrs. Frankweiler, running away is treated with insight and humor. During their escapade, Claudia and Jamie become real friends, rather than just siblings. Claudia learns that running away from a situation does not change her as an individual: her habits and personality have remained intact, even in another environment. She realizes, though, that the experience has altered her attitudes and perceptions in some important ways.

Ages 9-12

Also available in:
Braille—*From the Mixed-Up Files of Mrs. Basil E. Frankweiler*
Library of Congress (NLSBPH)

Cassette—*From the Mixed-Up Files of Mrs. Basil E. Frankweiler*
Library of Congress (NLSBPH)

Paperbound—*From the Mixed-Up Files of Mrs. Basil E. Frankweiler*
Aladdin Books

Talking Book—*From the Mixed-Up Files of Mrs. Basil E. Frankweiler*
Library of Congress (NLSBPH)

344

Konigsburg, Elaine Lobl

Throwing Shadows

Atheneum Publishers, 1988.
(168 pages)

MATURATION
Age: respect for
Responsibility: accepting

In the first story of this collection, "On Shark's Teeth," Ned tells about meeting a retired college president at his father's Florida fishing camp. President Bob, as he tells Ned to call him, is a braggart who pesters the boy into coming with him to hunt fossilized sharks' teeth. What Bob doesn't know is that Ned and his mother have collected fossils for years and are self-taught authorities on the fossils in the area. Soon the two are locked in competition to find outstanding specimens. When Ned finds several teeth still in a jawbone, an unusually exciting find, Bob becomes a picture of what Ned sees as "Jealousy and Greed." But Ned suddenly becomes aware of his own smugness, and he decides to give Bob the jawbone. In "The Catchee," Avery describes his young life: though shy and unassuming, he is always, and always will be, an innocent victim. For example, there was the time he was

K

accused of burglary while looking for a hose to water the azaleas he'd been hired to care for while their owner was on vacation. His experiences have shown Avery that the world is divided into catchers and catchees, and he will always belong to the second group. "In the Village of the Weavers" is narrated by Ampara, a novice guide in the mountains of Ecuador. She tells about a poor, proud boy named Antonio who sells weavings while his grandfather lays ill. Once the grandfather recovers, Antonio, feeling the need to continue to prove himself, begins singing on Ampara's tourist bus. Soon he brings on more children to sing and help him sell his weavings. Full of his success, Antonio becomes quite bossy. Then his changing voice cracks, and his singing and selling careers are through. He decides to ask Ampara to teach him English so he can be a guide. Philip is laid up with a broken arm in "At the Home." Needing new batteries for his tape recorder, he stops at the nursing home where his mother works. An old man, noticing the tape recorder, sings Ukrainian folk songs into it. Philip begins going to the home often, staying as long as he can. He is persuaded to record a Hungarian man's life story as it rambles from crisis to crisis on the theme "how being ugly saved my life." Fascinated almost in spite of himself, Philip wants to continue the recording. But because he now can't spend so much time at the home, he encourages the residents to listen to and record each other. In "With Bert and Ray," William explains how two antique dealers ask his mother to manage estate sales for them. They tutor her in the business and, loyal to her mentors, his mother gets them into house sales first so they can buy the choice items. Gradually, William's mother begins to surpass Bert and Ray in her knowledge and skill. After she makes a real find, buying a Chinese screen for about one hundred dollars and selling it for over twenty thousand, William resolves to convince his insecure mother—who feels that people won't love her if she is smarter than they are—that she has gone beyond her teachers.

These five stories, each narrated in the first person, all show the male main character coming to a sense of the world and his place in it. Sometimes this insight results from a sudden revelation, as when Ned discovers that his smugness is just as lamentable as Bob's greed and jealousy. Sometimes the realization comes as a summing up of the boy's whole life, as in Avery's tale. Readers will enjoy not only each boy's comprehension and appreciation of life, but the events leading up to the insight. The stories have an appeal and depth that should make them ideal for discussion.

Ages 10-12

Also available in:
Paperbound—*Throwing Shadows*
Collier Books

345

Kraus, Robert

Leo the Late Bloomer

Color illustrations by Jose Aruego.
HarperCollins Publishers, Inc., 1987.
(32 pages counted)

MATURATION

Leo, a young tiger, cannot do any of the things that his friends do: he cannot read, he cannot write, he cannot draw, he cannot talk, and he still has not learned to eat politely. Leo's father worries that something is wrong with his son, but his mother contends that he "is just a late bloomer." Leo's father watches for signs of blooming, but the young tiger does not bloom. Leo's father becomes increasingly worried until he is reminded by his wife that "a watched bloomer does not bloom." Finally, in his own good time, the young tiger begins to bloom: he reads, he writes, he draws, he eats neatly, and he speaks in complete sentences.

This charming story offers encouragement to children who may have difficulty—physical or mental—in keeping pace with their peers. It demonstrates that individual children develop skills and abilities at their own speed. The illustrations help expand the limited text.

Ages 3-7

Also available in:
Talking Book—*Leo the Late Bloomer*
Library of Congress (NLSBPH)

346

Krementz, Jill

How It Feels to Be Adopted

Black/white photographs by the author.
Alfred A. Knopf, Inc., 1982.
(107 pages)

ADOPTION: Feelings About
Adoption: explaining
Adoption: identity questions
Adoption: interracial

Adopted children consider their special circumstances. Jake doesn't think he'll ever search out his birth mother. Carla agrees that the family who adopted her is her real family, although she is black and they are white. Melinda wasn't adopted until she was seven. Now, at ten, she needs to have one of her parents around all the time because she feels so insecure. Timmy understands how impossible it would have been for his very young, unmarried parents to keep him. Sometimes, though, he's jealous of his younger sister, the child of his adoptive parents, because she's not adopted and doesn't have to answer questions about it. Sue's adoptive family encouraged her in her search for her birth mother, but she considers them her real family. Barbara feels jealous when her friends discuss their ethnic origins and she doesn't know what hers are. When Alfred was eight, he was adopted by a single man who had already adopted another son, Wayne. The family has since grown to include three more adopted brothers, one black (as are Alfred and Wayne), one Hispanic, and one Korean. Last year, Holly's birth mother phoned her. Although she now sees her occasionally, Holly still thinks birth mothers should approach children indirectly, through their adoptive parents. Quintana says she probably won't look for her birth mother, for fear of intruding on the woman's life. Jack says his friends think that because he's adopted, his parents treat him better. Gayle loves and admires the seventy-one-year-old woman who has raised her and her adopted siblings: one deaf and mute, one paralyzed, one only four months older than Gayle, who is fourteen. Jane has become much more self-assured since meeting her birth mother, and she and her adoptive family agree that the meeting has added a new dimension to their own relationship. Lulie was adopted along with her twin brother; having someone in the family who's actually related to her has made things easier. Soo-Mee feels her life began at the age of three when she came from Korea to live with Mommy. Joey's mother awarded him to the state because she couldn't handle him. He lived in an orphanage for a year until he came to the attention of Father Clement, a Catholic priest who was urging his parishioners to adopt kids who needed homes. Getting little response, Father Clement decided to set an example by adopting Joey himself. They've gotten a lot of publicity, but Joey knows that "as long as there's love and caring, that's all that matters."

Nineteen adopted children talk candidly about their feelings, including their differing outlooks toward their birth parents. The diversity and wisdom expressed in this beautifully written and photographed book should reassure readers who are adopted and inform others of the broad range of feelings that adoption can inspire. This outstanding book should be an excellent resource for discussion.

Ages 9 and up

Also available in:
Cassette—*How It Feels To Be Adopted*
Library of Congress (NLSBPH)

Paperbound—*How It Feels To Be Adopted*
Alfred A. Knopf, Inc.

347

Krementz, Jill

How It Feels When a Parent Dies

Black/white photographs by the author.
Alfred A. Knopf, Inc., 1988.
(128 pages, paperbound)

DEATH: of Father
DEATH: of Mother
Death: attitude toward
Mourning, stages of
Suicide: of parent

Twelve-year-old Laurie Marshall's father died in a plane crash. She handles her grief by talking to Ingrid, who lost her father two years ago, and by sharing feelings with her mother. One day Jack Hopkins's father, depressed because of an illness, paid all the bills; the next day he fatally shot himself. Although Jack, at eight, will never understand everything that went into his father's decision, he's not angry anymore. For the first three months, though, he didn't talk to anyone about his father's death—especially not his mother. Susan Radin's mother died when Susan was only six. Every now and then, just for a second, Susan can feel her mother's presence. Peggy Laird lost her father two years ago, when she was nine. Her mother has remarried, which was difficult for Peggy. She finds it helpful to write in her diary. Nine-year-old Alletta Laird believes the garage light that shines only in her window is her father's spirit. When Stephen Jayne, then eight, heard his father had died, the first thing he asked was if they could keep their dog and cat and house. He also worried about money and was afraid to ask for anything special the first Christmas. When he went to camp, he pretended to his new friends that his father was still alive. Helen Colon, now sixteen, whose mother died after years of illness, says, "You blame them for a very long time. You think that it's their fault that they died and left you." John Durning was nine when his mother died, and he drew her a picture and wrote a note to put in her coffin. Tora Garone still doesn't know the details of her father's hunting accident or even where he's buried. She thinks she could get over her grief more quickly if her mother wouldn't "spare" her. Meredith Meryman's mother was sick for two years, but Meredith never knew how sick until she died. She hasn't said the word "Mom" in five years. Gardner Harris was twelve when his mother contracted cancer. He still feels guilty about the things he didn't do for her. Father-child night at school is hard for Carla Lehmann, but memories of her father are very important to her. At the very moment Valerie Crowley's father, a firefighter, died, she and her friends were walking home from school talking about another firefighter who'd been killed. "They say that time makes it better, but it hasn't really. It's just made me think about it more. . . ." Nine-year-old Amira Thoron was only three when her father died. Sometimes she thinks it was better that way, because she doesn't miss him so much. David Harris's mother had cancer. Although he didn't want her to die, he did want her to be free of the pain. In some ways her illness made things easier; he spent more time with her that last year and had time to prepare for and, to some extent, accept her death. Seven-year-old Gail Gugle's father died just nine months ago. She believes she misses him more than her brother does. "A neighbor said Daddy would come to live in our hearts so he would keep living with us but in a different way."

Eighteen youngsters, aged seven to sixteen, tell what it's like to lose a parent. Supplemented by wonderfully vibrant and moving photographs, the text provides readers with an excellent opportunity to reflect on, discuss, or evaluate their own feelings about this sensitive subject. The author found that the children interviewed welcomed the opportunity to talk about their experiences. The book aims to solace and strengthen other children who may share the grief, anger, anxiety, and embarrassment of having lost a parent, to let them know they are not alone and that everyone reacts differently to such an event. The children frequently mention behavior of their peers that either helps or antagonizes them, making the book informative and useful for all children.

Ages 8 and up

Also available in:
Cassette—*How It Feels When a Parent Dies*
Library of Congress (NLSBPH)

348

Landis, James David

The Sisters Impossible

Alfred A. Knopf, Inc., 1979.
(172 pages, paperbound)

SIBLING: Younger
Appearance: concern about
Careers: dancer
Competition
Jealousy: sibling
Problem solving
Talents

Thinking herself clumsy and graceless, nine-year-old Lily is jealous of her older sister, Saundra, a promising ballet dancer. Their parents want curly-headed Lily to take ballet lessons with tall, long-haired, graceful Saundra. Reluctantly Lily agrees to take the lessons, and with equal reluctance "haughty" Saundra agrees to act as her coach. In private the girls agree that a single lesson should satisfy their parents and leave Lily free to quit. At first Lily is miserable, embarrassed by the casual nudity of the locker room and by the "toilet jokes" she hears, shocked by the dancers' bloody feet. Dance class is cruel: the teacher is abrasive, the work demanding. Yet somehow Lily loves it. After class she is taunted by Meredith, Saundra's only serious rival for a place in the school's professional company. Lily wins their verbal battle, but Saundra is furious with her for even talking to Meredith and won't let Lily explain. As audition time nears Saundra withdraws into herself, losing weight along with her confidence. Meredith again confronts Lily, and this time Saundra sees Lily slap her. The sisters leave class holding hands. At home Lily dances for Saundra, trying to draw her from her isolation. The truth comes out: Saundra is afraid that Meredith will beat her in the audition. Since she believes her parents' love depends on her success as a ballet student, she fears that if she loses the competition she'll lose their love. She also fears her future as a professional dancer. Saundra is afraid to win and afraid to lose. Now Lily understands that her sister's cool, aloof exterior is only a mask to hide her fears. Together they explain the situation to their concerned parents. Lily proposes to intimidate the intimidating Meredith, but her lawyer father helps her see that this tactic won't work. So Lily takes her father's advice and decides to give Meredith a false sense of security. She will allow the unkind, conceited rival to think that she and Saundra have given up the battle, that they believe Meredith to be the better dancer. Lavishly and openly, Lily praises Meredith, assuring her of easy victory in the audition. In private she bolsters Saundra's sagging will and watches her sister's confidence return. The audition is not yet won, but Lily knows she and Saundra, though different, are both very strong, especially as a team.

A young girl with a talented sister overcomes her jealousy, learns to accept herself as she is, and helps her sister cope with an aggressive rival and a temporary loss of will and self-confidence. Lily's mind is very subtle for her age, but her story remains believable. The keen, bitter battle for the coveted ballet position is well drawn, as is the relationship between the two sisters. The parents—the father a lawyer and the mother a lawyer and judge—are concerned and supportive. However, the father's aid in manipulating the other dancer, although realistically presented, could be construed as negative and undesirable by some readers and adults. The open ending should prompt discussion.

Ages 9-11

Also available in:
No other form known

349

Lasker, Joe

He's My Brother

Color illustrations by the author.
Albert Whitman & Company, 1974.
(37 pages counted)

LEARNING DISABILITIES
Sibling: loyalty

According to his older brother, eight-year-old Jamie does not have many friends his own age. He plays instead with little children. Sometimes, however, older children play with him when they have no one else to play with. Jamie sometimes gets into fights because he does not know how to react when he is teased. It has taken Jamie a long time to learn how to tie his shoes, and he still has trouble hanging up his clothes. Schoolwork is difficult for Jamie, especially when the room is noisy or when he is under pressure to perform well. There are times when Jamie's older brother becomes angry with him for being so slow, but then he feels sorry for Jamie and plays checkers with him. When Jamie comes home hating school, his mother hugs him and expresses regret over his "bad day." Jamie does some things very well: he plays the drums well enough to gain the admiration of the neighborhood children, and he draws pictures—sometimes as many as two hundred of the same object. But no matter what he does, his family loves him and tries to understand him.

In a note at the end of this first-person narrative, the author states that although "Jamie suffers from the invisible handicap," he is not retarded. Children like Jamie are confused by "their uneven growth and development," and this same uneven development leads "others to unrealistic expectations." This book presents realistic experiences of a child with learning disabilities. It also helps the reader to understand the feelings of the disabled child as he works and plays among children without learning problems.

Ages 4-9

Also available in:
Cassette—*He's My Brother*
Educational Enrichment Materials

Filmstrip—*He's My Brother*
Educational Enrichment Materials

350

Lasker, Joe

Nick Joins In

Color illustrations by the author.
Albert Whitman & Company, 1980.
(32 pages counted)

WHEELCHAIR, DEPENDENCE ON
Differences, human
Fear: of school
School: mainstreaming

Nick, about seven, is frightened at the prospect of going to school for the first time. Nick wears leg braces and gets around in a wheelchair; his teachers have always come to his home. Now he will attend a regular school and many questions plague him. How will he go up and down stairs? Will anyone want to play with him? Will there be others who cannot walk? Meanwhile, at school, a ramp is built and a special desk made to accommodate Nick's wheelchair. The big day arrives. A teacher's aide wheels Nick into the school. He is frightened by the noise and clamor, but as he enters the classroom his teacher, Mrs. Becker, welcomes him with a smile. After checking with Nick, she invites the other children to ask him questions. "Why do you use a wheelchair?" they ask. "Why can't you walk?" Shy at first, Nick gradually relaxes and answers the questions with growing confidence. Days pass, and Nick and the other children grow used to each other. People help Nick and he helps them. One day he even helps the gym teacher open windows with a long pole. Nick especially loves watching the other children run and jump during recess. To him, they seem to be flying. Then, during a basketball game, the ball accidentally lands on the roof. No one, not even the teachers, can get it down. But Nick can! He wheels off to get the window pole, returning to cries of "Nick to the rescue!" He pokes at the ball with the long pole, and as the ball drops to the ground everybody cheers. Now Nick feels *he* is flying.

A disabled child's initial fear of school dissolves with barely a ripple, thanks to understanding parents, sympathetic teachers, and his own outgoing attitude. The approach to the topic is matter-of-fact, the emphasis positive. Children, disabled or not, who face mainstreaming with some anxiety will find the story reassuring. The illustrations are delightful.

Ages 5-8

Also available in:
No other form known

351

Lasky, Kathryn

I Have Four Names for My Grandfather

Black/white photographs by Christopher G. Knight.
Little, Brown & Company, Inc., 1976.
(46 pages)

GRANDPARENT: Love for

Young Tom has four names for his grandfather: "Poppy," "Pop," "Grandpa," and "Gramps." The elderly man is the boy's best friend. They share hats, runs, an interest in old trains, fishing, hammering, planting, and games. When Tom feels low or angry he can call up his grandfather and talk to him. Then he feels better and much loved.

This attractive book, with its black-and-white photographs, sets forth a special, loving relationship between a boy and his grandfather. Their joyous companionship is shown to thrive on exploring, learning, even teasing. Although the boy mentions death and asks when the grandfather will die—grandfather replies, "How do I know?" The sunny disposition of the book includes no shadows.

Ages 3-6

Also available in:
No other form known

352

Le Guin, Ursula Kroeber

Very Far Away from Anywhere Else

Atheneum Publishers, 1976.
(89 pages)

BOY-GIRL RELATIONSHIPS
IDENTITY, SEARCH FOR
Loneliness
Self, attitude toward: feeling different

Seventeen-year-old Owen Griffiths is a loner, a reader, a thinker, and a social misfit. He wants to go to MIT and become a scientist, but his parents plan to send him to a local college. His efforts to imitate the other boys' preoccupations with sports, cars, and girls have been futile. One rainy day he meets Natalie Field, and for the first time, another person makes a difference in his life. Natalie is a musician, and like Owen, a loner and a thinker. The two spend hours discussing how the mind works, how music and thinking are alike, and how strong are social pressures to conform. Each feels the other is a true companion. Then Owen decides he is in love with Natalie, and begins to act toward her the way he thinks a person in love ought to act. One day at the beach he grabs her and kisses her. Natalie is angry. She says she does not want a romantic relationship with him, and embarrassed and confused, Owen takes her home. Afterwards, out driving, he has an accident that wrecks the car his father had given him for his birthday. When he wakes up in the hospital three days later, he remembers nothing. For several weeks he lives in a fog, refusing to see Natalie, or even do homework. One day he learns that some music composed by Natalie will be played at a concert. Owen attends and her music moves him to tears. Later they talk. Natalie confesses that she had been wrong to discipline her life so thoroughly as to shut out love. Their relationship resumes, stronger than before. Owen also takes a stand with his parents: helped by a scholarship and the insurance money from the car, he will go to the school of his choice.

Owen and Natalie's romance is unusual. The author shows the unique communication between these two people, and allows Owen to tell the story wittily. Through the discussing and sharing of dreams, plans, and limitations, the young people come to a better understanding of themselves and make realistic decisions for the future.

Ages 12 and up

Also available in:
Cassette—*Very Far Away from Anywhere Else*
Library of Congress (NLSBPH)

353

Lee, Harper

To Kill a Mockingbird

HarperCollins Publishers, Inc., 1961.
(296 pages) o.p.

VALUES/VALUING: Moral/Ethical
Family: unity
Justice/Injustice
Prejudice: ethnic/racial

Jean Louise (Scout) and Jeremy Atticus (Jem) Finch grow up in a small Alabama town in the 1930s. When they are eight and twelve years old, their lawyer father is appointed by the court to defend a young black man accused of raping Mayella Ewell, a white woman. The white members of the community feel it is disgraceful for Atticus Finch to defend a black accused of such a horrendous crime. In the summer weeks before the trial, the children are subjected to the bitter prejudice of many townspeople and even some long-time family friends. As the tension grows, Atticus tries to maintain a balance of understanding and patience toward the black community as well as the white community. Although his client is convicted, Atticus is threatened by Mayella's father. When Mr. Ewell seeks revenge through an attack on Scout and Jem, their lives are saved by a neighborhood recluse, the mysterious "Boo" Radley, whom the children never have seen before.

This compelling story is told by Scout. Although the children are surrounded by ignorance and racial prejudice, they are taught tolerance and acceptance by their father. Because of his influence, they do not realize how vicious the prejudice is until their father's client is convicted in spite of strong evidence that he is innocent and later is killed in prison awaiting an appeal. The community's hatred then is directed at their father and at them.

Ages 12 and up

Also available in:
Braille—*To Kill a Mockingbird*
Library of Congress (NLSBPH)

Cassette—*To Kill a Mockingbird*
Library of Congress (NLSBPH)

354

Lee, Mildred Scudder

The Skating Rink

Houghton Mifflin Co., 1979.
(136 pages) o.p.

INFERIORITY, FEELINGS OF
SPEECH PROBLEMS: Stuttering
Loneliness
Name-calling
Sibling: relationships
Stepparent: mother

When Tuck Faraday was three, he saw his mother drown in a flood, and since then he has stuttered. The people in the small Georgia community where he lives have always made fun of Tuck because of his speech problem, and so he has never said much to anyone, not even his family. Now, nearly sixteen, Tuck wants to quit school because he feels unhappy and unsuccessful there. Then he meets Pete Degley, who is building a roller-skating rink near Tuck's home. Mr. Degley doesn't seem to mind how long it takes Tuck to say something; he listens to him. One day Mr. Degley suggests that Tuck might want to try roller-skating and offers to train him to do exhibition work with Mr. Degley's young wife, Lisa. Tuck accepts but does not let anyone know and practices in secret. As he becomes a skilled skater, Tuck gains confidence in himself. He begins to appreciate his stepmother, Ida, whom he has always resented, even though she has tried to show her love for him. Also, he learns that his little sister, Karen, is just as lonely as he is. On the day of the rink opening, Tuck is nervous about his first performance, but he does well. He helps Mr. Degley teach skating, and although he still stutters, he has enough self-confidence to decide to continue at school.

Haunted with the recurrent nightmare of his mother's death, Tuck becomes the victim of his own sensitivity as well as the victim of the thoughtless actions of others. Mr. Degley's encouragement helps Tuck to develop other talents and to acquire confidence in himself—changes which occur naturally and smoothly.

Ages 10-13

Also available in:
Braille—*The Skating Rink*
Library of Congress (NLSBPH)

355

Lee, Virginia

The Magic Moth

Black/white illustrations by Richard Cuffari.
Houghton Mifflin Co., 1979.
(64 pages) o.p.

DEATH: Attitude Toward
DEATH: of Sibling
Family: unity

The children of the George Foss family are Stephen, fifteen; Barbi, fourteen; Julie, nine; Mark O, six; and Maryanne, ten. Maryanne has an incurable heart disease, and death is near. The story depicts the confusion and sadness the Fosses feel about their beloved Maryanne. As they stand at her deathbed, a white moth emerges from a cocoon Maryanne has kept through the winter. To the family, it represents the release of Maryanne's spirit. Mark O struggles to understand his sister's death. He asks why Maryanne had to die so young. In his search for answers, he has "the strange feeling that everything that was happening was part of a Big Law that had to be obeyed." He begins to understand that the whole family has gained much from Maryanne—love, consideration, the ability to share—even though her life was brief. Through love, Mark O and the rest of the Foss family accept the death of Maryanne.

A family experiences the trauma of losing a child. Their love for Maryanne and each other is vividly and poignantly portrayed. The white moth that "flutters to life" at the moment of Maryanne's death might be too abstract a symbol for some young readers to understand.

Ages 8-11

Also available in:
Talking Book—*The Magic Moth*
Library of Congress (NLSBPH)

356

Leggett, Linda Rodgers and Linda Gambee Andrews

The Rose-Colored Glasses: Melanie Adjusts to Poor Vision

Color illustrations by Laura Hartman.
Human Sciences Press, 1979.
(31 pages)

GLASSES, WEARING OF
VISUAL IMPAIRMENT
Empathy
School: classmate relationships
Self, attitude toward: accepting

Melanie, about ten, has impaired vision from a car accident. Her family has moved, and she is embarrassed about the round, thick, pink-tinted glasses she needs now. So she struggles along without them.

Unaware of her predicament, her new classmates consider her awkward and peculiar. Mrs. Davis, her teacher, asks Melanie and another student, Deborah, to work with her on a project that will help everyone understand and accept Melanie's vision problem. Afterwards, as the girls walk home together, Melanie begins to cry. She admits that she feels hideous in her glasses, that she wishes desperately her eyes were all right again. But Deborah, kind and concerned, assures her that people will like her regardless of her glasses. The next day Deborah and some other girls walk to school with Melanie. Mrs. Davis begins the morning by showing an out-of-focus film. Everyone has to strain to see and no one can follow it; only Melanie and Deborah know what the teacher's purpose is. After the film, students describe the uncertainty and nervousness they felt about watching the blurry screen. Then Melanie tells the class that fuzziness is what she always sees without her glasses. Deborah continues the presentation by having students read the blackboard through squinted eyes, and Mrs. Davis instructs a pupil to walk across the room while squinting. Participants all agree that they feel angry and unsure of themselves when they cannot see well. All—including Melanie—agree that she should wear her glasses rather than suffer unnecessarily the frustration of impaired vision.

A perceptive teacher recognizes that both Melanie and her classmates need to understand and accept her poor vision and the glasses she must wear because of it. Not only does Mrs. Davis encourage Melanie's self-acceptance and self-confidence, but she also helps the other students empathize with the girl's situation by having them actually experience the effects of damaged eyesight. Narrated by Deborah, this aptly illustrated account would be excellent both for visually impaired and visually normal children.

Ages 8-11

Also available in:
No other form known

357

Lerner, Marguerite Rush

Lefty: The Story of Left-Handedness

Illustrations by Rov Andre.
Lerner Publications Co., 1960.
(32 pages) o.p.

LEFT-HANDEDNESS

Seth is nicknamed "Lefty" because he is left-handed. He and his Uncle David, who is also left-handed, try to learn as much as they can about their special trait. When they visit the museum, Lefty learns that throughout history there have been tools and weapons specifically designed to accommodate left-handed people. Lefty later talks with a geneticist who tells him that left-handedness is a result of both inheritance and learning. A biologist tells Lefty that there is a right- and left-sidedness in plants and animals as well as in people. Lefty then decides to find out about famous left-handed people. Baseball players are at the top of Lefty's list because he is interested in the sport.

This clear, informative explanation of left-handedness by an authority on the subject is reassuring to the left-handed child and of interest to the right-handed child as well. The author includes an explanation of the term "southpaw" and information about famous left-handed people.

Ages 9-11

Also available in:
No other form known

358

Levine, Edna S.

Lisa and Her Soundless World

Color illustrations by Gloria Kamen.
Human Sciences Press, 1984.
(32 pages counted)

DEAFNESS
Education: special

Lisa, an extremely pretty eight-year-old girl, is deaf. Before her parents realized that her hearing was impaired, she was very unhappy. Since she could not hear, she did not speak, and other children would not play with her. Lisa's parents, worried about their little girl's lack of speech, took her to a physician. She was diagnosed as deaf. The physician added, however, that she could be helped with hearing aids. Lisa's hearing improved with the hearing aids, but she still cannot hear as well as other people, and so she attends a special school for persons who are hard of hearing. At school she learns to speak, to read lips, and to use sign language and finger spelling, which enable her to communicate with other deaf people. She is also taught regular school subjects. Lisa becomes increasingly happy with each new thing she learns, because now she can make friends and communicate with them.

With sensitivity and understanding, this book describes the challenges faced by a child who is hard of hearing. The purpose of the book is stated to be an effort to create "understanding attitudes to the deaf and by the deaf at a child level."

Ages 5-9

Also available in:
Paperbound—*Lisa and Her Soundless World*
Human Sciences Press

359

Levoy, Myron

A Shadow like a Leopard

HarperCollins Publishers, Inc., 1981.
(184 pages) o.p.

AUTONOMY
FRIENDSHIP: Meaning of
MATURATION
Delinquency, juvenile
Gangs: membership in
Gender role identity: male
Parental: absence
Puerto Rican-American
Violence

At fourteen, Ramon Santiago wants to be macho almost as much as he wants to be a writer. A gang member, Ramon lives a dangerous, complicated life. He and his friend Harpo steal a woman's Social Security money in a darkened hallway, but Ramon can't forget her eyes bulging with terror. Ramon's mother is in the hospital, and he believes nobody helps her because she's on welfare. "You're no person if you're on welfare. You're just a piece of junk." When he takes a plant to his mother, who has suffered a nervous breakdown, she confuses him with his father, Carlos, in prison for the past year for assaulting a policeman at a "Free Puerto Rico" riot. Carlos's anger and frustration have sometimes been directed at his son, the "sissy" who writes his feelings in a notebook the boy now keeps well hidden. Dopey Luis, a fellow gang member always looking for possible victims, tells Ramon that the artist Arnold Glasser, an old man in a wheelchair, is an easy mark. Ramon talks his way into Glasser's apartment and then pulls a knife. Wildly frightened, Glasser begs the boy to take all his money—twelve dollars. The gang refuses to believe Glasser doesn't have several hundred dollars, as Dopey Luis claims. Determined to get the money if it exists, Ramon puts the twelve dollars and an apology under Glasser's door. When Glasser invites him in, Ramon tears up the apartment looking for money. Only when he sees the pitiful bits of food in the refrigerator does he realize that Glasser truly is poor. But Ramon likes Glasser's paintings and offers to sell them and split the proceeds with the old man. He eventually does sell some of them and returns to Glasser's apartment to fix a celebration dinner. Glasser shows Ramon a book about artists of the 1930s that includes color reproductions of several of the large murals he did for important buildings around the country. Glasser and Ramon spend the next day at the Metropolitan Museum of Art. When Ramon sees Dopey Luis spying on them, he knows the gang is out to get him but refuses to be frightened. He is splitting his half of the painting proceeds with them, but they don't like him hanging around with one of "them." Ramon goes to the art galleries on Madison Avenue to sell more of Glasser's paintings but gets a poor reception everywhere. Then he spots a painting in the window of the Nielsen gallery that he thinks looks like one of Glasser's. Nielsen, citing a revival of 1930s paintings, agrees to hang some of Glasser's work. Ramon plans to surprise Arnold on Wednesday by bringing him in to Nielsen's to sign a contract. Delighted with himself, Ramon decides he has style and brains, which is a lot more than the other members of the gang have. But that night the gang ambushes Ramon and knifes him; a cut in his neck just misses his jugular. They also give him a bad cut in the shoulder, requiring stitches. Now Ramon wants revenge. First, though, he takes Glasser to the Nielsen gallery as arranged. To his amazement Glasser goes wild, ripping down his paintings and refusing to be part of the exhibition. Ramon accuses him of being afraid to be alive, afraid to keep painting, afraid to exhibit his work. Glasser countercharges that Ramon is afraid to go anywhere without his knife. The boy immediately drops his knife in Glasser's lap. "I'll trade you," he says. "My scared for your scared." Glasser agrees. On the street later Ramon sees Harpo, who slinks away, having evidently been part of the ambush. Ramon realizes there is no honor, no macho, in attacking someone four against one. When he arrives home his father is there, out on parole and determined to banish his anger. He's a new person, he says. He thinks Ramon's mother will be better in a few weeks, and the two of them can begin cleaning up the apartment for her. Then his father makes scornful remarks about a studious friend of Ramon's and about the "old bum" Arnold Glasser. He also wants to know if Ramon got his knife cuts with honor. Finally Ramon bursts out, "You want me always to win! To be macho! I'm gonna be macho my way, not your way!" Locking himself in the bathroom to write in his notebook, Ramon thinks, "Nobody's gonna tell me what to be. Not him. Not Harpo. Not Glasser. Nobody. I'm gonna be me, from inside."

A young Puerto Rican-American boy in New York City finds his own definition of macho with the help of an elderly artist and the discipline of keeping a journal. Ramon is a likeable, memorable protagonist who grows and defines himself in believable stages as the story progresses. The friendship between Ramon and the irascible but talented Glasser is based on respect and a growing understanding and sympathy. Although violence, poverty, and prejudice form a backdrop for the story, Ramon's choices are the central issue. He is ultimately true to his own instincts, and therein lies his strength. The colorful milieu includes street language with considerable profanity.

Ages 12 and up

Also available in:
No other form known

360

Levy, Elizabeth

Come Out Smiling

Delacorte Press, 1981.
(186 pages) o.p.

HOMOSEXUALITY: Female
PEER RELATIONSHIPS
Camp experiences
Communication: parent-child
Competition

Fourteen-year-old Jenny will be a senior at Camp Sacajawea this summer. As she says goodbye to her parents in Cincinnati and boards the train for New York, she anticipates all the special privileges that senior campers enjoy. Shortly after joining the other girls in the compartment they will share for the trip, she spots her favorite counselor, Peggy, the riding instructor. She has with her a tall, pretty girl named Ann whom she introduces as her assistant for the summer. Since Jenny will be training for the Midsummer Horse Show, she expects to see a lot of Peggy and Ann during the next eight weeks. The camp director believes that competition is a good and natural part of life. To emphasize this, she always divides the camp into two teams, the blues and the greens. They compete in weekend sports matches and earn points during the week for things like flagpole attendance and bed making. Jenny longs to be both color captain and the best rider at camp. She feels on the social borderline—not really popular at school or at camp, but not unpopular either. She has plenty of friends, but no best friend. Ever since her first year at Sacajawea she has wanted Marcie as her special friend, and she is immediately drawn to her again. Marcie is unaffected, noncompetitive, and easy to talk with. Among the things they discuss as they get reacquainted is how far each has gone with a boy during the past school year. When the color war competition begins, Jenny is delighted to come in second on the green team and get to serve as lieutenant. Marcie is placed on the blue team and, as the summer progresses, her dislike for the color war increases. She agrees with Ann, who says "it's insane to have color war all summer long." In fact, Marcie agrees with Ann about a lot of things. Jenny likes Ann too, finding that Ann understands her insecurities and her problems with a sarcastic father who embarrasses her and makes her feel inadequate. Early one morning, Jenny goes to the stable and sees Peggy and Ann holding hands and kissing. Terribly upset, she reasons that since these are two of her favorite people, maybe she is gay too. After all, she has never had a real boyfriend. During the next week as she practices for the Midsummer Show, Jenny can think of nothing but what she has seen. She's not even happy after she wins the blue ribbon. When she finally tells Marcie her secret, Marcie also begins to feel insecure about her sexual identity. Maybe they both will turn out to be lesbians. At the final campfire, each girl is given a candle float to wish on, light, and push out onto the lake. At first Jenny intends to wish that she won't be gay. Instead, however, she thinks about the many times her parents have sent her to her room with instructions not to come out until she is smiling. She places her candle on the water and asks the spirit of Sacajawea to "please give me courage. Give me courage to come out smiling."

A young girl worries about her ambivalent attitude toward boys. She wants to keep up with her friends in their experiments with the opposite sex, but sometimes doubts that she likes boys or thinks about sex as much as a normal girl should. Furthermore, the one man in her life whom Jenny does love, her father, is so sarcastic and insensitive that she's usually angry when she's with him. When she discovers that two of her favorite people are gay, Jenny's questions about her own sexuality intensify. Believable dialogue and skillful characterizations mark this thoughtful story of a girl's unresolved struggle to define herself.

Ages 12 and up

Also available in:
No other form known

361

Levy, Elizabeth

Lizzie Lies a Lot

Black/white illustrations by John Wallner.
Delacorte Press, 1976.
(102 pages) o.p.

HONESTY/DISHONESTY
Grandparent: living in child's home

Nine-year-old Lizzie often tells little lies to her Nana in self-defense against the old lady's carping criticism—and not only to Nana. She lies to her parents too, as when she says she is to star in a dance assembly at school, when no such assembly is planned. One day Lizzie and her best friend, Sara, find a stray cat in a vacant house. Lizzie longs to keep the cat and tells lies to Sara about her mother and about cats. When her parents refuse to let her keep the cat, Lizzie lies to Sara about letting the cat go—but Sara is beginning to sense her friend's dishonesty. The following Saturday, playing at Lizzie's home (Nana lives there too), the girls get into trouble with Nana, and when Lizzie lies to Nana, Sara is so upset she no longer wants to play. The next Monday is supposedly the day of the dance assembly at school. When Lizzie's parents question her about it, she confesses she made the whole thing up. In fact, she finally admits that she lies frequently. Her parents reprimand her but then talk to her about how she might stop lying. Lizzie admits she is more comfortable with the truth, and says she will try. She even confides some of her "whoppers" to Sara, and the two become best friends again.

A little girl becomes a compulsive liar—to impress people, to get out of trouble, but usually for no reason at all. Not until her best friend accuses her of lying does she see the trouble she is making for herself and decide to try telling the truth. Children who often lie will understand Lizzie, and may come to understand children around them who tell tales.

Ages 9-11

Also available in:
No other form known

362

Lexau, Joan M.

I Should Have Stayed in Bed!

Color illustrations by Syd Hoff.
HarperCollins Publishers, Inc., 1965.
(48 pages) o.p.

EMBARRASSMENT
Mistakes, making

One bright, sunny morning Sam gets out of bed. By lunchtime he wishes he had not bothered. First he puts his shoes on the wrong feet and then knots both shoelaces trying to untie them. Next he puts on his Cub Scout uniform and learns that it is the wrong day; "Cub Scouts" is the next day. Changing clothes, he breaks both shoelaces. On the way to school, Sam finds a nickel. As he bends down to pick it up, he accidentally kicks it into the sewer. At school Sam throws his notebook at his friend Albert, but instead it hits Amy Lou, who reports him to the teacher. In the classroom Sam gets caught clowning; later he is embarrassed because he reads poorly in front of the class. Then Albert sends him a note which the teacher makes him read to the class as punishment for note-passing. At lunchtime Sam runs home, gets into bed, and starts the day all over again.

This is an entertaining first-person narrative of a child who remains optimistic in spite of his problem-filled morning. Cartoon illustrations add to the humor of this beginning reader.

Ages 6-8

Also available in:
Braille—*I Should Have Stayed in Bed!*
Library of Congress (NLSBPH)

Talking Book—*I Should Have Stayed in Bed!*
Library of Congress (NLSBPH)

363

Lexau, Joan M.

Striped Ice Cream

Black/white illustrations by John Wilson.
Scholastic, Inc., 1971.
(95 pages) o.p.

SIBLING: Love for
SIBLING: Youngest
African-American
Family: unity
Pride/False pride
Sharing/Not sharing

Rebecca Jane, called Becky, is nearly eight years old, the youngest of five children. Becky often feels that being the youngest has many disadvantages. She never can be first to do anything, and all her clothes are hand-me-downs. During the last few days, she has felt unappreciated by her family and excluded from activities in her own home. It is mostly because her big sisters—fourteen-year-old Cecily, thirteen-year-old Flo, and ten-year-old Maud—keep suggesting things for her to do that will keep her away from the house. But her eleven-year-old brother Abe takes part in this ploy too, trying to keep her occupied outside so that the three older girls can be home alone. Mother works all day at a button factory. When she returns at night, things seem more or less normal again. But the next day it's back to "Becky, how would you like to take the fairy-tale book outside and read it in the park?" At last it is Becky's birthday, and the family not only has her favorite, "striped ice cream," but she receives a wonderful surprise. The creation of this surprise has taken the family's combined efforts during the days Becky felt rejected.

This story vividly depicts the pride of a black mother who resists welfare aid because of the crippling effect she believes it might have on her family. Despite material poverty, the family members are rich in generosity, mutual support, loyalty, and the sharing of excitement over little pleasures.

Ages 8-11

Also available in:
Braille—*Striped Ice Cream*
Library of Congress (NLSBPH)

364

Lifton, Betty Jean

I'm Still Me

Alfred A. Knopf, Inc., 1981.
(243 pages) o.p.

ADOPTION: Identity Questions
IDENTITY, SEARCH FOR
Family: relationships
Sex: premarital

Sixteen-year-old Lori Elkins gets an impossible assignment from her history teacher. As one of his "living" projects designed to help young people "feel" history, Mr. Innskeep asks his students to trace their family trees. Since Lori is adopted, the task raises feelings she has always tried to suppress. Her parents have never been forthcoming about either Lori's or her adopted brother Mike's backgrounds, and Lori has refrained from asking too many questions. But even as a small child she fantasized about her birth parents and their reasons for giving her away. Lori's friend Maggie has a similar problem. Her father died when she was a baby, and her mother has refused to tell her anything about him. Maggie thinks she can use her stepfather for the family tree assignment. But Lori decides she would feel like a "fraud" if she handed in her adoptive parents' tree. She confides her dilemma to Sue O'Brien, her former baby-sitter who lives next door. Sue's boyfriend, Tony Daley, is a law student who thinks Lori has the "human right to know how she got on this earth." He explains, however, that birth records aren't easy to get. Encouraged by Maggie, Lori searches her house and finds an Order of Adoption that gives her mother's name, Barbara Goldman, and the agency in New York City that handled her case. Lori is reluctant to continue the investigation for fear of hurting her parents, but Maggie insists she make an appointment with Ms. Barnes, the director of the adoption agency. What Lori learns from this meeting does not make her happy. Her nineteen-year-old birth mother was not married and did not divulge the father's name. Lori has never considered the possibility that she could be illegitimate. Her first reaction is to give in to her "bad blood" by getting drunk and letting her boyfriend, Chris, make love to her. After all, many of her friends are sleeping with boys. She is humiliated when Chris decides he doesn't want to have sex with her while she's intoxicated. Lori doesn't think she can talk to her mother about any of this, especially during her parents' latest troubles with Mike, always hard to handle both at school and at home. Lori wonders if he too could be troubled by the fact that he is adopted. She has learned by attending a Search and Find group meeting in New York that many adoptees are, like her, disturbed by their mysterious origins. Even Maggie discovers a need to visit her paternal grandparents, who she knows live nearby. Lori goes with her and is impressed by their kindness and delight in being "found." Lori begins to forgive her birth mother when she and Chris start to have sex regularly and she realizes how easy it would be to become an unwed mother herself. Meanwhile, Tony has managed to locate Barbara Goldman's wedding certificate, along with her current address and phone number. Lori phones and arranges a meeting. She finds Barbara to be a warm and sensitive woman who has suffered a great deal from giving up her baby. She tells Lori about her father and the circumstances surrounding her adoption. At last Lori feels she has "been born" and belongs "on this planet." When she returns home she tells her adoptive parents about her discoveries and is surprised by their understanding. They talk frankly about the possibility that some of Mike's problems might be caused by his uncertainty about his origins. Relieved and closer to her adoptive parents than ever, Lori finds that instead of changing her identity, her discoveries have strengthened it.

An adopted teenage girl seeks out her birth mother and learns about her past in this first-person narrative about the turmoil adopted children can face. Lori's search is successful on all fronts—her birth mother is warm and communicative, her adoptive parents completely supportive—not at all the norm, one feels, for such investigations. But the story is insightfully told and should be good reading for adopted young people, their adoptive parents, and other readers. Although the "modern," permissive view of teenage sex goes unquestioned, there is good discussion material for the opposite position.

Ages 12 and up

Also available in:
No other form known

365

Lindgren, Astrid

I Want a Brother or Sister

Translated from the Swedish by Barbara Lucas.
Color illustrations by Ilon Wikland.
Farrar, Straus & Giroux, Inc., 1988.
(29 pages counted)

SIBLING: New Baby
Attention seeking

Peter, now three, knows he once was a baby. He knows too that despite his almost constant crying back then, Mama and Papa loved him very much. One day in a park, Peter meets a friend pushing a carriage. "My baby brother," the friend exults, but Peter answers he would rather play with toys than with a baby. Once home, though, Peter promptly asks Mama for a brother or sister. To his surprise, Mama tells him he will soon have one. Peter likes the idea and for a time he even likes Lena, his baby sister. He watches Mama caring for her, and he approves. But soon Peter decides it is "not any fun to have a sister." How can Mama and Papa love Lena—even more than they love him—when all she does is cry? Peter grows furious at them and at Lena too. He throws a tantrum and when Mama comes, Peter is glad. "After all, she was Peter's mama first, and not Lena's." One day Peter confides his feelings to Mama and she replies, "First I loved my little Peter and now I love my big Peter." She confirms that he too was troublesome and required a lot of attention as a baby, and she asks him to help her tend Lena. Peter decides that maybe it is Lena's turn to be little and troublesome. He pushes her in a carriage, he plays with her, and he enjoys it. When he becomes older still and Lena is three, they both receive a little brother named Mats. The two are able to accept and love Mats right away.

Here is an excellent story for introducing a young child to the idea of a baby brother or sister, not as a rival for affection but as a future playmate. Parents will also discover tips for handling sibling rivalry by enlisting the older child's aid in caring for the baby. Colorful illustrations will charm young readers and listeners.

Ages 3-7

Also available in:
No other form known

366

Lindgren, Barbro

Sam's Car

Translated from the Swedish.
Color illustrations by Eva Eriksson.
William Morrow & Company, Inc., 1982.
(29 pages counted)

PLAY
SHARING/NOT SHARING

Sam is playing with his car when Lisa comes along and wants to play with it. Sam won't let her so "Lisa smacks Sam." "Sam smacks Lisa" in return, and now both Sam and Lisa hurt. They cry. Then their mother brings another car. Happiness is restored as each child plays with a car.

Two very young children fight over a toy until their mother provides a solution. This simple, whimsically illustrated book could be a useful discussion starter about sharing and playing together. Also worthy of discussion is the hitting portrayed. This is one of several books about Sam.

Ages 2-5

Also available in:
No other form known

367

Lindgren, Barbro

Sam's Cookie

Translated from the Swedish.
Color illustrations by Eva Eriksson.
William Morrow & Company, Inc., 1982.
(29 pages counted)

PETS
Sharing/Not sharing

Sam has a cookie and is just beginning to enjoy it when along comes his dog. The dog wants the cookie and ends up taking it away from Sam. "Sam is angry. Dumb doggie." When he pulls the dog's ear, the dog gets angry too and growls. When the dog begins to chase him, Sam becomes frightened and cries. This brings Mommy, who scolds the dog and tells him not to take Sam's cookie. Then she gives Sam another cookie.

A young child and his dog disagree about the ownership of a cookie. When the dog wins by greater might, Sam's mother has to step in and Sam gets another cookie. This extremely simple book could be used with very young children to stimulate discussion about sharing, pets, and when not to argue with an animal. The brief text and whimsical illustrations are encouraging and inviting. This is one of several books about Sam.

Ages 2-5

Also available in:
No other form known

368

Lionni, Leo

Fish Is Fish

Color illustrations by the author.
Pantheon Books, 1970.
(29 pages counted)

SELF, ATTITUDE TOWARD: Body Concept
Imagination
Maturation

A minnow and a tadpole living in the pond at the edge of the woods are inseparable friends. As the weeks pass, the tadpole develops into a frog, but the minnow refuses to believe that his friend is changing. During the same time, the minnow has been growing into a large fish. After the frog leaves the pond, the fish often wonders where his old friend has gone. One day the frog returns to the pond to tell the fish of his adventures around the world. He tells the fish about birds, cows, and people. The fish pictures these things as fish with wings, fish with horns, and fish with legs. After the frog has gone, the fish decides he must explore the frog's exciting world. With a mighty leap, the fish jumps out of the water and lands on the shore of the pond. He lies there, unable to breathe or to move, sure that this is the end of him. But the frog appears and helps him back into the water. With new appreciation of his beautiful natural surroundings, the fish tells the frog, "You were right...fish is fish."

Lured by enticing tales of the outside world, a fish becomes dissatisfied with his familiar environment and tries to escape. In the process, he endangers his life. This story graphically illustrates how mental images of the unknown drawn from someone else's personal experiences can be misleading.

Ages 4-8

Also available in:
Paperbound—*Fish Is Fish*
Alfred A. Knopf, Inc.

369

Lionni, Leo

Frederick

Color illustrations by the author.
Pantheon Books, 1990.
(30 pages counted)

VALUES/VALUING: Aesthetic
Creativity
Sharing/Not sharing

While the other mice are busy collecting stores of food, Frederick gathers sun rays for the cold winter days ahead. The others, curious about Frederick's activities, demand to know why Frederick is not hoarding food. Frederick tells them he is storing warmth instead. The mice are also puzzled when they observe Frederick sitting and staring in the meadow. But Frederick explains that he is only gathering color in preparation for the gray winter days that soon will follow. When his fellow mice catch Frederick snoozing, they accuse him of being lazy. Frederick insists that he is working hard collecting and storing words for silent winter days. When snow begins to fall, the mice move to their home in the gray stone wall. During the beginning of winter there is plenty of food, and the mice are content. But little by little they nibble up most of their stores, and because of their vastly depleted food supply and the icy weather, not one of the mice is warm or happy. Then they remember that Frederick has amassed unusual supplies for the winter, so they ask him to share with them. Frederick instructs the mice to close their eyes and as they listen, Frederick draws upon his stores of warmth, words, and color, captivating his friends with stories of summer. Soon the mice feel much warmer and happier.

In a fanciful manner, this book convincingly illustrates the belief that creative endeavors are as valuable as manual labor.

Ages 5-8

Also available in:
Braille—*Frederick*
Library of Congress (NLSBPH)

Cassette—*Frederick*
Library of Congress (NLSBPH)

Paperbound—*Frederick*
Alfred A. Knopf, Inc.

370

Lionni, Leo

Swimmy

Color illustrations by the author.
Pantheon Books, 1973.
(29 pages counted)

COOPERATION: in Play
COOPERATION: in Work
Problem solving

A little black fish named Swimmy lives with a school of red fish. One day, a large tuna fish eats all the little red fish in one gulp. Fortunately, Swimmy escapes. He is very sad and frightened as he swims alone, but he sees many strange and beautiful sights. Finally, he discovers another school of fish hiding in the weeds, afraid to swim and play for fear that a big fish will eat them. Swimmy tells them to swim together so that they will look like one large fish. They swim very close together, and because he is a different color, Swimmy takes the position of the fish's eye. Now they scare all the big fish away.

Alone, Swimmy is fearful and insecure. But when he organizes the other fish and they band together, they are all more secure in their unity. This story illustrates a mutual problem solved through cooperation and the wise guidance of a leader. Because of the difference in color between Swimmy and the little red fish, this book can be used to demonstrate the positive aspects of being different.

Ages 3-7

Also available in:
Paperbound—*Swimmy*
Alfred A. Knopf, Inc.

371

Lionni, Leo

Tico and the Golden Wings

Color illustrations by the author.
Alfred A. Knopf, Inc., 1975.
(29 pages counted, paperbound)

GIVING, MEANING OF
Differences, human
Friendship: meaning of
Ostracism

Tico the bird has no wings. His friends, the other birds, bring him berries and fruits since he cannot secure his own food. One summer night, a strange bird grants Tico a wish, and Tico receives golden wings. When his friends see this splendid change, they suddenly leave him alone. Tico feels shut out and does not understand why the other birds have rejected him so. Then, one day, he sees a man crying because his child is ill and he has no money to buy medicine to make the child well. Tico gives the man one of his golden wing feathers to purchase medicine. A black feather appears in its place. From that day on, Tico gives his golden feathers to those in need, and black ones appear to replace them. After his wings have turned completely black, Tico returns to his friends' tree, wondering whether they will accept him now.

This is a beautiful, first-person narrative about a bird who is considered more lowly than other birds because he looks different. In spite of his appearance, the other birds accept him until remarkable changes in his physical appearance bring about their distrust and fear. They also believe he feels superior in his splendor, and so they ostracize him. The story dramatizes the satisfaction and pleasure of giving to others in need.

Ages 4-8

Also available in:
No other form known

372

Lipsyte, Robert

The Contender

HarperCollins Publishers, Inc., 1967.
(182 pages, paperbound)

CAREERS: Planning
EDUCATION: Value of
GOALS
SELF, ATTITUDE TOWARD: Respect
African-American
Drugs: dependence on
Self-improvement
Values/Valuing: moral/ethical

Orphaned Alfred Brooks, a seventeen-year-old high-school dropout, lives with his aunt and three cousins in a Harlem tenement. Alfred is convinced that his job as a grocery store stock boy will be a "dead end," but he does not know what else to do. When the store is robbed, his best friend James is arrested for the robbery. The others in James's gang believe that Alfred "fingered" James and blame Alfred for the arrest. One night, when Alfred fears the gang is after him, he hides in Donatelli's Gym, a boxing club that has trained national champions. While he waits to see whether he is safe from the gang, he decides that becoming a boxer may be his only way out of the ghetto. While training toward that end, Alfred meets Mr. Donatelli and other people who help him recognize that he can make something of himself. He decides to finish high school while continuing to work at the store and training to fight. After he loses an amateur fight, he understands what Mr. Donatelli means when he says, "It's being a contender that makes the man."

This novel portrays the ghetto honestly. It focuses on the contrast between two close fiends: Alfred tries to rise above his circumstances, and James slips into the world of heroin addiction. The story gives glimpses of Black-American activism and Alfred's family life.

Ages 12 and up

Also available in:
Braille—*The Contender*
Library of Congress (NLSBPH)

Cassette—*The Contender*
Library of Congress (NLSBPH)

Talking Book—*The Contender*
Library of Congress (NLSBPH)

373

Lipsyte, Robert

One Fat Summer

HarperCollins Publishers, Inc., 1977.
(151 pages, paperbound)

L

INFERIORITY, FEELINGS OF
WEIGHT CONTROL: Overweight
Determination
Fear: of physical harm
Job

Mr. Marks has no confidence in his fat fourteen-year-old son, Bobby, and neither does Bobby himself. At Rumson Lake, where the family goes in summer, his father wants him to be a counselor at day camp like his older sister, Michelle, but what Bobby really wants to be is an athletic hero like Pete Marino, a college boy who dates Michelle. As things are, Bobby is only the butt of jokes and disapproval. Nagged by his friend Joanie, he takes a caretaking job at Dr. Kahn's. Then Willie Rumson, an ex-Marine and local bully who had the job and wants it back, warns him to quit—or else. It being tortuous physical work for a boy of more than 200 pounds, and Dr. Kahn being a demanding employer, Bobby is not sure himself why he is so determined to stay on. Willie abducts the boy and leaves him naked on an island, but Bobby is rescued by Willie's friend, who is trying to keep Willie out of trouble. Still Bobby stands firm. That he is losing weight and gaining strength from the work adds to his confidence—even when Willie comes after him with a rifle. The same friend talks Willie out of shooting, but Michelle's boyfriend leaps on Willie. A fight ensues in which Bobby almost drowns Willie, but Willie's friend breaks that up too. Remorseful, Bobby begins to see that the boyfriend Pete's swaggering toughness and Willie's bullying are alike poses. Being a man means something else.

This well-paced and sensible first-person narrative traces the formation of "a miserable fat boy into a fairly presentable young man," as Bobby's employer smugly puts it. But the job, though a catalyst for the change, is hardly its cause. As Bobby tells Dr. Kahn, "You didn't do it. I did it." Overweight children could find in this thoroughly credible story the link between overeating and undervaluing oneself.

Ages 12-14

Also available in:
Cassette—*One Fat Summer*
Library of Congress (NLSBPH)

374

Litchfield, Ada Bassett

A Button in Her Ear

Color illustrations by Eleanor Mill.
Albert Whitman & Company, 1976.
(32 pages counted)

DEAFNESS

Young Angela has trouble hearing people clearly. When her teacher says, "Tomorrow we're going to learn our letters," Angela thinks she has said, "Tomorrow we're going to burn our sweaters." Angela thinks people mutter. But her parents think otherwise and take her to an ear doctor. Unable to find a physical defect in her ears, he sends her to an audiologist. After testing, she goes to a hearing-aid dealer and is fitted with a hearing aid. Because the device helps so much, she does not mind wearing it. Her teacher, comparing the aid to glasses, asks her to show it to the class. Soon Angela is both accustomed to her "magic button" and hears almost every word spoken to her.

In this first-person narrative, a child talks about misunderstanding others because of poor hearing. The smooth movement of events, from discovery of the hearing loss to its correction, may skate over a child's fears of wearing an aid, of being "different." But this calm and clear exposition should reduce such fears while explaining to other children what a hearing aid is and does.

Ages 5-8

Also available in:
Cassette—*A Button in Her Ear*
Library of Congress (NLSBPH)

375

Litchfield, Ada Bassett

A Cane in Her Hand

Color illustrations by Eleanor Mill.
Albert Whitman & Company, 1977.
(32 pages counted)

VISUAL IMPAIRMENT

Very few fifth or sixth graders have to wear glasses as thick as Valerie has worn for years, and so when her vision worsens, her parents rush her to the doctor. He says he can hope to prevent blindness but cannot promise more. Meanwhile, although schoolwork is harder and harder for her, Valerie yearns to stay with her class. At last a specially trained teacher arrives to help her with her studies and to show her some ways her other senses can aid her more. She learns to differentiate sounds and to use a cane to prevent herself from bumping into things. Eventually, while still sensitive to people's comments about her handicap, she on the whole accepts the fact of it. "Seeing with your eyes is important, but it isn't everything."

The kindness and understanding of friends and family, as well as skilled professional help, all assist a little girl in coping with a severe visual impairment. As pointed out in the preface, children in similar situations will be able to identify with Valerie. Children with normal vision will better understand the feelings and difficulties of those who are visually impaired.

Ages 6-9

Also available in:
Braille—*A Cane in Her Hand*
Library of Congress (NLSBPH)

Talking Book—*A Cane in Her Hand*
Library of Congress (NLSBPH)

376

Litchfield, Ada Bassett

Words in Our Hands

Color illustrations by Helen Cogancherry.
Albert Whitman & Company, 1980.
(32 pages counted)

DEAFNESS
Change: new home
Self, attitude toward: feeling different

Michael Turner, age nine, and his two sisters, Gina and Diane, have learned several ways to communicate with their deaf parents. Mr. and Mrs. Turner attended schools for the deaf as youngsters, so they did learn to speak. Their speech, however, is often difficult for people outside the family to understand. Lipreading is another way for Mr. and Mrs. Turner to perceive the world around them. Most of the time, though, the Turner family communicates by talking with their hands. They use both finger spelling, in which every letter of the alphabet has a sign, and sign language, in which every sign has a more complete meaning. Sign language is faster and easier than finger spelling. The children began learning sign language as babies and are still learning new signs all the time. The Turner home also has a TTY, a teletypewriter that records messages on tape when attached to the telephone. Lights flash on and off when the telephone or doorbell rings. And Polly, the family dog, is especially helpful in alerting the parents to events like an alarm going off or a knock at the door. The Turners are a very happy family until the father's company relocates in a new town and they must move. The move is very difficult for everyone. Mrs. Turner feels strange and uncomfortable in the stores, where no one knows her. When the Turners talk with their hands, people stare at them. For the first time, the children are embarrassed by their parents' deafness. One day Michael sees three boys imitating his parents. Humiliated, he realizes that "just for a minute, I wanted to pretend my mother and father were not my parents." That evening Gina comes home with a note from her teacher inviting her family to attend a performance of the National Theatre of the Deaf. The Turners decide to go and are pleasantly surprised to find many people in the audience using sign language. Some of the actors are deaf, and the entire performance of The Wooden Boy is presented in sign. After the play, the Turners go backstage to meet and talk with some of the actors. Gina's teacher is there, and Gina is delighted to learn that she can sign. Michael is very proud of his parents, and the whole family becomes optimistic about their life in the new town. As Michael says, "Being deaf doesn't mean you can't hear or talk. If you have to, you can hear with your eyes and talk with your hands."

In this first-person narrative, Michael describes in both informative and emotional terms his life with his deaf parents. The illustrations include the finger spelling symbols for each letter of the alphabet and several examples of sign language. Deaf children will identify with the parents' problems and feelings, as well as their satisfying experiences. Hearing children will gain insight into the feelings, challenges, and abilities of deaf people.

Ages 7-9

Also available in:
No other form known

377

Little, Jean

From Anna

Black/white illustrations by Joan Sandin.
HarperCollins Publishers, Inc., 1972.
(201 pages) o.p.

IDENTITY, SEARCH FOR
Belonging
Change: new home
Education: special
Glasses, wearing of
Immigrants
Sibling: rivalry

Nine-year-old Anna, the youngest in her family, lives in pre-World War II Germany. Because she is always stumbling into things, she has earned the nickname "Awkward Anna." She is constantly teased by her brothers and sisters because she does not seem to want to learn the needlework her mother tries to teach her and because she has trouble reading. Anna becomes sullen and withdrawn in response to the taunts. Only her father believes that Anna is really an intelligent, lovable girl. Soon Anna's father decides it is unsafe to live in Germany because a person can no longer think "free thoughts." Despite the objections of his wife and children, he takes the family to Canada, where he has inherited his brother's small grocery store. There it is discovered that the reason Anna is so awkward is that she cannot see well. She is fitted with glasses and sent to a school that has a special class for pupils with similar problems. Anna gradually gains self-confidence in school, but at home she remains withdrawn because she still feels unsure of her place in the family. At Christmas, when her brothers and sisters decide to give their parents presents, Anna hopes to show them that her present can be just as good as theirs. With the help of her teacher, she makes a beautiful woven basket. Her parents' surprise and delight and her brothers' and sisters' recognition of her achievements finally help Anna feel that she is a valued member of the family.

The reader watches Anna change from a sullen, withdrawn child into a happy, contented one. The problems of uprooting an entire family are well described. The rivalry of the five children for their mother's affection is realistically depicted. The black-and-white illustrations capture the mood of the story.

Ages 9-11

Also available in:
Talking Book—*From Anna*
Library of Congress (NLSBPH)

378

Little, Jean

Home from Far

Black/white illustrations by Jerry Lazare.
Little, Brown & Company, Inc., 1965.
(145 pages, paperbound)

COMMUNICATION: Parent-Child
FOSTER HOME
Change: resisting
Death: of sibling

Both Jenny MacGregor and Mike Jackson have lost loved ones through death. Jenny's eleven-year-old twin brother, Michael, was killed six months earlier in a car accident. Mrs. MacGregor has packed all her son's possessions away and seldom talks about him. Mike is also eleven. His mother died several years ago. When his father can no longer provide for Mike and his little sister Hilda, they become foster children of Mr. and Mrs. MacGregor, who have three other youngsters besides Jenny. The Jackson children's arrival imposes a need for adjustments. Jenny must share her room with Hilda and deal with her resentment toward Mike: she feels he will try to take her deceased twin's place in the family. Jenny is also confused by her mother's actions and angry because her mother does not seem to miss Michael. Hilda soon adjusts happily to life with the MacGregors, but Mike still wishes he could go back to live with his own father. Mother and daughter finally talk out their mutual feelings of loss and hurt. With the help and understanding of the MacGregor parents, all of the children learn to accept themselves and each other.

Home from Far is an unsentimental account of the relationships among members of a family affected by death and the placement of foster children. Jenny's hurt and confusion and Mike's resentment are pictured clearly. A most satisfying aspect of this well-written story is the parents' respect for each child's individuality.

Ages 10-13

Also available in:
Braille—*Home from Far*
Library of Congress (NLSBPH)

379

Little, Jean

Kate

HarperCollins Publishers, Inc., 1971.
(162 pages, paperbound)

IDENTITY, SEARCH FOR
JEW
Friendship: meaning of
Marriage: interreligious

Kate Bloomfield, in her early teens, faces a choice between being a nominal Jew or one who proudly and formally practices her faith. Her Jewish father does not attend the synagogue, follow Jewish customs, or celebrate Jewish holidays. Her mother is an "independent" reared in an Anglican home. Kate knows that religion had something to do with her father's alienation from his parents, but she does not know exactly what happened. Kate herself does not think seriously about her Jewishness until Sheila Rosenthal moves into the neighborhood. Sheila is Jewish, proud of her faith and her family's traditions and customs. Kate experiences resentment and confusion about Sheila's Jewishness. At first, she explains away her bewilderment as dislike for Sheila, but she cannot fool herself for long: she envies the special joy and satisfaction Sheila gets from her faith. She also begins to appreciate the hurt and sadness her father has experienced since he shut out his past and married a non-Jewish woman. As Kate's awareness grows, she begins to search for answers about her family background and about her own beliefs. This search reveals the existence of a paternal grandfather, whom Kate unthinkingly alienates, and other relatives. Shortly after Grandfather's death, Kate decides to go to the synagogue. Her father joins her, and together they enter. It marks a beginning.

This convincing, first-person narrative, told in retrospect by Kate, has an important secondary theme concerning friendship and its problems. *Kate* continues the relationship between Emily and Kate begun in the book's precursor, *Look Through My Window.*

Ages 10-14

Also available in:
Cassette—*Kate*
Library of Congress (NLSBPH)

Talking Book—*Kate*
Library of Congress (NLSBPH)

380

Little, Jean

Listen for the Singing

HarperCollins Publishers, Inc., 1991.
(262 pages, paperbound)

VISUAL IMPAIRMENT
Blindness
Canada
Family: unity
Friendship: making friends
Sibling: love for
War

The time is 1939, the place Canada, and Anna Solden expects trouble in the ninth grade. Since coming with her family from Germany in 1934, she has attended a special class for children with limited vision. Now she fears her transfer to a new school, there to have new teachers, no special tutoring, and no friends. Normally she would confide in her father, but now he is preoccupied with political developements in Germany—his homeland still, though he has had to uproot his family to come to a place where people are "free to speak their thoughts aloud without fear." Soon Britain declares war on Germany. The news distresses Anna's parents and her older brother, Rudi; the war seems remote to Anna. School begins with pleasant surprises: she likes several of her teachers and almost immediately makes new friends. Even a notoriously harsh teacher treats her kindly, and later Anna learns that he has a visual handicap similar to her own. Anna's major obstacle is mathematics. Rudi, a genius in math, tutors her, and a special kinship grows up between brother and sister. But as the war spreads through Europe, Rudi determines to fight the Nazi regime. At the end of the school year he enlists—and while still in basic training is blinded in an accident. He returns home bitter and aloof. Anna hears him pacing his room at night, weeping. She recalls her own retreat "into some safe secret place where nobody can reach," and her sense that at the same time a handicap is "like being shut up inside a shell with no way out." She consults with her friends Dr. and Mrs. Schumacher, who had helped her sight, brings home records for Rudi, and learns Braille in order to teach him. With her encouragement, Rudi slowly returns to an almost normal life.

As a child, Anna had been stubborn and clumsy, afraid of school and all things new. Yet she becomes a young woman of determination, compassion, and confidence. Understanding so well the world of the visually impaired, she is able to help Rudi feel whole again. The whole family is portrayed with subtle sensitivity. This book is a sequel to *From Anna.*

Ages 10-14

Also available in:
Paperbound—*Listen for the Singing*
HarperCollins Publishers, Inc.

Talking Book—*Listen for the Singing*
Library of Congress (NLSBPH)

381

Little, Jean

Look Through My Window

Black/white illustrations by Joan Sandin.
HarperCollins Publishers, Inc., 1970.
(258 pages) o.p.

FRIENDSHIP: Making Friends
RELATIVES: Living in Child's Home
Change: new home
Jew
Prejudice: religious

Emily, a young adolescent, is dismayed to learn that her father is being transferred. She and her parents will be leaving their small apartment to move into an old eighteen-room house in Riverside, Ontario. Her four younger cousins will be living with the family until her aunt recovers from tuberculosis. When Emily arrives at the large, old house, she finds evidence that girls have played there while it stood empty, and she hopes to make friends with them. As she helps her mother take care of the house and the children, Emily finds that she likes her young cousins. When she meets Kate and Lindsay, the girls who had played in the house, she discovers that they share her interest in writing poetry. However, she is surprised and confused when Kate announces that she is part Jewish and apparently expects Emily and Lindsay to reject her. After a talk with her mother, Emily understands her friend a little better. She learns that some people accept or reject others because of race, religion, or ethnic background. Emily has never encountered these feelings before and tries to show Kate that she isn't concerned about her being Jewish. Kate and her parents are planning to take a trip during the Christmas holidays, but both Kate and Emily come down with chicken pox at that time. Emily's parents invite Kate to stay with them. In the excitement of the season and of creating a Christmas play, Kate becomes less sensitive about being Jewish. Throughout the spring, Emily must face more changes: her aunt's condition improves and her cousins will be leaving soon; the wonderful house—too big for three people—will be sold. Emily thinks this is the end of all good times until her mother points out that they will still live near Kate and that Emily will have a baby brother or sister in the fall.

This sensitively written story clearly depicts the feelings of a girl who suddenly becomes an older sister to several siblings. The confusion she feels when exposed to the existence of prejudice is dealt with sensibly and realistically in discussions with her mother. Kate's story continues in the sequel *Kate.*

Ages 10-14

Also available in:
Cassette—*Look Through My Window*
Library of Congress (NLSBPH)

Talking Book—*Look Through My Window*
Library of Congress (NLSBPH)

382

Little, Jean

Mine for Keeps

Black/white illustrations by Lewis Parker.
Little, Brown and Company, 1988.
(186 pages, paperbound)

CEREBRAL PALSY
Fear: of school
Pets: responsibility for
Self, attitude toward: pity

Ten-year-old Sarah Jane Copeland (Sal for short) is a victim of cerebral palsy and always has lived in an institution for handicapped children. Her family recently moved to a new house near a treatment center, which means that Sal can live at home and still receive therapy. The change will be quite an adjustment for Sal because she feels incapable of coping with all the challenges of living at home and attending a public school. Sal is not sure she can dress and feed herself and maneuver on crutches. But by learning to trust her own ability to care for and train her new pet—a helpless, frightened dog—she becomes able to cope with the demands of home and school. Sal meets a new girl at school named Libby who befriends her. After an awkward beginning, Sal, Libby, and Elsje, a Dutch girl, discover a warm friendship developing among them. Sarah learns about Piet, Elsje's brother who has a rheumatic heart which prevents him from participating in some activities. But the most serious of Piet's handicaps are his self-pity and his unwillingness to try. When Piet sees that, even with her handicap, Sal can train a dog, he finds the courage to become an active member of his family and class at school.

While Sal clearly is frustrated by her clumsiness, the reader does not pity her. Mr. and Mrs. Copeland are presented as strong individuals who strive to do what is best for all their children. Sal's handicap never is considered a major issue by anyone but the girl herself. This idealistic attitude is somewhat unrealistic.

Ages 10-13

Also available in:
Cassette—*Mine for Keeps*
Library of Congress (NLSBPH)

383

Little, Lessie Jones and Eloise Greenfield

I Can Do It by Myself

Color illustrations by Carole Byard.
HarperCollins Publishers, Inc., 1978.
(39 pages counted)

DEPENDENCE/INDEPENDENCE
Fear: of animals
Pride/False pride

Young Donny resents the help that older people continually press on him—as if they can do everything and he nothing. On his mother's birthday he awakens determined to walk to a nearby florist shop alone and buy a plant he has already picked out as her present. He turns down his older brother's offer of help and walks on, towing a wagon. Belatedly, Donny remembers a frightening bulldog ahead but vows not to walk another way and be laughed at. The dog barks at Donny, briefly scaring him, but is behind a fence, and the boy arrives at the store with his "cool" intact. Pleased that the storekeeper treats him like a grown-up customer, Donny confidently sets off for home with the plant. But this time the bulldog is outside the fence. Forgetting his vow to be brave, the boy cries and yells for Mama. He does remember not to run from a dog, but backing away, he falls. Now he is truly frightened—but the dog merely looks at him, turns, and goes back inside his yard. Donny quickly latches the gate and walks on home. There he gives Mama the plant and proudly tells his brother, "I told you I could do it by myself."

A young boy's self-reliance outweighs his courage, and his encounter with a dog shows the limits of that. Neither the boy nor the book draws lessons therefrom, but readers should be able to. The book features some Black English; the only difficulty for readers unfamiliar with it might be a sentence in which "bad" means "good": "You think you bad, don't you?"

Ages 5-7

Also available in:
Talking Book—*I Can Do It by Myself*
Library of Congress (NLSBPH)

384

Liu, Aimee

Solitaire

HarperCollins Publishers, Inc., 1979.
(215 pages) o.p.

ANOREXIA NERVOSA
GUILT, FEELINGS OF
SELF, ATTITUDE TOWARD: Body Concept
Boy-girl relationships: dating
Family: relationships
Friendship: making friends
Maturation

Aimee describes her early childhood as a "cupcake existence," "frosted with affluence, filled with adventure, and sprinkled generously with loving care." But her joy ended brutally at seven when she was raped by two twelve-year-old boys. When Aimee was nine, her grandmother called her "chubby," making the girl wonder for the first time if she was overweight. By twelve, Aimee is filled with doubts about herself, concern that her parents' bickering will end in divorce, and worries about her stormy relationship with her mother. That Christmas, weighing one hundred thirty pounds, Aimee decides to diet. She becomes obsessed with calorie counting, calisthenics, dancing, and schoolwork. In three weeks she loses fifteen pounds and feels great satisfaction at having total control over this one part of her life. With the weight loss comes the stopping of her periods and the constant feeling of being cold. But her friends admire her self-discipline and, despite her parents' concern, Aimee loves her sense of control. At fourteen she decides she wants to be a model, and her parents reluctantly agree to let her apply to various agencies in New York City. The Wilhelmina Agency signs her, pleased with her slender, tall figure and good looks, and she begins periodic modeling jobs on weekends and during the summers. But Aimee is still obsessed with her weight. She begins going on eating binges, after which she makes herself throw up and uses laxatives. At fifteen, Aimee weighs ninety-two pounds. She moves to the basement bedroom, seeking refuge from the parental battles. At sixteen, her picture begins appearing in magazines. Classmates admire her, especially the girls, and Aimee loves the attention. Dieting becomes gratification. It also serves as an escape from her problems—her parents, pressure to date, school, the future. In her senior year Aimee begins dating for the first time. She goes steady with Ken Webster, who is also obsessed with pushing himself to the limit: doing without sleep, driving fast cars. They take strength in each other, and when both enter Yale they begin living together. Aimee becomes a vegetarian and starts eating a little more regularly. After several months devoted solely to school and Ken, she begins to reevaluate her life. She realizes she and Ken are suffocating each other. She breaks up with him, moves into a dorm, cultivates a more varied social life, and even tries to eat better. In the process,

Aimee realizes she had been leading a sick, unnatural life; she had been afraid to grow up. Home for the summer, she even comes to discover that her parents really do love and care for her and each other. They are her support and "I was downright lucky to be their daughter."

In this deeply affecting first-person narrative, Aimee describes the true story of her struggle against anorexia nervosa and other eating disorders. Raped at seven, profoundly disturbed by her parents' constant arguing, Aimee's obsession with losing weight becomes her way to assume control. Overcoming her self-destructive behavior requires her to understand that what she fears most is growing up. In the end, Aimee triumphs over both anorexia and her feelings of worthlessness. The rape scene, though sensitively handled, is detailed and could upset some readers.

Ages 13 and up

Also available in:
No other form known

385

Lopshire, Robert

I Am Better Than You!

Color illustrations by the author.
HarperCollins Publishers, Inc., 1968.
(179 pages)

BOASTING
Pride/False pride

When two lizards named Sam and Pete meet on a vine, Sam demands the right of way, claiming to be the "best" lizard in the world. Pete wants to see proof of this claim, so Sam demonstrates his skills by catching a fly with one flick of his tongue. But Pete is able to do the same, so the two lizards go on catching flies until an angry Sam falls from the vine. Sam tells Pete that he did not really fall but merely came down to show how fast he could run. So the two lizards run abreast until Sam smashes into a tree. Once again, he makes an excuse, claiming that he stopped by the tree to show Pete his ability to turn brown. But Pete performs the same feat and then outdoes Sam by turning green and brown at the same time. So Sam crawls onto a sheet of newspaper comics and tries to become multi-colored. He can't, of course, and Pete tells him it was foolish to try because he is a lizard, and lizards only turn green and brown and catch flies. Then Pete stalks away to catch flies, and a humbled Sam quietly asks if he may come along.

This book for beginning readers humorously illustrates how boasting can lead to painful and humiliating consequences. It provides a good basis for discussing honest self-evaluation.

Ages 4-8

Also available in:
No other form known

386

Lowry, Lois

Anastasia Again!

Black/white illustrations by Diane de Groat.
Houghton Mifflin Co., 1981.
(145 pages)

CHANGE: New Home
Age: aging
Friendship: making friends
Moving

Twelve-year-old Anastasia Krupnik is alarmed and outraged at the prospect of her family's move from Cambridge, Massachusetts, to the suburbs. She dreads leaving her best friend and thinks suburban lives are played out much like those of the characters in soap operas. She envisions people with no integrity in houses decorated with matching furniture, bowls of fake fruit, and paint-by-number pictures. Her father, a university professor and published poet, cautions her against "premature assumptions." However, both he and her mother, a successful artist, along with her precocious little brother, Sam, suffer and share their own pre- and post-moving blues. But they find and buy an old house that is just right for the family, and having her own room makes Anastasia less resistant to the move. Her spirits rise further when she makes friends with a neighborhood boy who is actually taller than her five feet, seven inches. She determinedly befriends an eccentric old neighbor and, in the end, engineers a party during which she introduces this lonely woman to a group of older people. Helping her friend overcome her fear and shyness shows Anastasia the truth of her father's warning about "premature assumptions." The move to the suburbs hasn't been so bad after all.

In this sequel to *Anastasia Krupnik,* the precocious Anastasia weathers her anxiety about moving, learning, through her friendship with a lonely neighbor, how misconceptions and fear can close off happiness. Anastasia is a resilient, enthusiastic, affecting heroine with a delightful sense of humor. Witty, accurate descriptions and remarkably authentic dialogue give this story great appeal. A hasty summation of the whimsical mystery novel Anastasia is writing provides an amusing ending to the book.

Ages 9-12

Also available in:
Braille—*Anastasia Again!*
Library of Congress (NLSBPH)

Cassette—*Anastasia Again!*
Library of Congress (NLSBPH)

387

Lowry, Lois

Anastasia at Your Service

Black/white illustrations by Diane de Groat.
Houghton Mifflin Co., 1982.
(149 pages)

MONEY: Earning
Friendship: making friends
Job
Practical jokes/pranks
Prejudice: social class
Responsibility: accepting
Revenge

Anastasia Krupnik, twelve, recently moved, her only friend gone to camp, suffering from poverty, boredom, and depression, places advertisements around town offering her services as a Companion to a rich older woman. When she reports to her first employer, Mrs. Ferris Bellingham, she is a little surprised to be put to work polishing silver, but she assumes a Companion has to pitch in during emergencies. Then she accidentally drops a silver spoon into the garbage disposal. Mrs. Bellingham tells Anastasia she is to work as a maid at a birthday luncheon for her granddaughter, Daphne, the next day. As if being a maid weren't bad enough, Anastasia learns that the girl she'll be serving will probably be in her class this fall. Mrs. Bellingham also points out that the silver spoon cost thirty-five dollars and Anastasia will have to work another twelve hours to pay for it. The next day Anastasia disguises herself by wearing her mother's bra stuffed with panty hose, powdering her hair, and wearing makeup. But Daphne unmasks her when Anastasia's bosom falls into the platter of deviled eggs she's carrying, and the girls become friends. Daphne's father is a minister, she tells Anastasia, so she has had to become almost a juvenile delinquent in order to rebel. She's angry at her grandmother for insulting her with a doll on her birthday, and Anastasia is angry at being forced to do maid's work when she applied to be a Companion in the best tradition of Gothic mysteries and romances. Daphne proposes that they revenge themselves on Mrs. Bellingham by inviting a neighborhood drunk, a bag lady, two potheads, a couple of recently released psychotics, and people from the low-income housing units to Mrs. Bellingham's upcoming fund-raising party. Meanwhile, Anastasia's little brother, Sam, falls out of a window and is hospitalized with a head injury. While in the hospital, he makes friends with a Mrs. Flypaper, apparently imaginary. Anastasia is horrified when she hears that the money from Mrs. Bellingham's fund raiser is to go to the pediatric wing of Sam's hospital. She and Daphne resolve to head off trouble at the affair by spotting the people Daphne invited and asking them to leave. Unfortunately, Daphne doesn't remember what most of them look like. She asks one disreputable-looking guest to leave and he turns out to be the mayor of Boston. Finally, the girls confess their scheme to Mrs. Bellingham, also confiding their fear of her. She sends them home and soothes her guests. When Anastasia goes to collect her paycheck, she takes Sam along. To her surprise, he embraces Mrs. Bellingham and calls her Mrs. Flypaper. It turns out that Mrs. Bellingham works as a volunteer in the hospital. She is upset that both Anastasia and Daphne were angry with her but were too afraid to confront her with their feelings. Daphne, dealt with severely by her parents for the first time in her life, asks Anastasia's help in keeping out of trouble in the future; school detentions aren't much fun. Anastasia gladly agrees to help her new friend.

In this entertaining sequel to *Anastasia Krupnik* and *Anastasia Again!* the feisty young heroine learns not to prejudge people just because they are very rich. She also accepts the consequences of her actions and realizes, when he is badly hurt, how much she actually loves her precocious little brother. This is easy, appealing reading with several ideas worth thinking about—such as the tendency of revenge to backfire.

Ages 9-12

Also available in:

Braille—*Anastasia at Your Service*
Library of Congress (NLSBPH)

Cassette—*Anastasia at Your Service*
Library of Congress (NLSBPH)

388

Lowry, Lois

Anastasia Krupnik

Houghton Mifflin Co., 1979.
(113 pages)

MATURATION
SIBLING: New Baby
Age: aging
Loss: feelings of

At age ten, Anastasia suddenly finds herself possessed of an unpredictable temperament. In a little green book, she keeps two lists headed "Things I Love" and "Things I Hate." One day she loves Washburn Cummings, with his huge Afro; the next day, after he makes insulting remarks about her hairdo, she hates him. She decides to turn Catholic but changes her mind quickly at the idea of confession. She hates pumpkin pie at Thanksgiving, but by Christmas she loves it. Shortly after her tenth birthday, a small, pink wart had appeared on her left thumb. Anastasia loves her wart because her father has told her warts have a kind of magic about them. Angry when she learns that her mother is expecting a child, she immediately adds the baby to her "hate" list. To reconcile her to the loss of her only-child status, her father tells her she can name the baby. In anger, she secretly decides on a terrible name: One-Ball-Reilly, after a classmate she hates. She hates her grandmother for being old and confused and in a nursing home. At Thanksgiving she tries to talk to her, but the old woman lives only in the past and doesn't know Anastasia. The girl is saddened and frightened by the idea of old age. Then one day she learns from a poem by Wordsworth about "the inward eye," the solace of happy memories. Realizing that her grandmother has the inward eye, Anastasia is more sympathetic at Christmas when the old woman talks in the present tense of her deceased husband, Sam. One day, just as suddenly as it came, the wart disappears. Anastasia goes to tell her parents and finds them grieving for her grandmother, who has died. Anastasia is amazed to find herself crying with real feeling. That same day, her mother goes to the hospital to have the baby. Anastasia is convinced these upsetting events are related to the sudden disappearance of her wart. On the way to the hospital to see her baby brother, she crosses out the name she had planned for him and writes down a new one. The name she has chosen is Sam.

One of a series of books about Anastasia Krupnik, this is a sensitive and lively account of a bright young girl beginning the painful process of growing up. Anastasia learns to balance her brimming emotions by becoming attuned to others' needs, and so comes to understand herself a bit better. Told realistically and with humor, the story is consistently involving.

Ages 9-11

Also available in:
Braille—*Anastasia Krupnik*
Library of Congress (NLSBPH)

Cassette—*Anastasia Krupnik*
Library of Congress (NLSBPH)

389

Lowry, Lois

A Summer to Die

Black/white illustrations by Jenni Oliver.
Houghton Mifflin Co., 1977.
(154 pages)

FAMILY: Unity
SIBLING: Relationships
Death: of sibling
Illnesses: terminal
Leukemia

The Chalmers family has temporarily moved to a farmhouse in the country. Mr. Chalmers has been given a year's sabbatical from the university to finish writing his book. Thirteen-year-old Meg, plain and intellectual, hates being away from her painting class and her photography club, while fifteen-year-old Molly, pretty and popular, misses her boyfriends and cheerleading. But before long, Molly has a new boyfriend, and Meg has a new friend of a different kind. Will Banks is the elderly owner of the house the Chalmers rent, and lives nearby. Interested in photography, he allows Meg to photograph him, and, later in the winter, when Meg and her father build a darkroom, Meg teaches Will how to make photographic prints. Meanwhile, Molly has been ill, her frequent nosebleeds keeping her away from school. Briefly in the spring the nosebleeds stop, but one night she awakens to profuse bleeding. During a hospital stay her illness is diagnosed and an effective medication found. But back at home she is listless and depressed. Meg tries to cheer her, but Molly's illness troubles the whole family. When Will rents the third house on his land to a young couple about to have a baby, Meg and Molly befriend the new renters and enjoy them. But one day Molly is taken back to the hospital. Meg suddenly realizes that her sister will not get better—she is going to die. Her parents confirm her suspicion: Molly has leukemia. At first Meg avoids visiting Molly; but soon she goes to tell her of the birth of the neighbor couple's baby. Molly, connected to machines and heavily drugged, barely responds. Two weeks later she dies. The grieving Chalmers family leaves the farmhouse to return home.

Set in the rustic New England countryside, this book is at once refreshing and sad. It portrays the warmth of both family life and friendships. The narrator, Meg, who has always envied Molly's poise and prettiness, finally understands that she is beautiful, too, in her own way. Molly's illness and death are described with a realism and sympathy that avoid sentimentality.

Ages 10-14

Also available in:
Braille—*A Summer to Die*
Library of Congress (NLSBPH)

390

Luger, Harriett Mandelay

Lauren

Dell Publishing Company, Inc., 1981.
(157 pages) o.p.

DECISION MAKING
UNWED MOTHER
Boy-girl relationships: dating
Communication: parent-child
Friendship: meaning of
Parent/Parents: fighting between

Terribly afraid she's pregnant, seventeen-year-old Lauren Murray changes quickly from a carefree member of the Gruesome Threesome, with friends Judy and Stephanie, into an adult with burdens nearly too great to bear. After telling her boyfriend, Donny, she confides her apprehension to Judy and Stephanie. They accompany her to the Free Clinic where she learns she is twelve to fourteen weeks pregnant, too far along for a simple abortion. Desperately needing support and guidance, Lauren is soon disappointed by friends and family. Judy scoffs at her stupidity for not taking precautions; in response, Stephanie attempts to support Lauren by declaring that love cannot be so cold and calculating. Donny, though supportive, is frightened about his own future and wants Lauren to get an abortion. Lauren's parents, usually at odds, band together in support of their daughter, placing full blame on Donny, while his parents consider Lauren the culprit. Upset by the attitudes of both sets of parents, hurt by her friends' lack of understanding, feeling betrayed by Donny,

Lauren packs a bag and, with fifty dollars to her name, leaves home intending to solve her own problems. She goes to the beach, her favorite refuge, and cries out her fear, hurt, and anger. There she is befriended by Liz and Dawn, unwed mothers who offer her shelter in exchange for food and money. Lauren soon learns the difficulties of a life without parental support: Dawn, negligent and immature, eventually loses her child to the courts, and Liz finds herself unable to pay the rent. Through the two, Lauren meets Tom and Andrea, a married couple who have been trying for seven years to have a baby. She and Andrea become friends, but Andrea accuses Lauren of not taking seriously her responsibilities to her unborn child. For the first time, Lauren begins to contemplate what keeping her baby might mean. One day, the tense situation with her roommates explodes as Lauren (now penniless after losing her job in a hamburger joint) is accused by Dawn's boyfriend of leading him on. Depressed, despairing, and alone once more, Lauren packs her bag and again heads for the beach. Tempted by the soothing rhythm of the waves, she walks into the surf, half intending never to return. She comes to her senses in time and strikes out struggling for the shore. Once safe, she finds herself at a pay phone calling her mother to come for her. Her frightened, concerned family welcomes her home. Donny tells her he still loves her, and at first Lauren believes he will marry her. She tells her parents she will keep the baby, although she doesn't say that she and Donny will marry. When she talks to him of marriage, he reluctantly agrees. But Lauren realizes that he feels trapped and resentful, that their marriage would be much like her parents' unhappy one, and she lets Donny go. Then Carla, Lauren's fourteen-year-old sister, shyly but proudly confides that she and her boyfriend have had sex for the first time. Appalled, Lauren sees history repeating itself. Her thoughts turn to the childless Andrea and Tom and to the need of her unborn child for a family. Her decision is made.

This emotion-packed novel clearly depicts the agonizing decisions young people must face when burdened with premature parenthood. The various options available to Lauren—abortion, single parenthood, marriage, adoption—are sensibly, thoroughly, and impartially examined through the girl's own thoughts and actions. This is a strong, affecting story, filled with possibilities for discussion.

Ages 12 and up

Also available in:
No other form known

391

Lund, Doris Herold

Eric

HarperCollins Publishers, Inc., 1974.
(345 pages) o.p.

CANCER: Leukemia
Courage, meaning of
Death: attitude toward
Parent/Parents: respect for/lack of respect for

Seventeen-year-old Eric Lund, a college-bound champion athlete, is constantly on the go. When he is told that he has leukemia, he accepts the diagnosis but vows not to let the disease overcome him. Eric asks his parents to let him live his life as normally as possible between trips to the hospital and bouts with nausea induced by the anti-leukemic medication. Despite his mother's misgivings, Eric attends college part-time, plays varsity soccer, swims, and skin dives. He tries to keep himself in the best possible physical condition for the deadly battle he knows he must face. In his only acts of overt frustration, Eric lashes out at his mother's protective suggestions and her interference in his lifestyle. Eventually, Mrs. Lund accepts the fact that her son must fight the disease in his own way and that she is the "valve" through which Eric releases the frustration and anger he feels toward his fatal illness. As the leukemia progresses and Eric spends more and more time in the hospital, he loses none of his sense of humor. He tries to cheer and encourage the other "inmates," as he calls them. In the hospital Eric also meets MaryLou, a private-duty nurse, and the two fall in love. They have an affair but make no plans to marry. As several of his close friends from his hospital days die of their various types of cancer, Eric is forced to accept reality. He faces the inevitable by trying to hurry as many experiences as possible into his time away from the hospital, but soon he is unable to spend more than a few days away at a time. Near the end, Eric becomes calm and tells his mother he still wants to get the most out of the things around him—a sunny day, the laughter of children, the sound of rain, and his love for his family and for MaryLou. When Eric lapses into semi-consciousness, the family and MaryLou agree to refuse medical aid which will only prolong Eric's suffering.

This emotion-filled, first-person narrative by Doris Lund, Eric's mother, deals explicitly with the young man's attitude and behavior during the four years of his fatal illness. Mrs. Lund also gives the reader a profound understanding of the soul-searching and suffering of the family during Eric's battle with leukemia, and of their grief at his death. The descriptions of Eric's illness and treatment are very frank, giving the reader an almost shocking view of the extreme physical pain and mental anguish that Eric suffered.

Ages 12 and up

Also available in:
Talking Book—*Eric*
Library of Congress (NLSBPH)

392
MacLachlan, Patricia
Arthur, for the Very First Time
Black/white illustrations by Lloyd Bloom.
Charlotte Zolotow Children's Books, 1980.
(117 pages)

SIBLING: New Baby
Differences, human
Identity, search for
Reality, escaping
Relatives: living in home of

The summer that Arthur Rasby is ten years old, he's sure his mother is going to have a baby, but isn't sure he likes the idea. Because his mother isn't feeling well and he has no friends nearby, Arthur is sent to spend the summer with Great-Aunt Elda and Great-Uncle Wrisby. They live in a huge, rambling old house with a pet chicken, Pauline, who responds only to French. Great-Uncle Wrisby sings to the pig, Bernadette, and Arthur feels that his relatives are "scatty." But he does come to love Pauline and believes she is much nicer than a baby would be. Moira MacAvin, the veterinarian's granddaughter, insists on calling Arthur Mouse. She tells him that her parents have abandoned her. Arthur feels abandoned too and hasn't opened any of his parents' letters. Moira accuses Arthur of writing about things in his journal instead of experiencing them. She says he's like their social worker who comes to ask "meaningful" questions, writes in her notebook, and then does nothing about any of it. Since Bernadette will be giving birth in a few weeks, Moira lends Arthur a book about birthing sows. But when Arthur tries to tell Wrisby about the precautions they must take, Wrisby doesn't want his advice. Elda explains Wrisby's belief that if he doesn't think about bad things, they won't happen. Then Arthur and Moira decide Pauline looks sickly, so they dose her with Great-Uncle Wrisby's "tonic" while he and Elda are in town. In the course of tasting this brew, Moira, Arthur, and Pauline get drunk and reach Moira's house just as the social worker does. Moira's grandfather spanks her, proving to her that he really does love her. The social worker decides that Moira can stay with her grandfather instead of being put in a foster home. Following this, Arthur reads all twelve of his parents' letters. In one of them, his mother mentions that everything takes time. When Arthur tells Moira about the letters, she says his parents sound nice. He agrees. Bernadette starts to have her babies during a storm while Wrisby and Elda are in town. Moira and Arthur find her in the new pen Arthur built for the birthing, and they help until Wrisby comes home. Moira congratulates Arthur on really doing something at last, calling him Arthur instead of Mouse for the very first time.

Spending the summer with his whimsically unconventional great-aunt and great-uncle, a young boy slowly comes to terms with the fact that he will soon have a sibling. From being an observer of life, Arthur becomes a participant. In the process, he begins to know and accept himself and others. In the future he'll be more confident, better able to cope with life's uncertainties. Softly shaded illustrations capture the story's mood.

Ages 8-10

Also available in:
Cassette—*Arthur, for the Very First Time*
Library of Congress (NLSBPH)

Paperbound—*Arthur, for the Very First Time*
Charlotte Zolotow Children's Books

393
MacLachlan, Patricia
Cassie Binegar
Charlotte Zolotow Children's Books, 1982.
(120 pages)

CHANGE: Accepting
PRIVACY, NEED FOR
Belonging
Change: new home
Differences, human
Family: extended
Family: relationships
Guilt, feelings of

Cassie Binegar, about eleven, and her family have moved to an old house near the shore. Now her father and brothers can be closer to their fishing boat, and their mother can rent out the little cottages surrounding the house. But Cassie misses her old tree house and feels she now has no private space. She tries making a place for herself in the attic, but is moved out when more storage space is needed. For a while a closet under the stairs seems like a good place, but her father and brothers need it for their gear. Cassie feels so different from her casual, rough family that she's sure she must have been adopted. She likes her new friend's family because they are more formal and unchanging, but Margaret Mary is intrigued by Cassie's relatives and wishes she had some unusual family members. Cassie's Uncle Hat, who even wears a hat to bed, speaks in rhymes; Cousin Coralinda wears a feathered cape and other miscellaneous feathered items. One day Gran comes to visit, followed by Uncle Hat, Cousin Coralinda, and Baby Binnie. Guilty Cassie isn't sure she wants to see Gran; just before her grandfather died Cassie had yelled at him, and she's sure that if she had just apologized, he would be alive today. Gran brings a beautiful tablecloth for the dining room table; it extends to the floor and makes a wonderful hiding place for Cassie. Underneath the table she overhears talk about Cousin Coralinda's husband, who has left her and Baby Binnie. She also hears "the writer" when he comes in to rent a cottage. Cassie falls in love with him and talks to him about her space

M

problem. He says we all carry around our own private space. Gran tells Cassie that the hermit crab changes its space many times, that different kinds of spaces can shelter a person. Cassie begins to feel that perhaps she does have a space of her own after all. She talks to Gran about the time she yelled at her grandfather. Gran explains that Papa died because he was sick, and that he used to yell too. In fact, just before he died he sat up in bed and yelled, "Where in hell are my green socks!" Gran tells Cassie she has to let her guilt go. "The writer" and Cousin Coralinda begin spending a lot of time together. When they marry, Cassie is maid of honor and wears a dress worn by her mother and grandmother at their weddings.

In this rather low-key but delightful book, Cassie, "who wishes that things never changed," learns that things can change and still remain the same. When she wonders if Gran has changed after her husband's death, Cassie's mother explains that Gran is still the same person even though her life has taken on new patterns. Margaret Mary helps Cassie see that what may look static and secure on the outside can actually be very different on the inside. She provides counterpoint for Cassie's feelings; when Margaret Mary delights in the changing images in a kaleidoscope, Cassie wants to pick one picture and keep it the same always. Cassie is ashamed of her family, whom she considers odd, but begins to change her mind when Margaret Mary insists they are all "splendid."

Ages 9-12

Also available in:
Cassette—*Cassie Binegar*
Library of Congress (NLSBPH)

Paperbound—*Cassie Binegar*
Charlotte Zolotow Children's Books

394

MacLachlan, Patricia

Mama One, Mama Two

Color illustrations by Ruth Lercher Bornstein.
HarperCollins Publishers, Inc., 1982.
(30 pages counted)

FOSTER HOME
PARENT/PARENTS: Substitute
Mental illness: of parent

Young Maudie is awakened in the middle of the night by the baby's cries and goes to his room. Soon Katherine appears with the baby's bottle and lets Maudie feed him. Then Katherine comes to sit on Maudie's bed and together they tell the story of "Mama One, Mama Two," which Maudie has again requested. Maudie begins and tells about a girl and her mother, Mama One, and how happy they were together. Mama One painted bright pictures of trees and sunsets. But then, continues Katherine, Mama One became unhappy and did not know why. She painted dark pictures and did not cook or clean. The girl did all the chores, says Maudie. Mama One stayed in her room and the girl was lonely without her. Mama One asked a social worker for help—"Tom, who listens." He took Mama One to a place where she could talk about being sad and find out what it was that made her sad. Tom told the girl it was not her fault that Mama One was unhappy. Then he described a special place where she could live for a while with someone who had helped other children and knew all about Mama One. The girl was afraid, but she packed her things, including her blue quilt, and got in the car with Tom, wondering if she'd have a night-light in her new home. Maudie tells about how Tom spotted a bluebird and stopped his car. He told the girl the bird was going south but would be back in the spring, and maybe Mama One would also. At her new home the girl helped Mama Two with the baby, learned to make pancakes, and made new friends. When Maudie and Katherine finish the story, Katherine puts the sleeping baby in his crib and comes back to sleep with Maudie awhile. Then Maudie—the girl—and Katherine—Mama Two—talk about when spring will come. "Whenever Mama One comes home will be spring," says Katherine. Then they sleep under Maudie's blue quilt.

This gentle story-within-a-story reassures a little girl in a foster home about the eventual return of her mentally ill mother. Even more, it demonstrates the depth of love and understanding of the foster mother who willingly accepts the role of second mother so urgently required by the child. Significantly, little Maudie indicates by her part of the "Mama One, Mama Two" story that she realizes her need for help and recognizes how her life has improved since coming to her foster home. Pastel illustrations emphasize the caring, soothing tone of the book, which could be very helpful in preparing a child for a foster home.

Ages 4-7

Also available in:
No other form known

395

MacLachlan, Patricia

The Sick Day

Color illustrations by William Pene Du Bois.
Pantheon Books, 1979.
(29 pages counted) o.p.

ILLNESSES: Being Ill
Love, meaning of

Dragging Frederick, her blanket, into her father's writing room, little Emily says her head, stomach, and toe hurt. Put to bed, she asks for Moosie, a lost stuffed animal. While looking for Moosie and a thermometer, her father finds her rubber bands and he puts her hair into three ponytails, the one on top making her look like a fountain. When Emily says she may have to "swallow up," he bends down and talks her stomach out of it. Emily says she feels like a sandwich, and her father makes her laugh by saying she doesn't look like a sandwich. When she asks if she is going to die, he says she is going to read instead. She complains that she has read all her books, so he invents a story for her. Then he makes her some broth and draws a picture of a "gentle monster" to chase her sickness away. Emily smiles and says it is fun being sick with him. The next day Emily is better, but her father is sick. Her mother stays home from work and Emily sings to her father, draws him a picture, and finds beneath his bed the missing thermometer and Moosie.

The care and attention of a loving father inject happiness into Emily's day of sickness. Young readers and listeners will be cheered by the father's reassurance and charmed by the clever dialogue and illustrations. Emily's care for her father the next day is a satisfying turn of events.

Ages 4-7

Also available in:
No other form known

396

MacLachlan, Patricia

Through Grandpa's Eyes

Color illustrations by Deborah Ray.
HarperCollins Publishers, Inc., 1979.
(40 pages counted)

BLINDNESS
GRANDPARENT: Love for

Young John loves his grandpa's house. It isn't big or shiny-new like some houses he's seen. But John likes to go there because he can see the house through his grandpa's eyes. His grandpa is blind, but he still has a very special way of seeing and he helps John see this way too. Grandpa gets up when the touch of the sun warms him awake. He can smell the fried eggs and buttered toast Nana has fixed for breakfast and can even sense the fresh bouquet of marigolds in the kitchen. For John the smells are all mixed together until he closes his eyes and concentrates on distinguishing them. Grandpa and John play their cellos together. John uses written music, but Grandpa can play because the notes "are in his fingers." When Nana makes a clay sculpture of Grandpa's head, Grandpa can tell it's a good likeness just by running his fingers over it. When John pretends his fingers are water flowing down the clay head and filling all the spaces, he discovers the head does look like Grandpa. Grandpa sees some things through his memory. When he and his grandson walk across the field, he sees in his mind how the sun shines on the river and how the Queen Anne's lace looks in the meadow. Grandpa tells which direction the wind is coming from by "the feel of the meadow grasses and by the way his hair blows against his face." He can identify birds by their sounds. Grandpa smells lunch when it's ready and feels if John has washed the dishes clean enough to dry and put away. He reads Braille and listens to television. Of course, sometimes Grandpa makes mistakes and needs a little help. But it still seems to John a very special thing to use ears, hands, and nose as Grandpa does. When Nana says goodnight, John can hear the "smile" in her voice. Grandpa always says her voice smiles to him and John can see it too—if he looks through Grandpa's eyes.

The quiet, gentle tone of this book reflects the loving relationship between John and his grandparents. Young readers may become more aware of their senses and of the extra dimension of experience that can come from using each sense more carefully. They may also gain an appreciation for and understanding of the ways blind people can "see" their world. Delicate, subdued pictures add to the feeling that the reader too has had a chance to look through Grandpa's eyes.

Ages 5-8

Also available in:
Cassette—*Through Grandpa's Eyes*
Library of Congress (NLSBPH)

Paperbound—*Through Grandpa's Eyes*
HarperCollins Publishers, Inc.

397

Madler, Trudy

Why Did Grandma Die?

Color illustrations by Gwen Connelly.
Raintree/Steck-Vaughan Publishers, 1980.
(31 pages)

DEATH: of Grandparent
Death: funeral issues
Family: unity
Grandparent: love for

Young Heidi arrives home from school eager to go with her grandmother to the park for a pony ride. But her grandmother is lying down and promises to take her the next day. Instead, Heidi and her grandmother make horses out of clay. The next day when she comes home from school, Heidi sees her grandmother on a stretcher that is being placed in an ambulance. Heidi's mother explains that her grandmother is sick and is going to the hospital. Mrs. Kane, a neighbor, watches Heidi and her younger brother while her parents are at the hospital. The next morning Heidi's mother comes home and sadly tells her that her grandmother has died. "Death is a natural part of life," she explains. "Your grandma had a long and good life." That day the family stays home and everyone is sad. Heidi decides that if she wishes hard enough, maybe her grandmother will come back. But it doesn't work. She notices her father has also been crying, and the two of them talk about her grandmother. Heidi tells him of her distress over not getting to say goodbye. Her father reassures her: her grandmother knew Heidi loved her. At the funeral Heidi stares at her grandmother's body and says goodbye. Back at the apartment, Mrs. Kane tells Heidi she will now be her baby-sitter after school, but Heidi only wants her grandmother. The little girl and her father go for a walk in the park. There they talk about the grandmother's death and their fond memories of her. Heidi realizes that part of her grandmother will always be with her. She goes back to the apartment to apologize to Mrs. Kane and to water her grandmother's flowers.

A little girl struggles to accept her grandmother's death, coming to realize the value of her loving memories. Bright, detailed illustrations help convey the story, and the picture of the grandmother in her open casket could help prepare children for a funeral. The book handles a difficult subject tastefully.

Ages 4-9

Also available in:
No other form known

398

Magorian, Michelle

Good Night, Mr. Tom

HarperCollins Publishers, Inc., 1981.
(318 pages)

CHILD ABUSE
DEPRIVATION, EMOTIONAL
LOVE, MEANING OF
WAR
Death: of friend
Friendship: making friends
Friendship: meaning of
Orphan
Talents: artistic

Just prior to the Second World War, eight-year-old William Beech, pale, weak, and scared, is evacuated from London and sent to live in the town of Little Weirwold with irritable, crusty Thomas Oakley, a widower in his sixties who has decided to do his part for the war effort. Will knows he's a bad boy because Mum often tells him so. A religious fanatic for whom virtually everything is "evil," she even sends along a belt with instructions to whoever gets Will to watch him all the time. When the boy arrives, Tom discovers bruises and sores all over his arms and legs. Will can't read, he sleeps under the bed, and, when persuaded to sleep in it, wets the bed nightly. He suffers from malnutrition, can't keep more than a small amount of food in his stomach, and looks like a waif. Tom buys Will some clothes and boots; even, when Will displays some uncharacteristic interest in them, some paints and brushes. Tom hasn't been near the art supply store since his young wife, Rachel, died over forty years before. Nine-year-old Zacharias Wrench, as energetic and effervescent as Will is quiet, also an evacuee, befriends Will. Will is embarrassed to be placed in a class with younger children because he can't read, but he works industriously at his schoolwork and makes progress. On his ninth birthday he receives many gifts and cards, and Tom has a surprise party for him. He hardly knows how to react: he's never had a present or friends or praise. Meanwhile, his mother writes to repeat over and over that he is bad and that Tom must watch him all the time. After two months with Tom, Will keeps the sheets dry at night, his last sore is healing, and he's making progress in school. Tom himself is changing, coming out of himself into life again. With Will Tom is patient, caring, and reassuring. He changes the bed daily without reprimand, takes the boy to the library, and reads aloud to him every night. The villagers are delighted and amazed, even more so when Tom joins them more actively in the war effort. In March, Will's mother writes that she is ill and wants her son back for a while. For Will, being back with his mother is like drifting into a nightmare. He finds a baby in their apartment with her little mouth taped shut. When Will questions his mother, she beats him senseless. A month later, when Tom still hasn't heard from Will, he goes to London to investigate. He and a warden find the boy chained to a pipe in a closed alcove, clutching his dead sister's tiny body and nearly dead himself. Will is taken to a hospital, and Tom discovers that the authorities plan to put him in a children's home. Desperate, he kidnaps the sedated boy, wraps him warmly, and takes him back to Little Weirwold. He and Zach nurse Will through weeks of nightmares and fever. When he's better, Will, Tom, and Zach have a happy seaside holiday together. Back home, Will meets Geoffrey Sanderton, an established artist, who begins giving the boy lessons when he sees how talented he is. Authorities from London bring news that Will's mother has committed suicide. They still want to take Will to a children's home, but Tom finds a way to start adoption proceedings instead. The day before Will's tenth birthday, Zach's father is badly wounded in a London air raid and Zach goes to London to see him in spite of his mother's warnings. He is killed in the London bombings. For four months Will is inconsolable. Then Geoffrey tells him about a dead friend of his and how he feels better when he smokes his friend's pipe. Will repairs and learns to ride Zach's old bike, and he begins to heal. He sees that even without Zach it's good to be alive, especially living in Little Weirwold with his "dad."

A young victim of an unbalanced, murderously abusive mother finds a loving home with a reclusive widower in a small English town. In discovering a world he never knew existed, Will also discovers his own artistic talents and begins to emerge as a complete human being. The mutual love and need of the boy and the man are movingly described. Richly detailed, engrossing, and appealing, this story of rural England during World War II illuminates daily life in a small, generous community. The country dialect is easily understood and adds authenticity.

Ages 11 and up

Also available in:
Cassette—*Good Night, Mr. Tom*
Library of Congress (NLSBPH)

Paperbound—*Good Night, Mr. Tom*
HarperCollins Publishers, Inc.

399

Mann, Peggy

There Are Two Kinds of Terrible

Avon Books, 1979.
(132 pages) o.p.

DEATH: of Mother
MOURNING, STAGES OF
Cancer
Communication: parent-child
Illnesses: terminal

To fall off your bike on the first day of summer vacation when you are about twelve is perfectly terrible, as Robbie Farley finds out. You miss tennis lessons, baseball, and swimming. But that autumn, his arm healed, Robbie learns that "there are two kinds of terrible." His mother, to whom he is extremely close, tells Robbie she must have a minor operation and will be in the hospital for a few days. That is bad enough. The boy sees little of his always-aloof father, and spends his days and evenings alone. But when his mother does not come home after two weeks, he becomes suspicious. His father seems sad and more remote than ever. Finally his father admits that Mother is dying of cancer. When Robbie is at last permitted to visit her, he cannot believe how thin, pale, and weak his beautiful young mother has become. She dies soon afterward. Devastated, son and father avoid each other, and Robbie feels hurt and angry that his father will not reach out to help him. Then he finds a scrapbook under his father's pillow containing photographs of his parents, photographs his father must be poring over privately. For the first time he glimpses the pain of his father's loss. He writes a note saying as much, and his father answers gratefully. When his father buys Robbie a set of drums, the boy decides that the two of them can make a life together after all.

This sad but not melodramatic first-person story portrays a child's loneliness and grief at the loss of a parent after a frightening illness. Robbie must take a leap toward growing up in order to make a family of himself and his father.

Ages 9-12

Also available in:
No other form known

400

Marino, Barbara Pavis

Eric Needs Stitches

Black/white photographs by Richard Rudinski.
Addison-Wesley Publishing Company, Inc., 1979.
(32 pages)

HOSPITAL, GOING TO
SUTURES
Accidents

When young Eric has an accident on his bicycle, his father says he needs stitches in his knee. On the way to the hospital, a frightened Eric wants to know what will happen and if his father will stay with him. His father reassures him, saying he'll stay with Eric if it's all right with the doctor. He explains the procedure for anesthetizing the area and then stitching it, telling Eric why it's important to have some wounds stitched. When Eric tells the emergency-room nurse he's scared and might cry, she says it's okay to cry if it hurts, as long as he holds his leg still. When the doctor joins them he too is reassuring, explaining what he is doing as he proceeds to treat Eric's cut. After the knee is numb, the doctor stitches it up. He congratulates Eric for being such a good patient. The nurse wraps Eric's knee and gives him instructions for keeping it clean and dry so it won't become infected. On the way home, Eric's father takes him for a double-scoop ice-cream cone.

A young boy visits a hospital emergency room to have his knee stitched. Realistic, informative photographs and a simple, candid text give readers a good idea of exactly what's involved in this kind of injury. A note from the author, herself an emergency-room nurse, reports that children who are prepared psychologically for emergency-room care are usually less traumatized and more cooperative than other children. This book is written to help provide good preparation.

Ages 4-10

Also available in:
No other form known

401

Marshall, James

George and Martha Encore

Color illustrations by the author.
Houghton Mifflin Co., 1973.
(47 pages)

FRIENDSHIP: Meaning of
Consideration, meaning of

George and Martha, two hippos, demonstrate their close friendship by doing thoughtful things for each other. George thinks that he will hate a dance recital, but he goes to please Martha. Contrary to his expectations, he discovers that dancing is fun. When

George disguises himself as an Indian to fool Martha, she sees through the trick. Poor George is very disappointed that he couldn't fool Martha; but Martha tells him that she recognized him because he couldn't hide his "bright smiling eyes."

The tenderness and consideration of the two hippos are appealing. A young child could benefit from these examples of friendship.

Ages 3-7

Also available in:
Paperbound—*George and Martha Encore*
Houghton Mifflin Co.

402

Marshall, James

George and Martha—One Fine Day

Color illustrations by the author.
Houghton Mifflin Co., 1978.
(47 pages counted)

FRIENDSHIP: Meaning of
Anxiety
Consideration, meaning of
Privacy, need for

George the hippopotamus is amazed to see his friend Martha, also a hippo, walking a tightrope, and says that he could never do that: he might fall. Right then he notices that Martha is losing her balance and her confidence. He quickly restores both by complimenting her talent and skill, and soon she is walking smartly, just as before. In a second story Martha notices that George is trying to peek whenever she writes in her diary. George confesses that he does want to read the diary, and Martha says he should ask permission. When he does, Martha refuses it. In a third story George and Martha are eating lunch when George commences to tell an "icky" story. Martha asks him to stop, but George ignores her and finishes the story. That is when Martha tells an "icky" story of her own, causing George to feel queasy and turn green. In the fourth story Martha is working on her stamp collection when George frightens her. Martha vows she will scare George in return and he agrees that is only fair. But Martha says she will not scare him immediately. Thus George spends the day worrying and wondering when Martha will scare him until she remarks that she has forgotten all about it. In the final story George and Martha spend the evening in an amusement park. They have a wonderful time until Martha grows strangely quiet in the tunnel of love. Suddenly she shouts "Boo," frightening George out of his wits. Then she tells him that she had not, after all, forgotten to scare him.

By observing how the main characters behave toward each other, the young reader can discern some of the qualities and actions that go into building a strong friendship. Since Martha decides in two of the stories to teach George a lesson, discussion might be started about alternative ways to reform a friend. The illustrations here are no less delightful than the witty text.

Ages 3-6

Also available in:
Braille—*George and Martha—One Fine Day*
Library of Congress (NLSBPH)

Paperbound—*George and Martha—One Fine Day*
Houghton Mifflin Co.

403

Marshall, James

George and Martha Rise and Shine

Color illustrations by the author.
Houghton Mifflin Co., 1976.
(46 pages)

FRIENDSHIP: Best Friend

George and Martha are best of hippopotamus friends, but are not perfect. In two of the five stories in this book, George makes boasts: in one, that he can charm snakes; in the other, that he is not afraid of scary movies. But Martha sees how far he jumps at the sight of a stuffed snake and how white he turns at a scary movie. In two stories, Martha's curiosity embarrasses her: she does experiments with fleas and she disapproves of George's secret club. But the fleas make her itch and the club turns out to be The Martha Fan Club. In the remaining story, Martha pushes a sleepy and abed George, bed and all, to a picnic, which George then enjoys while Martha, exhausted, falls asleep.

These stories show how, when one friend is caught fibbing or being foolish, the other friend handles it in a considerate, often funny way. The drawings form a warm, integral part of the story. This book is one of the popular "George and Martha" series.

Ages 3-7

Also available in:
Paperbound—*George and Martha Rise and Shine*
Houghton Mifflin Co.

404

Maruki, Toshi

Hiroshima No Pika

Translated from the Japanese by Komine Shoten.
Color illustrations by the author.
Lothrop, Lee & Shepard Books, 1980.
(47 pages counted)

WAR
Death
Japan
Violence

On August 6, 1945, at 8:15 in the morning, seven-year-old Mii is eating breakfast with her parents in their Hiroshima home. Suddenly a terrible light, ever after known as the Flash, surrounds them. It is followed by shock waves, collapsing buildings, and violent flames. The United States has dropped its top-secret explosive, known as "Little Boy" by the crew of the plane that dropped it, on the city. Mii's father is caught in the flames but his wife rescues him somehow, lifts him onto her back, and sets off with him and Mii to reach the safety of the river. They join crowds of people with clothes burned away, swollen faces, weak voices. Many just drop where they are. Mii sees terrible, horrifying sights: a dead man floating down the river followed by a dead cat; a woman whose baby won't nurse because it's dead, whereupon she wades out into the river and out of sight; hundreds of dead and wounded people. They run through the burning, collapsing city and cross the river. On the beach outside Hiroshima they lie sleeping or dazed, shocked to learn that four days have passed. An old woman sits up, gives Mii a rice ball, and lies down, never to move again. Mii's father is left in a hospital that is little more than shelter—no doctors, medicine, or bandages—while Mii and her mother return to the wasteland that was their city. Since the day the bomb was dropped, Mii stopped growing. Her mother still must remove bits of glass embedded in Mii's skull that eventually work their way out. Her father recovered from the injuries suffered that day, but several months later his hair fell out, he began coughing blood, purple spots appeared on his body, and he died. Many other people later fell ill with this incurable radiation sickness. Some are still in hospitals. Every year on August 6, people from Hiroshima commemorate their dead. They set lighted lanterns afloat on Hiroshima's seven rivers, each with the name of a loved one. Mii's mother says the horror cannot happen again, as long as "no one drops the bomb."

The bombing of Hiroshima is seen through the eyes of a Japanese girl and her family. The vivid, nightmarish, rather surrealistic illustrations tell a story that is often stronger than the text, of death, destruction, horror. Although the material may seem too powerful for young readers, the treatment is factual without being offensive or overly frightening. Readers will understand that Hiroshima must never happen again. One paragraph that describes the bomb contains words children may need to have explained: explosive, impact, conventional, contaminated, radiation. This account can serve equally well as a read-aloud or as an independent reading selection for which younger children will need adult guidance. Older readers too will profit from guided discussion.

Ages 7 and up

Also available in:
No other form known

405

Mathis, Sharon Bell

The Hundred Penny Box

Color illustrations by Leo and Diane Dillon.
Viking Penguin, 1975.
(47 pages)

AGE: Respect for
African-American
Relatives: living in child's home

Young Michael loves his Great-great-aunt Dew very much, even though, at one hundred, she sometimes forgets and calls him John, his father's name. Michael likes to listen to her favorite record with her, and to hear her sing. But he especially likes her to tell stories of long ago, while he counts the pennies in her hundred-penny box. To Aunt Dew, each penny represents a year in her life, and the box where she keeps them all means everything to her. As she says, "Anybody takes my hundred penny box, takes me." But the over-tidy Ruth, Michael's mother, wants to burn Aunt Dew's big, scruffy penny box, and replace it with a smaller, prettier one. Michael, who knows how his aunt values the box, cannot understand such insensitivity. Ruth tries to tell Michael that Aunt Dew does not need just that box, but Michael knows she does. Angry with his mother, he begs his aunt to let him hide the box, but she will not let it out of her sight. Then Aunt Dew begins to sing her old gospel song again, and he knows she will not be persuaded. Michael respects her wishes.

Old age and its memories can change a person's perspective on life, as Michael learns. Ruth sees Dew as a childish old woman, partly because Ruth has not listened, as Michael has, partly because Dew forgets things. But at one hundred, one may have one's own idea of what is important to remember. Dew plainly states the source of the misunderstanding: "But me and Ruth can't talk like me and John talk—cause she don't know all what me and John know." This story, told mostly in dialogue, is beautifully written and the character of Aunt Dew skillfully developed.

Ages 8-10

Also available in:
Cassette—*The Hundred Penny Box*
Library of Congress (NLSBPH)

Paperbound—*The Hundred Penny Box*
Puffin Books

406

Mathis, Sharon Bell

Listen for the Fig Tree

Puffin Books, 1990.
(175 pages, paperbound)

BLINDNESS
African-American
Alcoholism: of mother
Parental: unreliability
Poverty

Marvina Johnson, a sixteen-year-old black girl who is called "Muffin" by everyone but her mother, is blind. Still, she manages household affairs and cares for her mother. It has been almost a year since last Christmas, when her father was brutally murdered. Mrs. Johnson, filled with despair over the memory of last year's holiday season, has started drinking. Muffin tries to prevent her, but strong-willed Mrs. Johnson is desperate in her grief and will not be dissuaded. The black pastor, Mr. Willie Williams, helps Muffin by giving her money, and her friend Ernie takes Muffin shopping and gives her rides to school. But Mr. Dale is Muffin's greatest source of encouragement. He taught Muffin to sew last year and is teaching her to be a lady now. Even Mrs. Johnson respects him. Muffin tries to plan a Christmas celebration in spite of her mother. She has gifts for everyone, makes preparations for Christmas dinner, and best of all, plans to attend her first Kwanza, a Black African holiday celebration to be held the night after Christmas. Mr. Dale gives her a lovely piece of lemon-yellow panne velvet, and Muffin sews a beautiful dress all by herself. When it is finished, she starts upstairs to model it for Mr. Dale. In the hallway she is stopped by a strange man, and before Muffin realizes what is happening, he attacks her. Suddenly Mr. Thomas, the old man down the hall who cannot speak, comes to help her. Then Mr. Dale appears, and the stranger runs away. The rape attempt was unsuccessful, but the dress is ruined. The girl is taken to the hospital, examined, and questioned by the police. Then she returns home feeling dead and hopeless. There will be no Christmas; she cannot go to the Kwanza. But Mr. Dale has a surprise; he has made her a new dress, more lovely than the first. She can go to the Kwanza with Ernie after all. Her strength is renewed; her spirits soar and she finds again the courage to face the future.

Muffin is a brave young girl who fights vigorously to bring peace and happiness into her world and to keep her mother from giving up. The characters are lifelike. Ernie, the boy she cares for, is sullen and discouraging; her mother is barely sane. Mr. Dale, a homosexual, gives her encouragement. But Muffin's real strength comes from within.

Ages 12 and up

Also available in:
Braille—*Listen for the Fig Tree*
Library of Congress (NLSBPH)

Talking Book—*Listen for the Fig Tree*
Library of Congress (NLSBPH)

407

Mathis, Sharon Bell

Sidewalk Story

Black/white illustrations by Leo Carty.
Viking Penguin, 1986.
(64 pages)

PROBLEM SOLVING
African-American
Friendship: meaning of
Resourcefulness

Nine-year-old Lilly Etta Allen cannot believe that Tanya Brown, her neighbor and best friend, is moving away. Mrs. Brown and her seven children are being evicted for not paying their rent. Lilly Etta believes that someone can help Tanya's mother. She remembers that when Mrs. Ruth, a blind lady in the neighborhood, was given an eviction notice, the eviction was halted by the police and TV and newspaper reporters. Lilly reasons that if these same people knew that Mrs. Brown could not go to work because her babies were sick and she had to spend her rent money for food, the movers might be stopped from putting the family's furniture on the sidewalk. Lilly calls the police, who say that there is nothing they can do. Then she calls the newspaper and talks to a reporter named Frazier, who tells her that there is nothing unusual about the eviction but that Lilly herself would make a very interesting story. Disheartened but not defeated, Lilly promises to watch the family's belongings while Mrs. Brown and the children stay at a cousin's house. Late that night it rains, and Lilly quietly slips outside with her mother's sheets and blankets to cover the furniture. Frazier appears later and finds Lilly asleep on the furniture. The story and a picture of the scene are printed in the paper, and Mrs. Brown and her children soon get help from sympathetic readers.

This memorable story depicts a problem of the urban poor but shows what can be accomplished with untiring effort. The strong friendship between the two black girls is warmly portrayed in the text and illustrations.

Ages 8-10

Also available in:
Cassette—*Sidewalk Story*
Library of Congress (NLSBPH)

Paperbound—*Sidewalk Story*
Puffin Books

408
Mathis, Sharon Bell
Teacup Full of Roses
Puffin Books, 1987.
(125 pages, paperbound)

PARENTAL: Overprotection
Drugs: dependence on
Sibling: loyalty

Mattie and Isaac Brooks have three sons: twenty-four-year-old Paul, a drug addict; seventeen-year-old Joe, a former high-school dropout who has returned to night school; and fifteen-year-old David, an excellent student and basketball player. Mr. Brooks is sick and unable to leave the house. When Paul, Mrs. Brooks's favorite son, comes home after seven months in a drug rehabilitation center, Mrs. Brooks pampers him so much that she has no time left for the other boys. David begs his mother to sign papers that will allow him to participate in a program for talented students. Mrs. Brooks says she doesn't have time to go to David's school and sign the papers; she must, she says, go to work instead. In spite of the love and support shown by his entire family, Paul begins taking drugs again. Realizing the futility of efforts to help Paul, Joe decides to join the Navy after graduation. He gives his savings to David for college. Paul discovers the money hidden in an old coat and spends it all on drugs. Hoping to recover some of the money, Joe tries to track down the pusher who sold Paul the drugs. David calls the police and follows Joe to the place of confrontation. David is shot when he gets in the way of a bullet meant for Joe.

This stark story, set in Washington, D.C., shows the devastating effect of drugs on the user and his family. The episodic nature of the plot, the authentic dialogue, and the well-drawn characterizations create a compelling tale.

Ages 12 and up

Also available in:
Talking Book—*Teacup Full of Roses*
Library of Congress (NLSBPH)

409
Matthews, Ellen
Getting Rid of Roger
Black/white illustrations by Pat Duffy.
The Westminster/John Knox Press, 1978.
(96 pages) o.p.

SIBLING: Older
Maturation
Parent/Parents: single

Nine-year-old Chrissy is mortified at school by the antics of Roger, her six-year-old brother. She is a model student; he is a terror, frequently in need of discipline. At school she can try to ignore him (it does not work), even pretending not to be his sister; but at home he pesters her constantly. She complains to her mother, who points out that Roger is not only younger but different even from most other boys his age: he needs to mature, "to grow inside." Chrissy listens but does not understand, and Mother suggests that both children may need some growing inside. But Chrissy fears that Roger will even ruin her mother's chances to remarry. Divorced, the mother is seeing Mr. Davis, whom they all like. Indeed, the boy causes so much trouble when Mr. Davis takes them out that Chrissy lies, saying he is adopted. Shamed anew to hear that Roger is to be held back in first grade, Chrissy tries to persuade her father to take him. But events conspire to draw the two children together. They spend a night alone when a snowstorm prevents Mother from getting home from work. Chrissy notices a classmate's little brother misbehaving in school. And it is to his sister that Roger turns for comfort after breaking two teeth in an accident. Chrissy even sees how much she depends on him for help and companionship. In the end she is inclined to say, "I won't get rid of him."

Unable to understand or tolerate her little brother, this youngster tries to ignore him or drive him away. Her mother's advice and her own awakening to the boy's worth gradually change her mind. Roger himself matures, though the book, mainly written from Chrissy's viewpoint, does not dwell on this. Neither child is now troubled by their parents' divorce. The single-parent household, visits to the father, and the mother's new suitor are presented as commonplace. Chrissy thinks her mother and father happier for divorcing.

Ages 8-10

Also available in:
No other form known

410
Mauser, Pat Rhoads
A Bundle of Sticks
Black/white illustrations by Gail Owens.
Atheneum Publishers, 1987.
(176 pages)

BULLY: Being Bothered by
Aggression
Courage, meaning of
School: classmate relationships
Self, attitude toward: accepting
Violence

When eleven-year-old Benjamin Tyler comes home from school with a badly beaten face and torn shirt again, courtesy of Boyd Bradshaw, Ben's angry father says the next time Ben comes home like that he's going to lock him out of the house. He accuses his wife of pampering the boy and says Ben needs lessons in courage. But Ben hates fighting—it makes him sick to his stomach—and only wants to be left alone. He can't understand why Boyd hates him and picks on him.

When Boyd calls Ben a faggot in school the next day, the substitute teacher, Miss Fletcher, makes Boyd read the dictionary definition of "faggot": a bundle of sticks. She gives Ben a ride home so he can avoid being attacked again. Then his mother drives him to his first kajukenbo lesson, a self-defense method that includes karate, judo, kenpo, and boxing. Ben is sure he will hate the lessons. But his Sifu (instructor) is patient and understanding, gently instructing Ben in the beginning movements. As the boy's skill grows, his father warns him not to tell anyone about it; then he'll be forced to demonstrate what he knows, like it or not. But Ben can't resist, and then is embarrassed when he falsely claims he has his yellow belt. He continues his kajukenbo lessons and befriends Roger Wilmer, the only other young boy in the class. Then Boyd has an emergency appendectomy, making Ben feel alternately delighted and guilty. With any luck, Boyd will be out until summer vacation. When Ben finally does earn his yellow belt, he is disappointed at his own reaction. He knows that inside he is still not a fighter; the yellow belt has really changed nothing. But his Sifu claims that if Ben ever needs to defend himself, the moves will come automatically. Boyd returns to school and teases Ben. Ben starts to fight back, using one of the kicks he's learned, but stops when he realizes he could seriously damage Boyd's new appendectomy scar. During the summer months, Ben earns his orange belt. His sixth-grade teacher is none other than Miss Fletcher, now married and teaching full-time. But when Boyd turns up in his classroom, still itching for a fight, Ben sees nothing has changed. One afternoon Boyd kicks Ben's dog, Daisy. When Ben sees Daisy lying there, he turns on Boyd and attacks him, winning the fight hands down. But he feels sick afterwards and worries about whether he's knocked out any of Boyd's teeth. He is not happy being the hero his classmates now think him. Ben earns his purple belt in a day-long test and awards ceremony. When he and another student, a brown-belt adult, encounter two characters who want to fight about a dented car door, Ben watches his fellow student use diplomacy to settle the dispute, even though he could also have "settled" it physically. Ben begins to understand what his Sifu means about the freedom never to have to fight. He feels different, yet still the same. He'll always hate fighting, but now knows it is absolutely right to be the Ben Tyler he is.

The young victim of a school bully learns both to defend himself and to accept himself as he is when he takes kajukenbo training. This attractively illustrated book subtly emphasizes the connection between self-image and how a person is perceived by others; as long as Ben felt like a helpless victim, he remained one. Self-defense, as his instructor points out, is partly in the fists and partly in the mind. But the Sifu also maintains that one might never have to use one's fists if one's attitude is right, a philosophy worthy of discussion.

Ages 10-12

Also available in:
Cassette—*A Bundle of Sticks*
Library of Congress (NLSBPH)

Paperbound—*A Bundle of Sticks*
Aladdin Books

411

Mauser, Pat Rhoads

How I Found Myself at the Fair

Black/white illustrations by Emily Arnold McCully.
Atheneum Publishers, 1990.
(58 pages)

LOST, BEING
Dependence/Independence
Problem solving

Since her mother is ill, nine-year-old Laura is going to the state fair with her best friend, Mary Denton, and the Denton family. On the way Laura, who sees most things as she thinks her mother would, reflects on "poor Mary, being stuck in a crazy family like this!" Laura is an only child, but the Dentons have six children, all of whom seem to Laura noisy, grubby, carelessly dressed (jeans and T-shirts), and reckless—they don't use seat belts. Furthermore, they don't look out for one another. Once they arrive at the fair they all scatter, leaving Mary and Laura on their own. First the girls get something to eat, and then they go to the 4-H barn where Laura's blue-ribbon painting and Mary's wild flower collection are displayed. From there, Mary runs off to use a restroom and doesn't come back. After wandering around the fairgrounds looking for her, Laura gets on the Ferris wheel, hoping to see at least one Denton face from the top. Instead she finds herself high in the air with a defective bar on her chair. It unhooks and she clings to it and screams all the way to the bottom. But just before the bar came unhooked she had seen Mr. and Mrs. Denton, so she hurries after them filled with misgivings: the Dentons haven't even missed her, she might throw up, she might have to spend the night sleeping on a bench without a blanket or pillow. When she can't find them, she tries to call her mother on a pay phone. After getting a recording about her call being long-distance and finally losing all her money in the phone, Laura gives up. She'll probably have to steal food eventually, she thinks, since her money is gone. She walks aimlessly through barns and exhibits and is allowed into the Mansion of Mirrors free when she tells the woman she's looking for her friend. But once inside, she becomes lost and disoriented: "I was lost inside of being lost." When she finally gets out, she goes back to the 4-H barn, takes down her painting, and hugs it. Then she has an idea. If she stays by Mary's wild flower collection, sooner or later Mary will have to come by to pick it up. Sure enough, Mary finally appears, demanding to know where Laura has been. She's heard that someone was nearly killed on the Ferris wheel! Laura tells Mary about that and everything else. When Mary discovers that Laura has never heard of calling collect and that she didn't get her money back for the uncompleted call, the two run back to the pay phone and collect Laura's money. Impressed by her friend's knowledge and quick action, Laura asks Mary if she's ever been lost and scared. Mary says she gets lost all the time. She usually just tells someone and gets taken to the information booth to wait for her parents. But Mary compliments Laura on the number of different solutions she tried. On the way home, various Dentons tell how they saw Laura at different times during the day, but didn't realize she was lost. Their concern gives Laura "a warm feeling." "What a great family," she thinks.

An only child, used to her mother's close supervision, goes to a state fair with the large, unruly family of a friend and gets lost. After a succession of frightening experiences, Laura uses her head and finds her friend again. Laura tells this story herself, and the panic of a child unaccustomed to being on her own comes through in her exaggerations and convictions of doom. But the style is light and the illustrations emphasize the humor of the situation. Laura gains some self-confidence when her good idea succeeds in reuniting her with her friend; perhaps she won't feel quite so helpless in the future.

Ages 7-9

Also available in:
Paperbound—*How I Found Myself at the Fair*
Aladdin Books

412

Mayer, Mercer

Just Me and My Dad

Color illustrations by the author.
Golden Press, 1977.
(24 pages counted, paperbound)

PARENT/PARENTS: Respect for/Lack of Respect for

A little boy and his father go camping together. Once they are settled in their campsite, the boy sets about launching their canoe—and sinks it. Father and son go fishing, and the boy cooks their catch—which is stolen by a bear. Father and son dine on scrambled eggs. After dinner, the boy roundly frightens his father with ghost stories—but takes care to hug him so he'll feel better. Then they settle in their tent for a good night's sleep.

The illustrations of this little boy's first-person narrative add much to a very simple text. They show, for example, that the characters are whimsical, furry animals. But they show too how understated the child's account is: when, for instance, he tells us, "I pitched the tent," we see him ensnared hopelessly in ropes, poles, and canvas. Above all, they show his adoring admiration for his father, who is a model of patience throughout.

Ages 3-6

Also available in:
No other form known

413

Mayer, Mercer

There's a Nightmare in My Closet

Color illustrations by the author.
Dial Books for Young Readers, 1968.
(31 pages)

FEAR: of Darkness
NIGHTMARES

A little boy is so afraid of the nightmare lurking in his bedroom closet that he faithfully closes the closet door every night before going to sleep. One night the boy decides to confront his nightmare. Wearing his army helmet, he waits, barricaded behind his pillow with his toy cannon, his pop gun, and his toy soldiers. The boy hears the nightmare creeping toward him as soon as he turns out the light. Snapping on the light, the boy catches a sheepish nightmare sitting at the foot of his bed. After commanding the timid monster to leave, the boy shoots it with his pop gun. Despite the boy's pleas for silence, the nightmare immediately begins to cry. The only way the boy finally quiets the "injured" monster is to take him by the hand, tuck him in bed, and at the monster's request, close the closet door. The boy then crawls into bed with the contented nightmare and is undisturbed by its presence.

This humorous first-person narrative imaginatively relates a boy's conquest of his fear of the dark and of the nightmares hovering there. By facing the situation, the boy learns that there is nothing to fear. The illustrations are an essential part of the story, but the ghoulish creatures may frighten some children.

Ages 3-7

Also available in:
Paperbound—*There's a Nightmare in My Closet*
Dial Books for Young Readers

414

Mazer, Harry

The Island Keeper

Dell Publishing Company, Inc. (Laurel Leaf Library), 1981.
(165 pages, paperbound)

AUTONOMY
IDENTITY, SEARCH FOR
Death: of sibling
Family: relationships
Nature: living in harmony with

At sixteen, wealthy Cleo Murphy is overweight and very unhappy. Her mother died nine years ago in a car accident and now her sister, Jam, "the only person she loved in the world," is dead too, having drowned in

M

a boating accident. Her father is emotionally distant, forever occupied with his business affairs. Her grandmother is no comfort, always sending her off to distant places where she's to learn how to conduct herself appropriately. With Jam gone there seems no reason for Cleo to go on enduring the "stiff and artificial" life at home or the endless procession of private schools and camps. Her only desire now is to "disappear completely." Cleo has written out an escape plan that allows her to shed her old identity and steal away to Duck Island, her father's uninhabited property in Canada where she and Jam spent one wonderful summer together. The plan succeeds, and from the first moment she steps onto the beach she feels her sister's presence all around her. Then, however, Cleo senses something else. Smelling ashes, she climbs up the slope and sees that their cabin has burned to the ground. She goes in search of other shelter and finds a small cave where she can sleep and keep her things. But a few days later a raccoon breaks into her knapsack and destroys most of her food supply. She knows she should give up, but she feels such a strong sense of Jam's presence in the "extraordinary emptiness and silence" of the island that she cannot leave. She starts to live on fish and vegetation, amusing herself by imagining her grandmother's reaction to her new way of life: "Pure savagery." She gets to know the animals—a doe with two fawns, a chipmunk, and an injured owl. One day when she is very hungry she knows she is ready to eat a frog as Owl does. She catches several and finds that with each one she kills, something inside of her hardens. She keeps a pot of soup at her camp, each day throwing in whatever she is able to forage. And each day that she survives, she feels happier. Her body becomes thin and strong. When the caretaker of the estate comes to look for her, she eludes him. Life on the island is "simple and real," and she is not ready to leave. One day, however, a bad storm seems to mark the beginning of winter, and Cleo goes to prepare her canoe for departure. She finds it crushed under a fallen tree. Since it will be at least three months until the lake freezes enough to cross on foot, she feels sure she will die on the island. Still, she builds a stone shelter around the opening of the cave and stores up as much food as she can find. She kills a porcupine, a raccoon, even a small, lame deer. Finally the lake freezes. Cleo straps on her hand-made snowshoes and struggles through the wind and snow to the mainland and her angry father and grandmother. She finds that even though she has changed, home is the same. After a time she decides to return to school, perhaps to become a naturalist. On her trip back to school she considers her previous unhappiness and decides that things don't have to be that way again. "Things had happened—the island had happened."

An unhappy young girl, mourning the death of her sister, embarks on a true voyage of discovery in this engrossing book. By becoming "part of the island," Cleo learns that she, like the animals she befriends, is a survivor. She finds enough inner strength to keep going against formidable odds, accepting and adapting to natural rhythms. The reader is drawn into Cleo's struggle and must applaud the serene, strong young woman who returns to her world not as a passive observer, but as a participant.

Ages 10-14

Also available in:
No other form known

415

Mazer, Norma Fox

Dear Bill, Remember Me? And Other Stories

Dell Publishing Company, Inc. (Laurel Leaf Library), 1978. (208 pages, paperbound)

ALCOHOLISM: of Father
DEPENDENCE/INDEPENDENCE
ILLNESSES: Terminal
SELF, ATTITUDE TOWARD: Confidence
Boy-girl relationships: dating
Death: attitude toward
Family: extended
Inferiority, feelings of
Love, meaning of
Parental: overprotection

In this collection of eight short stories, fifteen-year-old Jessie Granatstein, in the first story, experiences first love, yet strives to maintain her individuality. In the second story, fourteen-year-old Zoe Eberhardt, struggling to loosen the protective bonds linking her to mother, grandmother, and aunt, gains a measure of independence by disobeying a parental command. In the third story, Marylee Daniels discovers her mother's infidelity and says nothing. By remaining silent, Marylee judges herself a coward until she prevents a theft. Mimi Holtzer, a high school student in the fourth story, realizes that, despite her mother's hovering protection, she is moving "away from her mother, swimming toward her own life." In the fifth and title story, fifteen-year-old Kathy Kalman begins letter after letter to her sister's former boyfriend, trying to confess her love for him. Story six deals with Chrissy's efforts to make a pleasant life for herself while living in a dilapidated trailer with an uncle and father who are alcoholics. The seventh story brings eighteen-year-old Louise, who has had two mastectomies and had a leg amputated, to the realization that she is dying. Although she is in constant pain and bloated from drugs, her mother and sister refuse to confirm her suspicion. When the truth is finally told, Louise feels at peace with herself and what is to come. Fifteen-year-old Zelzah, of the final story, travels from turn-of-the-century Poland to the United States, where she is to marry her cousin. When the groom marries another, Zelzah makes a satisfying life for herself with her training and career as a school teacher.

In this collection of short stories, eight young women come variously to grips with the need for independence, an uncertain self-confidence, paternal alcoholism, serious illness, maturation, and relationships with young men. The first, third, fifth, and sixth stories are first-person narratives. All eight are well written, their protagonists easy to know and care about. Though the name of the disease in the seventh story is not mentioned, it may be cancer.

Ages 12 and up

Also available in:
Cassette for the Blind—*Dear Bill, Remember Me? And Other Stories*
Library of Congress (NLSBPH)

416

Mazer, Norma Fox

Up in Seth's Room

Dell Publishing Company, Inc. (Laurel Leaf Library), 1979.
(199 pages, paperbound)

BOY-GIRL RELATIONSHIPS: Dating
SEX: Attitude Toward
Autonomy
Communication: parent-child
Family: relationships
Maturation
Parental: control
Values/Valuing: moral/ethical

At fifteen, Finn Rousseau looks forward to sexual experiences but for now wants to remain a virgin. At the apartment her sister Maggie shares with a boyfriend, Jim, she meets and is attracted to Jim's brother, nineteen-year-old Seth, a handsome high school dropout. Finn's parents are furious with Maggie and Jim for living together, and her mother forbids Finn to date Seth when she learns that he is Jim's brother. Finn tells Seth of her mother's anger, revealing at the same time that she is only fifteen. Seth is shocked at how young she is, and they part. At a friend's suggestion, Finn considers seeing Seth and lying to her parents about it. Then the two meet by accident at a concert. Seth apologizes for their last encounter and kisses Finn, in sight of her mother, who has come to pick Finn up. At home there is an angry scene, Finn's parents claiming she is too young to know what she is getting into with Seth. When Seth calls, Finn's father tells him not to call again and hangs up on him. A few days later, Finn defiantly goes to him and returns home late, triggering another scene. During the next weeks they meet secretly at the restaurant where Seth works. Maggie learns of the relationship and takes her parents' side, leaving Finn increasingly cut off from her family. Seth takes her to Maggie and Jim's apartment, where he has been staying, but Jim will not let them remain. So Seth moves out, rents a cheap attic apartment, and takes Finn there. She is nearly as ardent as he, but insists they stop short of intercourse. Late getting home, Finn quarrels with her parents again. Her father slaps her and grounds her for a month. After some time and several calmer discussions, the parents relent and say Finn can see Seth—within limits they propose and she accepts. But when she goes to Seth, he tries to force himself on her. When she refuses he becomes physically aggressive and verbally abusive. Later, their quarrel mended, she learns that he had never taken her refusal to have intercourse seriously. He tells her that she has led him on and explains himself thus: "If at first you don't succeed . . . that's the male creed." This "insight" into the male mind is a major discovery for Finn. After a drive in the country, Seth tells her he is leaving home to work on a distant farm. Finn is heartsick. In a sunny meadow they make love, but again stop short of intercourse. Since Finn has heard that love without intercourse isn't really love, she asks, "Did we just make love?" Seth takes her home and they part tenderly.

Finn's struggle for love, sexual experience, and independence is described clearly and nonjudgmentally. The language is frank, the narrative candid. Strong characterizations enable readers to see the developing relationship between Seth and Finn from varied perspectives. There is much good discussion material here: Finn's emotions, her parents' attempts to control her, the pressures of her friends, and the sometimes aggressive behavior of the boys. Especially provocative is Seth's "male creed." Finn is a heroine with whom many readers will strongly identify.

Ages 13 and up

Also available in:
Cassette—*Up in Seth's Room*
Library of Congress (NLSBPH)

417

Mazer, Norma Fox

When We First Met

Scholastic, Inc., 1984.
(199 pages, paperbound)

BLAME
BOY-GIRL RELATIONSHIPS: Dating
LOVE, MEANING OF
Accidents: automobile
Death: of sibling
Guilt, feelings of
Mourning, stages of

March is a month when seventeen-year-old Jenny Pennoyer's spirits usually sink. It was in March, two years ago, that her sister, Gail, was killed by a drunk driver. Jenny is still tormented by having argued with Gail that dark, stormy night about who would ride her bike to the store; her mother, Amelia, still hates Nell Montana, the woman who hit Gail. Mrs. Montana had been charged with second-degree manslaughter. Amelia tells Jenny that she is sending a blood-red rose to Mrs. Montana, along with a note reminding her of her atrocity. Jenny is surprised when something good happens to her in the midst of all this sorrow; it is early in March when she first sees the handsome, blond boy with the rainbow suspenders and starts to fall in love. One Saturday morning, as Jenny and her best friend, Rhoda, are leaving a shopping mall, they see the boy and one of Rhoda's admirers approaching them. They meet, talk, and agree to have a pizza together. At the end of their lunch, Jenny's happiness disappears; she learns the boy's name is Rob Montana. When Rob learns her last name is Pennoyer, he asks, "Would you know anything about a red rose?" Jenny tries to persuade herself that they can't see each other again, but Rob is persistent and soon they are secretly dating. Then one day they stop in at Rob's house and forget about the time. When Mrs. Montana comes home from work, Jenny suddenly finds herself face-to-face with the woman her mother calls "Mrs. Killer." As they talk it becomes obvious that Nell has suffered a great deal because of the accident. She explains that she wasn't drunk, just a little relaxed by the "drink or two" she had at a party, and that the visibility was so bad she couldn't see Gail until the last moment. Though sympathetic, Jenny knows that out of loyalty to her parents she cannot allow herself to befriend Mrs. Montana. She stays away from their home and resists Rob's arguments for bringing their relationship into the open. Eventually she agrees to let him meet her family, but the resulting scene is as bad as she has feared. Her mother rushes from the room and her father orders Rob out of the house, telling Jenny to break off the relationship. At first she refuses, but can't ignore the pain she is causing everyone and finally gives in. During the weeks that follow, Jenny suffers a great deal. Then, by accident, she and her mother go into the shoe shop where Nell Montana works. Nell takes the opportunity to beg for forgiveness and, although she can't oblige, Amelia begins to see her daughter's "killer" as a human being, one who has the "tense, lined face of a woman in pain." Soon after, a newspaper article reports Nell Montana's near-fatal overdose of sleeping pills. Amelia wonders if she is to blame. She is finally able to dismantle Gail's room—until now, it had been left intact as a shrine. Meanwhile, Jenny sees that no one's life has been changed for the better because she has given up Rob. She goes to him and, after expressing some of his hurt and anger, he acknowledges that he wants her back. Jenny's parents are not overjoyed, but can see that Mrs. Montana is not a monster and that Jenny is still their daughter no matter whom she loves.

The love between a teenage girl and the son of the woman whose car struck and killed the girl's sister helps both families toward recovery from grief and guilt. Rob and Jenny's love begins with physical attraction and develops into a true appreciation of each other's character. This is an affecting story of the healing powers of love and the gradual reawakening to life of several people who have mourned for a long time. Readers will remember Jenny and her family from an earlier book, *A Figure of Speech,* and will be just as caught up in this second story about them.

Ages 12 and up

Also available in:
No other form known

418

McCaffrey, Mary

My Brother Ange

Black/white illustrations by Denise Saldutti.
HarperCollins Publishers, Inc., 1982.
(86 pages) o.p.

REJECTION: Sibling
Accidents: automobile
Baby-sitting: involuntary
Family: relationships
Guilt, feelings of
Sibling: older

Eleven-year-old Michael (Mick) Tooley often feels irritated with his younger brother, Angelo (Ange). He's tired of looking after Ange, tired of helping out at home, tired of his dull, gray life. He still misses Granny Mia dreadfully; things haven't been the same since she died. He tries not to think of his father either—it's been a year since he walked out and didn't come back. One day Mick's friend Leon gives him a souvenir pencil filled with sand from the Isle of Wight. In a scuffle over the pencil, Ange inadvertently knocks it out of Mick's hand and all the special sand spills out. Wild with rage and distress, Mick screams at Ange, calls him names, and tells him to get lost. When Leon tries to calm him down, Mick says the pencil incident has clinched months of frustration at Ange's following him everywhere, talking unceasingly, asking so many questions. The little boy runs off, and Mick lingers behind in spite of strict orders not to let Ange walk home alone from school in the dangerous London traffic. When he finally does head home, he hears a siren and a girl from school runs up to tell him his brother's been killed. Mick races to the scene and has to be restrained from going to Ange, who is underneath a van. A policeman tells him his brother is seriously injured, but not dead. Mick and his mother visit Ange in the hospital. He is bandaged all over except for his eyes and mouth. Mick cries and cries, telling Ange how sorry he is, what a creep he is. Ange accepts Mick's apology, saying they're both creeps. Mick promises to come back and read to Ange, vowing never to tell him to shut up again. A previously bad-tempered neighbor is the soul of comfort and hospitality during the crisis. Mick decides that if adults can change, so can kids. In the apartment that seems so empty without Ange, Mick begins to understand what his mother's lonely life must be like. He realizes that he doesn't need to fantasize anymore about Mr. Rivers, his teacher, becoming his father. When Leon gives Mick his own sand pencil, Mick decides to give it to Ange, even though he loves it himself. He goes to a church and lights candles for his brother's recovery. Walking out, he feels he is a different person.

When his clinging younger brother is seriously injured, Mick's hostility to Ange changes radically as he reconsiders his attitude toward his sibling. This simple, touching story, sparsely illustrated, does not examine the roots of Mick's antipathy toward his brother, but it may inspire some readers to reflect on their own sibling relationships. The dialogue is a bit British at times, but meaning is never obscured.

Ages 8-11

Also available in:
No other form known

419

McCloskey, Robert

One Morning in Maine

Black/white illustrations by the author.
Viking Penguin, 1952.
(64 pages)

TOOTH, LOSS OF
Maturation

Sal, about six years old, is excited. After her father has finished digging clams, he is going to take her to the town of Buck's Harbor. As she is getting ready, Sal discovers that she has a loose tooth. She is afraid it will hurt and force her to stay in bed for the day. Sal's mother assures her the tooth is supposed to fall out and make room for a new, bigger tooth. Mother says that a loose tooth shows that Sal is growing up. Sal asks her mother when the tooth will fall out because she wants to make a wish on it when it does. Sal goes down to the seashore to help her father dig for clams so that they may leave sooner for Buck's Harbor. She shows Father her loose tooth. While she is digging for clams, her tooth falls out and is lost in the muddy water. Sal and Father search for the tooth in vain. Disappointed, Sal is certain that her "tooth wish" has been lost with the tooth.

This story describes a child's first experience with a loose tooth. It emphasizes that the loss of a "baby" tooth is a sign of growing up. Outstanding illustrations enhance the text.

Ages 5-8

Also available in:
Braille—*One Morning in Maine*
Library of Congress (NLSBPH)

Paperbound—*One Morning in Maine*
Puffin Books

Talking Book—*One Morning in Maine*
Library of Congress (NLSBPH)

420

Melton, David

A Boy Called Hopeless

Black/white illustrations by the author.
Landmark Editions, 1986.
(231 pages, paperbound)

BRAIN INJURY
Cooperation: in work
Education: special
Family: unity
Helping
Love, meaning of
Perseverance
Success

Seven-year-old M. J. Rodgers and her younger brother, Josh, are less than thrilled to learn that their mother is pregnant. When Jeremiah is born, the family pronounces him "perfect in every way." But as time passes, they notice that he seems too perfect: sleeping a great deal and crying very little. When Jeremiah cannot crawl by his first birthday, Mrs. Rodgers begins taking him to specialists. Three years later, the family concludes that, beyond the fact that Jeremiah is now walking, the specialists have done little good. At the county medical center, Jeremiah is diagnosed as mentally retarded, but Mrs. Rodgers refuses to accept that finding. While reading a book by a man named Glenn Doman, she sees hope for her son in a place in Philadelphia called The Institute for the Achievement of Human Potential. The family votes to vacation in Philadelphia so that Jeremiah can be tested at the Institute. There the boy is diagnosed as brain-injured and the family is trained in an intensive daily program to treat Jeremiah at home: for twelve hours each day Jeremiah is scheduled through body exercises—crawling, rolling, somersaulting—eye exercises, reading instruction, tactile experiences, speech drill, and so forth. Volunteers are recruited from the neighborhood to keep up the hectic program. After a time, Jeremiah is showing gradual progress. When he returns to the Institute for a six-month checkup, the family is given a new program to train him in reading simple sentences, running, undressing himself, speaking in short sentences, and printing his name. Soon he is accomplishing these, and the family is told that with another year's training he will be well. When that time comes, Jeremiah enrolls in school.

A journal kept by Jeremiah's older sister tells this simple yet dramatic story of brain injury, its possible causes, and a detailed, concrete method of treating it. The book portrays candidly the emotional strain on the family and the love which holds the family. The Institute in Philadelphia is real and is headed by Glenn Doman, and the author, a parent of a brain-injured child, tells us that "the family in this story is a composite of many families." This powerful book educates without being didactic.

Ages 10 and up

Also available in:
No other form known

421

Meyer, Carolyn

The Center: From a Troubled Past to a New Life

Atheneum Publishers, 1979.
(193 pages) o.p.

DETENTION HOME, LIVING IN
SELF-IMPROVEMENT
Communication: importance of
Delinquency, juvenile
Drugs: abuse of
Guilt, feelings of
Homosexuality: male
Honesty/Dishonesty
Self-discipline
Values/Valuing: moral/ethical

Fifteen-year-old David Peterson is in trouble at school and at home, regularly gets high on drugs, and has now been picked up for stealing mail. His parents enroll him in the Center, a place where troubled teenagers are helped to change themselves. The first thing David sees there is a plaque with the word HONESTY on it. But David has vowed not to stay at the Center, hates everyone there, and has no compunction about lying to the staff and counselors. Meanwhile, David's father, Richard, thinks about his son, reflecting on his doubts about David's paternity and his unsatisfying marriage. Richard is very proud of his successful older son, Richie, and of his bright and pretty daughter, Susie. David's mother, Ellen, remembers all the conflicts between Richard and David, especially the one that led to her husband striking her. She has felt cold towards him ever since. In the privacy of his room, the "good" son, Richie, smokes pot, listens to acid rock, and thinks about how he wants to be a carpenter instead of the CPA his father expects him to be. Ellen begins attending the Center's Parents Club and learns that a delinquent child is often reflecting the troubles of the whole family. During his first months, David spends time with his counselor, Kevin Murphy, and gradually gives up the idea of escaping the Center. He lies a number of times, but is then subjected to brutal verbal confrontations in encounter groups and eventually confesses his dishonesty. He tells Kevin about his homosexual relationship with his friend on the outside, Billy. David says he doesn't feel homosexual and is ashamed of the relationship. After three months, David is determined to make it at the Center. He is raised to Intermediate status; his new counselor is Betsy Coleman. The first visit home is tense. Billy talks him into sneaking out at night, and they smoke a few joints. When he returns to the Center he lies to Betsy about having seen Billy. From that moment the pressure of his guilt builds until he finally tells a friend the truth about his home visit. As part of the consequences of his dishonesty, he must face the entire group and endure a loud, angry, verbal trimming. David cries and admits that he just wants his father to love him. When a newcomer teases him about his masculinity, David slams him against the wall. But a session with the Center's sexuality expert reassures him somewhat on that point. During his next visit home, David realizes that the real conflict in his home is between his parents. Ellen, who still attends the Parents Club, finally breaks down and tells the group that her marriage is disintegrating. On a family vacation in Maine, David celebrates his sixteenth birthday and learns that his parents are divorcing. Richie has decided to bum around rather than go to college. Susie has constant tantrums, and David worries about her choice of friends. When Doug, a good friend, drops out of the Center, David feels the bottom fall out of his world. Against regulations he goes after Doug. After they share a joint, David calls the Center and says he's coming back. As part of the stringent rules governing readmittance, David has to beg his Center "family" to take him back. His father has moved out, and David visits him in his small, depressing apartment. For the first time, the two express some of their feelings for each other. Moved up to a supervisory position at the Center, David gets a job at a restaurant. One day he finds the courage to ask Heather, one of the waitresses, if he can take her home. She invites him to attend a party with her—a party featuring marijuana, as it turns out. Heather sees nothing wrong with getting high once in a while, but David is now opposed to all drugs and from then on sees Heather only at work. After two years at the Center, David is favorably evaluated. When he graduates, his mother feels that what's happened to him is a miracle. The counselors know it's more a product of energy and hard work. Heather attends the graduation ceremony, telling David she's given up pot after thinking over what he told her. He asks her out again.

A badly troubled teenager enters a therapeutic community where patients are involved in their own treatment. David emerges two years later having internalized a set of values that will allow him to pursue his own goals and enter into nurturing relationships. Although the book offers a great deal of information and many psychological insights, it is primarily the story of the uneven, painful maturation of a likeable, well-delineated character. Based on reality therapy, treatment at the Center is a combination of psychotherapy and encounter groups. Some of it may seem incomprehensible or even brutal to the reader; in context, however, all the methods make sense and are shown to be effective for many young people. This earnest, involving account would be an excellent choice for discussion because of the broad range of adolescent thoughts and feelings it covers. Because of crude and scatological language and the subtlety of certain ideas and issues, however, the book should generally be recommended for older readers. David Peterson is a composite of the kind of boy found at Vitam Center in Norwalk, Connecticut. The author's own son's residence there led to the writing of this book.

Ages 13 and up

Also available in:
No other form known

422

Miklowitz, Gloria D.

Did You Hear What Happened to Andrea?

Delacorte Press, 1979.
(168 pages) o.p.

GUILT, FEELINGS OF
RAPE
Boy-girl relationships: dating
Family: relationships
Fear: of physical harm
Hitchhiking

Andrea Cranston, fifteen, and her boyfriend, David Hoffman, eighteen, have spent a hot August afternoon at the beach. When they miss their bus home, Andrea convinces David to hitchhike, even though her mother has told her many times not to. An ordinary-looking man in a green Dodge picks them up. He lets David off near his home, saying he will take Andrea on to hers; she agrees. But he passes her street, and when she protests he threatens to kill her if she does not cooperate. He drives to a wooded area in the hills and rapes her at gunpoint. Then he takes her back to the highway and pushes her out, warning her to tell no one or he will come back for her. Numbly she walks down the highway until some classmates pick her up and take her to the police. Andrea's shock and horror are intensified by the reactions of her family. Her mother is ashamed and wants to pretend nothing has happened; she will not permit Andrea to talk about the rape. Her father is angry and wants revenge. Her older sister, Sue, is quite matter-of-fact, encouraging Andrea to act tough. Her little brother is confused because no one will explain what has happened. Her mother questions her decision to go back to her part-time job, but Andrea feels she must take her mind off herself. Still, she fears going out, fears sleeping with her windows open, terrified that the rapist will find her and kill her as he said he would. She avoids David for several days, fearful of his reaction, but when she sees him and tells him she was raped he is grief-stricken and blames himself. He also becomes determined to find the rapist, spending much of his remaining vacation searching for the car. Gradually, Andrea learns to relax with David again. However, when he goes away to college and school starts for her, she fears the boys and isolates herself from everyone but Kim, one of the girls that found her on the highway. She receives some help by phone through a "Rape Hotline," but her mother doesn't encourage further counseling, nor does she want Andrea to press charges even if the rapist is caught. At Thanksgiving time, while shopping with Kim and Sue, Andrea is sure she sees the green Dodge go past her in the street. Later she recognizes the man—walking right toward her. She faints and when she regains consciousness, all she can do is scream. The rapist has vanished. Sue and Kim take her home and insist to her parents that not only Andrea but they too must have professional help. They begin seeing a counselor, who helps all of them deal with their anger and fear. Just before Christmas, Andrea is summoned to the police station for a line-up. She recognizes the rapist immediately and decides to press charges. Another young victim is also able to identify him; she too will testify. By the time of the trial, five months later, Andrea is feeling more confident and her family has better learned to cope. The rapist is convicted on several counts and gets a sentence of five years to life in prison. Though Andrea knows she will never be the same, she does feel relief and a new sense of freedom knowing the man will be behind bars.

This suspenseful first-person narrative gives a sensitive, perceptive look at the traumas of a young rape victim and her family. It makes clear that others to whom Andrea is important are also victims; they too have been hurt and must be helped to recover. The rape account is straightforward, and the police interrogation uses descriptive language and terms. The book requires a mature reader.

Ages 13 and up

Also available in:
No other form known

423

Miles, Betty

Around and Around—Love

Black/white photographs from various sources.
Alfred A. Knopf, Inc., 1975.
(42 pages) o.p.

LOVE, MEANING OF

Love is everywhere to be seen every day. Sharing flowers with one's grandmother, smiling at a friend, talking over a disagreement, helping someone do something all show love in action. Caring for pets, sharing a secret, sometimes even being sad or angry—all may be part of loving. Love is part of everyone's life for as long as one lives.

This photographic picture book suggests how many different ways people express love for each other every day, and how love changes yet endures as people grow. Young children may profit from having the photographs explained by an adult. Probably all children and most adults will find people resembling themselves in these pictures, so various are the classes and ethnic groups depicted. The accompanying rhymed verse considers what love is and how it feels.

Ages 3-8

Also available in:
No other form known

424
Miles, Betty
Just the Beginning
Alfred A. Knopf, Inc., 1976.
(143 pages)

INFERIORITY, FEELINGS OF
Embarrassment
Maturation
Parent/Parents: mother working outside home
Pride/False pride
Responsibility: accepting
Sibling: rivalry

Thirteen-year-old Cathy Myers is embarrassed over the work her mother is undertaking, but dreads even more telling her parents of her two-day suspension from school; such a thing could never happen to her brilliant sister, Julia. Sure enough, her parents behave as though the whole family has been disgraced, and Julia deepens Cathy's shame with a thoughtless remark for which she later apologizes. Adding insult to injury, Cathy's parents insist that she spend her two free days cleaning the house and helping her father paint his store. Only too eager to make amends, Cathy pitches in, and to her surprise discovers she likes the housework she had thought demeaning. Even more surprising to her, the clientele in the store treat her with a respect she is not used to. As they work, father tells daughter of some mischief he had made as a youngster and about his mixed feelings toward his more successful, financially secure older brother. That helps Cathy and her mixed feelings toward Julia. Back in school, Cathy finds that housework is not left behind: she must tell her more well-to-do friends that her mother plans to clean houses for extra income. Her friends are not put off—in fact, they seem a bit too understanding, and the girl's morale hits a new low. But life perks up when the Estys, a young couple Mrs. Myers cleans for, ask her—not Julia—to baby-sit. Cathy protests that she may not be up to the job but finally accepts, and the Estys like her so much they ask her again. When one night she calmly handles an emergency, the Estys ask her to go with them on vacation to Maine and look after the baby. This happy news comes on the same day as Julia's letter of acceptance from Yale. The family is as delighted by Cathy's news as by Julia's.

In this realistic first-person narrative, an adolescent feels better about some waywardness and resentment when she discovers that others have been through them too. And given a chance to apply herself responsibly, she finds that her sister is not the only capable person in the world. With this new confidence, it is easier for her to accept her mother's commonplace job. These characters, in themselves and as a family, are thoroughly convincing.

Ages 10-12

Also available in:
Braille—*Just the Beginning*
Library of Congress (NLSBPH)

425
Miles, Betty
Looking On
Alfred A. Knopf, Inc., 1978.
(187 pages)

IDENTIFICATION WITH OTHERS: Adults
IDENTITY, SEARCH FOR
Belonging
Boy-girl relationships: dating
Embarrassment
Height: tall
Maturation
Responsibility: accepting
Weight control: overweight

Fourteen-year-old Rosalie Hudnecker is tall, overweight, and self-conscious. Ever since her father abandoned the family eight years before, Rosalie has lived with her mother, Rita, a beautician, and, until recently, her older brother, Joe Pat, now married and living out of town. Rosalie has a close girlfriend, a boyfriend, and a regular baby-sitting job. Still, she is not really happy with herself or life. Her dissatisfaction finds some relief when a neighbor, Mrs. Cree, rents the trailer in her backyard to two newly married college students, Tony and Jill. At first, Rosalie watches only curiously while the pair move in, imagining how nice such privacy and independence must be. But when Tony comes over to introduce himself, Rosalie is taken with his beard and sophisticated manner. Suddenly she wants to become part of Tony and Jill's life, even if only in her daydreams. She becomes preoccupied with watching the couple's life day by day. She envies Jill her petite build, and watches out her window as the "perfect" couple play frisbee, go off to classes, have arguments, and prepare for a weekend party. Soon she is turning down invitations from her friends, just to watch Tony and Jill, just to muse on their perfect life together. Desperate to know more, she goes to the trailer one night uninvited while Tony and Jill are having a party. Though they are friendly and seem to like her, Rosalie feels out of place. Very well, she will spend more time with them—even if it means incurring the disapproval of her mother and friends, who have begun to notice how preoccupied she is. She has already missed a chance to work on the school play, turned down a date with her boyfriend, and been late for a baby-sitting job, just to keep a date with Jill. But guilt about all this eats away at her until, one day, she irritably hits the child she baby-sits for. That does it. She apologizes to her friends, makes a date with her boyfriend, goes on a diet, and cuts her hair. It is fun to talk to Jill, but for feeling easy and at home she will take her own friends and the interests they genuinely share.

Rosalie finds in her almost obsessive curiosity about Tony and Jill that getting married does not spell the end of change, dissatisfaction, or difficulty. She also realizes that she, and no one else, is responsible for directing her own life, but that to do that she must get along with her contemporaries as well as her admired elders, with whom she cannot, finally, have a great deal in common. This introspective story is eventful but leisurely in pace. Rosalie's maturing is natural, at times painful, and at last satisfying. Teenagers will identify with her desire to belong.

Ages 11-14

Also available in:
Cassette—*Looking On*
Library of Congress (NLSBPH)

Paperbound—*Looking On*
Alfred A. Knopf, Inc.

426

Miles, Betty

Maudie and Me and the Dirty Book

Alfred A. Knopf, Inc., 1980.
(144 pages, paperbound)

CENSORSHIP, LITERARY
Friendship: making friends
School: classmate relationships

Kate Harris quickly volunteers when her teacher, Ms. Plotkin, asks for sixth graders to read to first graders at an elementary school. But her excitement vanishes just as quickly when the only other volunteer is Maudie Schmidt. Kate and her friends think Maudie is "sort of a dope—one of those kids that everyone wants to avoid." The girls visit the school together and observe Ms. Dwyer's first-grade class. Reluctantly Kate agrees to go with Maudie to the library to pick out a book to read. She is surprised to discover that she and Maudie share a love of reading. After they make their selections, Kate goes to Maudie's house. As she comes to know her, Kate begins to feel more comfortable with Maudie. The following Friday the two girls return to Ms. Dwyer's class, both excited and nervous. Maudie reads *Little Bear* and then Kate reads *The Birthday Dog,* about the birth of a puppy. The children begin to ask questions about how the puppy was born, and soon Kate is stammering through an explanation of mating. Ms. Dwyer nods her approval and later tells Kate she handled the situation well. The following Monday, Kate, Maudie, and Ms. Plotkin are summoned to the principal's office. Over the weekend, it seems, certain parents called to complain about Kate's book and her explanation. Scared and confused, Kate is comforted by her teacher's calm support and acceptance of responsibility. The principal listens to Kate and agrees the incident was innocent, but she decides to suspend the reading project for the time being. Kate's parents are understanding and supportive. Her older brother is upset, however, because the incident almost causes a breakup with his girlfriend, whose parents are angered by what happened. Soon a public controversy begins, to Kate's extreme distress. Letters appear in the newspaper, both for and against the reading project, and an organization is formed called "Parents United for Decency." They want "smut" removed from the school and library bookshelves. Finally the school board calls a meeting, Kate included, to discuss what has happened and whether or not the project should continue. Upset by the discussion, Kate stands and defends the book, the discussion that followed, and the reading project. Her speech receives favorable applause, and the board votes to continue the project. The library begins to hold weekly adult discussions about children's books, more children volunteer for the reading project, and, best of all, Maudie is accepted into Kate's group.

Kate's first-person narrative looks humorously at a serious subject, censorship in school and library. Kate defends the book she read and the discussion that followed, and her courage leads to a defeat for the forces of censorship. Along the way, the friendship between Kate and Maudie blossoms. Some thought-provoking discussions may follow the reading here.

Ages 10-12

Also available in:
Braille—*Maudie and Me and the Dirty Book*
Library of Congress (NLSBPH)

Cassette—*Maudie and Me and the Dirty Book*
Library of Congress (NLSBPH)

427

Miles, Betty

The Trouble with Thirteen

Alfred A. Knopf, Inc., 1979.
(108 pages)

CHANGE: Accepting
Death: of pet
Divorce: of parents
Friendship: best friend
Loss: feelings of
Maturation
Menstruation
Moving

Annie Morrison and Rachel Weiss have been best friends since nursery school. On a perfect spring day, they both wish they could stay twelve forever. Annie doesn't like the way "things are always changing." But she is helpless when Rachel announces that her parents are getting a divorce and she will soon move to the city with her mother. Annie dreads the changes that Rachel's absence will bring. She also dreads the possibility of Rachel becoming a sophisticated New Yorker and leaving her, Annie, far behind. When Kate, one of their friends, announces she's getting her ears pierced, Annie again feels that everything is changing too fast for her. One day Rachel goes into the city with her mother to look at schools and misses the slumber party Kate has for her thirteenth birthday. When she returns, Rachel is excited about her new school, the city, and the friends she is making there; Annie wants to talk about the birthday party and learning how to dance. Rachel and Annie do resume most of their former closeness the next day, however, when Annie's old dog, Nora, dies. Annie grieves for a long time and wonders if the sadness will ever fade. When she gets her first period she wants to tell Rachel about it, but the right moment doesn't seem to come. One Saturday they decide to walk all around town, with Rachel taking pictures of Annie in the old familiar places. While acting silly in the dime store photo booth, Annie tells Rachel she got her period. Rachel says she did too, and their friendship seems stronger than ever. But when they go into New York for a day, their tensions and sadness erupt in a shouting match in front of a dress shop. They are reconciled when each begins yelling that the other is her best friend. They go into the shop and buy two look-alike dresses; now they feel like real New Yorkers. Rachel's young aunt further encourages them when she says that her best friend lives in Bloomington, Indiana, that people can remain best friends even if they don't live in the same city. But the day Rachel moves is a sad one for Annie. She reflects that although she'll probably have fun that summer, life will definitely be different—no Nora and no Rachel. Rachel gives Annie her prized dollhouse that they both have added to and tended over the years. They use the last precious hour left to them to start a quilt for one of the beds. Annie gives Rachel, who dreams of becoming a photographer, a photography book she's admired. On the flyleaf, Annie has written a poem. At the last minute, when Rachel's mother arrives to pick her up, Rachel gives Annie a picture of Nora that she'd taken shortly before the dog's death. Annie muses on how long ago that seems. "We were like children. I remembered how I wished we would never grow up and that things would never change. In the back of my mind I must have known they would."

In this first-person narrative, Annie, who hates changes, details the feelings of young teenage girls facing traumatic alterations in their lives—menstruation, divorce, changes in friends, the death of a beloved pet, separation from a best friend. Her candor adds depth to the characterizations as she and Rachel, about to live apart, manage to preserve the closeness they have always enjoyed.

Ages 9-13

Also available in:
Paperbound—*The Trouble with Thirteen*
Alfred A. Knopf, Inc.

428

Miles, Miska, pseud.

Aaron's Door

Black/white illustrations by Alan E. Cober.
Little, Brown & Company, Inc., 1977.
(46 pages) o.p.

ADOPTION: Feelings About
Fear
Loneliness
Rejection

Aaron, who is about eight years old, and his younger sister, Deborah, had been placed in a children's home by their mother after their father moved out. When a couple adopts them, Deborah takes easily to their new parents, but Aaron, refusing to believe that they want him or love him, locks himself in his room. Safe behind the door, he thinks of all that has happened that could show he has nothing and can expect nothing. And he finds reasons for hating everyone: he hates Deborah for hugging the new parents and calling them Mom and Dad; he hates the new parents, especially the man who, though he has built him a model ship, Aaron is sure wants to beat him. Though they set food outside the door, the parents do not try to force the boy to come out. But he decides that not only the food but the gifts they have given him are meant as bait. So he refuses the food, smashes the model ship, and remains locked in his room through the night and the following day. When the father returns from work, he breaks in the door, picks Aaron up and, holding him close, carries him toward the dinner table. Fearful of him, Aaron pushes away, and the father releases him. Yet the boy follows him to the table, thinking, "Maybe they want me."

Aaron's encompassing fear, loneliness, and shame are all too real: he is afraid to love or be loved and transforms all possibilities into threats. When the boy is forcibly freed from his own prison, the reader can feel that Aaron has been looking for just this—an active, physical proof of love.

Ages 5-9

Also available in:
No other form known

429

Miles, Miska, pseud.

Annie and the Old One

Black/white illustrations by Peter Parnall.
Little, Brown & Company, Inc., 1972.
(44 pages, paperbound)

DEATH: Attitude Toward
Grandparent: living in child's home
Grandparent: love for
Native American

Annie, a Navajo child, loves to sit at her grandmother's feet and listen to stories of long ago. She and her grandmother are very close; they enjoy the same jokes and ideas. Annie's mother is weaving a beautiful rug, and Grandmother encourages the girl to observe how the weaving is done. But Annie's thoughts wander as she watches her mother at work. One day Grandmother calls the family together and tells them she is going to "return to Mother Earth" when the rug has been completed and taken from the loom. Annie does not want her grandmother to die. She decides she must unravel the rug so that Grandmother will not die. When Grandmother discovers Annie unraveling the rug, she explains to her that all things come from the earth and later return to the earth. Annie understands and is awed by the wonder of life and death.

This book sensitively and effectively portrays the feeling of closeness between a child and her grandmother. The unity of life and death is dealt with in a simple and moving manner that will appeal to the young reader.

Ages 6-9

Also available in:
Braille—*Annie and the Old One*
Library of Congress (NLSBPH)

430

Moeri, Louise

First the Egg

Dutton Children's Books, 1982.
(99 pages) o.p.

RESPONSIBILITY: Accepting
Boy-girl relationships
Egocentrism
Family: relationships
Maturation
Rejection: parental
Values/Valuing: moral/ethical

High school senior Sarah Webster is as astonished as her classmates when the instructor in her Marriage and Family class pairs the students off, gives each couple a raw egg, and tells them they are to become the egg's parents for the next five days, applying all they've learned about caring for a newborn baby. They are never to leave the egg unattended, unless it is "sleeping" in an adjoining room. They are to keep a baby book, listing everything they do for the egg. Sarah is paired with David Hanna, a handsome but hostile transfer student with an icy personality and a caustic tongue. When Sarah explains her assignment at the dinner table, her father becomes inexplicably and deeply angry about it. Sarah begins to become involved with her egg, waking at two in the morning for its "feeding" and worrying when it's David's turn to watch over it. She's puzzled when her father makes remarks about there being too many babies in the world already. Then she finds her mother crying in the middle of the night and discovers that her father never wanted their last child, nine-year-old Julie. He'd been planning to start his own business when his wife became pregnant and has since blamed her for his failure to make a lot of money. He frequently threatens to leave her. Suddenly Sarah understands the distance she has always sensed between her father and Julie, and she realizes that Julie is a little too quiet, too unassuming. When David, a prospective doctor, turns the egg and the baby book over to Sarah the next day, she reads his entries. He refers to the egg as "the patient" and says it appears to be so severely retarded that several pediatricians have recommended it be institutionalized. Sarah ponders the dilemma of one parent wanting a child institutionalized and the other not. David stops over to say she'll have to finish the egg project alone; he's taking off for Baja with several friends. He's not going to graduate or go on to college. When her friend Becca tells Sarah to alert David's father, Sarah refuses. She suspects that David wants her to do just that, so he will be absolved of all responsibility for his decision. He's not in school the next morning but shows up later in the afternoon, telling Sarah that he left his friends and hitchhiked home. She's glad he's not going to ruin the egg project because she really needs the good grade she's working for. She has not worked up to her potential in high school, she realizes. Then her mother announces she has taken a job. Sarah will have to fix dinner every night and help out while her mother works an evening shift. When she complains that her older brother, Rob, should help, her mother points out that Rob is a full-time student working four hours a day. He's exhausted, and Sarah is shocked to realize that she hadn't even noticed Rob's fatigue. She hadn't really looked at her mother as a person either, until now. Becca calls Sarah in the middle of the night to report on a date she had with Bobby. He wanted to sleep with her and at one time she might have been tempted. But caring for the egg has helped her realize that she and Bobby could create a child between them, an act that would be totally irresponsible. The day the students are to return the eggs, Sarah confesses to David that this week of having to face reality has been terribly hard. David admits he has been shaken up too. They both feel a certain amount of grief at giving up their egg. The last entry in their baby book says, "We will be back to get you."

A school project serves as a catalyst for the maturation of two teenagers, one afraid of responsibility, the other too wrapped up in her own concerns to notice the problems and needs of her family. This is a book that can be read on two levels: as a story and as a study of human behavior and relationships, punctuated by reflections on the meaning and importance of life. Skillfully written in journal form, the story provides sensitive characterizations and believable situations, although some readers may wonder at the speed with which feelings emerge and attitudes change. The premise is based on an assignment that has been given in a number of U.S. schools.

Ages 12 and up

Also available in:
Cassette—*First the Egg*
Library of Congress (NLSBPH)

431

Moeri, Louise

The Girl Who Lived on the Ferris Wheel

Dutton Children's Books, 1979.
(117 pages)

CHILD ABUSE
FEAR: of Death
FEAR: of Physical Harm
MENTAL ILLNESS: of Parent

To eleven-year-old Clotilde Foerester, called Til, living in San Francisco in 1943, even riding the hated Ferris wheel with her mild-mannered father is better than staying home with the mother whose violence she fears more and more. Til's mother, Gertrude, was an unloved daughter and is now a compulsive nag and house cleaner, one for whom nothing in life is good enough. She has driven Til's father to divorce, and now she slaps and punches Til and knocks her down the stairs. Til's father, who avoids the details of his daughter's home life, takes Til to an amusement park every Saturday, his only free time. Til likes the bumper cars, feeling heroic and in control as she drives them, but secretly hates the Ferris wheel, something bigger and stronger that throws her around. Til's father plays his fiddle for her as they walk along the beach in Golden Gate Park, and Til feels cheated of a happy family life. At school a worried Til asks a friend if her mother ever hits her. The friend replies, "Of course not. What do you think my mother is—some kind of nut?" Til tries to attract attention at school by drawing on a math paper a face that calls "Help." Talking with the school nurse, she cannot bring herself to reveal her fears of her mother. Instead, she talks about hating the Ferris wheel because it throws her around. The nurse, concerned about Til's many bruises, constant headaches, and trouble with schoolwork, thinks the girl is complaining about her father. Til cannot correct her and unhappily leaves for home. There she finds a chilling sight: her own place at the dinner table is set as usual, but her mother's is set with butcher knives. Til takes some money and flees, but then tries to sneak back home, confused. She hears her mother calling her softly, knife in hand, and realizes her danger in time to get out of the house. On her way to her father's apartment she stops to eat, and a drunken sailor molests her. The Navy's shore patrol stops him and offers help, but Til runs away again. At her father's apartment she finds not him, but his friend Helga. Again Til flees, and a worried Helga calls Til's father and alerts the police. Bewildered and weary, Til goes home. Her mother is waiting in the shadows with a knife. The police arrive and Gertrude hides the knife, saying she can handle this bad girl who ran away. Til realizes at last that she must act to save her life. She goads her mother, calling Gertrude a slave, herself a princess. Gertrude loses the last shred of control and goes for Til with the knife. The police stop her. Then Til's teacher and the school nurse arrive. The nurse had alerted the teacher to Til's need for help, but they were delayed in coming to the house because of the wartime gas rationing. Til's father comforts the shaken girl, assuring her that the two of them had little to do with Gertrude's madness. Til begins to understand that she had been trying not to believe what she knew to be true about her mother, that her life has been saved by her independent action.

A young girl whose mentally ill mother abuses her and finally threatens her life must break out of her paralyzing fear and guilt and take action to save herself. Described clearly are the sources and signs of Til's mother's illness and the dangerous condition of Til's home life, a setting for disaster both before and after her parents' divorce. Til's difficulty in admitting to herself that her mother means to kill her is both painful and compelling. This book has unusual power and suspense—too much, perhaps, for some readers. Adult support and guidance may help keep the story in perspective. Mature readers will find much to discuss here.

Ages 13 and up

Also available in:
No other form known

432

Mohr, Nicholasa

Felita

Black/white illustrations by Ray Cruz.
Dial Books for Young Readers, 1979.
(112 pages) o.p.

MOVING
PREJUDICE: Ethnic/Racial
Death: of grandparent
Family: unity
Friendship: best friend
Grandparent: love for
Harassment
Puerto Rican-American

To get the children into better schools, the family of eight-year-old Felita Maldonado moves from an apartment in a Puerto Rican neighborhood to "a way better neighborhood" nearby. Felita is unhappy about the move. But the new apartment is larger and nicer, the area cleaner and quieter, and at first the neighbor girls are friendly. Adults are not so hospitable, however, and soon Felita is asked, "Why don't you stay with your own kind?" The girls, influenced by their parents' attitude, strike her and tear her dress. Johnny, her brother, is beaten and called a "spick." Her younger brother wants to fight back, but is restrained by his father. The family's mailbox is damaged, the mail scattered. Bags of water are dropped on Felita's mother from windows as she comes home with groceries. The Maldonados decide to move again for safety's sake. Their new apartment in the old neighborhood, across the street from the first, is small; Felita sleeps in a fixed-up storage area. She loves to stay overnight with her grandmother, Abuelita, who lives nearby. Abuelita tells her, "We Puerto Ricans are a rainbow of earth colors . . . like the many flowers of one garden." The two dream of visiting Puerto Rico together. When Felita's fourth-grade class prepares to do "The Courtship of Miles Standish," Felita and her best friend, Gigi, both want to play Priscilla. Felita talks about the play tryouts and her intentions, but Gigi does not. So Felita is amazed and hurt when Gigi tries out and does so well that she gets the part. Felita's teacher reminds her that she is already set designer and assistant stage manager, but the girl is not consoled. The play is a great success, as is Gigi. At the cast party she is friendly towards Felita, who remains resentful. After Thanksgiving dinner Felita again stays with her grandmother. She tells Abuelita that Gigi was sneaky about getting the part, but admits that she herself would not have played it so well. Abuelita's advice, to talk to Gigi, results in a reconciliation between the girls. In spring, Felita's grandmother lies near death. She summons the children for private talks. Always happy to be Felita's confidante and ever involved in family life, she encourages the girl to tell her how things have gone with Gigi. Then she dies. As a grieving Felita walks with her uncle through a park, listening to his proposal of a trip to Puerto Rico, Felita silently promises that if she ever gets there, she will make a big bouquet of the colorful Puerto Rican flowers for her grandmother.

Blind, inherited prejudice and the violence it spawns threaten a trusting young girl but show her the value of her close-knit family and neighborhood life. The large and small concerns of Felita's life will be easily understood and sympathized with by young readers. The story, appropriately illustrated, is enriched by details of Puerto Rican-American life and by the warmth of Felita's relationship with her old-world grandmother.

Ages 8-10

Also available in:
Cassette—*Felita*
Library of Congress (NLSBPH)

433

Mohr, Nicholasa

In Nueva York

Arte Publico Press, Inc., 1988.
(192 pages, paperbound)

NEIGHBORS/NEIGHBORHOOD
PUERTO RICAN-AMERICAN
Friendship
Homosexuality: female
Homosexuality: male
Loneliness
Love, meaning of
Poverty
Stealing

By now, Old Mary has lived in New York almost forty years, having left behind in Puerto Rico a baby. Now William is coming to New York to be with her, and Old Mary is elated, for William is her hope for her old age. To Old Mary's astonishment, William turns out to be a dwarf. But his gentle kindness wins over the neighborhood, and he takes a job at the hub of the neighborhood, Rudi's luncheonette. There he becomes the best friend of Lali, Rudi's young wife, also recently come from Puerto Rico, lonely and homesick. Old Mary's American-born son, Federico, in New York on a visit, also takes a job at the luncheonette when Rudi breaks his leg. Federico and Lali become lovers. Already lovers are two young men in the neighborhood, Johnny and Sebastian. When Johnny is drafted (the time is the late 1960s), he marries a lesbian who will turn over his dependent's allowance to Sebastian—all this with the neighborhood's blessing. Soon Rudi recovers, and Federico plans to move on. Lali begs to go with him. She even takes money from Rudi's savings to buy a car, but Federico leaves one night without her. Lali is heartbroken; Rudi is furious at her deception. Still, life returns to normal, and Lali and William continue to be friends. When the luncheonette is robbed and Rudi shoots one of the thieves, the excitement of a new adventure dims the older ones.

This book is a collection of short stories about everyday life in a poor ethnic neighborhood on New York's Lower East Side. Each character's story is told separately, and Rudi's diner provides the point at which the characters intersect. These accounts combine wry humor and pathos in a persuasive way. Mature readers will probably take street language and passages on sex in stride, though others may not.

Ages 13 and up

Also available in:
Talking Book—*In Nueva York*
Library of Congress (NLSBPH)

434

Mosel, Arlene

Tikki Tikki Tembo

Color illustrations by Blair Lent.
Holt (Henry) and Company, Inc., 1968.
(46 pages counted)

NAME, DISSATISFACTION WITH
SIBLING: Younger
Chinese
Parental: inconsistency

"Once upon a time, a long time ago, it was the custom of all the fathers and mothers in China to give their first and honored sons great long names. But second sons were given hardly any names at all." In this story, the first and honored son's name is Tikki Tikki Tembo-no sa rembo-chari bari ruchi-pip peri pembo, while the second son is simply called Chang. Each day their mother washes clothes in the stream near their house, and the boys play on the bank. There is an old well nearby, and mother warns, "Don't go near the well, or you will surely fall in." But the mischievous little boys do not mind their mother, and when each, in turn, falls into the well, Tikki Tikki Tembo-no sa rembo-chari bari ruchi-pip peri pembo's extraordinarily long name is almost his undoing.

Younger siblings might take special satisfaction in this humorous retelling of an old folktale that portrays partiality shown to an elder son. The fanciful color illustrations have a Chinese character and appropriately are in ink and wash.

Ages 4-9

Also available in:
Cassette—*Tikki Tikki Tembo*
Scholastic, Inc.

Paperbound—*Tikki Tikki Tembo*
Scholastic, Inc.

435

Murphy, Jim

Death Run

Clarion Books, 1982.
(174 pages) o.p.

DELINQUENCY, JUVENILE
GUILT, FEELINGS OF
Peer relationships: peer pressures
Values/Valuing: moral/ethical
Violence

Sophomore Brian Halihan steals a six-pack of beer to take to the park where he's meeting his friends Roger, Al, and Sticks, all older boys. While they're killing time waiting for a dance to start, they begin hassling a basketball player who's been practicing in the park, taking his basketball and playing keep-away. Roger pretends to throw the ball over the boy's head, but when the boy reaches up for it, Roger slams it into his face instead. When the boy falls, convulsing and bleeding, the others run away. The next day Brian learns that William Janowski, a basketball star, has been found dead in the park. Detective Sergeant Robert Wheeler, a former New York City detective who now works in Brian's suburb, senses something peculiar about Janowski's death—especially when he finds three full beer cans near the body and marks on Janowski's face that match the pattern on a basketball. Janowski had epilepsy and an autopsy shows a burst aneurism at the base of his brain, previously undetected. It ruptured as the result of a seizure, according to the medical examiner. The police consider the case solved, but Wheeler doesn't. The four boys decide to avoid being seen together until the whole thing blows over. But Brian finds himself walking past the Janowski house. Wheeler sees Brian and becomes suspicious. He files his report, but adds a supplementary page detailing his concerns. The police chief closes the case anyway. Then Wheeler's daughter, Susan, who attends the same high school as the boys, decides to do some detecting on her own. She and several of her friends discover that Sticks had a locker-room fight with Janowski several weeks earlier. Without asking her father, Susan copies his reports and shares them with R.R., editor of the school newspaper, who is writing an article on Janowski's death. R.R. decides the next step is to find out who Sticks's friends are. Meanwhile, Brian has seen Wheeler's name in the newspapers and calls the police station, giving a false name, to get his address. He doesn't want to meet Wheeler, just to observe him. When he does, Brian knows that Wheeler has not given up the case. After Susan spends a day trying to track down Sticks's friends, she is attacked and threatened at knifepoint but does not see her assailants. However, she hears one of them call another Sticks. The Janowski case is reopened, a file is begun on Susan's attack, and Wheeler is removed from both cases because of his daughter's involvement. Al and Roger tell Brian that they staged the attack on Susan in order to incriminate Sticks; when Brian gets angry they beat him up and warn him to keep quiet. Brian realizes he's trapped between Roger and Al on one side, Wheeler on the other. Disobeying his orders, Wheeler interrogates Sticks, hoping to make him nervous enough to implicate his accomplices. Seeing Sticks and Brian together, Wheeler decides to wait at Brian's home, but Brian sees his car and flees. Then Brian borrows money from his girlfriend so that Sticks can run away; because of a previous juvenile record in Michigan, Sticks is sure to bear the brunt of Janowski's death. Brian is tempted to run away too. But "as easy as it sounded, he knew he could never completely outrun Janowski's ghost or his own guilt." In studying her notes, R.R. discovers that one of Sticks's friends is Roger, whose former girlfriend broke up with him to date Janowski. In addition, if someone did hit Janowski with the basketball it had to be a left-handed person because of the side of his face that was bruised. Roger is left-handed. She calls the detective on the case with her information. When Roger and Al are found together and questioned, they admit their guilt. After seeing Sticks off on the train, Brian, unaware of Roger's and Al's confession, goes to Wheeler's house and knocks at the door. "I think we should talk," Brian says.

A teenager involved in a fatal incident is unable to live with his guilt. Brian tries to tell himself that he was only an innocent bystander, but knows that once he chose to flee and leave Janowski dying, he became part of the act. He eventually chooses to reveal himself to the detective, Wheeler, not only because he realizes Wheeler will get him anyway, but also because he needs to take responsibility for what he's done. The book presents three viewpoints: Brian's, Wheeler's, and a neutral narrator's. Wheeler's story gives glimpses into the man's job conflicts, self-doubts, even procedural matters. Brian's story, fast-paced and filled with action, is definitely written for adolescents. His parents remain in the background, concerned about the obvious changes in their son. This is a gripping story and a good book for discussion.

Ages 11 and up

Also available in:
No other form known

436

Myers, Walter Dean

Fast Sam, Cool Clyde, and Stuff

Viking Penguin, 1975.
(190 pages)

FRIENDSHIP: Meaning of
MATURATION
African-American Clubs
Empathy

At twelve-and-a-half years old, Francis moves to 116th Street, a black neighborhood in New York. Two days later he meets a bunch of local children: Cool Clyde, Fast Sam, Gloria, and others. They accept him immediately and nickname him "Stuff." But Stuff has barely time to get acquainted when he and others land in jail for trying to do good: during a fight between Binky and Robin, Robin has bitten a piece off Binky's ear. The kids take Binky to the hospital to have the piece sewn back on, and the police come and arrest them all for fighting. Soon after that, Clyde's father dies. Times look rough. The crowd decides to form a club to help one another out in time of need—to "dig each other's problems." They call themselves "The 116th Street Good People." But before long they are in trouble again, this time falsely accused of being thieves after recovering a woman's stolen purse and preparing to return it. Luckily, a witness exonerates them. Throughout the school year the club sticks together—through parties, basketball games, and troubles with school and parents. Everyone feels especially close when, together, they save Carnation Charlie from a drug overdose. (Later Charlie is shot to death in an attempted store robbery.) When Sam and Clyde graduate from high school, the club begins gradually to dissolve. Eventually, time separates the Good People, but Stuff will always remember the happy, rewarding times they had together, and he knows the others will remember too.

Stuff's tender, funny first-person narrative recaptures his life of five years earlier and conveys the warmth and safety friendship provides. The discussion here of premarital sex is both frank and unexceptionable, and the dialogue is at all times natural without being coarse. If anything, the plot and style may be thought prim by some readers.

Ages 11-14

Also available in:
Paperbound—*Fast Sam, Cool Clyde, and Stuff*
Puffin Books

Talking Book—*Fast Sam, Cool Clyde, and Stuff*
Library of Congress (NLSBPH)

437

Myers, Walter Dean

Hoops

Dell Publishing Company, Inc. (Laurel Leaf Library), 1981.
(183 pages, paperbound)

DETERMINATION
MATURATION
African-American
Boy-girl relationships
Crime/Criminals
Friendship: meaning of
Peer relationships
Sports/Sportsmanship
Talents: athletic
Violence

Springtime in Harlem finds Lonnie Jackson, seventeen, living part-time at home and part-time at the Grant Hotel where he works. Fulltime, he thinks about basketball. When all else in his confusing life fails, he has his basketball. "My game was my fame, and I knew it was together." At the gym one day, Lonnie and others are told about an upcoming city-wide basketball tournament. College scouts will be watching the games, especially the finals. This tournament is a chance for kids who did not play high school ball to be recognized. Lonnie is excited about the possibilities until he meets their coach, Cal Jones. Lonnie has seen Cal on the streets, considers him a wino, and refuses to be coached by him. So Cal challenges him to a six-point one-on-one game. If he loses, he will quit. When Cal beats Lonnie, he demands he come to practice the next day. From then on, Cal rides Lonnie constantly, demanding more of him than of the others. Lonnie resents it, yet he knows Cal thinks he has the potential to succeed. When they lose their first game, Cal says they're playing as individuals, not as a team. By now Cal and Lonnie are friends, and Cal invites the boy to his apartment. He shows Lonnie his scrapbook and for the first time Lonnie realizes that Cal is actually Spider Jones, a

M

former professional basketball player. Cal explains that he threw away his one gift, basketball, by getting involved in a point-spread gambling scheme. Meanwhile, Lonnie's girlfriend, Mary-Ann, discovers that her boss, Tyrone Giddins, has her brother Paul's name on an envelope. This worries her: Paul has had lots of money recently and she knows Tyrone can't be trusted. Paul confesses to Lonnie that he is stealing and selling welfare checks. At the same time, Mr. O'Donnel, the head of the basketball tournament, tells Cal he doesn't want any bad publicity and urges him to quit coaching. Lonnie learns that it was Tyrone's bodyguard who told Mr. O'Donnel about Cal's past. Cal fails to show up for the next two games, and Lonnie discovers he's in jail. When he's out on bail, Lonnie learns that he beat up a man who wanted him to shave points again. Then Cal is called back to Mr. O'Donnel's office and told that Lonnie, who was kicked out of one game for arguing with the referee, cannot play in the championship game. Lonnie is furious; Cal tells him he can suit up and watch. Then, in front of Lonnie, Cal calls in a bet against his own team. If he is going down, he tells Lonnie, he intends to take some people with him. The team loses badly in the first half. In the second half, when Cal knows all bets are placed, he sends Lonnie in to play. The team wins the championship by one point. Lonnie sees Cal leave for the locker room and runs after him. Too late, he sees Cal being beaten by Tyrone and his bodyguard. Lonnie tries to help, but Cal is shot and dies. A grieving Lonnie realizes that Cal has made his restitution and his comeback. Cal has taught him that if he keeps himself and his game together, he might have a chance in this world.

A Harlem teenager determined to have something better than the bleak environment of his childhood finds in basketball and in the courage of his coach the strength and self-confidence he needs. Surrounded by crime and coercion, Lonnie tries not to yield; he even avoids having sex with his girlfriend so their relationship can be special in their world. His first-person narrative is vivid and involving; the basketball sequences add excitement and are woven smoothly into the plot.

Ages 12 and up

Also available in:
Braille—*Hoops*
Library of Congress (NLSBPH)

438

Myers, Walter Dean

It Ain't All for Nothin'

Avon Books, 1985.
(217 pages) o.p.

CRIME/CRIMINALS
VALUES/VALUING: Moral/Ethical
African-American
Alcoholism: adolescent
Decision making
Deprivation, emotional
Guilt, feelings of
Honesty/Dishonesty
Parental: unreliability

Black, twelve-year-old Tippy, whose mother died when he was born, has lived with his kind, proud, religious maternal grandmother all his life. Now she has been sent to a nursing home, and he is sent to live with Lonnie, his father, whom he has scarcely seen. The two live in dirt and clutter, their meals irregular, and Tippy sleeps on a cot. He mistrusts Lonnie's friends, Bubba and Stone, and he notices that Lonnie, despite having no job, always has enough cash for food and liquor. One evening Lonnie confides that he steals for a living. Then he forces Tippy to take part in a robbery. For days afterward, the boy is tormented by guilt. No Catholic, he nevertheless goes into a church one day, finds a priest, and begins to unburden himself. The priest asks him to wait and makes a telephone call which Tippy overhears. Frightened, the boy makes for home. When he tells Lonnie what he has done, Lonnie beats him. Soon Tippy is drinking to forget the trouble he is in. One day he becomes so belligerently drunk that he starts a fight and blacks out. He comes to in the house of a man named Roland Sylvester, who, with his wife, shows genuine concern for Tippy, giving him their phone number and address, and telling him to reach them should he ever need help. When Lonnie, Bubba, and Stone involve him in an armed robbery, during which Bubba is wounded, concern for Bubba (and his own complicity should Bubba die) drives Tippy to brave a beating from Lonnie and Stone's drawn gun in order to make straight for Mr. Roland. He tells Mr. Roland all, and the police are called: Lonnie and Stone are arrested, and Bubba is taken to a hospital, where he later dies. Meanwhile, after eight days in a detention home, Tippy is cleared of all charges and becomes Mr. Roland's ward. Just before Lonnie is sent to the state prison, Tippy visits him in jail. Father and son promise to keep in touch, and Lonnie assures Tippy that he was right to go to Mr. Roland. As time passes, Tippy finds himself able to look forward to his father's release and a good life for both of them.

In this somber but melodramatic first-person narrative, Tippy learns that no one avoids choosing between right and wrong. With that knowledge, he begins to spurn the liquor he has started to depend on and tries to depend on his conscience. As a character,

Tippy is perceptive and remarkably rounded, a basically honest young man caught and gradually strengthened by rapidly changing circumstances and events, all during one summer vacation. The other characters are well developed and the black dialect will not prove difficult for readers unfamiliar with it.

Ages 11-13

Also available in:
Cassette—*It Ain't All for Nothin'*
Library of Congress (NLSBPH)

439

Myers, Walter Dean

Won't Know Till I Get There

Viking Penguin, 1982.
(176 pages)

AGE: Aging
FOSTER HOME
MATURATION
Adoption: feelings about
Age: respect for
Delinquency, juvenile
Sibling: rivalry

Fourteen-year-old Steve Perry's parents ask him if he has any objections to their adopting a child. He doesn't and so Earl Goins—thirteen, with a record of disturbing the peace, vandalism, and armed robbery—comes to live with them for a trial period. In an impulsive attempt to look as tough as he thinks Earl is, Steve writes on the side of a train with spray paint. Transit police take him, Earl, and two other boys to the station. When they appear in court, the judge offers them an alternative to the detention center: working six days a week all summer at Micheaux House for Senior Citizens. There Steve and his friends meet the janitor, London Brown, and the five residents left in the home, which is to be shut down at summer's end—Pietro Santini, Esther Cruz, Eileen Lardner, Jack Lasher, and Mabel Jackson. Steve doesn't know what to think about Earl, who tends to be sarcastic, cool, and remote, but also has nightmares and occasionally wets the bed. When this happens, Steve helps him change the bedding and wash it without his parents' knowledge. Still, Steve resents his loss of privacy. Meanwhile, the residents want to keep their home open and remain independent. Eileen decides they need a source of income. She has a three-thousand-dollar inheritance they can use for seed money. Pietro and Steve decide to set up a sandwich and coffee shop in the deli area of a local supermarket. London is advanced one thousand dollars to start a waxing business, and two others clean sidewalks for local businesses. Then Steve and Earl fight, and the family discusses sending Earl back to the agency. A camping trip suggested by a counselor seems to please Earl; later, Steve's father says the experience made him lean toward keeping Earl. But when they finally decide to adopt the boy, who cries with happiness and apprehension when he learns their intentions, Earl's mother arrives to make sure her son's adoptive home is all it should be. As she has twice before, she refuses permission for him to be adopted. However, the family is granted legal custody of Earl until he is eighteen. The city shuts down the House after all, declining to take responsibility for the residents' business activities. The group is split up, although Steve and Earl visit Mabel and the now-married Pietro and Esther. Steve decides that in trying to understand Earl during the summer, he has come closer to understanding himself. He has also learned a great deal from his association with the old people. At first they all seemed alike to him; now, they are individuals. He wonders what old age will hold for him: "I guess I won't know till I get there."

Written in the form of a diary, Steve's story shows him learning to see beyond preconceived notions about people to the real individuals beneath. The old people at the home and his troubled foster brother all touch Steve's life. Set in Harlem, the book moves as quickly as does its fresh, lively dialogue. The characterizations of the House's residents and their exchanges with Steve and his friends give readers superb insight into some of the problems, feelings, and concerns of older people.

M

Ages 11-14

Also available in:
Paperbound—*Won't Know Till I Get There*
Puffin Books

440

Myers, Walter Dean

The Young Landlords

Viking Penguin , 1989.
(208 pages)

NEIGHBORS/NEIGHBORHOOD
RESPONSIBILITY: Accepting
African-American
Boy-girl relationships
Cooperation: in work
Crime/Criminals
Friendship: meaning of
Ghetto
Problem solving

Paul Williams, in his mid-teens, lives in a run-down neighborhood of New York City. It is summer vacation and his friend Gloria wants to spend the time doing neighborhood projects. With Paul and three other friends she starts the "Action Group," whose main target will be to clean up "The Joint," a crumbling apartment building on the block. When they complain about the building's condition to its owner, the man turns to Paul and asks him to invest a dollar towards improving the place. Paul pays. About a week later, an amazed Paul receives the title to "The Joint," made out in his name. He is reluctant to accept the responsibility, but at Gloria's insistence and with his parents' approval he decides the group will try to make some improvements. First they meet the tenants, an odd and demanding bunch. The young people quickly learn that operating an apartment brings much more trouble than profit. They hire an eccentric little man, Mr. Pender, to do the bookkeeping. He shows them that after they make minor repairs and pay the insurance, taxes, and bills, they will have no money left to make any improvements. They will have to raise money, they decide, by doing extra projects. Meanwhile, a neighborhood boy, Chris, has been accused of stealing stereo equipment from the store where he works. The Action Group decides to help clear him, hoping to collect the thousand-dollar reward offered by the owner of the store for the recovery of the equipment. Paul, Gloria, and another group member, Bubba, check out a vacant warehouse for stolen merchandise, but are told by the police to stay out of the case. Mr. Pender suggests they spread the word through the neighborhood that they want to buy stereo equipment; maybe someone will approach them with the stolen goods. In the meantime, they decide to have a street fair to raise money. They set up booths and people donate food to sell. The fair is a great success, netting the group over four hundred dollars. During cleanup, a man who has been lingering in the area tells Paul that the kids should set up a little disco joint in the basement of the building; he can get them some stereo equipment, he says, at half price. Paul's ears perk up. He and Bubba, without asking Gloria or Mr. Pender, take the profit money and meet the man at a warehouse. They spend most of the money on the stereo equipment he shows them, but when they get home and compare the serial numbers of the stolen equipment with the numbers on the boxes of the equipment they've bought, they begin to think they've made a mistake—that this is not, after all, the equipment Chris was accused of stealing. Depressed, Paul tells his father what he's done. His father suggests they recheck the numbers and, sure enough, those on the actual equipment do match the list of stolen numbers. Chris is cleared, but the Action Group refuses the reward money. Chris, they have learned, knew about the theft and was paid to keep quiet. "We didn't feel right taking the reward money. . . . We would just try to do more of the work ourselves and to get by the best we could." But their finances deteriorate even more during the winter, and they realize they can't afford to keep the building. Then the man who heads the local numbers racket, a benevolent soul, buys the building and hires the group to run it. The kids are sure that with a little luck they'll be making a profit in two years.

Five friends attempt to improve living conditions in their depressed neighborhood. Paul tells this warm, realistic story with wit, authentic dialogue, and lively characterizations. The conclusion, in which they must surrender ownership of the building, is credible, but out of their determination to improve "The Joint" comes much good. The group members learn to appreciate each other, the tenants begin to help one another, a crime is solved, and a tentative romance is born between the two leaders, Paul and Gloria.

Ages 11-14

Also available in:
Cassette—*The Young Landlords*
Library of Congress (NLSBPH)

Paperbound—*The Young Landlords*
Puffin Books

441

Ness, Evaline Michelow

Sam, Bangs, and Moonshine

Color illustrations by the author.
Holt (Henry) and Company, Inc., 1966.
(39 pages counted)

REALITY, ESCAPING
Honesty/Dishonesty
Imagination

Young Samantha lives near the ocean with her father and her cat Bangs. Her mother is dead, but Sam likes to say that her mother doesn't live with them because she is a mermaid. Sam falsifies so many things that people feel they cannot believe anything she says. One day, after Sam's father has warned her about lying, Sam sends her friend Thomas to a cave near the shore to look for a baby kangaroo that she claims is nearby. A storm blows in and Sam fears for Thomas's safety. When her father comes home, she tells him what she has done, and he rushes to the cave to rescue Thomas. Later that evening, Sam's father tells her she must "learn the difference between REAL and MOONSHINE," and before she goes to bed, Sam admits to herself that she already knows the difference. The next day, when her father brings home a gerbil, Sam wants to call it a kangaroo, but her father insists that she call it by its real name. Sam feels remorseful about the distress she caused Thomas. To try to make up for what she did, she takes the gerbil to him and tells him what it really is.

This story depicts a girl who prefers her fantasies to reality. A near tragedy forces her to admit that some things must be accepted as they really are. She continues to have a vivid imagination but manages to control her desire to falsify things to other people.

Ages 4-8

Also available in:
Braille—*Sam, Bangs, and Moonshine*
Library of Congress (NLSBPH)

Filmstrip—*Sam, Bangs, and Moonshine*
BFA Educational Media, a division of CBS Inc.

Paperbound—*Sam, Bangs, and Moonshine*
Trumpet Book Club

Videotape—*Sam, Bangs, and Moonshine*
Newbery Award Records/Random House Inc.

442

Neufeld, John

Edgar Allan

S.G. Phillips, Inc., 1968.
(95 pages)

ADOPTION: Interracial
Peer relationships: peer pressures
Prejudice: ethnic/racial

Twelve-year-old Michael, son of the Reverend and Mrs. Robert Fickett, tells the story of his family's adoption of Edgar Allan, a three-year-old black child. The family lives in a small, all-white town, and the community reacts negatively to the adoption. However, not until Edgar Allan enrolls in nursery school does the negative community reaction become vicious. Teen-aged Mary Nell Fickett is influenced by peer values that reflect the prejudices of the rest of the town. She has resisted Edgar Allan's adoption from the first. When a cross is burned on the Ficketts' lawn and Reverend Fickett is threatened with the loss of his church, Mary Nell issues the ultimatum, "...if he stays...I'll just leave." The Reverend Fickett returns Edgar Allan to the adoption agency. The security of the youngest Fickett children, six-year-old Sally Ann and three-year-old Stephen Paul, is shaken when their new little brother is "given away." The injustice done to Edgar Allan is felt keenly by both Mother and Michael. Mary Nell and others in the community demonstrate a lack of conviction as they change their position on the adoption and censure Reverend Fickett for giving way under pressure.

Honest, vivid, and moving, this first-person narrative effectively captures the feelings that can develop when a black child is adopted into a white family living in a white community. It is a poignant, contemporary novel about the pain caused by prejudice.

Ages 10 and up

Also available in:
Braille—*Edgar Allan*
Library of Congress (NLSBPH)

Paperbound—*Edgar Allan*
New American Library/Penguin USA

443

Neville, Emily Cheney

Berries Goodman

HarperCollins Publishers, Inc., 1965.
(178 pages, paperbound)

FRIENDSHIP: Meaning of
PREJUDICE: Ethnic/Racial
Jew
Values/Valuing: moral/ethical

Bertrand "Berries" Goodman, about a fourth grader, is not Jewish, although he has grown up in a predominantly Jewish neighborhood in New York City. He has been taught by his family to be tolerant of other people's values and lifestyles. When the Goodman family moves to a New York suburb, Berries is confronted for the first time with an insidious, covert prejudice directed at the Jewish families in the community. Puzzled by the discrimination, Berries asks, "How am I supposed to remember some kid is Jewish, when we're catching polliwogs or climbing a tree?" Eventually, Berries becomes close friends with Sidney Fine, a Jewish schoolmate. When Berries questions his family after he hears anti-Semitic remarks made about Sidney, his father explains, "Some people are prejudiced. That means they dislike another whole group of people without there being any sensible reason for it." The boys' friendship is resented by Berries's next-door neighbor, a young girl named Sandra, who had been Berries's constant companion before he met Sidney. One day, Sandra dares Sidney to jump the outlet culvert at the pond. Sidney makes the leap but slides back down on the frozen ground and is seriously injured. Because Mrs. Fine feels that Berries should have prevented the accident, she sees to it that the two boys are separated. Sidney is sent to a different school and forbidden to see Berries. Soon the Goodman family moves back to New York City, and there is no apparent way that the friendship can continue.

This first-person narrative is told in retrospect by Berries following a reunion with Sidney, whom he has not seen for six years. Told directly and candidly, the story captures the meaning of friendship through its realistic development of individual characters. Prejudice, the major theme of the story, is not explained away but is placed in perspective and dealt with honestly and sensitively. This is a powerful, engrossing book that may provoke discussions of the meaning of friendship and the problems of prejudice.

Ages 11 and up

Also available in:
Braille—*Berries Goodman*
Library of Congress (NLSBPH)

Cassette—*Berries Goodman*
Library of Congress (NLSBPH)

Talking Book—*Berries Goodman*
Library of Congress (NLSBPH)

444

North, Sterling

Rascal: A Memoir of a Better Era

Black/white illustrations by John Schoenherr.
Dutton Children's Books, 1984.
(189 pages)

PETS: Love for
PETS: Responsibility for
PETS: Substitute for Human Relationship
Nature: appreciation of
Parent/Parents: single

Eleven-year-old Sterling lives alone with his father. His mother has been dead for four years, his two older sisters have their own homes, and his brother is in the Army. The boy is encouraged to be independent, and he is allowed to keep any kind of pet, even a skunk. Sterling's father has helped him develop an appreciation for nature. He and his father love wildlife and the outdoors. In the spring, Sterling finds a baby raccoon, brings it home, and names it Rascal. Sterling is fascinated by Rascal's curiosity, intelligence, and dexterity. The boy and the raccoon become inseparable; they even eat and sleep together. As Rascal matures, he begins raiding the neighbors' corn fields, and the neighbors demand that the raccoon be caged. Sterling is unwilling to make his pet a prisoner, but he realizes that the animal might be shot if he is allowed to run loose. Sterling's sisters each come to visit, and each voices the opinion that Sterling and his father need a housekeeper to keep the house in order and look after Sterling; but no one is hired. During the winter, Rascal spends most of his time sleeping, but when spring comes, he learns to escape from his cage and raids a nearby henhouse. When a housekeeper is finally hired, Sterling realizes that to keep his pet, he would need to padlock Rascal's cage and keep him from roaming the house and getting into mischief. So he takes Rascal deep into the woods and returns the raccoon to the freedom of his natural habitat.

The boy in this autobiographical book, set in 1918, is very sensitive, independent, and self-reliant. He takes complete responsibility for the care of his many pets, and he is often totally responsible for his own welfare as well. His absent-minded father works to instill important values in his son but ignores many of the details of everyday life.

Ages 11 and up

Also available in:
Braille—*Rascal: A Memoir of a Better Era*
Library of Congress (NLSBPH)

Talking Book—*Rascal: A Memoir of a Better Era*
Library of Congress (NLSBPH)

445

O'Connor, Jane

Yours Till Niagara Falls, Abby

Black/white illustrations by Margot Apple.
Scholastic, Inc., 1982.
(128 pages) o.p.

CAMP EXPERIENCES
MATURATION
Friendship: making friends
Friendship: meaning of
Separation anxiety

Having convinced her parents to send her to summer camp with Merle, her best friend, ten-year-old Abby must go alone when Merle breaks an ankle. Abby's misadventures begin almost immediately. Her bunkmates, veteran campers Bonnie and Phyllis, collapse her bed, soak her hand in water as she sleeps, and tease and taunt her at the slightest provocation. Abby forgets to lock the food chest, and seagulls eat the girls' picnic lunch. Abby gets poison ivy. When mice nest in her pajamas her sympathy is awakened and she adopts them as pets, but she still wants to go home. "You must learn to make the best of situations even when they don't turn out like you want," her mother maintains. With the arrival of a new camper, Roberta, Abby finds someone clumsier and more of an outsider than she is. Abby's sympathy for Roberta is strengthened by the overt hostility of Bonnie and Phyllis. The dauntless Roberta leads Abby on a spy mission to the counselor's cabin, and the two girls turn the tables on Bonnie by running off with her robe and towel while she showers. Slowly, Abby's confidence returns, but certain fears persist. Though a good swimmer, she is afraid of diving and pleads with her parents to get her excused from diving lessons. She enjoys her assignment of teaching younger girls to swim, but feels ashamed of her refusal to dive. Then, in an accidental fall from the diving board, she discovers she can indeed dive. She even stars as Dracula in a skit. As camp ends, Abby learns that Merle is spending an extra week away from home with a new friend. At first Abby is hurt, but soon she realizes that change is part of friendship. Her own new friendship, with Roberta, will also be tried by separation. She realizes too that, in spite of everything, she has enjoyed camp and is sorry to see it end.

On her own for the first time at summer camp, a young girl must cope with separation from her home and best friend, harassment by difficult bunkmates, and her own lack of confidence. She sides with several shy girls and holds back from testing or trusting herself until sympathy for another outsider and success in teaching younger girls enhance her self-esteem. Abby comes to realize that her worth is independent of the people and places she had thought its source. Although Abby's financial security will seem alien to some readers, most will identify with her easily. Her story is told with humor and illustrated invitingly.

Ages 8-10

Also available in:
No other form known

446

O'Dell, Scott

Island of the Blue Dolphins

Houghton Mifflin Co., 1960.
(184 pages)

RESOURCEFULNESS
Abandonment
Courage, meaning of
Death: of sibling
Gender role identity: female
Loneliness
Native American

Karana is twelve when a boat with red sails comes to her island off the coast of California. It brings Aleuts who ask her father, chief of the Ghalas-at Indian tribe, for permission to hunt otter. Her father agrees on a price, and when the price is not paid, he confronts them. In the ensuing fight, Karana's father and most of the other men of the village are killed. The rest of the villagers decide to move to a new island. A ship comes for them. Karana already is aboard when she realizes that her six-year-old brother Ramo has returned to the village for his fishing spear. The boat will not wait for him, and rather than leave him alone, she jumps over the side and swims ashore. The next morning, Ramo goes off to launch a canoe and is killed by a pack of wild dogs. Karana waits alone for the ship, which is supposed to return in a few days. However,it takes eighteen years for a ship to return to the island. In that time, Karana teaches herself to build shelters, hunt for food, and make weapons, a task forbidden to the women of her tribe. She resolves to destroy the pack of wild dogs that killed her brother. After seriously injuring the pack's leader, Karana nurses him back to health and tames him for a pet. When the ship finally comes, Karana, now a young woman, is ready to sail across the sea.

This compelling first-person narrative is based on the true story of an Indian girl who lived alone on the tiny island of Saint Nicholas, off the California coast, from 1835 to 1853. Karana exhibits great resourcefulness and courage in overcoming the many problems she must solve to survive.

Ages 10 and up

Also available in:
Braille—*Island of the Blue Dolphins*
Library of Congress (NLSBPH)

Cassette—*Island of the Blue Dolphins*
Library of Congress (NLSBPH)

Talking Book—*Island of the Blue Dolphins*
Library of Congress (NLSBPH)

447

O'Dell, Scott

Kathleen, Please Come Home

Houghton Mifflin Co., 1978.
(196 pages)

DRUGS: Abuse of
RUNNING AWAY
VALUES/VALUING: Moral/Ethical
Crime/Criminals
Death: of fiancé/fiancée
Dependence/Independence
Judgment, effect of emotions on
Peer relationships: peer pressures
Pregnancy

When fifteen-year-old Kathy meets Sybil, a new girl at school, she is attracted by Sybil's glamour and boldness. Sybil uses drugs—marijuana, uppers, downers, even heroin—and she teases the inexperienced Kathy for being "chicken." Still, she invites Kathy and two other girls to go into the California desert for a weekend camp-out, and while the others are getting high, Kathy goes for a walk. She meets a young Mexican named Ramón, who has illegally entered the United States from Mexico. Kathy speaks fluent Spanish and offers him a ride back to town, where she helps him find a place to live and takes him to Mr. Diaz, who finds him a job for a percentage of the wages. Kathy and Ramón fall in love, and Ramón proposes. When Kathy tells her mother, her mother quietly says she would like to think it over. Secretly, her mother notifies the immigration authorities, and Ramón and several other illegal immigrants are arrested and returned to Mexico. Kathy gives Mr. Diaz money to bring Ramón back, but the truck is ambushed by the authorities as it crosses the California line: Ramón is shot and dies a few days later. Kathy is grief-stricken. In time, she questions her mother about Ramón's capture, and her mother admits to giving Ramón's name to the authorities. She had felt Kathy too young to marry, especially someone she hardly knew. Kathy runs away to Tijuana with Sybil and there gets a waitress job. Her mother locates her there a few days later, but Kathy flees again, sticking with Sybil, earning her living by waitressing. She visits Ramón's family, who receive her warmly. By now Sybil has persuaded Kathy to try uppers and downers, even heroin. Then Kathy learns she is pregnant. Thrilled to be carrying Ramón's child, she is told by a doctor that she cannot take heroin. Sybil is going to another part of Mexico to buy a load of heroin to sell back in the States, but Kathy stays behind to avoid Sybil's influence. Later she does agree to drive back to California with her $10,000 worth of heroin in the car. On the way, there is a terrible accident, and Sybil is killed. Kathy is not seriously injured, but she loses the baby. She is also arrested for possession of some heroin that is found in her purse, and she is sent to Tranquility House, a detoxification facility. Confused and uncertain about what to do with herself, Kathy takes a job to pass the time. Months later, she

O

has decided to go home and see her mother, but she finds their house sold and her mother gone in search of her daughter. Kathy and a girlfriend go to the ocean and throw in the remaining heroin; it is washed out to sea.

In this thought-provoking story a teenage girl is so influenced by a peer that, in the name of friendship, she loses all common sense and all regard for the values she has grown up with. Though the story's open ending implies that she will go straight, the attraction to heroin is still with her. The book is written in three parts: the first and third from Kathy's diary, and the second is a first-person narrative by her mother.

Ages 12 and up

Also available in:
Cassette—*Kathleen, Please Come Home*
Library of Congress (NLSBPH)

448

O'Hara, Mary, pseud.

My Friend Flicka

HarperCollins Publishers, Inc., 1973.
(253 pages) o.p.

PETS: Love for
RESPONSIBILITY: Accepting
Communication: parent-child
Daydreaming
Family: unity
Maturation

Ten-year-old Ken has done so poorly at school that he will have to repeat the fifth grade at the boarding school that he and his older brother Howard attend. Because Ken daydreams so much, he forgets instructions and becomes lost in thought at critical times. Although Ken wants a colt of his own, his father refuses to give him one until Ken proves that he can assume responsibilities. However, Ken's mother intervenes and persuades his father to give him a colt. Ken chooses a wild yearling filly, and he names the horse Flicka. When she is caught, the horse crashes through a barbed wire fence in an attempt to escape and is badly injured. Ken spends every free moment talking to Flicka, trying to gentle her, but not until her wounds become infected does the horse permit Ken to touch her. Although Ken's father orders Flicka destroyed, Ken, trying to break the horse's fever, spends the night with her in the creek, holding her head to prevent her from drowning. Flicka begins to recuperate, but Ken contracts pneumonia and is very sick for a long time. When he recovers, the boy and horse have a joyous reunion.

Family relationships, the lack of understanding between father and son, the intense longing of a boy for his own horse, and the boy's maturation are realistically and sympathetically portrayed themes in this moving classic. The story is enhanced by beautiful descriptions of the range, the mountains, and the animals. It presents a vivid picture of ranch life and its problems.

Ages 11 and up

Also available in:
Braille—*My Friend Flicka*
Library of Congress (NLSBPH)

Cassette—*My Friend Flicka*
Library of Congress (NLSBPH)

Talking Book—*My Friend Flicka*
Library of Congress (NLSBPH)

449

Okimoto, Jean Davies

Norman Schnurman, Average Person

Putnam Berkley Group, Inc., 1982.
(125 pages) o.p.

EXPECTATIONS
PARENTAL: Interference
Communication: parent-child
Courage, meaning of
Gender role identity: male
Sex: attitude toward

Sixth-grader Norman Schnurman, who has absolutely no interest in or aptitude for sports, is the son of Mad Dog Dave Schnurman, a former college football star. When Norman's father begins coaching the junior league Bears team, he promises to turn Norman into a first-rate running back. Sure Norman will soon love the game as much as he does, he buys his protesting son a complete football outfit with his old number, 33. Meanwhile Norman, whose main interests are garage sales and video games, has accidentally broken three hula-lady lamps at Reasonably Honest Al's. To repay Al the twelve dollars for the broken lamps, Norman and his friend P.W. repair one of the lamps and then hold a tent show after school. They charge admission to watch the hula-lady lamp light up, look at a poster of a woman in a wet T-shirt, and other raucous goings-on. A mother finds out and tells Norman's parents. For his punishment he has to show the mother the lamp and apologize. Then, at a garage sale, Norman meets Carrie Koski and her grandfather. She's new in school and attractive, and Norman offers to show her around. Since Norman has never seen a naked woman, he decides to hide in his older sister Sally's closet and watch her undress. Instead, he leaps out and scares her. He and his mother talk, Norman blaming his current antics on the pressure to play football. His mother sympathizes, explaining that his father simply wants to relive his happiest times through Norman. Norman helps Carrie find her way around on the first day of school, braving his friends' teasing to sit with her at lunchtime. He goes to his first football practice with much anxiety, and during it he throws up. On his way home in disgrace he meets Mr. Koski, who invites him for tea and tells him that being a man does not depend on size or aggressiveness. During the first football game, Norman makes a touchdown—for the other side. Then P.W. reports that his neighbors have installed a hot tub and use it nude. The two plan to peek from a tree in P.W.'s yard. One day Mr. Koski takes Carrie and Norman to the zoo. When they see a monkey "fooling around with himself in front of all the people and all the other monkeys and everything," Mr. Koski points out that the monkey is not ashamed or unhappy with himself. Norman's father tries with growing desperation to turn his son into a football player. Finally, Norman tells his father he is not cut out for football and is quitting the team. He recommends, though, that his father continue coaching, since it gives him so much pleasure. When Norman tells Mr. Koski he's quit the team, Mr. Koski rewards him with a medal. Whenever he finds an outstanding example of everyday human courage, he bestows a medal; this is the second one he's ever given. Norman takes Carrie out and enjoys their time together: "It sure had been a good day for me, Norman Schnurman, son of Mad Dog."

With the help of his sympathetic mother and understanding friend, Norman arrives at a better understanding of who he is and is not when he's pressured to play football against his own inclinations. Torn between wanting to please his father and needing to be himself, Norman finally finds the courage to make the right choice. Along the way, this funny first-person narrative includes the language and preoccupations of sixth-grade boys, giving it great appeal for the intended audience. But it is also a warm, perceptive story of family relationships and growing up.

Ages 10-12

Also available in:
No other form known

450

Oneal, Zibby

A Formal Feeling

Viking Penguin, 1982.
(162 pages)

DEATH: of Mother
MOURNING, STAGES OF
Emotions: accepting
Emotions: identifying
Family: relationships
Guilt, feelings of
Parent/Parents: remarriage of

When sixteen-year-old Anne Cameron returns home from boarding school for Christmas vacation, she has to face an upsetting reality: her mother has been dead for a year and now her father has remarried. She can't understand how her father could have remarried so soon. When her older brother, Spencer, tells her she'll like having Dory around, Anne considers him disloyal. To forget her grief, Anne has taken up running; sometimes even hours later she still feels pleasantly isolated in a crystal shell. As she talks to her father, Dory, and Spencer, she feels detached, as though they are all characters in a play. Even when Eric calls she feels remote, although they'd dated the previous summer. She remembers how she listened to her father read Dante all that summer, how she and Eric dated and kissed, how the heaviness that had been with her since her mother's death began to lift. But since August, since Dory's arrival on the scene, the bleakness has set in again. Spencer believes that getting on with their lives doesn't mean they are forgetting their mother, but to Anne it seems they're all doing just that. She feels obligated to remember her, although Spencer questions, but doesn't correct, Anne's "memory of perfection." Anne envies her best friend Laura's spontaneous warmth and understanding. When a puppy dies and Laura's mother feels bad, Laura hugs and comforts her, something Anne would have hung back from doing. Seeing the blue sweater her mother knit for her the summer before she died reminds Anne that her mother always provided her with blue clothes because blue was her mother's favorite color. Anne suddenly realizes she hates blue. She begins to remember something about a train trip. When she questions Spencer and he adds to her recollections, she remembers the time when Mother went away to live by herself because she needed time to think. Anne had screamed at her shortly before she left. While living with her grandmother during her mother's absence, Anne had decided that if you lose control, people won't love you anymore. So when her mother did return home, Anne ignored the whole incident and immediately buried the memory. Then Anne sprains her ankle ice skating. When she asks the doctor's permission to go caroling on Christmas Eve, he doesn't think it's a good idea. Anne protests, but he tells her, "Some things you have no control over." His words strike a chord in Anne. She refuses pain medication because, she tells Dory, she wants to feel the pain and be sensitive to her own healing. Now Anne begins to realize that she's always felt responsible for her mother's death. Painful as it is, she must ask herself: Did she actually love her mother? She remembers anger, repressed feelings, and constant efforts to please, but she also recalls their good times. In sum, "they had loved each other in their imperfect ways." Anne finally knows her mother is dead and can say goodbye to her at last.

A teenage girl who has for years denied her feelings about her mother must confront them in order to live and feel again after her mother's death. In the beginning Anne takes a protective, belligerent attitude toward her mother's memory; she was perfect. Anne finally realizes that this willful blindness hides guilt and resentment that must be acknowledged if she is to recover from her grief. This beautifully written, gently suspenseful novel offers little action, but its complex examination of a difficult emotional problem invites and should gain the reader's empathy.

Ages 12 and up

Also available in:
Paperbound—*A Formal Feeling*
Puffin Books

451

Oppenheimer, Joan Letson

Gardine vs. Hanover

HarperCollins Publishers, Inc., 1982.
(152 pages) o.p.

PARENT/PARENTS: Remarriage of
STEPBROTHER/STEPSISTER
Arguing
Differences, human
Family: relationships
Rejection: parental

When Frances Gardine marries Berkley Hanover, their children have varied reactions. Young Abby Gardine and Drew Hanover are pleased, but Jill Gardine, fifteen, hates the whole idea and especially dislikes her new stepsister, Caroline Hanover, sixteen. Jill hadn't been overly happy about her mother remarrying, but she was particularly distressed to learn Berk's two children would live with them. For her part, Caroline has new reason to resent her mother, a famous cancer specialist who claims not to have a maternal bone in her body. It was her mother's idea that she and her brother be sent from New York City to California to live with their father. Then Caroline meets Jason Emery and falls in love for the first time. When she overhears sharp-tongued Jill making fun of her first encounter with Jason, Caroline responds in kind. By the time their parents return from their honeymoon, the battle lines are drawn. Jill's boyfriend, Gary, feels Jill is needlessly hard on Caroline, just as she is on him. Frances and Berk call a family conference to discuss the incessant arguing between Jill and Caroline. Jill becomes very emotional and says she can't live with Caroline. In response, Caroline leaves the room, accusing Jill of being melodramatic. The tension spreads. When Jill and Abby return from a visit with their father, they find strained relations between Frances and Berk and between Frances and Caroline. Even Abby and Drew have their first falling-out. That night, Frances and Berk announce their separation. Drew blames Caroline for the breakup and spends every free minute with Abby at the Gardine house. Meanwhile, Caroline makes her first real friend, Michelle, and learns from her that she intimidates people with her beauty, intelligence, and sophistication. Michelle herself had simply decided to act on her suspicion that Caroline was basically shy and insecure. Then Caroline has a talk with her biology teacher, a career woman like Caroline's mother. The girl begins to see that her mother is simply a limited person, that she doesn't really dislike her daughter. Caroline, who had considered and rejected the idea of becoming a doctor because of her mother's attitude, now realizes she could become one without turning into her mother. Human relationships are important to her; they are not to her mother. Jill's mother is suffering a great deal from the breakup, losing weight and sleep. Jill wants to help mend fences but when Gary says that will mean talking to Caroline, she balks. Then Frances falls seriously ill with the flu and Jill nurses her. When Jill also becomes very sick, Abby, in desperation, calls Caroline. For several days Caroline takes care of them both, and she and Jill have several talks. They agree that they want the families to reunite. When Jill becomes insulting Caroline quietly leaves the room, proud that she hasn't indulged in her usual knee-jerk reaction to Jill's sharp tongue. They talk again, though, and each admits to a secret admiration of the other. Caroline confesses that her mother's rejection has always made her feel like a loser. They decide to call another family conference, confident that this time they can all live together in harmony.

The antagonism between two teenage stepsisters breaks up their new family, but it is the girls' decision to work at resolving the conflict that eventually reunites it. In the process, both Caroline and Jill learn quite a bit about themselves, allowing them greater understanding of the roots of their difficulty. This well-written book, with strong, believable characters and a suspenseful story line, alternates viewpoints between Caroline and Jill so that readers can appreciate both sides of the conflict. There is insight here into the little, everyday habits and routines that can cause friction and must be considered in such a family merger.

Ages 11-14

Also available in:
No other form known

452

Oppenheimer, Joan Letson

Working On It

Dell Publishing Company, Inc., 1986.
(136 pages) o.p.

INFERIORITY, FEELINGS OF
SHYNESS
Boy-girl relationships
Friendship: best friend
School: classmate relationships
School: pupil-teacher relationships
Self, attitude toward: accepting

Tracy Ayres is convinced "fifteen is the pits" as she joins teacher Eden Lindsay's drama class. She has been talked into taking the class by family members and by Carla, her best friend—they've heard wonderful things about the class and think it will help improve Tracy's sense of herself. But the painfully shy Tracy dreads it. Suffering from a "rotten self-image," a "superwoman" mother, and a bright, popular older brother, Tracy is dismayed when her appointed class partner for improvisations is the popular, good-looking Wylie Babcock. Each student must keep a personal "Character Notebook" about an emotion frequently felt: Tracy writes about shyness and Wylie writes about "like" because he really has no one to love. At the end of six weeks, each improvisation team is to do a presentation illustrating the feelings in their notebooks. Tracy is at first resentful at being chided for her shyness, goaded to express her real feelings, and analyzed mercilessly by Wylie as they work together. But slowly the girl's "work in progress" becomes a process of building her confidence and self-acceptance. She is almost paralyzed with fright before each class presentation but gradually comes to relax and act freely, the class forgotten. She begins to see how adept both Wylie and her mother are at manipulating responses from her; she works out her frustrations by describing her feelings in the class log, able to recognize changes in herself as the class progresses. As Tracy blossoms, she and Wylie are drawn together. There is one casualty of Tracy's maturation, however: Carla is resentful and hurt when Tracy stops sharing every thought with her and their friendship ends. By the end of "miracle worker" Miss Lindsay's class, many students have grown in self-acceptance and tolerance for others. Tracy especially benefits from her teacher's advice: "Stop and think when you put yourself down. Become aware of what you are doing to yourself."

A painfully shy teenage girl blossoms under the guidance of a wise teacher and the discipline of improvisational acting. In the process, Tracy learns how much people can help one another to gain self-knowledge. Plot development is logical and although the ending is rather tidy, it does not appear contrived. Characterizations lack some depth, but relationships are realistic and the dialogue natural. Readers will easily identify with Tracy and her classmates and will be left hopeful that their growth will continue beyond the class.

Ages 11-13

Also available in:
No other form known

453

Park, Barbara

Don't Make Me Smile

Alfred A. Knopf, Inc., 1981.
(114 pages)

DIVORCE: of Parents
Anger
Change: resisting
Communication: parent-child
Lifestyle: change in

Charlie Hickle, almost eleven, has had his life turned upside down by the breakup of his parents' marriage. He is angry with both of them and deeply frustrated about his own helplessness: "Divorce is like watching your mother back the car over your brand new bicycle. You know what's about to happen, but there's nothing you can do about it." He's sure he'll never smile again and suspects he might even lose his mind. Life becomes more and more chaotic as Charlie refuses to go to school, tries running away from home to live in a tree, and rejects all his father's overtures during their Saturday visits. Worried about his son, Charlie's father takes the boy to a child psychologist, Dr. Girard, whom Charlie at first resents. But when he learns that Dr. Girard's parents divorced when he was a boy and he didn't let it ruin his life, Charlie decides the doctor might just understand how he, Charlie, feels. Dr. Girard suggests that Charlie share his feelings with his parents. His first attempts are clumsy: during an Easter visit from his mother's cousin, he manages to hurt both her feelings and his mother's. For his eleventh birthday, Charlie wants to have things normal again and convinces his parents to go on a family picnic. But the afternoon ends with the mother and father quarreling bitterly and Charlie, in desperation, calls Dr. Girard and asks what he should do. Advised again to make his feelings known, Charlie returns to his parents and politely asks his father to leave. This his father does, without anger. Over the next two months, Charlie continues to meet with Dr. Girard. The psychologist helps the boy grapple with sinking grades, disruptive school behavior, and the conviction that he will never be truly happy again. At the story's end, Charlie has begun to believe he will survive the divorce. He even catches himself smiling now and then.

P

A boy troubled and alienated by his parents' divorce is helped to cope by a skillful, sympathetic psychologist. Charlie's sometimes-humorous narration lends his story credibility and saves it from sentimentality. His painful struggle to adjust to the breakup of his family moves believably to his realization that, while the sadness is not completely gone, he is learning to live with his new situation.

Ages 8-11

Also available in:
Paperbound—*Don't Make Me Smile*
Alfred A. Knopf, Inc.

454

Pascal, Francine

My First Love & Other Disasters

Viking Penguin, 1979.
(186 pages)

BABY-SITTING
BOY-GIRL RELATIONSHIPS
Decision making
Dependence/Independence
Maturation
Responsibility: accepting
Values/Valuing: moral/ethical

Victoria, nearly fifteen, has spent her whole freshman year madly in love with seventeen-year-old Jim, who doesn't even know she's alive. Worse yet, he has a clingy girlfriend named Gloria. Determined to win him over, Victoria convinces her parents to let her work as a mother's helper on Fire Island, where Jim will be spending the summer without Gloria. After much pleading and arguing, her parents consent. Their main stipulation is that Victoria must tell Cynthia, the divorced woman she will be working for, that she cannot stay alone overnight with Cynthia's two children. During her first day on the island, Victoria is kept busy helping unload and unpack. When she finally gets down to the pier with the children, she runs into another boy from school, Barry, who she has heard likes her. He is waiting for Jim, soon to arrive on the ferry, so Victoria waits with him, anxious to see her true love. The first meeting goes badly. Jim thinks she is Barry's girl, which Victoria flatly denies. Then later, Barry surprises her by confessing his love for her. Nervous, she laughs, and her later apologies cannot undo the hurt he suffers. Back at the house, Victoria must tend to the children until their bedtime. Coming downstairs from her small, hot, third-floor bedroom, hoping to slip away for a while, she is intercepted by Cynthia, who tells her not to let the children talk to their paternal grandfather if he should call—at least not until his son, her ex-husband, starts paying some of their bills. Uneasy about this situation, Victoria hopes the grandfather will not call. The next day, Victoria stops at the restaurant where Jim works. She surprises herself by telling him she'll be at the local disco on her night off, a place Cynthia has asked her to avoid. He responds rather noncommittally. The next day, Victoria meets several other mother's helpers and soon realizes that she is doing much more and being paid less than any of the others. Still, she feels Cynthia needs and appreciates her. Besides, she leaves Victoria such cute, clever instructions. Later, Jim actually invites Victoria to meet him at the disco that night, but Cynthia has plans for the evening and tells Victoria to stay home with the children. Around midnight, Victoria discovers Cynthia home asleep and, hoping to salvage her long-awaited date, sneaks out. After a few dances, Jim takes her out to the pier where she agrees to the heaviest petting she has ever allowed. She returns home to find that she's locked out and must wake up a furious Cynthia. Soon after, the children's grandfather does call and Victoria allows them to talk to him, swearing them to secrecy. Several days later, at the disco, she refuses Jim's invitation to go outside and he walks off, ignoring her pleading apology. The next morning, after Cynthia leaves for a day in the city, the grandfather arrives and wants to take the children out fishing. Victoria agrees, certain they'll be back before Cynthia returns. Then Cynthia calls and says she'll be gone for the night also, if that will be all right with Victoria. Again she agrees, certain her parents will never find out. Everything catches up with her when Cynthia unexpectedly returns after learning from Victoria's mother, whom she happened to see and talk to, that Victoria is forbidden to stay alone. Searching for the grandfather and children, Cynthia and Victoria discover that their boat is the only one still out on the bay, now filled with whitecaps. Barry takes Victoria and Jim out in his boat to search for them. It is difficult going and Jim wants to turn back, but Victoria begs Barry to keep looking despite the danger and he willingly obliges. They finally spot the lost boat, and it is Victoria and Barry who risk their lives to rescue the children and the old man. Back on shore, all is soon forgiven as Cynthia learns of their bravery and reconciles with the grandfather. The next morning, when Jim delivers one of his customary take-it-or-leave-it ultimatums, Victoria realizes how spoiled he is. She leaves it. The next time she finds one of Cynthia's clever notes listing extra work for her, she writes a clever note of her own, playfully asking for many outrageous favors in return. And then she calls the person she wants to see—Barry.

In this entertaining first-person story, an engaging, realistic girl finds being in love and on her own more complicated than she had ever imagined. Victoria compromises herself time and again, making ill-considered decisions she soon regrets. In the end, when everything catches up with her, she is relieved, mature enough now to recognize the shallowness of her "love," to assert herself with her employer, to seek out the boy she genuinely likes, and to realize she still values the security of parental supervision. Victoria is an appealing heroine, her story enriched by authentic-sounding dialogue.

Ages 12 and up

Also available in:
Cassette—*My First Love & Other Disasters*
Library of Congress (NLSBPH)

Paperbound—*My First Love & Other Disasters*
Puffin Books

455

Paterson, Katherine Womeldorf

Bridge to Terabithia

Black/white illustrations by Donna Diamond.
HarperCollins Publishers, Inc., 1977.
(128 pages)

DEATH: of Friend
FRIENDSHIP: Best Friend
Imagination
Ostracism
Prejudice: social class
Sibling: relationships

Fifth grader Jesse Aarons, a quiet, introspective farm boy in a rural community, plans on being the fastest runner in his school, but on the first day of the new term, he is bested by a girl—his new neighbor and classmate, Leslie Burke. Shunned by the class because she wears jeans to school and sports a short haircut, Leslie tries to make friends with Jesse, but he avoids her at first. Soon, though, they are riding home on the bus together, Leslie confiding that she and her parents moved to the country to escape the pressures of city living. Several days later while they are playing, Leslie suggests they stake out a secret place in the woods behind her house. Leslie names their magical kingdom Terabithia. They must enter it by swinging on an old rope swing across a dry creek bed and into the woods. They build a castle in Terabithia from old boards; Leslie teaches Jesse how to speak and act like a ruler, and tells him stories from the many books she has read. The two become close friends. Jesse helps Leslie and her father fix up their old farm house; Jesse persuades Leslie to put aside her own sense of isolation to befriend an unhappy, belligerent seventh-grade girl; and Leslie, whose parents do not attend church, goes with Jesse and his family to church on Easter Sunday. During Easter vacation it rains heavily, and the creek bed bordering Terabithia becomes a deep, fast waterway. Leslie swings fearlessly across, but Jesse follows cautiously. In the following days the rain continues and Jesse's fear mounts with each crossing, until he privately decides they should give up their kingdom for a time. Then his music teacher invites him to spend the day with her in Washington, D.C., touring the National Gallery. Jesse returns home full of news after a wonderful day and is told that Leslie is dead. The rope has broken over the stream and she has drowned. Dazed, angry, grieving, and feeling somehow responsible, Jesse withdraws for several days. One morning he returns to Terabithia. Crossing the creek on a fallen branch, he makes a funeral wreath for his departed queen and places it in their sacred grove. He hears his younger sister, May Belle, crying for help, and rescues her from the branch on which she has tried to follow him. A few days later he leads her into Terabithia across a bridge he has built and crowns her its new queen.

A friendship flourishes between a country boy and a girl from the city as each opens new experiences to the other. Leslie introduces Jesse to the world of imagination and books, and Jesse teaches Leslie compassion and regard for other people. As the only boy in his family, Jesse has learned to live with others by avoiding conflicts; Leslie inspires him to assert himself. The girl's death is as much of a shock to the reader as it is to Jesse. His recovery, while fairly abrupt, shows the legacy of strength and resourcefulness Leslie has left him. This beautifully written, moving story won the 1978 Newbery Award.

Ages 9-12

Also available in:
Braille—*Bridge to Terabithia*
Library of Congress (NLSBPH)

Cassette—*Bridge to Terabithia*
Library of Congress (NLSBPH)

Paperbound—*Bridge to Terabithia*
HarperCollins Publishers, Inc.

456

Paterson, Katherine Womeldorf

The Great Gilly Hopkins

HarperCollins Publishers, Inc., 1978.
(148 pages)

FOSTER HOME
Deprivation, emotional
Hostility
Love, meaning of

At eleven, Gilly Hopkins scarcely remembers her mother, who left her eight years earlier. But she is obsessed to rejoin a lovely, gracious mother she imagines. Now at her third foster home in less than three years, the ramshackle house of Maime Trotter (called simply "Trotter"), Gilly confidently sets out to establish supremacy over her latest foster parent, over seven-year-old William Ernest (another foster child), and over Mr. Randolph, an aged, blind man who lives next door. She thinks herself too tough and too clever for them. But Trotter effortlessly handles her worst sallies as though her great bulk absorbed them. Gilly then replies to an almost impersonal postcard from her mother that she must be rescued from mistreatment. Aware of her mother's long inattention, however, she steals money from Mr. Randolph and Trotter and buys a transcontinental bus ticket for San Francisco, where her mother lives. The police, alerted by a clerk, stop her. Trotter refuses to press charges for theft but lays down her own law—return the money and help William Ernest with his schoolwork. Gradually Gilly realizes Trotter's goodness to her, to the boy, to Mr. Randolph, and comes to love her foster family. Then out of the blue arrives the girl's unknown maternal grandmother, encouraged by her estranged daughter to take Gilly home to Virginia. Once there, Gilly has a visit from her mother, and a final disillusionment—her mother will not take her back. Heartbroken, the girl begs Trotter on the phone to let her return. But they lovingly agree that it is her grandmother who both loves and needs her, who will otherwise be all alone.

Each time Gilly has offered love, she has seen the other person withdraw. Better to square off against the world reserving "soft and stupid" feelings for an unknown mother far away. Yet Gilly's separations from those she does come to love do not break her. Recognizing that "life has no happy endings," as Trotter points out, she begins again, without fantasies. The theme of this book is serious; the telling and the characters are richly humorous. Gilly uses mild profanity for pungency—and to annoy people.

Ages 10-13

Also available in:
Cassette—*The Great Gilly Hopkins*
Library of Congress (NLSBPH)

Paperbound—*The Great Gilly Hopkins*
HarperCollins Publishers, Inc.

457

Paterson, Katherine Womeldorf

Jacob Have I Loved

HarperCollins Publishers, Inc., 1980.
(216 pages)

TWINS: Fraternal
Age: aging
Grandparent: living in child's home
Jealousy: sibling
Maturation
Self, attitude toward: feeling different

Louise Bradshaw, thirteen, strong and healthy, resents the attention given her frail, musically talented twin, Caroline, by their parents and other inhabitants of Rass Island in Chesapeake Bay. The tiny island, at this time (the late 1930s) populated almost entirely by fishermen, offers Louise few escapes from Caroline and their acid-tongued, Bible-quoting grandmother who lives with the family. Pointedly, the grandmother recites the verse ending "Jacob have I loved, but Esau have I hated." Louise is certain she is Esau. "Progging for crab" with Call Purnell, her only friend, provides Louise with an outlet and a way to contribute to the family's income. When Louise is about fifteen, Captain Wallace returns to the island after a fifty-year absence. The legendary captain had left as a young man, after his behavior during a severe storm resulted in the islanders calling him a coward. Louise and Call quickly befriend the man, but Louise is bitterly jealous when Caroline does so also. Following a hurricane, the Captain briefly moves in with the Bradshaws, causing Louise to feel keenly her need for affection and her embarrassed attraction to the old man. Noticing Louise's emotional turmoil, the insensitive grandmother increases her verbal attacks. Then the Captain uses his inheritance to send Caroline to a Baltimore boarding school to study music. Betrayed, tormented by her grandmother, Louise quits school and joins her father on his fishing boat. Her mother, a former teacher, tutors her at home. Call is drafted early in World War II; when he is discharged, Louise learns to her sorrow that he and Caroline plan to marry. After passing her high school exams, Louise decides to build a life for herself away from Rass Island. Her mother accepts her decision, but tells Louise that they will miss her even more than they miss Caroline. Convinced now of her parents' love, Louise is able to leave the island "and begin to build myself as a soul, separate from the long, long shadow of my twin." The years pass. Louise becomes a nurse-midwife in rural Appalachia, marries, and has a child. Her story comes full circle when she delivers the twins of one of her mountain patients. The first twin is vigorous, the second frail. Secure now about herself and her own family, Louise can advise the mother and grandmother about the special needs of both infants.

Set in the late 1930s and early 1940s, this beautifully written first-person account, told by Louise in retrospect, presents some of the timeless dilemmas of growing up. With its realistic, fully developed characters and its depiction of the slow, painful ways human relationships mature, the story is touching without being sentimental.

Ages 12 and up

Also available in:
Braille—*Jacob Have I Loved*
Library of Congress (NLSBPH)

Cassette—*Jacob Have I Loved*
Library of Congress (NLSBPH)

Paperbound—*Jacob Have I Loved*
HarperCollins Publishers, Inc.

458

Paulsen, Gary

The Foxman

Viking Penguin, 1990.
(125 pages)

MATURATION
Death: of friend
Friendship: meaning of
Nature: respect for
Relatives: living in home of

Abused by alcoholic parents, an unnamed fifteen-year-old boy is remanded to the custody of his Uncle Harvey and family, who live in the Minnesota north woods. As the summer and fall pass, the boy almost feels like a member of the family, especially with his teenage cousin, Harry. Often at night they all sit around the wood-burning stove, listening to the war stories of Harvey's father and uncle. The old men find humor in every tale, but the boy sees nothing funny in discomfort and death. One day, while tracking deep into the woods on a weekend hunting trip, the young cousins seek shelter from an approaching snowstorm and come upon an isolated cabin inhabited by a man with a frighteningly deformed face. Wearing a mask to put the boys more at ease, the Foxman, as they come to think of him, shelters the two until the storm passes. Returning home, they tell no one of the recluse—sensing that he does not want to be found. Alone, the protagonist makes a return visit to the Foxman, and senses the pleasure this second visit brings. The boy and the man speak of science and how it "kills beauty," of war and how it destroys life. When the boy expresses his distaste for the war stories he has heard, the Foxman, his own face a casualty of battle, excuses the old men for "trying to find some use in all that waste." The boy returns again and again, learning how to hunt foxes and partaking of long and searching discussions. Then, on one such visit, the boy becomes snow-blind and hopelessly lost—and the Foxman rescues him from certain death. As a result, the Foxman falls mortally ill. To seal his anonymity, even in death, he instructs the boy that when he is dead the boy is to burn the cabin, his body, and all his belongings except some valuable hides and books, which the boy is to keep. The boy complies, but in the end saves only one fox pelt, to remind him of his friend.

In this haunting first-person narrative, a teenage boy experiences with an adult an abiding friendship precious to both, a bond forged in free-ranging conversation, in which the boy learns to trust his own mind.

Ages 11-14

Also available in:
Paperbound—*The Foxman*
Puffin Books

459

Payne, Sherry Neuwirth

A Contest

Color illustrations by Jeff Kyle.
Carolrhoda Books, Inc., 1982.
(37 pages counted)

DIFFERENCES, HUMAN
SELF, ATTITUDE TOWARD: Feeling Different
WHEELCHAIR, DEPENDENCE ON
Cerebral palsy
School: classmate relationships
School: mainstreaming

In fifth grade Mike, confined to a wheelchair because of hemiplegic cerebral palsy, which "means his legs don't work," changes from a special school to a public one. He finds his new school very difficult. He needs help in the cafeteria and in entering the bathroom but is afraid to ask for it. After the first day he tells his father about a kid who took his hat and called him a "spaz." His father says, "It's not easy. . . . But you have to live with all kinds of people. And a good place to start learning about them is in school." The youth center next door to the school is accessible to wheelchairs, and when Mike goes there he finds many of the kids in his class playing pool. He often plays pool at home with his father by leaning against their pool table and would like to play with the kids, but they seem afraid of him. So he just watches. Mike can easily keep up with his classwork, but the loneliness is harder. Then his teacher, noticing his sadness, decides they need to show his classmates the ways he is not so different. The next day she announces an arm wrestling contest. Randy, the strongest boy in the class, beats everyone until Mike is the only one left. Afraid to hurt him, Randy lets Mike win. Then they play again and Mike wins for real. To avoid alienating Randy, he tells him that he has an advantage because pushing his wheelchair has strengthened his arms. Later, Randy is surprised to learn that Mike swam nearly every day at his old school. At lunch the next day, one of the girls from Mike's class sits by him. After lunch there is another classroom contest, this time checkers, and Mike beats Randy again. Randy, friendly and interested, wants to know what else Mike can do. Mike tells him about pool. Randy wonders why he never said anything before. "Because I was afraid no one would want to play with me. Besides, who would stand next to me?" asks Mike, who needs someone there in case he loses his balance. "I will," Randy replies. When they enter the game room that afternoon, some kids make fun of Mike and say he cannot play. Randy only grins and says, "Try him." Mike's second year at his new school is much easier. He has people he can ask for help, and even though some still stare, many have discovered he is not so different from them.

A wheelchair can isolate a person emotionally as well as physically. In this smoothly written story, a sensitive teacher recognizes that the key to understanding and acceptance of her new disabled student is to make his wheelchair "disappear" by structuring contests in which Mike can demonstrate his strengths. Stereotypes are forgotten as Mike and his classmates discover their common interests and forget about the wheelchair. The difficult transition of the main character, portrayed as an average boy who likes sports and competition, from a special to a mainstreamed school and the positive change in his self-concept will be helpful reading for similarly afflicted children, their teachers, parents, and new classmates. Expressive illustrations aptly capture Mike's feelings.

Ages 8-10

Also available in:
No other form known

460

Peck, Richard

Are You in the House Alone?

Viking Penguin, Inc., 1976.
(156 pages)

RAPE
Boy-girl relationships: dating
Fear: of physical harm
Sex: premarital

Gail Osburne, seventeen, lives comfortably with her parents in Oldfield, Connecticut, a gracious town, some of whose families have lived there since early colonial times. Gail's best friend, Alison, dates Phil Lawver, son of one of the most distinguished families. Gail dates Steve Pastorini, also from an old family, but less eminent for Mr. Pastorini's being a plumber. On some of their dates, Gail and Steve have met secretly at the Pastorini lake cottage for sex. Gail takes birth-control pills. One day she finds an obscenely threatening note on her school locker. Shaken, Gail tells Alison, who dismisses it as a prank. But Gail is soon getting nasty phone calls at home and at the house where she regularly baby-sits. When a second note is left on her locker, she is frightened enough to tell the school counselor, who offers little help or comfort. More and more terrified and wary of men, Gail is nevertheless ashamed to tell anyone else about the notes, which mention her secret meetings with Steve. Finally determined to tell her father, she goes to his New York office, only to find that he has been fired, and her parents have not told her. Clearly, she cannot confide this new worry to him. Yet while doing her usual Saturday-night baby-sitting for Mrs. Montgomery, she gets another threatening call, this time an eerie voice intoning, "Are you in the house alone?" Desperate, she leaves a message at Steve's house for him to come over, and when the doorbell rings, rushes to open the door. Instead of Steve, she finds Phil Lawver, saying he is looking for Alison, wanting to use the phone. "Are you in the house alone," he asks, once inside. He assaults her, and she resists; he knocks her unconscious. She awakens in the hospital with a concussion. She has been beaten and raped. Later, under questioning, Gail is told by the police chief that she deserved what she got, and that accusing Phil Lawver is asking for trouble. Worse, her lawyer explains all too clearly what will happen in the courtroom should she decide to prosecute. Concluding that violation of another kind lies ahead if she presses charges, she finally decides not to. Phil remains at large, and, in time, rapes and nearly kills another girl. He is not convicted—but is sent away by his parents for psychiatric treatment.

This honest, harrowing story is told by Gail herself, with sharp characterizations and impressive detail down to the medical examination following the rape. The victim, the victim's family, the social and legal ramifications of the crime, and police and judicial procedures apt and otherwise are all scrutinized candidly but without sensationalism. Much is to be found here for thoughtful discussion.

Ages 12 and up

Also available in:
Cassette—*Are You in the House Alone?*
Library of Congress (NLSBPH)

Paperbound—*Are You in the House Alone?*
Dell Publishing Company, Inc.

461

Peck, Richard

Close Enough to Touch

Dell Publishing Company, Inc. (Laurel Leaf Library), 1981. (133 pages, paperbound)

DEATH: of Friend
MOURNING, STAGES OF
Boy-girl relationships: dating
Loss: feelings of
Love, meaning of

During the Fourth of July fireworks, sixteen-year-old Matt Moran gets up his courage and tells Dory Gunderson he loves her. She wants to know what took him so long; she loves him too. The following March, Dory dies suddenly and unexpectedly of a ruptured aneurysm. Matt is one of six pallbearers. After the funeral, he stops by the Gundersons' home at Mrs. Gunderson's invitation. Wealthy and snobbish, she tells Matt things would never have worked out between him and Dory anyway, and that he'll soon forget her. His father and stepmother attempt to comfort him, but Matt refuses to eat that day. The next day he goes to school, but "by lunch I'm only about 10 percent there." A locker-room acquaintance, Joe Hoenig, tries to comfort him and tells him he should cry. Matt decides that a "simple solution" to his pain would be to get roaring drunk. He does so. Police pick him up and call his father, who continues to be sympathetic. "Something had to happen. You wouldn't grieve." Matt says he was grieving but his father insists, "You didn't grieve. You just got quiet. That's the way I was when your mom died." Matt's next solution is to drop out of school. Over spring break, he announces that he's going up to the family's lake cottage for a few days. He doesn't intend to return. When he's jogging the first day, however, he finds an injured girl lying in a ditch. A horse with a sidesaddle stands nearby. Matt takes the girl to the local emergency room, where her dislocated shoulder is bandaged, and then drives her home. He learns her name is Margaret and she's a senior at his school. Matt returns to school and seeks out the Hopkins poem that Margaret says she was named after. When he suggests they get together to talk about it she refuses, saying they would just be talking about Dory, since the poem concerns death. Matt doesn't see Margaret again for several days, but he's not looking too hard. "I'm making a pretty good adjustment to being miserable. I may be able to make a lifetime career out of it." He does drive past Margaret's house and around the block several times until her father comes outside and signals him into the driveway. Margaret explains why she doesn't want to talk about Dory: "She meant too much to you. She can't mean enough to me." Some friends of Dory's tell Matt that instead of going to the junior dance, they plan to spend the evening together in memory of Dory. Matt has just asked Margaret to the junior dance, but she's refused because it's the same night as the senior prom, which she's attending with Joe Hoenig. So Matt decides to join the memorial. He now suspects he loves Margaret, but feels guilty since he once told Dory he would love her forever. The memorial evening is uncomfortable and Matt leaves early. He goes to the country club where the senior prom is being held and finds Margaret and Joe. He explains to Joe that he's crazy about a senior girl and plans to abduct her. Joe thinks it's a great idea until he finds out the girl is Margaret. However, Joe is interested in another girl anyway and agrees to leave the prom with Margaret and go with Matt to the lake cottage. Once there, Joe goes straight to sleep. Matt and Margaret walk down to the beach to watch the sunrise.

A teenage boy whose girlfriend has died tries to cope with his grief and make a new beginning. Written in the first person, this beautifully crafted story is moving, witty, and grounded in reality. Matt has trouble identifying his own feelings and conveying what he feels to others. Defending himself from the pain of losing Dory, he shuts off his emotions for periods of time. But he makes progress in self-knowledge and in reaching out to others, leaving readers hopeful for him at the end. Several stereotypical and undeveloped characters don't detract from the impact of the story.

Ages 12 and up

Also available in:
Cassette—*Close Enough to Touch*
Library of Congress (NLSBPH)

462

Peck, Richard

Father Figure: A Novel

Dell Publishing Company, Inc. (Laurel Leaf Library), 1988.
(192 pages, paperbound)

COMMUNICATION: Parent-child
Death: of mother
Gender role identity: male
Maturation
Parental: absence
Responsibility: accepting
Sibling: older
Suicide: of parent

Jim's mother, terminally ill and in increasing pain, has committed suicide by carbon monoxide poisoning. At seventeen, Jim must somehow surmount this second blow, the first having been his father's abrupt departure eight years earlier, never quite explained, never quite forgiven. Since that time, Jim has assumed the role of father to his brother, Byron, now eight; they live with their grandmother. As Jim struggles with his own feelings about his mother's death, he is also concerned about his brother. The night before the funeral, Byron comes to him, embarrassed and frightened at his sudden regression to bed-wetting. Jim talks reassuringly, helps him change the bed, and invites Byron to sleep with him. At the funeral Jim notices a tanned stranger, whom Grandmother acknowledges as their father. Later Jim introduces himself, aware first of his father's curious lack of excuses for his "eight-year coffee break." Jim also physically positions himself between his brother and father to prevent their talking. The following day, Dad is gone again and routine is restored until Byron is hurt by a street gang while walking home from school. Jim's self-reproach at not having somehow prevented the incident and his pain at seeing Byron injured bring him to the point of tears for the first time since his mother's death, but he explodes in anger instead during a confrontation with Byron's principal. The episode is witnessed and reported to Grandmother who, unwilling to assume parental responsibility for the boys, calls upon their father to take them for the summer. In Florida, Jim and his father manage to sidestep a showdown until Jim awakens one night to find his father caring for the still healing Byron, and he explodes in anger. Seeing no tolerable summer but in coexistence, Jim and his father agree on ground rules for future conversations. The agreement avoids conflict, but it also prevents Jim from asking the lingering questions about the past. Suffering tension with his father that polite conversation cannot resolve, and angered by the growing rapport between his father and Byron, Jim verbally strikes out at a woman who has been a good friend to them all. Ashamed, he seeks out his father for the discussion so long overdue. His father's honest explanation of why he left eases them into a more trusting relationship, although that is soon tested by Byron's wanting to stay in Florida with his father. Jim decides to allow Byron some responsibility for his own life and to allow their father to be a father to Byron. He goes back to New York, to school, to his grandmother's house. For the first time, he can tend his own needs, grieve for his mother, and begin to form relationships with people his own age.

In the eight years since his father's departure, Jim has been a father figure to his little brother, Byron, trying tirelessly to provide Byron a security he himself never knew. Jim's attempt to protect Byron is shattered by his inability to prevent their mother's death, and Byron's misfortune further questions the idea that Jim, or anyone, can successfully shield another person from all pain. During the summer with their father, Jim learns to accept the people around him as they are, and in so doing, is free to accept himself as well. His father was not a "family man," yet he cares for his sons; Byron is not simply his little brother but a person with distinct opinions and needs, and one who has now developed his own unique relationship with his father. In deciding to allow Byron to stay with his father, Jim also chooses to renounce both the security and the confinement of his own role as a substitute parent, and begins assuming greater responsibility for his own life.

Ages 11 and up

Also available in:
Cassette—*Father Figure: A Novel*
Library of Congress (NLSBPH)

463

Peck, Robert Newton

A Day No Pigs Would Die

Alfred A. Knopf, Inc., 1972.
(150 pages)

MATURATION
Communication: parent-child
Death: of father
Death: of pet
Pets: love for

Robert Peck, a thirteen-year-old Vermont farm boy, has been raised in the "Shaker Way." When Robert sees Apron, Mr. Tanner's prize cow, giving birth, he helps her and is badly mauled by the cow. Mr. Tanner shows his gratitude for Robert's aid by giving the boy a small pig. Robert raises the pig as a pet and shows her at the county fair. During this time Robert's father, Haven Peck, teaches him how to run the family farm; Mr. Peck is ill and knows he has not long to live. When fall comes and the pig has not had her first heat, Robert recognizes that the family cannot afford to keep a pig incapable of producing a litter. Mr. Peck, a hog butcher by trade, and Robert kill the pig. When Robert understands the difficulty his father had killing the pet, he realizes how much he admires his father. Shortly afterward, Mr. Peck dies, and Robert must arrange his father's funeral.

This moving first-person narrative deals with the strong bond between a father and a son who appreciate and respect each other. Both birth and death are handled in a low-key manner. Frank descriptions of animal breeding and birth are included in the book.

Ages 12 and up

Also available in:
Talking Book—*A Day No Pigs Would Die*
Library of Congress (NLSBPH)

464

Perl, Lila

Hey, Remember Fat Glenda?

Clarion Books, 1981.
(168 pages)

SELF, ATTITUDE TOWARD: Body Concept
WEIGHT CONTROL: Overweight
Friendship: best friend
School: classmate relationships
School: pupil-teacher relationships

By the time school starts in the fall, eighth-grader Glenda Waite has lost sixteen pounds by dieting all summer. Her best friend, Sara, who just recently moved away, writes Glenda encouraging notes about losing weight and thinking thin. Glenda is really trying, especially now that she has a crush on Mr. Hartley, her English teacher. She is determined to eat less and jog more. Glenda's mother, also overweight, encourages her to join a "dancercise" group. Glenda refuses, preferring to jog. Besides, her mother isn't a great recommendation for dancercise, since she eats the moment she returns from class. One Sunday, two school friends, Mary Lou and Patty, come to Glenda's house to study. They notice some of Sara's encouraging notes about losing weight and laugh. Hurt, Glenda begins to eat more and more. But when Mr. Hartley announces he will be directing the school's musical review, Glenda decides to try to lose weight again. She joins dancercise and discovers that Patty is in her class. Soon people begin to notice a thinner, more attractive Glenda. By the time of the class's Halloween costume party, Glenda feels thin enough to go as a dance-hall queen. No one recognizes her, and she notices the admiring glances and whispered appreciation. When a classmate grabs her mask and reveals who she is, everyone is surprised. Mr. Hartley arrives to judge the costumes, and Glenda ties for first. Then she and Patty decide to try out for the musical review. They ask their dancercise teacher, Miss Esme, to help them with a routine. Miss Esme, who knows Mr. Hartley, warns the infatuated girls that he is a selfish "user." But when Mr. Hartley asks Glenda to help him with auditions, she works very hard. When the players are announced, however, Glenda and Patty are not on the list. Disappointed, Glenda still agrees to be Mr. Hartley's assistant director. She works hard, continually misses dancercise, and begins eating more. After Christmas she realizes he is simply using her, and she quits. Angry at herself and at Mr. Hartley, Glenda decides she will always be fat. Then fat Robert Fry tells Glenda that with her as his inspiration, he is beginning to lose weight. Glenda begins to put her life in perspective. She may never be skinny, she tells Sara, but maybe she can be somewhere between fat and thin.

A young teenage girl struggles to lose weight, hampered by a mother who can't control her own eating. Glenda must also cope with changing relationships among her classmates and a crush on her glamorous but exploitative English teacher. Slightly exaggerated characterizations add humor to this first-person narrative, a sequel to *Me and Fat Glenda.*

Ages 9-12

Also available in:
Paperbound—*Hey, Remember Fat Glenda?*
Pocket Books, Inc.

465

Perl, Lila

Me and Fat Glenda

Clarion Books, 1979.
(185 pages)

COMMUNICATION: Parent-Child
Lifestyle
Loneliness
Peer relationships
Weight control: overweight

In a garbage truck that carries their belongings, nine-year-old Sara and her parents move from California to New York, where her father has accepted a college teaching position. At their new home, Sara meets Glenda Waite, a friendless, overweight girl who eats a lot when she is unhappy. At times Sara feels that her parents' lifestyle is too different and too noticeable: her home has no furniture, the family sleeps in sleeping bags, and her father creates "junk sculpture" in the yard. Sara eats what she likes, but her parents' vegetarian diet becomes an embarrassment when Glenda's mother brings them a homemade stew. Although Glenda considers Sara her friend, conservative Mrs. Waite is shocked and annoyed by Sara's family and causes them considerable trouble when she gets other neighbors to sign a petition asking them to leave. At school, Sara feels that the unpopular Glenda is too possessive of her friendship. On Halloween the "junk sculpture" is torn apart, and an old argument among the other neighborhood children reaches a crisis as damaging accusations are made by all sides. Following the argument, an understanding is reached, with promises of friendship for the future. The next day, Glenda resolves that she will, with Sara's help, lose weight and try to be a more likable person.

After examining her feelings about her parents' lifestyle and discussing it with them, Sara is better able to accept their individualistic ways. This often humorous, first-person narrative shows the genuine love and respect Sara and her parents feel toward each other. The lack of such a relationship between Glenda and her mother is equally apparent.

Ages 9-12

Also available in:
Paperbound—*Me and Fat Glenda*
Pocket Books, Inc.

466

Perl, Lila

The Telltale Summer of Tina C.

Scholastic, Inc., 1984.
(160 pages) o.p.

INFERIORITY, FEELINGS OF
Appearance: concern about
Clubs
Grandparent: living in home of
Parent/Parents: remarriage of

Tina Carstairs, in her "thirteenth year on this planet," is intensely aware of her height, her thinness, and her nose—which "twitches" uncontrollably when she is nervous. She and her friends belong to the Saturday Sad Souls, a club Tina has founded for members' mutual personal aid. But during the summer Tina's worries multiply to include the club itself: her divorced mother has married someone a little puzzling; her father is planning to remarry too; and a new girl, Karla, with whom the other girls seem to be smitten, has become a probationary club member over Tina's objections. When Tina's grandmother, with whom she and her father and younger brother, Arthur, live, begins an extended European vacation, Tina declines an invitation to stay in New York City with her mother. She wants neither to leave the club under Karla's sway nor live with her mother and the new husband, Peter, who keeps house while his wife has a job. Arthur accepts and is soon gone. After an argument with her girlfriends and telling her father she dislikes the woman he intends to marry, Tina goes to New York too. There, in a museum with Arthur, Tina meets sixteen-year-old Johann, a visitor from Holland. The three agree to meet at the museum the next day. But on the way, Tina has second thoughts: Johann is not like the American boys she knows, her hair is a frizzy disaster, and her nose is twitching. She sends Arthur on alone, promising to meet him later. In fact she meets Johann later, but neither can locate Arthur. After a frantic search, Tina becomes panic-stricken and calls her mother. Sobbing too hard to talk, she gives Johann the phone, whereupon the news comes that Arthur is with his mother. Walking back with Johann, Tina realizes that she has not once thought of her appearance, nor has her nose twitched.

This life-like, sometimes funny first-person narrative takes us inside a twelve-year-old's intense self-concern without making it seem unnatural. Tina exaggerates her least favorite features, is swift to disapprove of her parents, and thinks little of others' feelings. Only when she must concern herself with the very welfare of another does she accept herself unquestioningly and see what is important. A secondary theme, the remarriage of divorced parents, is dealt with instructively.

Ages 10-13

Also available in:
No other form known

467

Perrine, Mary

Nannabah's Friend

Color illustrations by Leonard Weisgard.
Houghton Mifflin Co., 1989.
(29 pages)

P

LONELINESS
Friendship: making friends
Native American
Resourcefulness
Responsibility: accepting

Nannabah, a young Navajo girl, is entrusted for the first time with the job of taking her grandmother's sheep to the canyon for grazing. Even though Nannabah knows how to take the herd to the canyon, it is a big responsibility for such a young girl. One day Nannabah begins to feel very lonely thinking about her family, so she makes herself a doll from the red mud around a nearby pool. She fashions a second doll and then an Indian dwelling, or hogan, for the two mud figures, "Baby Brother" and "Little Sister." Nannabah wishes her grandfather were present to sing a traditional blessing for her little hogan. Since he is not, and she is too shy to sing, she recites the words of the song instead. The day passes quickly, and soon Nannabah returns home with the sheep. The next day she sets out again, and at the canyon she meets a girl who has seen her dolls and hogan. While sharing Nannabah's dolls, the girls soon become friends and are no longer lonely.

This simple story shows how closely the Navajo Indians live with nature. The friendship that develops between the two girls, fulfilling their need for companionship, is depicted with sympathetic understanding.

Ages 7-10

Also available in:
Paperbound—*Nannabah's Friend*
Houghton Mifflin Co.

468

Perry, Patricia and Marietta Lynch

Mommy and Daddy Are Divorced

Black/white photographs by the authors.
Dial Books for Young Readers, 1985.
(30 pages counted, paperbound)

DIVORCE: of Parents

Ned and his little brother, Joey, live with their divorced mother and are awaiting their father's regular Wednesday morning visit. Daddy arrives and they play awhile, then work on Ned's model airplane. But when Daddy must leave, Ned loses his temper, shouting that he never wants to see him again. Daddy reassures the boy that he loves him and will see them again Saturday. Later, no longer angry but still unhappy, Ned questions his mother about the divorce. She reminds him about the arguments she and Daddy used to have and how they decided that a divorce would make them happier. Saturday arrives and once again the boys are with their father. And once again they are sad to have him say good-bye—but know that they will soon see him again.

Very young children enduring the aftermath of their parents' divorce will recognize Ned's feelings—his anger, his divided loyalties—through this candid first-person narrative and the accompanying large photographs. Children whose absent parents do not visit regularly may, however, be confused or envious.

Ages 3-6

Also available in:
No other form known

469

Petersen, P. J.

Would You Settle for Improbable?

Dell Publishing Company, Inc. (Laurel Leaf Library), 1983.
(160 pages, paperbound)

FRIENDSHIP: Meaning of
Delinquency, juvenile
Maturation
School: classmate relationships
School: pupil-teacher relationships

Ms. Karnisian, the ninth-grade English student-teacher, asks Mike, Warren, and Harry a favor they consider impossible. She replies that it is not impossible, just improbable. She wants the three to befriend Arnold Norberry, a boy from the county juvenile hall where she works nights. Arnold will soon be getting out of juvenile hall and into Marshall Martin Junior High. The boys reluctantly agree to meet Arnold and Ms. Karnisian at the bowling alley that Saturday afternoon. The two are an hour late and after Ms. Karnisian leaves, things don't go well. Trying to befriend Arnold, Mike invites him to his house. Arnold promptly steals Mike's calculator and makes a joke of it when he's caught. At school, most of the ninth graders avoid Arnold with his swaggering walk and cocky attitude. Then one day Warren cuts the wires to the class intercom and Arnold takes the blame, to Mike's puzzlement. Why would Arnold want to protect Warren? Deciding to give friendship another try, Mike rides his bike to Arnold's home in the run-down section of town. There he meets Arnold's drunken mother and sees the kind of life Arnold must contend with every day. As ninth-grade graduation nears, Ms. Karnisian says Arnold can graduate if he passes the eighth-grade constitution test. His friends help him cram, but Arnold doesn't show up to take the test when he is scheduled. So Warren tricks him into taking it another day, and Arnold passes. Elated, he asks Jennifer to the graduation dance. She accepts, making Arnold happy and excited. But then Jennifer's parents plan a family party that Jennifer must attend instead of the dance. Arnold is convinced her father simply didn't want the girl to date him, and he tells Mike he will seek revenge. When Arnold's mother is arrested, he stays with Mike's family for several days, talking to Mike about stealing a car and going to Canada. As the school year ends, the class plans a party and gift for Ms. Karnisian. Mike is treasurer of the fund. When the books they'd intended to buy are sold, Arnold volunteers to get something else and Mike gives him the money. Arnold promptly disappears. Then Mike hears that Jennifer's father's sports car has been vandalized. He's sure Arnold has had his revenge. When Ms. Karnisian reports that Arnold was arrested in a stolen car and will return to juvenile hall, the class, especially Mike, feels hugely let down. Arnold writes a letter to the class explaining his troubles, but Mike doesn't believe the explanation. He still suspects that Arnold took the money and the car to go to Canada. After talking with Ms. Karnisian, however, Mike feels better. He can't stay angry; Arnold needs his support, no matter what really happened.

Despite Arnold's tough-guy attitude, Mike and his friends like and try to help him. When Arnold gets into trouble again anyway, the sympathetic Ms. Karnisian convinces Mike to stand by the incorrigible boy. Mike tells the story with wit and warmth. It is punctuated with excerpts from individual class notebooks that provide in-depth portraits of the main characters. A serious novel about a serious problem, this story's realistic ending leaves open the possibility of Arnold's changing and maturing some day.

Ages 11-13

Also available in:
No other form known

470

Peterson, Jeanne Whitehouse

I Have a Sister—My Sister Is Deaf

Black/white illustrations by Deborah Ray.
HarperCollins Publishers, Inc., 1977.
(32 pages counted)

DEAFNESS
Sibling: older

The girl who narrates this story has a little five-year-old sister who loves to leap and roll and swing like other children but never hears a warning shout. She loves to play the piano but never hears the tune. She is deaf. The two usually—but not always—understand each other; the hearing sister speaks slowly and uses her hands, face, and eyes to show what she is saying; the deaf sister can have trouble speaking, but she "speaks" too, in facial expressions and in sign language. The hearing girl plugs her ears and wonders if the effect is the same as being deaf. (It is not, for her sister will never hear noises of any kind.) The littler girl even sleeps on when thunder frightens her sister. When friends ask if it hurts to be deaf, the older sister replies, "No, her ears don't hurt, but her feelings do when people do not understand."

In telling about her deaf sister in this perceptive first-person narrative, a hearing girl shows the ways in which a deaf child differs from a hearing one. Perhaps the most puzzling difference to a hearing child is that a deaf child never reacts to noises, as is shown here several times. Numerous tips are given on how to act toward a deaf child: speak slowly and expressively; stamp the ground or else wave to attract their attention; and so on. The author writes from experience, for she has a younger sister who is deaf. Since this is not an instructional book, and its text resembles verse, discussion will likely be needed to emphasize these lessons.

Ages 4-7

Also available in:
Paperbound—*I Have a Sister—My Sister Is Deaf*
HarperCollins Publishers, Inc.

471

Pevsner, Stella

And You Give Me a Pain, Elaine

Houghton Mifflin Co., 1979.
(192 pages) o.p.

SIBLING: Relationships
Boy-girl relationships
Death: of sibling
Love, meaning of
Maturation
Running away

The only way thirteen-year-old Andrea Marshall can cope with her sixteen-year-old sister, Elaine, is by retreating to another room to practice gymnastics. Her mother tries to change Elaine, but her efforts end in furious bickering. Elaine remains Elaine—willful, contentious, sarcastic, and selfish. Finally, Andrea turns to Joe, her loving and beloved older brother now in college, for advice. He tells her to leave Elaine to their parents. For a time Andrea's work on a school play and her worries about Joe's girlfriend, Cassie, who is cooling towards him, divert her attention from Elaine. She is further distracted by the attentions of a boy named Chris, also involved with the play. Her mother, however, continues to worry about Elaine and becomes frantic after the girl withdraws her bank savings and refuses to say why, asking only to be left alone. Shortly after that, Elaine runs away, and soon telephones from Arizona, where she is living with her boyfriend, who has moved there. The news does not disturb Andrea unduly. It is Elaine's return several weeks later that upsets her, all the more so because her parents then refuse to let Andrea date Chris, after the example Elaine has set. Yet relations improve, perhaps because of the professional counseling Elaine and her parents take. Elaine begins to change and even does small favors for Andrea. Andrea learns of the pressures on her sister, especially Mom's desire that the younger girl emulate the elder's high school successes. Then Andrea's life is shattered when Joe, driving home on a motorcycle to see the play, is killed. For a time, Andrea drops everything, including Chris, and even blames herself for Joe's death: had she not made so much of the play, he would not have made the trip. But, reminded by Cassie of how highly Joe thought of her, Andrea resolves to set aside her grief: "Step by step, move by move, I'd make it."

This first-person narrative shows the effects of a girl's maturing on her relations with a troublesome sister. As Andrea becomes confident in herself, she sees that Elaine must also work things out her own way. There are numerous subplots here—school activities, the vagaries of Joe's romance—that contribute to the realism of the story as well as show the experiences that inform Andrea's growing awareness of herself and others. The Marshall family, though troubled, is a close one, and their dialogue rings true. Humor leavens the whole.

Ages 10-13

Also available in:
Cassette—*And You Give Me a Pain, Elaine*
Library of Congress (NLSBPH)

472

Pevsner, Stella

Keep Stompin' Till the Music Stops

Houghton Mifflin Co., 1979.
(144 pages) o.p.

LEARNING DISABILITIES
Age: respect for
Great-grandparent
Self-esteem

Richard, entering seventh grade in the fall, suffers from dyslexia and cannot follow complicated reading matter or conversation. When his family attends a reunion at his great-grandfather's home, Richard's cousin, Alexandra, tells him that she suspects the overbearing Great-aunt Violet of having some secret plan up her sleeve. To discover that plan, Richard—concentrating as never before—learns by eavesdropping that Aunt Vi, convinced that Great-grandpa Ben is too old to go on living in his large house, wants to take her father to Florida. This and additional clues gathered over days persuade the cousins that their great-aunt plans to deposit Grandpa Ben in a senior citizens' trailer court. Richard tells all to his father, extracting his promise to stand up for Grandpa Ben. But when family discussion concerning his welfare becomes heated, Ben announces that he will not be made to move and has made arrangements to rent part of his house to the local historical society, which will allow him to go on living there and help maintain the place. Richard is both relieved that his great-grandfather has thwarted Aunt Violet and more hopeful, after his detective work, that he can conquer his learning disability.

Richard's dyslexia has made him extremely sensitive to criticism, real or imagined, and generally unsure of himself. His father, ambitious and demanding, resents his son's disability. Sensing this, the boy has difficulty trusting or even liking his father. Tempering her husband's impatience, Richard's mother tries to help the boy. Vivid characterizations enliven this leisurely narrative, not least Richard's courage in bewilderment—courage which readers who share his disability may well identify with. Other readers will come away knowing more about dyslexia than before.

Ages 9-12

Also available in:
Cassette—*Keep Stompin' Till the Music Stops*
Library of Congress (NLSBPH)

473

Pevsner, Stella

A Smart Kid Like You

Houghton Mifflin Co., 1979.
(192 pages) o.p.

DIVORCE: of Parents
SCHOOL: Pupil-Teacher Relationships
STEPPARENT: Mother
Maturation

Twelve-year-old Nina Beckwith's parents are recently divorced, and she still has difficulty accepting their separation. She resents her father's remarriage even more. Nina is also worried about starting junior high school. Her first school day goes well, until she enters the mathematics class and finds that her teacher is her father's new wife. Nina wants to transfer to a different class, but her friends convince her to try another approach to force the teacher to quit. For several days the students harass Mrs. Beckwith until she finally puts her foot down. In a private talk, Mrs. Beckwith and Nina agree to work together as best they can. Meanwhile, Nina has other troubles. Her mother works as a secretary and has little time to talk with her. Nina is even more annoyed when her mother starts dating Phil. On Saturdays, Nina goes out with her father; slowly she learns to understand him as an individual with needs of his own. She begins to warm toward his new family and accept his new wife. When communication with her mother improves and Nina comes to know Phil better, she starts to feel that things may work out after all.

Nina not only faces the usual adolescent worries—school, boys, clothes, relationships with parents—she must also learn to accept her parents' divorce. Her initial feelings of resentment, fear, and loneliness give way to an understanding of her parents' desires to make new lives for themselves, apart from each other, but not excluding her.

Ages 10-13

Also available in:
No other form known

474

Pfeffer, Susan Beth

About David

Dell Publishing Company, Inc. (Laurel Leaf Library), 1980.
(167 pages, paperbound)

SUICIDE
Adoption: feelings about
Boy-girl relationships
Communication: lack of
Death: of friend
Death: murder
Friendship: best friend
Guilt, feelings of
Mourning, stages of
School: classmate relationships

Even as her father tells her the tragic story, seventeen-year-old Lynn Epstein cannot believe it. Her friend for thirteen years is dead. More than that, David Morris has murdered his parents and then committed suicide. Lynn loved David like a brother and felt she knew him well. Why would he do this? David knew he was adopted, and he hated the birth parents who gave him up. He also didn't get along with his adoptive parents, who had great expectations for him but expressed little love, praise, or encouragement. Lynn tries to reconstruct the last conversation she had with David in the school cafeteria, but she draws a blank. After several days she returns to school, but all David's other friends are as confused and grief-stricken as she. Lynn becomes obsessed with that last, forgotten conversation, wondering if it holds the key, wondering if she could have stopped David. Her parents become so concerned about her guilt, nightmares, insomnia, shaking fits, loss of appetite, and shifting moods that a month after the tragedy they suggest she see a psychologist. She readily agrees, knowing she needs to talk to someone. Then Lynn finds and reads David's four notebooks, left to her in his own personal will which was found by Lynn's father, acting as solicitor for the family. The closer she comes to the end of the last notebook, the more she dreads finding out why David murdered his parents and took his own life. When she finally confesses this to her psychologist, he tells her she must finish the notebook and start living her life without David. Back home Lynn finishes the notebook. David wrote that his mother, who had longed for a child of her own, was pregnant. Yet Lynn learns this was not true. An autopsy proved his mother was not pregnant; this was a figment of David's imagination. Her questions unanswered, Lynn remains haunted by that final lunchtime conversation. Back at school, she walks fearfully into the cafeteria she has been avoiding and finally remembers what David said. The conversation was mundane, except that David told her he had a surprise planned for his mother's birthday. The murder/suicide occurred two days before her birthday. Lynn realizes there was no way she could have prevented the tragedy, that David "lived in a world of such misery that the only way he could be happy was by destroying it all, and himself with it." Six months later Lynn stops seeing the psychologist and believes she has successfully adjusted to David's death. She is looking forward to college, knowing she will never forget David but feeling stronger and more mature because of what happened.

Shocked and baffled by her friend's murders and suicide, Lynn struggles to understand the events and to overcome her crushing guilt at failing to predict and avert them. With the help of her parents, friends, and psychologist, she comes through her grief a stronger person as she finds some answers. Told by Lynn in diary form and including some profanity, this is a tense, memorable, emotion-charged story that is neither melodramatic nor morbid. There is much to discuss here, particularly the varied reactions and interactions of classmates and friends, all perceptively presented.

Ages 13 and up

Also available in:
No other form known

P

475

Pfeffer, Susan Beth

Just Between Us

Color illustrations by Lorna Tomei.
Delacorte Press, 1980.
(116 pages) o.p.

FRIENDSHIP: Meaning of
SECRET KEEPING
Adoption: feelings about
Divorce: of parents
Trust/Distrust

Cass Miller, eleven, cannot keep a secret. When her best friend, Jenny, confides that she has bought her first bra, Cass's weakness threatens their friendship. Cass's mother, a psychology student, devises a way to teach Cass to be silent: she will be paid for the secrets she keeps. Cass agrees to the arrangement, but then reveals a secret almost immediately. Determined to keep the next secret told to her, she tries not talking at all. Then her second-best friend, Robin, tells Cass that her parents were divorced and that she was adopted by her mother's second husband. Cass keeps this secret, then five others, and feels very good for a little while. Soon, though, she tells three of the secrets. Robin invites Cass and Jenny to dinner and Jenny, resentful since her parents' recent divorce and looking for a way to hurt Robin, whom she dislikes, notices that Robin does not resemble her parents. She becomes convinced Robin is adopted and tries to think of a way to reveal this news. Meanwhile, Cass manages to reveal no secrets during a visit to relatives by keeping quiet, eating, and coughing a lot. Jenny confesses that her mother is short of money since the divorce. Robin advises her to call her father for help. But when Jenny calls, she repeats her mother's angry remarks about her father's new girlfriend, infuriating her father into hanging up on her. Since the call was

Robin's idea, Jenny vows revenge. Cass is sure that if Robin just apologizes to Jenny, all will be well, but Robin refuses. Knowing none of this because Cass, though increasingly distressed, hasn't revealed the secret, Cass's mother takes the girl to her psychology class to show her off; her classmates know about their agreement. When Jenny announces her intention to spread the word that Robin is adopted, Cass threatens to lie and say Jenny is a bed-wetter. The blackmail works. Jenny confesses that she'd really like to stop being mean and losing friends. Cass realizes that the secret to keeping secrets is to consider, "Would she want other people to know about this?" The tension breaks, the three girls become friends again, and Cass treats Robin and Jenny to lunch with the money she has earned keeping secrets.

Three young girls learn how important it is to keep secrets in this warm, funny first-person narrative. Cass sets out her problem clearly—she simply talks without considering the consequences—and her realistic attempts to change could be useful to readers. The reasons why some secrets shouldn't be told warrant discussion. Clever illustrations complement the text.

Ages 10-12

Also available in:
No other form known

476

Pfeffer, Susan Beth

Kid Power

Black/white illustrations by Leigh Grant.
Scholastic, Inc., 1982.
(121 pages) o.p.

JOB
Friendship: best friend
Resourcefulness
Responsibility: accepting
Values/Valuing: materialistic

Eleven-year-old Janie Golden has never given much thought to money nor held onto it long. Just when her mother loses a job, she and her sister, Carol, at thirteen a junior miser, find they need money to buy new bicycles. Carol already has a newspaper route, and Janie decides to advertise for odd jobs under the name of "Kid Power." Soon she is so busy working and so fascinated by making money that she is neglecting her best friend, Lisa, who accuses her of forsaking everything for the almighty dollar. In fact the dollar is plaguing the whole household. When Mrs. Golden stops looking for a new job, she and her husband stop talking to each other. When Mr. Golden and Carol blame Janie for the family disruption, she worries that they may be right. The glitter of all her new money dims. Matters only worsen when a newspaper article about Janie and her business brings in many more job offers than she can fill—baby-sitting, gardening, walking dogs, helping at yard sales. Soon she is sharing jobs with friends, asking for 10% of their earnings as her agent's fee. Janie has found her true calling, management, and Mrs. Golden employs herself by starting her own agency—a Kid Power for adults.

This first-person narrative shows the delights and pitfalls of making money. Inventive at solving problems on the job, Janie is not prepared for the stress her work causes her family and friends. By becoming an agent, she finds time for them and takes 10% to boot. Children bent on summer jobs should enjoy this story, filled with interesting characters, humor, unexpected troubles, and intelligent, believable solutions.

Ages 9-12

Also available in:
Cassette—*Kid Power*
Library of Congress (NLSBPH)

477

Pfeffer, Susan Beth

Starring Peter and Leigh

Delacorte Press, 1979.
(200 pages) o.p.

DECISION MAKING
IDENTIFICATION WITH OTHERS: Peers
IDENTITY, SEARCH FOR
Divorce: of parents
Hemophilia
Parent/Parents: remarriage of
Stepbrother/Stepsister

Leigh Thorpe, sixteen, has chosen to leave Los Angeles and her career as a television actress to move to Long Island with her divorced mother, who has recently remarried. After spending four years playing the part of Chris Kampbell on "The Kampbell Kids," a family program, Leigh feels she has missed out on normal teenage life. Her new stepbrother, Peter, one year older than she, has hemophilia. Like Leigh, Peter has missed out on much of the usual teenage social scene. Because of his illness he is frequently confined to home, sometimes to bed, and has not been in school for months. He now plans to enjoy a social life vicariously, through his stepsister. The two discuss how Leigh should dress and behave in order to be accepted by the right crowd and to overcome her "star" status. Leigh is soon befriended by Anna, an eccentric loner who is not intimidated by Leigh's television career. Gradually the two girls are accepted by a popular group of students. But when a movie Leigh made before leaving California is televised, some of her new friends have difficulty separating the real Leigh from the runaway alcoholic prostitute she portrayed. The school drama teacher, impressed with her performance, pressures Leigh to star in the class play, *Antigone.* But she decides not to audition, and Anna gets the lead. Coaching Anna and several other actors and then seeing *Antigone* performed make Leigh miss acting. A visit to her actor father and his live-in girlfriend in New York City, where she spends a day on the set of his soap opera and has her picture taken for a fan magazine, stirs more restlessness in Leigh.

Back at home, she decides she still prefers a "normal" life. But she finds it increasingly difficult to juggle ex-stardom and her new friendships: she has yet to be asked on a date and her friends, with the exception of Anna, are still somewhat uncomfortable in her presence. Peter, whose intermittent bouts with internal bleeding are often brought on by routine colds and infections, comes down with the flu, and his father, Ben, argues with Leigh's mother about his care. Seeing that the argument bothers Peter, Leigh reminds him that all married people fight. But Peter believes his parents divorced because of his illness, and he fears he may destroy this marriage too. Leigh begins dating the class president, but finds that Peter is not interested in hearing about her newfound romance. Realizing she is now living the life she has always dreamed of, Leigh decides to let the future take care of itself for a while. Then she is offered the role of Anne Frank in a four-month tour. Her father, now out of work, is offered a job with the touring company if Leigh will play Anne. The girl, conscious of her responsibility to her father, decides to take the job. Her mother and stepfather support her decision, but Peter is upset. Ill again, the boy confesses his love to Leigh, who finally perceives that his affection for her has for some time been more than brotherly. He compels her to consider her own feelings, which she finds she doesn't fully understand. She tells him time will help them both sort things out. Peter decides to go to California for some specialized and intensive physical therapy. When he is better he plans to visit his mother to try to reconcile some of the anger and guilt that has alienated them since the divorce.

Although few readers will be able to identify with Leigh's specific plight—that of choosing between a regulated home life and a career as a successful actress—many will sympathize with her wish to be accepted by her peers, her search for stability, and her undefined love for her stepbrother. Although the story line at times seems shallow and the heroine's first-person narration is less than sparkling, themes are clearly developed and the hemophiliac Peter is an interesting character. His guilt and alienation resulting from his parents' divorce are not explored in great depth. But Leigh's philosophical, almost jaunty, attitude toward her parents' breakup certainly presents the case that divorce is something to which teenagers can adjust. The dialogue includes some profanity.

Ages 12-14

Also available in:
Cassette—*Starring Peter and Leigh*
Library of Congress (NLSPBH)

478

Pfeffer, Susan Beth

What Do You Do When Your Mouth Won't Open?

Black/white illustrations by Lorna Tomei.
Dell Publishing, Inc. (Yearling Books), 1981.
(114 pages, paperbound)

FEAR
Family: relationships
Friendship: best friend
Jealousy: sibling
Perseverance
Problem solving
Success

It started in kindergarten when she forgot her lines in a play. Since then Reesa Nathan, now twelve, has had a fear of talking in public. Her teachers respect her phobia and do not call on her to speak in class. One day Reesa's language arts teacher tells her she has won the school's writing contest on "What I Like Best About America." Delighted, Reesa happily tells her family at dinner. But her older sister, Robby, informs her that she will have to read her essay at the countywide contest. If that is true, Reesa declares, she will drop out of the contest. The principal confirms Reesa's fears: in two weeks she will read her essay in front of five hundred people. Her presentation will constitute fifty percent of the final judging. Terrified, Reesa turns to her best friend, Heather, for advice. Heather tells Reesa to see a psychiatrist who will cure her of the phobia. Reesa sees a psychologist, Dr. Marks, and asks her, "What do you do when your mouth won't open?" Dr. Marks is sympathetic, but can't promise to cure the girl's phobia in two weeks. Several days later Dr. Marks calls Reesa and tells her to pick up some library books about public speaking. She also asks the girl to return to her office that Friday to learn some relaxation techniques. Reesa learns from the books that fear of public speaking is normal and that it helps to become very familiar with one's speech. She begins practicing diligently, even summoning the courage to read her essay to Heather. Robby, though, tells Reesa she will freeze up and embarrass the family and urges her to quit. That Friday at Dr. Marks's office, Reesa learns breathing exercises and other ways to relax. That weekend Robby persuades Reesa to practice by reading to her language arts class. So that Monday Reesa volunteers to read part of a play aloud. Unfortunately, she freezes and is unable to speak. Furious at her sister, Reesa messes up Robby's file cabinets, Robby slaps her, and soon both girls are crying. Each confesses she is jealous of the other: Reesa of Robby's extra privileges, Robby of Reesa's prettiness and their mother's view of her as a talented writer. They make up and Reesa reads her essay to Robby, who encourages her. The night of the contest arrives, and a frightened Reesa practices her relaxation techniques. But when it is her turn, she begins to panic. Seeing her family and Dr.

P

Marks helps her regain control, and she concentrates on looking at Robby. Reesa begins reading her essay, but ends up speaking extemporaneously; she has changed since she wrote the essay, and the attitudes expressed have changed too. She decides to put forth her new ideas and feels good about herself when she's done. Although she doesn't win, "I'd won what I wanted to win." Tremendously encouraged, Reesa begins to consider the upcoming auditions for the school play.

A young girl with a deep fear of public speaking is helped to overcome her phobia in this lively first-person narrative. Although it seems odd that Reesa has never gotten help from parents or teachers and must seek it out herself, her encounters with the psychologist are convincing and the book's other relationships and situations ring true. Despite unattractive illustrations, this is a most appealing story.

Ages 10-13

Also available in:
No other form known

479

Philips, Barbara

Don't Call Me Fatso

Color illustrations by Helen Cogancherry.
Raintree/Steck-Vaughan Publishers, Inc., 1980.
(31 pages)

NAME-CALLING
WEIGHT CONTROL: Overweight
Responsibility: accepting
Self, attitude toward: feeling different

Rita, about seven, is the heaviest child in her class. At school she quickly eats a big lunch and then tries to trade her carrots for cookies. When the children line up to be weighed, someone whispers, "Let's see if Fatso breaks the scale!" Rita weighs seventy-five pounds, and the nurse quietly says they may have to come up with a diet for her. Embarrassed, Rita thinks she will feel better in art class. But when they are assigned to draw someone in the class, two boys draw "Fatso" and snicker. The teacher scolds them, saying, "People come in all shapes and sizes, and that's no reason to make fun of them." At home Rita's stepfather asks what's bothering her, and she tells him that everyone at school calls her names. He suggests they both diet by not eating sweet things or drinking soda pop. She hesitates, but then runs to ask her mother to leave the cookies out of tomorrow's lunch. "I don't want to be fat anymore." Her mother also likes the idea of losing weight and suggests they go jogging together. Rita hates even thinking about exercise, much preferring to watch TV, but she agrees to take swimming lessons with a friend. When she jumps off the board for the first time she hears a whisper: "She's so fat that she sinks when she dives!" In frustration, she eats three candy bars on the way home. Her stepfather reassures her, saying that losing weight takes time and she will feel better about herself if she keeps trying. So Rita decides to continue her diet. Her parents thank her for changing the eating habits of the whole family. Some weeks later, when she is again weighed at school, she has lost only five pounds. But the nurse is enthusiastic. Rita has also grown an inch and "a growing girl shouldn't lose too much weight." Rita runs off to join her friends, too happy to notice that no one is calling her names.

An overweight young girl, teased at school, finds the determination to lose weight. Although Rita's family's attitude may seem idealized and her success a bit too easy, readers will sympathize with her hurt feelings as the victim of name-calling. Overweight children will be cheered by Rita's story; others may gain understanding. The text is enriched by colorful illustrations that reflect the characters' emotions.

Ages 5-9

Also available in:
No other form known

480

Piper, Watty

The Little Engine That Could

Retold from *The Pony Engine* by Mabel C. Bragg.
Color illustrations by George & Doris Hauman.
Platt & Munk Publishers, 1990.
(39 pages) o.p.

DETERMINATION
Consideration, meaning of
Problem solving

A small train is carrying dolls, toys, books, and good food for boys and girls who live on the other side of the mountain. Suddenly, at the foot of the mountain, the engine breaks down. Worried that the children will be disappointed, the toys and dolls look for another engine to pull their train. A large, shiny new engine refuses because he pulls only passenger trains. A freight engine will carry only cargo for adults. An old rusty engine is too weary to pull anything over a mountain. The dolls and toys are about to lose hope when a pretty, new engine comes down the tracks. She does not know if she can pull so heavy a load over a mountain, but is eager to help. She is hitched to a train and starts slowly up the slope repeating, "I think I can—I think I can. . . ." Just in time, and barely, she gets over the mountain. The children are delighted with the joyous freight.

This 50th-anniversary edition of a classic is larger than the original and has been reillustrated in the style of the 1920s. The larger size is convenient to use with read-aloud groups. The unchanged text will continue to satisfy youngsters with its message of consideration, perseverance, and willingness paying off.

Ages 3-7

Also available in:
Talking Book—*The Little Engine That Could*
Library of Congress (NLSBPH)

481

Platt, Kin

The Ape Inside Me

HarperCollins Publishers, Inc., 1979.
(117 pages) o.p.

ANGER
Aggression
Peer relationships
Self-discipline

Ed Hill is a fifteen-year-old boy with a problem. He has a terrible temper that rises up inside him and explodes "like a volcano." Since he feels incapable of controlling it, he thinks of this temper as a separate being, an ape he calls "Kong." No amount of reasoning by Eddie's rational side can bring Kong into line. On several occasions his temper almost gets him killed because it will not let him back down when the odds are against him. But in spite of the trouble Kong causes, Ed is not sure he really wants to control him. After all, Ed likes to fight and Kong is good at finding opportunities—in fact, the boy dreams of becoming a professional boxer. But he is small and doesn't really think he has a chance. Besides, Ed without Kong is a very nice person. He loves his divorced mother and wants to earn a lot of money so he can give her nice things. He tries to put up with Les, who lives with them, although Les dislikes Eddie and deliberately irritates and berates him. Eddie works hard at Sal's Body Shop and tries to justify Sal's faith in him. He chooses friends like Debbie Donaldson, the shyest girl in school, and Bobby Penna, gentle and studious. When Debbie wins a national poetry contest and learns she must give a speech to the student body, she's sure she will die of fright. She wishes she could be more like Eddie; Sal and Bobby, however, do not admire Eddie's irascible ways. They both try to convince him that anger starts in the mind and his mind must control Kong. Sal, however, realizes that part of Ed's problem is that he likes to fight. So he sends the boy to see Phil Sierra, a friend who runs a gym and can tell Eddie if he has what it takes to become a professional fighter. Phil watches Eddie in the ring and concludes that he is "a fighter already," that fighting is obviously part of his nature. But he warns the boy that he must learn to control his temper. "Otherwise, when your temper is up, you're like a runaway car with no brakes. You got no steering power either, because the control is gone." He explains that when a person is angry he isn't thinking clearly; "and it's easy to pick him apart and then put him away." Phil tells Eddie to come back when he has Kong under control. Eddie resolves to subdue his temper and soon has a chance. During Debbie's speech in the school auditorium, Mike Boyd, sitting behind Eddie, starts to disrupt the assembly by making fun of the girl. Kong roars, "You letting him get away with this? . . . Kill the bum, hit him!" But even after Boyd jams the heel of his hand into Eddie's face, Eddie remains calm. He is in charge now. Determined to control himself, he thinks, "No more, Kong. I'm boss. Get back in your tree."

A teenage boy gives his uncontrollable temper a separate identity but realizes he'll never get anywhere until he takes charge of "Kong." Eddie's first-person narrative is peppered with his conversations with other characters and his dialogues with Kong. Thought-provoking and full of discussion possibilities, the story makes a valuable distinction between the discipline required for prizefighting and untempered anger. Ed's story may help readers with similar temperaments and should have special appeal for the reluctant reader.

Ages 12 and up

Also available in:
No other form known

482

Platt, Kin

Brogg's Brain

HarperCollins Publishers, Inc., 1981.
(123 pages) o.p.

AMBIVALENCE, FEELINGS OF
EXPECTATIONS
Boy-girl relationships: dating
Communication: parent-child
Competition
Maturation
Sports/Sportsmanship
Talents: athletic

Fifteen-year-old Monty Davis runs the mile for the school track team because he enjoys running, not because he wishes to compete or loves to win. The adults around him, however, don't accept what they consider his lack of drive. His coach thinks he should demand more of himself. His father, who had also been a runner in high school, wants him to work harder. Even his English teacher urges him to be more ambitious, suggesting that most people need to win. Monty disagrees. In fact, he is irritated by all these demands to excel, telling himself that all he has ever wanted to do is run for fun. Then, in contradiction of his own philosophy, he starts training harder. He begins running a course around a park near his home and there sees a blonde girl with a ponytail who can outrun him every time. He begins dating a school friend, Cindy, a marathon runner and Japanese-American, although his father would much prefer him to date an "American" girl. He takes her to a movie called "Brogg's Brain," in which a talking brain dominates the other characters. Afterwards, the two discuss the possibilities of Monty's controlling his running by sending positive messages to himself. One night Monty's father again prods him about doing better. Angrily Monty leaves the house and heads for the park. There he speaks with the ponytail girl, Julie Mars, a champion marathon runner. She suggests they run together and gives him some pointers. The day of the big meet with arch-rival Culver arrives. Monty

P

will compete with his own teammates, Cott and Rose, and with a runner from Culver named Bunny Ellison. Now the coach, after all his lectures about winning, tells Monty that today he is to be a "rabbit"—he is to run hard in order to wear out Ellison, letting Cott and Rose take first and second place so their school can win the meet. But a voice inside Monty tells him that today he can run better than he ever has before. He runs for all he is worth, yet is unable to "wear out" Ellison. Monty beats him by less than ten yards, with Cott and Rose left behind.

A boy who runs for the pleasure of it resists adult demands that he run to win and then discovers that he has a competitive spirit after all. Furthermore, once he begins competing he decides he wants to win. Monty's first-person narrative will compel the attention of readers, especially budding athletes. His discovery of the joys of competition merits discussion.

Ages 12 and up

Also available in:
No other form known

483

Polushkin, Maria

Bubba and Babba

Color illustrations by Diane de Groat.
Crown Publishers, Inc., 1986.
(30 pages counted) o.p.

RESPONSIBILITY: Avoiding

Bubba and Babba are two very lazy bears who always argue about the housework. Bubba says Babba should make the beds, but Babba says that is pointless since they will only muss them again at night. When Babba says Bubba should sweep the floors, Bubba declines, saying they will only get dirty again. While out walking one day, they are offered a dozen eggs by a farmer if they will help with his mowing. They both decline, saying that should they break the eggs on the way home, all that work would have been for nothing. Instead, they sit under a tree and watch the farmer work. At suppertime, because they cannot think how to avoid it, they chop wood for a fire and prepare some porridge. At the end of the meal, however, they have a loud, long argument over who should do the dishes. Finally Babba suggests that they leave the dishes and go to bed—and whoever gets up first will do them. They agree. But in the morning, both bears stay in bed feigning sleep. Most of the day passes and neither gets up. In the late afternoon, their raccoon friend comes by for a visit, and is appalled by the awful mess in the kitchen. He decides to surprise the bears by cleaning it up. Hearing noise, both bears leap out of bed and run into the kitchen, where Raccoon is so startled he drops a bowl. At that Bubba and Babba laugh and laugh. They see their own silliness and promise to try to be less lazy in the future.

Young children will get the point of this funny story, based on an old Russian folk tale, and see how laughing at oneself can be the beginning of change. The book is especially fun when read aloud.

Ages 3-8

Also available in:
No other form known

484

Potter, Beatrix

The Tale of Peter Rabbit

Color illustrations by the author.
Frederick Warne & Company, Inc., 1902.
(59 pages)

DISCIPLINE, MEANING OF
Risk, taking of

Peter Rabbit lives under the roots of a large fir tree with his mother, his brother, and his sisters. One morning, Mrs. Rabbit sends the children out to play, sternly admonishing them to stay away from Mr. McGregor's garden, where their father met his untimely end. The other Rabbit children gather blackberries, but Peter decides to visit McGregor's garden. He slips under the garden gate and manages to have a large meal, which makes him ill. Peter decides to look for some parsley to calm his upset stomach, but his search leads him not to the parsley, but to Mr. McGregor. Mr. McGregor chases Peter around the garden, and during the chase Peter loses his shoes and new jacket. He finally hides in a watering can—quite full of water—and is safe until he sneezes. Again Mr. McGregor begins the chase, but Peter eludes him, slips under the gate, runs all the way home, and falls asleep on the floor. That evening, while Peter rests in bed and receives medicine because he is ill, his brother and sisters have a delicious supper which includes freshly picked blackberries.

This timeless story depicts Peter's foolhardiness in disobeying his mother's instructions and the danger that results. Although animal characters are used, children always have and always will relate to Peter.

Ages 3-7

Also available in:
Braille—*The Tale of Peter Rabbit*
Library of Congress (NLSBPH)

Cassette—*The Tale of Peter Rabbit*
Library of Congress (NLSBPH)

Cassette—*The Tale of Peter Rabbit*
Frederick Warne & Company, Inc.

Paperbound—*The Tale of Peter Rabbit*
Frederick Warne & Company, Inc.

Talking Book—*The Tale of Peter Rabbit*
Library of Congress (NLSBPH)

485

Power, Barbara

I Wish Laura's Mommy Was My Mommy

Black/white illustrations by Marylin Hafner.
HarperCollins Publishers, Inc., 1979.
(47 pages) o.p.

FAMILY: Relationships
Love, meaning of
Parent/Parents: mother working outside home

Jennifer thinks her friend Laura's mother is just about perfect. As a matter of fact, she wishes she could have Laura's mommy for her own. After-school snacks at Laura's house consist of things like punch and donuts. Her own mother thinks that "snacks should be real food, not just sugar." Laura's family eats in the dining room, sometimes by candlelight. But Jennifer's little brothers are messy eaters, so her family has to eat in the kitchen. When Jennifer eats at Laura's the girls are served seconds of dessert, and then they are allowed to leave the table and play. At her house Jennifer has to help clear the table and get her own seconds of dessert—if there are any. When Jennifer sleeps over at Laura's house, Laura's mother lets the girls stay up late and gives them a breakfast of pancakes shaped like little people. Jennifer's mother makes them go to bed early and be quiet so they won't disturb the boys. In the morning they have to make the beds and fix their own breakfast. One day everything changes. Jennifer's mother goes back to work, and Laura's mother begins baby-sitting for Jennifer and her brothers. Jennifer is sure life will be wonderful now. But instead of donuts after school, the children are given apples. "Donuts are fine for a treat once in a while, but fruit is much better for you," says the new baby-sitter. Then, since Laura's mother is busier now, Jennifer is asked to teach Laura how to make her own bed. When Jennifer and her brothers have to stay late one evening, the family eats in the kitchen, "the way they had when Laura was little." The girls are asked to help clear the table; Laura has to learn how to scrape and stack the plates. By the end of the first week of this new arrangement, Jennifer is delighted to go out for pizza with her own family. On Saturday she and her mother bake a chocolate cake together. Mommy even calls her "Pumpkin Princess," as she did when Jennifer was little. A happy Jennifer decides that even though Laura's mother is nice, she's glad her mommy is still her mommy.

Jennifer comes to appreciate her own home and mother when the "perfect" mother of a friend becomes Jennifer's baby-sitter, rather than her hostess. This amusing story allows children to compare two lifestyles and to evaluate the old adage, "The grass is always greener." Expressive illustrations add to the humor of this easy reader.

Ages 4-7

Also available in:
No other form known

486

Quigley, Lillian Fox

The Blind Men and the Elephant: An Old Tale from the Land of India

Color illustrations by Janice Holland.
Charles Scribner's Sons, 1959.
(24 pages counted) o.p.

COOPERATION
Blindness

Six blind men who live together in India have often heard about elephants but have never seen one. One day when they go to visit the Rajah (the ruler of the people), they come upon an elephant in the courtyard, and each man touches it. One blind man feels the elephant's ear and infers an elephant must be wide, like a fan. Another man feels the trunk and concludes an elephant must be round, like a snake. The third man feels the elephant's leg and decides an elephant is tall, like a tree. Each of the other three men feels another part of the elephant—the side, the tail, and the tusk. On their way home, the men argue about what an elephant must look like. The Rajah overhears them and explains that each person has touched only a single part of a big animal—and that they must, therefore, put all the parts together to find out what an elephant really is.

This Indian fable shows the necessity of working together to solve a problem. More important, it points out the value of different perspectives in developing a full view of anything.

Ages 6-9

Also available in:
Braille—*The Blind Men and the Elephant: An Old Tale from the Land of India*
Library of Congress (NLSBPH)

487

Rabe, Berniece Louise

The Balancing Girl

Color illustrations by Lillian Aberman Hoban.
Dutton Children's Books, 1981.
(32 pages counted, paperbound)

SCHOOL: Classmate Relationships
Braces on body/limbs
School: mainstreaming
Wheelchair, dependence on

Margaret, a first grader, gets around either in a wheelchair or with leg braces and crutches. Even so, she is an expert at balancing. She can balance her books on her head, can balance a high tower of blocks, can balance her body on her crutches. Her classmate Tommy ridicules Margaret's balancing skills and frequently destroys the towers and castles she builds. Now Margaret's school is planning a carnival to raise money for gym equipment. The first grade will have a "fish pond" operated by Tommy and his father. William, another classmate, will dress up as a clown and sell balloons. Margaret decides that for her booth she will make an entire village of dominoes, each standing on end and properly spaced so that when the first domino is tipped, the next will fall and the next until the whole village topples. People will pay to have their names placed in a hat; the person whose name is drawn the night of the carnival will get to push the first domino. Margaret works on her village for days, using all the dominoes in the school. Her teacher watches Tommy carefully so he doesn't succeed in tipping the dominoes. The night of the carnival, Margaret buys three balloons from William and catches a big spider in Tommy's fish pond. Soon it is time to draw the name of the person who will push the first domino. Tommy's name is drawn, and he is thrilled at the opportunity to destroy something of Margaret's with permission. The domino village falls, according to Margaret's design, and her booth earns the most money for the carnival.

Margaret's disability is illustrated, but not mentioned in the text. She is shown to be a happy child functioning normally in a typical classroom. Even Tommy's continual provocation does not upset Margaret, and his characterization adds reality to a simply told story.

Ages 5-7

Also available in:
Talking Book—*The Balancing Girl*
Library of Congress (NLSBPH)

488

Radley, Gail

Nothing Stays the Same Forever

Crown Publishers, Inc., 1988.
(148 pages) o.p.

PARENT/PARENTS: Remarriage of
Age: aging
Change: resisting
Death: of mother
Friendship: meaning of
Loss: feelings of
Maturation

Everything seems to be changing for twelve-year-old Carolyn (Carrie) Moyer. Her father seems very serious about Sharon, the first time he's been serious about a woman since Carrie's mother died of cancer four years ago. Carrie is unhappy about the developing relationship and feels her older sister, Phyllis, is disloyal to their mother's memory because she likes Sharon. Carrie's friend Bridget tells her about an art workshop in New York. Carrie's father isn't encouraging about the possibility of her attending, but since he says that money is one of the obstacles, she begins looking for jobs. She works in the garden of Grace Stebbins, an elderly neighbor, and gets a few other odd jobs. She also enrolls in an art class at the recreation center, even though she feels it's beneath her. Her teacher appreciates her caricatures and cartoons. When Sharon comes for dinner, Carrie is antagonistic; when her father tries to talk to her about including Sharon in their lives, she refuses to listen. Only with Grace can Carrie talk about her feelings. When her father takes her, Sharon, Phyllis, and her boyfriend, Al, out for dinner, Carrie feels lonelier and lonelier as everyone else seems happier. Then her father announces that he and Sharon will be married in September. Carrie dashes into the restroom. Sharon follows her, but Carrie rudely rebuffs her overtures. Then Grace has a heart attack. Carrie visits her often in the hospital, becoming so absorbed in her friend's illness that the New York workshop seems unimportant and Carrie sees Bridget off on the train without a qualm. When Carrie next goes to visit Grace in the hospital, she's told the woman has been moved to a nursing home. Carrie is very upset, but Grace reassures her. As Carrie watches Grace's belongings being carried out of her house, she feels that familiar sense of loss. Sharon understands and is kind and supportive. Carrie makes a small gesture of goodwill toward Sharon when she brings her some of Grace's flowers. Al and Phyllis also announce their engagement. When Bridget returns from her workshop, Carrie can tell her that all is well.

Carrie stops fighting the changes in her life with the help of an elderly woman who knows how to listen and how to accept whatever life deals her. Carrie tells her own story and it is well written, with perceptive characterizations. Children whose parents are remarrying or whose classmates are going through family realignments will empathize with Carrie's resistance, anger, fear, and loneliness.

Ages 9-12

Also available in:
No other form known

489

Raskin, Ellen

Figgs & Phantoms

Black/white illustrations by the author.
Dutton Children's Books, 1977.
(152 pages)

DEATH: of Relative
IDENTITY, SEARCH FOR
MOURNING, STAGES OF
Love, meaning of
Shame

Mona Lisa Newton is an overweight, self-conscious adolescent who is ashamed of her vaudeville family, the Fabulous Figgs. Her mother, Sister Figg Newton, is a tap-dancing baton twirler, and her father, Newton Newton is a used-car dealer. Several other members of the Figg family reside in the town of Pineapple: Uncle Truman, a human pretzel and sign painter who cannot spell; twin Uncles Romulus and Remus; Uncle Kadota, a dog trainer; his wife Gracie Jo, the dog catcher; their son Fido; and Uncle Florence Italy, a four-foot six-inch former child dancing star. The only relative Mona respects is Uncle Florence, who is now a dealer in rare books. Mona loves this uncle very much, but he is gravely ill, and Mona fears he will soon leave her and go to "Capri," the Figg heaven discovered in a vision by an ancestor. When Uncle Florence dies, Mona refuses to accept his death and resolves to find the legendary Capri so that she can join him there. Searching Uncle Florence's books for a clue to Capri's location, Mona discovers that a newly purchased volume has disappeared from his collection. Undaunted, she finds a book of maps, including one of an island called Caprichos. Mona now believes she knows the way to the Figg heaven, and she sets off to find Uncle Florence. She discovers her uncle located happily in Caprichos, but Mona learns that because she is unable to make a contribution to the community and therefore does not yet belong on Caprichos, she cannot stay there. Returning home, Mona awakens in a hospital. She has been very ill. Has Capri been a dream? When Mona sees Mr. Bargain, the old bookseller—an old friend of Uncle Florence—she is convinced that she has been to Capri! Yet, "Mona had a lot of remembering to do, a lot of living and learning and loving to do, before she left once more for Caprichos."

The clever names and delightfully whimsical drawings add much humor to this unusual and memorable story. Until the end of the book, some readers may not realize that Mona is ill and that her journey to Caprichos is a dream sequence.

Ages 12 and up

Also available in:
Braille—*Figgs & Phantoms*
Library of Congress (NLSBPH)

490

Raskin, Ellen

Spectacles

Color illustrations by the author.
Atheneum Publishers, 1988.
(48 pages)

GLASSES, WEARING OF

Iris Fogel sees things. She has seen a fire-breathing dragon, a giant nuthatch, an Indian making funny faces, a friendly looking bull dog, a fat kangaroo, and a fuzzy green caterpillar. The things that Iris sees are not really what they appear to be, so Iris's mother takes her to an "eye doctor." When the doctor tells Iris that she needs glasses, Iris says, "NO!" She keeps saying no as she is picking out her frames, but stops resisting once she looks through her new glasses.

Iris is accused of misbehaving because of the things she says she has seen. When her mother takes her to have her eyes examined, she balks at the idea of having to wear glasses. However, once she tries them out, she realizes that she has an advantage over other people: she is able to see things not just one way, but two.

Ages 4-9

Also available in:
Paperbound—*Spectacles*
Aladdin Books

Talking book—*Spectacles*
Library of Congress (NLSBPH)

491

Rawlings, Marjorie Kinnan

The Yearling

Color illustrations by N.C. Wyeth.
Charles Scribner's Sons, 1985.
(416 pages)

LONELINESS
Death: of pet
Family: unity
Friendship: meaning of
Nature: appreciation of

Twelve-year-old Jody Baxter lives in the seclusion and security of Baxter's Island, his family's homestead in northern Florida. Ma Baxter is a no-nonsense, work-hardened woman. Penny Baxter, Jody's father, struggles to provide for his family. Although the safety of home provides some comfort and pleasure for Jody, he is lonely and longs for affection from outside the family circle. Jody's father understands his son's need for other friendships and allows Jody to keep a fawn as a pet. Although the acquisition of a pet is against Ma's better judgment, the fawn fills a void in Jody's life. As the fawn matures to a yearling, it begins to destroy crops. There seems no way to prevent the deer from continuing his destruction. Penny tells Jody to destroy the fawn, and Jody goes through the heart-rending ordeal of killing his beloved pet. Although at first he feels betrayed by his father, Jody eventually begins to understand the necessity of the act.

Florida frontier life is described movingly, and the feelings of the three main characters are well defined. The reader gains a respect for wildlife through Penny's sensitivity to it. Women are treated as second-class citizens, in keeping with the times, and disparaging terms are casually used to refer to black people.

Ages 12 and up

Also available in:
Braille—*The Yearling*
Library of Congress (NLSBPH)

Paperbound—*The Yearling*
Collier Books

Talking Book—*The Yearling*
Library of Congress (NLSBPH)

492

Reiss, Johanna

The Journey Back

HarperCollins Publishers, Inc., 1976.
(212 pages)

CHANGE: Accepting
Belonging
Jewish
Maturation
Stepparent: mother
War

A young Jewish girl, Annie de Leeuw, and an older sister, Sini, have spent the last two-and-a-half years of World War II hidden in the upstairs bedroom of Johan and Dientje Oostervel's farmhouse in Usselo, Holland. With the war over, Annie, now thirteen, and Sini rejoin their father and another sister, a convert to Christianity, in their home village. (Their mother had died early in the war.) Annie, who has grown to love Johan, his mother, and Dientje, is unhappy at home. Everyone and everything has changed. Her two older sisters have other interests and eventually move to the city. Father is gone much of the time, trying to rebuild his business. None of Annie's pre-war friends return to the village, and Annie is slow to make new friends. Even physical recovery comes slowly, with daily visits to the masseur to strengthen legs weak and painful from her long confinement. She longs to return to Johan and Dientje. Her father remarries, and her stepmother brings to the household, along with many lovely possessions, a critical eye for whether Annie is behaving "like a lady." Annie longs for her stepmother's approval, but that seems reserved for her own daughter, away at boarding school. At last Annie is allowed to visit Johan and Dientje—but once there she is bored by the routine of farm life. Though Johan and Dientje still love her, she feels like a misfit. Returning home, she can only hope one day to win her stepmother's favor.

In this first-person account, a Jewish girl describes the spiritual hardships of rebuilding one's life after war has destroyed all that was familiar and secure. Annie's own quiet struggle is complicated by her father's remarriage. But after repeated disappointments, she waits patiently for signs that she has come to where she belongs. This sequel to the autobiographical *The Upstairs Room* is a bittersweet picture of the aftermath of war, with its reunions, fragmented families, shortages, ravaged villages, determination, and hope.

Ages 10-14

Also available in:
Braille—*The Journey Back*
Library of Congress (NLSBPH)

Paperbound—*The Journey Back*
HarperCollins Publishers, Inc.

Talking Book—*The Journey Back*
Library of Congress (NLSBPH)

493

Reuter, Margaret

My Mother Is Blind

Color photographs by Philip Lanier.
Children's Press, Inc., 1979.
(31 pages)

BLINDNESS
Family: unity

A mother and father and their son, about eight, have prepared a picnic lunch to take to the park. The mother has recently gone blind. She must hold her husband's arm as she walks. When she first became blind, the boy and his father had to do all the housework because the mother was sad and fearful. Then a special teacher began coming to the house. He taught Mother new ways to perform household tasks. Now she listens to recipes on a tape recorder and is able to cook and bake. She cleans and even does the grocery shopping again. She reads Braille and labels foods with Braille labels. She uses a special cane to walk outside, and at the park she distinguishes each plant by its smell and the shape of its leaves. Various sounds help her know where she is and what and who might be around her. The boy is glad his mother has learned to do so much, but "I wish she could see."

A boy describes his mother's and the family's adjustment to her blindness. The emphasis is on the woman's strengths and growing independence. Photographs illustrate the steps of her progress; illustrations of a Braille book and of writing in Braille with a stylus are of special interest. The text can be easily understood by young children.

Ages 5-8

Also available in:
Cassette—*My Mother Is Blind*
Library of Congress (NLSBPH)

494

Rey, Margret Elisabeth Waldstein and Hans Augusto Rey

Curious George Goes to the Hospital

Color illustrations by the authors.
Houghton Mifflin Co., 1973.
(48 pages)

HOSPITAL, GOING TO
Surgery

George, a monkey, lives with a man who wears a yellow suit. When George swallows a piece of a puzzle, he is sent to the hospital, first to have an X-ray and then to have the puzzle part surgically removed. George is put to bed. The man in the yellow suit stays with him. When the man has to leave for the night, George cries. He feels better when the man returns the next morning as he said he would. George is kept busy having his temperature and blood pressure taken. Before the operation he is given a pill to make him sleepy and a shot to make him unconscious. After surgery, George feels sick and dizzy, so he sleeps most of the day. The next day, George feels better and gets out of bed. He entertains the children in the playroom and causes much confusion when the mayor visits the hospital.

This book was written in collaboration with the Children's Hospital Medical Center in Boston. It depicts a common hospital experience, including descriptions of injections, nurses, X-rays, operating rooms, feeling sick after anesthesia, and being afraid when left alone in the hospital.

Ages 4-9

Also available in:
Braille—*Curious George Goes to the Hospital*
Library of Congress (NLSBPH)

Paperbound—*Curious George Goes to the Hospital*
Houghton Mifflin Co.

495

Riley, Jocelyn

Only My Mouth Is Smiling

William Morrow & Company, Inc., 1982.
(222 pages)

FAMILY: Relationships
MENTAL ILLNESS: of Parent
Boy-girl relationships: dating
School: classmate relationships
Violence

Thirteen-year-old Merle Carlson has learned how to paste on a smile that has nothing to do with how she's feeling inside, a handy device when you have a frequent mental patient for a mother. Elaine Carlson has stayed well for so long this time, however, that Merle and her younger brother and sister are beginning to believe she's cured. She has kept the same job for nearly two years and has been paying rent all this time to Grandma. Her face is even fairly clear; it is always covered with "red zits" just before she has a nervous breakdown. The children are not, therefore, prepared for what happens one Saturday morning in July when Grandma gets home from having her hair done. She and their mother get into a fight over the rent money that culminates in Grandma pushing Mrs. Carlson onto the floor and kicking her. Even though the scene has been violent, the children leave the house with their mother thinking they are just accompanying her on her usual Saturday escape to the movie theater. They end up at the Chicago bus depot buying one-way tickets to northern Wisconsin. After riding all afternoon and night, they finally arrive at Lake Lune, where last spring their mother made the down payment on a lakefront lot. Mrs. Carlson buys a tent, a few clothes, and other necessities. With the exception of a once-a-week hike into town for supplies, the family stays in this secluded spot for the rest of the summer. Their lives are uninterrupted except for one visit from Grandma, who has traced their whereabouts. The women have a loud argument during which the children feel torn in their loyalties to both adults. Merle later wonders why, "if Grandma is so sane," she can't see that "she always sets Mother off with the things she says." As autumn approaches, Mrs. Carlson rents a small house in town. At least now they have running water. The children sleep on a mattress and box-spring set left on the floor of one of the bedrooms. Their mother finds a part-time job as bookkeeper for a feed-and-grain company and brings home bags of free oatmeal for them to eat. On the first day of school, Merle walks to the junior-senior high feeling happy about the few hours she will have each day to live her own private life. She makes friends and meets Ricky Ellesen, to whom she's very attracted. Eventually she discovers that Ricky's apparent interest in her is only his way of making a former girlfriend jealous. One day Mr. Hall, the school counselor, calls Merle in for a conference. He explains that he has had a letter from her grandmother detailing her mother's mental problems and expressing concern for the children's welfare. Reluctant to confide anything that might get back to her mother, Merle does her best to make him think everything is fine. Then Merle returns home after the Homecoming Dance to find her mother sitting alone in the dark, smoking two cigarettes at one time, and talking about the evil forces that wish her ill. Her skin lately has become "pasty white" with "big red zits popping out," so Merle knows something bad is about to happen. Elaine behaves strangely all weekend and on Sunday afternoon Merle calls her grandmother; returning to Chicago seems "the least worst of all the possible terrible solutions." Grandma promises that she and the children will go to family counseling sessions while Elaine is in the hospital. By Monday morning, Mrs. Carlson is completely irrational. Early in the morning, a social worker comes to the door with two policemen. They take Mrs. Carlson away in a straitjacket. Shortly afterward, Grandma arrives to take the children home. She explains that part of the reason for their mother's relapses is her reluctance to take antipsychotic drugs. When she stops taking them she can't sleep, her skin breaks out, and she eventually has a breakdown. Even with this explanation, there are many questions left in Merle's mind. She can only hope the family therapy sessions will help them all understand mental illness a little better.

Three children live at the mercy of their mother's eccentric whims and occasionally psychotic behavior in this serious, believable first-person narrative. They can't argue with her because she becomes irrational, and they can't always turn to their grandmother because her brutality with her daughter only makes things worse. They know that confiding in anyone or acknowledging that anything is wrong will ultimately reinforce their mother's paranoia. The only alternative is to pretend that everything is fine. The story offers considerable insight into the trauma of being part of a family touched by mental illness. Merle's tone is rather matter-of-fact, never maudlin, but the terror of her life comes through clearly.

Ages 12-14

Also available in:
No other form known

496

Roberts, Willo Davis

Don't Hurt Laurie!

Black/white illustrations by Ruth Sanderson.
Atheneum Publishers, 1978.
(166 pages)

CHILD ABUSE
Guilt, feelings of
Loneliness
Mental illness: of parent
Stepbrother/Stepsister
Stepparent: father

Eleven-year-old Laurie Kolman lives with her mother, Annabelle, and her stepfather, Jack, and Jack's son, Tim (nine), and daughter, Shelly (five), by an earlier marriage. Annabelle's first husband had deserted her when Laurie was three, and the mother has been physically abusing Laurie ever since. Tim knows this, knows that Laurie is not "clumsy," as Annabelle insists to friends, neighbors, and hospital staff, every time Laurie "bumps herself." Neither Tim nor Laurie will tell anyone about the abuse for fear of Annabelle taking revenge. Besides, Laurie feels that no one would believe her. Annabelle is always on her best behavior when Jack is home, and always lies so convincingly about Laurie's injuries that Laurie thinks her mother really believes them to be accidents. Laurie has no friends to talk to; every time she finds one, and every time someone in the hospital emergency ward notices the frequency of her visits, Annabelle moves to a new neighborhood. In a rage one day, Annabelle threatens to kill Laurie, and as usual the girl can tell no one, feeling that somehow these rages are her own fault. It is not until Annabelle attacks Amigo, the puppy Laurie and her only friend have been secretly keeping, that Laurie turns on her mother. Annabelle is so infuriated that, forgetting Tim is watching, she beats Laurie unconscious with a poker. When Laurie comes to, she knows she cannot live with her mother anymore. Tim, who had feared his stepsister was dead, insists they tell his grandmother, Nell. All three children make the long bus trip across town, and Nell is told the shocking story. To Laurie's amazement and relief, Nell believes every word. Jack and Annabelle come, but Nell refuses to let the children go back with Annabelle, and urges Jack to get help for his wife. For the first time in her life, Laurie is free of fear. While Laurie's mother receives treatment, the children stay with Nell. Laurie learns both to trust and to love.

This tense story untangles the inner lives of an abused child, including her reasons for not seeking help. Sometimes Laurie tries to escape with books, without which she would have no idea what normal families are like. Her fantasy about her real father coming to save her only prolongs her silence to others. Each time she does decide to tell someone, her own fear or circumstances beyond her control stop her. Such incidents are so convincingly told that we come to share Laurie's bafflement and despair. But we come as well to believe Jack: Annabelle's derangement is connected with her having been beaten herself as a child, and never having told. Jack will stay with her and help her get well.

Ages 10-14

Also available in:
Paperbound—*Don't Hurt Laurie!*
Aladdin Books

497

Robinet, Harriette Gillem

Ride the Red Cycle

Black/white illustrations by David Brown.
Houghton Mifflin Co., 1980.
(34 pages)

HANDICAPS: Multiple
PERSEVERANCE
Brain injury
Courage, meaning of
Sibling: relationships
Success
Wheelchair, dependence on

Eleven-year-old Jerome Johnson wears thick eyeglasses, special shoes, and leg braces. He speaks slowly and his speech is slurred. Because his legs have been paralyzed since a viral infection left him with brain damage at the age of two, Jerome has spent most of his life in a wheelchair. Now he has convinced himself that he can make his legs work again. He has shared his secret dream of owning a three-wheel cycle with his older sister, Tilly, who helps him ask Mama and Papa about buying one. Mama, who Jerome knows fusses and fumes to hide her fears for him, is angered by his request, but Papa is sympathetic. He asks Mama what the physical therapists say, and she answers softly that they think a cycle would strengthen Jerome's legs. So Papa takes Jerome and Tilly to buy a large, red, three-wheel cycle. He puts a special seat on it and alters the pedals. The first time Jerome sits on the cycle, the whole neighborhood comes to watch him. His legs tremble, he's nervous, and he drools, but Jerome cannot make the pedals go. His audience slowly drifts away. Every day Jerome sits on the cycle for hours, but nothing happens. One day he has an idea. He asks Tilly to take him up by the alley where the pavement slopes to the street. Here the cycle can build some momentum, and his legs can learn the motions of pedaling. All summer long Tilly takes Jerome to this secret place, and little by little his legs begin to work as the muscles grow stronger. Jerome has another secret too, something that not even Tilly knows about, something that he practices nightly in his room. Summer ends, and the neighborhood plans a Labor Day block party. One of the events is a talent show, and Tilly enters Jerome. At the time of his performance, she brings Jerome out to the sidewalk on his cycle. Slowly he pedals to the middle of the block. There he stops, bows, and climbs off the cycle. Standing alone, he haltingly stammers a thank-you to Tilly, Papa, and Mama. Then he takes the few cautious steps toward his wheelchair, showing family and friends what he has practiced late at night. His family is ecstatic, his neighbors overjoyed. For Jerome, it is the greatest victory of his life—so far!

A brain-damaged boy makes great progress because of his courage and determination. Jerome's handicaps, limitations, and perseverance are all realistically portrayed, and readers will empathize with him and cheer him on. Especially well described are Jerome's relationships with his loving family. Pencil drawings further illustrate the rare qualities of this special boy, whose dreams and frustrations match those of the author's son.

Ages 7-11

Also available in:
No other form known

498

Rockwell, Anne F. and Harlow Rockwell

Can I Help?

Color illustrations by the authors.
Macmillan Publishing Company, Inc., 1982.
(24 pages counted)

HELPING

A little girl often asks, "Can I help?" She likes, for example, to "squish the suds in the sponge" and "squirt the hose all over the car," polishing it "until it shines in the sun." Sometimes she helps set the table or wash clothes. Sometimes she helps with the grocery shopping, picking out cereal and the kind of peanut butter she likes best, even pushing the big, heavy shopping cart. The next-door neighbors like the way the little girl helps them by entertaining their baby when they're busy. In the fall she rakes leaves, in the winter she shovels snow, and she's always ready to make cookies. There are some jobs, however, that her parents won't let her help with until she's bigger. One is mowing the lawn; another is painting the walls; another is slicing onions. The little girl's parents help her too. As a matter of fact, when they ask if they can help her tie her shoes, make her bed, or pick up her toys, she likes to say, "Yes!"

This first-person account, engagingly illustrated, captures the joy young children feel when adults have the patience to let them help. One of the Rockwells' My World series, the book could inspire the read-aloud audience with some new ideas for "helping."

Ages 3-6

Also available in:
Talking Book—*Can I Help?*
Library of Congress (NLSBPH)

499

Rockwell, Anne F. and Harlow Rockwell

I Love My Pets

Color illustrations by the authors.
Macmillan Publishing Company, Inc., 1982.
(24 pages counted)

PETS: Responsibility for
Pets: love for

A little boy has two pets, a dog and a goldfish. He feeds the dog three times a day and never bothers him while he's eating. When they play in the backyard, the boy throws a stick and the dog brings it back. He plays with his goldfish in a very different way, by making funny faces and watching the fish make them in return. The boy has to be careful when he feeds the goldfish because too much food would make him sick. The goldfish has a plant, a castle, and a mermaid in his bowl. "He likes to hide in his castle and swim around his mermaid." The boy brushes his dog and tucks him into bed at night with a blanket that used to be his. When it is time to clean the fishbowl, the boy and his father fill a pitcher with cold water and let it stand overnight. Then, in the morning, they put the goldfish in a paper cup with some of the old water while they wash the bowl and fill it with water from the pitcher. When they're finished, the boy empties the cup into the clean bowl. Whenever the dog drinks water, he gets his whiskers wet and drips onto the floor. The boy wipes up after him. On the dog's red collar are a license, a rabies tag, and a silver name tag that says Mac. These tags jingle when he walks. The goldfish's name is Goldie and he "wiggles and waves his tail when he swims." Mac wags his tail whenever he sees the boy. The boy loves his pets and agrees with his friend next door who thinks he's very lucky to have two.

A little boy tells how he cares for and loves his pets. Listeners and readers will learn some basics of pet care in this cheerful, vibrantly illustrated book, another in the Rockwells' My World series.

Ages 3-5

Also available in:
No other form known

500

Rockwell, Anne F. and Harlow Rockwell

Sick in Bed

Color illustrations by the authors.
Macmillan Publishing Company, Inc., 1982.
(24 pages counted)

ILLNESSES: Being Ill
Doctor, going to

A little boy comes home from school cranky and unable to eat his supper. He goes to bed early but wakes in the middle of the night shivering and feeling sick all over. His parents take his temperature, rub him down with warm water and alcohol, and stay with him until he goes back to sleep. In the morning he sucks on ice to soothe his sore throat until it is time to go to the doctor, who examines him thoroughly. Later, at home, his mother explains that the throat culture the doctor took is a way of finding out what kinds of germs are causing the sore throat. Then the doctor will know what medicine to prescribe. The rest of the day the boy drinks ginger ale and sucks cracked ice while his mother reads to him or he watches television in his room. The next morning his mother calls the doctor's office and learns that he has to go back and get a "big shot." It hurts, but he is very brave and doesn't cry. By that evening the boy feels well enough to eat, and the next day he plays in his room. On the weekend he goes outside with his dog and on Monday morning is ready to return to school. His teacher and friends all tell him how much they missed him.

This charmingly illustrated book moves step-by-step through a typical bout of childhood illness and a trip to the doctor. The examination is described and pictured and could help prepare a child for something other than a routine physical. The young narrator includes reassuringly familiar objects and experiences that enhance this addition to the Rockwells' My World series.

Ages 3-6

Also available in:
No other form known

501

Rockwell, Harlow

My Dentist

Color illustrations by the author.
Greenwillow Books, 1975.
(32 pages counted)

DENTIST, GOING TO

A little girl describes a routine visit to her dentist—the chair that goes up and down, the X-ray camera, his little mirror on a handle, the tools for taking tartar off her teeth, and his drill and its attachments. She has no cavities today, but she has her teeth cleaned and explains how that is done. After the dentist has brushed her teeth with a special drill attachment, he has her rinse her mouth, then polishes her teeth, and tells her to rinse again. Afterwards he checks each tooth, even the loose one and the space where she had lost one a week before. She is finished. The dentist lowers the chair, removes the plastic bib, and reminds her to take care of her teeth. The girl chooses a prize from the prize drawer and goes home.

This book is an informative preparation for a child's first visit to the dentist. Both the text and the illustrations are straightforwardly factual. No mention is made of a dental assistant, who in life often does the dentist's preliminary work. But the detailed drawings accurately show the tools and equipment.

Ages 4-7

Also available in:
Braille—*My Dentist*
Library of Congress (NLSBPH)

Paperbound—*My Dentist*
Greenwillow Books

502

Rockwell, Harlow

My Doctor

Color illustrations by the author.
Macmillan Publishing Company, Inc., 1973.
(24 pages counted)

DOCTOR, GOING TO

The five- or six-year-old boy who narrates this book goes to the doctor's office for a checkup. He notices the physician's equipment: a scale, a stethoscope, a blood-pressure gauge, an eye chart, a rubber mallet, and other interesting items. He tells the reader what each piece of equipment is used for and describes the examining table. The boy also mentions the thermometer, the medicines, the bandages, and finally the needle. He is told that he does not need a shot today. Saying goodbye to the physician, he comments "She is a nice doctor."

Briefly and clearly, this simple book describes the equipment routinely used during a physical checkup. It may be read to reassure a very young child who fears going to the doctor.

Ages 2-7

Also available in:
Braille—*My Doctor*
Library of Congress (NLSBPH)

503

Rockwell, Harlow

My Nursery School

Color illustrations by the author.
Greenwillow Books, 1990.
(24 pages counted, paperbound)

NURSERY SCHOOL

A little girl takes the reader along for a typical day at her nursery school. After introducing the two teachers and the nine other children, she describes the materials in the room and how the children use them: Susan builds a tower with blocks; Olly works on a puzzle; the girl herself molds clay; and so on. The children are also shown playing games, exercising, and reading.

Vivid pictures combine with a simple text to show what nursery school is like. The tone throughout is one of enjoyment and interest, and will encourage children approaching nursery school for the first time.

Ages 3-5

Also available in:
No other form known

504

Rodgers, Mary

Freaky Friday

HarperCollins Publishers, Inc., 1972.
(145 pages)

COMMUNICATION: Parent-Child
Empathy
Responsibility: accepting

Annabel Andrews, thirteen, wakes up one morning and discovers that her mind is in her mother's body. She thinks the change-about is terrific. As her mother, Annabel arranges for the family to spend the month of July with Grandmother, overlooking the fact that her father will not want to go. She breaks the washing machine, forgets to meet her younger brother at the bus, and prepares for her father's clients to come to dinner. She plans to meet with her "daughter's" principal, school psychologist, and homeroom teacher to discuss her "daughter's" poor grades and rude behavior in school. When mother/Annabel arrives at school, she is told that her "daughter" has skipped classes. Returning home, she finds that her "son" has been kidnapped by a beautiful stranger, her "husband's" clients have arrived, Annabel is still missing, and the police will not believe the story she is telling them. When Annabel, as her mother, recognizes that she is unable to cope with her situation, she retreats. In desperation, she begs her mother to return things to normal and her mother complies.

In this frantically funny first-person narrative, Annabel experiences several of the duties and troubles her mother must cope with daily. Annabel dislikes her brother until she sees him from her mother's point of view. Although the situation is fanciful, the insights Annabel gains in this story are realistic. She comes to understand her relationship with other family members and friends, and develops a greater appreciation of people.

Ages 10-13

Also available in:
Cassette—*Freaky Friday*
HarperCollins Publishers, Inc.

Paperbound—*Freaky Friday*
HarperCollins Publishers, Inc.

Talking Book—*Freaky Friday*
Library of Congress (NLSBPH)

505

Rodowsky, Colby F.

H. My Name Is Henley

Farrar, Straus & Giroux, Inc., 1980.
(184 pages)

PARENTAL: Unreliability
Belonging
Change: new home
Decision making
Parent/Parents: single
Security/Insecurity

Twelve-year-old Henley and her mother, Patti, are always on the move. Patti is eternally restless, believing that each of her jobs stifles her creativity. The next move, she's always sure, will make them both completely happy. On a casually extended, unthinking invitation from acquaintances, Patti uproots them once again to move to New York City, though Henley begs her not to, reminding Patti that this time she promised to stay put for a while. But Patti uses the thousand dollars sent to Henley by her paternal grandparents when her father died, although on Henley's insistence she leaves fifty dollars for "emergencies." When they arrive in New York, they find that Roger, a hard-working law student, and his wife, Margery, a nurse, are hardly the free-living, "creative," relaxed people Patti was expecting. Patti promises she'll look for an apartment and a job, but she insists on showing Henley around New York first. Henley is extremely uncomfortable about imposing on their unwilling hosts, but Patti begs Henley to trust her; this time things are going to be different. After all, Patti reminds her daughter, she gave up her job and everything just to bring Henley to New York where she could have "advantages." Despairing, Henley feels she is wearing away like a snake shedding skin after skin. Then Roger asks them to leave. Patti decides to return to Baltimore, although she changes her mind again at the bus depot and Henley must urge her on. In Baltimore they stay with a friend, Angel, who lectures Patti about being immature and unfair to Henley. Patti resents the lectures and soon leaves. Henley is torn between wanting to defend Patti and needing to agree with Angel. They drive south of Baltimore, wildly, and Henley's "head throbbed with Patti's refrain: round and round and round she goes—where she stops, nobody knows." They drive endlessly, aimlessly, stopping at hotels and eating in restaurants. When they have less than one hundred dollars left and their car breaks down, they head for Aunt Mercy, a woman Henley's heard many stories about. Aunt Mercy is a doctor in a small town and lives with Booshie, an old, slightly demented woman. Aunt Mercy accepts their arrival calmly. As the summer days go by, Henley comes to love the stability of the small town. But Patti begins complaining about feeling trapped. After two weeks in a job Aunt Mercy got for her, she is already bored. She admits what Henley has suspected all along: she's not a real niece

R

of Aunt Mercy's, just an old friend of one of her nieces. Patti teases Booshie, and Henley doesn't like the meanness she feels coming from her mother. One day Henley is enjoying herself at the Fourth of July carnival when Patti pulls her away and tells her to grab a few things so they can catch a train out of town. She makes all her usual promises, but this time Henley refuses to go along. She spends the time until Patti's train leaves with Slug, a girl her own age. The rest of the summer is solid contentment for Henley. When school starts that fall, she feels close to Aunt Mercy, Booshie, and the others. But she always remembers that it was Patti who brought her here.

In this tense and memorable first-person narrative, a young girl plays mother to her own restless, immature parent, following her unwillingly from town to town until the girl finally makes the break to achieve the security she needs. Henley's situation is an agonizing one, and readers will get deeply involved in her plight. Her sense of coming home after she realizes she can't survive with Patti any longer provides a satisfying conclusion to a very affecting book.

Ages 10-13

Also available in:
No other form known

506

Rodowsky, Colby F.

P.S. Write Soon

Farrar, Straus & Giroux, Inc., 1987.
(149 pages)

BRACES ON BODY/LIMBS
REALITY, ESCAPING
Attention Seeking
Boasting
Honesty/Dishonesty
Inferiority, feelings of
Sibling: youngest

Tanner McClean, a sixth grader, is the youngest of three children in a successful, talented, and busy family, and she wears a waist-to-ankle brace on her paralyzed leg, the result of an auto accident four years earlier. But Tanner writes her pen pal, Jessie Lee, none of this—preferring to fabricate tales of her athletic ability. When Tanner's older brother, Jon, elopes, she writes Jessie of being a bridesmaid at Jon's beautiful wedding, and neglects to tell her that she dislikes her new sister-in-law, Cheryl. She also dislikes the fact that Jon and Cheryl have settled in the third-floor apartment of the family home while Jon continues law school. When Tanner visits the apartment, she learns that Cheryl has inherited a small house in Virginia from which she has brought some things with her. In Tanner's next letter to Jessie this fact becomes Cheryl owning a very grand house indeed, from which she has brought precious antiques. In ensuing letters, Tanner brags that Jon and Cheryl have bought a house and are remodeling it with her help and that Cheryl is pregnant. But Cheryl accidently discovers what Tanner has written and confronts her. She reminds Tanner that she is not pregnant and that they have bought no house—in fact she and Jon will be moving to the small house in Virginia. She then encourages Tanner to tell Jessie the truth, to let her meet the real Tanner. But Tanner does this only after Jessie writes that she and her parents will be taking a vacation trip and would like to drop in on the McCleans for a visit. When at last Tanner receives a reply to her confessional letter, she happily shows it to Cheryl: her pen pal still wants to visit and wants Tanner to visit her during the summer.

A handicapped youngster improves reality in letters to a pen pal, while her feelings of inferiority and anger go unrecognized by her otherwise considerate, understanding family. To compensate, Tanner lies, falls down on purpose, speaks rudely to her sister-in-law, even steals to impress a friend. Only her new sister-in-law has the insight to recognize Tanner's unhappiness and help her do something about it. Despite the predictability of the plot, readers will empathize with Tanner and may want to discuss similar feelings and experiences.

Ages 10-12

Also available in:
Cassette—*P.S. Write Soon*
Library of Congress (NLSBPH)

Paperbound—*P.S. Write Soon*
Farrar, Straus & Giroux, Inc. (Sunburst Books)

507

Rodowsky, Colby F.

What About Me?

Farrar, Straus & Giroux, Inc., 1989.
(136 pages)

DOWN SYNDROME
JEALOUSY: Sibling
Ambivalence, feelings of
Death: of sibling
Guilt, feelings of
Talents: artistic

Dorie, fifteen, lives in New York City with her parents and her eleven-year-old brother, Fred, who has Down's Syndrome. Dorie is a talented artist planning to make art her career. She has always gotten along well with her parents and liked her brother, but lately it seems to her that the older Fred gets, the harder he is to manage, and the more often her mother asks her to change her plans and "help out" with him. The boy's heart condition requires particular caution in the choosing of baby-sitters. Dorie has to miss a party because of him, and her parents miss seeing art shows where Dorie's works are displayed, because there is no one to baby-sit for Fred. Usually affable and well-received even by strangers, Fred is nevertheless becoming an embarrassment to Dorie. She tells us, "I hated him Honest-to-God hate. Not all the time, not every day, but enough to scare me sometimes." Just when she thinks her life could not possibly be worse, her father tells her that the family will be moving to Maryland so that he can join his brother's law firm—but primarily to be near relatives who can lend a hand with Fred. Dorie sees her career plans going up in smoke. She is so desperate to stay in New York that she gives up an internship teaching art so that she can teach at Fred's school, hoping that her show of interest in her brother will make her parents want to stay. But they are steadfast in their decision. After several explosive scenes with her parents and an unfortunate incident in which Fred breaks her best ceramic piece, Dorie's mother and father arrange for her to stay with Guntzie, her art teacher, mentor, and friend, while Dorie finishes her last two years of high school. With that settled, Dorie begins to soften toward her brother. She agrees to baby-sit one night while her parents go to dinner. But when she looks in to check on Fred, she sees that his lips are blue and he is gasping for air. She calls the doctor, and an ambulance takes Fred to the hospital, where he dies. Dorie is amazed to find that her parents had been worried about her being alone in so frightening a situation. She sees they do think of her. Fred's funeral is held in Maryland, and on her way back to New York, having watched her mother grieving, Dorie realizes how much a part of their lives Fred has become, and how much she will miss him.

In this first-person narrative, a girl, jealous of the attention given her handicapped brother, alternately loves and hates him. Because she never fully expresses her feelings, including her guilt about those feelings, she becomes increasingly confused, resentful, and lonely. The relationship with her teacher affords her some opportunity to vent emotions and, toward the end of the story, she has gained some insight into her family's relationships. But it is not until Fred's death that she understands what her brother has meant to all of them and that she loved him. The stress of a family coping with a retarded child is dramatized realistically here, and Dorie's confusion is of a kind readers will sympathize with.

Ages 11-13

Also available in:
Paperbound—*What About Me?*
Farrar, Straus & Giroux, Inc. (Sunburst Books)

508

Rosen, Lillian D.

Just Like Everybody Else

Harcourt Brace Jovanovich, Inc., 1981.
(155 pages)

COMMUNICATION: Importance of
DEAFNESS
Family: unity
Friendship: meaning of

After a bus accident, fifteen-year-old Jenny is left totally deaf. Angry and resentful, she is not convinced she even wants to live. She does begin taking lessons in lip-reading, practicing with family and friends. Still, the first time after the accident that Jenny goes to a party, she leaves in despair after realizing how impossible it is to read lips in a group and still keep up with what's going on. Wondering if anyone will ever want her, she briefly thinks about killing herself. In the summer her world shrinks even more when a good friend moves away and other friends take summer jobs. She can't use the phone, no one asks her to baby-sit anymore, and when a new girl her age moves into the neighborhood she rejects Jenny when she discovers she's deaf. One day Joe Benton comes to visit her; they have mutual friends. Joe has been deaf since birth and his "deaf" speech is sometimes difficult for hearing people to understand. But Jenny can read his lips. He begins to teach her to sign and takes her to her first captioned movie. She enjoys meeting other hearing-impaired people, so encouraging and accepting, and she's relieved to be able to communicate again. She and Joe spend a lot of time together, sharing ideas and practicing signing. He takes her to his house where a number of special electronic devices make life easier for him and his deaf parents. One night when she's there, the police call and ask his father to come see if a child found by the highway is deaf. Jenny goes with them and watches the relief on little Mary's face when Mr. Benton begins signing to her. She has run away from an abusive foster home and a school where no allowances are made for her deafness. Mr. Benton comforts her, suggesting the police call the state deaf association's hotline. Joe has told Jenny how difficult school is for him. He understands very little and faces continual frustration, yet he's learning more in a regular school than he did in the too-easy school for the deaf. He intends to go on to college. When Jenny's parents tell her she must return to school in a month, she is distressed at having to go through the motions of attending school when she will understand so little. Then Joe comes over and says he's been accepted at several colleges, including two that are just for the deaf. He tells Jenny to continue her education, suggesting that she can help change the current unworkable system. Jenny's parents discover that under the law she has a right to a proper education, and they are prepared to stand behind her and work for a solution. With the support and encouragement of her parents and Joe, Jenny feels ready to return to school.

This first-person narrative of a teenager who loses her hearing is an appealing story in itself, but it also contains a great deal of information about living with this disability. At times the need to convey information overpowers the story line, but this doesn't happen often enough to alienate the reader. Jenny's insistence on her need for human contact, which her deafness has radically affected, will be illuminating for hearing readers, as will her hatred of pity and her desire to show she can function in a hearing world, given half a chance. She reproaches hearing people for not even trying to meet her special needs—small things such as facing her when they talk and speaking more slowly. This readable and informative book offers the special insight of an author who is deaf.

Ages 11 and up

Also available in:
No other form known

509

Sachs, Marilyn

Amy and Laura

Black/white illustrations by Tracy Sugarman.
Scholastic, Inc., 1984.
(160 pages) o.p.

PARENTAL: Overprotection
Communication: parent-child
Illnesses: of parent
Sibling: relationships

Amy is ten and her sister Laura is twelve. Their mother, hospitalized for a year following an auto accident, has returned home in a wheelchair. Daddy asks Amy and Laura to keep things peaceful and pleasant for Mama; they are not to worry her with problems until she is well. The girls must learn to adjust to the changes in their mother's behavior—changes resulting from the trauma and from her long separation from home. Laura, who has always been very close to her mother, feels the changes most deeply. She stays away from home as much as possible to avoid the sight of her invalid mother. Laura is also kept from pursuing her own interests and activities; she must stop being a monitor at school because of her mother's overprotection. Family tension mounts after weeks of catering to Mama's needs and it erupts in a fight between the two sisters. This crisis leads Mama to discover that the family has been shielding her from all unpleasantness. She reveals how unhappy she has been in her helpless dependence on the others. She has not felt comfortable with the quiet restrained atmosphere since her return home, unaware that her husband told the rest of the family to shelter her. From now on things will be different! Mother and the girls begin to renew their earlier relationships, enjoying each other's confidences.

Amy and Laura experience anger, hurt, and frustration, which they finally displace onto each other. Their relationships with both parents are realistically detailed, and the crisis that precipitates their mother's return to full family life is natural and satisfying.

Ages 9-12

Also available in:
Braille—*Amy and Laura*
Library of Congress (NLSBPH)

Cassette—*Amy and Laura*
Library of Congress (NLSBPH)

510

Sachs, Marilyn

The Bears' House

Black/white illustrations by Louis Glanzman.
Dutton Children's Books, 1987.
(81 pages)

REALITY, ESCAPING
Abandonment
Mental illness: of parent
Responsibility: accepting
Thumb sucking

Fourth-grader Fran Ellen Smith sucks her thumb and smells bad. She skips school to care for her seven-month-old sister, Flora. She is also the target of classmates' ridicule. Fran Ellen's home life is deplorable. Her father has left the family—Mrs. Smith, four daughters, and one son. The abandonment leads Mrs. Smith to withdraw and sleep or cry most of the time. Fran Ellen's only joy is in the fantasy world she has built around the beautiful dollhouse in her classroom. Here she can escape her shoddy world and be the heroine, respected and accepted by the bear family in the dollhouse. Her teacher, Miss Thompson, persists in trying to see Mrs. Smith to discuss Fran Ellen's truancy. Meanwhile, the Smith children have agreed to keep their family troubles a secret to prevent being split up and placed in foster homes. When Miss Thompson visits the Smith home, she is appalled at the mess and the neglect of the children. Fran Ellen tries very hard to overcome her "bad habits," hoping to keep Miss Thompson from interfering further. Eventually Fran Ellen is awarded the dollhouse because of her efforts to stop playing hooky and sucking her thumb. When Miss Thompson helps Fran Ellen take the dollhouse home, she discovers that the situation there is deteriorating. The reader is left with the impression that the teacher will try to find help for the family.

This open-ended story presents a family in which the parents' behavior results in their children's having to assume responsibilities and worries far beyond their capabilities. This story could be very depressing for some readers.

Ages 9-12

Also available in:
No other form known

511
Sachs, Marilyn
Class Pictures
Dutton Children's Books, 1980.
(138 pages)

FRIENDSHIP: Best Friend
MATURATION
Grandparent: living in child's home
Loyalty

Patricia Maddox (Pat) and Lorraine Scheiner (Lolly) become best friends in kindergarten. In first grade, they attend each other's birthday parties, which are as different as the girls themselves—Lolly with all the advantages an affluent family can provide, Pat living in a small apartment above a store with her widowed mother, her grandmother, and two brothers. In second grade, it is popular, outgoing Pat who protects funny, artistic, unpopular Lolly. That year, Pat learns that the man she always thought of as her daddy was not really her father, that her mother was married once before. By fourth grade the girls are in separate classrooms, since Pat has been placed in the gifted class. She talks to Mr. Evans, her third-grade teacher, about her dislike of the class. When the girls are in sixth grade, Pat's grandmother has a romantic interest, Mr. Nagel. Although Pat and her mother do not get along, they both dislike Mr. Nagel. He and Grandma eventually marry; Pat's mother does not attend the wedding. Pat becomes extremely interested in rocketry and begins spending time at Mr. Evans's house using his tools to build a reflecting telescope. She baby-sits for his young son, Luke, and becomes friendly with his wife, Meg. When seventh-grade class pictures come out, Pat realizes that "Lolly had become a beauty." As an eighth grader, Lolly blossoms socially and is very popular. But she refuses to go to a party unless Pat is invited. Pat thinks of herself more and more as a scientist, but it is Lolly who manipulates a teacher into allowing Pat to enroll in a metal shop class. "There was a reshuffling in our friendship too. After all those years of looking after Lolly and protecting her, suddenly she didn't need my protection anymore. Suddenly, it looked as if I might need hers. And I hated it." In ninth grade, Lolly and Pat admit they have each been jealous of the other over the years: Lolly envying Pat's firmness of purpose, Pat envying Lolly's beauty. In tenth grade, Pat confides more in Mr. Evans than in Lolly, becoming almost a part of the Evans family. When Pat and Lolly double-date, Pat's date has eyes only for Lolly. Lolly's picture is all over the yearbook, but Pat is considered "a brain." Sometimes their friendship seems finished, but they still retain ties to each other. As a junior, Pat has "shameful daydreams" about Meg dying and herself ending up in Mr. Evans's arms. That year Lolly is president of the Ecology Club. It starts with five members but swells to many more under her leadership; most are boys. As seniors, both girls want to demonstrate against a nuclear power plant, but Lolly's mother won't permit her to take part. Pat does, and Mr. Evans picks her up at the detention center after she is arrested. Pat is accepted by both Stanford and MIT. She and Mr. Evans have an emotional scene when he tells her Meg is pregnant and she cries and says she can't bear to leave him. The summer after graduation, Lolly prepares to move away from home and Pat to leave for MIT. They are still best friends, but both admit they are glad to be going away from each other for a while. They share their fears about the future and the changes it might bring. Lolly suggests that, instead of the dire things Pat thinks might happen to their friendship, "maybe it will be even better than it's ever been."

Pat narrates these fourteen chapters that chronicle her fourteen-year and continuing friendship with Lolly. The complementary nature of friendship, the give-and-take, the enduring loyalty are all part of Pat and Lolly's relationship. Each becomes an individual in her own right, their friendship having to change and adapt as they grow; sometimes keeping pace, sometimes not. Giving strength to Pat's lyrical reflections on a childhood friendship is the well-drawn story of two girls and how they grew.

Ages 10-13

Also available in:
No other form known

512
Sachs, Marilyn
Hello. . . . Wrong Number
Black/white illustrations by Pamela Johnson.
Scholastic, Inc., 1984.
(106 pages, paperbound) o.p.

BOY-GIRL RELATIONSHIPS
Appearance: concern about
Self, attitude toward: accepting

When Angie calls Jim McCone to apologize for telling him to get lost at the dance Saturday night, she misdials and gets another Jim, beginning her apology before she realizes her mistake. She quickly hangs up, but then calls the boy back for his promise not to tell Jim McCone of her intention to apologize. She has reconsidered: Jim McCone had his hands all over her while they were dancing. The next night Angie calls Jim again to make him promise not to say a word to Jim McCone. He promises, after supplying his own evidence that McCone is not worth her attention. The next night, Angie asks Jim to tell her all the bad things he knows about McCone so she won't be tempted to call him. Jim does—and also tells Angie a little about himself. The next night they talk again, but not about anything that would allow them to identify each other. Angie says she'd just be a pest, bringing all her problems to him. And she likes being able to tell him things she can't tell anyone else. She muses about why people treat her as a helpless, silly blonde, deciding it's partly because she plays that game. Jim plays

S

and sings some sad songs he's written. He tells Angie about breaking up with his last girlfriend, who crowded him and tried to change herself to be more what he wanted. When Angie asks if he only writes sad songs, he sings her a bouncy tune that he recently composed. But he won't tell her the occasion for it. The next time she calls him, Jim sings her "Angie's Song." Now she wants them to meet, but Jim refuses. Maybe there are things about him that Angie wouldn't like. Nobody is perfect, she replies, mentioning a funny-looking boy who followed her around in school that day and even asked someone who Angie was. Jim points out that even such a funny-looking boy might be beautiful on the inside. But Angie insists that this boy with the big nose couldn't be anything like Jim. When Angie calls again, she says she saw the short, funny-looking boy with the big nose again. She's discovered that he is Lisa Franklin's former boyfriend named Jim, that he is musically talented but was too shy to sing any of his songs for Lisa, that he and Lisa broke up because he was crowding her and trying to change himself to be more what she wanted. Angie and Jim both admit that the time they spent talking to each other on the phone was the happiest of their lives, but Angie says she can't continue now that she knows he has lied to her. In their last phone call, they review the nine hours they have just spent together, decide to go dancing soon, and make plans to meet the next day. They finish by telling each other the love they feel.

Two teenagers begin their relationship entirely over the phone and get to know a great deal about each other. Both learn not to judge on externals. Written entirely in dialogue, the book focuses on the things that are really important in a relationship: kindness, sharing, support, encouragement. Considering that they only picture nightly phone calls, the illustrations are well done, although the characters appear younger than their ages. Cleverly, Jim is seen only from the back until the end. This is a Skinny Book, part of a series designed for older readers with limited reading skills. These well-written books focus on the interests and concerns of today's young people and should have great appeal.

Ages 12-16

Also available in:
Braille—*Hello. . . . Wrong Number*
Library of Congress (NLSBPH)

Cassette—*Hello. . . . Wrong Number*
Library of Congress (NLSBPH)

513

Sachs, Marilyn

Peter and Veronica

Black/white illustrations by Louis Glanzman.
Scholastic, Inc., 1987.
(176 pages, paperbound)

FRIENDSHIP: Meaning of
PREJUDICE: Religious
Boy-girl relationships
Inferiority, feelings of
Jew

Peter Wedemeyer, twelve years old, is an intelligent and well-liked boy who expects to do well in Hebrew school. His schoolmate and friend Veronica Ganz is clumsy, sloppy, and large for her age. To hide her feelings of inferiority and shyness, Veronica often is aggressive and belligerent. Peter is her only friend. Their friendship is frowned upon by both their mothers because of religious differences. Peter argues and fights with his family for weeks before his Bar Mitzvah because he wants to ask Veronica, a gentile, to the celebration. When she finally is invited, Veronica dreads having to mingle with other people and decides not to go. Later, when she apologizes for turning down the invitation, Peter is so angry that he mocks her and refuses to accept her apology. His anger lasts most of the summer. When school begins, Peter approaches Veronica, wanting to be friends again. Before he can say anything, Veronica says, "I didn't owe you an apology. You owed me one... You were thinking about you... It had nothing to do with me." Peter admits the truth of her accusations and they resume their friendship.

The problems of prejudice and friendship are conveyed sensitively through the main characters' realistic, often humorous, dialogue. The characterizations of Peter and Veronica give the book, a sequel to *Veronica Ganz*, a lively quality. The third book in this series is *The Truth about Mary Rose.*

Ages 10-12

Also available in:
Paperbound—*Peter and Veronica*
Scholastic, Inc. (Apple Paperbacks)

Talking Book—*Peter and Veronica*
Library of Congress (NLSBPH)

514

Sachs, Marilyn

A Secret Friend

Scholastic, Inc., 1987.
(111 pages)

FRIENDSHIP: Making Friends
FRIENDSHIP: Meaning of
Parental: interference
Rejection: peer
School: classmate relationships

Jessica Freeman and Wendy Cooper, fifth graders, have been best friends for many years. Now something has gone wrong, for reasons unknown to Jessica. Wendy says she is not Jessica's friend any more, but has chosen to be best friends with a classmate named Barbara. Jessica hopes a note written to herself, signed "A. S. F." will make Wendy curious, even jealous. And Wendy is curious—the note says Jessica has a better friend in the class than Wendy—but she is not jealous and refuses Jessica's plea to renew their friendship. Jessica confides in her mother. Finding no way to reconcile the two girls, Mother advises Jessica to find a new friend. Despite this advice and despite her dislike for Wendy's cruelty, Jessica desperately pursues the reconcilation by writing her more more notes from "a secret friend." She even sets up a meeting with the "friend" at the library, across from Wendy's house, but Wendy sends her new friend, Barbara, to tell her to stop spying on them. At a loss to find another friend among her classmates, Jessica asks Helen, her teenage sister, how friendship is made. Reciting the things that go into it, Helen remarks that she and Wendy share none of these: their mothers have pushed them into being friends. Yet even after a talk with Barbara about Wendy's meanness, Jessica returns to her quest of her former friend, who is such fun to be with. One day, failing to prevent Wendy from going home with Barbara, and then mistaking Wendy's mockery of Barbara for mockery of herself, Jessica stops her pursuit abruptly and begins to look seriously elsewhere. Her next friend turns out to be Barbara, who has seen Wendy for what she is.

A girl's quest to restore friendship after a friend has scorned her ends when she understands what a friend really is. Her realization that her goal is "disgusting" marks not only her new wisdom about friendship but her recognition of her mother's interference. Previously Jessica has accepted her mother's advice indiscriminately, but she now sees that her mother tries to impose her own values and wishes on others.

Ages 10-12

Also available in:
Paperbound—*A Secret Friend*
Scholastic, Inc. (Apple Paperbacks)

515

Sachs, Marilyn

A Summer's Lease

Dutton Children's Books, 1979.
(124 pages)

EGOCENTRISM
JEALOUSY: Peer
SCHOOL: Pupil-Teacher Relationships
Cooperation: in work
Determination
Friendship: lack of
Maturation
School: classmate relationships
Talents

It is June, 1943, the end of the school year, and fifteen-year-old Gloria Rein wants one thing only: to be appointed next year's assistant editor of Wings, the school literary magazine. As one of the most talented writers in her class, she would appear to be a likely candidate. But her adviser, Mrs. Horne, feels Gloria is not qualified to do the job alone, for the girl does not get along well with others. When Gloria learns that Mrs. Horne plans for her to share the coveted editorial job with Jerry Lieberman, she becomes physically ill. Burningly jealous of other writers, Gloria is filled with hatred at the very sight of other students' writing and tells herself that she is more "versatile," more "extraordinarily talented" than anyone else. She gets little understanding from her widowed mother, who works in a factory and aims to save Gloria from that fate by convincing her to take a "commercial" course so she can get a job in an office. Gloria, however, considers herself a "genius" and is determined to go to college. Mrs. Horne invites both Jerry and Gloria to spend their vacation helping take care of a group of children at her family's summer home in the Catskills. Never having spent time out of the city, Gloria is enchanted with the mountain retreat. She basks in nighttime conversations with Mrs. Horne, who treats Gloria as a friend and equal and is one of the few people the girl admires and respects. But when Mrs. Horne speaks to Jerry with similar intimacy, Gloria storms out of the room. She glories in being the leader of a group of young boys who admire her skills in punchball and wrestling. For Jerry, who is clumsy and has no stomach for rough play, Gloria has only taunts and disdain. She takes Jerry's kindness and his patience in the face of her own rudeness as signs of his weakness. After witnessing an incident in which Gloria leads the others in ridiculing Jerry, Mrs. Horne cuts off her confidential nightly chats with the girl. Aching for her teacher's approval, Gloria apologizes to her for treating Jerry unkindly. But Mrs. Horne tells her it's too late for being sorry. She reminds her that Jerry should no more have to be "locked inside of being a boy" than Gloria should into being a girl. After this, Gloria begins at last to warm up to Jerry, and one night the two openly discuss their feelings. Gloria admits that she hates feeling jealous all the time, that she knows she has no friends. Jerry tells her that many people like her and would befriend her if she would only show an interest. Then Dorothy, a little girl who has shared a special relationship with Jerry during the summer, falls into a coma. While Mrs. Horne calls frantically for a doctor, Jerry sits paralyzed and Gloria tends to the child. But later, in the hospital, Dorothy dies, and Jerry and Gloria each confess a regret: Jerry that he was unable to help Dorothy while she was dying, and Gloria that she was never kind to the girl while she was living. During the next school year, Gloria and Jerry work together as co-editors, though not without "disputes and differences." Gloria is even able to respond without jealousy to a poem of Jerry's. Shortly before the end of the term, the two quarrel over a submission to Wings. Jerry, busy with other projects and perhaps weary of quarreling, resigns. They reestablish a relationship after this, but it's never what it was. Gloria knows their real friendship is over, but she looks forward to being sole editor-in-chief of Wings in the fall. "I gloated. . . . It was all mine now, . . . all mine!" She understands herself a bit better, though: "It was still there, to my shame—my need to contend against him."

Wrapped up in her talent, eager for recognition, a teenage girl has immersed herself in lonely, bitter isolation. A perceptive teacher recognizes Gloria's need for love and friendship, and a gentle friend helps her begin to find them. Although Gloria matures and mellows through her experiences with Jerry and Mrs. Horne, her basic personality doesn't change. But she is able to consider the feelings of others upon occasion, discovering "it's a better world . . . if you let your compassion grow bigger than your jealousy." The plot proceeds logically, and character development is strong. Much of this first-person account is in the form of a diary.

Ages 11-14

Also available in:
No other form known

516

Sachs, Marilyn

The Truth about Mary Rose

Black/white illustrations by Louis Glanzman.
Scholastic, Inc., 1987.
(159 pages)

EGO IDEAL
Identity, search for
Imitation

Eleven-year-old Mary Rose is named after her mother's sister Mary Rose, who died thirty years earlier in a fire. Her Aunt Mary Rose died saving the lives of everyone else in her building. Mary Rose idolizes her namesake and has reconstructed in her mind her aunt's personality and the dramatic night of her death. When Mary Rose's father accepts a teaching position in New York, the family temporarily moves in with Grandmother. Living nearby is cousin Pam, who soon becomes Mary Rose's best friend. Pam's father Stanley is the younger brother of the dead Mary Rose and one of the people Mary Rose saved from the fire. Listening to Grandmother, Stanley, and her mother, Mary Rose learns even more about her heroine. Grandmother tells her that Stanley saved one box belonging to the first Mary Rose, and the younger Mary Rose searches the house until she finds it. Inside the box are cut-out paper pictures of jewelry and gold rings from cigar wrappers. The contents of the box prompt a discussion between Pam's parents and Mary Rose's parents, in which Stanley tells how selfish the first Mary Rose had been and how mean she always was to him. He confesses that he rang the fire warning bells the night of the fire, and that Mary Rose had not died trying to save anyone, but attempting to rescue her own precious boxes. Young Mary Rose, a chronic eavesdropper, hears the entire conversation from a closet where she is hiding. The truth is shattering to her, and she begins to sob hysterically. Her father takes her home, and after the two talk, Mary Rose calms down. She finally decides to remember the first Mary Rose realistically, as a person with both good and bad points.

Mary Rose learns two valuable lessons in this first-person narrative: first, she perceives that she is her own person, and that regardless of her namesake, she is a unique and valuable individual; second, she realizes that no two people see another person or situation in the same way.

Ages 10-13

Also available in:
Paperbound—*The Truth about Mary Rose*
Scholastic, Inc. (Apple Paperbacks)

517

Sachs, Marilyn

Veronica Ganz

Black/white illustrations by Louis Glanzman.
Scholastic, Inc., 1987.
(156 pages)

BULLY: Being a
Appearance: concern about
Boy-girl relationships
Height: tall

An eighth-grader named Veronica is a bully and the largest girl in her class. She has intimidated most of the children at school so badly that they cower from her. But little Peter Wedemeyer, a new boy in class, refuses to let Veronica boss him around. He even composes malicious verses and dares to dedicate them to her. Veronica makes plans to get even. But Peter outsmarts her whenever she tries to chase him home or pounce on him. In a last attempt to squelch Peter, Veronica waits for him after school one day, intending to thrash him. But Peter has two friends along, and the three boys "gang up on" her. When a passerby comes to Veronica's aid, she is impressed that someone has, at last, taken her side. Several days later, Peter feels guilty about his unfairness and offers

Veronica a chance to hit back. But she discovers she really doesn't want to hit Peter. Surprisingly, new feelings of respect grow between the two. Veronica admits to herself that Peter is the one person she likes and admires.

Veronica's problems at school are compounded by the actions of her divorced parents. Her mother screams at her much of the time, and her father makes promises he fails to keep. The breezy humor of the dialogue adds a light touch to this realistic novel. *Veronica Ganz* is followed by *Peter and Veronica* and *The Truth about Mary Rose.*

Ages 10-12

Also available in:
Braille—*Veronica Ganz*
Library of Congress (NLSBPH)

Paperbound—*Veronica Ganz*
Scholastic, Inc. (Apple Paperbacks)

Talking Book—*Veronica Ganz*
Library of Congress (NLSBPH)

518

Sallis, Susan Diana

Only Love

HarperCollins Publishers, Inc., 1980.
(250 pages)

BOY-GIRL RELATIONSHIPS
LOVE, MEANING OF
WHEELCHAIR, DEPENDENCE ON
Amputee
Death: attitude toward
Nursing home, living in
Paraplegia
Reality, escaping

Frances (Fran) Adamson is sixteen, high-spirited, mischievous, strong-willed, and paraplegic. Newly at Thornton Hall, the last in a series of institutions she has lived in since being abandoned as an infant, Fran meets "Aunt" Nell and "Uncle" Roger, a childless couple who befriend youngsters at Thornton. They enlist her help with another resident, Luke Hawkins, who recently lost both legs in a motorcycle accident. The eighteen-year-old son of wealthy parents, he has withdrawn from all human contact. Fran invites Luke to attend a planning meeting for the upcoming Fete Day at Thornton, but he doesn't appear; instead, Fran learns, he listens to the proceedings from next door. In time, she and Luke begin talking frequently on the telephone, but Luke doesn't want her or anyone to see him. Meanwhile, Fran helps keep things lively at Thornton Hall. She plays matchmaker. She befriends Granny Gorman, full of life despite being crippled by arthritis. Then Fran has a long bout with pneumonia that saps her vitality and drains her spirits. When she is somewhat recovered, Luke finally agrees to meet her—outdoors, after everyone is asleep. When he demands to know why he should respond to her urgings and begin thinking about crutches and artificial legs and walking again, Fran informs him jauntily that he has to have legs to carry her over the threshhold. Fran doesn't hear from Luke again for the next two weeks. On the day of the Fete, he appears triumphantly on crutches with one artificial leg in place. After that, their relationship deepens, impelling Dr. Beamish, the head of Thornton, to advise Fran to tell Luke about her serious heart and lung condition, about the fact that she hasn't long to live. She is not being fair to Luke, the doctor warns. All Fran wants is a year or two of happiness, but she decides to stay away from Luke. That night, however, she can't resist meeting him and returning his embraces. He talks about marriage, but all Fran can see is a future in which everyone but she can walk. Luke invites his parents to visit Thornton for the first time so they can meet Fran. They are shocked at the idea of marriage between a paraplegic girl and a boy with no legs. Fran's disclosure that she can't have children doesn't dissuade Luke, but she is still unable to tell him she is dying. To Granny Gorman, though, she expresses her "calm certainty that it was a privilege to die young. . . . Something to do with a journey; a journey toward something pretty good. And I would get there early." That night, in the garden, Fran tells Luke her secret. He wheels away, devastated. Then Nell and Roger fail to appear as usual on Sunday, and Fran discovers that Roger has left Nell. Fran spends three days with Nell, and the two make plans to swim in the Channel the next weekend. When their scheduled day for the swim arrives, Fran waits for Nell but instead sees Roger and Luke drive up. Gently they break the news: Nell has drowned. Roger seems to think she has killed herself because he left her, but a sorrowful Fran convinces him that Nell was probably just testing the Channel waters in preparation for their swim. When she returns to her room, Luke is waiting outside her door. He lifts the blanket over his legs and she sees jeans and shoes. Awkwardly and with difficulty, he carries Fran over the threshhold of her room. Nobody disturbs them, and they talk together until they fall asleep. In the middle of the night, Luke goes back to his room and telephones Fran, saying that he will always hold her hand on this side and Nell will surely hold her hand on the other. Luke narrates the last chapter of the book. Two years have passed since the six months he knew Fran. She is buried next to Nell. Luke now works in the family business and goes back to Thornton once a week to help out.

Fran's poignant and unforgettable first-person narrative, set in England, is both a love story and a perceptive, useful, and sometimes lyrical view of life from a wheelchair. Her candid storytelling gives vivid life to all the characters. Although the book deals with heavy and sometimes depressing subjects and ends sadly, it has such authenticity and Fran such an irrepressible spirit that it can't be put down. One of the helpers in the institution asks, "What has she got to laugh about? What have any of us here got to laugh about?" But Fran knows what there is to laugh about and shares her laughter with others.

Ages 12 and up

Also available in:
Talking Book—*Only Love*
Library of Congress (NLSBPH)

519

Sargent, Sarah

Secret Lies

Crown Publishers, Inc., 1981.
(118 pages, paperbound)

IDENTITY, SEARCH FOR
MATURATION
Abandonment
Change: accepting
Fantasy formation
Loneliness
Parental: absence
Relatives: living in home of

One day Elvira Judson, thirteen, comes home from school in Chicago and discovers a note from her mother that makes her furious. Elvira's mother has run off to marry her boyfriend and has left Elvira money to go to her Aunt Carrie's in Charlottesville, Virginia. Elvira has no intention of leaving Chicago, but when school officials discover her situation they turn her over to a social worker who makes the arrangements for her. Elvira must resign herself to the fact that while her mother is gone, she will have to stay with relatives. "She was a deserted daughter going to stay with an old aunt back in the bushes, and she might as well start facing up to it." Elvira's passion has always been to fantasize about the father she never knew and knows nothing about. Now, traveling by train to her aunt's, she dreams of him. Aunt Carrie, a semi-retired nurse, meets Elvira and drives her to her home thirty miles outside of Charlottesville. Living with her also is Cousin Henry, past eighty and an invalid. The next day Elvira goes for a hike in the woods and comes upon a deserted, dilapidated old plantation. There she discovers Michael, about sixteen, who has run away from his nearby home. Elvira falls in love with the old house that fits so well the life she imagines with her handsome, rich father. She begins asking her aunt about her parents. Aunt Carrie is vague, saying only that they were too young to face up to family life. She does mention that Elvira's father's sister lives in Charlottesville. Elvira begs to see her and a meeting day is set. But Aunt Joyce is a bitter disappointment. The visit is made even worse when Elvira is shown a recent picture of her father. He is fat and bald. Her dreams of him fade, and she realizes how alone she really is. She begs Michael to let her go with him when he leaves the plantation. He tells her the tragedy of Aunt Carrie's childhood and why Cousin Henry is an invalid. Aunt Carrie's "deranged" father, discovering that his young wife and Cousin Henry loved each other, had shot and killed his wife and himself. Henry too was shot and crippled. Suddenly Elvira feels great sympathy toward these two who have suffered as she has and who also keep secrets. Back at the house, Aunt Carrie warns Elvira to stay out of the woods; the sheriff thinks someone is staying at the old plantation. That night Elvira sneaks away and warns Michael. He asks her to join him in his escape, but she refuses: Aunt Carrie and Cousin Henry are her family now.

Abandoned by both parents, a young teenage girl must leave her home in Chicago to live with an aging aunt and cousin. When her fantasy life with her glamorized father is shattered by the truth of his appearance and nature, Elvira comes to see that the security and love she longs for can be found with her relatives in her new home. Enhancing the story are the sympathetic tone, strong characterizations, and vividly described setting; detracting a bit is the superficially handled relationship with the runaway, Michael.

Ages 11 and up

Also available in:
No other form known

520

Schlein, Miriam

The Way Mothers Are

Color illustrations by Joe Lasker.
Albert Whitman & Company, 1963.
(31 pages)

LOVE, MEANING OF

A small male kitten asks his mother whether she loves him, and she assures him that she does. Then he asks how she can love him when he escapes while she tries to dress him. Mother explains that she does not stop loving him when he is naughty. Next, the kitten wants to know if his mother loves him when he screams, even after being told to quiet down. Mother tells her son that she loves him even then. Amazed, the little kitten asks if Mother loves him when he is naughty all day long. Mother firmly states that she loves him, even though she may not like one single thing he does. The little kitten demands to know why, so Mother asks him to give *his* ideas about why she loves him. He answers that Mother loves him because he is smart, draws nice pictures, is sometimes sweet to his sister...and he eats what he should, brushes his teeth, sits still in the car, and sometimes puts his toys away. His mother explains that all these things are very nice, but they are not the reason she loves him. From the moment he was born, she cared for him and wanted him. And she loves him all the time, because he is hers.

This simply told story might help an anxious child understand that, although a parent may not like what a child does, the parent still loves the child. However, a child who has been rejected by a parent might be confused by this mother's total acceptance and love.

Ages 3-6

Also available in:
No other form known

521

Schuchman, Joan

Two Places to Sleep

Color illustrations by Jim LaMarche.
Carolrhoda Books, Inc., 1979.
(31 pages counted)

DIVORCE: of Parents
Anxiety
Change: accepting
Guilt, feelings of

David's parents are divorced and the seven-year-old spends weekdays with his father, weekends with his mother. During the week, David is in the family home: familiar surroundings. His father's kindly housekeeper assures him that he can and will get over his parents' breakup, but David is uncertain and fearful, continuing to hope his parents will be reunited. Despite the patience and reassurance of both parents, David dreads losing their love and feels that he is somehow the cause of the family's troubles. One Saturday his mother buys him a kite and races him through the park. At dinner after this happy afternoon, David spills his malt. Although his mother does not scold him, the episode lingers in the boy's mind. Finally, he asks his mother if she will "get undivorced from Dad" if he is careful not to spill anything and keeps his room clean. She assures David that he is not the cause of the divorce, that he need not change—he is loved by both parents just as he is. After she tucks him in bed, reads him a story, and kisses him goodnight, David decides he is getting used to having two places to sleep.

Despite patient, supportive, reassuring parents, a young boy needs time and abundant love to accept the breakup of his family. The first-person narrator is convincing, even touching, a figure young readers should find easy to understand and trust. The characters, though lightly developed, are deftly drawn. Handsome illustrations complement the compact text. David's insights—that divorces happen but that parents don't "get divorced from their children," that he can get used to his new life—have wide application and should provoke useful discussion between parents and children.

Ages 5-7

Also available in:
No other form known

522

Schulman, Janet

The Big Hello

Color illustrations by Lillian Hoban.
Greenwillow Books, 1976.
(32 pages)

FRIENDSHIP: Making Friends
Moving
Transitional objects: toys

The little girl who tells this story is moving to California with her parents and her doll, Sara. By reassuring the doll, the girl is able to convince herself that the plane ride is all fun and California an ideal place to live. But she wonders if she will find new friends. Two days after the family arrives, she loses Sara, with whom she has always slept. As a surprise, her father gives her a dog, which she names Snoopy. That night, Snoopy sleeps with her. The next day is doubly happy. She finds Sara and meets her first new friend.

The young narrator finds that moving to a new home brings her adventures and new friendships. Color illustrations add to this cheerful story, which young readers can read alone easily.

Ages 3-7

Also available in:
Braille—*The Big Hello*
Library of Congress (NLSBPH)

Paperbound—*The Big Hello*
Dell Publishing Company, Inc.

523

Schultz, Gwendolyn

The Blue Valentine

Black/white illustrations by Elizabeth Coberly.
William Morrow & Company, Inc., 1979.
(64 pages) o.p.

SCHOOL: Transfer
Friendship: making friends

Cindy and her parents move to a new house, and Cindy enters first grade in a new school. Although none of the children in her class seem friendly, the teacher, Miss Kelly, tries to make her feel welcome. Cindy discovers that she and Miss Kelly share a favorite color: blue. A week before Valentine's Day, Cindy works hard to make a beautiful blue card for Miss Kelly. She is the first in the class to put her card into the classroom box, and for a week she anticipates the opening. When the valentines have been distributed, Cindy feels sad because she received very few, but she feels especially hurt because Miss Kelly does not hang up the blue valentine with her others. The next morning Miss Kelly explains that after all the children went home, she found Cindy's card stuck to the bottom of the box. She tells the class it is so beautiful that she wants Cindy to show how the card was made. After school one of the girls in her class walks Cindy home.

A young girl seeks to win her teacher's approval and her classmates' acceptance through the use of her artistic talent. An understanding mother and a sensitive teacher give her gentle encouragement. Updated illustrations make the book more timely and give new appeal for young readers. Detailed instructions for making the valentine card are included.

Ages 5-8

Also available in:
No other form known

524

Scoppettone, Sandra

The Late Great Me

Bantam Books, 1984.
(256 pages, paperbound)

ALCOHOLISM: Adolescent
Boy-girl relationships: dating
Mental illness: of parent
Peer relationships: peer pressures

Seventeen-year-old Geri Peters has always been a lonely, quiet girl, with only two girlfriends, until Dave Townsend becomes her boyfriend and introduces her to drinking. Geri discovers that drinking gives her the social confidence her mother has always preached. By mid-May of her junior year, Geri cannot complete a school day without a drink of milk and vodka from the thermos in her locker or the bottle in her purse. Blackouts assail her; periods of time blank in her memory; she cannot concentrate in class; she keeps a bottle of Scotch in her closet at home. Her older brother notices changes in her, but the family ignores him: Mrs. Peters's mind is failing, and that and his work absorb Geri's father. It is Kate Laine, a nondrinking alcoholic who is Geri's humanities teacher, who, observing Geri, candidly suggests to her that she may be an alcoholic. Worried that Kate may be right, Geri limits her drinking. But when her mother is institutionalized, Geri again drinks heavily. While drunk she takes her mother's car and some time later, having blacked out, recovers from her blackout in a rented room where she is beaten by a stranger whose sexual advances she has resisted. Geri now sees her severe drinking problem and calls on Kate for help. At the teacher's urging, Geri attends meetings of Alcoholics Anonymous and, to better understand Geri's illness, Mr. Peters and his son attend meetings of Alanon. By December of her senior year, Geri has gone without drinking for ninety days and is learning to like and understand herself.

In this first-person narrative, a teenage alcoholic graphically describes her blackouts and the physical discomfort and mental anguish of withdrawal from alcohol dependence; her sexual encounters are only touched on. Kate Laine, a nondrinking alcoholic, is contrasted with Dave Townsend's mother, an alcoholic whose drinking leads directly to her own death. Mrs. Peters's mental illness is portrayed convincingly but from her alcoholic daughter's perspective. More attention is given to Geri's perilous drinking than to her recovery and consequent self-knowledge; this, then, is an account of teenage alcoholism more vivid than moralizing.

Ages 12 and up

Also available in:
No other form known

525

Scott, Ann Herbert

Sam

Black/white illustrations by Symeon Shimin.
McGraw-Hill, Inc., 1967.
(30 pages counted) o.p.

SIBLING: Youngest
Belonging

Preschooler Sam is bored and wants someone to play with. But everyone in his family is too busy to pay any attention to him. Mother is making an apple pie, so she sends him outside to play. Outside, his brother George is studying, and when Sam picks up one of George's school books, George yells and tells him to go inside. Sam's big sister Marcia is busy playing with her paper dolls, so she sends him to find Daddy. But Daddy is reading the newspaper. Sam punches one of the keys on the typewriter to get Dad's attention, and Dad shouts at him, telling him to go find Mother. Feeling hurt and unwanted, the boy sits down and cries. The whole family comes to see what is wrong, and they realize that they have rejected Sam. Mom picks him up and finds a job for him in the kitchen making a raspberry tart for himself as the rest of the family watches.

Sam faces a problem which is common for the youngest member of a family. The drawings beautifully convey the mood of this story.

Ages 3-7

Also available in:
Braille—*Sam*
Library of Congress (NLSBPH)

Talking Book—*Sam*
Library of Congress (NLSBPH)

526

Seredy, Kate

The Good Master

Color illustrations by the author.
Viking Penguin, 1986.
(196 pages, paperbound)

CHANGE: Accepting
Maturation
Parent/Parents: substitute
Relatives: living in home of

Ten-year-old Kate Nagy, spoiled and headstrong, has come to live with her eleven-year-old cousin Jansci and his parents on their ranch in Hungary. Kate's mother is dead, and her father feels that Kate should live with a family. Although Jansci has heard that his cousin is "delicate," he finds that she is just the opposite. She pushes him off the horse-drawn wagon and drives the team home by herself; she even climbs up to the rafters of the house to eat the sausages stored there. Wanting to wear trousers so that she can ride horses, she cuts her skirt up the middle. In addition, she ridicules the rural customs, the native costumes, and the lack of conveniences. As the months pass, Kate hears Hungarian legends from one of the herders, and she begins to understand and appreciate the rich cultural heritage of the area. She also comes to accept the native way of dressing as well as the more primitive lifestyle. During this time, she receives love and guidance from her aunt and uncle. By Christmas, Kate is "just another country girl," but she misses her father terribly, for she has not seen him since spring. When her father—who teaches school in Budapest—visits her at Christmas, Kate and the Nagys persuade him to come live on the ranch and teach in the country school, which is in great need of a new teacher.

This touching classic, set in 1911, describes a girl's adjustment from city to country life. Characterizations, though somewhat idealistic, are credible, and the sense of security that envelops Kate is nicely conveyed. Under the influence of the good master and his family, Kate adjusts to her situation and becomes less self-centered. This is the first of two books about the Nagy family. The second is *The Singing Tree.*

Ages 9-12

Also available in:
Braille—*The Good Master*
Library of Congress (NLSBPH)

Cassette—*The Good Master*
Library of Congress (NLSBPH)

Paperbound—*The Good Master*
Puffin Books

Talking Book—*The Good Master*
Library of Congress (NLSBPH)

527

Sharmat, Marjorie Weinman

A Big Fat Enormous Lie

Color illustrations by David McPhail.
Dutton Children's Books, 1978.
(32 pages counted, paperbound)

HONESTY/DISHONESTY

It begins as the smallest of lies, the little boy telling his father, then his mother, then his sister, that he did not eat all the cookies in the jar. If he tells the truth, he is sure, they will all be angry. He certainly regrets having eaten the cookies, but that is no help. However much he pretends that the lie is nothing, it remains monstrously with him. He is stuck with it. He wonders how a boy as smart as he is could be so stupid as to lie. Finally, unbearably oppressed by the lie, he confesses to his parents and is instantly loosed from its hold. Wherever it has gone, it has gone forever. And that, we are told, is "the absolute and total truth."

S

The lie is first depicted as a small, harmless, snouted green creature. As the boy continues to worry about it, the monster grows and grows and finally sits on him. Once the boy confesses, the monster grows smaller and smaller, and finally disappears. This first-person narrative whimsically shows how one thing leads to another. Seemingly harmless at first, the lie eventually affects the boy terribly. The humorous illustrations accompanying this story text make this a fine book for reading aloud.

Ages 3-7

Also available in:
No other form known

528

Sharmat, Marjorie Weinman

Goodnight, Andrew; Goodnight, Craig

Color illustrations by Mary Chalmers.
HarperCollins Publishers, Inc., 1969.
(32 pages)

BEDTIME
Imaginary friend

It is eight o'clock and Father has just said goodnight to Andrew and Craig. The boys wish each other "pleasant nightmares" and have a pillow fight until Dad firmly tells them to go to sleep. From his bed, Andrew tells his older brother Craig about the boy next door. Craig reminds Andrew that there is no boy next door and then tries to go to sleep. But Andrew persists. Crawling into Craig's bed, Andrew tells Craig what he and the boy next door are planning to do the next day. Again Dad comes into the bedroom. He chases Andrew into his own bed and very sternly tells the boys to go to sleep. After Dad has left, Andrew asks Craig to check the lump under Andrew's covers.

Craig finds that the lump is underwear that Andrew forgot to throw into the hamper. Dad comes in again and insists that it is time both boys were sleeping. As soon as Dad leaves the room, Andrew begins to chatter again. It is only when Craig promises to play ball with him the next day that Andrew settles down to sleep.

The older brother, who wants to sleep, is continually disturbed by his younger brother, who invents an imaginary friend in order to keep his sibling's attention. This short, engaging picture story, written completely in dialogue, has universal appeal in its natural, child-like theme.

Ages 3-7

Also available in:
No other form known

529

Sharmat, Marjorie Weinman

I'm Terrific

Color illustrations by Kay Chorao.
Holiday House, Inc., 1977.
(30 pages counted)

PRIDE/FALSE PRIDE
Boasting
Identity, search for

Jason Everett Bear is a little bear who lives in a tidy house in the forest with his mother. Jason thinks himself "terrific" and awards himself with gold stars for especially superior deeds. His friends Raymond Squirrel and Marvin Raccoon see him differently. Marvin thinks Jason a goody-goody and calls him a "mama's bear." One day a new bear moves into the forest. Jason decides he will make the new bear his friend. He goes to her house and introduces himself: "I'm Jason Everett Bear. I suppose you've heard of me." When he goes on bragging, the new bear, Henrietta, calls him a show-off and slams the door in his face. Jason is depressed, doubtful about himself, and decides that he wants to try acting entirely different. The next day, not to seem a goody-goody, he acts mean. He ties knots in Marvin's hair and kicks over Raymond's pile of nuts. Then he goes over and tells Henrietta what he has done. Once again she calls Jason a show-off and slams the door in his face. Jason broods about his behavior some more. He goes back to Marvin and Raymond and apologizes. He brings a flower to Henrietta. But he is still unsure who he is and spends the rest of the day thinking. The next day he throws away all the gold stars. Jason's friends decide they like him when he is just Jason, not trying to impress anyone.

Jason's effort of self-discovery is long and painful. He finds that by being vain and boastful he loses friends, just as he does when acting mean. Only when he starts thinking about others more than himself does he discover who he is.

Ages 4-7

Also available in:
Paperbound—*I'm Terrific*
Scholastic, Inc.

530

Sharmat, Marjorie Weinman

Mitchell Is Moving

Color illustrations by Jose Aruego and Ariane Dewey.
Macmillan Publishing Company, Inc., 1978.
(46 pages)

MOVING
Friendship: best friend

Mitchel the dinosaur has decided to move as far away as he can walk in two weeks' time. Marge, his best friend and next-door neighbor, begs him to stay, but he staunchly insists he wants to change old routines by moving. Afraid that Mitchell no longer likes her, Marge threatens him with ingenious methods of imprisonment. He, insisting that he still likes Marge, counters with equally clever means of escape. And so Mitchell leaves, walks for two weeks, and builds himself a house. But he finds life lonely and writes Marge a letter, inviting her to visit. When she arrives, both decide that, since they are neighborless and miss each other very much, Marge will build a house next door.

Two friends, in this humorous and easy-to-read story, decide to remain together despite a move by one, something that does not usually happen in life. For moving need not signal the end of a friendship, nor does it mean the friends do not like each other.

Ages 5-8

Also available in:
Paperbound—*Mitchell Is Moving*
Aladdin Books

531

Shreve, Susan Richards

The Bad Dreams of a Good Girl

Black/white illustrations by Diane de Groat.
Alfred A. Knopf, Inc., 1982.
(92 pages, paperbound)

FAMILY: Relationships
Daydreaming
Parent/Parents: mother working outside home
School: classmate relationships
Sibling: rivalry

Fourth-grader Carlotta McDaniel is, by default, the good girl in her family. With three teenage brothers who steal street signs, lie, and even smoke cigarettes, all Lotty can do is dream about being bad. At Lotty's new school for gifted children, Kathy Sanders—class president, all-around leader, and former friend—has started the I Hate Lotty Club. When Lotty's family finds out, her brothers are unexpectedly supportive and comforting. But Lotty's schoolwork worsens, and she feels an academic failure as well as a social one. Her brother Nicholas suggests that she herself join the hateful club, but after she requests membership it loses members and folds. When Lotty's mother returns to work after twelve years at home, the girl feels like an orphan. She daydreams about running away from home and how her family will beg her to come back. She is somewhat comforted by a note her mother leaves under her pillow, reminiscing about Lotty as a toddler. Growth is always painful, her mother suggests, but eventually welcome. That evening Lotty makes dinner, cleans the house a little, and makes a valentine to put on her mother's bed. Then her father's week of bed rest for a back injury coincides with a day off from school for Lotty, who doesn't feel she knows her father very well. She fixes him a special breakfast, he writes her little notes, they talk. When her brothers come home and monopolize their father, Lotty fantasizes about burning up all his nice little notes; he only seems to like her when nobody else is around. Then the doorbell rings. It's the florist with roses for Lotty and a note from her father thanking her for one of the nicest days he's had in years. Although Lotty spars with all her brothers, most of her fights are with Philip. After one incident in which she dumps a can of tuna on his head and he dumps a pan of lumpy white sauce on hers, Lotty dreams about Philip's upcoming camping trip and how she rescues him when he breaks his leg. When he actually does break his arm, she and he promise not to have any more bad dreams about each other. Sometimes bad dreams come true.

A young girl daydreams to work out feelings she can't express as a real-life good girl. Lotty details several situations that mark her year as a fourth grader: peer rejection, her mother returning to work, getting to know her father, and a fight with one of her brothers. These separate episodes flow together smoothly in this entertaining first-person narrative. Charming drawings illustrate both Lotty's real world and her dreamworld.

Ages 8-10

Also available in:
Cassette—*The Bad Dreams of a Good Girl*
Library of Congress (NLSBPH)

532

Shreve, Susan Richards

The Masquerade

Alfred A. Knopf, Inc., 1980.
(184 pages) o.p.

FAMILY: Relationships
IMPRISONMENT
Ambivalence, feelings of
Lifestyle: change in
Mental illness: of parent
Parental: weakness
Responsibility: accepting

Eighteen-year-old Rebecca Walker is making fudge in the kitchen when her older brother, Eric, tells her that two policemen are leading their father away from the house; he is being arrested for embezzlement. The anguished days that follow are particularly difficult for Rebecca, who must assume even more responsibility for the family than she already has. Because of her remote, genteel mother's emotional fragility, Rebecca's father, a lawyer and accountant, has always depended on her. Eric has always been the difficult child; Sarah, now sixteen and a talented dancer, the self-centered child; and Eliza, now seven, the favorite. It's been up to Rebecca, the "good" child, to hold the family together. Now the four must read about their father in the newspaper. They are forced to sell their beautiful house on the Sound in Greenwich, Connecticut, and move to a two-bedroom apartment over a drugstore. Their mother takes a job in the drugstore as a cashier, the first job she has ever had. Eric returns abruptly to medical school and to Gayatri, the Pakistani woman he lives with. Through the turmoil of their lives their mother moves like someone untouched, but her behavior becomes increasingly bizarre. Then Sarah does not come home from a gymnastics tournament, and the family hears nothing of her for many days. One night during Sarah's absence, their mother dresses up in her high school prom dress and tells the children her date will be picking her up at eight. The owner of the drugstore has spoken to Eric about his mother, afraid that something is wrong with her. Sarah finally returns home. She has been in New York, pursuing her dream of becoming a professional dancer, but makes Rebecca promise not to ask her anything about her stay there. Soon after, Sarah quits dancing. Their father seems to have lost all interest in his children. Their mother is put in the state mental hospital after she is found wandering around one night in her prom dress. Their father has her transferred to a private institution, but will not explain to Rebecca how they can afford it. Then a representative from a local church group organized to "support the Walker children" approaches Rebecca about putting Sarah and Eliza in two local homes. She refuses. The frustrated representative promises to come up with another solution. She returns and asks Rebecca and Sarah to attend a benefit dance at the country club. There they discover

S

halfway through the evening that the "benefit" is for their mother's stay in the private hospital and that their father has okayed it. Still, Rebecca clings to the belief that her father will be found innocent. She tells herself she can tolerate anything, now and in the future, if he is exonerated. When her father pleads guilty at his trial, Rebecca turns "mean," as Eliza puts it. She talks about sleeping with everyone she meets. She begins running with a wild crowd, staying out until nearly dawn night after night. Although she doesn't actually sleep with any of the boys, she thinks often of her father's reaction should he see her with them. When summer comes, Eric and Gayatri move into the small family apartment while both work at the local hospital. Eric is sick a great deal, primarily psychosomatic illnesses culled from his medical textbooks. Sarah receives a ballet scholarship, but refuses it. Rebecca herself is getting a "bad reputation." Their mother is soon to be released from the hospital and her psychiatrist suggests they rent a house so she will feel more at home. Their father is also due out on parole before too long, but Rebecca says she can't live in the same house with him; she has not been able to visit him since the trial. They find a modest but comfortable house to rent and begin to fix it up. The day her mother is due home, Rebecca drives to the prison to see her father. As she walks into the visiting room she says, "I'm finally here."

Caught in a complex web of needs and emotions, four strikingly individual young people try to keep their equilibrium during a stressful, tragic time in their lives. Eric, Sarah, and Eliza are all shown reacting to the turmoil in various ways, but the book focuses on Rebecca: the family mainstay, the strong one, the surrogate mother. As long as she clings to her unrealistic beliefs about her father, she avoids reality. When reality comes, it crushes and disorients her. At the end, Rebecca's visit to the prison seems a step toward peace—with her father and with herself. No easy solutions are proposed. But it's clear that Rebecca and her family have come through some unusually difficult months with tattered bits of their family flag still flying. Strong characterizations make for an absorbing story.

Ages 12 and up

Also available in:
No other form known

533

Shura, Mary Francis Craig

The Barkley Street Six-pack

Black/white illustrations by Gene Sparkman.
Putnam Berkley Group, Inc., 1979.
(159 pages) o.p.

FRIENDSHIP: Best Friend
PEER RELATIONSHIPS: Peer Pressures
Animals: love for
Change: new home
Friendship: meaning of
Honesty/Dishonesty
Manipulation: peer
Neighbors/Neighborhood

When Natalie Lowery moves in across the street from thirteen-year-old Jane Todd, the shy, lonely Jane doesn't like her at all. But she finds herself drawn to fascinating Natalie, who claims she knows how to use magic. Both girls are new to the neighborhood and soon are friends. But Natalie will allow Jane no other friends. New young families keep moving in and the children of each, it seems, discover some reason to distrust Natalie and, by extension, Jane. The Jarvis boys, for example: Natalie tangles her kite strings with those of Steve Jarvis's very special, much-admired kite, making his kite fall into a tree. Later, the younger Jarvis boy's roller skate disappears. When Tracy moves in, Natalie loses a special ring and allows suspicion to fall on Tracy and her little brother. Always Natalie denies guilt, always she accuses others of lying and picking on her, and always she seeks affirmations of Jane's trust. Soon nobody in the neighborhood will even speak to Jane. Then Natalie's father is transferred and her family moves to Germany. One night a lonely Jane sees a dark shape moving on the porch of Natalie's empty house. It is a dog, alone and starving. Jane names it Stilts because of its long legs, feeds it and loves it, but keeps it a secret because she knows her parents won't let her keep it. Winter nears and she worries about the dog's safety. When Mr. Garvic, divorced and with a young son who visits on weekends, moves into the Lowery house, Jane is frantic because Stilts sleeps beneath the house. Trying to sneak a visit, she meets the son, Duke Garvic, who knows Jane's reputation in the neighborhood as Natalie's friend and already dislikes her. Jane realizes that Duke is a bit afraid of her too because his father's lease forbids children in the house. Seeing a way to get rid of the Garvics and protect Stilts, Jane writes to Natalie, telling her of Duke so Natalie's parents will evict the Garvics. Natalie's response speaks only of a new friend: "I've taken her under my wing, just like I did you." Slowly, Jane begins to suspect that there was no magic, that Natalie did all the things she denied and blamed on others. Then one day Jane glances into the Garvics' house and sees Stilts, happy, healthy, and obviously loved. She worries about her letter to Natalie, now that she has begun to like the Garvics and especially when Duke tells her he will be living permanently with his father. Her fears about Natalie are confirmed when Natalie's ring, missing since the episode with Tracy, is found behind the lattice enclosure under Natalie's house. Then Natalie writes to Jane again, telling about her new best friend and adding that her father no longer owns the house; he has accepted Mr. Garvic's recent offer to buy it. Duke invites Jane to a skating party with the two Jarvis boys, Tracy, and her brother. The Barkley Street Six-pack, as Jane's father calls it, begins to be a real team.

Complex emotions and ambiguous situations force a young girl to admit some unpleasant truths about her manipulative friend and her own judgment in this first-person study of relationships. Jane's loneliness in a new neighborhood, her love for Stilts, her initial ambivalence about Natalie and later the control Natalie exerts over her are all realistically described, as is the resolution of her problem and her happy return to the neighborhood children. The book will amply reward discussion about friendship, manipulation, and peer pressures.

Ages 9-12

Also available in:
No other form known

534

Shyer, Marlene Fanta

My Brother, the Thief

Charles Scribner's Sons, 1980.
(138 pages) o.p.

STEALING
Adoption: feelings about
Family: unity
Self-esteem
Sibling: relationships

Carolyn Desmond, twelve, and her fifteen-year-old brother, Richard, spend most of their summer vacation in each other's company, since both parents work. Richard is really Carolyn's half-brother. His father walked out when he was two; when he was three his mother married Dr. Desmond. Richard is an angry, hostile boy, but Dr. Desmond, who has adopted him, thinks of him as his own son. He is a loving but demanding parent who makes sure both children have plenty of chores to keep them busy. Since he worked his way through high school, college, and dental school, he believes in the merits of hard work; as a dentist, he hates junk food and concerns himself greatly with his children's diets. When Carolyn begins to notice that Richard is hiding things in his room that do not belong to him, she feels she should tell her parents. She knows, however, that if she does, Richard will reveal to her friends her hated middle name of Frankfurter. So she decides to keep quiet. One day she overhears Richard's friend, nicknamed Flim Flam, asking him to hide some more stolen property in their house. When Richard refuses, Flim Flam threatens to tell a special girl named Cookie that Richard can't swim. Since he is very ashamed of this fact, Richard agrees to do what Flim Flam wants. Preoccupied with guilt and the fear of being caught, Richard becomes careless about his chores, angering Dr. Desmond. Their relationship worsens when Richard takes the key Carolyn is using to care for the neighbor's cat and lets himself into their house. Mrs. Desmond thinks it might help if Richard saw his father. She makes arrangements for them to meet, but when the time arrives, his father fails to show up. After this Richard begins to steal. When the neighbors return from their vacation, they find a silver cream pitcher, an antique silver whistle, and forty-five dollars in cash missing from their home. Dr. and Mrs. Desmond cannot believe that Richard has had anything to do with this, but Carolyn discovers that her brother has given both the missing silver items to Cookie. She also finds a trunk full of stolen goods in their attic. When she asks Richard why he has taken these things, he replies, "Because I'm no good. . . . Because I'm just like my father." He'll never be "great, super, excellent, wonderful" like Dr. Desmond, "Mr. Perfect." Carolyn decides she must try to return a penlight and five dollars stolen from a member of the family's swim club. When she squeezes these things under the door of the appropriate beach locker, she is caught in the act by the club manager. They discover her family's locker filled with stolen goods; Flim Flam apparently stowed them there. The manager assumes Carolyn is the thief, compelling Richard to confess and explain his recent behavior. Flim Flam is apprehended and sent to jail. His eyes opened, Dr. Desmond lets Richard know that he is not "Mr. Perfect." In fact, he gives the boy specific examples of his imperfections. The judge dismisses Richard's case and, though they must give up their club membership and withstand some ostracism and harassment, the family comes through this painful time with a deeper understanding of and commitment to each other.

In this first-person narrative, it is clear that Carolyn hates what her brother is doing and even at times believes she hates him. But as she attempts to help him without betraying him, she knows deep down that she will "always love him." When her father realizes that his high standards have contributed to Richard's poor self-image, he tries to be gentler with his children. Richard begins to see that he does not have to win trophies or love chores to be a good person, that one mistake does not make him irresponsible like his birth father. Readers will sympathize with these very human characters as they live through a critical time in their family relationship.

Ages 10-13

Also available in:
No other form known

535

Shyer, Marlene Fanta

Welcome Home, Jellybean

Charles Scribner's Sons, 1978.
(152 pages)

MENTAL RETARDATION
Sibling: love for

Geraldine Oxley is one year older than her twelve-year-old brother, Neil, but has only now been toilet-trained and learned to tie her shoes. Gerri is mentally retarded. After a stay in a residential training center, she is moving back home, though Mr. Oxley, wary of her return, tells Neil it is not going to be easy living with her. Sure enough, she disturbs and angers other tenants in their apartment house when, out of anger or disappointment, she beats her head against the wall at night. And she makes messes of her parents' and Neil's belongings. She even causes Neil trouble at school. New there and without close friends, the boy sees a chance to be befriended by some popular fellow students by playing the piano for a show; Gerri continually interrupts not only his practicing but also his homework. Eventually he is near to being expelled, until his father explains the home situation to the principal. Mr. Oxley maintains that Gerri's actions make no sense, but by now Neil thinks they do; he begins to understand and protect his sister, encouraging her to learn. Mr. Oxley, however, moves out, unable to tolerate Gerri any longer. Neil refuses to leave with him. Then Gerri creates chaos during the school show, and he feels he must leave, though Gerri piteously tries to stop him. Only when Mr. Oxley arrives to pick him up does Neil reconsider. He realizes that Gerri is his sister no matter what she does. His father has quit, and one quitter in the family is enough.

A retarded girl tries to show her love for her family, but her misunderstood efforts—often noisy and disruptive—anger and bewilder others, and thus herself. But when her brother, who narrates this story, learns to perceive the intentions behind what she does, he can genuinely like and accept her. Readers will learn from the logic he discovers in Gerri's actions and can share his joy in her accomplishments. Good humor is by no means the least of virtues in this sympathetic, realistic story.

Ages 10-13

Also available in:
Paperbound—*Welcome Home, Jellybean*
Aladdin Books

536

Silverstein, Shel

The Giving Tree

Black/white illustrations by the author.
HarperCollins Publishers, Inc., 1964.
(52 pages)

GIVING, MEANING OF

A large apple tree and a little boy have great affection for each other. The boy picks the tree's leaves and wears them like a crown. He climbs her trunk, swings from her branches, and eats her fruit. When he is tired, he takes a nap in the tree's shade. The tree is very happy because of all the attention the little boy gives her. But as time passes and the boy grows up, he visits her less often. When the boy is a young man, he needs money; at the tree's suggestion, he takes her apples and sells them. Years later when the boy becomes a man, he comes and tells the tree that he wants a house for his family. The tree offers him her branches as timber to build his house, and she is happy because she is able to help her friend. The next time the "boy" appears, he is a sad old man who wants a boat to carry him far away. The tree gives him her trunk and is happy. But she is not really happy, because her friend seems so miserable. Finally the "boy" returns as a very old man. The tree has nothing left except her stump. But that is just fine because the old man just wants a quiet place to sit and rest.

This is a tender story of a tree that gives everything, asks for nothing in return, and remains happy simply because she is able to give. The boy appears thoughtless in his relationship with the tree. A discussion of the joy or meaning of giving could easily be encouraged after reading this story aloud. This story is appropriate for all ages.

Ages 4 and up

Also available in:
No other form known

537

Simon, Norma

All Kinds of Families

Color illustrations by Joe Lasker.
Albert Whitman & Company, 1976.
(37 pages counted)

FAMILY: Relationships
FAMILY: Unity
Belonging
Family: extended
Lifestyle

Almost everyone is a member of a family. Families share good and bad times. They may have any number of children, or none at all, and may have one, two, or no parents. Families gather from far-apart places to celebrate or mourn together. In any case, families—some including grandparents, aunts, uncles, and cousins—are a unit. That unit is added to by births, adoptions, and marriages and is subtracted from by death, separation, and divorce. The members of some families are not close and do not communicate with each other. Others when apart, keep in touch through letters, visits, and telephone calls. These latter families share stories, work, visits, sadness, and fun. In fact, the thing that makes a family unit is not its size, but the care and love members show one another.

This story, speaking directly to the reader, discusses the differences and similarities in families. Through illustrations and text, the reader learns that families vary but are to be found everywhere. We also learn that the family unit is steady and fertile, nurturing the emotional and physical growth of the child.

Ages 5-8

Also available in:
Talking Book—*All Kinds of Families*
Library of Congress (NLSBPH)

538

Simon, Norma

How Do I Feel?

Color illustrations by Joe Lasker.
Albert Whitman & Company, 1970.
(37 pages)

EMOTIONS: Accepting
Grandparent: living in home of
Twins: identical

Carl and Eddie, about seven, are twins who live with their grandparents and their big brother, Mike. Carl feels lazy when the alarm clock rings in the morning, and he is slow in getting dressed. But Eddie is always ready to start a new day, and he gets ready for school quickly. Grandma knits Carl a new sweater, and he feels cozy wearing it. But when other children make fun of it, he becomes angry and sad. Although Carl feels bright because he can write his full name correctly, he feels stupid when it rains and he leaves his rainhat at school. He wonders if Eddie—who remembered his hat—ever forgets anything. Carl feels strong when he helps Grandma carry grocery bags, and he feels brave when he rescues his cat from a dog. But when the dog barks at Carl, he becomes afraid until Mike demonstrates that the animal is friendly. Carl feels grown-up like Mike when his team wins its ball game, but later he feels dirty and tired. After taking a bath, Carl sits down to dinner with the family. Grandpa and Grandma have a fight at the table, and all three boys are worried. When the grandparents make up, however, everyone feels better. The next day is Eddie and Carl's birthday, and both twins feel excited and special. But what they feel most of all is "happy!"

This book describes the various feelings of a boy who is an identical twin. At times Carl is unhappy with himself—especially when he compares himself with his twin. This book would be helpful in showing a child that all types of emotions are normal and acceptable. This book could be used to stimulate group discussion.

Ages 4-8

Also available in:
Talking Book—*How Do I Feel?*
Library of Congress (NLSBPH)

539

Simon, Norma

I Was So Mad!

Color illustrations by Dora Leder.
Albert Whitman & Company, 1974.
(37 pages counted)

ANGER

Several children share stories about things that make them angry. One child is angered when he is unable to tie his shoes. When a building she has been working on is knocked down by another child, a young girl feels angry enough to hurt the boy who destroyed it. Other boys and girls become angry when they cannot do tricks that other children are able to do, when friends laugh at them for wetting their pants, when they must take a nap, when their pets misbehave, or when they must go to bed at night. They become angry when they are not allowed to do the same thing an older sibling does or when relatives dote on a new baby in the family. They also feel angry when planned outdoor activities are postponed because of weather, when a child is unjustly accused of wrongdoing, or when a favorite toy is broken. The story emphasizes that anger is a normal response to these situations and that adults also become angry.

The text and illustrations of these first-person narratives relate situations in which a child may experience frustration, anxiety, jealousy, humiliation, or loss of emotional control. The book includes a forward that suggests ways for parents to help a child accept and cope with emotions.

Ages 4-8

Also available in:
Cassette—*I Was So Mad!*
Educational Enrichment Materials

Filmstrip—*I Was So Mad!*
Educational Enrichment Materials

Paperbound—*I Was So Mad!*
Albert Whitman & Company

540

Simon, Norma

I'm Busy, Too

Color illustrations by Dora Leder.
Albert Whitman & Company, 1980.
(32 pages counted)

FAMILY: Relationships
Day-care center, going to

Mikey, Sara, and Charlie are all members of active, working families. When Monday morning comes, these preschool children and others like them must wake up and get ready for their own busy day. There is "stretching, yawning, grumbling, tumbling, tossing covers off, all over town." Soon everyone is on the way to work or school. The teachers are ready for the children, and the children are ready for their school day. Parents also work hard. Mikey's mother helps a dentist clean and repair teeth. Sara's mother works in their house; her father works in their restaurant. Charlie's father fixes broken television sets. When the day is over, everyone goes home. Now is "a time to talk together." Mikey tells his mother about the Halloween pirate's mask he made. She promises to help him make his costume. Sara's family admires her paintings, and her sister hangs them in their room. Charlie tells his father about building a garage for Mikey's truck. His father promises to visit school soon so he can see everything. Then there are "sleepy people, tired people, washing up to go to bed. . . . Happy dreams, all over town."

Three children of working parents are themselves "working playing, playing working, all day long." But when adults and kids come home, everyone's adventures during the day are taken seriously and shared. Realistic illustrations complement the happy, positive tone as the notion is quietly conveyed that close family relationships are still the norm in today's day-care-dependent society. The use of rhythmic repetition makes the book especially pleasant for reading aloud.

Ages 3-5

Also available in:
Large Print—*I'm Busy, Too*
Macmillan/McGraw-Hill School Publishing Company

541

Simon, Norma

Nobody's Perfect, Not Even My Mother

Color illustrations by Dora Leder.
Albert Whitman & Company, 1981.
(32 pages counted)

PERSEVERANCE
Encouragement
Self, attitude toward: confidence

Various young narrators tell of things they can do well, such as putting together puzzles or doing somersaults, and things they can't manage, such as baking birthday cakes. One admits, "When I really try to do something right and it comes out all wrong, I feel awful. Just awful!" But each child notices that parents, grandparents, and teachers have shortcomings too. One boy's mother is good at repairing cars, but she can't seem to stop smoking. A father yells at his children and frightens them, but he acknowledges the situation and is trying to change. A grandfather doesn't play his guitar very well, but he practices every night. In sum, "You're good at some things—I'm good at some things. Everyone's good at some things. But nobody's perfect!"

A cast of ethnically and racially varied children and adults, many shown pursuing untraditional tasks and occupations, helps young readers understand that everyone is good at something and that even adults fall far short of perfection. Children made anxious both by their own shortcomings and by the limitations of the adults in their lives will find reassurance in the examples of grown-ups facing everyday failures and weaknesses, just as children do. Illustrations are exceptionally realistic and appealing.

Ages 4-8

Also available in:
No other form known

542

Simon, Norma

Why Am I Different?

Color illustrations by Dora Leder.
Albert Whitman & Company, 1976.
(31 pages)

DIFFERENCES, HUMAN
Autonomy

Children of the most varied backgrounds, and with the most varied appearances and skills, talk about the ways they are different. Some are tall, others short. One child is the only one in his family with red hair. Another is allergic to chocolate, shrimp, and clams, and dislikes the difference that makes. As for skills, one is good at drawing, another at writing. Having no TV set at home, one child wonders why his parents should be different. Another child's family owns no car: he and his mother take the bus to "lots of places." Parents differ too in their occupations. And having a grandmother living at home makes a delightful difference to a boy who likes his grandmother. Some children are adopted. One boy is an only child. One youngster sums it up: "We're different, but alike, too. We eat and play and wear clothes and live in houses. But I'm not you, and you're not me. I think different things, I feel different things. I know different things, and I do different things. I look different. I *am* different. That's good!"

This book encourages young children to recognize and accept differences in themselves and others. The author's introductory note speaks of helping "children feel pride in the specialness of 'Being me!'" Questions scattered throughout the text encourage thought and promote discussion. The last page is written for adults, and offers suggestions on how the book may be most helpfully used.

Ages 4-8

Also available in:
No other form known

543

Singer, Marilyn

It Can't Hurt Forever

Black/white illustrations by Leigh Grant.
HarperCollins Publishers, Inc., 1978.
(186 pages) o.p.

SURGERY: Heart
Death: attitude toward
Friendship: making friends
Hospital, going to

Eleven-year-old Ellie Simon is to enter the hospital, where she will have tests to confirm and surgery to repair a "patent ductus arteriosus"—an open duct on her heart. Though her parents and physician have thoroughly explained the procedure, and her mother has promised that she will not die, Ellie is deeply worried. Admitted to the hospital, Ellie meets another patient, Sonia, a girl about her own age who takes her to meet the other children in the ward. This helps Ellie to relax and to stop feeling alone—but then she meets May, who terrifies her with wild stories about her own heart catheterization and surgery. Sure enough, Ellie is badly scared when she is taken for her heart "cath," but finds that, though painful, the procedure is not debilitating. In any case, surgery approaches, and the team that will operate on Ellie comes to her to discuss it. Despite honest answers from all concerned, Ellie remains fearful all the way into the operating room. She survives as promised, but in the recovery room finds she is in extreme pain. Mercifully, shots relieve that. When the pain lessens and she is again allowed to walk through the ward, Ellie meets Melissa, a girl also scheduled for heart surgery. Melissa is so frightened that she has bitten a doctor and repeatedly attempted to run away. Ellie persuades her to have mock surgery—a kind of rehearsal—in the recreation room. Having learned what is ahead, Melissa is far less frightened and Ellie is pleased that she, like Sonia, was able to help someone be less afraid.

This first-person narrative, based on the author's own experience with heart surgery at eight, is filled with candid observations concerning serious surgery and lengthy hospital stays. When the main character meets other patients in the children's ward, they display a multitude of feelings about surgery and serious illness. Truthfulness is shown to be the best antidote to children's fears about surgery. Because the main character candidly expresses her own feelings, this book could be of great use and comfort to children facing surgery, and to those friends and siblings who want to understand what a hospital stay and an operation are like.

Ages 9-12

Also available in:
Cassette—*It Can't Hurt Forever*
Library of Congress (NLSBPH)

S

544

Slepian, Jan

The Alfred Summer

Macmillan Publishing Company, Inc., 1980.
(119 pages)

DEPENDENCE/INDEPENDENCE
FRIENDSHIP: Meaning of
SELF, ATTITUDE TOWARD: Accepting
Cerebral palsy
Epilepsy
Limbs, abnormal or missing
Mental retardation
Peer relationships
Rejection: parental
Stealing

At fourteen, Lester Klopper, who has cerebral palsy, wants friends and a full life. He is stymied by an over-protective mother and an aloof, uninterested father. Then he meets Alfie and Myron and his summer takes on new dimensions. Alfie is retarded and has a deformed hand and foot; Myron, who has recently lost his father, feels dominated and interfered with by his family. The friendship among the three boys begins at the beach one Sunday when Lester sees Alfie caught in rocks and in danger from the waves and incoming tide. Alfie never thinks to call for help, so Lester tries frantically to alert someone to the situation. But he is unable to speak when excited, and his gestures succeed only in drawing an uncomprehending crowd. Then Lester's father arrives and the boy calms down enough to explain the situation. His father and Myron rescue Alfie. Afterwards, the three boys go off together for ice cream. Lester has to concentrate on getting the spoonfuls of ice cream to his lips, but soon realizes that he is enjoying the normality of eating ice cream and talking with friends. Myron tells them a secret; he is building a rowboat in his basement. In it he plans to escape from all the people who dominate his life. Excitedly, Alfie and Lester convince Myron to let them help him find materials for the boat, and the three quickly warm to the project. They are joined by another outcast, Claire. Myron decides they must all go to a park to examine the construction of rowboats. Lester's anxious mother is at first very reluctant to let him go without her, but she consents when she understands that Myron and Claire will be going also. At the park, Myron studies the boats and is dismayed to find that he has made no provision for oarlocks. Claire urges him to steal some. He tries, but is seen by an attendant who tells the four to leave the park. Only Claire has the courage to ask strangers for directions out, and the others admire her confidence. Later she admits that talking to people she doesn't know unnerves her. After much planning, Lester and Alfie return to the park and succeed in stealing a pair of oarlocks. But this triumph is forgotten when, on their way home, they ride a commuter train together and Alfie has a seizure. Nobody on the train makes a move to help and so, gathering composure and strength he didn't know he had, Lester gets Alfie off the train, forgetting the oarlocks in the process. People finally help the two, taking Alfie to a hospital and Lester home. Once there, Lester locks himself in his room. He is devastated by the limitations of his handicap, angry at the lack of sympathy and understanding he encounters all the time. His mother tries to draw him out of his room, but he bitterly rejects his attachment to her: "The strings are gone," he tells her. She accuses his father of never being home long enough to get to know his son, and the father replies angrily that she has pushed him away by preferring Lester. Finally, Lester's father knocks on the boy's door and Lester admits him. Told what he has lived to hear, that rescuing Alfie was the act of a man, Lester is now too embittered to care. But his father is able to console him and together they go to dinner. News of the rescue has spread, they discover, and Lester is a hero. Everyone but Alfie, who is still in the hospital, comes to the launching of Myron's boat, which he has renamed "Alfred." As he rows from shore, the boat begins to sink. But he keeps rowing until the boat is completely submerged, at which he stands up and raises his hands in victory. The laughing crowd begins applauding, and Lester is filled with triumph, pride, affection for his friends—many emotions he has never known before.

In this special book about special people, four friends, two outcast because of their disabilities and two because of personality and circumstance, find strength and self-acceptance through their relationship. Lester, who tells the story, gives reality and urgency to the people, emotions, and events he describes. He injects humor too, often leavening the seriousness of the story. The sequel to this richly rewarding book is *Lester's Turn.*

Ages 11-13

Also available in:
Cassette—*The Alfred Summer*
Library of Congress (NLSBPH)

545

Slepian, Jan

Lester's Turn

Macmillan Publishing Company, Inc., 1981.
(139 pages) o.p.

FRIENDSHIP: Best Friend
Boy-girl relationships
Cerebral palsy
Death: of friend
Determination
Love, meaning of
Mental retardation
Self, attitude toward: accepting

When sixteen-year-old Lester, who has cerebral palsy, visits his retarded friend Alfie in the hospital where he lives now that his mother has died, he's appalled at how fat and pasty Alfie looks. Although Alfie has always loved the outdoors, the hospital staff finds it easier to keep him indoors so that if he has an epileptic seizure he won't get hurt. Lester feels an urgent need to get Alfie out of the place. But when his attempt to smuggle his friend out is foiled, Mrs. Brenner, the hospital director, explains to him what caring for Alfie would mean, why people can't just remove patients from the hospital. She realizes she has not convinced him, however, and says she recognizes an obsession when she sees one. Lester visits his good friend Claire, who introduces him to her upstairs neighbors, Lena Lensky and her violinist son, Alex. Lester tells them about Alfie, but Lena thinks it would be a mistake to remove him from the hospital. She asks Lester if he really cares that much about Alfie and Lester reflects, "It was not the caring I knew so much about, but the needing." He remains determined to devote his life to Alfie, the only person, he believes, who really needs him. Later that day he walks down to the beach and meets Tillie-Rose, a hospital volunteer. She and some friends are having a cookout and she invites Lester to join them. At first he refuses, unable to visualize himself with normal kids, afraid to eat with them because he often makes a mess. But Tillie-Rose persists, and Lester enjoys himself. Later, the group pairs off under blankets and Tillie-Rose kisses Lester, his first kiss. This experience awakens him to a "secret treasure—he likes Tillie-Rose, but he really loves Claire. The next day the principal tells Lester that he could get a college scholarship if he would just try a little harder. But Lester thinks he knows what his future holds, and it doesn't include college. That afternoon he gets a part-time job making deliveries for a drugstore, but after several days, one of his uncontrollable movements brings down a stack of pill bottles and he loses the job. Tillie-Rose offers to let Alfie live in her basement, and Claire offers to keep him with her family. But Lester wants to care for Alfie himself. Still, he accepts Lena's offer of a benefit violin concert performed by Alex. He also gets permission from Mrs. Brenner for Alfie to spend the weekend of the concert with Claire's family. Claire, Tillie-Rose, and Lester take Alfie around the hospital grounds, and Lester is amazed at how popular Alfie is. Too bad that such a beautiful place isn't good for Alfie, who appears to have gotten more forgetful and fanciful during his stay. Tillie-Rose reassures Lester that Alfie will be his old self again once they get him out of there. The afternoon of the violin concert, Lester and Alfie explore Claire's neighborhood and remember old times. After several hours, however, Alfie asks to go home. He looks sick—bent over, gray lips, a yellowish cast to his eyes. Lester leaves him with Claire, as they've arranged, planning to return after dinner. Claire's family discovers that Alfie is running a high temperature. Although they rush him to the hospital and he has emergency surgery, his appendix bursts and he dies. In the middle of the night, Lester creeps into Tillie-Rose's basement. She finds him there, calls Claire, and the three grieve together. Lester is guilt-ridden at the thought that he had been using Alfie just as he accused everyone else of doing. He goes to see Mrs. Brenner. She tells him he can either use his guilt as an excuse for failure, or he can use the example of Alfie's life to make something of himself. On Lester's way out of the hospital, Alfie's friends tell how they miss him and how special he was. Noticing a man with cerebral palsy in a wheelchair, Lester realizes that, unlike this man, he himself has choices, choices he intends to make wisely.

A teenager with cerebral palsy is forced to examine his relationship with a retarded friend, and in so doing learns quite a bit about love and friendship. The sequel to *The Alfred Summer,* this first-person narrative set in 1939 is universal in its emotions and especially rich in settings and characters. Lester's mother is overprotective and his father all but invisible, so the boy fastens on Alfie as a reason for living. Gradually, he sorts out his obligations to his friends and to himself. The book is powerfully effective in conveying the richness and complexity of the lives of disabled people. Lester and Alfie are very real, human, and likeable. The story makes good dramatic use of the ways love can highlight the similarities among all people.

Ages 11-14

Also available in:
Cassette—*Lester's Turn*
Library of Congress (NLSBPH)

546

Slote, Alfred

Matt Gargan's Boy

HarperCollins Publishers, Inc., 1985.
(160 pages, paperbound)

PARENT/PARENTS: Single
Little League
Prejudice: sexual

Eleven-year-old Danny lives in Arborville, Michigan, with his divorced mother. Danny's father, Matt Gargan, is a well-known catcher for the Chicago White Sox, and Danny pitches for a recreational league baseball team in Arborville. Against all his mother says to the contrary, Danny believes his parents will reunite when his father retires in another year. Pitching his first game of the season, Danny notices that in the stands his mother is enjoying the company of a new escort. Distracted, he pitches badly—recovering only when the man leaves early. The man is Herb Warren, his mother's new boss at the library, a widower with two daughters. Susie, the eleven-year-old, plans to try out for Danny's baseball team. Against all the boys' efforts to keep a girl from qualifying, Susie passes—and Danny quits the team just before a tough game. He reasons that with no games to attend together, Mr. Warren will leave his mother available for his father. When he tells her this, Danny's mother responds that she is going to the big game anyway. Danny calls his father for advice—and Matt Gargan tells his son that he is getting married. He dons his uniform and bikes over to the game. The team is doing badly. Finally, after explaining everything to the coach, Danny gets to pitch. He strikes two players out; then he and Susie execute another play for a third out and victory. Later that evening, Danny tells his mother of his talk with his father: "I admire him, Mom. I'm his son. I'm always going to be his son, aren't I?" His mother replies, "Of course you are. You always will be."

This believable first-person narrative perceptively describes a boy's resentment of his parents' divorce and his unfounded hope for reconciliation. His father's planned remarriage shocks Danny into seeing clearly that his parents are individuals with their own lives. Even if both parents remarry, Danny won't lose his identity; he will always be "Matt Gargan's boy."

Ages 9-11

Also available in:
Braille—*Matt Gargan's Boy*
Library of Congress (NLSBPH)

547

Slote, Alfred

Tony and Me

HarperCollins Publishers, Inc., 1974.
(156 pages) o.p.

FRIENDSHIP: Meaning of
Change: new home
Decision making
Sports/Sportsmanship
Stealing: shoplifting

Fifth-grader Bill Taylor is not content with his new home in Arborville, Michigan. He anxiously awaits his family's planned return to California. Arborville does have something to recommend it, though—several baseball teams. Bill plays for the Miller Laundry team. Although they placed last in the league the previous year, the "Laundries" are confident they can improve their record. Another team has disbanded, and the Miller Laundry team plans to draft some of its best players. Tony Spain, a superb player, is immediately chosen. The "Laundries" all vie for the attention and friendship of their new star, but Tony chooses Bill as his special friend. After being with Tony only one afternoon, Bill is sure the boy will become one of the greatest friends he has ever had. But during the same afternoon, Bill also discovers that Tony shoplifts. Tony dupes Bill into being a decoy while he steals a baseball from a sports store. Bill is caught while Tony escapes. Bill faces the choice of either revealing Tony's name and losing a friend or withholding Tony's name and going against his own better judgment. His mother and father finally convince him to report the truth. When Bill and his father go to see Tony and Mr. Spain, they are shocked to learn that Tony is going to be sent away by his father to live with Tony's older married brother in Kentucky. Although he loves Tony, Mr. Spain cannot cope with him. This time, Tony's father pays for the stolen merchandise and the charges are dropped. When Bill's dad is offered a permanent job in Arborville, Bill decides he no longer wants to return to California. Instead, he will help the "Laundries" become a winning team. Bill knows that he and the rest of the team will remember Tony's good qualities—especially his talent for baseball.

This first-person narrative uses the sport of baseball as a background for an appealing story of two boys' friendship. The boys' personalities and home lives are well portrayed in this fast-paced novel.

Ages 10-13

Also available in:
Braille—*Tony and Me*
Library of Congress (NLSBPH)

Cassette—*Tony and Me*
Library of Congress (NLSBPH)

548

Smith, Doris Buchanan

Kelly's Creek

Black/white illustrations by Alan Tiegreen.
HarperCollins Publishers, Inc., 1975.
(71 pages)

LEARNING DISABILITIES
Self-esteem

Nine-year-old Kelly O'Brien is worried. For two months he has been in the special class for children with learning disabilities, but his progress report shows no progress: his hands and feet will not obey his brain. Knowing his parents will be disappointed, he escapes to the one place where no one thinks him clumsy or slow, the marshland down the bluff from his home. There he meets his friend Phillip, a biology student who has taught Kelly much about the science of the marsh life they both love so much. Sure enough, Kelly's mother is angered by his absence and rules Phillip and the marsh off limits. Kelly must stay home and practice drawing basic shapes. But the next day Kelly sneaks off to the marsh, on his way finding an empty ice-cream container. He traces its roundness over and over, only to find Phillip watching him. He feels more stupid than ever. At home he tries drawing the circle on paper unaided—and for the first time draws not only a circle but a square. His parents, his teacher, even his schoolmates are happy for him. Phillip comes to Kelly's house and offers a suggestion: that the boy share with his classmates what he has learned about the marsh. The next day Kelly takes two pairs of fiddler crabs to class and talks about them. His classmates are astounded by how much he knows, and for once, Kelly feels the warm self-respect of having excelled in front of others.

The author has created a charming, vigorous little boy, whose spirit is not suffocated by all those who expect too much of him too quickly. Kelly's disability is described only as "an eye-to-hand problem."

Ages 8-13

Also available in:
No other form known

549

Smith, Doris Buchanan

Kick a Stone Home

HarperCollins Publishers, Inc., 1974.
(152 pages) o.p.

IDENTITY, SEARCH FOR
MATURATION
Boy-girl relationships: dating
Death: of pet
Divorce
Parent/Parents: single

Fifteen-year-old Sara Jane is more interested in sports and animals than in school or dating. Because of her love for animals—especially for her dog Tally—Sara aspires to become a veterinarian. Her mother does not understand the girl's interests or her hopes for the future. Sara's parents were divorced three years earlier, and although her father has remarried, Sara refuses to accept the reality of her parents' divorce. She dreads the visits she and her brothers must make to Dad and Joyce's house. Her stepmother is very kind, but Sara's feelings make it difficult for her to respond to this kindness. When she returns home after one such visit, she learns that Tally has been struck by a car. When he dies, Sara feels that she has lost her only real friend. Later in the story, she befriends a homeless wild dog, and this helps ease her grief. She even finds a summer job as a veterinarian's helper. Sara is comfortable around dogs, but with boys it is another matter. Bill, whom she dislikes, invites her out for a date, but she does not accept until her mother prods her. Sara is uncomfortable with Bill. She wishes that her companionable football-playing friends would take her out, but they do not seem to think of her in terms of dating. On the last day of school, she impulsively invites a boy named Francis to a party. Although they have been in class together all year, she does not really know him. She is delighted when he not only accepts but also proves to be charming company. Sara concludes that "it has really been a good year."

The girl in this book is struggling to sort out her confused feelings about her parents' divorce, her grief at the death of her dog, and her growing interest in boys. As she matures, she finds that "you have to understand yourself before you can understand other people."

Ages 11 and up

Also available in:
Braille—*Kick a Stone Home*
Library of Congress (NLSBPH)

550

Smith, Doris Buchanan

Last Was Lloyd

Viking Penguin, 1981.
(124 pages)

SELF-ESTEEM
Friendship: making friends
Parental: overprotection
School: truancy
Talents: athletic
Weight control: overweight

Unhappy and overweight, twelve-year-old Lloyd is pampered, almost smothered, by his overprotective, divorced mother. She cooks whatever he wants, insists on driving him everywhere he goes, has allowed him to miss sixty-four days of school, and defends him from the truant officer, Mr. Duggan. Lloyd is a crackerjack baseball player, the star hitter on his mother's softball team. But no one at school knows of his prowess because his mother, fearing for his safety, insists that he play only under her watchful eye. Always the last chosen for the school team, he never tries to hit the ball and refuses to run when he accidentally does hit it. The kids make fun of him, but Lloyd thinks of himself as a turtle whom names and jeers cannot reach. Then Kirby, a classmate, sees Lloyd at one of his mother's practice sessions and discovers his hitting ability. Dismayed, and further embarrassed when Kirby learns that he is not allowed to ride a bike or walk to the ball park by himself, Lloyd still refuses to make any effort when Kirby chooses him for the school team. He does notice that Ancil, the spirited, "spaghetti-haired" new girl in class, is now the last to be chosen. Meanwhile, Mr. Duggan tries to learn why Lloyd is so often truant, what is bothering him. Lloyd confides in him and is surprised by the truant officer's sympathy and his concerned insistence that Lloyd attend school regularly. Touched by Mr. Duggan's interest and by Kirby's continuing attempts to befriend him, Lloyd begins to come out of his shell. Kirby refuses a birthday party invitation unless Lloyd is invited; Lloyd, in turn, refuses to go unless Ancil is invited. Then he convinces the friendless Ancil to attend. During the party baseball game, Ancil gets a hit. Rather than strand her at first base, Lloyd hits the ball and runs. Pleased by his classmates' approval, he even resolves to begin his diet—he will have only a small portion of cake and ice cream.

A lonely, overprotected boy responds quickly but credibly to the friendship and encouragement of several classmates and a truant officer. As his self-image improves, Lloyd can assert himself for the benefit of another outcast classmate and begin to loosen his dependence on his mother. Although sympathetically portrayed, Lloyd's complete metamorphosis may seem a bit too smooth and sudden.

Ages 8-11

Also available in:
Paperbound—*Last Was Lloyd*
Puffin Books

551

Smith, Doris Buchanan

A Taste of Blackberries

Black/white illustrations by Charles Robinson.
HarperCollins Publishers, Inc., 1973.
(58 pages) o.p.

DEATH: of friend
Friendship: meaning of
Loss: feelings of
Mourning, stages of

This is a first-person account of the emotions, memories, and actions of an eleven-year-old boy whose best friend Jamie dies of an allergic reaction to a bee sting. The boy struggles to overcome his shock, denial, and anger as well as his feelings of guilt for not trying to help Jamie when the bee stung him. When he attends the funeral, he can no longer deny his friend's death. In his search to discover "why Jamie had to die," he learns that some difficult questions do not have answers.

This is a touching and vivid story. Death is given no pat explanation but is presented as a fact that must be dealt with and accepted. Grief is seen as a natural outcome of losing someone dear. The boy's thoughts about death are realistically presented. Because the story depicts only the first few days following a death, the total mourning process is not portrayed.

Ages 8-11

Also available in:
Talking Book—*A Taste of Blackberries*
Library of Congress (NLSBPH)

552

Smith, Doris Buchanan

Tough Chauncey

Black/white frontispiece by Michael Eagle.
Puffin Books, 1986.
(222 pages, paperbound)

REJECTION
Child abuse
Deprivation, emotional
Grandparent: living in home of
Parent/Parents: single
Self-esteem

Thirteen-year-old Chauncey looks no older than eleven, but he is so "tough" that he can beat up any other boy in school except Jack. Chauncey lives with his maternal grandparents and visits his mother only occasionally. Grandpa is very strict and whips Chauncey with a belt or locks him in a closet for the slightest offense. Grandma approves of Grandpa's harsh discipline, and Mama is too intimidated by her parents to be willing to defend her own child. After a particularly bad encounter with Grandpa, Chauncey runs away to Mama and pleads with her to keep him—but to no avail. In fact, he overhears Mama and his grandparents talking about filling out papers to give his grandparents legal custody of him. He runs away again and meets up with a person named Jack, who helps him hide out for several days. Jack tells Chauncey about his own life, which has included several years in a foster home. Chauncey concludes that living in a foster home is the solution to his own problem, and he decides to tell his story to a social worker.

This book describes a boy who is mistreated both physically and emotionally. His home life has taught him to be tough and distrustful of his schoolmates and teachers. Since he knows his family cannot provide for his needs, he makes a mature decision to seek outside help. The book portrays several incidents of cruelty to animals, including the shooting of some kittens by the grandfather. Some children might be upset after reading this graphic description.

Ages 12 and up

Also available in:
Braille—*Tough Chauncey*
Library of Congress (NLSBPH)

Talking Book—*Tough Chauncey*
Library of Congress (NLSBPH)

553

Smith, Janice Lee

The Monster in the Third Dresser Drawer and Other Stories about Adam Joshua

Black/white illustrations by Dick Gackenbach.
HarperCollins Publishers, Inc., 1981.
(86 pages)

CHANGE: Resisting
Age: respect for
Baby-sitter
Fear: of darkness
Friendship: making friends
Moving
Sibling: new baby
Tooth, loss of

Young Adam Joshua strongly objects to the move his family is planning. But the move takes place nevertheless, and he ends up in a new town, a new house, and a new room. While climbing a tree, he sees into a bedroom hung with Spiderman posters. He yells hello and gives his name, but the boy in the room slams down the window. Then he lifts it up a crack and says his name is Nelson. Later, Adam Joshua writes on his bedroom wall that moving is moving and there's not much he can do about it. Nobody asks Adam Joshua if he wants a baby in the family either. But Amanda Jane arrives all the same. Suddenly Adam Joshua is "too loud. And too babyish. And too in the way." While Amanda Jane's bedroom is readied she sleeps in her brother's room, waking him up repeatedly when she cries. Nelson, with whom he's become friends, has already warned him that babies get all the attention. One night, after Adam Joshua gets a little kiss and a little hug from his parents and Amanda Jane gets a big hug and a big kiss, he cuts up her teddy bear with a scissors. His parents respond by hugging him and reading him a story. After they leave, Adam Joshua makes amends by tucking Amanda Jane in. When Adam Joshua gets a loose tooth, he and Nelson try to make it fall out with string, bubble gum, pounding on the back, and other ineffective measures. In due time, Adam Joshua swallows the tooth while eating cereal. The baby-sitter who comes one night does not understand about the monster hiding in Adam Joshua's third dresser drawer. As many times as he turns on the light, she turns it off. When Amanda Jane wakes up, the baby-sitter pats her back and takes her downstairs, but she tells Adam Joshua to get to sleep and keep the light off. When his parents return, he explains the monster to his mother. She tells the monster to scat, waves her arms around, and assures her son that it's gone. Adam Joshua is not happy when Great-Aunt Emily comes to visit. She is old, wears black, smells like lavender, and loves Amanda Jane. But this time she brings Adam Joshua a present—a very old picture of her family standing by their sod house in Kansas. The more she tells him about the old days, the more he likes her and the more she appreciates him. He is sorry to see her go. Adam Joshua's parents finally begin working in earnest on Amanda Jane's bedroom. He takes care of her while they carpet, paint, and wallpaper. When he complains about how much nicer her new room is compared with his, his father says he can choose between the two rooms. After sitting in both rooms Adam Joshua decides to remain in his own, and he paints stars and a moon on the ceiling and some flowers on the wall. The first night Amanda Jane sleeps in her new room, Adam Joshua worries she will be lonely. He brings her to his room and tucks her in bed with him, saying, "Now you don't have to worry, I'm right here."

In these anecdotal chapters, young Adam Joshua, helped by understanding parents, copes with a move, a new baby sister, and several less dramatic but very familiar events. Young readers will appreciate the humor of the little boy's escapades as he makes new friends and learns to love his baby sister. Delightful illustrations capture the lighthearted mood.

Ages 5-8

Also available in:
Braille—*The Monster in the Third Dresser Drawer and Other Stories about Adam Joshua*
Library of Congress (NLSBPH)

Cassette—*The Monster in the Third Dresser Drawer and Other Stories about Adam Joshua*
Library of Congress (NLSBPH)

Paperbound—*The Monster in the Third Dresser Drawer and Other Stories about Adam Joshua*
Library of Congress (NLSBPH)

554

Smith, Nancy Covert

The Falling-Apart Winter

Walker & Co., 1982.
(112 pages) o.p.

DEPRESSION
MENTAL ILLNESS: of Parent
Change: new home
Change: resisting
Family: relationships
Reality, escaping
School: classmate relationships

Twelve-year-old Addam Hanley misses his dog, his grandparents, and the friends he left in Ohio when his father's new job took him and his parents to an apartment (no pets allowed) in Virginia. He also misses the way his mother used to be. These days she's listless, apathetic, and cries a lot. She's too tired to do the housework or fix meals, and Addam's father won't take care of those chores either. Months after their move, boxes still sit unpacked. Addam's parents fight often, his mother crying that nobody understands, his father calling her crazy. A new friendship with a classmate named Bryan is hindered when Addam's mother makes a scene in front of Bryan. In response to all this, Addam's schoolwork suffers. Moose, the football team captain, compounds his misery by teasing him. One day Addam comes home to find that his mother has been hospitalized. Angry with his father for not averting the situation, partly relieved, anxious, guilty, he runs out of the house. He tells friends that his mother works for the State Department and travels a lot, fantasizing about the wonderful gifts she brings when she returns home. When his father asks him to come along on the nightly visits to his mother, Addam refuses. He "didn't want to think about his real mother. His made-up mother was better." When Addam's mother finally returns home, she is somewhat better but still not herself. She will visit a mental health clinic daily as an outpatient. As part of her treatment, Addam and his father must also attend sessions with her therapist, Dr. Collier. Dr. Collier explains that his mother is suffering from depression. She asks Addam if he is willing to help his family be happy. He doesn't know. In subsequent visits, Dr. Collier helps Addam understand human psychology and family dynamics a bit better. Thanksgiving approaches, and Addam bemoans the TV turkey dinner he's expecting. However, his mother does fix the traditional dinner while Addam and his father watch the parade. While she does all the dishes, they watch the football game. Then an essay contest on freedom is announced at school, and Addam begins a paper about the freedom to be mentally healthy. Dr. Collier arranges a conference with all three Hanleys, during which Mrs. Hanley reports that on Thanksgiving she was once again taken for granted, doing all the cooking and cleaning up while her husband and son enjoyed their own pursuits. Addam watches as his parents assume their familiar postures: his father turning away from the problem, his mother crying. Mr. Hanley refuses to attend any more sessions with Dr. Collier and forbids Addam to also. Addam works hard on his essay and becomes one of six semi-finalists. All are to read their essays to the entire seventh grade, and the whole class will help choose the winner. Addam is horrified. He imagines the jeers when Moose and his other classmates learn his mother has been mentally ill. The night before the contest, Addam reads his essay to his parents, figuring his father will forbid him to read it in public. His father storms out of the apartment, and Addam isn't sure what his reaction is. His mother cries, this time with the relief of feeling that Addam actually understands some of what she's been going through. The next day, just before the essay reading, Addam tries to intercede when Moose bullies his friend Joanne. Furious with Moose, Addam, after reading his essay, lashes out extemporaneously at bullies who not only refuse to help others, but actually aggravate their problems. Addam's classmates choose his essay as the winner. Then Addam discovers that Moose's mother is an alcoholic; they may never be friends, but a truce is declared. Mr. Hanley finally admits to being wrong-headed, and the family resumes therapy sessions with Dr. Collier. When the question of returning to Ohio for Christmas comes up, all three agree that "home" is where they are. They know they can look forward now, not backward.

A young boy tries to make sense of his changed family situation while his mother suffers from acute depression. He must also cope with the loss of his dog, friends, and former home; a new school; a bully; and his father's tendency to offer less support, rather than more, in times of trouble. The book is never didactic, but does offer a number of suggestions to readers who live with mentally ill family members. Familiarizing themselves with mental illness in general and the person's condition in particular is a first step, and the book defuses anxiety about counseling, therapists, group sessions, and mental health clinics. Addam's negative feelings about his mother's illness—fear, shame, guilt, hostility, selfishness—are all shown to be natural, although he learns how to turn them around. This well-written story takes readers into the troubled Hanley home and leaves them with more empathy, understanding, and knowledge than they had before.

Ages 10-13

Also available in:
Large Print—*The Falling-Apart Winter*
Library of Congress (NLSBPH)

555

Smith, Robert Kimmel

Jelly Belly

Black/white illustrations by Bob Jones.
Dell Publishing Company, Inc. (Yearling Books), 1981.
(155 pages, paperbound)

WEIGHT CONTROL: Overweight
Camp experiences
Determination
Family: relationships
Grandparent: living in child's home
Self-discipline

Eleven-year-old Ned Robbins is thirty pounds overweight. Ned used to be skinny until his grandmother came to live with his family five years ago. His grandmother loves to cook; Ned loves to eat. Now the kids call him names like Blimpie, Tubby, Piggy, Lard-Butt, and Jelly Belly. Ned's parents have put him on a diet but he has not lost any weight in four months—because he sneaks food and his grandmother helps him. One day in May, Ned's parents inform him he will be spending two months at Camp Lean-Too. Ned thinks the camp sounds "like a jail for fat kids." Jamie, his older brother, tells a depressed Ned that he must not want to lose the weight badly enough; if he did, he would try. By the first day of camp, Ned has gained seven pounds. Dr. Skinner, the camp dietician, tells him he should expect to lose twenty pounds in eight weeks. He encourages all the campers to think sports, not food. Ned meets his roommates: Richard, Max, Hog, Fred, and Brian. He immediately takes to Richard, the only one who managed to sneak food into camp. The regular camp food is so bad that Ned, Richard, Max, and Hog raid the kitchen one night, stealing cheese and bread to make sandwiches. After three weeks Ned has only lost three pounds. Then Richard sneaks into town and buys large quantities of snack foods and candy. They stash the food and eat it each night after dinner. By the end of camp Ned is only fourteen pounds lighter. He feels guilty and regretful when an award is given to a boy who has lost forty-four pounds. Back home, Ned again begins to eat his grandmother's food heartily. His father makes a deal with him. If Ned can get down to seventy-five pounds by Easter, the family will go to Disney World. Ned is not sure he can do it. But while sitting in the school cafeteria, he comes to the realization that he indeed eats too much. He decides to lose weight. That afternoon he tells his grandmother to stop feeding him so much. He then tells Jamie of his determination, and Jamie encourages him to jog. By January Ned is down to seventy-nine pounds and cannot seem to lose any more. At his checkup, the doctor informs him that since he has grown one-and-a-half inches, his ideal weight is now seventy-nine pounds. Ned is elated; his father makes reservations at Disney World. Shortly thereafter, Ned receives a letter from Richard saying he will see him at Camp Lean-Too. Ned vows never to see Camp Lean-Too again.

Until Ned makes up his mind to lose weight, even sending him to a weight-loss camp doesn't solve his eating problem. When he becomes determined to win a coveted trip by losing weight, he succeeds. Ned's first-person narrative offers considerable insight into the struggle involved in losing weight, especially when one's grandmother plies the family with good food. Clever illustrations enhance the humor of the story.

Ages 10-12

Also available in:
Cassette—*Jelly Belly*
Library of Congress (NLSBPH)

556

Snyder, Anne

My Name Is Davy—I'm an Alcoholic

Black/white illustrations by the author.
New American Library, 1986.
(144 pages, paperbound)

ALCOHOLISM: Adolescent
DECISION MAKING
Boy-girl relationships
Loneliness
Responsibility: accepting
Responsibility: avoiding
Sex: premarital

Lacking friends or interested parents, fifteen-year-old Davy has been drinking steadily for the past year to ease his loneliness. While sneaking a drink at school one day, he is discovered by Mike—the leader of the crowd Davy most envies—and invited to join a lunch-time drinking party. That evening the glow of being accepted deserts him when Mike and his friends, finding that Davy is sexually inexperienced, get him drunk and force him on Maxine, a girl whose willingness to share herself and her liquor have earned her a reputation as "everybody's pal." Overcome by embarrassment and drink, Davy passes out and later cannot remember what, if anything, happened. The next day Davy learns that Maxine had been beaten by her alcoholic father for coming home late, and he apologizes to her. They become friends, spending many hours at her secret hideaway, a dried-up creek in a park, talking and drinking. During a party at Maxine's house, Mike and his friends trick Maxine into losing a game of strip poker. She protests and looks to Davy for help, but he stands by mutely while they rip her clothes off. Then he comforts her and tells the others to leave. After this the two stay away from the group, needing only each other and the bottle. Soon, however, Maxine's liquor supply runs out. They drive to a liquor store and give three tough-looking men some money to buy them a bottle of Scotch, but the men keep both the bottle and the change. Davy angrily demands both and is brutally beaten. Shunning the police or an ambulance, Maxine takes him to her father's camper to recuperate. Frightened and disgusted with themselves, Davy and Maxine decide to quit drinking. The first few days of withdrawal are painful for both of them, but Maxine, a heavier drinker than Davy, experiences frightening convulsions. That settles it: Davy decides to attend Alcoholics Anonymous meetings with her. Maxine accepts the A.A. program wholeheartedly, but Davy is more skeptical. Increasingly bored with the meetings, and seeking to regain their former closeness, he persuades Maxine to skip a session and go with him to the beach, where they meet Mike and his crowd. Davy joins their drinking party; Maxine protests, but eventually gives in. From a drunken stupor Davy watches as Maxine and the others go swimming nude and thinks himself dreaming when he sees Mike carry a girl's body out of the water. The next morning when he regains consciousness he finds it was not a dream—Maxine is dead. He goes home, fights with his parents, and runs away when they threaten to send him to an institution. Too guilty to go on living and afraid to die, he retreats to the hideaway, drinking himself to oblivion. When he runs out of money and is unable to beg any more drinks off passing derelicts, Davy sneaks home for clean clothes and money, then heads for a liquor store. There a young boy asks him to buy a bottle of wine for him. Davy explodes. He chases the boy until he can no longer run, then sinks down exhausted and begins to cry. "He couldn't fight any longer. He couldn't think anymore. He could only hurt." Finally, he walks to the A.A. clubhouse, enters, and says, "My name is Davy—I'm an alcoholic."

In this story, a teenage alcoholic goes through many of the well-known rationalizations to avoid the truth about his addiction. His final decision to seek help, precipitated by the death of his girlfriend, affirms the idea that it is necessary for an alcoholic to hit rock bottom before he can begin to change. Much A.A. philosophy is included in this book, often at the expense of plot and characterization. Some readers may be unprepared for the profanity, subject matter, and explicit sex scenes to be found here.

Ages 12 and up

Also available in:
No other form known

557

Sobol, Harriet Langsam

My Brother Steven Is Retarded

Black/white photographs by Patricia Agre.
Macmillan Publishing Company, Inc., 1977.
(26 pages)

MENTAL RETARDATION
Ambivalence, feelings of
Emotions: accepting
Sibling: relationships

Eleven-year-old Beth has an older brother, Steven, who is mentally retarded. Although she knows that the term means "you can't understand things like everyone else," she does get angry with Steven when he breaks things. She feels sorry for him because his condition is permanent, but wishes her parents could spend more time with her. She also knows that mental retardation is not "catching," and that Steven's brain damage is not her mother's fault. During the day, Steven goes to a special school and has friends there. But Beth enjoys her own time with him and they often play a special game of ball. When her own friends come over, she explains Steven's condition to ease their nervousness. Beth says, "I guess I love Steven because he's my brother, but many times I think he's hard to love." In fact, Beth feels relieved that it is Steven who is retarded and not she, but feels guilty about this relief. After examining her feelings about him, though, she realizes that her deepest wish for Steven is that he be happy.

This first-person narrative follows Beth's exploration of her mixed feelings toward her retarded brother. Her self-inquiry shows maturity, frankness, and compassion. The black and white photographs communicate her feelings well and portray Steven as a happy boy.

Ages 7-10

Also available in:
No other form known

558

Sonneborn, Ruth A.

Friday Night Is Papa Night

Color illustrations by Emily A. McCully.
Puffin Books, 1987.
(29 pages counted, paperbound)

PARENTAL: Absence
Family: unity
Work, attitude toward

Four-year-old Pedro is very excited; he is looking forward to his father's homecoming tonight. Mama explains that Papa does not come home every night because he must work at two jobs far away in order to earn enough money to support them. Pedro promises Mama that when he is old enough, he will work so that Papa can quit one of his jobs. When Pedro's sister and two brothers come home from school, Mama has work for all of them to do in preparation for their father's arrival. Soon everything is ready, but Papa still has not come. Finally, Mama tells the children to eat. But Pedro, who is very disappointed, goes to bed. Waking up in the dark, he goes to the window and sees someone moving toward the house. It is Papa! Pedro turns on the lights and wakes everyone up. While Mama gives Papa his supper, Papa explains that he is late because he had to take a sick friend to the hospital. The children examine the small gifts Papa has brought them, and everyone rejoices because Papa is finally home.

This book is about the members of a loving family who miss their father during the week and enjoy having him home on weekends. Without preaching or moralizing, it demonstrates the value of working hard. The brown-and-yellow illustrations enhance the text.

Ages 5-8

Also available in:
No other form known

559

Sperry, Armstrong

Call It Courage

Color illustrations by the author.
Macmillan Publishing Company, Inc., 1940
(95 pages)

COURAGE, MEANING OF
Fear
Resourcefulness

Fifteen-year-old Mafatu, a South Sea Islander, has grown up with a great dread of the big water. His mother died in an ocean when Mafatu was three. Because the sea is the way of life for the men of Mafatu's tribe, they ridicule the boy for his fear. Mafatu attempts to conquer his fright by setting sail with his only true companions, an albatross and a mongrel dog. He encounters a terrible storm but manages to land safely on another island. There Mafatu proves his courage by surviving on his own. With considerable resourcefulness he provides himself with food, shelter, and clothing. Eventually Mafatu sails back to his own island, now a brave and socially acceptable young man.

This dramatic story has become a children's classic. It is both suspenseful and inspirational.

Ages 9 and up

Also available in:
Braille—*Call It Courage*
Library of Congress (NLSBPH)

Cassette—*Call It Courage*
Library of Congress (NLSBPH)

Paperbound—*Call It Courage*
Aladdin Books

Paperbound—*Call It Courage*
Collier Books

Talking Book—*Call It Courage*
Library of Congress (NLSBPH)

560

Stanek, Muriel Novella

I Won't Go Without a Father

Color illustrations by Eleanor Mill.
Albert Whitman & Company, 1972.
(28 pages)

ANXIETY
PARENT/PARENTS: Single
SELF, ATTITUDE TOWARD: Feeling Different
SELF, ATTITUDE TOWARD: Pity

Young Steve Blakeman does not want people to know he is fatherless. Unwilling to attend his school's open house with only his mother, he decides not to mention the date. But she learns of the event anyway. Steve defends his silence on the subject by maintaining that he will be the only child there without a father. But Mother reminds him that many other children are fatherless and must get along with the family and friends they have. As the two talk, Steve imagines he sees his father's face. The next morning, Mother proposes that Steve's Uncle John come up from his Army base to attend the open house. But even though he likes Uncle John, Steve complains that this would not be the same as going with a father. Mother must work late that day, so Steve goes to Grandpa's after school. Continuing to brood about the open house, Steve confesses to Grandpa that he still does not want to go. Nevertheless, Steve does attend the open house, and there he sees many other students with single parents. When everyone goes to find seats, Uncle John, Grandpa, and a neighbor, Mr. Green, come to join Steve. He is pleased that no one can tell now whether he has a father or not. Looking around, Steve realizes that, except for his relatives and Mr. Green, everyone is too busy to notice him anyway. Being without a father does not seem to hurt so much.

Steve is envious of children who have fathers and pities himself for being fatherless. He fears that with only one parent, he will be considered different. The book portrays Steve's emotions and behavior with an understanding that builds sympathy for the boy.

Ages 8-10

Also available in:
Cassette—*I Won't Go Without a Father*
Educational Enrichment Materials

Filmstrip—*I Won't Go Without a Father*
Educational Enrichment Materials

561

Stanek, Muriel Novella

Starting School

Color illustrations by Betty and Tony DeLuna.
Albert Whitman & Company, 1981.
(32 pages counted)

SCHOOL: Entering

Mama tells her son that since he'll start school next fall, it's time to get ready. She shows him how to walk to school and they explore the school building. All summer long, the boy prepares for school: he counts to ten, says his address and telephone number, and practices writing his name. He gets a physical and has his teeth checked. He shops for new shoes and shows his father how he can tie them and zip his jacket. On the first day of school, his mother walks him to the classroom door. She cries, but he doesn't. The teacher greets him, as do his friends Mary and Timmy. One boy tries to return to his mother, but the teacher brings him back. Timmy's dog comes in, but is sent home. The teacher gives the children paper and crayons and shows them the science table and the hamster. Then she reads them a story and they all sing a song. When they line up to go to the water fountain, the narrator and Danny disagree about who's first. They are both told to go to the end of the line. When it's time to work, however, he and Danny work together. At dismissal time, his mother is waiting for him. He tells her the teacher must like him because she calls him "honey" just as his mother does. The next day he asks for permission to walk to school by himself. After he promises to be careful, his mother consents.

A little boy narrates in considerable detail his preparation for school and his first-day experiences. His attitude is positive and practical, the book useful for preparing preschoolers. Softly colored illustrations present a multi-ethnic class and characters.

Ages 3-5

Also available in:
Braille—*Starting School*
Library of Congress (NLSBPH)

Talking Book—*Starting School*
Library of Congress (NLSBPH)

562

Stanton, Elizabeth and Henry Stanton

Sometimes I Like to Cry

Color illustrations by Richard Leyden.
Albert Whitman & Company, 1978.
(32 pages counted)

EMOTIONS: Accepting

Young Joey likes to laugh. But sometimes he cries: when he cuts his finger, or feels left out, or grieves for his pet hamster, killed by the cat. In fact, he decides, everybody cries once in a while: his cat, his dog, even grownups, as when his sister got married and his father cried at the ceremony. Sometimes people even cry when they are happy.

A young boy discovers—and his parents agree—that crying is sometimes necessary and right. Both girls and boys can recognize Joey's experiences, and his relief when he accepts his emotions without embarrassment.

Ages 4-7

Also available in:
Cassette—*Sometimes I Like to Cry*
Educational Enrichment Materials

Filmstrip—*Sometimes I Like to Cry*
Educational Enrichment Materials

563

Stein, Sara Bonnett

About Dying: An Open Family Book for Parents and Children Together

Color photographs by Dick Frank.
Walker & Co., 1984.
(47 pages)

DEATH: Attitude Toward
DEATH: of Grandparent

Three- or four-year-old Eric and four- or five-year-old Jane love their bird, who is named Snow. One day Eric and Jane find that Snow has died. Eric wants to keep Snow because he is "interested in dead animals," but Mommy says that they must bury him. The children put Snow in a box. Their older brother Michael and their friends come to see the funeral. They put the box in a hole in the ground and mark the place with a flower. Then Grandpa, who gave Snow to the children and often plays with them at home and in the park, becomes ill. When he dies, Mommy cries. Grandpa is put into a coffin. Eric wants to keep the coffin, but it is placed in the ground in a cemetery. After gathering up some of Grandpa's belongings and eating all of Grandpa's cookies, Michael "still felt empty inside." Jane is angry with Grandpa for dying, and she cries. One rainy day, Eric observes that men's umbrellas are black. Black reminds him of Grandpa's funeral. Eric asks his mother to buy him a red umbrella because a red umbrella will make him feel safe. The next time the children go to the park, Grandpa is not there. But the children feel comforted as they "remember when he was."

This book introduces the idea of death gently, first with the loss of the bird and then with the death of the grandfather. Through the reactions of the mother and her children, the story describes common responses to the death of loved ones. This book is one of the Open Family Series, written to help parents prepare children for the "common hurts of childhood" and to facilitate communication between parents and children. A guide for parents, explaining how the contents may be used in relation to a child's feelings, is included on each page along with the text for the child. Illustrations are found on the pages facing the text. These books are primarily read-aloud books for parents, but both the adult and the child texts could be read by an older child.

Ages 3-8

Also available in:
Paperbound—*About Dying: An Open Family Book for Parents and Children Together*
Walker & Co.

564

Stein, Sara Bonnett

About Handicaps: An Open Family Book for Parents and Children Together

Color photographs by Dick Frank.
Walker & Co., 1984.
(47 pages)

HANDICAPS
Cerebral palsy
Limbs, abnormal or missing

Matthew and Joe, who are about six years old, are friends. But Matthew is afraid of Joe because Joe has cerebral palsy and cannot walk right. Because he is afraid his legs will become like Joe's, Matthew runs and jumps to prove that his limbs are strong and healthy. He worries that his little toe, which is crooked and sticks up, will cause him to walk funny. He wears heavy boots, a big belt, and an army hat to make himself look strong. When Joe wants to wear his hat, Matthew pushes him down. When Matthew's daddy sees them arguing, he realizes something is wrong. Later at a store, Matthew and his daddy see a man with a hook for a hand. Matthew wants to leave immediately, but Daddy introduces him to Mr. Bello, who shows Matthew how his artificial arm works and lets him touch it. Gradually, Matthew and his daddy are able to discuss Mr. Bello, Joe, and Matthew's toe. When Joe comes to play at Matthew's house, the boys talk about Joe's legs, and Matthew shows Joe his toe. Then, with Matthew doing the legwork and Joe using his hands, they begin to build something together.

This book shows a young child's reactions to handicaps such as cerebral palsy. It also illustrates how a healthy child might fear that someone else's handicap could be contagious. Matthew's understanding father helps him overcome his fear of handicaps. This book is one of the Open Family Series, written to help parents prepare children for the "common hurts of childhood" and to facilitate communication between parents and children. A guide for parents, explaining how the contents may be used in relation to a child's feelings, is included on each page along with the text for the child. Illustrations are found on the pages facing the text. These books are primarily read-aloud books for parents, but both the adult and the child texts could be read by an older child.

Ages 4-8

Also available in:
Paperbound—*About Handicaps: An Open Family Book for Parents and Children Together*
Walker & Co.

565

Stein, Sara Bonnett

The Adopted One: An Open Family Book for Parents and Children Together

Black/white photographs by Erika Stone.
Walker & Co., 1979.
(47 pages)

ADOPTION: Explaining
ADOPTION: Feelings About
ADOPTION: Identity Questions
Family: relationships
Identity, search for

Joshua, about four, is celebrating Thanksgiving with all his relatives. He realizes that everyone resembles everyone else and they all have dark hair—all except him. Blond Joshua is adopted. He does not know where he came from. When he asks his mother who his "real" mother is, she tries to reassure him, explaining that his birth mother loved him but could not care for him. She also mentions that she herself wanted to love a baby, but could not have one. Then she tells of the excitement of adopting Joshua and how all the relatives came to visit. The little boy has some trouble accepting the story. He thinks maybe his real mother would let him stick his fingers in the cranberry jelly. Maybe his real father would not make him eat asparagus. Maybe he wouldn't be in trouble for spilling milk. When his aunt and uncle both comment about Joshua's behavior at the dinner table, Joshua yells that his parents are not really his mother and father. His father yells back that Joshua is not their real child. But, his father says as he hugs Joshua, he is their special surprise gift.

Written and photographed with compassion and understanding, this book shows the confusion and doubt of an adopted child. Although reassured of his "real" mother's love and also of the love of his adoptive parents, Joshua still wonders if life would be better were he not adopted. At the close of the story Joshua once again is assured of his special value to his adoptive parents, but the emphasis here is on the child's unwillingness and inability to accept his adoption and his place in the adoptive family and to reconcile his feelings of rejection by his birth parents. This focus could be viewed as a negative, and therefore undesirable, point of view by some parents. This book is one of the Open Family Series, written to help parents prepare children for the "common hurts of childhood" and to facilitate communication between parents and children. A guide for parents, explaining how the contents may be used in relation to a child's feelings, is included on each page along with the text for the child.

Ages 4-8

Also available in:
Paperbound—*The Adopted One: An Open Family Book for Parents and Children Together*
Walker & Co.

566

Stein, Sara Bonnett

A Hospital Story: An Open Family Book for Parents and Children Together

Color photographs by Doris Pinney.
Walker & Co., 1984.
(47 pages)

SURGERY: Tonsillectomy
Hospital, going to

Jill, who is about four or five years old, does not feel well. The doctor says that her tonsils must be removed. Jill's doll Dodie becomes sick too, and Jill "operates" on her. After the "surgery," Jill patches Dodie with Band-Aids. Mommy tries to help Jill understand what operations are really like, but Jill continues to worry. When Jill and her parents arrive at the hospital, Jill gets her hospital identification bracelet and gives Dodie a ride in a wheelchair. She meets the nurses and puts on hospital clothes. A nurse takes a sample of her blood, and a doctor checks her throat. Jill rides to the operating room on a bed with wheels. A doctor gives her an anesthetic to make her unconscious. When Jill wakes up, her throat hurts, and Mommy is not with her. Mommy is waiting in Jill's room. Jill stays at the hospital all night and goes home the next day. She eats chicken, potatoes, and red jello when she gets home. Jill is well now, but "Dodie still needs operations."

This book shows what a child might expect before, during, and after surgery. The child's fears are clearly and sympathetically described, and sensible ways for parents to deal with these fears are suggested. This book is one of the Open Family Series, written to help parents prepare children for the "common hurts of childhood" and to facilitate communication between parents and children. A guide for parents, explaining how the contents may be used in relation to a child's feelings, is included on each page along with the text for the child. Illustrations are on the pages facing the text. These books are primarily read-aloud books for parents, but both the adult and the child texts could be read by an older child.

Ages 3-8

Also available in:
Paperbound—*A Hospital Story: An Open Family Book for Parents and Children Together*
Walker & Co.

567

Stein, Sara Bonnett

Making Babies: An Open Family Book for Parents and Children Together

Color photographs by Doris Pinney.
Walker & Co., 1974.
(47 pages)

SEX: Education

The children in this book are curious about many things, but especially about how seeds and babies grow. They notice that cats sometimes have fat bellies, and that when a woman is pregnant, she has a fat belly. A baby starts as an egg that has been joined by a sperm. First it grows inside its mother, and it continues to grow after birth. A boy who feels a baby kicking inside his mother wonders how it will get out. He finds out that human babies are born in much the same way as kittens are born, and that dogs reproduce in the same way. From the time it begins to grow, a baby is either a boy or a girl. "Every girl has a vagina. Every boy has a penis." Only females can nurse babies, only boys can become fathers, and only girls can become mothers.

This book is very explicit in its explanations and in its photographs, which include a series showing the birth of kittens, another showing dogs mating, and several pictures of fetuses. The text for adults is especially useful because it gives alternate ways of explaining some of the material, and it cautions the adult about children's fears of these subjects. It also suggests further topics to discuss with children, such as menstruation. This book is one of the Open Family Series, written to help parents prepare children for the "common hurts of childhood" and to facilitate communication between parents and children. A guide for parents, explaining how the contents may be used in relation to a child's feelings, is included on each page along with the text for the child.

Ages 4-8

Also available in:
Paperbound—*Making Babies: An Open Family Book for Parents and Children Together*
Walker & Co.

568

Stein, Sara Bonnett

On Divorce: An Open Family Book for Parents and Children Together

Black/white photographs by Erika Stone.
Walker & Co., 1979.
(47 pages)

DIVORCE: of Parents
Communication: parent-child

Becky, about four, loves to play house with her friends Heather and Tom. She is always the baby and they play the mother and father. One day during the game, Heather and Tom pretend to fight. Tom leaves and Heather says they will get a divorce. This upsets Becky and she tells the two to go home. At lunch that day Becky asks her mother where her father is. He's at work, her mother replies. After cartoons she asks again and is again told. At supper, she asks a third time. When her father is not home at Becky's bedtime, the little girl becomes frightened and, during the night, has a bad dream. She calls for her father, but he's still not home. Her mother comforts her, saying that her father is still at work but will return soon. Both parents are there as usual for breakfast, and Becky's mother tells her father that Heather and Tom's parents are divorcing. A frightened Becky cuddles up to her father and asks for a baby doll. Her parents argue when he agrees to buy her the doll, and Becky runs off and hides. When they find her, the alarmed child asks if they are getting a divorce. They explain to Becky that being angry does not mean hating, that people often quarrel with the ones they love. In the days that follow, Heather and Tom come over and the three again play house. Whether they pretend they are married or divorced, they still care for their baby as usual. Several days later, Becky's father brings her a doll and her mother a dress. While a sitter cares for Becky, her parents go out for the evening.

A little girl, hearing that her friends' parents are divorcing, fears her father will leave her. When her parents argue, Becky is sure they will divorce too. Reassured that even people who love each other can disagree, Becky's fear is alleviated. Photographs accompany and complement the text. This book is one of the Open Family Series, written to help parents prepare children for the "common hurts of childhood" and to facilitate communication between parents and children. A guide for parents, explaining how the contents may be used in relation to a child's feelings, is included on each page, along with the text for the child.

Ages 4-8

Also available in:
Paperbound—*On Divorce: An Open Family Book for Parents and Children Together*
Walker & Co.

569

Stein, Sara Bonnett

That New Baby: An Open Family Book for Parents and Children Together

Color photographs by Dick Frank.
Walker & Co., 1984.
(47 pages)

SIBLING: New Baby

Three- or four-year-old Charles and six- or seven-year-old Melissa have been told that a new baby is soon coming to their family. Mommy's lap is crowded when Charles tries to sit on it. When Melissa touches Mommy's abdomen, she can feel the baby kick. Melissa wants to have a baby of her own. Charles, pretending he is pregnant, walks around with a pillow under his shirt. When Mommy goes to the hospital, Grandma comes to stay with the children. When Mommy comes home with a baby boy, Grandma admires him, and friends and neighbors come to visit and welcome him. Charles and Melissa learn to help care for the baby, although Mommy must watch them to be sure that they are very careful. As Mommy watches the two older children play in ways that reveal their ambivalent feelings about the baby, she interprets their actions to help them understand—sometimes they do not like the new baby. . .or they wish the baby would "fly away." The children learn that they can do things the baby cannot do, and that they have some special needs while the baby has others. The children learn that Mommy has enough time and "love for everyone."

This book candidly describes the feelings of happiness, uncertainty, and jealousy that young children might have before and after a new baby enters the family. The parents demonstrate their love and concern for the whole family as they help the older children understand how fragile and dependent a newborn baby is and how each family member is important to the family unit. This book is one of the Open Family Series, written to help parents prepare children for the "common hurts of childhood" and to facilitate communication between parents and children. A guide for parents, explaining how the contents may be used in relation to a child's feelings, is included on each page along with the text for the child. Illustrations are found on the pages facing the text. These books are primarily read-aloud books for parents, but both the adult and child texts could be read by an older child.

Ages 3-8

Also available in:
Paperbound—*That New Baby: An Open Family Book for Parents and Children Together*
Walker & Co.

570

Steptoe, John Lewis

Daddy Is a Monster . . . Sometimes

Color illustrations by the author.
HarperCollins Publishers, Inc., 1980.
(30 pages counted, paperbound)

PARENTAL: Control
Discipline, meaning of
Family: relationships

Javaka and Bweela think their daddy is nice most of the time. But sometimes he turns into a monster. For example, once he bought them each an ice-cream cone to eat while he did the grocery shopping. Later he decided to get one for himself but would not buy them a second cone because "one . . . is enough for one day." That's when it happened. Right in front of their eyes, "hair started comin' out of his face" and he began turning into a monster. Then a woman came into the store and saw the children pouting. She thought Daddy was treating himself to ice cream but making them go without. Their father tried to stop her, but before he could explain she bought two large strawberry cones for the delighted children. Their daddy was very angry and "his teeth started growing out like Dracula's." He even laughed when Bweela's cone dropped onto the sidewalk. Sometimes Daddy is a monster at bedtime when Javaka or Bweela ask for one more drink, make another trip to the bathroom, or have an argument that keeps them awake. Daddy also becomes a monster when he takes them to a restaurant. He warns them to stop playing with their food, and he turns into a scary creature right there at the table—but only a little bit so nobody sees him doin' it." Sometimes he's a monster when they are messy, make noise, or have an accident. When the children ask him why he turns into a monster, Daddy replies, "Well, I'm probably a monster daddy when I got monster kids."

Most children find their parents to be monsters sometimes. These feelings find humorous and loving expression here as Javaka and Bweela discuss and recall several transformations of their usually quite human father. The idea that children can be monsters too will interest the young reader or listener, and the familiar, everyday occurrences and realistic relationships are appealing. Exceptional, surrealistic illustrations give the book special artistic value for children. Modified black dialect is used. Another story about Bweela and Javaka is *My Special Best Words.*

Ages 5-7

Also available in:
No other form known

571

Steptoe, John Lewis

Marcia

Color illustrations by the author.
Puffin Books, 1991.
(69 pages, paperbound)

SEX: Attitude Toward
African-American
Boy-girl relationships: dating
Sex: premarital

Fourteen-year-old Marcia lives in a Brooklyn housing project with her mother. She is dating Danny, and they are deeply fond of each other, but Marcia is worried that Danny wants to make love to her. She feels altogether unready to take that step and to risk becoming pregnant. She worries the matter around, and unable to find a solution, discusses it with her best friend, Millie. To her relief, she finds that Millie is worried about the same thing. The two acknowledge that they eventually want to make love with their boyfriends; that seems to them only natural, given their feelings. But when Danny comes to visit while Marica is home alone and wants to make love to her, she rebuffs him. He storms from the apartment and Marcia is sure they are finished. It is then that she discusses the situation with her mother and says fully what she thinks: "There ain't nothin' wrong with sex—there ain't nothin' wrong with loving somebody—it's just that you have to defend yourself against the stupidity of the world and realize that the *world* is screwed up, not you." *And* she does not want a baby until, as she puts it, "I can give my child the things I want easily." Soon Danny returns and the two are going steady again.

This first-person narrative is told largely in dialogue, mostly in Black English, changing into something nearer standard English when a conversation is serious. Marcia's dilemma lies in wanting to make love with Danny, yet feeling unready for and afraid of pregnancy. The book also airs her mother's views, Danny's, and those of her best friend. The young people in this novel take themselves seriously, plan for success, and scorn drugs. These subjects are discussed along with the central subject of sex. Plot and character run second to ideas here.

Ages 12 and up

Also available in:
No other form known

572

Stevens, Margaret

When Grandpa Died

Color photographs by Kenneth Ualand.
Children's Press, Inc., 1979.
(31 pages)

DEATH: of Grandparent
Death: attitude toward
Death: funeral issues
Grandparent: love for

A young girl, about eight, spends lots of time with her grandfather, who lives with the family. The two enjoy reading, storytelling, walking, and working in the garden. When they find a dead bird in the yard, the girl wonders aloud why it has died. Grandpa tells her there are many reasons things die: they become sick, they are hurt, or their bodies grow very old and weak. The two bury the bird in the garden. After its death, Grandpa says, the bird will continue to contribute to the earth's life cycle. The bird's body will change underground, and it will help the flowers grow. Soon afterwards, Grandpa becomes ill and goes to the hospital, where the girl's parents visit him every day. When they return from visiting one day, upset and crying, the girl feels frightened. Her father tells her Grandpa has died. At first she is angry with Grandpa because she wants him to come back home and play with her. Soon, though, she goes to his bedroom, puts on his sweater, and cries and cries. Her father comforts her, telling her it is all right to cry, but she still regrets not having said goodbye to Grandpa. Her father explains that there will be a funeral and that funerals allow people to say goodbye to those they love. He takes her to see the dead man's closed casket, and the next day the girl and her parents attend the funeral. The girl says she now knows her grandfather will never return. She plans to tell her little sister all about Grandpa, as soon as the younger child is old enough to understand.

In this simple, first-person narrative, a young girl learns to see the death of her beloved grandfather as part of the continuing life cycle. Sensitive photographs help keep the story straightforward and realistic. The text conveys a sense of grief and the assurance that it is natural to experience and express sorrow. The photograph of the closed casket might be helpful in preparing a child for a visit to a funeral home.

Ages 4-8

Also available in:
No other form known

573

Stolz, Mary Slattery

The Bully of Barkham Street

Black/white illustrations by Leonard Shortall.
HarperCollins Publishers, Inc., 1963.
(194 pages)

BULLY: Being a
Encouragement
Loneliness
Name-calling
Pets: love for
Reputation
Weight control: overweight

Martin is a lonely, overweight sixth grader. He talks back to adults and picks fights with younger children, especially his next-door neighbor Edward. Whenever Edward calls him "fatso," Martin makes him holler "uncle." Martin and his sister are constantly arguing. Only his dog Rufus seems to love him. Because the neighbors complain about Martin's treatment of their children and property, his parents threaten to give Rufus away in punishment if Martin does not reform. Although he tries hard in his own way to be good, he comes home one day to find that Rufus has been taken away. Martin stops trying to be good and eats more to ease his hurt. This pattern is broken only when Mr. Foran, his teacher, finds things about him to praise. When Martin is scheduled to play the bugle at a school assembly, his mother makes a special effort to change her plans for the evening to hear him. With his parents giving him more encouragement, Martin feels more like going on a diet and really trying to change. He finds that it is not easy to live down his reputation, but now that he is getting good words from grownups—even from his father—he is determined to succeed.

This book clearly shows the frustrations of a lonely boy who has become a bully. Although he sometimes enjoys his role, he also wishes he could be friends with other boys. When his teacher and parents take the time to understand him and to help him understand himself, he finds his hostile manner no longer necessary. This is a realistic story with no simple solutions. The same tale is told from Edward's standpoint in a companion book entitled *A Dog on Barkham Street.*

Ages 8-11

Also available in:
Braille—*The Bully of Barkham Street*
Library of Congress (NLSBPH)

Cassette—*The Bully of Barkham Street*
Library of Congress (NLSBPH)

Paperbound—*The Bully of Barkham Street*
HarperCollins Publishers, Inc.

574

Stolz, Mary Slattery

A Dog on Barkham Street

Black/white illustrations by Leonard Shortall.
HarperCollins Publishers, Inc., 1960.
(184 pages)

RESPONSIBILITY: Accepting
Bully: fear of
Loss: feelings of
Pets: love for

Fifth-grader Edward Frost has several problems. He longs to have a dog for a pet, but since he is not dependable—he loses things, forgets things, and leaves his belongings scattered around—his parents refuse to get him a dog. Edward's other problem is his next-door neighbor Martin, the Barkham Street Bully. Martin teases Edward and starts fights with him whenever possible. One day Uncle Josh arrives with a beautiful collie named Argess. Josh is an irresponsible, happy-go-lucky wanderer whose experiences Edward admires and whose freedom he envies. To prove to his parents how responsible he can be, Edward offers to care for Argess. He does a good job. One day, encouraged by Uncle Josh, Edward decides to face Martin instead of running from him. The resulting fight is going strong when Argess joins in to defend Edward. The boys' parents and neighbors also join the scuffle and begin to take sides, yelling and screaming at each other. The two embarrassed boys leave the scene and go home. For a period of time after this, all is quiet on Barkham Street. One morning, Edward is shattered to find that Uncle Josh has left, taking Argess with him. Edward's parents try to help him accept the departure. But in his anguish, he decides to skip school with a friend so that the two of them can sort out their problems. They wander near a freight train and climb into one of the empty cars. The train starts moving. Three hours later, they are found by a baggage man and sent to a police station until their parents can come for them. When he arrives home, Edward finds Uncle Josh and Argess waiting for him. Uncle Josh has decided that Argess belongs with Edward. Now, with a dog of his own and some understanding advice from his father on how to handle Martin, Edward discovers that his problems—both the lack of a pet and the Bully of Barkham Street—have been overcome.

This absorbing and convincing story portrays a boy's problem with a bully and his anguish over losing something he loves. It also illustrates Edward's growing sense of responsibility and his learning to cope effectively with everyday situations. A companion book, *The Bully of Barkham Street,* relates the story from Martin's viewpoint.

Ages 8-11

Also available in:
Braille—*A Dog on Barkham Street*
Library of Congress (NLSBPH)

Cassette—*A Dog on Barkham Street*
Library of Congress (NLSBPH)

Paperbound—*A Dog on Barkham Street*
HarperCollins Publishers, Inc.

575

Strang, Celia

Foster Mary

McGraw-Hill, Inc., 1979.
(162 pages) o.p.

FAMILY: Unity
RESPONSIBILITY: Accepting
Abandonment
Child abuse
Education: value of
Foster home
Love, meaning of
Migrant workers
Work, attitude toward

In the fall of 1959, fifteen-year-old Wallace (Bud) Meekin comes with his adoptive family to pick apples in Yakima, Washington. Bud, Bennie, and Ameilla were each abandoned by their parents and taken in by "Aunt" Foster Mary and "Uncle" Alonzo. Mary and Alonzo, migrant workers, have recently taken in another abandoned boy, Lonnie, about seven, who was beaten and left by his father, also a migrant worker. The brutalized Lonnie is at first violently hostile, even pointing a gun at Bennie and Bud. But once installed in Aunt Mary's care, Lonnie adapts easily to his new home. Mary has "a way of making a home out of any old place," but she clings to her dream of a permanent home where her children can attend school regularly. The picking over, the Meekin family stays on in Yakima so Alonzo can apply to Mr. Ransome, the orchard owner, for the job of caretaker. Bud is happy at the prospect of a settled life, but does not look forward to attending school regularly. Never having stayed in one school very long, he finds schoolwork difficult and is still in the eighth grade. He cannot imagine that he will ever go to college, although this is Mary's goal for all the children. Alonzo gets the job and he and Mary prepare to spend the winter, buying the necessary food, clothing, and supplies. A heavy snowfall necessitates an early opening of Christmas gifts—they need the warm clothing packed inside—and Alonzo and the children surprise Foster Mary with a sewing machine. Soon after, Alonzo goes to get a sled down for the kids and falls from the ladder, breaking his leg. Bud must go for help and, finding the snow too deep to accommodate car or truck, has to make his way to a neighbor's on foot. He gets through, and an ambulance comes and takes Alonzo to the hospital. It is soon learned that Alonzo's leg will require surgery, that it will be months before he will be able to walk or use his strength again. Together, Foster Mary and Bud must hang on to the caretaking job. Bud is daunted by the prospect, but Mary is confident they will find a way. Bud sees that keeping the job—and their settled life—is so important to Alonzo and Mary that he must help them succeed. He and Mary begin doing all the work they can by themselves, planning to have Alonzo supervise and teach them the rest after he comes home from the hospital. At the same time, Bud works on his schoolwork with a friend, Liz Holbrook. Liz, formerly a migrant worker with her mother, helps Bud see that education is the only way out of the migrant's hard life. Alonzo is released from the hospital in time to see all the children in their Christmas pageant at church. With a new confidence, Bud resolves that next summer Aunt Foster Mary will have the flower garden she has always wanted.

Bud narrates this story of a family's struggle to escape the hard life of migrant workers. His colloquial storytelling style and flair for using language inject humor into a rather slow, predictable account with more than a touch of unreality. The undiluted goodness of Mary and Alonzo's world may put some readers off; others may be encouraged and cheered. Characterizations are generally believable and complete, and the book offers some insight into a way of life that may be unfamiliar to many.

Ages 10-13

Also available in:
No other form known

576

Strasser, Todd

Angel Dust Blues

Coward–McCann, 1979.
(203 pages) o.p.

DRUGS: Abuse of
Boy-girl relationships: dating
Communication: lack of
Crime/Criminals
Drugs: dependence on
Friendship: meaning of
Parental: negligence
Rebellion
Sex: premarital
Wealth/Wealthy

When wealthy, seventeen-year-old Alex Lazar, a good student and state tennis champ, becomes bored and rebellious, he turns to drug dealing for excitement. Alex's father, a retired businessman, and his mother, a former county executive, spend their time in Palm Beach, Florida, leaving Alex at home in suburban New York City with only Lucille, the housekeeper, for supervision. Alex's friend Michael, a dropout and a junkie, teaches him how to make big money in drugs. While picking up a kilo of marijuana in Brooklyn one morning, Alex, nervous and hungry, mistakenly walks into G. Schapmann & Sons, the office of a commercial bakery, where he is impressed with the cool attractiveness of Schapmann's daughter, Ellen. He begins to cultivate a friendship with her. Becoming the number-one dealer in school gives Alex a certain satisfaction because he's reached this pinnacle through his own efforts—and because his parents would be shocked if they knew. When Michael informs Alex of a deal on angel dust (PCP-phencyclidine), a more potent drug than marijuana, the lucrative project appeals to him. Still, he can't help but notice Michael's deterioration as he grows more and more dependent on drugs. When Michael disappears, Alex, certain he has been arrested, is frightened into burying his share of the angel dust and marijuana. At this time his friendship with Ellen deepens. Her determination to attend the University of Southern California and become a film director makes him aware of how uncertain his own future is. All he knows is that he doesn't want to go to Columbia University and become a businessman like his father. When Alex learns that Michael has been at Hillcrest, a mental institution for drug abusers, he relaxes somewhat. But he discovers he no longer enjoys drug dealing and doesn't care for the feeling that people only like him for what they can get from him. He prefers getting high on his love for Ellen, and they become lovers. Michael finds a buyer for the angel dust buried in Alex's backyard, and Alex is only too glad to be rid of it. He is not aware that Michael has turned state's evidence and that the buyer is an undercover police officer. The next morning, a shocked, frightened Alex is arrested. His parents return from Palm Beach and Alex, arraigned and released on bail, confronts his mother angrily. "You managed to run a whole county filled with people, but you don't want to bother with me." But he knows he cannot change his parents and when they return to Palm Beach, planning to come back in two weeks to check up on him, he decides to take his lawyer's advice and get a summer job. He also applies to a small Maine college with a poor tennis team, where he is required to work for his acceptance rather than take an easy tennis scholarship. Then one day Alex finds Michael in his garage, stoned and very sick. He cares for him as best he can, but by the next afternoon Michael's condition worsens. Alex notifies the police. Soon after, he is summoned home from school to find that Michael has gotten into the house, ransacked it, found and taken prescription drugs, and collapsed. A blood test reveals angel dust in Michael's blood. He remains in a coma. The charges against Alex are reduced and he knows he has "crossed the line for good. Why he had made it and Michael hadn't he didn't know."

This is a taut, believable portrayal of teenage alienation and drug abuse. Character development and the portrayal of relationships, especially the one between Alex and Ellen, are well done, and readers will readily understand and sympathize with various characters as the story unfolds. The bitterness Alex feels toward his parents is vividly portrayed. Several brief, explicit sexual encounters between Alex and Ellen are included. This is strong, candid, informative, but not didactic, material.

Ages 14 and up

Also available in:
Braille—*Angel Dust Blues*
Library of Congress (NLSBPH)

Cassette—*Angel Dust Blues*
Library of Congress (NLSBPH)

Paperbound—*Angel Dust Blues*
Dell Publishing Company, Inc.

577

Strasser, Todd

Friends till the End

Dell Publishing Company, Inc. (Laurel Leaf Library), 1987.
(224 pages, paperbound)

FRIENDSHIP: Meaning of
ILLNESSES: Terminal
Boy-girl relationships: dating
Careers: planning
Death: attitude toward
Leukemia

High school senior David Gilbert doesn't have much time in his life for a new friend. He is goalie for his school's soccer team and until last spring had planned to go to college on a soccer scholarship and eventually become a professional player. Recently, however, he has decided to enter pre-med and is studying hard. His remaining time is taken up by his independent and strong-willed girlfriend, Rena Steuben. David first meets Howie Jamison at a bus stop. Howie has just moved to Long Island from Florida and hasn't yet learned to dress and act like the typical Gold Coast teenager. But David finds him refreshing. Then, suddenly, after the first week of school, Howie is hospitalized for a form of leukemia called AML and his mother asks David to visit him. At the hospital he finds Mrs. Jamison upset over the move north and pessimistic about her son's illness. Howie, anxious to talk to someone more objective, tells David how sick the chemotherapy makes him. After leaving the hospital, David remembers hearing how smoking marijuana can help reduce the side effects of chemotherapy and decides to tell Howie about this. When he returns to the hospital a week later, David learns that Howie has contracted an infection. Howie's distraught mother talks about taking him back to Florida for Laetrile treatments. By now David is becoming quite preoccupied with Howie's problems and is upset that his classmates don't want to get involved. He tries to express his feelings to Rena, but finds her also uninterested—in him as well as in Howie. She's upset because he has given up his plans to become a pro soccer player. The following weekend David goes to Howie's house for dinner. Howie tells David he is in remission now. But his mother seems to believe that everything that goes wrong is part of a "big plot" against them. She still wants to return to Florida. David brings up the marijuana idea and both parents become very upset. He realizes he has probably lost their approval of his and Howie's friendship. The soccer team wins its ninth straight game, but instead of being elated, David worries about Rena's increasingly distant behavior. The next day he gets a note from her, breaking off their relationship. The team continues undefeated and is assured a place in the sectionals. When one of the team members gives a party to celebrate, David invites Howie to come along. Both boys lose track of the time, getting back late. Also, Howie has violated his doctor's instructions not to drink. His parents hold David responsible. Soon Howie returns to school. To David's surprise, Rena, who is in most of Howie's classes, offers to help him get caught up with his work. The next time he goes into the hospital, she organizes a blood drive. She admits to David that part of the reason she broke up with him was because of the pressure he was putting on her to "join the Howie Jamison bandwagon." Later, another friend tells him that he has resented David's "sister of mercy" attitude about Howie. David decides, however, that some things are "more important than being Mr. Cool Popular Nice Guy." David and Rena visit Howie in the hospital on the day before the soccer championship and learn from the doctor that he is getting worse. Later, Rena tells David that his involvement with Howie has made it impossible for her to think of him as just a fun, safe boyfriend whom she can drop at the end of high school. She knows she must take him seriously. For the first time in months, they make love. Two days later, after winning the championship, David returns home to find that the Jamisons are moving back south and that Howie has already been transferred to a hospital in Florida. Both David and Rena feel that something special has been taken away from them. Over the next couple of months David writes to his friend three times, but Howie never writes back.

It is a life-changing experience for David to realize that no one, regardless of age, is invulnerable to sickness and death. As his friendship with Howie grows, he is forced to ask the same searching questions his friend does: Why do these things happen to some people and not to others? Is there a God who punishes sin by letting people get sick? What happens to a human being after death? Since David does not believe in God or in life after death, the only persistent question for him is "Why?" He finally concludes that there is no answer: "Sometimes things just happen. The toughest part is learning to accept that." This is a convincing, substantive first-person narrative that skillfully integrates various issues—friendship, love, illness, career goals, attitudes toward life and death—within a compelling story line.

Ages 12 and up

Also available in:
No other form known

578

Stretton, Barbara

You Never Lose

Alfred A. Knopf, Inc., 1982.
(237 pages) o.p.

DEATH: Attitude Toward
ILLNESSES: Terminal
Ambivalence, feelings of
Anger
Boy-girl relationships: dating
Cancer
Change: resisting
Communication: parent-child
Friendship: meaning of
Guilt, feelings of
Maturation
Sports/Sportsmanship

Jim Halbert is not looking forward to the first day of his senior year. He's known for five weeks that his father, the popular football hero and coach, is dying of cancer. Soon everyone knows, and emotions run high throughout the school. Jim's English teacher, Dundee, begins a unit on "Death, the Final Taboo." Jim freezes up; the other students are shocked. One of Jim's problems in responding to people's sympathy is that he has ambivalent feelings about his father, who has always ridden him harder than anyone else. Most of his life, Jim has tried to stay out of his father's way. He remembers a game last year when he carried the ball ninety-five yards for a touchdown. Afterwards his father swore at him and benched him, calling him a Saturday hero. Jim's mood is lifted by a brash, noisy new girl from West Virginia, Gus (Agnes), but he's still looking forward to seeing Mimi again. They dated last year, although they've been out of touch this summer. By noon, Mimi has begun organizing a campaign to make the school the best in the state as a tribute to Coach Halbert. She's proud to be Jim's girl, but mainly because everyone is talking about his father. At football practice, Coach Halbert (who insists on coaching the team this year although he doesn't need to) lashes into Jim as usual. He has never, in his eleven years of coaching, praised anyone. During practice, he falls as he's running across the field. He accepts the help of Jim's younger sister, Liz, but just yells at Jim. As always, Jim is puzzled and hurt by his father's rejection. At the next football practice, Coach Halbert harasses his son again. When he tells Jim to throw him the ball, Jim puts everything he has into it: "A lifetime of being told to be a man and somehow never quite making it, rode on the leather of that ball, in the power of that pass." The ball hits the coach in the stomach and knocks him out. He's taken to the hospital where he remains for several days. The first thing he says to Jim as soon as he can get the words out is that Jim's throw was a great pass. But Jim never again wants to feel the kind of anger that made him throw the ball that way. One afternoon Gus, who's become a good friend, skips school with Jim to visit the coach in the hospital. While Gus waits, Jim goes looking for his father. He finds him in a restroom, sobbing. Jim doesn't want his father to be discovered in his weakness, so he leaves. He and Gus make love, leaving Jim exhilarated at first but then depressed, wondering if he's just using her. Friends and family offer information and advice. Jim's mother talks about his father's defenses and how he can't ever admit to weakness. Then Dundee decides to shelve the death unit. He himself has unresolved feelings about his own father's suicide and, after being approached by a delegation of students about the way he's picked on Jim, admits he hasn't handled the situation well. But he tells Jim that anger is an important part of grief. At the first football game of the season, Mimi, a cheerleader, leads a cheer about Coach Halbert. Jim continues to believe she just wants to be part of all the attention and fame. After the game she's anxious to get to a favorite hangout, even though Jim wants to go to the hospital to tell his father about their victory. He's beginning to realize that he's probably the most important thing in his father's life, that his father loves him and that he loves his father. He promises the coach that he can die at home and not in a hospital, understanding at last what playing football means to his father, his need for the love that surges from the crowd in their cheers. Coach Halbert replies that his deepest wish has been that Jim would know that same feeling. Jim picks up Gus, who's been suspended for three days for skipping school to go to the hospital with him; he only received a reprimand. Jim knows Mimi isn't for him anymore and he lets Gus know they have a future together. He recalls his father's old saying after a lost game: "You didn't lose. The damned clock ran out, that's all."

When a young man learns that his football-coach father, whom he both loves and resents, is dying of cancer, he begins learning a lot about love, courage, and staying true to oneself. Relationships are more important than plot in this powerful book, which is not so much the story of a father's dying as of a son coming to understand some of the mystery that is his father. Another focus is change, inevitable whether it results from a death or from the growing human spirit. The reader is offered considerable insight into various attitudes toward impending death; also part of this narrative are profanity and some descriptive sexual passages, as Jim turns for comfort from the superficial Mimi to the down-to-earth Gus.

Ages 12 and up

Also available in:
No other form known

579

Sunderlin, Sylvia

Antrim's Orange

Color illustrations by Diane de Groat.
Charles Scribner's Sons, 1976.
(57 pages) o.p.

SHARING/NOT SHARING

In wartime England, the only abundance is of shortages. So when Granny, visiting eight-year-old Antrim and his mother, gives the boy an orange, he treasures it like a rare gem. He proudly shows the large orange to friends, saying he will keep it a long, long time. Mr. Grove, an aged gardner, advises against this, lest it rot. But Antrim wants to show it at school before eating it, does so the next day, and loses the orange when the teacher misunderstands and accepts it as a gift. The boy's sense of courtesy will not let him correct her. Later she sees her error and returns the orange. Joyously, Antrim dashes home, tossing the orange high in the air, only to see it crash to the earth as it slips from his grasp. Mother, joking that there is no use crying over split orange, peels it, and Antrim gives a section to Mr. Grove and each of his other friends. While doing this, he drops and steps on the section saved for himself. Mother suggests he take the piece saved for his teacher, but Antrim staunchly refuses. Remembering the small navel in the orange, Mother gives it to him: "It was a little orange, but every drop was delicious."

The accurate description of wartime shortages here, and the to-do made over Antrim's orange builds a convincing case for the value of the orange at any time and thus for the boy's generosity in sharing it. The illustrations, whose only color is that of the orange, also convey the importance of this once scarce, though now common, fruit and of the exhilaration of sharing when times are hard.

Ages 7-9

Also available in:
No other form known

580

Swartley, David Warren

My Friend, My Brother

Black/white illustrations by James Converse.
Herald Press, 1980.
(102 pages, paperbound)

CHILD ABUSE
FAMILY: Unity
Adoption: feelings about
Communication: importance of
Friendship: meaning of
Mennonite
Religion: faith

When twelve-year-old Eric refuses the challenge of his classmate Jon Simon to enter the local pool hall on a hot Indiana summer day, Jon scornfully attributes Eric's refusal to his being a Mennonite. One day Jon tells Eric that his father gives him money all the time. Eric is therefore surprised to learn from his own father that Jon's parents were killed when Jon was an infant, that he lives with an aunt and uncle who are under investigation after complaints by neighbors about their poor treatment of the boy. A membership meeting for Boy Scouts during which Eric declines to join is another occasion for Jon to call attention to Eric's "strange" religion. Even so, Eric thinks about Jon often and hopes everything will work out well for him. One day as they're walking home from school together, Eric tells Jon that he knows about his tough time at home. Immediately defensive and angry, Jon shoves Eric into a snowbank. Eric forgets his own distress when he gets home and learns that his beloved grandfather has died. A few days before Christmas Jon gives Eric a present, with a card apologizing for his behavior and telling Eric he wants to be friends. During the vacation, the boys become better acquainted. One night Eric invites Jon to sleep over. As they prepare for bed, Eric asks Jon about the bruises on his back. After swearing Eric to secrecy, Jon tearfully tells him that his uncle beats him nearly every day and his aunt often puts the man up to it. Eric longs to help but doesn't know how. However, after he witnesses the uncle's dangerous and unreasonable anger directed at Jon, he feels he must tell his father about the beatings. Then, when Jon is absent from school for the next three days, Eric takes his father's advice and tells the teacher about the incident he saw. It is discovered that Jon has run away; the police find him unconscious and severely beaten in an abandoned railroad car. Jon spends several weeks in the hospital and then stays with Eric's family before he's moved to a foster home. Eric invites Jon to a weekend church retreat during which Jon reveals his unhappiness with his new school and foster family. Then Eric is distressed to learn that his grandmother plans to sell her home. His outlook brightens a bit when, told to choose a keepsake, he picks his grandfather's 1957 Oldsmobile, a car he had always treasured even though it hasn't run in years. Eric is delighted when his parents agree, at the request of a social worker, to have Jon come stay with them. At first the two boys feel awkward around one another. Then one day while they are polishing the Oldsmobile, Jon admits that he used to feel jealous of Eric's close family but that now he feels differently about Mennonites. That evening Eric's father announces that they have applied to adopt Jon, now a ward of the court, if the boy consents. Jon enthusiastically does. A newspaper article about his uncle's trial prompts Jon to tell Eric that he now feels sorry for his aunt and uncle. The last day of school, the family learns that Jon's adoption has been approved.

A friendship develops between a Mennonite boy and his hardened, abused detractor, who eventually is accepted into the loving Mennonite family. The most important aspect of this book is its emphasis on family togetherness and communication. Information about the Mennonite religion and way of life adds interest. The fast-moving plot is advanced mainly by narration, occasionally by stilted dialogue. Characterization lacks depth. Still, the book has a refreshingly wholesome tone, and the restricted vocabulary qualifies it as an easy reader for older children.

Ages 9-11

Also available in:
No other form known

581

Taylor, Mildred D.

Roll of Thunder, Hear My Cry

Dial Books for Young Readers, 1978.
(276 pages)

AFRICAN-AMERICAN
PREJUDICE: Ethnic/Racial
Family: unity
Justice/Injustice

Like some other black Southern families, eight-year-old Cassie Logan's family raises cotton on a four-hundred-acre farm in Mississippi in 1933. The land, purchased by Cassie's grandfather years before, makes the Logans more secure than the nearby black sharecroppers, but it also arouses the covetousness of Harlan Granger, descendant of the family whose plantation it had been part of before the Civil War. Granger longs to rebuild the original plantation, and would seize any opportunity to force the Logans off. When the Wallaces, owners of the local store, attack and badly burn some sharecroppers, the Logans try to organize a boycott. Able to enlist only a few families, they prove more of an irritation to the Wallaces than a financial threat—but for that, Cassie's father, David, is physically injured by the Wallaces and loses his job with the railroad. It is only with financial aid from his brother up North that David keeps their land out of Granger's clutches. While David is recuperating from his injuries, thirteen-year-old T. J., a friend of Cassie's brother, makes friends with the white, shiftless Simms boys, who are older than he is. When the

Simmses and T. J. rob a store and the Simmses murder the owner, T. J. is recognized while the brothers escape. That night the Wallaces and the Simmses (who have gone undetected) gather a lynching party and storm T. J.'s house. To create a distraction, David sets fire to his own cotton field and the fire threatens the Grangers' adjoining forest. T. J. is saved from the mob and turned over to the sheriff. And as David explains the ways of white justice at that time, the Logan children realize they will never see T. J. again. He and he alone will be convicted, because he is black.

The story Cassie tells shows how her family faces unrelenting humiliation and hardship without compromising their values or losing self-respect. This story, skillfully paced, candid, and rich in characterization, affords discussable lessons in American black history. If persecution of blacks is usually less blatant now, the spirit behind it is by no means dead, and this story will be understood.

Ages 10 and up

Also available in:
Braille—*Roll of Thunder, Hear My Cry*
Library of Congress (NLSBPH)

Cassette—*Roll of Thunder, Hear My Cry*
Library of Congress (NLSBPH)

Paperbound—*Roll of Thunder, Hear My Cry*
Bantam Books

582

Terris, Susan Dubinsky

No Scarlet Ribbons

Farrar, Straus & Giroux, Inc., 1981.
(154 pages)

FAMILY: Relationships
PARENT/PARENTS: Remarriage of
SECURITY/INSECURITY
Death: of father
Reality, escaping
Self-esteem
Stepbrother/Stepsister
Stepparent: father

Before Rachel's father died of cancer some years ago, he said people must make things happen, that they shouldn't live passive lives. Now Rachel is thirteen and obsessed with following that advice. When her mother marries Norm, Rachel feels triumphantly responsible, since it was she who introduced them. Delighted with her new family, which includes Norm's son, Sandy, Rachel wants family closeness to blossom instantly and keeps engineering events to create those feelings. Even her mother, Ginger, who understands and often shares Rachel's enthusiasm, grows weary of her continual suggestions for family happenings: a Halloween sand-sculpture day at the beach, a roller-skate across the Golden Gate Bridge. At first Sandy is overwhelmed by Rachel. He dislikes her tireless attempts to befriend him, her needling, the embarrassing comments in front of his friends. Gradually, though, Sandy begins to warm to Rachel a bit. She tells him that the song she often sings and plays on her harp, "Scarlet Ribbons," reminds her of her father. He was the kind of man, she remembers, who would fill her bed with scarlet ribbons, as in the song. Sandy assures her that color-blind Norm never would. Norm himself is perplexed by his new stepdaughter. Once she asks him, "If something happens to Mom, Norm—if she dies, do I belong to you?" When he pauses to think of the proper answer to this and other questions, she changes the subject, refusing to be serious with him for long. One evening Ginger and Norm go out to dinner and leave an unhappy and jealous Rachel to fix dinner for herself and Sandy, who is confined to bed with a broken leg. She goes into Sandy's room to keep him company, and they begin an innocent conversation about sex. Hearing her mother and Norm return, Rachel suddenly jumps into bed with Sandy, telling her angry mother that they were talking about sex. Then Rachel flees to her grandmother's house nearby, where her mother and Norm decide she should spend a few days. Afraid that she is losing her mother and unsure of how Norm feels about her, Rachel does the forbidden and asks Sandy to come over and talk with her, meeting her that night in her grandmother's car. He reluctantly agrees when she says there will be a chaperone. The "chaperone" turns out to be an inflated plastic doll. When Norm discovers them, Rachel again says their conversation was about sex. The girl's behavior causes a tremendous strain between Norm and Ginger, Norm steadfastly trying to understand the cause of it and Ginger increasingly angry. When Rachel returns home the following day, she is sullen and belligerent. Christmastime arrives, a painful season for Rachel since it coincides with the day of her father's death and her own birthday. Everything comes to a head when Rachel refuses to join in her birthday outing to the movies but goes out alone after everyone leaves, returning to find they have all been frantic with worry about her. She hears Norm and Ginger argue bitterly and feels awful when she hears the front door slam. Assuming Norm has left and hearing loud, desperate sobs, she goes to comfort her mother. Instead she finds Norm crying—her mother has left the house. He speaks plainly and honestly to her about how she uses her dead father as an excuse, how he enjoys her enthusiasm but dislikes her pushiness, how he will always take care of her. Chastened, realizing that Norm, though angry, does love her, Rachel wants to make up and play her harp for him as he has so often asked her to. But Norm says she must first prove herself. The next morning Rachel apologizes to her mother. She begins making wild plans for atonement but checks herself, remembering her resolve to be less pushy and extravagant. Still, she tells her mother how marvelous it would be if Norm would fill her bed with red ribbons. That afternoon, Christmas Eve, after Rachel has surprised her family with a harp concert of Christmas carols at the Golden Gate Bridge, she returns home to find a small bundle of green ribbons on her bed. She knows the ribbons could only be from one person: her color-blind stepfather.

A young teenager still mourning the death of her father and anxious about her new stepfather hides behind a facade of unpredictability and extravagance. Only when she comes close to harming her mother's recent marriage does Rachel accept her stepfather's affection and her own need to make peace with her family and herself. Believable characterizations distinguish this realistic view of the challenges faced by two families merging into one. One caution: although this is probably a contemporary story, the jacket illustration looks old-fashioned and could mislead potential readers.

Ages 11-13

Also available in:
No other form known

583

Thomas, Ianthe

Willie Blows a Mean Horn

Color illustrations by Ann Toulmin-Rothe.
HarperCollins Publishers, Inc., 1981.
(22 pages) o.p.

IDENTIFICATION WITH OTHERS: Adults
TALENTS: Musical
Parent/Parents: respect for/lack of respect for

Willie's young son describes how his father, "The Jazz King," plays his horn: "people start moving and swaying. Then I know Willie's brought the sunshine in." After Willie plays to thundering feet and nodding heads, sweat runs down his face. Sitting in the audience, his son knows when Willie has finished playing and it's time to head backstage. There he wipes the sweat off Willie's face with a clean white rag. When his father hands him his horn and invites him to play a little blues, the boy does, feeling "warm and dizzy inside." He admits, "My music isn't smooth and easy, but everybody stops and listens. And when I'm finished, Willie tells me that one day I'll play a lullaby to the wind." After they drive home together, Willie carries his sleepy son into the house, undresses him, and tucks him in bed. Half asleep, the boy wants to know what it means when people talk about blowing a mean horn. Willie says it means the musician is making beautiful music, just as the boy did when he played for Willie. The boy asks his mother if he can keep the white rag that he used to wipe Willie's face. His mother tucks it under his pillow and whispers goodnight. As he falls asleep the boy thinks, "Willie says someday I'll play a lullaby to the wind. And he should know, 'cause Willie blows a mean horn."

A young boy greatly admires his jazz-musician father and is encouraged by him to pursue his own music. This strong, lyrical, first-person narrative subtly conveys the boy's unsentimental attachment to his father. It also reflects the father's love and the many ways he helps build his son's self-esteem and confidence. The illustrations provide a sensitive counterpoint to the upbeat, spirited text.

Ages 5-8

Also available in:
No other form known

584

Thomas, Jane Resh

The Comeback Dog

Black/white illustrations by Troy Howell.
Clarion Books, 1981.
(62 pages)

ANIMALS: Love for
Expectations
Responsibility: accepting

Daniel, a nine-year-old farm boy, is still grieving over the recent death of his dog, Captain, when he finds a female English setter nearly dead in a culvert. Doc, the veterinarian, says the dog is close to starvation and predicts she won't last the night. He offers to put her away, but Daniel won't hear of it. His parents help him as he warms her with rags and feeds her broth. He takes time out to do his chores, but spends the night with the dog, calling her Lady. He imagines her herding cows as Captain used to do and playing Captain's old games. In the days that follow, Lady begins to regain her weight but reacts strangely to Daniel: she cringes or hides from him, even bares her teeth and snarls. Pa speculates that she's been beaten. Daniel tries to force her to accept his caresses and his company, but she generally ends up evading him. His mother reminds him he can't squeeze blood out of a turnip. Lady isn't a bit like Captain, and Daniel, grieving and angry, finds himself wishing she had died that first night. One day while checking fences, he puts Lady on a choke chain. His father suggests the choke chain can be cruel, and Daniel finally gets so exasperated with Lady's cringing ways that he removes the chain. Somewhat to his relief, she runs away. He watches for her every day, but it is nineteen days later when she returns, porcupine quills stuck all over her face. She snarls at Daniel's father when he tries to help her, but then approaches Daniel with imploring eyes. An angry Daniel kicks a bucket, hitting a cow in the shin and frightening all the cows in the barn. His father tells him to take a good look at himself, that it's now or never if he wants the dog. Tears running down his cheeks, Daniel hugs Lady and painstakingly removes the porcupine quills. With a swollen, infected face and sore paws, her ribs showing, Lady has nearly returned to the condition she was in when Daniel first saw her. But he plans to fatten her up again; maybe this time she'll stay.

In this warm story of Midwestern farm life, a boy grieving for his dead dog comes to love another animal with a very different temperament. Lady isn't at all what Daniel expected, but he can still accept responsibility for her once he's won her trust. Accompanied by illustrations that evoke the rural setting, this is a simple, well-told story that reflects traditional values: hard work, responsibility, satisfaction in a job well done.

Ages 7-9

Also available in:
No other form known

585

Thompson, Jean, pseud.

Don't Forget Michael

Black/white illustrations by Margot Apple.
William Morrow & Company, Inc., 1979.
(64 pages)

FAMILY: Unity
SIBLING: Youngest
Family: extended
Privacy, need for

Seven-year-old Michael is the smallest and quietest of the McBrides, a very large family that includes his parents, five brothers and sisters, three grandparents, various aunts and uncles, twenty-five cousins, and a host of pets. Sometimes the boy feels lost and overlooked in the middle of this noisy, busy brood. One day, when the family goes on a picnic, Michael wanders off by himself for a while and returns to find he has been left behind. He is just about to cry when he realizes that he is hearing silence for the first time in his life. He enjoys nature's little noises until suddenly, with horns and loud voices, the family returns for him. Everyone is so happy to see him that, although he enjoyed his time alone, he is glad to know he's been missed. Another day, several members of the family go to a farm to buy produce. Michael's older brother, Kevin, puts a bushel of very ripe tomatoes in the back seat with Michael. Then, while driving, he swerves to avoid another car and puts the front end of their car in the ditch. The tomatoes hit against Michael and split open, covering him with red pulp. Great-Aunt Olivia, thinking he is covered with blood, passes out. When she comes to, she hugs him and calls him her "own dear little Matthew." This is not the first time Michael has been called by his cousin's name, but now he doesn't mind because he knows Aunt Olivia loves him. Grandma Cameron cares about him too, he soon finds. One evening, when the rest of the family is out, she and her parrot, Captain Kid, come to stay with Michael and nine-year-old Connie. Grandma is tired because she stayed up late the night before reading a murder mystery called *The Empty Grave*. The scary title captures the children's imaginations, and later, when Grandma falls asleep and Captain Kid escapes into the night, they are at first afraid to go after him. But they do, and when they finally get him back into the house, Grandma wakes up and shows them how pleased she is with their "nice, quiet evening" together by giving them big scoops of ice cream. One day the McBride children decide to have a volleyball game. While getting the ball from the shed, Kevin drops the shed key through a crack in the porch. They all hurry around trying to devise ways to get the key back. They ignore Michael when he tells them he has a plan and are amazed when he retrieves the key all by himself, using a magnet attached to a yardstick. They call him a genius and promise to listen to him from now on. Reassured, the boy knows that no one will "ever really forget Michael again."

Life in a big family is realistically portrayed in four short episodes. Sometimes Michael feels that if he hears any more noise, he is "going to short out like a computer on TV, lights flashing wildly on and off, sparks flying out, and finally grind to a stop." The boy also frequently feels ignored. But once in a while he is reminded that he is a special part of the family, and then he feels very happy. The book should be appealing to the intended audience and can be read as a novel or as individual short stories. Clever illustrations help depict the hustle and bustle of the McBride household.

Ages 7-9

Also available in:
No other form known

T

586

Tobias, Tobi

Moving Day

Color illustrations by William Pène du Bois.
Alfred A. Knopf, Inc., 1976.
(28 pages counted) o.p.

MOVING
Transitional objects: toys

It is moving day for a little girl and her toy bear. Bear is afraid, she says, but she is not. She tells how she and Bear prepare for their departure. She packs some things and throws some others away—but not Bear, who must always be by her side. She observes how everything in the house is carefully sorted, boxed, and loaded into the moving van. For an unsettling moment, Bear is lost in the shuffle. But he is found, just in time to help his owner say good-bye to the old neighborhood. After a long ride, the little girl and Bear arrive at their new house. It is so big that she worries Bear may get lost in it. She eats her first meal in the new house with Bear beside her. Seeing family objects arranged in the new surroundings, she finds that the big house feels more like home. Next day, the little girl and Bear find a new friend and begin to feel happy in the new neighborhood.

Written in free verse, this book shows a child successfully getting used to a major change in her life by projecting some of her own fears onto her toy, and by holding onto that toy as a friend when other friends must be left behind. The story is told as much in the illustrations as in the simple verse.

Ages 3-6

Also available in:
No other form known

587

Udry, Janice May

Let's Be Enemies

Color illustrations by Maurice Sendak.
HarperCollins Publishers, Inc., 1961.
(32 pages counted)

ANGER
Friendship: meaning of

John and James usually are good friends, but today John is upset with James. He says that James is too bossy and always wants his own way. James also takes all the toys and throws sand. John explains how things were when he and James were friends: they were together at a birthday party; they had chicken pox together; and the two of them once watched a horned toad together. John decides to go to James's house and tell James that they are now enemies, and James will no longer have anyone to play with. The two boys agree to be enemies and angrily say goodbye. But they soon reconsider and share pretzels as they roller-skate together.

Childhood anger is often short-lived. John and James have too close a friendship to hold a grudge for long. This first-person narrative is illustrated cleverly and should serve as a model to help children consider their anger and overcome it.

Ages 3-7

Also available in:
Paperbound—*Let's Be Enemies*
HarperCollins Publishers, Inc.

588

Udry, Janice May

What Mary Jo Shared

Color illustrations by Eleanor Mill.
Albert Whitman & Company, 1966.
(30 pages counted)

SHARING/NOT SHARING
SHYNESS
Encouragement

First-grader Mary Jo has never brought anything for sharing time at school. It is not that Mary Jo does not want to share; she is afraid to be in front of the class. When it rains one day, Mary Jo decides to share her new pink umbrella with the class until she sees many new umbrellas drying in the hall. The next week, after Mary Jo's brother helps her catch a grasshopper, she decides to show it to the class—until she hears that Jimmy, a classmate, has caught six grasshoppers all by himself and intends to display them during sharing time. Now Mary Jo is quite determined to share something, but something no one else has shared. So Mary Jo decides to share her father with the class. She invites him to come to school, and he readily agrees. On the day her father attends school with Mary Jo and is "shared," Mary Jo feels proud; what she shares is unique and quite a success.

This picture book, illustrated with drawings of a racially integrated classroom, shows how a young girl overcomes her shyness and displays her individuality at the same time. The reader also senses the security and supportive nature of the girl's home environment.

Ages 5-8

Also available in:
Filmstrip—*What Mary Jo Shared*
Phoenix Films and Videos

Paperbound—*What Mary Jo Shared*
Scholastic, Inc.

Videotape—*What Mary Jo Shared*
Phoenix Films and Videos

589

Van Leeuwen, Jean

Seems Like This Road Goes On Forever

Dial Books for Young Readers, 1979.
(214 pages) o.p.

COMMUNICATION: Parent-Child
IDENTITY, SEARCH FOR
MENTAL ILLNESS: of Adolescent
Accidents: automobile
Deprivation, emotional
Expectations
Guilt, feelings of
Parental: control
Reality, escaping
Religion: questioning
Stealing: shoplifting

Seventeen-year-old Mary Alice Fletcher lies in a hospital bed feeling completely detached from what is going on around her. She doesn't speak, eat, or react to anyone or anything. Even the car accident that brought her to the hospital with a head injury and broken leg does not seem real. She cannot tell whether or not she is in pain. But her parents do not believe in "such things as emotional breakdowns and psychiatrists." Her father, a minister, believes Mary Alice is going through a spiritual crisis that can only be healed by prayer. Her mother thinks there is nothing wrong with her mind at all, except the shock of the accident. However, they do agree to let their daughter talk to Dr. Nyquist, a psychologist who works with young people. Even though Mary Alice feels she has "had no life" and therefore has nothing to discuss, Dr. Nyquist patiently helps her probe her feelings and memories to understand why she has found it necessary to retreat from the world. Most of Mary Alice's childhood memories center around her parents. She feels from all she has observed that her father is "a completely good person." She, by contrast, is very imperfect, and his penetrating eyes seem to look into her head and "see the bad thoughts there." She remembers that when he punished her, which was often, he never spanked her or even raised his voice. Instead, he would quote the Bible and make her think about how she had sinned against God. Since he always had all the answers, Mary Alice never talked back. She recalls how her older brother, Peter, used to make their father very angry by questioning him. But by the time Peter was fifteen he had learned to keep his thoughts to himself. Mary Alice sees her father as "a silent reproachful shadow" looming over her hospital bed and her life. Her mother is also unapproachable, in a different way. She is not the warm and caring person she pretends to be, not even with her children. Since her father frowns on worldliness, Mary Alice has always worn homemade clothes of her mother's choice or clothes bought at rummage sales. Pretty accessories were not allowed. When Peter left for college, Mary Alice was panic-stricken at the thought of being without him. He advised her to remember that she would be leaving soon too, but that while still at home she must "buck the tide—they've got a strong tide going—but it's got to be done." About the time Peter left, their father was becoming more extreme in his religion. He had become a follower of Bob Parker, an evangelist who preached about the Power of Prayer and the Healing of the Holy Spirit. Mary Alice didn't understand any of this. Yet when it was time for her to think about college, her parents insisted that she apply only to Bob Parker University. She felt extremely uneasy when she "thought of turning herself over like a lump of clay to be molded—body, mind, and spirit—into a total Christian woman." In high school Mary Alice had felt invisible. At one point she had begun to think of herself as a good student. But when she wrote an exceptionally fine book report, her teacher accused her of plagiarism. After that, she didn't think good grades were worth the effort. Her job as a salesclerk gave her a sense of identity for a while, but this was ruined by her compulsion to take small, pretty items from the store. The breaking point came when a boy she thought was interested in her asked out her friend instead. Then Mary Alice started "spinning a cocoon" around herself. Shortly after this, she stole a sweater from the store and fled in her parents' car. She had an accident and was brought to the hospital. As Dr. Nyquist helps Mary Alice better understand herself and her family situation, she decides that with his and her brother's help, she may be able to take charge of her own future. She knows it won't be easy to "buck the tide," but she will try.

This book describes the inner life of a sensitive girl who is given no freedom to explore her own personality or ideas in a home dedicated totally to a stern, impersonal religion. Her brother is strong enough to survive his stifling home life, but Mary Alice, paralyzed by guilt and fear, does not have the willpower to resist her forceful parents. It is only after much painful self-analysis, helped by a skillful psychologist, that she begins to understand how her seemingly irrational behavior has been an expression of anger and despair. Not a fast-paced narrative, this study of a troubled girl is convincingly realistic but won't appeal to all readers.

Ages 12 and up

Also available in:
Cassette—*Seems Like This Road Goes On Forever*
Library of Congress (NLSBPH)

Paperbound—*Seems Like This Road Goes On Forever*
Dell Publishing Company, Inc.

590

Veglahn, Nancy Crary

Fellowship of the Seven Stars

Abingdon Press, 1981.
(175 pages) o.p.

CULTS
Family: relationships
Rebellion
Religion: questioning
Running away

V

Mazie Ffoulke, a plump high school senior who is "good" at home and at school, attends her first meeting of a religious organization, the Fellowship of the Seven Stars, after a particularly bad day. She has been replaced on the "A" debate team by Harrison Baker, and her older brother, Rich, who is continually in trouble, has stolen the family car. Nick Sorenson is the magnetic, good-looking leader of the Fellowship, and Mazie is drawn to him. At the first meeting she hears that members of the Fellowship never use each other selfishly, as other people do. Founded five years ago by a former Chicago businessman now known as Malakh, the Fellowship exists to spread the messages he receives from God. The next evening Mazie and Paul Clough, whom she's casually dated, attend another meeting. Everything the speakers say seems logical, and Mazie likes the feeling of unity and the kindness members show each other. The following morning, Mazie stays home from church—her father is a Methodist minister and, although she enjoys being in church, her religious feelings aren't deep—and hears Rich sneaking in. He's come to steal their grandfather's coin collection and warns Mazie not to say anything. Always full of get-rich-quick schemes, Rich is sure this stake will start him on the road to riches. After church Mazie's parents are so happy to see the returned car that she doesn't tell them about the coin collection. She knows they'll just make more excuses for Rich. All her life she's watched them argue about her brother and bail him out of trouble. Paul's distressed parents come by and report that Paul is joining the Fellowship. Mazie announces that she is joining too. Suddenly she wants to get away from everything, to be "free from all those answerless questions." She moves into the Fellowship house, a place of constant prayer and Bible reading. To her distress, she is told that every day she must try to sell forty dollars' worth of cheap ballpoint pens. But eventually she settles into her new routine. She promises her parents that she will finish high school and will call home once a week; in return, they are to leave her alone. One day Harrison sees her selling pens in a mall. He wonders how such an intelligent, analytical person could join a group like the Fellowship; Mazie replies that he simply doesn't understand. Then it's announced that the great Malakh is coming for a rally, and Mazie joins the publicity committee. When Harrison calls her at the Fellowship house to discuss debate, Nick tells Mazie that relationships outside the Fellowship are discouraged. Then Paul quits school to become an orderly in a nursing home so he can contribute more money to the Fellowship. His move shocks Mazie; Paul was in line for several top college scholarships. One of the girls, Ellen, who shares a bunk in Mazie's room suffers from severe headaches. After she faints one day, a healing service is held and Ellen says her headache is gone. But Mazie finds her very ill in the middle of the night and begs Nick to get a doctor for her. Nick insists that too little faith can make a person ill; Ellen will be all right if she has enough faith. But Ellen goes to a doctor who puts her in a hospital for tests. When Nick discovers where she is, he brings her back to the Fellowship house before all her tests are run. Malakh arrives in town, and Mazie accompanies him and his assistants to an interview she has set up with a local journalist. The reporter illustrates his story with photographs of a luxurious set of buildings in Chicago where only the elite of the Fellowship ever go, wondering how the Fellowship's huge income can come from teenagers working menial jobs and selling ballpoint pens. Harrison has kept in touch, and Mazie invites him to attend Malakh's upcoming rally. But when Mazie sees Paul wrapping up a scorpion to send to the skeptical journalist, something in her snaps. She leaves the Fellowship house and spends the night in her father's church. When she returns to pick up her things, Nick tells her she will leave the next morning for a rural retreat where troubled members can be helped. Mazie realizes it may not be easy to leave the Fellowship. During the rally, Mazie is kept close to Fellowship members. She sees her parents and Harrison in the audience, but is only able to break away and go to them when some bleachers collapse and cause a diversion. Back at home again, Mazie misses the sense of belonging. But when she learns that Ellen died of an operable brain tumor, her anger quells her desire to return to the Fellowship. She's dating Harrison and that helps. But she's "still bugged sometimes by having to think and decide—by not being sure of anything much."

In this first-person narrative, a teenager looks back at the time she spent with a religious cult, what drew her to join and then compelled her to leave. She also acknowledges the part of herself that is still vulnerable to the group's appeal. Readers will come away from the book knowing a little more about cults and how they operate. However, the story seems fuzzy because the one-dimensional characters exist only to further the plot. Readers will recognize the typical—perhaps stereotypical—cult tactics of poor food, little sleep, repetitive teachings, and no outside contacts. Many will also understand the implications of the Fellowship's finances.

Ages 12 and up

Also available in:
No other form known

591

Vigna, Judith

She's Not My Real Mother

Color illustrations by the author.
Albert Whitman & Company, 1980.
(32 pages counted)

PARENT/PARENTS: Remarriage of
STEPPARENT: Mother
Change: resisting

Miles, about five, lives with his divorced mother. He likes to visit Daddy in the city, but he doesn't like Daddy's new wife because "she's not my REAL mother." He's afraid that by befriending his stepmother, he may anger his mother. "Suppose Mommy found out and got mad and left me just the way Daddy did?" When Daddy's wife buys Miles a balloon at the zoo, Miles refuses to thank her. When she tells Miles she'd like to be his friend, he responds that he does not want to be hers. One Sunday afternoon, Miles and his stepmother go alone to the Ice Show. Though Miles enjoys the show he worries about being too nice to Daddy's wife, so he hides behind a column at the giant stadium just to scare her. But he quickly loses sight of his stepmother and grows frightened, fearing Daddy's wife has left him in the crowded arena and gone home. Actually, she has gone to the lost children department, and soon Miles hears his name over the loudspeaker. Reunited with his stepmother, Miles is now very happy to see her. When he realizes she is not going to tell his father "the bad thing" he did, he decides he can be friends with Daddy's wife after all without feeling disloyal to his mother.

A little boy tells in his own words how hurt and bewildered he is by his parents' divorce and his father's remarriage. His stepmother's kindness helps Miles realize he can be friends with her and still maintain his relationship with his mother. Although written in language that some children will be able to read on their own, this convincing and realistic story is also a good read-aloud selection and may stimulate discussion. The illustrations nicely complement the text.

Ages 4-8

Also available in:
No other form known

592

Viorst, Judith

Alexander and the Terrible, Horrible, No Good, Very Bad Day

Color illustrations by Ray Cruz.
Atheneum Publishers, 1972.
(32 pages)

ANGER

Young Alexander knows right from the start that it is going to be a very bad day. He wakes up with chewing gum in his hair, trips over his skateboard, and drops his sweater into a sink full of water. He knows for sure that it is a bad day when he does not find a toy in his breakfast cereal, and his brothers do. Riding in the car pool on his way to school, he asks for a seat next to the window but is refused. In school, he makes a counting mistake, sings too loudly, and discovers that Paul does not want to be his best friend. Alexander's lunch is a disappointment too: Mother forgot to pack dessert. After school, Alexander and his brothers go to the dentist, and Alexander is the only one with a cavity. Leaving the dentist's office, Alexander falls in the mud, gets into a fight with one of his brothers, and is scolded by his mother. At the shoe store, the clerk does not have the sneakers Alexander wants, and when they go to pick up his father, Alexander makes a shambles of the office. The evening is just as bad as the day: lima beans for supper, kissing on TV, a bath that is too hot, having to wear railroad pajamas to bed, and not being able to have the cat sleep with him. But it makes him feel better when his mother tells him that some days are like that for everyone.

In a simple yet amusing manner, this first-person narrative conveys the anger Alexander feels when everything goes wrong. The reader will empathize with the boy.

Ages 3-8

Also available in:
Cassette—*Alexander and the Terrible, Horrible, No Good, Very Bad Day*
Library of Congress (NLSBPH)

Paperbound—*Alexander and the Terrible, Horrible, No Good, Very Bad Day*
Aladdin Books

Talking Book—*Alexander and the Terrible, Horrible, No Good, Very Bad Day*
Library of Congress (NLSBPH)

593

Viorst, Judith

I'll Fix Anthony

Color illustrations by Arnold Lobel.
HarperCollins Publishers, Inc., 1969.
(32 pages counted)

SIBLING: Youngest
Daydreaming
Sibling: rivalry

Anthony can read, but he will not read to his five-year-old brother. He plays checkers with his friends but will not do this with his little brother, either. Their mother consoles the younger boy by telling him that Anthony loves him "deep down in his heart, where he doesn't even know it." But Anthony says that "deep in his heart" he thinks his brother "stinks," and with this he chases the youngster away. So the five-year-old daydreams about getting even with Anthony someday when he is six...and when Anthony gets sick, the little brother will go places with his parents and will not bring anything home for Anthony...and he will beat Anthony at games, he will read better and swim better than Anthony, and he will be taller than Anthony ever will be. The five-year-old also imagines that he will be smart, know his complete address, ride his bicycle well, and receive money from the tooth fairy—while Anthony achieves nothing. Thus the little boy imagines that when he is six he will have no reason to envy his big brother.

The older sibling's unkind behavior toward his younger brother frustrates the little one, who then relieves this frustration through fantasy formation. The younger sibling wants to be best at things which will make him the more dominant of the two—things he expects will bring him power, admiration, and respect. The open ending of this story offers opportunities for discussion.

Ages 3-6

Also available in:
No other form known

594

Viorst, Judith

My Mama Says There Aren't Any Zombies, Ghosts, Vampires, Creatures, Demons, Monsters, Fiends, Goblins, or Things

Black/white illustrations by Kay Chorao.
Atheneum Publishers, 1974.
(43 pages counted)

FEAR: of Darkness
Imagination
Trust/Distrust

A little boy states that his mama has said there is no mean-eyed monster with slimy hair and pointy claws outside his bedroom window—but sometimes even mamas make mistakes. His mother has also told him there is no vampire flying over the house, no thing oozing along in the yard, no fiend lying in the lower bunk, and no tall white ghost going "hoo!" from a hole in its mouth. But Mama has been mistaken about other things. She once made him carry a grocery bag he knew he would drop, and he dropped the bag. She once said he would not be carsick, but he was. She scolded him for leaving his skates on the sidewalk (although they were not his) and accused him of not flushing the toilet (when it was someone else who hadn't). Mama's errors make the boy think that if Mama was wrong about those things, perhaps she is mistaken about the monsters as well.

In this first-person narrative a little boy's fear of darkness is vividly illustrated. The child accepts the fact that mothers are not always right but realizes that most times they are. He reaches the conclusion that perhaps Mama is right this time and the monsters exist only in his imagination.

Ages 4-7

Also available in:
Paperbound—*My Mama Says There Aren't Any Zombies, Ghosts, Vampires, Creatures, Demons, Monsters, Fiends, Goblins, or Things*
Aladdin Books

595

Viorst, Judith

Rosie and Michael

Black/white illustrations by Lorna Tomei.
Atheneum Publishers, 1974.
(39 pages counted)

FRIENDSHIP: Best Friend
Loyalty

Young Rosie and Michael are best friends. Rosie likes Michael even though he worries about pythons and puts Kool Whip in her sneakers. Michael is fond of Rosie even when she is grouchy and when she lets the air out of his basketball. Rosie comforts Michael when his parakeet dies and when he cuts his head. Michael offers Rose consolation when her dog runs away and when her bike is stolen. The two children trust and understand each other, share each other's secrets, and will always be loyal.

This picture book describes qualities of true friendship: trust loyalty, and complete acceptance of the other person. The illustrations are cartoon-like in nature.

Ages 4-7

Also available in:
No other form known

596

Viorst, Judith

The Tenth Good Thing about Barney

Color illustrations by Erik Blegvad.
Atheneum Publishers, 1971.
(25 pages)

DEATH: of Pet
Mourning, stages of

A little boy, heartbroken because his cat, Barney, has died, refuses to eat or watch television; he would rather cry. When he goes to bed, his mother tells him that they will have a funeral for Barney the next morning, and she asks him to think of ten good things about Barney. He thinks of nine—Barney was brave, smart, funny, clean, cuddly, handsome, and "he only once ate a bird." He also "purred in my ear, and sometimes he slept on my belly and kept it warm." At the funeral, Mother, Father, the boy, and his friend Annie bury Barney, put flowers on the grave, and sing a song for him. While having a snack after the funeral, Annie and the boy debate whether or not Barney is in heaven. Father resolves the discussion by saying that if there is a heaven, Barney may be there. Later, the boy still finds it hard to accept that Barney is dead and in the ground. Father understands his son's sadness but tells him that his grief will lessen in time. That afternoon while the boy helps his father in the garden, they discuss how seeds and animals change when they are put in the ground. When the boy accepts that "Barney is in the ground and he's helping grow flowers," he sees that as the tenth good thing about Barney and he begins to accept his sorrow.

This touching first-person narrative expresses the sadness a child experiences when a beloved pet dies. The parents understand their son's sorrow and do not downplay the extent of his grief. The reader is immediately drawn into the situation and is able to empathize easily with the boy. Because of the subject matter of the story, and because the author does not indicate an age for the main characters, the book appeals to a wide age range.

Ages 4-8

Also available in:
Paperbound—*The Tenth Good Thing about Barney*
Aladdin Books

Talking Book—*The Tenth Good Thing about Barney*
Library of Congress (NLSBPH)

597

Voigt, Cynthia

Dicey's Song

Atheneum Publishers, 1982.
(196 pages)

FAMILY: Relationships
Death: of mother
Grandparent: living in home of
Love, meaning of
Parental: absence
School: achievement/underachievement
School: classmate relationships
Sibling: relationships
Talents: musical

Dicey Tillerman, thirteen, and her younger brothers and sister have been living with Gram since their mother abandoned them and later entered a mental institution. To help out, Dicey gets an after-school job. Gram plans to adopt the children and will register for welfare because she must, although she hates taking charity. Maybeth, eight, has always been considered retarded by everyone but the family. As usual, she's not doing well in school. Dicey believes Maybeth is only shy and slow, but even long, hard hours of studying don't improve her reading. However, Mr. Lingerle, the music teacher, considers Maybeth extremely talented, and he wants her to take piano lessons. So Dicey uses the income from her job to pay for the lessons. Later, Mr. Lingerle offers to give Maybeth an extra lesson each week at no charge. Dicey herself is prickly with everyone except her family. A classmate, Mina, picks Dicey for her science lab partner and tries in vain to make friends with her. After school Dicey often sees Jeff, a tenth grader, sitting on the steps playing his guitar and singing. But when he makes overtures to her, she always finds some excuse to leave. Dicey also chafes at having to take home ec. instead of the mechanical drawing she wanted. After school conferences, Gram decides that she and Dicey will go into the city, do some necessary winter shopping, and discuss the conferences. She buys Dicey a beautiful dress, definitely a luxury, and then reports what she learned at school. James, ten, is extremely intelligent, but he turned in an inferior paper to avoid his peers' teasing and seems to have trouble making friends. Seven-year-old Sammy's "problem" is that he is too well-behaved in school; he's not being himself, and Gram and Dicey worry about him. Maybeth is still not learning, and her teacher mentioned special tutors. Gram is a little concerned about Dicey too, but Dicey assures her that she knows what she needs to about sex and isn't interested in boys yet. At Dicey's request, James begins researching reading methods to find out why Maybeth can't read and if another teaching method would help her. He decides that she probably could learn if he taught her phonetically. He spends evenings tutoring her, and gradually Maybeth begins reading more easily and fluently. Sammy begins coming home looking as if he's been in a fight, but nobody can find out why he's fighting. Then Dicey gets an F in home ec., although she's done all the assignments. Her attitude seems to have hurt her. Even more of a shock is her C+ in English. She discovers that the English teacher believes she plagiarized an essay she wrote about Momma. Mina defends Dicey and the teacher eventually apologizes, giving her an A+ on the paper and an A on her report card. When Dicey tells Gram about the experience, Gram asks her not to stop reaching out to people just because she got her hand slapped this time. Sammy's fighting continues. Mina suggests that Sammy is defending Gram's name. Gram has something of a reputation as an eccentric and if Sammy's friends have been making fun of her, he may be fighting them over it. One day Gram shows up at the schoolyard with a bag of old marbles she found in the attic. She teaches Sammy and his friends how to really play, winning all their marbles from them. The troublemakers are impressed by Gram, and Sammy's fighting ends. That night at dinner Gram announces that the adoption papers have gone through and they are now officially her children. Mina and Dicey discuss the future; Dicey is impressed with Mina's determination to choose her future freely, not fall into something because she is black and female. Then they get word that Momma is dying. Gram and Dicey go to Boston to see her. They hold the sick woman's hand and talk to her, although Momma is unconscious. When she dies, they can't afford to have her body taken back home and so have her cremated. At home, they bury her ashes under the old mulberry tree. Dicey ponders Gram's reflection that, although Momma is gone, she's home at last.

Four children living with their grandmother learn the give-and-take of family life. The oldest, Dicey, learns what it means to let go, to reach out, and to hold on to those she loves. In this sequel to *Homecoming* (the story of the children's long, hard walk to Gram's house), all four children meet school and family problems with courage, humor, and perseverance. When Gram decides to adopt them with all the attendant worry, fear, and inconvenience, she does so determined to hold on to her grandchildren as she didn't her own three children. Readers familiar with the first book will be delighted to meet the Tillerman children again, and newcomers will be drawn into their world of strong values and family commitment. This is a richly rewarding story.

Ages 11 and up

Also available in:
Braille—*Dicey's Song*
Library of Congress (NLSBPH)

Cassette—*Dicey's Song*
Library of Congress (NLSBPH)

598

Voigt, Cynthia

Homecoming

Atheneum Publishers, 1981.
(312 pages)

ABANDONMENT
DEPENDENCE/INDEPENDENCE
Change: accepting
Determination
Family: unity
Grandparent: living in home of
Relatives: living in home of
Sibling: relationships

The last thing Momma says to the children before she abandons them in a shopping mall parking lot in Peewauket, Connecticut, is that they should mind Dicey. After waiting a night and a day for Momma to return, thirteen-year-old Dicey and her younger brothers and sister—James, Sammy, and Maybeth—begin walking to Bridgeport where their Great-Aunt Cilla lives. They have only a few dollars and a map that Dicey buys. James remembers that their father left them just before Sammy was born. He wonders if "we're the kind that people go off from." Through summer days of hot, hungry walking, their nights spent in parks, Dicey cares for her family. When all the money is gone, they earn more by carrying bags of groceries for shoppers. One rainy night a college student named Windy treats them to a meal and becomes interested in their story. His roommate, Stewart, offers to drive them the remaining distance to Bridgeport. But first the matter of James stealing twenty dollars from Stewart must be resolved. The boy has turned to stealing several times, despite Dicey's disapproval, and defiantly resists seeing it as wrong. Stewart says James owes it to himself, not to anyone else, to be honest. When they arrive in Bridgeport they discover that Great-Aunt Cilla is dead. Her daughter, Cousin Eunice, doesn't know quite what to do with the children. She calls in her friend, Father Joseph, who makes plans for them. He will arrange to have someone check on their only other living relative, their maternal grandmother. He'll also contact the police so a missing-person report can be filed on their mother. In the meantime, James will go to a school camp and Maybeth and Sammy to a day camp. Although James is very bright and the school is pleased with him, the nuns find Maybeth slow and Sammy hostile. The priest tells Dicey she should think about adoption or foster homes for herself and the children. Cousin Eunice, who has been on the point of becoming a nun, says she will sacrifice her wishes and adopt the children herself. Dicey makes a little money from the sale of the car Momma abandoned along with the children. She also finds work washing windows. When the question of putting Maybeth in a special school and Sammy in a foster home becomes more immediate, Dicey decides she must go to their grandmother, apparently an acid-tongued recluse living in Crisfield, Maryland. The other children insist on going with her. With the money Dicey has saved, they set off on a bus. After various adventures, including traveling with a circus for a time, they finally arrive in Crisfield. Their grandmother is anything but welcoming, but Dicey is determined to stay and makes her plans. They begin immediately to work on their grandmother's badly neglected farm, pulling down overgrown honeysuckle bushes, repairing the screens and the back steps. Each night their grandmother acts as if it's their last, and each day the children find more work to do. Dicey refuses to let their grandmother mistreat the children: Sammy is not to be sent to bed without supper; Maybeth is not to be referred to as retarded. The grandmother seems to accept Dicey's stand, although she is not used to being crossed. Eventually, she explains to Dicey why she won't keep the children. She was married to an extremely domineering man for a long time and always obeyed him. Now she's gotten a taste of freedom and likes doing things her own way. She also feels she failed her own three children, and she doesn't want any more failure. However, she "temporarily" registers the children for school. Dicey is to start junior high, James is put in a program for gifted students, and Sammy will be in second grade. Maybeth has already repeated first grade, and her former school had strongly suggested she repeat second. But the Crisfield school counselor decides to test her in an effort to move her into third grade. While Maybeth is taking her tests, James suggests to his grandmother that she raise something to support them and pay the taxes on her farm: Christmas trees, chickens, pigs, or vegetables. Grandmother and Dicey go to the grocery store and Grandmother abruptly asks Millie, the widowed store owner, if she gets Social Security, something Grandmother has never applied for. Millie convinces Grandmother that there's nothing shameful about a widow's pension. On the way home, they all congratulate Maybeth for being promoted to third grade, and Dicey advises their grandmother to let them live with her. The old woman finally capitulates. She'll check into adoption procedures, Social Security pensions, and the possibilities of growing Christmas trees. The children are home at last.

Four children, led by the exceptionally resourceful Dicey, cope with the practical and emotional problems of being abandoned by their mother. Dicey loves her siblings, defends them, and finally wins them all a home with their sharp-tongued grandmother, whose life is changed through the children's determination to be accepted. Deft, strong characterizations and superbly developed relationships distinguish this story. Particularly noteworthy is the forcefully independent character of Dicey. This memorable odyssey is one of those rare books that can truly inspire readers. The story of Dicey and her family is continued in the sequel, *Dicey's Song.*

Ages 11 and up

Also available in:
Braille—*Homecoming*
Library of Congress (NLSBPH)

Cassette—*Homecoming*
Library of Congress (NLSBPH)

599

Waber, Bernard

Ira Sleeps Over

Color illustrations by the author.
Houghton Mifflin Co., 1972.
(48 pages)

TRANSITIONAL OBJECTS: Toys
Decision making
Visiting

Ira is happy about staying overnight with his friend Reggie. Yet he is also perplexed, for he does not know whether he should take his teddy bear along. Although his parents say he should take it, his big sister insists he should not. Ira is worried that Reggie will laugh and say he is a baby, and so after much indecision, Ira decides to leave the teddy at home. At Reggie's house, the boys have fun playing and the teddy bear is forgotten. However, when bedtime comes and they begin to tell ghost stories, Reggie gets out of bed, opens a dresser drawer, and takes something out of it. Once Ira sees what Reggie has removed from the drawer, he gets out of bed and walks next door; he returns to Reggie's house with his teddy bear.

Ira lets his older sister talk him out of his decision to take his teddy bear to Reggie's house. When he sees what Reggie takes out of the dresser drawer, he gains the courage to stand by his original decision. This book for young readers is written with humor and understanding.

Ages 6-8

Also available in:
Paperbound—*Ira Sleeps Over*
Houghton Mifflin Co.

Talking Book—*Ira Sleeps Over*
Library of Congress (NLSBPH)

600

Waber, Bernard

You Look Ridiculous, Said the Rhinoceros to the Hippopotamus

Color illustrations by the author.
Houghton Mifflin Co., 1973.
(32 pages)

APPEARANCE: Concern About
Self, attitude toward: body concept

A rhinoceros tells a hippopotamus that she looks ridiculous because she does not have a horn. Disturbed by the comment, the hippopotamus asks a lion, a leopard, an elephant, a monkey, a giraffe, a turtle, and a nightingale whether she does indeed look ridiculous. Each animal agrees that she does and suggests how she might improve her appearance. The lion tells her she should have a mane. The leopard suggests spots. The elephant suggests larger ears; the monkey, a tail; and the giraffe, a long neck. The turtle says the hippo should have a shell, and the nightingale tells the hippo that she needs a beautiful voice. The hippopotamus feels she is a ridiculous creature because she has none of the suggested attributes. She finds a place to hide and decides never again to show herself to anyone. Later, after imagining herself with all the features the animals have suggested, the hippopotamus decides she is happy with her own appearance.

The humorously absurd illustrations help point out the consequences of wishing to be what one is not. Children will be captivated by the ridiculous situation in this thought-provoking story.

Ages 5-8

Also available in:
Paperbound—*You Look Ridiculous, Said the Rhinoceros to the Hippopotamus*
Houghton Mifflin Co.

601

Walker, Mary Alexander

Year of the Cafeteria

Bobbs-Merrill Company, Inc., 1971.
(144 pages) o.p.

GRANDPARENT: Love for
GRANDPARENT: Respect for
Change: accepting
Change: resisting
Death: of grandparent
Friendship: making friends
Maturation
Mourning, stages of

A high-school senior named Azure has moved with her parents from Louisiana to California. Azure is not happy about the move. She is equally unhappy about working in the school cafeteria, which is run by her grandmother, Miss Abby. But Azure finds that working in the cafeteria has one advantage: it is easy to meet students and make friends since many of them pop in and out of the kitchen to have a few cookies or talk with Miss Abby. The biggest disadvantage of working in the cafeteria is that Gran is constantly giving Azure advice, telling her where to go, who to date, and how to conduct herself. Aggravated by Gran's interference, Azure defiantly accepts a date to go motorcycle riding with Zack, a flamboyant ladies' man and a reckless driver. Zack "stands her up" for another girl, and both Zack and the girl are hurt when Zack has a motorcycle accident. When he returns to school, Zack convinces Azure to lend him the key to the cafeteria storeroom so that he and some friends can use the room for a club meeting. When Gran discovers what Azure has done, she warns her to never let it happen again. After Zack takes the key again, Gran blames Azure and fires her. Azure now realizes how much she values Gran's companionship, and she asks to be rehired. Gran consents on one condition: Azure must try out for the school play. Azure agrees to this and begins working again in the cafeteria. One morning when Gran fails to show up at work, Azure becomes frightened, and she asks Mr. Gale, the school principal, to find Gran. He returns with terrible news: Miss Abby is dead. Azure refuses to believe him until she hears him notify the student body of Miss Abby's death. Then the truth hits the girl: she will no longer be able to turn to Gran for help. As she works on the play, in which she has one of the female leads, Azure finds comfort talking with friends who also loved Miss Abby.

This first-person narrative portrays the development of a warm, yet conflicting, relationship between a teen-age girl and her grandmother. Azure's grief and mourning are sympathetically and realistically portrayed.

Ages 12 and up

Also available in:
Talking Book—*Year of the Cafeteria*
Library of Congress (NLSBPH)

602

Wallace, Bill

A Dog Called Kitty

Holiday House, Inc., 1980.
(153 pages)

COURAGE, MEANING OF
FEAR: of Animals
PETS: Love for
Death: of pet
Fear: of physical harm

Bitten and mauled by a rabid dog when he was small, Ricky, now in fifth grade, has been terrified by all dogs ever since. Though he has suppressed memories of the attack, he recalls vividly the pain of the rabies shots. Ricky's friend Brad admits he is afraid of spiders and invites Ricky to make friends with his own gentle dog. Ricky will not. When a puppy appears on Ricky's farm, a bedraggled, hungry stray, the boy reacts in panic to the little dog's friendliness. Later he finds the puppy in the barn, obviously starving. Though he decides to let it die, he cannot sleep. He takes the puppy table scraps and somehow makes himself touch it, moving the animal nearer the food. Soon he is feeding the dog by hand three times a day, never admitting he is going to keep it. His parents are aware of the situation, but keep silent. Soon the puppy chases the farm cats from their food, coming whenever anyone calls "Kitty." Ricky cannot admit his love for the dog, now named Kitty, but they are inseparable. He and his father build a pen to protect Kitty from the poisoned meat that area ranchers have left for the wild dogs preying on their livestock. But the puppy climbs out of the pen and, when they cover the top, digs beneath the walls. Ricky realizes Kitty will eat the poisoned meat if he is not taught to eat only from his dish. So he trains the puppy by scattering meat filled with hot peppers. Then Ricky's father is called away from the farm, and Ricky and his mother undertake the chores. One day Ricky finds a heifer and her newborn calf surrounded by wild dogs. Kitty challenges the pack but Ricky flees, the old panic overwhelming him. He trips and hears his dog in a fight for its life. Without thinking, he grabs a large stick and races to save Kitty. He breaks one dog's back and cripples another, but then is pulled down from behind. Kitty and Ricky manage to drive the dogs off, but Ricky is sure his savagely bitten dog is dead. Suddenly Kitty wags his tail and licks the boy's face. The two are bandaged and treated like returning heroes. Fortunately, the wild dogs were not rabid. Soon after, Ricky makes friends with oil drillers working nearby. One day, when they're unloading a pipe from a truck, Kitty runs underneath and the pipe falls and crushes him. Ricky feels a part of him has died too, but he hides his feelings. His parents give him a birthday party but he is uninterested, eager for it to end so he can be alone with his sorrow. Suddenly they hear dogs fighting in the barn and find a large dog mauling a puppy—another hungry, unwanted puppy. Ricky drives the big dog off. Later, he hears the cats attacking the puppy and sees it run for the barn. He laughs heartily, for the first time since Kitty's death, and takes food to the puppy.

A boy of good sense and good heart overcomes his fear of dogs when a stray wins his loyalty and affection. This first-person narrative is convincing: Ricky's changing emotions seem realistic, his concern for the new puppy touching and believable. Dog lovers especially will enjoy this exciting and affecting story.

Ages 9-11

Also available in:
Paperbound—*A Dog Called Kitty*
Archway Paperbacks

603

Warburg, Sandol Stoddard

Growing Time

Color illustrations by Leonard Weisgard.
Houghton Mifflin Co., 1975.
(44 pages)

DEATH: Attitude Toward
DEATH: of Pet

Jamie is a preschool-age boy who lives in the country with his parents, Granny, Uncle John, and his dog King. King has become old, stiff, and tired, and one morning Mother tells Jamie that King is dead. Mother and Uncle John try to comfort the boy by showing him where King is buried, and together Mother and Jamie plant flower seeds around the grave. Then Uncle John tries to explain to Jamie that all things die. Jamie comforts himself by thinking about all the good times he had with King. Finally, Granny invites Jamie to sit in the rocking chair with her, and explains that King is not gone: "The spirit of something you really love can never die, it lives in your heart." That evening, Mother and Uncle John go in the truck to meet Dad. When they come home, they bring a puppy for Jamie, but he does not want it: he only wants King. Once asleep, he dreams of all the flowers and plants growing and finally of the "thump-thumping" of King's tail hitting the floor, but a noise in the kitchen awakens him. The new puppy has upset King's water dish, and he is wet, cold, shivering, and crying. Jamie bundles the puppy in King's old blanket, and together they sit in Granny's rocking chair. Soon the puppy is comforted, and Jamie talks to him for a long time.

This story could serve as a good introduction to the concept of death. Although it might be painful for a child who has just lost a beloved pet, this book could help the child to deal more successfully with his or her loss. The illustrations are striking.

Ages 7-9

Also available in:
Paperbound—*Growing Time*
Houghton Mifflin Co.

604

Wartski, Maureen Crane

A Boat to Nowhere

Black/white illustrations by Dick Teicher.
New American Library, 1982.
(160 pages, paperbound)

COURAGE, MEANING OF
LOVE, MEANING OF
REFUGEES
VIETNAM
Age: respect for
Belonging
Maturation

Mai, about twelve, and her younger brother, Loc, are Vietnamese war orphans. Years ago, the two fled their city with their grandfather, Van Chi, and came to live in a small village at the southern tip of Vietnam. Now fourteen-year-old Kien has arrived at the village, living "by his wits," traveling from town to town just a few steps ahead of the New Government officials. Van Chi, who has become the revered teacher and headman of the isolated village, listens uneasily while Kien tells of resettlement camps, economic zones, and dislocation. Bewildered by Kien's stories, Mai senses that her people's simple way of life is threatened. She resents the attention and credence her grandfather gives Kien; unlike her brother, who is Kien's friend immediately, Mai is suspicious. But gradually she comes to trust him, and the three young people become friends. One day, returning from a fishing trip, they find that officials of the New Government have arrived, bringing turmoil to the village. The officials accuse Van Chi of treason, set fire to the old man's books, and announce that he will be taken away to be "reeducated." With Kien's help, the grandfather, Mai, and Loc escape through the forest and set sail for Thailand in the village fishing boat, the *Sea Breeze.* Van Chi navigates the boat by the stars and sun, but they are beset by storms and thrown off course. Lost and without food, the four grow weak. Grandfather develops a serious cough and fever. Their joy at sighting Thailand is quickly squelched when Thai officials turn them away, refusing to accept more refugees. They must set sail for Malaysia, but their journey seems hopeless. As Van Chi's sickness worsens, Kien recognizes that he alone is responsible for the crew's fate. Overtaken by the worst storm yet and attacked by pirates, the four manage to survive and to reach land once more. But Outcast Island proves to be an evil place, controlled by Bac Thong, headman of a small band of Vietnamese refugees, who pretends kindness but actually covets their boat. The children narrowly escape with the dying old man. At sea again, the four are without food or medicine. Mai sickens. When Kien, weak and discouraged, spots a ship on the horizon, he swims toward the vessel but finds that the sailors on board intend to save only him. Unable to desert his helpless friends, Kien lets go of the lifeline and swims back to the *Sea Breeze.* Van Chi, dying, asks Kien to remain with Mai and Loc and see that they return someday to Vietnam. Kien declares that he owes allegiance to no one, but Van Chi insists that Mai and Loc are Kien's family now. "None of us choose to be born into a family," says the old man. "Nor do we choose those we come to love." Van Chi dies, and the three children bury him at sea. Mai is now delirious. Disheartened, Kien lets the *Sea Breeze* drift aimlessly. He prays that he, Mai, and Loc may die together, quickly and painlessly. But an American ship sights the craft and rescues them. After the ship's doctor reassures Kien that Mai will recover from her illness, the boy at last feels safe. He falls asleep between clean sheets, happy that he has not failed Grandfather Van Chi.

Victims of the dislocation of war, four people search for a haven in this engrossing, fast-paced account. Along the way, a solitary young man gains a family he can love and respect. Somewhat stilted dialogue and intrusive English translations of Vietnamese phrases (the glossary provides translation enough) mar the story's impact at times. But young people will learn much here about the plight of Vietnamese refugees. Evocative illustrations depict Vietnamese culture; especially valuable is a map of the characters' journey. The story of Kien, Mai, and Loc continues in the sequel, *A Long Way from Home.*

Ages 9-12

Also available in:
Cassette—*A Boat to Nowhere*
Library of Congress (NLSBPH)

605

Wartski, Maureen Crane

A Long Way from Home

New American Library, 1982.
(144 pages, paperbound)

REFUGEES
VIETNAM
Belonging
Bully: being bothered by
Hostility
Immigrants
Prejudice: ethnic/racial

Kien Ho, a fifteen-year-old Vietnamese refugee now living in the United States, struggles to adapt to American attitudes and habits. As a consequence of his promise to their dying grandfather during a sea crossing, Kien has become the adopted brother of Mai and Loc, two orphaned Vietnamese children. The three live with their sponsor family, the Olsons, in Bradley, California. Though Mai and Loc have readily adjusted to their new home and school, Kien cannot confide in the Olsons and is the target of the taunts and harassment of a racist bully at school. When he is physically attacked for the second time by the bully and two other boys, Kien, reverting to the fighting tactics that helped him survive when fleeing Vietnam, throws a rock at the bully, hitting his eye and injuring him seriously. Later, a witness verifies to the police and to the boy's furious—and equally racist—father that Kien had acted in self-defense. Still, Kien is sure he has ruined his chances in Bradley and with the Olsons. Convinced that everyone will be better off without him, he decides to move to another, more congenial, place. An old newspaper account of a happy Vietnamese settlement in the California fishing town of Travor leads him there. Instead of the peaceful existence Kien expects, however, he and all the Vietnamese in Travor encounter intolerance and hatred from the local fishermen. Wealthy, influential Paul Orrin convinces the American fishermen in the town that they cannot make a living if the Vietnamese continue selling their catches at lower prices. Amid the resulting violence directed at the Vietnamese, Orrin sets fire to his own boat and then sees that a Vietnamese man is charged with arson. With a promise not to press charges, Orrin forces the Vietnamese fishermen to sell their boats to him. Only Kien knows of Orrin's blackmail and arson but feels powerless to prove it: he was out walking near the boats that night and heard a deep laugh just as the flames burst out. Later, when he heard Orrin laugh, he recognized him as the arsonist. On the night before the Vietnamese are to leave Travor, Kien rescues Orrin from a burning boat that had been struck by lightning, getting injured in the process. Hospitalized, Kien uses his new status as hero and his secret knowledge about Orrin to bring the leaders of the warring groups together in an attempt to work out their differences. After the turmoil ends, Kien finds himself thinking of Mai, Loc, and the Olsons. With life back to normal in Travor, he feels something is missing in his own life. As warm memories flood over him, he decides to return to Bradley, his home.

A young Vietnamese refugee, struggling to find a place for himself in an often-inhospitable America, comes to accept and draw strength from the love of his adopted family in this exciting, if at times melodramatic, sequel to *A Boat to Nowhere.* Occasionally stilted dialogue doesn't always ring true, but the characters are believable and the accounts of bigotry realistic. The story evokes sympathy and understanding for the plight of America's Vietnamese immigrants.

Ages 11-13

Also available in:
No other form known

606

Wartski, Maureen Crane

My Brother is Special

The Westminster/John Knox Press, 1979.
(152 pages) o.p.

FAMILY: Relationships
MENTAL RETARDATION
Animals: love for
Change: new home
Honesty/Dishonesty
Peer relationships
School: transfer
Sibling: love for
Success

Noni Harlow is an eighth-grade girl with a talent for running. She has recently joined the track team at Conan Junior High in Conan, Massachusetts. She and her family, originally from California, had first moved to another east-coast town, Lincoln. But both Noni and Kip, her nine-year-old retarded brother, had disliked their schools. Kip had even tried to run away. When their father was transferred to Conan, Noni hoped life would soon be good again. But then she met Denise Baxley—popular, pretty, smart, and the captain of the track team. Noni had sought Denise's friendship, but from their first meeting Denise made cutting remarks about Kip. Now it is the morning of the interscholastic meet with Franklin. Noni wakes up knowing she is going to beat Denise in the 100-yard dash. When she arrives at the track, Red Balkans, the girls' coach, is telling her team about the Special Olympics for handicapped and retarded children. Denise and her friends do not lose this opportunity to taunt Noni about her "special" brother. An angry Noni is very pleased when she does beat Denise in the race. When Kip sees her ribbon he insists on having it, and Noni realizes that Kip believes he'll never win anything. She decides that Kip must compete in the Special Olympics. The local meet will be held in a few weeks at the school for retarded children at Haymarket. Noni gets some pamphlets from her coach and waits for a chance to discuss the idea with her parents. They have had a growing conflict about Kip since his bad school experience in Lincoln. The father wants to push Kip out into the world and make him achieve. Mrs. Harlow wants to protect him and keep him from getting hurt again. On one issue, however, they agree: Kip should not compete in the Special Olympics. They don't want to subject him to such an experience. But Noni is determined to give Kip his moment of victory. She will train him herself. Kip's secret workouts start at the beach, where he finds a gull caught in an oil spill. He loves birds and insists on taking it home. With the help of Denise, whose mother heads the local ecology group, and Neill Oliver, Denise's sympathetic boyfriend, Noni and Kip clean the oil off the bird and devise a hammock in which to suspend it until its broken legs heal. Noni continues Kip's training, often in the garage so he can stay with Bird. Then a newspaper article about Mrs. Baxley, "A Lady with a Heart," reveals Noni's plan for Kip and compares Kip's efforts to those of the bird trying to get well; the Baxley children had told the reporter the story in their mother's absence. Noni's angry parents grow even more incensed when they discover she has forged both her father's and their doctor's signatures on the entry form. But when they realize how desperately Noni wants to do this for her brother and what a good runner he has become, they forgive and support her. This change, along with the increasing attentions of Neill Oliver, makes Noni very happy. Her pleasure is marred only by Denise's continuing harassment. Noni knows exactly whom to blame when, on the morning of the race, Kip discovers Bird's hammock torn to shreds and the gull flapping its wings on the floor. This so upsets Kip that he must be medicated to calm him down. The family takes him to Haymarket, but does not plan to let him race. Kip, however, sneaks away and runs the course behind the others. His determination wins him everyone's admiration; he is a "real winner." Noni wins too when she comes to see Denise as a lonely girl who can only please her demanding parents by being best at everything. She even hopes that someday they'll be friends. Bird survives and the family makes plans to set him free.

A young teenage girl loves her retarded brother and cannot understand those who talk about handicapped and retarded people as though they are "creatures from another planet." Noni wants to prove to everyone, including Kip himself, that he can be a winner too. Along the way she comes to understand the reasons behind a classmate's hostility. Character development is slight here and the dialogue, situations, and conclusion are somewhat contrived. But the book has value in its emphasis on ways retarded people can succeed and in its examples of the varied responses retarded people can evoke from others. Sound information is given about the Special Olympics.

Ages 10-12

Also available in:
Cassette—*My Brother Is Special*
Library of Congress (NLSBPH)

Paperbound—*My Brother Is Special*
New American Library

607

Watanabe, Shigeo

How Do I Put It On?

Color illustrations by Yasuo Ohtomo.
Philomel Books, 1979.
(28 pages) o.p.

AUTONOMY

A young bear says, "I can get dressed all by myself." He then holds up a shirt and asks, "Do I put it on like this?" He puts the shirt on his legs, answers "No!" and then demonstrates the correct way. He repeats his question and answer with pants, cap, and shoes, putting his arms in the pants, the cap on his foot, and the shoes on his ears. Finally, he gets dressed properly.

A bear illustrates the right and wrong way to put on shirt, pants, cap, and shoes in this first book of a series. Large, clear, softly colored illustrations will amuse and encourage children who are just learning to dress themselves. Many will enjoy "reading" the book independently.

Ages 2-5

Also available in:
No other form known

608

Watanabe, Shigeo

I Can Ride It!

Color illustrations by Yasuo Ohtomo.
Translated from the Japanese.
Philomel Books, 1982.
(28 pages) o.p.

GOALS
Perseverance
Success

Little Bear can ride his tricycle by himself. He can also ride his two-wheeler with training wheels. Bear can even ride a skateboard—if he sits on it. He can roller skate just fine when he puts skates on his feet and on his hands. Bear can even drive a small toy car. Someday he hopes to drive a bus and maybe fly an airplane.

Bear tells and shows the read-aloud audience how he "masters" certain vehicles in this funny, colorful book, part of a series called "I Can Do It All By Myself." Each line of text faces a full-page illustration that shows Bear persisting in his attempts to keep from falling down. He never gives up and cheerfully continues to dream of further accomplishments.

Ages 2-5

Also available in:
No other form known

609

Waterton, Betty Marie

A Salmon for Simon

Color illustrations by Ann Blades.
Salem House, 1987.
(28 pages counted, paperbound)

NATURE: Respect for
Animals: love for
Animals: responsibility for
Freedom, meaning of
Native American
Resourcefulness

In September, near the west coast of Canada where young Simon lives, the salmon return from the sea to lay their eggs in the rivers and streams where they were born. Although Simon enjoys clam digging with his sisters, he wants more than anything to catch a salmon. All summer, every day, he tries and fails. So he decides to stop fishing, maybe forever. One day while walking along the beach digging clams, Simon looks up and sees a bald eagle with a salmon glistening in its talons. Excitedly, he flaps his arms and hops while screeching seagulls circle overhead. In all the excitement, the eagle drops the salmon and it lands with a splat in Simon's clam hole. Simon thinks Sukai, as he calls the salmon (from an Indian word meaning "king of the fish"), is the most beautiful thing he's ever seen. He watches with pity as Sukai tries to find his way out of the clam hole; he must find a way to save the salmon. So Simon decides to dig a channel to the sea. For hours he digs while his hands grow red and blistered and Sukai waits quietly. At last, when he can dig no more, he reaches the sea. He watches as Sukai feels the cold freshness and swims slowly down the channel. The salmon dives deep into the cool, green water and then gives one mighty leap as if to say thank-you to Simon. Exhausted, Simon returns to his home and supper. He decides he will go fishing tomorrow after all. "But not for a salmon."

This warm and simple story of a Canadian Indian boy who traps and then releases a salmon come to spawn speaks clearly of a child's sensitivity toward a living creature and the great satisfaction of having saved a life. The richly colored, full-page illustrations add much to the appealing tale.

Ages 4-7

Also available in:
No other form known

610

Watson, Jane Werner, Robert E. Switzer, and J. Cotter Hirschberg

My Friend the Dentist

Color illustrations by Hilde Hoffman.
Crown Publishers, Inc., 1987.
(29 pages counted) o.p.

DENTIST, GOING TO

A young child does not remember when he got his first teeth, but he does remember that his mother taught him how to brush them. When he has several baby teeth, she takes him to the dentist. In the examining room he sees a wonderful chair that goes up and down...a bright light...a little faucet and bowl...and sharp, frightening tools. The sympathetic dentist shows the child his little mirror and lets him hear the motor on his machine. He explains that in spite of good dental care, occasionally a spot will appear on a tooth. The dentist deadens the area, then quickly cleans out the decay with a special tool and "fills the hole with cement." The dentist gives the "brave and good" child a reward and tells him to return in six months for another checkup.

In a "Note to Parents," the authors stress the importance of introducing good oral hygiene at a very young age. Between the ages of two and three, children love to imitate and should be taught to brush their teeth correctly. Most will be so proud to have their own toothbrushes that they will learn quickly. Regular examinations are necessary to prevent minor cavities from becoming major problems. This first-person narrative is "A Read-Together Book for Parents and Children created in cooperation with the Menninger Foundation."

Ages 3-6

Also available in:
Braille–*My Friend the Dentist*
Library of Congress (NLSBPH)

611

Watson, Jane Werner, Robert E. Switzer, and J. Cotter Hirschberg

My Friend the Doctor

Color illustrations by Hilde Hoffman.
Crown Publishers, Inc., 1987.
(29 pages counted, paperbound)

DOCTOR, GOING TO

A preschool child knows that his doctor has been his friend for a long time—even before he can remember. Before he was born, his mother went to a doctor "to make sure I was growing well inside her." Now his mother takes him to see the doctor every six months for a checkup. After they have read books and played with the toys in the waiting room, the nurse calls them into the examining room. The friendly doctor checks the child all over, including his height and weight, his heart, eyes, mouth, and nose. When the doctor must give him a shot, he tells the boy that although it will hurt, it will keep him from becoming ill; and when the frightened boy cries, the doctor understands. Sometimes the boy does not feel well. Then his mother takes him to see the doctor, who takes his temperature rectally. It does not hurt. One day the doctor comes to the boy's house, examines him, and tells his mother what medicine to buy. The boy takes it even though it tastes bad, so that he will feel better and be able to play doctor with his toy doctor bag.

In a "Note to Parents," the authors emphasize that young children should regard the doctor as a friend who can help them regain and maintain their health. If children understand about illness, say the authors, they will be less fearful and anxious. This first-person narrative is "A Read-Together Book for Parents and Children created in cooperation with the Menninger Foundation."

Ages 2-5

Also available in:
Braille—*My Friend the Doctor*
Library of Congress (NLSBPH)

612

Watson, Jane Werner, Robert E. Switzer, and J. Cotter Hirschberg

Sometimes I Get Angry

Color illustrations by Hilde Hoffman.
Crown Publishers, Inc., 1986.
(32 pages counted, paperbound)

ANGER

A young, exuberant child wants to have his own way. If his mother says "no" to him, he might kick or throw something. He likes to explore, and if his mother stops him, he might stamp his foot. Even when his parents tell him to be quiet, he likes to make a lot of noise. Sometimes he plays a quiet game with his father. He prefers to do things at his own speed; if he must hurry, he will probably resist. Still young enough to cry, he nevertheless quiets down quickly when mother picks him up. He wants to please, but also must show that "I'm me, me, me!"

In a "Note to Parents," the authors stress that children's anger helps them grow and does not necessarily lead to battles with their parents. Anger needs to be understood and must not go unchecked. Parents should make rules, enforce them, and help children control their anger. When they encounter a difficult new task or concept, anger may result; when they feel better about themselves, it will disappear. This first-person narrative is "A Read-Together Book for Parents and Children created in cooperation with the Menninger Foundation."

Ages 3-6

Also available in:
No other form known

613

Watson, Jane Werner, Robert E. Switzer, and J. Cotter Hirschberg

Sometimes I'm Afraid

Color illustrations by Hilde Hoffman.
Crown Publishers, Inc., 1986.
(32 pages counted, paperbound)

FEAR

Although a three-year-old child has learned many things, he is afraid in new situations and while his parents are away. When loud noises or shadows scare him, it is comforting to be held by one of his parents; they can banish the fear caused by television shows or bad dreams. Parents also explain many things such as thunder and lightning, thus making them seem less fear-provoking. But when his parents are angry with each other, he fears they are also angry with him. Even a child's own anger can alarm him until he calms down. Though it is necessary to be cautious of things like busy streets and strange animals, the more one learns about one's world, the less frightening it will be.

In a "Note to Parents," the authors stress that parents can help minimize a child's fear. The child must be made aware of their love and should not feel left out of the family circle. Realistic fear of dangerous situations should be encouraged when it is necessary to make a child safety-conscious. As much as possible, children should be prepared for new experiences and their fears should be dealt with directly. This first-person narrative is "A Read-Together Book for Parents and Children created in cooperation with the Menninger Foundation."

Ages 2-5

Also available in:
No other form known

614

Watson, Jane Werner, Robert E. Switzer, and J. Cotter Hirschberg

Sometimes I'm Jealous

Color illustrations by Hilde Hoffman.
Crown Publishers, Inc., 1986.
(29 pages counted, paperbound)

SIBLING: Jealousy
Attention seeking
Sibling: new baby

A little child always has received the attention he needed. Occasionally he feels jealous when another child comes to visit and wants to play with his toys. Now he learns there will be a new baby in his family.

At first he thinks the baby will be a new toy for him, but soon he notices that his mother does not want to play with him so much, and his parents are buying lots of new things for the baby. He can feel the baby kicking in his mother's tummy. Although he knows his mother will go to the hospital, he feels excluded when she leaves. His parents call to tell him about the baby and say they still love him, but he feels jealous. When his mother and the new baby come home and he sees people bringing presents and talking about the baby, he tries to act like a baby himself. Soon, however, he learns that he can do many things the baby cannot, a source of pride for him, especially when he sees that his parents have enough love for both of them.

A "Note to Parents," explains that young children's egocentric outlook and dependence on parents cause them to resent anything that seems to diminish their own importance. Children especially are concerned that they will be displaced by a new baby. Plenty of love will help a child weather this crisis and learn to share. This first-person narrative is "A Read-Together Book for Parents and Children created in cooperation with the Menninger Foundation."

Ages 3-6

Also available in:
No other form known

615

Wells, Rosemary

Benjamin & Tulip

Color illustrations by the author.
Doubleday, 1973.
(30 pages counted)

AGGRESSION: Active
Bully, fear of
Friendship: meaning of

Tulip is an aggressive, whimsical little woodland creature who gets the best of Benjamin, another young woodland creature, whenever she can. Every time Benjamin passes her home, Tulip pounces on him and threatens to beat him up. One day, Benjamin walks past Tulip with the watermelon he has just bought at the store. Tulip fights Benjamin, and Benjamin, as usual, gets the worst of it. When Benjamin's watermelon is broken open, however, he finally stands up to Tulip. The two are momentarily stunned by the turn of events. Then they smile as they begin to eat the broken watermelon and spit the seeds.

At first Benjamin is afraid of Tulip, but when he defies her, he is able to overcome his fear. Once the two become equals, they are able to establish a friendship. This very brief story lightly touches upon how friendships can develop in spite of first impressions and differences in personalities. The child-like attitudes and reactions are competently and delightfully portrayed in the text and colorful illustrations.

Ages 3-7

Also available in:
No other form known

616

Wells, Rosemary

Noisy Nora

Color illustrations by the author.
Dial Books for Young Readers, 1973.
(38 pages)

ATTENTION SEEKING
Sibling: middle

Young Nora, the middle child in the mouse family, slams doors and knocks down lamps and chairs trying to get the attention of her mother and father. But Mother is always busy with Baby Jack, and Father is occupied with Nora's older sister, Kate. Finally Nora runs away. Nora's parents and sister become very worried and search the house and yard looking for her. But noisy Nora does not stay hidden long; she comes crashing out of the broom closet, much to her family's pleasure and surprise.

This delightful tale, written in rhyme, shows the extreme methods a child might use to attract attention.

Ages 4-7

Also available in:
Paperbound—*Noisy Nora*
Dial Books for Young Readers

617

Wells, Rosemary

Timothy Goes to School

Color illustrations by the author.
Dial Books for Young Readers, 1981.
(30 pages counted)

SCHOOL: Entering
Friendship: making friends
Jealousy: peer
School: classmate relationships

On his first day of school, Timothy excitedly hurries off in a new sunsuit with a new book and pencil. His teacher introduces him to a classmate, Claude. Claude promptly tells Timothy that nobody wears sunsuits on the first day of school. Upset, Timothy wishes Claude would fall in a puddle. At home Timothy tells his mother what Claude said. She makes him a new jacket for the second day of school, but Claude tells him he should not wear party clothes on the second day. Timothy goes home dejected. The next day Timothy wears his favorite shirt. But he is upstaged when Claude arrives wearing the same shirt. Timothy informs his mother that he won't be returning to school because he'll never measure up to Claude. Timothy does return to school, however, and there he meets Violet. Violet is mumbling, "I can't stand it anymore." When Timothy asks her what's wrong, she tells him she can't stand Grace, who can do anything. Timothy knows how she feels. During the day Timothy and Violet play together. Violet says, "I can't believe you've been here all along!" After school she invites Timothy home for a snack. On the way they laugh together about Claude and Grace.

Continually upstaged and second-guessed by a classmate, little Timothy is happy to make friends with Violet, who shares his feelings. Winning little animal characters in brightly colored illustrations add to the charm of this touching, funny story about some of the trials of entering school. Small children may find the book reassuring as they approach their own first days.

Ages 3-5

Also available in:
Paperbound—*Timothy Goes to School*
Dial Books for Young Readers

618

White, Elwyn Brooks

Charlotte's Web

Black/white illustrations by Garth Williams.
HarperCollins Publishers, Inc., 1952.
(184 pages)

FRIENDSHIP: Meaning of
Death: of friend
Loyalty

Wilber, a pig, is bottle-fed by Fern Arable and kept in his own little house because he is the runt of the litter. When he becomes too large to handle easily, Fern sells Wilber to her uncle, Homer Zuckerman. At the Zuckermans' farm, Wilber lives in the barn cellar with a comfortable manure pile for his bed. Wilber very much wants a friend but finds the other animals either too busy to pay attention to him or unwilling to befriend a manure-covered pig. One day while weeping and feeling sorry for himself, Wilber meets Charlotte, a gray spider. At first he is repulsed by her habit of eating insects, but after getting to know her, he decides he likes her. When Wilber discovers that he is going to be butchered in the fall, Charlotte decides that she must save his life. She spins a web interwoven with the words "some pig" near Wilber's pen. Homer and his neighbors are sure this is a sign that they "have a very unusual pig" and decide not to butcher Wilber. Meanwhile Charlotte, to ensure Wilber's safety, rewords her web, describing Wilber as "terrific" and then "radiant." When the Zuckermans decide to exhibit Wilber at the county fair in the fall, Charlotte, who now tires with the least exertion, goes with Wilber by hiding in his crate, as does Templeton the rat. In Wilber's stall at the fair, Charlotte spins a web which says "humble." She then crawls to the rafters, fashions a sac filled with spider eggs, and prepares to die. Wilber, heartbroken at his friend's impending death, resolves to take the sac to the farm with him and care for Charlotte's children. Templeton climbs to the sac and releases it from its moorings. Wilber gently scoops the sac into his mouth, carries it back to the farm, and cares for it during the cold winter months. When Charlotte's five hundred fourteen children hatch in the spring, three daughters take up residence in the barn. Wilber is overjoyed, for he has Charlotte's children to remind him of his dearest friend; he also has new friends of his own.

Charlotte's death late in the story and the subsequent birth of her children help explain how the cycle of life continues through children. The story describes sorrow after the death of a close friend and shows how memories of a dead friend can keep that person alive in one's mind. This touching classic is an excellent read-aloud book for a younger child or for a group.

Ages 8-12

Also available in:
Braille—*Charlotte's Web*
Library of Congress (NLSBPH)

Cassette—*Charlotte's Web*
Library of Congress (NLSBPH)

Paperbound—*Charlotte's Web*
HarperCollins Publishers, Inc.

Talking Book—*Charlotte's Web*
Library of Congress (NLSBPH)

619

White, Elwyn Brooks

The Trumpet of the Swan

Black/white illustrations by Edward Frascino.
HarperCollins Publishers, Inc., 1970.
(120 pages)

MUTENESS
Compensation
Honesty/Dishonesty
Responsibility: accepting

Louis, a trumpeter swan, was born without a voice. Everyday communication is a problem, but attracting a beautiful lady swan is almost impossible. To help himself, Louis learns to read and write. But this sort of communication works only with people; it has no effect at all on other swans. Louis's concerned father has another idea: he robs ("only because he hasn't any money") a music store and presents Louis with a trumpet. Louis learns to play the trumpet so well that he is able to earn a lot of money with it. He wins the heart of a beautiful lady swan and gives his earnings to his grateful father so that he can repay the music store and redeem his honor.

Louis's willingness to deal with his handicap leads him into a life rich in adventures and social relationships. This delightful book develops many wholesome themes, among them personal integrity, respect for wildlife, and the responsibility of one living thing for another.

Ages 9-13

Also available in:
Braille—*The Trumpet of the Swan*
Library of Congress (NLSBPH)

Cassette—*The Trumpet of the Swan*
Library of Congress (NLSBPH)

Paperbound—*The Trumpet of the Swan*
HarperCollins Publishers, Inc.

Talking Book—*The Trumpet of the Swan*
Library of Congress (NLSBPH)

620

Wilder, Laura Ingalls

By the Shores of Silver Lake

Black/white illustrations by Garth Williams.
HarperCollins Publishers, Inc., 1953.
(291 pages)

FAMILY: Unity
Blindness
Moving

During the 1870s, the Ingalls family is living near Plum Creek. Everyone but Pa and Laura has scarlet fever. One morning, while the family is recovering, Pa's sister, Aunt Docia, suddenly arrives with a job offer for Pa; she asks if he can come to work for the railroad in the Dakota Territory. Pa accepts the job and sells their farm. He goes on ahead, leaving the rest of the family to follow when daughter Mary is strong enough. The scarlet fever has left her blind, and she is still too weak to travel. When Mary is strong enough, Ma and the four girls take their first train ride to join Pa. Thirteen-year-old Laura functions as Mary's sight. The family lives temporarily in railroad camps, but as winter approaches and the camps disband, the family moves into the company surveyor's large house. When spring arrives, they take in travelers for room and board. Pa finds a homestead he likes, files a claim for it, and puts up part of a house. The family is happy and hopes to live there always.

This children's classic, the fourth in a series of eight books, depicts the life of a pioneer family whose strength and courage are shown most clearly in its matter-of-fact acceptance of one member's blindness. The story's main appeal lies in its depiction of the love and unity existing in the Wilder family, who do everything together.

Ages 8-11

Also available in:
Braille—*By the Shores of Silver Lake*
Library of Congress (NLSBPH)

Cassette—*By the Shores of Silver Lake*
Library of Congress (NLSBPH)

Paperbound—*By the Shores of Silver Lake*
HarperCollins Publishers, Inc.

Talking Book—*By the Shores of Silver Lake*
Library of Congress (NLSBPH)

621

Wilkinson, Brenda Scott

Ludell

HarperCollins Publishers, Inc., 1975.
(170 pages, paperbound)

AFRICAN-AMERICAN
GRANDPARENT: Living in Home of
Asthma
Boy-girl relationships
Friendship: best friend
Maturation
Parent/Parents: substitute
Poverty
School: pupil-teacher relationships
Self, attitude toward: respect

We first meet Ludell Wilson, a black girl living in Waycross, Georgia, when she is in fifth grade during the 1950s. Ludell lives with her grandmother; since her best friend, Ruthie Mae Johnson, lives next door, the two girls are often together. At school they often share lunch, for Ludell is one of the few children in her class who usually has lunch money. One afternoon Ruthie May feels a craving for cookies and candy and decides to try charging them on her mother's account at the neighborhood store. It works and Ruthie Mae goes on charging treats and sharing them with Ludell. At school the only day Ludell enjoys at all is Friday, when one can buy hot dogs for lunch. Other days, school bores her, and she does not like her teacher. Not at all boring is the day when she learns that her mother, living in New York since Ludell was a baby, is sending a television set. Her grandmother warns the girl not to talk about it to anyone because the set may be a long time coming, but very soon Ludell has told the whole Johnson family next door. The set finally does arrive in time for Christmas, but it has been broken. Once her grandmother settles the claim with the shippers, she and Ludell go shopping for a new set, which the girl likewise expects for Christmas. It does not appear, but some other good presents do, including the blue jeans she has wanted so badly. She surmises that her grandmother needed the money to straighten out some tax problems. A chance to earn money herself arrives that summer, when Ludell joins Ruthie Mae, her older brother Willie, and the two younger Johnson boys on a cotton-picking crew. But during her first week out, as has happened before, she has an asthma attack, and that is the end of her cottonpicking. Instead, she helps with the laundry her grandmother takes in. That fall Ludell and Willie, the latter held back unfairly, are in the sixth grade together, and Ruthie Mae, no luckier than her brother, is in fifth grade again. Soon Ludell is baby-sitting and doing light cleaning for several white women. In seventh grade she has the school principal for her teacher and, finding her less frightening than other teachers, begins to enjoy school. In fact, Ludell finds herself chosen for many favored tasks and becomes known as the teacher's pet. That year, too, she starts going with Willie and experiences the excitement of a boyfriend, a first kiss. And her grandmother buys the long-awaited television set. At school Ludell develops skill in writing and finds she wants to become a writer. By the end of seventh grade, she is filled with the twin joys of discovery and promise.

This warm, candid story, based on the author's girlhood in a small Southern town, unfolds the fears, interests, frustrations, and dreams of a young black girl approaching adolescence. While racial prejudice is not a central theme, the author shows how Ludell's experiences differ from other children's because she is black. A skillful use of black dialect adds interest and authenticity to the book, but may also be hard for some readers to follow. Reading the dialogue aloud may both vivify and clarify the more confusing words. Ludell's story is continued in the sequel, *Ludell and Willie.*

Ages 10-14

Also available in:
Cassette for the Blind—*Ludell*
Library of Congress (NLSBPH)

622

Wilkinson, Brenda Scott

Ludell and Willie

HarperCollins Publishers, Inc., 1977.
(181 pages)

BOY-GIRL RELATIONSHIPS: Dating
African-American
Age: senility
Death: of grandparent
Grandparent: living in home of
Parent/Parents: substitute
Poverty
Responsibility: accepting

Ludell, a high school senior in the early 1960s, in Waycross, Georgia, plans to marry her boyfriend, Willie, after their graduation. Both are from poor, fatherless families, and both realize the importance of finishing high school. Ludell's grandmother, who has cared for her since Dessa, her mother, went to New York to find work, keeps a tight rein on the girl; Ludell has therefore never been to a football game or a dance. She resents such restrictions, but tolerates them because Willie, a thoughtful and patient young man, does not wish to anger his future in-law. On top of all this, Ludell must spend her Saturdays cleaning house for a white woman, a job she finds demeaning. Only the thought of her upcoming marriage and her secret desire to become a writer keep her going. Suddenly, to her surprise and delight, her grandmother begins to ease up and allow her a dance and an evening out now and then. Just as unexpectedly, however, Grandma's health begins to fail and soon Ludell is spending most of her time caring for an old woman both bedridden and incontinent. Burdened by the extra work, Ludell is nevertheless relieved that her now childlike grandmother can no longer boss her around. But she is shocked and grieved when Grandma dies. Helpful neighbors make the sad time bearable—but when Dessa arrives for the funeral and announces she plans to take Ludell back to New York City with her, the girl is plunged into despair. She and Willie try their best to dissuade Dessa, and a kind neighbor offers to house Ludell for the six weeks left before she finishes school; but Dessa stubbornly insists, and Ludell, broken-hearted, goes off to finish school in a strange city. Ludell and Willie write to each other, vowing to be reunited and to marry after graduation.

Two adolescents, forced by the harsh circumstances of their lives to grow up quickly, cling to a love that appears strong enough to survive their separation. Ludell and Willie talk not only about love and marriage but about their families and missing fathers as well. The lively dialogue is written in Southern black dialect whose phonetic spelling may prove difficult for some readers. This is a sequel to *Ludell,* and, like it, is a sensitively written story based on the author's girlhood, telling of adolescent fears, disappointments, joys, and expectations.

Ages 12 and up

Also available in:
Cassette for the Blind—*Ludell and Willie*
Library of Congress (NLSBPH)

623

Williams, Barbara Wright

Kevin's Grandma

Black/white illustrations by Kay Chorao.
Dutton Children's Books, 1975.
(30 pages counted, paperbound)

GRANDPARENT: Love for

Two small boys have much about grandmothers to compare notes on. The narrator's grandma brings him crayons, coloring books, and ice cream when he's sick; his friend Kevin's grandma brings Kevin *Mad* magazine and homemade peanut-butter soup. The narrator's grandma drives an air-conditioned blue station wagon and takes him to Florida; Kevin's grandma drives a Honda 90 and they hitchhike to California. The narrator's grandma belongs to a bridge club, a garden club, and a music club; Kevin's grandma belongs to a karate club, a scuba-divers club, and a mountain-climbing club. Kevin's grandma used to work in a circus and goes skydiving. The narrator is not sure he believes everything he hears about Kevin's grandma.

This delightful story shows one grandma embarked on surprising and exciting adventures which she shares with her grandson. The other grandma leads a more conventional life but is no less prized by her grandson, cheering him when he's sick, treating him on his birthday, taking him on a vacation. The narrator tells the story of his times with his grandmother simply and lovingly. Kevin has obviously embellished the truth. The two grandmothers are presented alternately with charming black-and-white illustrations contrasting the two from page to page.

Ages 4-7

Also available in:
No other form known

624

Williams, Margery Bianco

The Velveteen Rabbit: Or, How Toys Become Real

Color illustrations by William Nicholson.
Henry Holt & Company, Inc., 1983.
(33 pages) o.p.

LOVE, MEANING OF

Soon after he is given to the boy as a Christmas present, the Velveteen Rabbit is put away in the nursery cupboard with the other toys. There in the cupboard, the more expensive toys look down on the Rabbit, and the mechanical toys point out how much better they are than he. The only toy that is friendly to Velveteen Rabbit is the Skin Horse, who is very old and wise. The Skin Horse has become "real" because he was once loved by the boy's uncle. The Velveteen Rabbit wants to be "real" like the Skin Horse, even though he realizes that this may make him shabby from having his fur loved off. Finally the Velveteen Rabbit is granted his wish. The boy, who has been taking the Velveteen Rabbit to bed every night since he lost his china dog, shares confidences with the Rabbit and plays with him in the yard. The boy loves the little Rabbit as a source of security, and he even tells his nanny that the Velveteen Rabbit is "real." From that day on, the Velveteen Rabbit is so very happy that he has become "real" and so glad to return the little boy's love that he does not notice how shabby he is becoming. It is only after the Rabbit has waited patiently under the bedclothes during the boy's bout with scarlet fever that he realizes how he looks. Because he is now old and shabby and "full of scarlet fever germs," he must be burned with the other contaminated articles. The Velveteen Rabbit is discarded on a trash heap behind the garden, and there in the dead of night he sheds a real tear for his loss of love. This tear turns into a flower from which a fairy emerges. She changes the Velveteen Rabbit into a real rabbit—the reward for all toys that are loved by children.

This enchanting, fanciful children's classic reveals the magical effects of love. Love is something that transcends physical appearance and social standing. And although it may grow out of pain and sacrifice, love is the bringer of life that transforms the toy rabbit into something "real."

Ages 5-10

Also available in:
No other form known

625

Willoughby, Elaine Macmann

Boris and the Monsters

Color illustrations by Lynn Munsinger.
Houghton Mifflin Co., 1980.
(32 pages)

BEDTIME
FEAR: of Darkness
Pets: love for

Though little Boris is assured by his parents that there are no monsters, he cannot overcome his dread of bedtime. Every night he finds excuses to stay up later. He must feed his goldfish, work on his airplane, pump up his football. Despite his efforts, though, bedtime always comes and in the darkness he sees shapes that form and dance. Certain the shapes are monsters, Boris shuts his eyes tightly and whispers, "There are no monsters." It doesn't help, but luckily the monsters don't grab him. In the morning he searches his room, finding no sign of the strange nighttime shapes. One evening his father helps him look, but even together they find nothing. Boris decides he needs something ferocious to frighten the monsters away—like a tiger or at least a big, fierce dog. So he and his father bring Ivan the Terrible home from the pet shop. Although Ivan is only a small puppy, he will grow to be big and ferocious. Boris puts a soft rug beside his bed for Ivan, and then his mother turns off the light. Boris says firmly, "There are no monsters in this house." Suddenly loud, mournful sounds pierce the darkness. It is Ivan. Boris takes the puppy under his covers. "I shall just have to protect him until he isn't afraid of the dark anymore!" says Boris. "Like me."

A small boy masters his fear of the dark when he moves to protect something more helpless than he is, his frightened puppy. This amusing and reassuring story is enhanced by softly colored, cartoonlike illustrations. Young children will enjoy the funny resolution of Boris's and Ivan's fears.

Ages 4-7

Also available in:
Paperbound—*Boris and the Monsters*
Houghton Mifflin Co.

626
Winthrop, Elizabeth
Marathon Miranda
Puffin Books, 1990.
(155 pages, paperbound)

ASTHMA
DETERMINATION
FRIENDSHIP: Meaning of
Adoption: feelings about
Fear: of failure
Helping
Running away

Suffering her third asthma attack in a week, an embarrassed Miranda has to leave her ninth-grade gym class accompanied by her best friend, Katherine. The next day, when her neighbor and friend Margaret, an elderly widow, takes Miranda to the zoo, she sees Katherine with "nerdy old Viola" who has made unkind remarks about Miranda and her asthma. Feeling deserted, Miranda decides Margaret is now her best friend. But while walking her dog, Miranda meets and befriends an enthusiastic jogger, Phoebe. She also meets—and jealously resents—Margaret's friend Steven Delaney, a young television actor. Phoebe invites Miranda to dinner, during which Phoebe, an only child, gets the constant, undivided attention of her well-to-do, formal parents. At Phoebe's urging, Miranda reluctantly agrees to try jogging, thinking it may strengthen her lungs. She enjoys running more than she expected and becomes devoted to the routine. Soon Phoebe encourages her to train for an upcoming marathon. Miranda hesitates, whereupon Phoebe and Miranda's older brother hint that she uses her asthma to keep from having to risk failure. One day, while the girls are running, Miranda has a severe asthma attack. Phoebe calls the police, who rush Miranda to the hospital for adrenalin. She recovers swiftly and runs again the next day, but Phoebe now has doubts that this is wise. In the park Miranda sees Steven with a young woman. When Miranda visits Margaret, who is haggard and depressed, the woman shows her a picture of her adopted son, now dead, and admits that she hasn't seen Steven since he met the younger woman. Miranda's sympathetic family invites Margaret to join them on a visit to Miranda's grandfather's farm in Vermont. Before they leave, Miranda tries several times to see Phoebe but is told that her friend has a mysterious illness and is being kept isolated. When at last the girls meet, Phoebe tells Miranda she has suddenly, during a parental argument, learned a terrible truth about herself: she is adopted. She has been sick about the news, and her parents will not discuss it with her. The girls part, Miranda to the farm, Phoebe to Connecticut for a vacation. Then Phoebe's mother calls the farm to say that Phoebe has run away. Soon the girl appears at the farm and begs Miranda and her brother to hide her. They do, but she is discovered and runs away again. The family finds her and returns her to the farm, where Margaret, who has found much in common with Miranda's grandfather, befriends her. When Phoebe's parents come for her, they are persuaded to let Phoebe stay for a while with Margaret in a little cottage at the farm. Order is restored; the girls stay an extra week on the farm and then return to the city. Phoebe's parents agree to talk with her about her adoption, and she and Miranda successfully complete the marathon.

Miranda, a forthright and objective girl, narrates this warm story about friendship and relationships. She tells of refusing to allow her asthma to limit her unnecessarily, of confronting and overcoming her fear of failure. Miranda also makes a new friend, strengthens her ties with an old one, and unites both. Readers will find her a believable, caring protagonist. Miranda's story continues in the sequel, *Miranda in the Middle.*

Ages 9-11

Also available in:
No other form known

W

627
Winthrop, Elizabeth
Miranda in the Middle
Puffin Books, 1990.
(128 pages, paperbound)

FRIENDSHIP: Meaning of
VALUES/VALUING: Moral/Ethical
Asthma
Friendship: best friend
Honesty/Dishonesty

When thirteen-year-old Miranda met her best friend, Phoebe, an avid jogger, she too took up jogging. Miranda runs with her dog, Frisbee, in hopes of curing her asthma. Recently Phoebe, who is angry with her parents for not telling her until now that she was adopted, has developed a rebellious attitude. When Phillip, a boy her parents wouldn't approve of because he smokes and drinks, asks her out, she begs Miranda to cover for her. Miranda does. One day, while she's jogging without Phoebe, Miranda meets ten-year-old Michael Oliver. Although she doesn't realize it, he is the unwitting guinea pig for a class experiment that Miranda's older brother, Alex, is conducting. Alex has observed Michael Oliver sitting on his fire escape day after day, apparently taking notes on the Methodist church below. When he informs Miranda of his suspicions that the church is being sold to a development corporation to be torn down for a high-rise, Miranda tells her father. Since a high-rise building will completely block their river view, Miranda's father forms a neighborhood committee to check into Michael Oliver's suspicions. When these suspicions are confirmed, the committee takes steps to prevent the destruction of the church. A member of this committee, an older friend of Miranda's family named Margaret, has recently become romantically involved with Miranda's grandfather. Miranda is nervous about this romance, because she's afraid that if they marry she will lose her two favorite people. Meanwhile, Alex learns that his "subject" is Miranda's friend, and he connives to become Michael Oliver's extra-special friend so he can observe him better. The lonely, unsuspecting boy becomes very attached to Alex. Miranda, feeling guilty at her position in the middle, wishes Alex would drop the project and tells him so, but even though Alex too is conscience-stricken, it's too late for him to start another paper on another person. Michael Oliver is crushed the day he enters Miranda's apartment alone and discovers Alex's report. Neither Alex nor Miranda can console him. Now Miranda feels lost: Phoebe is dating and Michael Oliver is angry. When Phoebe wants Miranda to lie for her again, she refuses, telling Phoebe's mother the truth when she calls asking for Phoebe. Phoebe is furious; Miranda feels she's lost another friend. Then Alex and Miranda together ask Michael Oliver to be their friend again—Alex gives his report to Michael Oliver instead of handing it in. The boy forgives them. As a Christmas gift and peace offering, Miranda sends Phoebe the pedometer she's been wanting and their friendship resumes. Phoebe confides that Phillip hasn't called since their last fatal date and that she has been grounded for life. Miranda recommends building up her parents' trust by following all rules, and Phoebe agrees to try. It is finally decided that the church will be preserved as an architectural monument. To cap Miranda's happiness, when her grandfather and Margaret announce their engagement and then marry, Miranda realizes she is not losing two friends—she is gaining a grandmother.

In this humorous first-person sequel to *Marathon Miranda,* Miranda must choose between her principles and her friendships. She finds to her relief and satisfaction that a true friend will appreciate her integrity. This story of friendship lost and restored will appeal to the intended audience.

Ages 9-13

Also available in:
Braille—*Miranda in the Middle*
Library of Congress (NLSBPH)

Cassette—*Miranda in the Middle*
Library of Congress (NLSBPH)

628

Winthrop, Elizabeth

Sloppy Kisses

Color illustrations by Anne Burgess.
Puffin Books, 1983.
(28 pages counted, paperbound)

PEER RELATIONSHIPS: Peer Pressures
Communication: parent-child
Embarrassment

"Emmy Lou's family loved to kiss." This doesn't disturb little Emmy Lou until the day her friend Rosemary sees Emmy Lou's father kissing her goodbye at school. Rosemary informs Emmy Lou that kissing is for babies. The next time Emmy Lou's father wants to kiss her, she tells him what Rosemary said. From then on her parents kiss only her younger sister, Dolly, giving Emmy Lou pats on the shoulder. One night, Emmy Lou finds it hard to fall asleep. She tiptoes into her parents' room. They ask her if she wants some juice, another blanket, or a story, but each time she answers no. "I know what you need," says her father. He grabs her up and gives her a great big sloppy kiss. Then her mother kisses her softly. Tucked back into bed, Emmy Lou falls right to sleep. The next morning her father drops her off at school. Spying Rosemary, he pats Emmy Lou's shoulder and turns to leave. Emmy Lou begs him for her goodbye kiss as Rosemary watches, disgusted. Emmy Lou tells her, "Kissing is for everybody." She gives the surprised Rosemary a quick little kiss on the cheek.

This appealing story gives a humorous account of the need children have for physical affection. The disarming Emmy Lou discovers this for herself and then teaches it to her doubting friend. The catchy title and small size of the book will delight young children, as will the bright pictures of the characters, a family of pigs.

Ages 4-7

Also available in:
No other form known

629

Wittels, Harriet and Joan Greisman

Things I Hate

Color illustrations by Jerry McConnel.
Human Sciences Press, 1973.
(35 pages counted)

ANGER
Fear

An unnamed boy about eight years old hates to go shopping with his mother, but he likes to run for the bus and get a treat after shopping. The possibility of getting lost while shopping in a big store gives the boy a "scare." The boy doesn't like to go to bed before his parents do; it doesn't seem fair that they can stay up and watch more television. Also, the shadows on the walls in a dark room at bedtime can be scary. He finds it pleasant to fall asleep, however, and to have good dreams in a bed where the pillow and sheets feel cool, soft, and clean. The boy hates leaving in a rush for school, and he doesn't like the fact that he cannot talk in class, must stay at his desk, and must sometimes wait in line. But he does enjoy seeing his friends at school. Going to the dentist and sitting in the oversized chair with the dentist breathing in his face makes the boy quite unhappy. All the other kids in the dentist's office are "shaking with fear," too, though. His favorite part of the visit comes when the dentist has finished and the boy's toothache disappears. The boy concludes that when his parents and teachers are proud of him, it has been worth putting up with all the things he hates.

This first-person narrative reminds children that there are positive aspects to things that they dread or find distasteful. According to the authors, the book could be used to help children "overcome fear or stubbornness in anxiety-provoking situations." This is one in a series of books by this publisher dealing with important psychological themes.

Ages 4-8

Also available in:
No other form known

630

Wittman, Sally

A Special Trade

Color illustrations by Karen Gundersheimer.
HarperCollins Publishers, Inc., 1978.
(32 pages, paperbound)

AGE: Respect for
FRIENDSHIP: Meaning of

Bartholomew is an old man when he first meets Nelly, the baby next door. He takes her for daily walks in her stroller, stopping so they can pat friendly dogs and the two of them occasionally racing through the neighbor's sprinkler. When Nelly learns to walk, Bartholomew is careful to offer her help only when she needs it. They are so often together the neighbors call them "ham and eggs." Nelly grows older and goes to school, while Bartholomew grows older and sometimes needs her help crossing the street. One day, while out alone, he falls and is taken to the hospital. Nelly writes to him every day, urging him to come home so they can go for walks again. But he returns in a wheelchair and says to Nelly, "I guess our walks are over." Nelly does not agree. She now takes him for walks, just as he once took her. "Now it's my turn to push," she says, "and Bartholomew's turn to sit . . . kind of like a trade."

This story of friendship through time and change is exceptionally well written and illustrated, and makes for amusing reading at any age. In a few brief pages, the author gives two characters vibrant life, persuades us of their strong friendship, and effects a logical role reversal, all this without affectation or sentimentality. The witty illustrations are consistent with the naturalness of the text.

Ages 2-5

Also available in:
No other form known

631

Wojciechowska, Maia Rodman

Shadow of a Bull

Black/white illustrations by Alvin Smith.
Atheneum Publishers, 1964.
(165 pages)

COURAGE, MEANING OF
Determination
Expectations
Fear: of failure
Maturation

Manolo Olivar lives in the shadow of his father's greatness. His father, the greatest bullfighter in Spain, was killed in a bullring at age twenty-two. The little Spanish town where Manolo lives still basks in the glory of his father's past. All the townspeople expect Manolo to be exactly like his father. Manolo, however, feels he is a coward because he is afraid of bullfighting. He doesn't want to go into the ring, nor does he wish to kill bulls. Yet Manolo feels that he cannot fail his community, so at the age of ten, he begins to train. His tutors insist that he follow his father's development as a bullfighter exactly. As his twelfth birthday approaches, Manolo is supposed to kill his first bull just as his father did. Manolo struggles between his fear of the bull, his fear of failure, and his desire to fulfill the dreams of his father's admirers. Fighting his first bull, Manolo faces and conquers his fear. As he exults in the beauty of his movements and in the way the bull follows his cape, Manolo realizes that he does not have to be a bullfighter, for he has proven to himself that he can handle himself well in the ring. He tells his sponsors his decision not to become a bullfighter. He then is free to leave the bullring and pursue his own choices in life.

In quiet, powerful prose, the author perceptively depicts a young boy's agony as he fights and conquers cowardice and accepts the freedom and responsibility of determining his own career. Much information about bullfighting is included in the story, and there is a glossary of bullfighting terms.

Ages 11 and up

Also available in:
Braille—*Shadow of a Bull*
Library of Congress (NLSBPH)

Cassette—*Shadow of a Bull*
Library of Congress (NLSBPH)

Paperbound—*Shadow of a Bull*
Aladdin Books

632

Wojciechowska, Maia Rodman

Tuned Out

HarperCollins Publishers, Inc., 1968.
(125 pages) o.p.

DRUGS: Dependence on
Maturation
Reality, escaping
Sibling: love for

Summer has come, and sixteen-year-old Jim joyfully awaits the arrival of his brother Kevin, who has been away at college since the previous September. Jim idolizes Kevin and has a great summer vacation planned for him. But when Kevin arrives, Jim is shocked to see him so changed. Kevin has turned against the "Establishment" and, seeking new meaning and values in his life, he has taken to smoking marijuana and using LSD. The two brothers go to Greenwich Village and there Kevin buys some acid. One Saturday, when his parents are away, he takes it. Jim is with him, and when Kevin starts to "freak out," Jim calls the family doctor and an ambulance. Kevin is admitted to Sweetmountain Hospital and committed to the care of Doctor Given. For weeks he is not permitted visitors, and Jim thinks the doctor is trying to turn Kevin against the family. When Jim goes to the hospital intending to help Kevin escape, he learns that Kevin doesn't even want to see him. Jim is crushed to think that the brother to whom he has been so devoted doesn't love him anymore. The rest of the vacation drags by. One day in late summer, Kevin calls; he wants to see Jim. Jim then realizes that he has selfishly nursed hurt feelings all summer while Kevin has been sick. At the hospital, he and Kevin talk. Kevin has recovered and matured. Jim is glad to see his brother looking so healthy and normal but still is sad to think that things can never be as they were when they were boys.

Through a diary Jim tells this intense, candid story of a summer of disbelief, anguish, and maturation. It is the account of a young man who feels unable to live up to standards set by his family and who turns to drugs to solve his problems. Through Jim's bitterness and pain, he struggles to understand the changes in his life and his family and matures in the process. The scenes involving drugs and their effects on a young person are traumatic.

Ages 12 and up

Also available in:
No other form known

633

Wolde, Gunilla

Betsy and Peter Are Different

Translated from the Swedish by Alison Winn.
Color illustrations by the author.
Random House, Inc., 1979.
(23 pages counted) o.p.

DIFFERENCES, HUMAN

Although little Betsy and Peter are the same age, they are different from each other. Peter lives in a small house; Betsy lives in a large apartment building. Betsy's mother and father take turns staying home with her; Peter has no father but does have his grandmother living with him and his mother. Betsy has a baby brother but no dog, and Peter has a dog but no baby brother. Betsy gets bored playing by herself, but when she plays with Peter they think up exciting games. Even when they dress up to look the same, they end up looking different. Betsy and Peter like being different from each other. They know it wouldn't be nearly as much fun if they were exactly alike.

Two preschoolers discover the advantages of human differences. Cheerful, attractive illustrations accompany the simple text and down-to-earth examples of the variety among human beings. This is one of a series of books about Betsy, her family and friends.

Ages 3-6

Also available in:
No other form known

634

Wolde, Gunilla

Betsy and the Chicken Pox

Translated from the Swedish.
Color illustrations by the author.
Random House, Inc., 1990.
(23 pages counted)

COMMUNICABLE DISEASES: Chicken Pox
Illnesses: of sibling
Jealousy: sibling

Betsy's baby brother is cranky, covered with spots, and feverish. When the doctor arrives and examines him, she neglects to say hello to Betsy. Even after she has finished diagnosing chicken pox and prescribing medication for the brother, the doctor says nothing to Betsy. After the doctor has gone, Betsy paints spots on herself. Her parents, busy caring for the baby, ignore Betsy—even with spots. Suddenly Betsy begins to yell, calling her father "mean," her mother "horrible," and her brother "stupid." Everyone gets angry; everyone quiets down; and mother, father, and Betsy care for the baby brother. That evening, when Betsy's painted spots are washed off, Daddy discovers real spots all over her. Now Betsy has the chicken pox—but doesn't want them any more.

A little girl, ignored when her brother falls ill, attempts—through imitation and anger—to gain attention. The anger generates anger in return. But thoughtful parents can recognize jealousy and reassure the child against the fears that cause it. This is one in a series of books about Betsy.

Ages 3-7

Also available in:
No other form known

635

Wolde, Gunilla

Betsy and the Doctor

Translated from the Swedish.
Color illustrations by the author.
Random House, Inc., 1990.
(23 pages counted)

HOSPITAL, GOING TO
Accidents
Doctor, going to
Sutures

Little Betsy has fallen on her head from the climbing tree on the nursery-school playground. Blood is trickling down her face and she is crying. Robert, a nursery-school employee, comes, picks her up, and says she must see a doctor. When they arrive at the hospital, Robert and Betsy must wait their turn, and Betsy wonders what the doctor will do to her. When her turn comes, a nurse bathes her forehead and the doctor checks for broken bones. The doctor explains that he will close the cut with stitches after he gives her a shot so the stitching won't hurt. After the shot, which pricks a little, Betsy no longer feels any pain at all, and the doctor makes three stitches, applies lotion to them, and bandages the cut. Now Betsy is eager to tell her parents and friends all about what has happened. A week later, when the stitches are removed, she feels only a little tickle on her forehead and sees a tiny red mark where the cut has been.

All young children could benefit from having this simple little book read aloud to them. They would be somewhat prepared and less anxious if an accident someday necessitates an emergency visit to the doctor. The presentation is honest and reassuring, and invites group discussion. This is one in a series of books about Betsy.

Ages 3-7

Also available in:
No other form known

636

Wolde, Gunilla

Betsy and the Vacuum Cleaner

Translated from the Swedish by Alison Winn.
Color illustrations by the author.
Random House, Inc., 1979.
(23 pages counted) o.p.

CHORES
Curiosity
Fear: of vacuum cleaner
Helping

When Betsy's father vacuums, she likes to sit on the vacuum cleaner and pretend it's an animal making a whirring sound. She knows her father turns on a switch to make it go, and she also knows she's not to turn it on herself. Sometimes, though, he lets her help him. The vacuum sucks up all sorts of dust and sand and even a button, a Lego block, and a piece of paper. Betsy discovers that her teddy bear is too big to be vacuumed up. So is she, although some of her hair gets sucked into the tube of the vacuum. When she pretends to vacuum up her baby brother, he gets scared and yells for his father. So Betsy vacuums up his sock instead. In an attempt to retrieve the sock, Betsy takes the cover off the vacuum cleaner after her father has shut it off and unplugged it. She finds a bag full of dust and dirt, which she empties onto the floor. She also finds sand, the button, the Lego, the piece of paper, and the sock. Her brother is glad to have his sock back, but Betsy wonders how happy her father will be with the pile of dirt on the floor. She also wonders how the vacuum works. As she replaces the vacuum cleaner cover, she decides that some things shouldn't be vacuumed up. Next time she'll be more careful. She then cleans up the pile of dirt she made on the floor. Her little brother is afraid of the vacuum when it's on, but when it's turned off he sits on it, pretending he's riding an animal. However, he makes his own whirring sound.

A little girl's interest in an ordinary household chore leads her to help with the vacuuming and eventually to become curious about how the vacuum cleaner works. Betsy's father is apparently in charge of the vacuuming and at least some of the child care in this family; no mother is seen. Some safety guidelines about working with an electrical appliance are included in the story line. Included also is a diagram of a vacuum cleaner that will interest many preschoolers and may prove especially valuable in consoling youngsters who are afraid of vacuum cleaners. The illustrations are attractive and lighthearted, reflecting the touch of whimsy in the text. This is one of a series of books about Betsy, her family and friends.

Ages 3-6

Also available in:
No other form known

637

Wolde, Gunilla

Betsy's Baby Brother

Translated from the Swedish.
Color illustrations by the author.
Random House, Inc., 1990.
(23 pages counted)

SIBLING: New Baby

Little Betsy has a cute, much littler baby brother. Asleep, he is quiet, but awake he often cries. When he cries to be fed, their mother feeds him. The truth is, Betsy resents the amount of attention her baby brother receives and sometimes wants to give him away, so as to have her mother all to herself. But at other times Betsy likes her baby brother and is glad to be his helpful older sister. She can help give the baby a bath and can change his dirty diaper and put soothing ointment on his bottom. But the baby—like all babies, according to Mother—likes to grab Betsy's hair, and that hurts. But like all babies, this one gets sleepy, too, and when he does, Betsy likes to talk to him quietly until he falls sound asleep. On the whole, Betsy thinks baby brothers are annoying and lovable, mostly lovable.

This simple, colorfully illustrated book shows candidly an older child's feelings when a new baby is brought into the home. It is one in a series about Betsy.

Ages 2-5

Also available in:
No other form known

638

Wolde, Gunilla

Betsy's First Day at Nursery School

Translated from the Swedish.
Color illustrations by the author.
Random House, Inc., 1982.
(24 pages counted) o.p.

NURSERY SCHOOL

Although Betsy doubts nursery school will be any fun, she goes along with her mother and baby brother. She does not speak to the man who greets them there, because the other children are staring at her, and she chooses to keep her snowsuit on while the man shows them around. In one room filled with pillows she feels like jumping but is too ill at ease with the other children. Betsy's brother likes the youngest children's room but Betsy goes on to see the bathroom where each child has a specially marked place to keep a towel and toothbrush. Betsy's place is marked with a carrot. In the kitchen a lady is cooking food in large pots, and in the cloakroom there are specially marked hooks, Betsy's marked with a carrot again. The man tells her she can hang up her things, but she takes off only her boots. While her mother is talking to the man, Betsy and another girl make faces at each other. Soon they are laughing and the girl tells Betsy her name. Her coat hook is right next to Betsy's, and Betsy takes off her snowsuit so the two can go to the pillow room to jump. Playing so long with her friend, Betsy suddenly remembers her mother and brother and runs to find them. The brother has been playing too and is tired, so her mother says it is time to go home until tomorrow. Betsy waves good-bye to her friend and decides that nursery school is fun after all.

This book, one in a series about Betsy, usefully anticipates the new experiences of nursery school. The colorful illustrations show fun-loving, energetic children who often create a happy disorder.

Ages 2-5

Also available in:
No other form known

639

Wolde, Gunilla

This Is Betsy

Translated from the Swedish.
Color illustrations by the author.
Random House, Inc., 1990.
(23 pages counted)

AUTONOMY

Young Betsy is sometimes happy, sometimes sad. Usually, she puts her jeans and sweater on the right way, but sometimes she puts her jeans on her head and her sweater on her legs to be funny. Most of the time she brushes her hair nicely and drinks cocoa from a mug, but sometimes she prefers messy hair and drinks cocoa from a saucer. She enjoys playing with blocks but gets angry when they fall down. She often shares her teddy bear with her baby brother but may suddenly grab it away from him. Betsy likes to take a bath and get clean all over; she also likes to play in the mud and get dirty all over. She hears her father perfectly when he announces bedtime, but sometimes she pretends she cannot. When she is sleepy, Betsy puts on her pajamas and gets into bed. True, she sometimes asks for a drink of water or a story. But always, eventually, she falls asleep.

With the aid of colorful pictures the author shows a little girl's often contradictory yet perfectly normal feelings and actions. This is one is a series of books about Betsy.

Ages 2-5

Also available in:
No other form known

640
Wolf, Bernard
Anna's Silent World
Black/white photographs by the author.
HarperCollins Publishers, Inc., 1977.
(48 pages)

DEAFNESS

Six-year-old Anna, though she lives in clangorous New York City, is not bothered by noise: she was born deaf and hears only the loudest sounds. Four years' training have taught her to read, write, and talk, and she and her teachers continue to work diligently at this. Anna attends school with hearing children, and ballet classes as well, for two hearing aids help her follow the basic rhythms of music. On Saturday she plays with a hearing friend who does not always understand what she says. Anna's mother explains to the friend how difficult talking is when one has never heard speech; she also shows her the hearing aids and explains lip reading. On Christmas day Anna is delighted to receive a recorder, with which she can make her own music.

This informative book describes a week in a deaf child's life. It also examines one way of teaching the deaf, the aural-oral method. But it says nothing about another way, which depends heavily upon sign language. Since the two methods are in contention among educators, this book might be instructively supplemented by one discussing sign language, as does Edna Levine's *Lisa and Her Soundless World* (See THE BOOKFINDER, Vol. 1, 1977). The present book describes honestly the special needs of a deaf child without dwelling on the child's limitations.

Ages 5-9

Also available in:
No other form known

641
Wolf, Bernard
Don't Feel Sorry for Paul
Black/white photographs by the author.
HarperCollins Publishers, Inc., 1988.
(96 pages) o.p.

LIMBS, ABNORMAL OR MISSING
Braces on body/limbs
Encouragement
Prosthesis

This is a real-life photographic account of the challenges seven-year-old Paul Jockimo must face every day because his hands and feet are incompletely formed. Paul overcomes the difficulties by wearing a prosthesis on his right arm and one on each leg. The book includes clear descriptions of the three prostheses. It tells how they are fitted and how they operate. Paul's family does not protect him unduly. They encourage him to do things on his own. Paul is involved in horseback riding, football, biking, and other activities. Sometimes he encounters unkind remarks from his classmates, and some people treat him with pity. These reactions hurt Paul's feelings, but he is able to overlook them. Paul's mother is realistic when she says, "Don't feel sorry for Paul. He doesn't need it."

The book makes impressive use of black-and-white photographs to illustrate a typical two-week period in the life of this child. The book is appropriate for people of all ages, whether physically handicapped or not.

Ages 8 and up

Also available in:
Cassette—*Don't Feel Sorry for Paul*
Library of Congress (NLSBPH)

642
Wolff, Angelika
Mom! I Broke My Arm!
Color illustrations by Leo Glueckselig.
Lion Books, 1969.
(45 pages)

FRACTURES: of Arm
Accidents

When Steven trips on a roller skate, his arm becomes swollen and sore from the fall, so his mother takes him to the pediatrician for an X-ray. The doctor takes two different X-rays, which show that Steven's arm is broken. The pediatrician sends the boy to a bone specialist, Doctor Rose, who sets the bone and puts it in a cast. The cast is to remain on Steven's arm for about six weeks. At home, Steven wears his older brother's shirt since the cast will not fit through his own shirt sleeve. The next day at school, Steven feels very proud and important when he tells the class about his broken arm. For the next five weeks, Steven visits Doctor Rose once a week to see how the bone is healing. During this time he learns how to play checkers and receives a new jigsaw puzzle. He also discovers how to take a bath without getting the cast wet. When the cast finally is removed, Steven's arm is "pale and pinched" from being covered for so long. But soon his arm is back to normal, and his family has a party to celebrate the healed arm.

This book is written to help any parent or child who might have to deal with the problem of a broken arm. The X-raying and the setting of the bone in a cast are discussed in detail, and the pain involved is also described. Steven's adjustment to using only one arm is also described.

Ages 5-8

Also available in:
Talking Book—*Mom! I Broke My Arm!*
Library of Congress (NLSBPH)

643

Wolff, Angelika

Mom! I Need Glasses!

Color illustrations by Dorothy Hill
Lion Books, 1970. (40 pages)

GLASSES, WEARING OF

Seven-year-old Susan Monti has difficulty seeing the ball during games of catch, dislikes jumping rope because she cannot see the rope, and is unable to perceive words on the chalkboard from her seat in the back of the classroom. After Susan's teacher moves her to the front of the room, she sends a note to Susan's mother suggesting that the girl have her vision tested. Mrs. Monti agrees and sets up an appointment with an oculist, Doctor Sugarman. During Susan's examination, Doctor Sugarman has her read an eye chart, fits her with corrective lenses, and explains how the eye functions. He also gives Mrs. Monti a prescription for the lenses to take to the optician. Susan picks out her frames and is pleased with how she looks in them. Once she receives her glasses, Susan sees clearly, moves back to her regular classroom seat, and improves in sports.

This book may help calm children's fears of going to the eye doctor and their anxieties about the change that wearing glasses will have on their appearance. It emphasizes the pleasure of being able to see clearly with the aid of glasses.

Ages 5-9

Also available in:
No other form known

644

Wolitzer, Hilma

Out of Love

Farrar, Straus & Giroux, Inc., 1976.
(147 pages)

DIVORCE: of Parents
MATURATION
Boy-girl relationships
Love, meaning of
Parental: overprotection
Stepparent: mother

Thirteen-year-old Teddy Hecht can recall incidents leading up to her parents' divorce—quarrels and silences and slammed doors—but she cannot understand how they fell out of love. She lives with her mother and her eleven-year-old sister, Karen, but she regularly sees her father and wonders how his love, shown in letters she has found, could shift from her mother to his new wife, Shelley. Teddy herself is unable to see much to like in Shelley and concludes that Mother simply let her appearance go. She sets out to persuade Mother to lose weight and spruce up. Mother tries but ends up joking about her failure to improve. Teddy's best friend, Maya Goldstein, brings over some boys one day, but the visit only further sours Teddy on the whole boy-girl business. She thinks herself too plain to attract boys anyway. An aunt, finding out about her plans to reconcile her parents, admonishes Teddy that they did not divorce because of looks, that it takes much more to dissolve a marriage than fading good looks. Teddy's earlier resolve to forget about boys weakens when one of the boys who had come over calls her up. Advised by Shelley, Teddy gets a new and attractive haircut. Then friend Maya runs away to protest her parents' overprotection and Teddy successfully negotiates between parents and daughter. But her newfound confidence is shattered when she learns that Shelley is pregnant. How can the family reunite now? But then, she thinks, why pretend? Divorce is divorce. Her mother, even though alone, is "brave and kind and loving," and a person could do worse than to turn out like her.

This first-person narrative records a spirited girl discarding youthful illusions for a more mature assessment of her life and memories. The changes do not come easily, and Teddy sometimes backslides. But in the end she seems to know how things stand and to be looking ahead to future changes. This author's wit and gentle humor should help adolescents take their daily trials less seriously.

Ages 10-13

Also available in:
Paperbound—*Out of Love*
Farrar, Straus & Giroux, Inc. (Sunburst Books)

Talking Book—*Out of Love*
Library of Congress (NLSBPH)

645

Wolitzer, Hilma

Toby Lived Here

Farrar, Straus & Giroux, Inc., 1978.
(147 pages)

EMOTIONS: Accepting
FOSTER HOME
Mental illness: of parent

Though taken to a mental hospital, Toby's mother lingers with her twelve-year-old daughter in spirit. After her husband's death the mother had lived calmly, uncomplainingly, even cheerfully, doing what she had always done. Her motto: "You just have to live." Toby applies this dictum cheerlessly to living in the foster home where she and her six-year-old sister, Anne, are placed. She does not cry; she does not complain; she only silently yearns for her mother's release and attempts to ignore the present situation. Little Anne, however, takes readily to the Selwyns, a sympathetic older couple whose many foster children love them; but Toby holds back, even concealing from her new friend, Susan, where her mother is, and why. Particularly unhappy on her birthday, Toby blurts out to Mrs. Selwyn that she hates her mother for leaving them. On Mrs. Selwyn's insistent advice, a social worker arranges for the girls' first visit with their mother, who until now was allowed to see no one. At the reunion, the mother explains that she had broken down because, fearing her own emotions, she had bottled them up. Realizing that she, too, has done this, Toby tells all to Susan and calls herself a dope. Several months later, released from the hospital, her mother plans to move back to their former neighborhood. Toby would now love to stay in the new one but accepts her mother's decision, understanding that she will always be a welcome visitor at the Selwyns.

Toby, like her mother, must learn to express her emotions. The barriers she puts between herself and her foster family are formidable and come down only when Toby stops deluding herself and others about the important things in her life. Her eventual confession to Susan and recognition of what the Selwyns have done for her suggest a healthier acceptance of life. This realistic, perceptive story offers no pat answers. Toby knows life has been painful and will be again. But she will be better prepared to meet difficult times when they arise.

Ages 10-12

Also available in:
Paperbound—*Toby Lived Here*
Farrar, Straus & Giroux, Inc. (Sunburst Books)

646

Wolkoff, Judie

Happily Ever After . . . Almost

Dell Publishing Company, Inc., 1984.
(215 pages) o.p.

FAMILY: Extended
PARENT/PARENTS: Remarriage of
Divorce: of parents
Family: relationships
Parental: custody
Stepbrother/Stepsister
Stepparent: father
Stepparent: mother

Kitty Birdsall, eleven, and her sister, Sarah, nine, are not surprised when they overhear Seth Krampner propose to their mother, Liz. They like Seth, a photographer who met their mother in her job of designing book jacket layouts. On weekends the girls visit their father, a pediatrician, who lives with his new wife, Linda, in a New York suburb much like their own. Seth's eleven-year-old son, R.J., lives with his difficult mother, Kay, an heiress and a manipulator. Seth and Liz want their children to meet and get along, but R.J. and Kitty immediately dislike each other. Seth explains to Kitty that R.J. has been seeing a psychiatrist since his parents' divorce. He asks Kitty to be tolerant of the boy. For New Year's Eve, Seth, Liz, and the children, with numerous relatives, gather at Seth's parents' house. Kitty overhears R.J. on the phone in the bedroom, begging his mother not to give away the guinea pig he's just bought, and she begins to realize just what life must be like for him. Then her father and Linda announce they are expecting a baby. After Seth and Liz are married, they and the girls move into the loft of a huge old shoe factory and begin renovation. During the summer, R.J. attends camp and he and Kitty begin writing to each other. When he returns in time to celebrate his twelfth birthday, Kitty gives him an album of photographs she's taken. R.J., who was shaken by the sight of the bums on the Bowery, gives his generous birthday check from his wealthy maternal grandfather to the Bowery Home for the Homeless. While Kitty and Sarah are visiting their father and Linda one weekend, the girls' half-brother, Josh, is born. Kitty desperately wants a special vest for her birthday—a neighbor makes them for thirty dollars. However, she is so moved by reports of starving children in Zaire that she tells her mother she'd rather have the money to send to Africa. Her mother and Seth promptly double the amount; her father and Linda add to it. Then Kitty's mother, harassed by the renovation and worried about a lump in her breast, shows signs of depression and emotional strain. After surgery, which shows the lump to be benign, Seth and the girls take her from the hospital to a hotel for four days of rest and recreation. Seth accidentally discovers that R.J.'s mother has had his school records sent to a boys' prep school in London. A Christmas trip to London has been planned, and Seth and R.J. both fear that Kay means to remain in London—which is against the custody ruling. Seth immediately sets a custody battle in motion. The judge denies the trip to London, keeping R.J.'s passport so his mother can't take him anyway, and awards custody to Seth. Kay appeals. The resulting legal fees leave little money for Christmas, so they all start making gifts for each other. Sarah and R.J., with the neighbor's help, make the vest for Kitty. Christmas Day finds all the children together with Linda and the girls' father, joined by Linda's two children from her previous marriage and baby Josh. Kitty enjoys this gathering of all her brothers and sisters. Before the final custody hearing, R.J. tells Kitty that he now likes her; he wants her to know that in case they lose and he has to go to London. But the judge finds for Seth. Kay becomes abusive when she hears the verdict, and R.J. runs away in the middle of the night to the loft where he stays for good. Eventually, his mother begins working with a psychiatrist (just as R.J. stops seeing his), and their relationship improves slightly. Now Liz is pregnant and the children are delighted. Kitty thinks back to the most unhappy day of her life—when her father left them—and realizes that from it has come the happy beginning of a new life.

In this first-person view of the upbeat side of changing family configurations, Kitty records the confusing relationships she has with her sister, her stepbrother, her half-brother, extra grandparents, and various unrelated people who are still "family." Sharply drawn characters people this fast-moving, funny, vivid chronicle of family members jockeying for position. Although there are trials and troubles, the emphasis here is on the advantages and stimulation of family changes. Kitty would have counseled her unhappy younger self, "You'll live through today. And tomorrow. And the next. But you won't stay sad. Just wait! Around the corner is a happy beginning."

Ages 11-13

Also available in:
Braille—*Happily Ever After . . . Almost*
Library of Congress (NLSBPH)

Cassette—*Happily Ever After . . . Almost*
Library of Congress (NLSBPH)

647

Wolkoff, Judie

Where the Elf King Sings

Macmillan Publishing Company, Inc., 1980.
(178 pages) o.p.

FAMILY: Relationships
VIETNAM
Age: aging
Alcoholism: of father
Violence

At twelve, Marcie Breckenridge watches her world fall apart. Her father, Billy, a Vietnam veteran haunted by flashbacks of his combat experiences, has lost his job and the family's car because of his violent, drunken behavior. At a slumber party, Marcie is taunted by some of the girls about her father's drinking. It is caused, they tell her, by the curse of a murdered servant girl who had worked for the store from which Marcie's father has just been fired. Determined to investigate this curse, Marcie goes to the old cemetery where the murdered girl is buried. There she meets the town eccentric, Mrs. King, who is wearing a bizarre outfit of hip boots and white gloves. At first Marcie finds the tales she's heard about the "town loon" confirmed. But soon she realizes that Mrs. King wears the boots and gloves to protect herself from the snakes and poison ivy in the graveyard. She goes there often to care for her brother's grave. Intrigued by the sharp-witted woman, Marcie accepts an invitation to tea. That night, unable to sleep, she recalls her family's happier times. In the middle of the night her father arrives, noisily drunk, having spent her mother's tip money from the diner where she works, not to redeem the car, but to buy liquor. Offended by the "racist" cast-iron black jockey on his neighbor's lawn, Billy drags it into the gutter. The next day Marcie takes her younger brother with her to have tea with Mrs. King. When they return home they find the house a shambles. Their grandmother, always willing to deny the truth, tries to blame the destruction on vandals, but the children know their father is responsible. Their mother had poured his liquor down the sink before she left for work. They spend that night at their grandmother's house. Next morning their father arrives, followed closely by their mother. She tells him, "You destroyed everything there ever was between us. You're not coming back. I won't let you." Billy promises to seek counseling at the V.A. hospital, but he's not allowed near the children. For a while the therapy seems to be working. Then Billy disappears and Marcie, her brother, and their grandmother search for him in vain. They go back home and find their mother with Curt, a member of Billy's therapy group. Curt, understanding what Billy could never tell his family, the horror of his Vietnam experiences, has found the tormented man at the grave of his best friend, killed in Vietnam while trying to save Billy, who had stepped on a mine. Mrs. King, aware that Billy goes to the cemetery on each anniversary of his friend's death, brings hot soup to comfort him. After this, Billy returns to the V.A. Alcoholic Unit and shows rapid improvement. The family looks forward to his return.

The unending agony of Vietnam, the terrible price still being paid by many veterans, and the impact of their traumas on their families are vividly conveyed in this powerful book. The story moves swiftly, the characters so well developed that each becomes an individual to whom the reader is closely drawn. This is a book rich in discussion possibilities.

Ages 12 and up

Also available in:
No other form known

648

Wood, Phyllis Anderson

This Time Count Me In

The Westminster/John Knox Press, 1980.
(119 pages, paperbound)

BOY-GIRL RELATIONSHIPS: Dating
SCHOOL: Transfer
African-American
Fear: of physical harm
Friendship: making friends
School: classmate relationships
Values/Valuing: moral/ethical

For her sophomore year Peggy Marklee transfers from her private girls' school to a public high school so she can make some nonwhite friends and have classes with boys in them. Shy and used to wearing uniforms, she worries about her clothes and whether the students will accept her. She is assigned to a Reading Lab and there meets Walter and Alfred, class troublemakers; Roxanne and Cheryl, stylish black girls she admires on sight; and Ron, who seems just the kind of boy she's hoped to meet. But trouble with Walter and Alfred begins almost immediately. They disrupt the class and pelt her with wadded paper. Alfred takes the folder and special gold pen from her desk, replacing the folder with a test answer key inside. His efforts backfire when Roxanne confronts him and demands that he return Peggy's pen. The teacher knows Peggy didn't steal the answer key—Alfred is already on probation. Although order is soon restored, Peggy feels unsettled and uneasy. All during her first week she has spent her lunch hour in the library because she was afraid to approach the busy, confusing cafeteria. When Ron, who has only been at the school for a short time himself, notices her plight, he walks her through the lunch line and soon they are eating together every day. One day they have lunch at a hamburger stand and overhear a conversation about two young men who have knocked a woman down and stolen her purse. From the descriptions, Peggy and Ron believe the thieves to be Walter and Alfred. Then in Reading Lab, Peggy sees Alfred steal the teacher's wallet. She knows that by reporting him she will make enemies, but she likes the teacher and feels compelled to speak up. Adding to her account of the theft at school, Ron tells the police about the episode at the hamburger stand. Later, two girls who are friends of Alfred's threaten Peggy with notes and phone calls, but Roxanne and Cheryl defend and protect her. In court several days later, Peggy testifies ably, despite her fears and self-consciousness. Later that day, in the school cafeteria, Alfred's two friends confront Peggy, call her a "snitch," and threaten to start a food fight with her as their target. Suddenly Peggy is surrounded protectively by twenty-five black girls, who face down her tormentors and the young tough who has come to help them. The crisis passes. Roxanne and Cheryl invite Peggy and Ron to a celebration dinner that evening at Cheryl's house. There they meet two more black friends. Returning to Peggy's house, they talk about the possibilities ahead when Ron gets his driver's license. He mentions that he wants to spend a day taking a friend up the coast. Shyly, Peggy realizes he means her.

An inexperienced girl hoping to make black friends and meet boys by attending a public high school for the first time overcomes her apprehensions and shyness, deals decisively with lawbreakers, and begins a first romance. Simply told with no complete characterizations other than Peggy's, this high-interest, low-vocabulary account rings true in its presentation of the trials of transferring schools and the joys of new friendships.

Ages 12 and up

Also available in:
No other form known

649

Wortis, Avi

Sometimes I Think I Hear My Name

Pantheon Books, 1982.
(144 pages) o.p.

BOY-GIRL RELATIONSHIPS
MATURATION
REJECTION: Parental
Deprivation, emotional
Love, meaning of
Relatives: living in home of

Since his parent's divorce three years ago, thirteen-year-old Conrad Murray has lived in St. Louis with his Uncle Carl and Aunt Lu. They have told him that his parents wanted him to have a good home life with a stable family. Conrad loves his aunt and uncle but is increasingly concerned that his parents, both living in New York City, are forgetting him. Just before spring vacation, Conrad's aunt and uncle tell him they are sending him to England by himself to visit relatives. But Conrad tells them he would rather go see his parents. They don't consent. Asked to pick up his tickets at the travel agency, he meets Nancy Sterling, about his age, who is also buying a ticket. A boarding-school student in St. Louis, she is going to New York City to see her parents and is less than excited about it. The next day Conrad stops at Nancy's and offers to trade tickets. Nancy declines, but she does give him her New York telephone number. Conrad resigns himself to a trip to England. But in talking over the plans with his aunt and uncle, he discovers there will be a layover and change of planes in New York City. Accordingly, when he gets into the New York airport terminal, he slips past the stewardess who has been asked to look after him and calls Nancy. Nancy's sister gives Conrad their address. He takes a bus there and is surprised to see that Nancy and her sister live in one apartment, their parents in another. After some initial fabrications about his own situation, Conrad admits that his parents don't even know he's in town. He calls both but neither is home, so he spends that night at Nancy's apartment. The next day he and Nancy go to his mother's apartment and are let in by a neighbor. The phone rings and when the answer tape goes on automatically Conrad hears his Aunt Lu as she leaves a message for his mother. Mortified, he realizes from her words that his mother did not want him to visit. When he goes to see his father, he notes the man's embarrassment. Suddenly he misses his aunt and uncle. The next morning he calls his mother and is invited over. After an uncomfortable visit, Conrad understands that his aunt and uncle were trying to protect him from his parents' indifference. That evening Conrad is invited to Nancy's parents' apartment for dinner. He sees the superficiality of their relationship with their daughters and understands why Nancy is so withdrawn and unemotional. Compelled to admit the truth to himself—his parents do not want him—Conrad flies back to St. Louis, glad to be home. Spring vacation ends and Nancy is still in New York, partly because her parents consider Conrad a bad influence on her. In a letter, she suggests that they "think each other's name. Hard." Maybe their "thoughts can connect." And each day at five o'clock, Conrad does just that. Sometimes he thinks he hears his name.

A young teenage boy abandons a trip to England to search for his divorced parents in New York City. With the help of a quiet, withdrawn girl who is similarly distanced from her parents, Conrad finds that the love and security he so desperately wants from his parents are already his from his aunt and uncle. Conrad tells this fast-paced story; readers will readily sympathize both with his hurt and longing and with Nancy's alienation and desire to separate completely from her own frustrating, unsatisfactory relationship with her parents. (The symbolism of the butterfly tattoo used to represent her feelings may elude some readers.) No reason is given for the emotional desert these young people face, but Conrad's loving aunt and uncle and his promising relationship with Nancy make the ending bittersweet.

Ages 10-13

Also available in:
No other form known

650

Wright, Betty Ren

I Like Being Alone

Color illustrations by Krystyna Stasiak.
Raintree/Steck-Vaughan Publishers, 1981.
(31 pages)

PRIVACY, NEED FOR
Emotions: identifying
Problem solving
Relatives: living in child's home

While showing her new friend Jason around her busy house, Brenda, about eight, feels vaguely out of sorts. Jason, an only child, admires the bunk bed she shares with her sister, her large and noisy family, the ready supply of constant companions. Brenda realizes that she feels just the opposite. "I'd like to be alone sometimes . . . I love my family, but they are always right there. Every minute." That night at dinner, surrounded by her family, not one of whom notices her sadness, the girl feels even more unhappy. Aunt Rose, a boarder and the only member of the household with a room of her own, finally does notice Brenda and invites her to her room. As Brenda admires her aunt's homemade furnishings, she happens to glance at the single tree in their backyard and gets an idea. Using her aunt's leftover lumber, she builds a platform and puts it in the tree. When her father comes along, she tells him, "This is my very own place, Dad. I made it." He goes to get some rope to secure the platform in place. Then the whole family comes to see the tree house, including Aunt Rose who brings more lumber to build walls. Brenda happily spends that entire day in her tree house with only her books and the birds for company. When she wants to sleep there, Aunt Rose's encouragement overrides her parents' objections. Brenda stays awake for a long while, listening to the peaceful night sounds. In the middle of the night, however, she awakens to darkness and a strong wind. Hearing a noise beneath the tree, she summons all her courage, leans over, and shines the flashlight—onto Aunt Rose who has come to check on her. Relieved, Brenda settles back down and her aunt returns to the house. Tomorrow she will let her siblings and Jason take turns in her tree house. "But it will always be my place, when I want to be alone," she thinks before drifting back to sleep.

A need to escape from her large and ever-present family, to have a place of her own, is the impetus behind a girl's decision to build her own tree house. With the help and emotional support of an understanding aunt, Brenda creates her hideaway, a place she will share occasionally but will also reserve for herself when she wants it. There is good discussion material here on how people can balance their need for privacy with their need for social contact. Radiant, colorful illustrations emphasize the sense of emotional well-being Brenda achieves.

Ages 6-9

Also available in:
No other form known

651

Wright, Betty Ren

My New Mom and Me

Color illustrations by Betsy Day.
Raintree/Steck-Vaughan Publishers, 1981.
(31 pages)

CHANGE: Accepting
STEPPARENT: Mother
Loss: feelings of
Parent/Parents: remarriage of
Pets: substitute for human relationship

A girl of about nine is comforted by the thought that Cat, once her mother's special pet and now hers, remembers the good times as well as the bad. The worst time for her was two summers ago when her mother suddenly became ill and died. The girl remembers feeling very angry at her mother for leaving; "If she knew how sad I was going to be, she would have found a way to stay alive." Cat seems lost also, searching the house for the absent woman and wary of the girl and her father. "He doesn't want to love us, because he's afraid we might die too," says the girl. But soon the cat begins to sleep with her, and she tells him of her sadness and loneliness. Then the girl's father decides to remarry. Certain she will not like this new woman named Elena, the girl thinks, "We don't need her." She says nothing to her father, but demonstrates her unhappiness by refusing to let Elena hug her when she comes to live with them. Cat too keeps his distance, waiting for Elena to leave the room before approaching the food she has put in his bowl. Sometimes when Elena watches Cat and the girl her smile seems to fade, making the girl glad. Then one night her father must go out of town. After dinner the girl goes to her room and sprawls on her bed, regretting how different everything is now. Soon she hears Cat, meowing frantically. Although the sound seems to be coming from her closet, she cannot find him. Upset, she calls Elena, who comes into her room and searches the closet. They decide that somehow Cat is stuck inside the wall. The girl remembers a loose board at the back of her closet shelf, and Elena discovers a hole in the wall where Cat must have slipped through. Using a hammer the girl brings, Elena cracks open the wallboard and pulls the boards loose to the floor. Although the girl insists the cat will scratch, Elena softly and patiently calls to it and the frightened animal jumps right into her arms. For the first time, the girl really looks at Elena and thanks her for her help. Outside on the back steps Elena holds Cat, who buries his head under her arm. The girl tells Elena that he used to do that to her mother. Elena says, "Your mother taught Cat how to love. He'll never forget her, but maybe he's tired of keeping all that love locked inside." They sit quietly together. Elena puts her arm around the girl and she leans against her stepmother, surprised at how good the closeness feels.

In this first-person story of loss and change, a bereaved young girl withdraws from the affection her stepmother offers, clinging instead to the past as represented by her cat. Only when the cat needs rescuing and the stepmother acts quickly to provide it does the girl begin to accept the love of her new mother. This gentle story, appropriately illustrated, could serve as a starting point for a discussion of death and grief.

Ages 8-10

Also available in:
No other form known

652

Wright, Betty Ren

My Sister Is Different

Color illustrations by Helen Cogancherry.
Raintree/Steck-Vaughan Publishers, 1981.
(31 pages)

MENTAL RETARDATION
SIBLING: Younger
Sibling: love for

Whenever Carlo goes out to play he must take his mentally retarded sister, Terry, with him. Terry, though older and taller than he is, is slow to learn, usually drops the ball or gets the rules wrong, and is laughed at by the other children. Sometimes Carlo dislikes her. He even made a birthday card for her that expressed just those sentiments, but he decided not to give it to her. His grandmother tells him to love Terry. "Is your heart so dried up and scrawny that it can't love?" she asks. At Christmastime, Carlo takes Terry shopping to get a present for their grandmother. Terry wants to buy her a powder puff doll; Carlo quickly agrees because he is embarrassed by Terry and wants to move on so the clerk will stop staring at them. When Terry has to go to the bathroom, Carlo gives her hasty directions rather than accompanying her. He sees her stumble as she walks away, excited to be on her own. Ten minutes pass. Then Carlo, first thinking how very slow Terry is, goes to find her, enlisting the aid of a helpful clerk. Finding the bathroom empty, the clerk reassures him that his older sister can certainly take care of herself. But Carlo knows better. Searching the store, he considers how his family will blame him, thinking he lost Terry on purpose. He then remembers the good things about Terry—the birthday card that said "To my dearest Brother"; the way she can always make the baby laugh; the times she wanted to take his turn doing the dishes. Remembering how people often laugh at her, Carlo begins to cry and starts to run—nearly tripping over Terry, who is sitting on the floor playing with a baby while the mother shops nearby. The woman compliments Terry on her help with the fussy child. Carlo resists the urge to yell at Terry and hugs her instead. Then they go home. After that, although he still feels annoyed at his sister sometimes, Carlo remembers the day she was lost and how he felt. On Terry's birthday he gives her a card, "To a wonderful sister," that she carries around for a week. His family is pleased, even his grandmother: "Your heart is in better shape than I thought it was."

A young boy's resentment toward his mentally retarded sister, who is often made his responsibility, changes when he loses track of her in a department store. Though it doesn't entirely eliminate his resentment, the episode does help him see his sister's special talents and qualities. Once Carlo perceives Terry as a person rather than a burden, he can acknowledge and express his love for her. Young readers may be helped to see that mentally retarded people are more similar to them than different. Illustrations clearly show the girl's warm, gentle, loving personality.

Ages 6-9

Also available in:
No other form known

653

Yep, Laurence Michael

Kind Hearts and Gentle Monsters

HarperCollins Publishers, Inc., 1982.
(175 pages) o.p.

MENTAL ILLNESS: of Parent
Autonomy
Boy-girl relationships: dating
Differences, human
Empathy
Guilt, feelings of
Self, attitude toward: confidence

High school sophomore Charley Sabini angrily confronts Chris Pomeroy with a Poison Chain Letter she wrote about how despicable he is. He soon discovers that eccentric Chris is more human than he'd expected, and Chris finds Charley isn't as stuffy as she'd thought. Chris has a knack for unsettling Charley and making him doubt things he's always accepted. Before Charley meets her mother, though, Chris remarks that her mother is the real monster of the family. Charley then discovers that Chris's mother has been in a mental institution, and he watches in horror as she saws at her wrist with a nail file until Chris stops her. He admires Chris's strength and courage in dealing with the explosive Mrs. Pomeroy every day. But Chris avoids Charley once he knows about her mother's condition. Finally, he goes to talk to her at the library where she works. Chris says her mother has chased away every friend she's ever had. They go to the zoo together, the place Chris and her father used to escape to when things were bad at home. Then nine-year-old Duane visits the library to look for books about Godzilla. He seems to need a "protector" and is very involved in his monster fantasies. Chris and Charley "adopt" him, but when Chris mentions the actor who plays Godzilla, Duane, who thinks Godzilla is real, turns on her in a rage. Upset by the boy's abuse, Chris remarks that Duane is as vicious and sick as her mother. Charley supports her, telling her not to believe her mother's and now Duane's criticisms and insults. Chris does try to lead her own life, as her mother's psychiatrist advised her to do. When she mentions spending Christmas Eve with Charley's family, her mother appears unhappy but refuses to go with her, even though Charley invites her. Chris demands that her mother pull herself together, accusing her of eating her husband alive (he died of a heart attack three years ago) and announcing that she'll not do the same thing to Chris. "I'm drowning, mother, and I've only got the strength to save myself." Chris gets into the Christmas spirit with a vengeance, intending to enjoy herself since her mother has made her last ten Christmases a misery. When Charley calls her Christmas morning, she says her mother's been hospitalized after a suicide attempt. They are in a hopeless cycle, Chris explains. Her mother always appears to get better, but then as soon as Chris tries to pull away she regresses. She has tried to kill herself once before. Chris says she can feel her mother reaching out to her, but she finds such emptiness inside herself. Charley comforts her. They visit the zoo; Chris talks about the daily appointment she and her mother will have with the psychiatrist and the line she'll have to walk between supporting her mother and living her own life. Charley promises to stay around long enough to convince Chris she's really a good person.

Chris's struggles to live with her emotionally fragile mother are narrated by her new friend, Charley, who learns from her to empathize with other people's pain and confusion. He helps encourage Chris, whose sense of worth has been damaged by her critical, obsessive mother. Chris's mother isn't a monster but a suffering human being, making the situation more confusing and painful for both Chris and Charley. This is a gripping, realistic story of growth and courage in the face of an insoluble, anguishing problem. The book may alert readers to the possibility that a cocky facade can hide a heartbreaking story, and it emphasizes the importance of understanding and empathy in human relationships.

Ages 12 and up

Also available in:
No other form known

654

Young, Helen

What Difference Does It Make, Danny?

Black/white illustrations by Quentin Blake.
André Deutsch Ltd., 1980.
(93 pages) o.p.

EPILEPSY
SELF, ATTITUDE TOWARD: Accepting
School: classmate relationships
School: pupil-teacher relationships

Danny Blane, about nine, is a perfectly ordinary English schoolboy, except that he has epilepsy. His teachers and classmates know he has it and readily accept him. They also know he is on medication to control his seizures. Danny loves gym and all sports, especially swimming. At the school's sports day in the country, he comes in second in three running events. In a new event, swim races, he wins first place. One day in class Danny feels a seizure coming. He tells his teacher and then lies down. The children watch as Danny has a *grand mal* seizure. The teacher, who puts her folded jacket under his head, explains what is happening. Afterwards, the students ask Danny questions about his experience. Soon a new games master, Mr. Masterson, joins the school. Danny, because of his athletic ability, becomes one of Mr. Masterson's prized students—until he discovers that Danny has epilepsy. Then he refuses to let the boy participate in any sports. Any competitive stress, he fears, could cause Danny to have a seizure. Danny's teacher must tell him that his activities in gym will now be restricted to vaulting and mat routines. Hurt and bitter that Mr. Masterson didn't even bother to talk to him himself, Danny becomes extremely uncooperative in school. Soon he is "determined to behave as badly as he dared." His parents become increasingly distressed by his moods. Finally, his mother goes to talk with the principal. While the two converse, truant Danny is walking along a canal he's forbidden to go near. Suddenly he sees a small boy fall into the water. Danny dives in and, struggling to stay above water and reach shore, pulls the boy out. The boy's mother and neighbors rush both youngsters to the hospital, and soon Danny is a hero. Several days later he receives the Royal Humane Society Award at his school assembly. After the assembly Mr. Masterson apologizes to Danny. He also challenges the boy to prepare for the championship games.

A young epileptic boy proves his capabilities as an athlete in this well-written, informative book that emphasizes Danny's special needs rather than his limitations. Danny accepts and can freely discuss his condition, the information about which comes through clearly without didacticism. Lively pencil sketches add interest to this valuable book.

Ages 9-12

Also available in:
No other form known

655

Zalben, Jane Breskin

Maybe It Will Rain Tomorrow

Farrar, Straus & Giroux, Inc., 1982.
(181 pages)

REJECTION: Parental
Belonging
Change: accepting
Parent/Parents: remarriage of
Sex: premarital
Stepparent: mother
Suicide: of parent

When Beth Corey's mother commits suicide, sixteen-year-old Beth goes to live with her father, his wife, Linda, and their new baby. Beth's father left when she was ten, and Beth has never liked Linda. Starting at a new high school in April of her sophomore year, she meets Jonathan Schein, a good-looking, intelligent boy who has a scholarship at Juilliard for his Saturday morning flute lessons. One Saturday, when Beth takes the same train into New York City with him for a visit with her Aunt Ellen, they talk and make arrangements to meet. Beth wants to know from Ellen why her parents divorced and why her mother killed herself: "Wasn't I a good enough reason for Mom to stay around?" Her aunt sighs. "Of course you were, Beth." After her visit, Beth joins Jonathan and his friends as they play music for passersby, collecting money for it. Later in the week, Beth has dinner at Jonathan's house. She likes his family and plays one of her original songs for Jonathan. She also tells him about her mother's suicide and her own feelings of anger and guilt. One afternoon Beth and Jonathan skip school and go to the beach, where they make love, Beth for the first time. The next Saturday when Beth again joins Jonathan and his friends to play music on the New York sidewalks, they play one of her compositions. She and Jonathan decide to stay in town for a concert, and Beth declines to inform Linda; her father is out of town. They go to Jonathan's father's store and make love, falling asleep and not catching a train until very late. When Beth walks in, an angry Linda is waiting for her. Things are so uncomfortable between Linda and Beth all weekend that Beth packs a bag on Monday and arrives on her Aunt Ellen's doorstep. Beth tells Ellen about her involvement with Jonathan; Ellen matter-of-factly says she hopes they were careful and offers Beth her gynecologist's number. Beth confesses to her aunt her fears of being left alone again, as she was first by her father, then by her mother. What if Jonathan also abandons her? Ellen takes Beth home and talks to Linda, who resents being forced to deal with problems that her husband and his first wife should have dealt with. Beth accuses her father of keeping himself emotionally distant from everyone. She and Jonathan visit the country club, which isn't open for the season yet, and make love in one of the cabanas. Afterwards, Jonathan tells Beth he's going to spend the summer working in the Catskills. She feels betrayed; she'd never have made love with him if she'd known he wasn't going to be around. In the days before he leaves, Beth cannot bring herself to speak to him or respond to his notes. But they correspond during the summer, and Beth's life at home gets easier. When she visits Jonathan at the resort, she suspects he's seeing other girls. They make love and she knows, although she can't quite accept it, that it's the last time. By summer's end, Beth has made two new friends and is feeling more at home with her father and Linda. Then, in spite of several overtures from Jonathan, Beth decides not to resume any kind of relationship with him. "Alone no longer felt bad. It didn't mean loneliness; it meant I belonged to myself."

A teenage girl feels helpless in the face of relentless changes in her life: her mother's suicide, a new home with her father and his family, a new school, a first love affair. She learns that she must turn to herself for the sense of belonging and security she covets. This first-person account of a young woman struggling with feelings of rejection never provides a satisfying explanation for Beth's mother's suicide. But Beth's eventual response is to take charge of her own life and acknowledge that she has no control over other people's behavior. Beth's sexual relationship with Jonathan is presented as a fact, one of many things happening in Beth's life, of no great import or meaning; the book includes some rough language and sexual description. Beth's interaction with Linda, her stepmother, is something of a barometer of her increasing maturity. Toward the end, the reader knows there is hope for the relationship and for Beth as a competent, maturing person.

Ages 12 and up

Also available in:
No other form known

Z

656

Zelonky, Joy

I Can't Always Hear You

Color illustrations by Barbara Bejna and Shirlee Jensen.
Raintree/Steck-Vaughan Publishers, 1980.
(30 pages)

DEAFNESS
DIFFERENCES, HUMAN
School: classmate relationships
School: mainstreaming
Self, attitude toward: feeling different

Kim, a hearing-impaired girl of about ten, is attending a regular school for the first time. On the first day, her teacher, Mr. Davis, speaks loudly to her until she tells him he doesn't need to shout. Although she cannot always hear, she usually can. During arithmetic, Kim's best subject, she answers a question with "Eight tickery three is five," whereupon the whole class laughs. Reassuring Kim that her answer was indeed correct, Mr. Davis repeats the problem and solution. Kim clearly hears the words "take away" and repeats them to herself. Then, removing his glasses, Mr. Davis points out to the class that many people need glasses to see better, just as Kim needs a hearing aid to hear better. During lunch, when Erik, a classmate, taunts Kim, she makes a sarcastic retort about his dental braces and runs out of the room. At home that night, she tells her mother that she is "the only one in the world with a hearing aid" and that people always treat her differently. Her mother responds that each person is unique in some way and that people just need to get used to one another. But the next day brings an intensely embarrassing mistake for Kim. She notices several students lining up and so joins them, unaware that the teacher has asked all the boys who need to use the lavatory to form a line. After school that afternoon, Kim tells Mr. Davis that she doesn't plan to come back anymore. She hates being made fun of, she explains. He suggests that it might have helped if she had laughed along with the others about the washroom incident, but Kim replies that she didn't find it funny. Taking the girl by the hand, Mr. Davis escorts her to the principal's office. Ms. Pinkowski reveals to Kim that she too wears a hearing aid and that she also had trouble being accepted in school. Being friendly and patient makes things easier. "Expect a lot from yourself," she tells the girl. "Soon others will too." The following day on the playground, Erik's ball lands at Kim's feet. Rather than make an accusing remark, she simply tosses the ball back to him with a courteous comment. He asks to see her hearing aid and she removes it to give him a look. After he examines it, Erik tells Kim that now he is pleased she is in his class. When Kim begins to explain how she is different from the others, Erik points out that her hearing aid is no stranger than his braces. Sasha, a very tall girl who has come up beside Erik and Kim, adds that her height makes her different. Others join in, confessing their own special differences: one is adopted, another has no television set at home, another is a twin, another learned to read at the age of four, another gets a rash from eating chocolate. When the bell rings, the children all run back into the school, laughing together.

Kim tells how she learned to adjust to a mainstreamed classroom and how her classmates learned to accept her. The girl has obviously managed to overcome her physical disability, but now must struggle with the way others treat her. An introductory note for parents and teachers points out that the book can not only help break down the walls between disabled and nondisabled people, but can also prompt readers to consider the special qualities of all people. Illustrations show children of various sizes, shapes, and ethnic backgrounds.

Ages 7-10

Also available in:
No other form known

657

Zelonky, Joy

My Best Friend Moved Away

Color illustrations by Angela Adams.
Raintree/Steck-Vaughan Publishers, 1980.
(31 pages)

CHANGE: Accepting
FRIENDSHIP: Best Friend
Moving

Young Brian does not like hearing that his best friend Nick's parents have bought a new house. As soon as his house is sold, Nick will be moving across town and will transfer schools. Hoping to obstruct the sale, Brian rips the For Sale sign in Nick's yard off its post and hurls it into the street. The next day Nick tells Brian that someone played a dirty trick and stole their For Sale sign, almost losing them some potential buyers. Brian realizes his gesture was wrong and futile. One morning Nick meets Brian on the way to school and announces that his house has been sold and they will move in a month. Miserably unhappy, Brian can't bring himself to say anything in the face of Nick's obvious happiness. On moving day, Brian presents Nick with a bag of his best marbles as a going-away present. Then he retreats to his room, feeling miserably lonely. His father comes in to comfort him, but Brian is sure he will never again have a friend like Nick. "No two people are alike," agrees his father. "That's why each friend is special." One day Nick calls and invites Brian to visit. While there, Brian suggests that the two of them play marbles or fly kites. But Nick pooh-poohs the ideas, declaring that none of the kids in this new neighborhood do such things. Instead, he takes Brian, who is sworn to secrecy, to a construction site. Scoffing at Brian's worry that this is a dangerous place to play, Nick proceeds to walk across a narrow board straddling a deep, muddy hole. Brian hesitates to follow, but Nick goads him. The board is unsteady and Brian marvels that Nick, who wears a leg brace, managed to cross it so easily. Brian, on the other hand, slips and falls into the mud. As she helps Brian clean up, Nick's mother reprimands her son for the escapade and grounds him for the next day. Nick blames Brian for his punishment and a distressed Brian runs outside, where he meets his father who has come to pick him up. On the way to the subway, Brian tells what happened and how different Nick seems. Brian's father points out that Nick has been through a lot of changes and that he is probably not as happy as he appears to be. Riding the subway, Brian thinks this over. He does not like the fact that people have to change. His father suggests that he remember all the good times he had with Nick. Brian decides that eventually he might change too, "but if I'm careful, maybe the good things about me will get better." When he suddenly remembers that he has promised to play marbles with some kids on his block, father and son disembark to buy replacement marbles for the ones Brian gave Nick.

In this first-person narrative, young Brian explains how time and his father's support help him accept his best friend's moving and changing. Brian's confusion and sense of loss come through clearly, enhanced by the bright, appealing illustrations. Especially noteworthy is the close father-son relationship. A note encourages parents and teachers to help children express and work through their feelings of personal loss.

Ages 6-9

Also available in:
No other form known

658
Zindel, Paul
I Love My Mother
Color illustrations by John Melo.
HarperCollins Publishers, Inc., 1975.
(31 pages counted) o.p.

LOVE, MEANING OF
Parent/Parents: single

A little boy can have fine times with his mother, whether catching butterflies or going to the zoo. The presents she gives him are also occasions, especially the genuine boa constrictor he got for his birthday. He thinks of the future—of the ring, the collie, the farm, and the flowers he will give to her someday. The two of them comfort each other, too, at times when he has nightmares about gorillas, at times when she is lonely. True, they have differences as well: for instance, she will not let him drive the car. Sometimes the boy wishes his father were back, and his mother assures him that his father misses him, too.

Love is strong between this little boy and his mother, now single. They enjoy each other's company, but there are hard, lonely times as well. No reason is specified for the father's absence. This sensitive first-person narrative is powerfully illustrated in vibrant colors, the illustrations occupying full, sometimes double pages interspersed with brief text. The text appears on two pages at the front of the book. Especially striking are pictures of nightmares and one of the family, with the father drawn in blue to suggest his absence. Read aloud, this book could open up discussion between a single parent and her child.

Ages 3-7

Also available in:
No other form known

659
Zindel, Paul
The Pigman
HarperCollins Publishers, Inc., 1968.
(182 pages)

GUILT, FEELINGS OF
Death: of friend
Loneliness
Love, meaning of

Teenagers John and Lorraine discover in Mr. Pignanti, whom they nickname Mr. Pigman, the love and companionship they have long sought. They come from homes where love is often absent, and both find little meaning in their lives until they meet Mr. Pignanti, who is a gentle, lonely, and naive friend. Though he fills some of the emptiness in their lives, he is also someone they can easily take advantage of. Soon John and Lorraine begin to accept money and other gifts from the lonely old man, and when Mr. Pignanti is hospitalized with a heart attack, the teenagers use the Pigman's house for a wild party. During this party, many of his treasured belongings are ruined. John and Lorraine regret their actions, but it is too late—Mr. Pignanti is brokenhearted. Their thoughtless and careless behavior precipitates Mr. Pignanti's death, a death which leaves John and Lorraine feeling bewildered and guilty.

Z

This is a moving story of two young people who pursue a destructive course, caring little for anyone but themselves, excusing their inadequacies, and blaming others for their own ineptitudes. However, when their friend dies, they finally recognize the tragic consequences of their behavior; the reader is left with the feeling that they will change.

Ages 12 and up

Also available in:
Cassette—*The Pigman*
Library of Congress (NLSBPH)

Talking Book—*The Pigman*
Library of Congress (NLSBPH)

660
Zolotow, Charlotte Shapiro
Big Sister and Little Sister
Color illustrations by Martha Alexander.
HarperCollins Publishers, Inc. (Charlotte Zolotow Books), 1966.
(29 pages)

SIBLING: Love for
SIBLING: Relationships
Autonomy

Big sister takes care of her little sister, watching that she does not go in the street, taking her for a bike ride, helping her cross the street, and making sure she does not get lost when they play in the field. When little sister cries, big sister is there, putting an arm around her, giving her a handkerchief, and making her feel better. Big sister tells little sister to "sit here, go there, and do it this way." But one day, little sister decides she does not want to listen to what big sister has to say, so she slips out of the house while her sister is getting cookies and lemonade, goes to the meadow, and hides in the daisies and tall grass. She stays there even when she hears big sister calling her. Suddenly big sister is so close that little sister could touch her. Unable to find her, big sister sits down in the grass nearby and cries, the way little sister has often done. No one comforts big sister, so little sister gets up, puts an arm around her, gives her a handkerchief, and makes her feel better. From that day on, "little sister and big sister take care of each other because little sister has learned from big sister and now they both know how."

This story illustrates a loving relationship between two sisters. The younger sister finds a place to be alone when she does not want to be told what to do, and the older sister, feeling a sense of responsibility toward her younger sister, becomes worried when she cannot find her. The reader's empathy shifts from one sister to another throughout the book, making the story appealing for both older and younger siblings.

Ages 3-7

Also available in:
Paperbound—*Big Sister and Little Sister*
HarperCollins Publishers, Inc. (Charlotte Zolotow Books)

661

Zolotow, Charlotte Shapiro

A Father Like That

Color illustrations by Ben Shecter.
HarperCollins Publishers, Inc. (Charlotte Zolotow Books), 1971.
(32 pages counted)

PARENT/PARENTS: Single
Fantasy formation

The narrator, a boy six or seven years old, tells his mother that he knows what his father, whom he has never seen, would be like and what they would do if his father were there. (His father "went away" before the little boy was born.) The boy talks about all the time he would spend with his father: they would leave the house together in the morning; they would eat supper together; and they would play a game of checkers before bed. His father would always be there if he became sick or if he had a nightmare. His father would be present at parent-teacher meetings; would always stand up for him, right or wrong; and would be kind to him even when he was angry. The father would also play games with the boy and his friends. When the boy finishes, his mother tells him that although he may never have a father like that, "when you grow up, you can be a father like that yourself."

This is a touching story of a little boy who wants a father so much that he fantasizes about having a perfect dad. The mother is loving and perceptive.

Ages 4-6

Also available in:
No other form known

662

Zolotow, Charlotte Shapiro

The Hating Book

Color illustrations by Ben Shecter.
HarperCollins Publishers, Inc. (Charlotte Zolotow Books), 1969.
(32 pages)

ANGER
Communication: misunderstandings
Friendship: keeping friends
Problem solving

A little girl hates her friend who refuses to sit with her on the school bus and borrows Peter's pencil instead of hers. The little girl's mother suggests that she ask her friend why she is angry. But the girl will not take her mother's advice because she is afraid of what her friend might say. So her friend continues to snub her, and the little girl continues to hate her friend. Again the little girl's mother suggests that she ask her friend what is wrong, but the little girl says she would rather die. Finally, with more prodding from her mother, she goes over to her friend's house to discuss the problem. When the two talk it over, the little girl finds that her friend is feeling hurt after she misinterpreted something the little girl had said.

This first-person narrative skillfully explores a small girl's feelings of rejection and anger and the way in which she learns to confront and solve the communication problem responsible for these feelings. The child-like emotions are portrayed naturally and the situation is realistic.

Ages 3-7

Also available in:
Paperbound—*The Hating Book*
HarperCollins Publishers, Inc. (Charlotte Zolotow Books)

Talking Book—*The Hating Book*
Library of Congress (NLSBPH)

663

Zolotow, Charlotte Shapiro

If You Listen

Color illustrations by Marc Simont.
HarperCollins Publishers, Inc. (Charlotte Zolotow Books), 1980.
(29 pages counted)

PARENTAL: Absence
SEPARATION FROM LOVED ONES
Communication: parent-child
Imagination

A little girl whose father has been away for a long time asks her mother how she can tell if someone far away loves her. Admitting she means her father, she wonders, "If I can't see him, or hear him, or feel his hugs, how can I know he loves me when he isn't here?" Her mother explains a special way of listening, like listening to the faraway church bells or feeling the night outside her dark bedroom, with the distant foghorn and the dog barking in the hills. This listening is like the flash of lightning on a still summer day when you hear the thunder coming behind it; like when a petal from the vase of roses in the living room falls onto the coffee table. Her mother advises the girl to listen hard inside herself so she can feel someone far away sending his love to her. The little girl isn't quite convinced. "I will listen hard, but I wish he'd come home."

A mother reassures her little daughter that her father loves her, even though he is far away. Young readers may need help understanding the rather fragmented and abstract text. No explanation is given for the father's absence, so this could fit a variety of family circumstances. Beautiful illustrations help convey the thoughtful, lyrical tone.

Ages 5-7

Also available in:
Cassette—*If You Listen*
HarperCollins Publishers, Inc

664

Zolotow, Charlotte Shapiro

It's Not Fair

Color illustrations by William Pène du Bois.
HarperCollins Publishers, Inc. (Charlotte Zolotow Books), 1976.
(32 pages)

JEALOUSY: Peer
Friendship: best friend
Lifestyle

The girl who tells this story wishes that she had long, black hair like her friend Martha and thinks it unfair that Martha never gets freckles from the sun or gains weight, as she does. She also thinks it unfair that Martha has a homeroom teacher who is witty, a house made to play in, a mother who likes rock and roll, and a grandmother who bakes. Her own homeroom teacher is strict; her house has fancy, breakable furniture and decorations; her mother likes classical music; and her grandmother is a lawyer who lives far away. How puzzling, then, that Martha envies her stern homeroom teacher, her curly hair and freckles, her opera-loving mother, and a grandmother who is a lawyer rather than a cook. Can life have been unfair to *both* of them?

Two good friends in this first-person narrative envy each other's way of life. The fact that the girls in the illustrations appear to be teenagers seems at variance with the text. Over all, the book is superficial but does make clear how children often feel about each other, their homes, and their family lives.

Ages 5-7

Also available in:
No other form known

665

Zolotow, Charlotte Shapiro

Janey

Color illustrations by Ronald Himler.
HarperCollins Publishers, Inc. (Charlotte Zolotow Books), 1973.
(24 pages)

LONELINESS
Friendship: meaning of
Moving

The young girl thinks about her friend Janey, who has recently moved, and admits to herself that she is lonely. When she walks home from school in the rain, the girl thinks back and remembers how Janey liked to touch the things they passed on the way home, the pebble Janey found on the playground, and how Janey skipped stones on the water. Playing with other children, the girl recalls Janey's voice—no one else sounds like her. She also remembers how she and her friend could sit together without talking, and how they would talk on the phone after dinner. The girl reminisces about last Christmas when they gave each other the same book for a present. She thinks of Janey every time she reads the stories in that book. When the wind blows at night, it brings back memories of how she and Janey used to listen to the wind when Janey stayed overnight. She sadly remembers that she did not want her friend to leave and that Janey did not want to leave either, and the girl goes to sleep wishing Janey had not had to move away.

The loneliness a child experiences when her friend moves away, and her ensuing feelings of sadness are described as acceptable, normal reactions. The reader can clearly sense the child's loneliness.

Ages 4-7

Also available in:
Braille—*Janey*
Library of Congress (NLSBPH)

666

Zolotow, Charlotte Shapiro

My Friend John

Color illustrations by Ben Shecter.
HarperCollins Publishers, Inc. (Charlotte Zolotow Books), 1968.
(32 pages)

FRIENDSHIP: Best Friend
FRIENDSHIP: Meaning of
Cooperation: in play
Sharing/Not sharing

The narrator, a boy five or six years old, and his friend John know everything about each other. The narrator is afraid of the dark but can fight well; John is afraid of cats but can dive off a high board. They know and respect each other's strengths and weaknesses. They know each other's secret hiding places and all about each other's houses, how to get into them when they are locked and what is in the refrigerators. John cannot go out when it rains, but the narrator can go and play with him. The two best friends cooperate whenever possible, "and everything that's important about each other they like."

This slim book briefly and persuasively tells what friendship means to children. Each boy knows everything about the other and likes everything he knows. The friends complement each other—where one is weak the other is strong.

Ages 4-6

Also available in:
Cassette—*My Friend John*
Library of Congress (NLSBPH)

667

Zolotow, Charlotte Shapiro

My Grandson Lew

Color illustrations by William Pène Du Bois.
HarperCollins Publishers, Inc. (Charlotte Zolotow Books), 1974.
(32 pages)

DEATH: of Grandparent

Six-year-old Lewis wakes up one night and calls to his mother. He misses his grandpa, even though he has not seen him for several years. Lew remembers Grandpa's beard, his kind eyes, and his comforting voice when he hummed to Lew at night. He remembers going to the museum with Grandpa, the way Grandpa carried him, and the smell of Grandpa's pipe tobacco, and he wants to see Grandpa again. Mother does not understand how Lew can remember so much since Grandpa lived far away and did not often come to visit. She has never discussed Grandpa's death because Lew had never talked about him before. Mother then tells Lew that she remembers how happy Grandpa was when Lew was born, and that although Grandpa is dead, his family will always remember him and the things they did together.

This book touchingly describes the keen memory very young children may have for people and events that are important to them. The mother's willingness to share her memories encourages the child to cherish his own memories.

Ages 3-7

Also available in:
Paperbound—*My Grandson Lew*
HarperCollins Publishers, Inc. (Charlotte Zolotow Books)

668

Zolotow, Charlotte Shapiro

The New Friend

Color illustrations by Emily Arnold McCully.
HarperCollins Publishers, Inc., 1981.
(31 pages counted) o.p.

FRIENDSHIP: Best Friend
Loss: feelings of

A little girl has a close friend with long brown hair. The two girls play together often. They walk in the woods, pick wild flowers, and wade in the brook. They play in the attic when it rains and go barefoot in the grass when the rain stops. They share apples under the trees and talk together. One day the girl calls for her friend, but she is not home. The girl finds her in the woods with another friend. The girl watches as her friend shares the wild flowers and brook with this new friend. At home she sees them enjoying the activities she and her friend enjoyed, singing their songs and jumping rope. The girl goes home and cries herself to sleep. She dreams she finds a new friend and walks with her in the woods. The new friend shows her new paths and new flowers. When she wakes up she decides to look for this new friend. When she finds her she's sure to remember her other one with the long brown hair. "But maybe then I won't care!"

In this gentle first-person tale, a little girl feels hurt and disappointed when her friend forsakes her. Her dream shows her that new, different, perhaps even better friends await her. In time she will forget the hurt, but she will always remember the friend. Soft, pastel illustrations complement the spare, lyrical text.

Ages 3-7

Also available in:
No other form known

669

Zolotow, Charlotte Shapiro

One Step, Two . . .

Color illustrations by Cindy Wheeler.
Lothrop, Lee & Shepard Books, 1981.
(30 pages counted) o.p.

COMMUNICATION: Parent-Child
SHARING/NOT SHARING
Nature: appreciation of

One spring morning a mother and her little daughter start out on a walk to the corner. The girl shows her mother a yellow crocus and a fat gray cat. Then the child sees a blue jay and stops to pick up a white stone that gleams like the moon. Walking on, she sees clothes dancing on a clothesline. Then she hears the garbage truck grinding up the garbage, and the church bells ringing. Going on, they pass a yellow school bus. When they reach the corner, the mother says it is time to go home for lunch. On the way the child stops to pick some daffodils, but her mother reminds her that the flowers do not belong to them. So she bends to smell the flowers instead and, when she stands up, discovers yellow powder on her nose. Mr. Peabody and his big dog approach, and the friendly dog licks the powder right off. Mother and child walk past a house with plants in the window, and the mother names them for the girl. Then they are home. The little girl stops at the bottom of the steps, holds up her arms, and is carried in by her mother. Fast asleep, she does not hear her mother thanking her for showing her so many lovely things on their walk.

For a young child and her mother, a spring walk becomes an occasion for sharing and appreciating many little discoveries and wonders. The charming, rhythmic text conveys the pleasures of a companionable stroll. Originally published in 1955, this is newly illustrated with warm, pastel pictures that emphasize mother and child.

Ages 2-5

Also available in:
No other form known

670

Zolotow, Charlotte Shapiro

The Quarreling Book

Black/white illustrations by Arnold Lobel.
HarperCollins Publishers, Inc. (Charlotte Zolotow Books), 1963.
(30 pages counted)

HOSTILITY
Aggression, displacement of
Communication: misunderstandings

It is a rainy day and the James family feels cranky and quarrelsome. Mr. James starts a chain reaction of unpleasantries when he forgets to kiss Mrs. James goodbye on his way to work. Mrs. James passes her hurt feelings on to her son Jonathan, who passes his feelings on to his sister Sally. Finally, the feelings reach the family's pet dog. The dog, unaffected by weather and sharp words, responds with playfulness, and reverses the situation by starting a chain of pleasant events. Each person speaks kindly to another, and eventually the kind words reach Mr. James, who kisses his wife hello at the end of the day.

The characters' reactions of irritation or cheerfulness parallel the ways in which they are treated by "significant others." The story provides an example of unconscious displacement of hostile feelings, as each character unwittingly passes along these feelings rather than examine their meanings.

Ages 4-7

Also available in:
Talking Book—*The Quarreling Book*
Library of Congress (NLSBPH)

671

Zolotow, Charlotte Shapiro

The Storm Book

Color illustrations by Margaret Bloy Graham.
HarperCollins Publishers, Inc. (Charlotte Zolotow Books), 1952.
(30 pages counted)

FEAR: of Storms

In the summertime, a young farm boy notices the dry earth, the dusty plants, and the "special, hot stillness over everything." Then a storm gathers. During the storm, the boy's mother answers his questions about lightning and thunder. The storm's effect on people in the city, at the seashore, and on the mountains are also described. After the storm is over, the earth is left refreshed and a rainbow appears. The little boy seems intrigued with the beauty of these natural phenomena.

This book gives a picturesque and understandable explanation of a summer rainstorm. Because the illustrations, the descriptions, and the little boy's comments leave the reader with positive feelings, this book could be read to children who are afraid of storms.

Ages 3-7

Also available in:
Paperbound—*The Storm Book*
HarperCollins Publishers, Inc. (Charlotte Zolotow Books)

672

Zolotow, Charlotte Shapiro

The Three Funny Friends

Color illustrations by Mary Chalmers.
HarperCollins Publishers, Inc. (Charlotte Zolotow Books), 1961.
(32 pages)

IMAGINARY FRIEND

When a little girl moves to a new town, she is not lonely because she is accompanied by three funny friends, invisible to everyone but her. Guy-guy does all the things that the little girl would never do: he scatters books on the floor and tears the fringe off Mother's new curtains. Mother never sees Guy-guy; she sees only the things that he does. Bickerina does all the things the little girl would like to do: she brings home a wild white horse and helps Mother with the mending. Mother never sees Bickerina, nor the things Bickerina does. Mr. Dobie does the things the little girl is supposed to do: he takes her bath, eats her meat, and goes to bed when she is told. When the little girl meets the little boy who lives next door, she gains a friend her family can see, and her three funny friends disappear.

The little girl creates imaginary friends to cope with stress and to keep herself from being lonely. Her fantasy friends help her and accept the blame whenever something bad is done. When the little girl meets a real friend, however, her imaginary friends are no longer needed.

Ages 4-6

Also available in:
No other form known

673

Zolotow, Charlotte Shapiro

A Tiger Called Thomas

Color illustrations by Kurt Werth.
Lothrop, Lee & Shepard Books, 1988.
(30 pages counted)

FRIENDSHIP: Making Friends
Change: new home
Shyness

Thomas and his parents have just moved to a new house, and Thomas presumes that none of the people in his new neighborhood will like him. Although Thomas's mother encourages him to play with little Marie or visit the old lady with the cat, Thomas is so sure that they will not like him that he refuses to budge from the porch. From his lonely perch, Thomas watches the activities of people in his neighborhood: Gerald, the tall boy who looks lonely; the woman across the street who works in her garden; and the old man who walks his poodle each day. When Halloween comes, Thomas's mother buys a tiger suit for him to wear for trick-or-treating. Thinking no one will recognize him, Thomas goes to the houses of all the people he has watched. To his surprise, each of them gives him a nice treat, calls him by name, and invites him to return. Marie and Gerald even ask him to play with them sometime. When he returns home, Thomas tells his mother that his costume did not fool anyone and that everyone was nice. He realizes that the people all like him, and in return he likes them.

Thomas has no apparent reason to assume his new neighbors will not like him. Even though he is terribly lonely and without friends in his new home, his timidity prevents him from approaching anyone. His mother's support and encouragement help him decide to venture out in a disguise.

Ages 4-7

Also available in:
Cassette—*A Tiger Called Thomas*
Library of Congress (NLSBPH)

674

Zolotow, Charlotte Shapiro

The Unfriendly Book

Black/white illustrations by William Pène du Bois.
HarperCollins Publishers, Inc. (Charlotte Zolotow Books), 1975.
(32 pages) o.p.

FRIENDSHIP: Lack of
FRIENDSHIP: Meaning of

Little Judy has lots of friends. She is always ready to see the best in each of them, despite their faults. But Bertha, who has always considered herself Judy's best friend, likes none of the other girls. She sees only their faults and therefore has no friends. She criticizes Judy for liking everyone, but Judy sets her straight: she does not like everyone—she likes everyone but Bertha!

The story, enhanced by the clever illustrations, provides an opportunity for young children to recognize the importance of looking for the good in others. Each friend is pictured first as Bertha sees her, with unattractive traits exaggerated, then as Judy sees her, with the best foot forward.

Ages 4-8

Also available in:
No other form known

675

Zolotow, Charlotte Shapiro

The White Marble

Black/white illustrations by Deborah Kogan Ray.
HarperCollins Publishers, Inc., 1982.
(32 pages) o.p.

FRIENDSHIP
Nature: appreciation of
Sharing/Not sharing

One hot, still summer's night, John Henry and his parents walk to the park. John Henry picks up something from the grass. When his father asks him what he found, John Henry replies, "Nothing." Sitting between his parents on the bench, the only child in the park, John Henry feels lonely, even though he knows it is special to be allowed out late like this. Then he sees Pamela, a girl from school, arrive with her mother. He and she smile at each other and seem to understand that only children can know what a night like this really means. They run together, kicking off their shoes and enjoying the sweet, fresh-smelling air. Lying on the soft grass, John Henry shows Pamela the white marble he found. She thinks it's beautiful. "No grown-up would have known." They drink from the white, foamy fountain and let the icy water run down their necks. Their parents call them to the ice-cream man's cart and buy them pineapple sticks. When it's time to go, John Henry presses the white marble into Pamela's hand and tells her to keep it.

A young boy and girl share a special evening in the park, made magical by their sensuous appreciation of the soft breezes, fresh-smelling grass, icy fountain, and starry sky. Their friendship is a spontaneous one, formed from the simple bond of childhood. In this newly illustrated version of the story, soft, shaded pictures reinforce the lyrical mood established by the text.

Ages 4-8

Also available in:
No other form known

676

Zolotow, Charlotte Shapiro

William's Doll

Color illustrations by William Pène Du Bois.
HarperCollins Publishers, Inc. (Charlotte Zolotow Books), 1972.
(32 pages)

GENDER ROLE IDENTITY: Male

Because William wants a doll to care for and be a father to, his older brothers tell him he is a creep, and the boy next door calls him a sissy. William's father responds by buying his son a basketball and hoop. William practices and becomes very good at shooting baskets, but he still wants a doll. His father buys him an electric train. William and his father put up miniature trees and buildings to use with the train, but the boy still wants a doll. When William's grandmother comes to visit, he shows her his train set and how well he can play basketball. She seems very interested in him and his accomplishments, and so William tells her that he wants a doll. Grandmother then buys him one because "he needs it...to hug and to cradle and to take to the park so that when he's a father...he'll know how to take care of his baby."

This is an endearing story which completely captures the concept that there is nothing wrong with a boy who plays with dolls. The warmth and tender understanding expressed in the story will go far in proving to children the truth of this idea.

Ages 4-7

Also available in:
Paperbound—*William's Doll*
HarperCollins Publishers, Inc. (Charlotte Zolotow Books)

SUBJECT INDEX

To locate a book through the Subject Index, find the desired subject; titles of relevant books are listed under each subject. Numbers refer to annotation numbers.

A

Abandonment

See also: *Loss: feelings of; Rejection; Separation from loved ones*

Byars, Betsy Cromer. THE HOUSE OF WINGS.
Ages 9-12. 91
Childress, Alice. A HERO AIN'T NOTHIN' BUT A SANDWICH.
Ages 12 and up. 108
Hill, Margaret. TURN THE PAGE, WENDY.
Ages 10-14. 272
O'Dell, Scott. ISLAND OF THE BLUE DOLPHINS.
Ages 10 and up. 446
Sachs, Marilyn. THE BEARS' HOUSE.
Ages 9-12. 510
Sargent, Sarah. SECRET LIES.
Ages 11 and up. 519
Strang, Celia. FOSTER MARY.
Ages 10-13. 575
Voigt, Cynthia. HOMECOMING.
Ages 11 and up. 598

Abortion

See also: *Pregnancy*

Beckman, Gunnel. MIA ALONE.
Ages 12 and up. 32
Head, Ann. MR. AND MRS. BO JO JONES.
Ages 13 and up. 262

Absent Parent

See: *Divorce: of parents; Parental: absence*

Abuse

See: *Child abuse*

Accidents

See also: *Guilt, feelings of; Hospital, going to*

Marino, Barbara Pavis. ERIC NEEDS STITCHES.
Ages 4-10. 400
Wolde, Gunilla. BETSY AND THE DOCTOR.
Ages 3-7. 635
Wolff, Angelika. MOM! I BROKE MY ARM!
Ages 5-8. 642

Automobile

Bates, Betty. PICKING UP THE PIECES.
Ages 10-13. 29
Jordan, Hope Dahle. HAUNTED SUMMER.
Ages 11 and up. 320
Kingman, Lee. HEAD OVER WHEELS.
Ages 12 and up. 335
Mazer, Norma Fox. WHEN WE FIRST MET.
Ages 12 and up. 417
McCaffrey, Mary. MY BROTHER ANGE.
Ages 8-11. 418
Van Leeuwen, Jean. SEEMS LIKE THIS ROAD GOES ON FOREVER.
Ages 12 and up. 589

Achievement

See: *Competition; School: achievement/underachievement; Success*

Addiction

See: *Alcoholism; Drugs; Marijuana; Peer relationships: peer pressures; Smoking*

Adolescence

See: *Maturation; Menstruation; Puberty*

Adoption

See also: *Children's home, living in; Identity, search for; Orphan*

Explaining

Bunin, Catherine and Sherry Bunin. IS THAT YOUR SISTER? A TRUE STORY OF ADOPTION.
Ages 4-8. 75
Caines, Jeannette Franklin. ABBY.
Ages 3-7. 95
Fitzgerald, John Dennis. ME AND MY LITTLE BRAIN.
Ages 9-12. 182
Krementz, Jill. HOW IT FEELS TO BE ADOPTED.
Ages 9 and up. 346
Stein, Sara Bonnett. THE ADOPTED ONE: AN OPEN FAMILY BOOK FOR PARENTS AND CHILDREN TOGETHER.
Ages 4-8. 565

Feelings about

Adler, Carole Schwerdtfeger. THE CAT THAT WAS LEFT BEHIND.
Ages 9-12. 2
Krementz, Jill. HOW IT FEELS TO BE ADOPTED.
Ages 9 and up. 346
Miles, Miska, pseud. AARON'S DOOR.
Ages 5-9. 428
Myers, Walter Dean. WON'T KNOW TILL I GET THERE.
Ages 11-14. 439
Pfeffer, Susan Beth. ABOUT DAVID.
Ages 13 and up. 474
Pfeffer, Susan Beth. JUST BETWEEN US.
Ages 10-12. 475
Shyer, Marlene Fanta. MY BROTHER, THE THIEF.
Ages 10-13. 534
Stein, Sara Bonnett. THE ADOPTED ONE: AN OPEN FAMILY BOOK FOR PARENTS AND CHILDREN TOGETHER.
Ages 4-8. 565
Swartley, David Warren. MY FRIEND, MY BROTHER.
Ages 9-11. 580
Winthrop, Elizabeth. MARATHON MIRANDA.
Ages 9 11. 626

Identity questions

Krementz, Jill. HOW IT FEELS TO BE ADOPTED.
Ages 9 and up. 346
Lifton, Betty Jean. I'M STILL ME.
Ages 12 and up. 364
Stein, Sara Bonnett. THE ADOPTED ONE: AN OPEN FAMILY BOOK FOR PARENTS AND CHILDREN TOGETHER.
Ages 4-8. 565

Adoption (cont.)

Interracial
Bunin, Catherine and Sherry Bunin. IS THAT YOUR SISTER? A TRUE STORY OF ADOPTION.
Ages 4-8. 75
Krementz, Jill. HOW IT FEELS TO BE ADOPTED.
Ages 9 and up. 346
Neufeld, John. EDGAR ALLAN.
Ages 10 and up. 442

Affluence

See: *Prejudice: social class; Wealth/Wealthy*

Africa
Greenfield, Eloise. AFRICA DREAM.
Ages 3-6. 231

African-American

See also: *Ghetto*
Butterworth, William Edmund. LEROY AND THE OLD MAN.
Ages 12 and up. 86
Childress, Alice. RAINBOW JORDAN.
Ages 12 and up. 109
Clifton, Lucille. EVERETT ANDERSON'S NINE MONTH LONG.
Ages 4-7. 128
Greenfield, Eloise. AFRICA DREAM.
Ages 3-6. 231
Grimes, Nikki. SOMETHING ON MY MIND.
Ages 5-9. 238
Hamilton, Virginia. ZEELY.
Ages 10-12. 249
Hansen, Joyce. THE GIFT-GIVER.
Ages 9-12. 250
Lexau, Joan M. STRIPED ICE CREAM.
Ages 8-11. 363
Lipsyte, Robert. THE CONTENDER.
Ages 12 and up. 372
Mathis, Sharon Bell. THE HUNDRED PENNY BOX.
Ages 8-10. 405
Mathis, Sharon Bell. LISTEN FOR THE FIG TREE.
Ages 12 and up. 406
Mathis, Sharon Bell. SIDEWALK STORY.
Ages 8-10. 407
Myers, Walter Dean. HOOPS.
Ages 12 and up. 437
Myers, Walter Dean. IT AIN'T ALL FOR NOTHIN'.
Ages 11-13. 438
Myers, Walter Dean. THE YOUNG LANDLORDS.
Ages 11-14. 440
Steptoe, John Lewis. MARCIA.
Ages 12 and up. 571
Taylor, Mildred D. ROLL OF THUNDER, HEAR MY CRY.
Ages 10 and up. 581
Wilkinson, Brenda Scott. LUDELL.
Ages 10-14. 621
Wilkinson, Brenda Scott. LUDELL AND WILLIE.
Ages 12 and up. 622
Wood, Phyllis Anderson. THIS TIME COUNT ME IN.
Ages 12 and up. 648

African-American Clubs

See also: *Clubs*
Myers, Walter Dean. FAST SAM, COOL CLYDE, AND STUFF.
Ages 11-14. 436

Age

See also: *Family; Grandparent; Great-grandparent; Retirement*

Aging
Clifford, Ethel Rosenberg. THE ROCKING CHAIR REBELLION.
Ages 11-13. 127
Hentoff, Nat. DOES THIS SCHOOL HAVE CAPITAL PUNISHMENT?
Ages 11 and up. 265
Herman, Charlotte. OUR SNOWMAN HAD OLIVE EYES.
Ages 9-11. 267
Hughes, Dean. SWITCHING TRACKS.
Ages 10-14. 296
Lowry, Lois. ANASTASIA AGAIN!
Ages 9-12. 386
Lowry, Lois. ANASTASIA KRUPNIK.
Ages 9-11. 388
Myers, Walter Dean. WON'T KNOW TILL I GET THERE.
Ages 11-14. 439
Paterson, Katherine Womeldorf. JACOB HAVE I LOVED.
Ages 12 and up. 457
Radley, Gail. NOTHING STAYS THE SAME FOREVER.
Ages 9-12. 488
Wolkoff, Judie. WHERE THE ELF KING SINGS.
Ages 12 and up. 647

Respect for
Bates, Betty. PICKING UP THE PIECES.
Ages 10-13. 29
Bond, Nancy Barbara. THE VOYAGE BEGUN.
Ages 12 and up. 49
Cleaver, Vera and Bill Cleaver. QUEEN OF HEARTS.
Ages 10-13. 124
Irwin, Hadley, pseud. THE LILITH SUMMER.
Ages 9-13. 310
Konigsburg, Elaine Lobl. ALTOGETHER, ONE AT A TIME.
Ages 9-11. 342
Konigsburg, Elaine Lobl. THROWING SHADOWS.
Ages 10-12. 344
Mathis, Sharon Bell. THE HUNDRED PENNY BOX
Ages 8-10. 405
Myers, Walter Dean. WON'T KNOW TILL I GET THERE.
Ages 11-14. 439
Pevsner, Stella. KEEP STOMPIN' TILL THE MUSIC STOPS.
Ages 9-12. 472

Amputee

See also: *Hospital, going to; Limbs, abnormal or missing; Prosthesis;Surgery; Wheelchair, dependence on*
Sallis, Susan Diana. ONLY LOVE.
Ages 12 and up. 518

Amyotrophic Lateral Sclerosis
Dixon, Paige, pseud. MAY I CROSS YOUR GOLDEN RIVER?
Ages 12 and up. 166

Anger

See also: *Aggression; Depression; Hatred; Hostility; Tantrums*
Fitzhugh, Louise. THE LONG SECRET.
Ages 9-12. 184
Goff, Beth. WHERE IS DADDY? THE STORY OF A DIVORCE.
Ages 4-8. 209
Greene, Constance Clarke. YOUR OLD PAL, AL.
Ages 9-13. 229
Hogan, Paula Z. SOMETIMES I GET SO MAD.
Ages 5-8. 285
Kingman, Lee. HEAD OVER WHEELS.
Ages 12 and up. 335
Park, Barbara. DON'T MAKE ME SMILE.
Ages 8-11. 453
Platt, Kin. THE APE INSIDE ME.
Ages 12 and up. 481
Simon, Norma. I WAS SO MAD!
Ages 4-8. 539
Stretton, Barbara. YOU NEVER LOSE.
Ages 12 and up. 578
Udry, Janice May. LET'S BE ENEMIES.
Ages 3-7. 587
Viorst, Judith. ALEXANDER AND THE TERRIBLE, HORRIBLE, NO GOOD, VERY BAD DAY.
Ages 3-8. 592
Watson, Jane Werner, Robert E. Switzer. SOMETIMES I GET ANGRY.
Ages 3-6. 612
Wittels, Harriet and Joan Greisman. THINGS I HATE.
Ages 4-8. 629
Zolotow, Charlotte Shapiro. THE HATING BOOK.
Ages 3-7. 662

Animals

See also: *Pets; Transitional objects*

Fear of. *See: Fear: of animals*

Love for
Adler, Carole Schwerdtfeger. THE CAT THAT WAS LEFT BEHIND.
Ages 9-12. 2
Hall, Lynn. DANZA!
Ages 9-12. 245
Shura, Mary Francis Craig. THE BARKLEY STREET SIX-PACK.
Ages 9-12. 533
Thomas, Jane Resh. THE COMEBACK DOG.
Ages 7-9. 584
Wartski, Maureen Crane. MY BROTHER IS SPECIAL.
Ages 10-12. 606
Waterton, Betty Marie. A SALMON FOR SIMON.
Ages 4-7. 609

Responsibility for
Holmes, Efner Tudor. AMY'S GOOSE.
Ages 8-11. 293
Waterton, Betty Marie. A SALMON FOR SIMON.
Ages 4-7. 609

Anorexia Nervosa

See also: *Mental illness*
Hautzig, Deborah. SECOND STAR TO THE RIGHT.
Ages 12 and up. 256
Liu, Aimee. SOLITAIRE.
Ages 13 and up. 384

Anxiety

See also: *Fear; Separation anxiety*
Asher, Sandra Fenichel. JUST LIKE JENNY.
Ages 10-12. 22
Beckman, Gunnel. MIA ALONE.
Ages 12 and up. 32
Blume, Judy Sussman. IT'S NOT THE END OF THE WORLD.
Ages 10-12. 41
Blume, Judy Sussman. THEN AGAIN, MAYBE I WON'T.
Ages 12 and up. 46
Byars, Betsy Cromer. GOODBYE, CHICKEN LITTLE.
Ages 9-11. 90
Delton, Judy. MY MOTHER LOST HER JOB TODAY.
Ages 3-7. 164
Evans, Mari. JD.
Ages 4-8. 175
Fassler, Joan. DON'T WORRY DEAR.
Ages 4-6. 177
Greenberg, Jan. A SEASON IN-BETWEEN.
Ages 11-13. 219
Hamilton, Virginia. M. C. HIGGINS, THE GREAT.
Ages 12 and up. 248
Helmering, Doris Wild. I HAVE TWO FAMILIES.
Ages 6-8. 263
Marshall, James. GEORGE AND MARTHA—ONE FINE DAY.
Ages 3-6. 402
Schuchman, Joan. TWO PLACES TO SLEEP.
Ages 5-7. 521
Stanek, Muriel Novella. I WON'T GO WITHOUT A FATHER.
Ages 8-10. 560

Apartheid

See also: *Prejudice: ethnic/racial*
Jones, Toeckey. GO WELL, STAY WELL.
Ages 12 and up. 319

Apathy

See: *Depression*

Appalachia
Bulla, Clyde Robert. DANIEL'S DUCK.
Ages 5-8. 72

Appalachia (cont.)
Cleaver, Vera and Bill Cleaver. TRIAL VALLEY.
Ages 12 and up. 125
Cleaver, Vera and Bill Cleaver. WHERE THE LILIES BLOOM.
Ages 11 and up. 126

Appearance
See also: *Height; Weight control*

Body concept. *See: Self, attitude toward: body concept*

Concern About
Andersen, Hans Christian. THE UGLY DUCKLING.
Ages 4-8. 12
Blume, Judy Sussman. DEENIE.
Ages 10-12. 38
Brown, Marc Tolan. ARTHUR'S EYES.
Ages 4-7. 68
Danziger, Paula. THE PISTACHIO PRESCRIPTION: A NOVEL.
Ages 11-13. 154
Greene, Constance C. THE UNMAKING OF RABBIT.
Ages 10-13. 228
Guy, Rosa Cuthbert. THE DISAPPEARANCE.
Ages 12 and up. 243
Landis, James David. THE SISTERS IMPOSSIBLE.
Ages 9-11. 348
Perl, Lila. THE TELLTALE SUMMER OF TINA C.
Ages 10-13. 466
Sachs, Marilyn. HELLO. . . . WRONG NUMBER.
Ages 12-16. 512
Sachs, Marilyn. VERONICA GANZ.
Ages 10-12. 517
Waber, Bernard. YOU LOOK RIDICULOUS, SAID THE RHINOCEROS TO THE HIPPOPOTAMUS.
Ages 5-8. 600

Deformities. *See: Deformities*

Freckles. *See: Freckles*

Glasses. *See: Glasses, wearing of*

Appendectomy
See: *Hospital, going to; Surgery*

Appetite
See: *Weight control*

Apple polishing
See: *Attention Seeking*

Approach-Avoidance Conflict
See: *Ambivalence, feelings of*

Arguing
Burningham, John Mackintosh. THE FRIEND.
Ages 2-5. 81
Byars, Betsy Cromer. THE ANIMAL, THE VEGETABLE, AND JOHN D JONES.
Ages 10-12. 87
Oppenheimer, Joan Letson. GARDINE VS. HANOVER.
Ages 11-14. 451

Arthritis, Juvenile Rheumatoid
Jones, Rebecca Castalldi. ANGIE AND ME.
Ages 9-11. 317

Artificial Limbs
See: *Prosthesis*

Asthma
Danziger, Paula. THE PISTACHIO PRESCRIPTION: A NOVEL.
Ages 11-13. 154
Wilkinson, Brenda Scott. LUDELL.
Ages 10-14. 621
Winthrop, Elizabeth. MARATHON MIRANDA.
Ages 9-11. 626
Winthrop, Elizabeth. MIRANDA IN THE MIDDLE.
Ages 9-13. 627

Athletics
See: *Competition; Little League; Sports/Sportsmanship*

Attention Seeking
See also: *Boasting*
Brandenberg, Franz. I WISH I WAS SICK, TOO!
Ages 3-7. 61
Duvoisin, Roger Antoine. VERONICA.
Ages 4-7. 171
Giff, Patricia Reilly. FOURTH GRADE CELEBRITY.
Ages 8-10. 200
Lindgren, Astrid. I WANT A BROTHER OR SISTER.
Ages 3-7. 365
Rodowsky, Colby F. P.S. WRITE SOON.
Ages 10-12. 506
Watson, Jane Werner, Robert E. Switzer. SOMETIMES I'M JEALOUS.
Ages 3-6. 614
Wells, Rosemary. NOISY NORA.
Ages 4-7. 616

Attitude
See: *Self, attitude toward; Work, attitude toward*

Aunt
See: *Relatives: living in home of*

Autism
Gold, Phyllis. PLEASE DON'T SAY HELLO.
Ages 7 and up. 210

Autonomy
See also: *Dependence/Independence*
Danziger, Paula. CAN YOU SUE YOUR PARENTS FOR MALPRACTICE?
Ages 10-14. 151
George, Jean Craighead. MY SIDE OF THE MOUNTAIN.
Ages 11-14. 199

Autonomy (cont.)
Greenberg, Jan. THE PIG-OUT BLUES.
Ages 12 and up. 218
Hansen, Joyce. THE GIFT-GIVER.
Ages 9-12. 250
Kerr, M. E., pseud. LITTLE LITTLE.
Ages 11 and up. 331
Levoy, Myron. A SHADOW LIKE A LEOPARD.
Ages 12 and up. 359
Mazer, Harry. THE ISLAND KEEPER.
Ages 10-14. 414
Mazer, Norma Fox. UP IN SETH'S ROOM.
Ages 13 and up. 416
Simon, Norma. WHY AM I DIFFERENT?
Ages 4-8. 542
Watanabe, Shigeo. HOW DO I PUT IT ON?
Ages 2-5. 607
Wolde, Gunilla. THIS IS BETSY.
Ages 2-5. 639
Yep, Laurence Michael. KIND HEARTS AND GENTLE MONSTERS.
Ages 12 and up. 653
Zolotow, Charlotte Shapiro. BIG SISTER AND LITTLE SISTER.
Ages 3-7. 660

Avoidance
See: *Peer relationships: avoiding others; Responsibility: avoiding*

B

Baby, New
See: *Sibling: new baby*

Baby-Sitter
Smith, Janice Lee. THE MONSTER IN THE THIRD DRESSER DRAWER AND OTHER STORIES ABOUT ADAM JOSHUA.
Ages 5-8. 553

Baby-Sitting
See also: *Job; Sibling: older; Sibling: oldest*
Byars, Betsy Cromer. THE NIGHT SWIMMERS.
Ages 10-12. 92
Gilson, Jamie. DO BANANAS CHEW GUM?
Ages 9-11. 205
Pascal, Francine. MY FIRST LOVE & OTHER DISASTERS.
Ages 12 and up. 454

Involuntary
Bonsall, Crosby Newell. THE DAY I HAD TO PLAY WITH MY SISTER.
Ages 3-8. 52
McCaffrey, Mary. MY BROTHER ANGE.
Ages 8-11. 418

Voluntary
Byars, Betsy Cromer. GO AND HUSH THE BABY.
Ages 3-6. 89

Banned Books
See: *Censorship, Literary*

Battered Child
See: *Child abuse*

Beauty, Personal
See: *Appearance*

Bed-wetting
See: *Enuresis*

Bedtime
Crowe, Robert L. CLYDE MONSTER.
Ages 3-6. 148
Hoban, Russell Conwell. BEDTIME FOR FRANCES.
Ages 3-7. 279
Sharmat, Marjorie Weinman. GOODNIGHT, ANDREW; GOODNIGHT, CRAIG.
Ages 3-7. 528
Willoughby, Elaine Macmann. BORIS AND THE MONSTERS.
Ages 4-7. 625

Belonging
See also: *Clubs; Gangs: membership in; Loneliness; Peer relationships; Rejection*
Adler, Carole Schwerdtfeger. THE CAT THAT WAS LEFT BEHIND.
Ages 9-12. 2
Ashley, Bernard. A KIND OF WILD JUSTICE.
Ages 12 and up. 23
Burnett, Frances Hodgson. THE SECRET GARDEN.
Ages 10 and up. 78
Fitzhugh, Louise. THE LONG SECRET.
Ages 9-12. 184
Freeman, Don. CORDUROY.
Ages 3-8. 192
Greene, Constance C. THE UNMAKING OF RABBIT.
Ages 10-13. 228
Hill, Margaret. TURN THE PAGE, WENDY.
Ages 10-14. 272
Kent, Deborah. BELONGING: A NOVEL.
Ages 11-14. 328
Little, Jean. FROM ANNA.
Ages 9-11. 377
MacLachlan, Patricia. CASSIE BINEGAR.
Ages 9-12. 393
Miles, Betty. LOOKING ON.
Ages 11-14. 425
Reiss, Johanna. THE JOURNEY BACK.
Ages 10-14. 492
Rodowsky, Colby F. H. MY NAME IS HENLEY.
Ages 10-13. 505
Scott, Ann Herbert. SAM.
Ages 3-7. 525
Simon, Norma. ALL KINDS OF FAMILIES.
Ages 5-8. 537
Wartski, Maureen Crane. A BOAT TO NOWHERE.
Ages 9-12. 604
Wartski, Maureen Crane. A LONG WAY FROM HOME.
Ages 11-13. 605

Belonging (cont.)
Zalben, Jane Breskin. MAYBE IT WILL RAIN TOMORROW.
Ages 12 and up. 655

Best Friend
See: *Friendship: best friend*

Black
See: *African-American*

Blame
See also: *Guilt, feelings of; Justice/Injustice*
Mazer, Norma Fox. WHEN WE FIRST MET.
Ages 12 and up. 417

Blindness
See also: *Education: special; Pets: guide dog; Visual impairment*
Butler, Beverly Kathleen. LIGHT A SINGLE CANDLE.
Ages 10 and up. 85
Keller, Helen Adams. THE STORY OF MY LIFE.
Ages 11 and up. 324
Kent, Deborah. BELONGING: A NOVEL.
Ages 11-14. 328
Little, Jean. LISTEN FOR THE SINGING.
Ages 10-14. 380
MacLachlan, Patricia. THROUGH GRANDPA'S EYES.
Ages 5-8. 396
Mathis, Sharon Bell. LISTEN FOR THE FIG TREE.
Ages 12 and up. 406
Quigley, Lillian Fox. THE BLIND MEN AND THE ELEPHANT: AN OLD TALE FROM THE LAND OF INDIA.
Ages 6-9. 486
Reuter, Margaret. MY MOTHER IS BLIND.
Ages 5-8. 493
Wilder, Laura Ingalls. BY THE SHORES OF SILVER LAKE.
Ages 8-11. 620

Boarding Schools
See: *Schools, private*

Boasting
See also: *Attention seeking*
Blume, Judy Sussman. OTHERWISE KNOWN AS SHEILA THE GREAT.
Ages 9-11. 43
Bonsall, Crosby Newell. MINE'S THE BEST.
Ages 3-8. 53
Greene, Bette. GET ON OUT OF HERE, PHILIP HALL.
Ages 9-12. 220
Lopshire, Robert. I AM BETTER THAN YOU!
Ages 4-8. 385
Rodowsky, Colby F. P.S. WRITE SOON.
Ages 10-12. 506
Sharmat, Marjorie Weinman. I'M TERRIFIC.
Ages 4-7. 529

Body Concept
See: *Name-calling; Self, attitude toward: body concept*

Boy-Girl Relationships
See also: *Friendship; Peer relationships; Sex*
Angell, Judie. RONNIE AND ROSEY.
Ages 11 and up. 14
Asher, Sandra Fenichel. JUST LIKE JENNY.
Ages 10-12. 22
Bates, Betty. PICKING UP THE PIECES.
Ages 10-13. 29
Brancato, Robin Fidler. WINNING.
Ages 12 and up. 58
Bridgers, Sue Ellen. HOME BEFORE DARK.
Ages 12 and up. 64
Calhoun, Mary Huiskamp. KATIE JOHN AND HEATHCLIFF.
Ages 9-11. 98
Cleaver, Vera and Bill Cleaver. TRIAL VALLEY.
Ages 12 and up. 125
Cohen, Barbara Nash. THE INNKEEPER'S DAUGHTER.
Ages 11-14. 131
Danziger, Paula. THE DIVORCE EXPRESS.
Ages 11-14. 153
Danziger, Paula. THE PISTACHIO PRESCRIPTION: A NOVEL.
Ages 11-13. 154
Danziger, Paula. THERE'S A BAT IN BUNK FIVE.
Ages 10-14. 155
Foley, June. IT'S NO CRUSH, I'M IN LOVE!
Ages 11-13. 185
Frank, Anne. ANNE FRANK: THE DIARY OF A YOUNG GIRL.
Ages 11 and up. 191
Greenberg, Jan. THE PIG-OUT BLUES.
Ages 12 and up. 218
Greene, Bette. GET ON OUT OF HERE, PHILIP HALL.
Ages 9-12. 220
Greene, Sheppard M. THE BOY WHO DRANK TOO MUCH.
Ages 12 and up. 230
Guest, Elissa Haden. THE HANDSOME MAN.
Ages 12 and up. 241
Hallman, Ruth. BREAKAWAY.
Ages 12 and up. 247
Hamilton, Virginia. M. C. HIGGINS, THE GREAT.
Ages 12 and up. 248
Hansen, Joyce. THE GIFT-GIVER.
Ages 9-12. 250
Hogan, Paula Z. I HATE BOYS I HATE GIRLS.
Ages 5-8. 283
Hopkins, Lee Bennett. I LOVED ROSE ANN.
Ages 6-9. 294
Irwin, Hadley, pseud. MOON AND ME.
Ages 11-14. 311
Kerr, M. E., pseud. I'LL LOVE YOU WHEN YOU'RE MORE LIKE ME.
Ages 12 and up. 330
Kerr, M. E., pseud. LITTLE LITTLE.
Ages 11 and up. 331
Kingman, Lee. BREAK A LEG, BETSY MAYBE!
Ages 12 and up. 334

Boy-Girl Relationships (cont.)
Le Guin, Ursula Kroeber. VERY FAR AWAY FROM ANYWHERE ELSE.
Ages 12 and up. 352
Moeri, Louise. FIRST THE EGG.
Ages 12 and up. 430
Myers, Walter Dean. HOOPS.
Ages 12 and up. 437
Myers, Walter Dean. THE YOUNG LANDLORDS.
Ages 11-14. 440
Oppenheimer, Joan Letson. WORKING ON IT.
Ages 11-13. 452
Pascal, Francine. MY FIRST LOVE & OTHER DISASTERS.
Ages 12 and up. 454
Pevsner, Stella. AND YOU GIVE ME A PAIN, ELAINE.
Ages 10-13. 471
Pfeffer, Susan Beth. ABOUT DAVID.
Ages 13 and up. 474
Sachs, Marilyn. HELLO. . . . WRONG NUMBER.
Ages 12-16. 512
Sachs, Marilyn. PETER AND VERONICA.
Ages 10-12. 513
Sachs, Marilyn. VERONICA GANZ.
Ages 10-12. 517
Sallis, Susan Diana. ONLY LOVE.
Ages 12 and up. 518
Slepian, Jan. LESTER'S TURN.
Ages 11-14. 545
Snyder, Anne. MY NAME IS DAVY—I'M AN ALCOHOLIC.
Ages 12 and up. 556
Wilkinson, Brenda Scott. LUDELL.
Ages 10-14. 621
Wolff, Angelika. MOM! I NEED GLASSES!
Ages 10-13. 643
Wortis, Avi. SOMETIMES I THINK I HEAR MY NAME.
Ages 10-13. 649

Dating
Angell, Judie. WHAT'S BEST FOR YOU.
Ages 11-14. 15
Bridgers, Sue Ellen. NOTES FOR ANOTHER LIFE.
Ages 12 and up. 65
Dacquino, Vincent T. KISS THE CANDY DAYS GOOD-BYE.
Ages 10-14. 150
Danziger, Paula. CAN YOU SUE YOUR PARENTS FOR MALPRACTICE?
Ages 10-14. 151
Girion, Barbara. A HANDFUL OF STARS.
Ages 12 and up. 207
Girion, Barbara. A TANGLE OF ROOTS.
Ages 12-16. 208
Hinton, Susan E. THAT WAS THEN, THIS IS NOW.
Ages 12 and up. 275
Kerr, M. E., pseud. LOVE IS A MISSING PERSON.
Ages 12 and up. 332
Liu, Aimee. SOLITAIRE.
Ages 13 and up. 384
Luger, Harriett Mandelay. LAUREN.
Ages 12 and up. 390
Mazer, Norma Fox. DEAR BILL, REMEMBER ME? AND OTHER STORIES.
Ages 12 and up. 415
Mazer, Norma Fox. UP IN SETH'S ROOM.
Ages 13 and up. 416
Mazer, Norma Fox. WHEN WE FIRST MET.
Ages 12 and up. 417
Miklowitz, Gloria D. DID YOU HEAR WHAT HAPPENED TO ANDREA?
Ages 13 and up. 422
Miles, Betty. LOOKING ON.
Ages 11-14. 425
Peck, Richard. ARE YOU IN THE HOUSE ALONE?
Ages 12 and up. 460
Peck, Richard. CLOSE ENOUGH TO TOUCH.
Ages 12 and up. 461
Platt, Kin. BROGG'S BRAIN.
Ages 12 and up. 482
Riley, Jocelyn. ONLY MY MOUTH IS SMILING.
Ages 12-14. 495
Scoppettone, Sandra. THE LATE GREAT ME.
Ages 12 and up. 524
Smith, Doris Buchanan. KICK A STONE HOME.
Ages 11 and up. 549
Steptoe, John Lewis. MARCIA.
Ages 12 and up. 571
Strasser, Todd. ANGEL DUST BLUES.
Ages 14 and up. 576
Strasser, Todd. FRIENDS TILL THE END.
Ages 12 and up. 577
Stretton, Barbara. YOU NEVER LOSE.
Ages 12 and up. 578
Wilkinson, Brenda Scott. LUDELL AND WILLIE.
Ages 12 and up. 622
Wood, Phyllis Anderson. THIS TIME COUNT ME IN.
Ages 12 and up. 648
Yep, Laurence Michael. KIND HEARTS AND GENTLE MONSTERS.
Ages 12 and up. 653

Braces On Body/Limbs
See also: *Limbs, abnormal or missing*
Blume, Judy Sussman. DEENIE.
Ages 10-12. 38
Rabe, Berniece Louise. THE BALANCING GIRL.
Ages 5-7. 487
Rodowsky, Colby F. P.S. WRITE SOON.
Ages 10-12. 506
Wolf, Bernard. DON'T FEEL SORRY FOR PAUL.
Ages 8 and up. 641

Bragging
See: *Boasting*

Brain Injury
See also: *Cerebral palsy; Epilepsy; Learning disabilities; Mental retardation*
Melton, David. A BOY CALLED HOPELESS.
Ages 10 and up. 420
Robinet, Harriette Gillem. RIDE THE RED CYCLE.
Ages 7-11. 497

Bravery
See: *Courage, meaning of*

Broken Bones
See: *Fractures; Surgery*

Brother
See: *Sibling*

Buddhist
Coutant, Helen. FIRST SNOW.
Ages 7-9. 147

Bully
See also: *Harassment; Teasing*

Being a
Sachs, Marilyn. VERONICA GANZ.
Ages 10-12. 517
Stolz, Mary Slattery. THE BULLY OF BARKHAM STREET.
Ages 8-11. 573

Being bothered by
Alexander, Martha G. MOVE OVER, TWERP.
Ages 5-8. 7
Chapman, Carol. HERBIE'S TROUBLES.
Ages 5-7. 107
Conford, Ellen. THE REVENGE OF THE INCREDIBLE DR. RANCID AND HIS YOUTHFUL ASSISTANT, JEFFREY.
Ages 10-12. 142
Mauser, Pat Rhoads. A BUNDLE OF STICKS.
Ages 10-12. 410
Wartski, Maureen Crane. A LONG WAY FROM HOME.
Ages 11-13. 605

Fear of
Cleary, Beverly Bunn. MITCH AND AMY.
Ages 9-11. 114
Stolz, Mary Slattery. A DOG ON BARKHAM STREET.
Ages 8-11. 574
Wells, Rosemary. BENJAMIN & TULIP.
Ages 3-7. 615

C

Camp Experiences
See also: *Separation anxiety*
Angell, Judie. IN SUMMERTIME IT'S TUFFY.
Ages 11-13. 13
Brown, Marc Tolan. ARTHUR GOES TO CAMP.
Ages 5-8. 67
Danziger, Paula. THERE'S A BAT IN BUNK FIVE.
Ages 10-14. 155
Jones, Ron. THE ACORN PEOPLE.
Ages 10 and up. 318
Levy, Elizabeth. COME OUT SMILING.
Ages 12 and up. 360
O'Connor, Jane. YOURS TILL NIAGARA FALLS, ABBY.
Ages 8-10. 445
Smith, Robert Kimmel. JELLY BELLY.
Ages 10-12. 555

Canada
Little, Jean. LISTEN FOR THE SINGING.
Ages 10-14. 380

Cancer
See also: *Hospital, going to; Surgery*
Donnelly, Elfie. SO LONG, GRANDPA.
Ages 9-11. 167
Hermes, Patricia. YOU SHOULDN'T HAVE TO SAY GOOD-BYE.
Ages 10-13. 270
Mann, Peggy. THERE ARE TWO KINDS OF TERRIBLE.
Ages 9-12. 399
Stretton, Barbara. YOU NEVER LOSE.
Ages 12 and up. 578

Leukemia*See also: Leukemia*
Lund, Doris Herold. ERIC.
Ages 12 and up. 391

Careers

Dancer
Landis, James David. THE SISTERS IMPOSSIBLE.
Ages 9-11. 348

Planning. *See also: Education; Work, attitude toward*
Clifford, Ethel Rosenberg. THE ROCKING CHAIR REBELLION.
Ages 11-13. 127
Lipsyte, Robert. THE CONTENDER.
Ages 12 and up. 372
Strasser, Todd. FRIENDS TILL THE END.
Ages 12 and up. 577

Catholic, Roman
See: *Roman Catholic*

Censorship, Literary
Miles, Betty. MAUDIE AND ME AND THE DIRTY BOOK.
Ages 10-12. 426

Cerebral Palsy
See also: *Brain injury*
Fassler, Joan. HOWIE HELPS HIMSELF.
Ages 5-8. 178
Little, Jean. MINE FOR KEEPS.
Ages 10-13. 382
Payne, Sherry Neuwirth. A CONTEST.
Ages 8-10. 459
Slepian, Jan. THE ALFRED SUMMER.
Ages 11-13. 544
Slepian, Jan. LESTER'S TURN.
Ages 11-14. 545
Stein, Sara Bonnett. ABOUT HANDICAPS: AN OPEN FAMILY BOOK FOR PARENTS AND CHILDREN TOGETHER.
Ages 4-8. 564

Change

Accepting

Alda, Arlene. SONYA'S MOMMY WORKS.
Ages 4-7. 6
Angell, Judie. WHAT'S BEST FOR YOU.
Ages 11-14. 15
Bates, Betty. PICKING UP THE PIECES.
Ages 10-13. 29
Bennett, Jack. THE VOYAGE OF THE LUCKY DRAGON.
Ages 11 and up. 33
Blaine, Margery Kay. THE TERRIBLE THING THAT HAPPENED AT OUR HOUSE.
Ages 3-7. 36
Bond, Nancy Barbara. THE VOYAGE BEGUN.
Ages 12 and up. 49
Bradford, Richard. RED SKY AT MORNING.
Ages 13 and up. 57
Brandenberg, Aliki Liacouras. WE ARE BEST FRIENDS.
Ages 3-6. 60
Bunting, Anne Evelyn. THE BIG RED BARN.
Ages 4-7. 76
Byars, Betsy Cromer. THE ANIMAL, THE VEGETABLE, AND JOHN D JONES.
Ages 10-12. 87
Byars, Betsy Cromer. THE NIGHT SWIMMERS.
Ages 10-12. 92
Cleary, Beverly Bunn. RAMONA AND HER MOTHER.
Ages 7-10. 117
Dacquino, Vincent T. KISS THE CANDY DAYS GOOD-BYE.
Ages 10-14. 150
Danziger, Paula. THE DIVORCE EXPRESS.
Ages 11-14. 153
Delton, Judy. THE NEW GIRL AT SCHOOL.
Ages 4-7. 165
Greenfield, Eloise. GRANDMAMA'S JOY.
Ages 4-8. 232
Hansen, Joyce. THE GIFT-GIVER.
Ages 9-12. 250
Holland, Isabelle. NOW IS NOT TOO LATE.
Ages 10-13. 291
Hunt, Irene. WILLIAM: A NOVEL.
Ages 12 and up. 302
Jones, Rebecca Castalldi. ANGIE AND ME.
Ages 9-11. 317
Kerr, Judith. WHEN HITLER STOLE PINK RABBIT.
Ages 10-12. 329
MacLachlan, Patricia. CASSIE BINEGAR.
Ages 9-12. 393
Miles, Betty. THE TROUBLE WITH THIRTEEN.
Ages 9-13. 427
Reiss, Johanna. THE JOURNEY BACK.
Ages 10-14. 492
Sargent, Sarah. SECRET LIES.
Ages 11 and up. 519
Schuchman, Joan. TWO PLACES TO SLEEP.
Ages 5-7. 521
Seredy, Kate. THE GOOD MASTER.
Ages 9-12. 526
Voigt, Cynthia. HOMECOMING.
Ages 11 and up. 598
Walker, Mary Alexander. YEAR OF THE CAFETERIA.
Ages 12 and up. 601
Wright, Betty Ren. MY NEW MOM AND ME.
Ages 8-10. 651
Zalben, Jane Breskin. MAYBE IT WILL RAIN TOMORROW.
Ages 12 and up. 655
Zelonky, Joy. MY BEST FRIEND MOVED AWAY.
Ages 6-9. 657

New home. *See also: Lifestyle: change in; Moving*

Blume, Judy Sussman. SUPERFUDGE.
Ages 8-10. 44
Brandenberg, Franz. NICE NEW NEIGHBORS.
Ages 6-8. 62
Conford, Ellen. ANYTHING FOR A FRIEND.
Ages 9-11. 140
Danziger, Paula. THE DIVORCE EXPRESS.
Ages 11-14. 153
Garrigue, Sheila. BETWEEN FRIENDS.
Ages 9-12. 198
Giff, Patricia Reilly. THE WINTER WORM BUSINESS.
Ages 8-10. 204
Guy, Rosa Cuthbert. THE FRIENDS.
Ages 12 and up. 244
Hughes, Shirley. MOVING MOLLY.
Ages 3-5. 299
Hurwitz, Johanna. ALDO APPLESAUCE.
Ages 7-9. 305
Hurwitz, Johanna. TOUGH-LUCK KAREN.
Ages 10-13. 308
Kerr, Judith. WHEN HITLER STOLE PINK RABBIT.
Ages 10-12. 329
Litchfield, Ada Bassett. WORDS IN OUR HANDS.
Ages 7-9. 376
Little, Jean. FROM ANNA.
Ages 9-11. 377
Little, Jean. LOOK THROUGH MY WINDOW.
Ages 10-14. 381
Lowry, Lois. ANASTASIA AGAIN!
Ages 9-12. 386
MacLachlan, Patricia. CASSIE BINEGAR.
Ages 9-12. 393
Rodowsky, Colby F. H. MY NAME IS HENLEY.
Ages 10-13. 505
Shura, Mary Francis Craig. THE BARKLEY STREET SIX-PACK.
Ages 9-12. 533
Slote, Alfred. TONY AND ME.
Ages 10-13. 547
Smith, Nancy Covert. THE FALLING-APART WINTER.
Ages 10-13. 554
Wartski, Maureen Crane. MY BROTHER IS SPECIAL.
Ages 10-12. 606
Zolotow, Charlotte Shapiro. A TIGER CALLED THOMAS.
Ages 4-7. 673

Resisting

Adler, Carole Schwerdtfeger. IN OUR HOUSE SCOTT IS MY BROTHER.
Ages 10-13. 3
Bridgers, Sue Ellen. NOTES FOR ANOTHER LIFE.
Ages 12 and up. 65

Change (cont.)
Conford, Ellen. ANYTHING FOR A FRIEND.
Ages 9-11. 140
Fox, Paula. A PLACE APART.
Ages 12 and up. 188
Greene, Constance Clarke. I AND SPROGGY.
Ages 9-11. 226
Hogan, Paula Z. WILL DAD EVER MOVE BACK HOME?
Ages 7-10. 286
Kerr, Judith. WHEN HITLER STOLE PINK RABBIT.
Ages 10-12. 329
Little, Jean. HOME FROM FAR.
Ages 10-13. 378
Park, Barbara. DON'T MAKE ME SMILE.
Ages 8-11. 453
Radley, Gail. NOTHING STAYS THE SAME FOREVER.
Ages 9-12. 488
Smith, Janice Lee. THE MONSTER IN THE THIRD DRESSER DRAWER AND OTHER STORIES ABOUT ADAM JOSHUA.
Ages 5-8. 553
Smith, Nancy Covert. THE FALLING-APART WINTER.
Ages 10-13. 554
Stretton, Barbara. YOU NEVER LOSE.
Ages 12 and up. 578
Vigna, Judith. SHE'S NOT MY REAL MOTHER.
Ages 4-8. 591
Walker, Mary Alexander. YEAR OF THE CAFETERIA.
Ages 12 and up. 601

Chemical Dependency
See: *Alcoholism; Drugs; Marijuana; Reality, escaping*

Chicken Pox
See: *Communicable diseases: chicken pox*

Child Abuse
See also: *Cruelty*
Greene, Sheppard M. THE BOY WHO DRANK TOO MUCH.
Ages 12 and up. 230
Guy, Rosa Cuthbert. THE FRIENDS.
Ages 12 and up. 244
Hill, Margaret. TURN THE PAGE, WENDY.
Ages 10-14. 272
Hunt, Irene. THE LOTTERY ROSE.
Ages 11 and up. 300
Magorian, Michelle. GOOD NIGHT, MR. TOM.
Ages 11 and up. 398
Moeri, Louise. THE GIRL WHO LIVED ON THE FERRIS WHEEL.
Ages 13 and up. 431
Roberts, Willo Davis. DON'T HURT LAURIE!
Ages 10-14. 496
Smith, Doris Buchanan. TOUGH CHAUNCEY.
Ages 12 and up. 552
Strang, Celia. FOSTER MARY.
Ages 10-13. 575
Swartley, David Warren. MY FRIEND, MY BROTHER.
Ages 9-11. 580

Children's Home, Living in
See also: *Adoption; Foster home; Orphan*
Hill, Margaret. TURN THE PAGE, WENDY.
Ages 10-14. 272
Hunt, Irene. THE LOTTERY ROSE.
Ages 11 and up. 300

Chinese
Mosel, Arlene. TIKKI TIKKI TEMBO.
Ages 4-9. 434

Choice Making
See: *Decision making*

Chores
See also: *Job; Responsibility*
Wolde, Gunilla. BETSY AND THE VACUUM CLEANER.
Ages 3-6. 636

Cigarettes
See: *Smoking*

Cigars
See: *Smoking*

Classmate Relationships
See: *School: classmate relationships*

Clowning
See: *Attention seeking*

Clubs
See also: *African-American clubs; Belonging; Gangs*
Bonsall, Crosby Newell. THE CASE OF THE DOUBLE CROSS.
Ages 6-8. 51
Greene, Bette. GET ON OUT OF HERE, PHILIP HALL.
Ages 9-12. 220
Hogan, Paula Z. I HATE BOYS I HATE GIRLS.
Ages 5-8. 283
Perl, Lila. THE TELLTALE SUMMER OF TINA C.
Ages 10-13. 466

Communicable Diseases
See also: *Illnesses*

Chicken Pox
Wolde, Gunilla. BETSY AND THE CHICKEN POX.
Ages 3-7. 634

Communication

Importance of
Dacquino, Vincent T. KISS THE CANDY DAYS GOOD-BYE.
Ages 10-14. 150
Meyer, Carolyn. THE CENTER: FROM A TROUBLED PAST TO A NEW LIFE.
Ages 13 and up. 421
Rosen, Lillian D. JUST LIKE EVERYBODY ELSE.
Ages 11 and up. 508
Swartley, David Warren. MY FRIEND, MY BROTHER.
Ages 9-11. 580

Lack of
Arrick, Fran. TUNNEL VISION.
Ages 12 and up. 20
Evans, Mari. JD.
Ages 4-8. 175
Hall, Lynn. THE LEAVING.
Ages 12 and up. 246
Pfeffer, Susan Beth. ABOUT DAVID.
Ages 13 and up. 474
Strasser, Todd. ANGEL DUST BLUES.
Ages 14 and up. 576

Misunderstandings
Hopkins, Lee Bennett. I LOVED ROSE ANN.
Ages 6-9. 294
Zolotow, Charlotte Shapiro. THE HATING BOOK.
Ages 3-7. 662
Zolotow, Charlotte Shapiro. THE QUARRELING BOOK.
Ages 4-7. 670

Parent-child. *See also: Family: unity*
Adler, Carole Schwerdtfeger. THE SILVER COACH.
Ages 9-12. 4
Alda, Arlene. SONYA'S MOMMY WORKS.
Ages 4-7. 6
Alexander, Martha G. WHEN THE NEW BABY COMES, I'M MOVING OUT.
Ages 2-5. 9
Angell, Judie. WHAT'S BEST FOR YOU.
Ages 11-14. 15
Blaine, Margery Kay. THE TERRIBLE THING THAT HAPPENED AT OUR HOUSE.
Ages 3-7. 36
Blume, Judy Sussman. IGGIE'S HOUSE.
Ages 10 and up. 40
Blume, Judy Sussman. IT'S NOT THE END OF THE WORLD.
Ages 10-12. 41
Blume, Judy Sussman. TIGER EYES.
Ages 11 and up. 47
Cleaver, Vera and Bill Cleaver. GROVER.
Ages 9-12. 122
Danziger, Paula. THE DIVORCE EXPRESS.
Ages 11-14. 153
Delton, Judy. MY MOM HATES ME IN JANUARY.
Ages 3-6. 163
Delton, Judy. MY MOTHER LOST HER JOB TODAY.
Ages 3-7. 164
Fox, Paula. BLOWFISH LIVE IN THE SEA.
Ages 11 and up. 187
Fox, Paula. PORTRAIT OF IVAN.
Ages 11 and up. 189
Frank, Anne. ANNE FRANK: THE DIARY OF A YOUNG GIRL.
Ages 11 and up. 191
Graeber, Charlotte Towner. MUSTARD.
Ages 4-10. 213
Greenberg, Jan. THE PIG-OUT BLUES.
Ages 12 and up. 218
Guest, Judith. ORDINARY PEOPLE.
Ages 13 and up. 242
Hall, Lynn. THE LEAVING.
Ages 12 and up. 246
Hentoff, Nat. DOES THIS SCHOOL HAVE CAPITAL PUNISHMENT?
Ages 11 and up. 265
Hentoff, Nat. THIS SCHOOL IS DRIVING ME CRAZY.
Ages 11-15. 266
Hogan, Paula Z. WILL DAD EVER MOVE BACK HOME?
Ages 7-10. 286
Hurwitz, Johanna. THE LAW OF GRAVITY.
Ages 10-13. 306
Johnson, Annabel Jones and Edgar Raymond. THE GRIZZLY.
Ages 10-13. 316
Kenny, Kevin and Helen Krull. SOMETIMES MY MOM DRINKS TOO MUCH.
Ages 5-8. 327
Levy, Elizabeth. COME OUT SMILING.
Ages 12 and up. 360
Little, Jean. HOME FROM FAR.
Ages 10-13. 378
Luger, Harriett Mandelay. LAUREN.
Ages 12 and up. 390
Mann, Peggy. THERE ARE TWO KINDS OF TERRIBLE.
Ages 9-12. 399
Mazer, Norma Fox. UP IN SETH'S ROOM.
Ages 13 and up. 416
O'Hara, Mary, pseud. MY FRIEND FLICKA.
Ages 11 and up. 448
Okimoto, Jean Davies. NORMAN SCHNURMAN, AVERAGE PERSON.
Ages 10-12. 449
Park, Barbara. DON'T MAKE ME SMILE.
Ages 8-11. 453
Peck, Richard. FATHER FIGURE: A NOVEL.
Ages 11 and up. 462
Peck, Robert Newton. A DAY NO PIGS WOULD DIE.
Ages 12 and up. 463
Perl, Lila. ME AND FAT GLENDA.
Ages 9-12. 465
Platt, Kin. BROGG'S BRAIN.
Ages 12 and up. 482
Rodgers, Mary. FREAKY FRIDAY.
Ages 10-13. 504
Sachs, Marilyn. AMY AND LAURA.
Ages 9-12. 509
Stein, Sara Bonnett. ON DIVORCE: AN OPEN FAMILY BOOK FOR PARENTS AND CHILDREN TOGETHER.
Ages 4-8. 568
Stretton, Barbara. YOU NEVER LOSE.
Ages 12 and up. 578
Van Leeuwen, Jean. SEEMS LIKE THIS ROAD GOES ON FOREVER.
Ages 12 and up. 589

Courage, Meaning of (cont.)
Jones, Ron. THE ACORN PEOPLE.
Ages 10 and up. 318
Kherdian, David. THE ROAD FROM HOME: THE STORY OF AN ARMENIAN GIRL.
Ages 12 and up. 333
Lund, Doris Herold. ERIC.
Ages 12 and up. 391
Mauser, Pat Rhoads. A BUNDLE OF STICKS.
Ages 10-12. 410
O'Dell, Scott. ISLAND OF THE BLUE DOLPHINS.
Ages 10 and up. 446
Okimoto, Jean Davies. NORMAN SCHNURMAN, AVERAGE PERSON.
Ages 10-12. 449
Robinet, Harriette Gillem. RIDE THE RED CYCLE.
Ages 7-11. 497
Sperry, Armstrong. CALL IT COURAGE.
Ages 9 and up. 559
Wallace, Bill. A DOG CALLED KITTY.
Ages 9-11. 602
Wartski, Maureen Crane. A BOAT TO NOWHERE.
Ages 9-12. 604
Wojciechowska, Maia Rodman. SHADOW OF A BULL.
Ages 11 and up. 631

Courtesy
See: *Etiquette*

Cousin
See: *Relatives; living in home of*

Creativity
See also: *Curiosity; Fantasy formation; Imagination; Problem solving; Resourcefulness*
Bulla, Clyde Robert. DANIEL'S DUCK.
Ages 5-8. 72
Byars, Betsy Cromer. THE CARTOONIST.
Ages 8-12. 88
Byars, Betsy Cromer. GO AND HUSH THE BABY.
Ages 3-6. 89
Lionni, Leo. FREDERICK.
Ages 5-8. 369

Crime/Criminals
See also: *Death: murder; Delinquency, juvenile; Detention home, living in; Guilt, feelings of; Imprisonment; Prostitution; Rape; Stealing; Vandalism*
Bonham, Frank. DURANGO STREET.
Ages 11 and up. 50
Butterworth, William Edmund. LEROY AND THE OLD MAN.
Ages 12 and up. 86
Guy, Rosa Cuthbert. THE DISAPPEARANCE.
Ages 12 and up. 243
Hassler, Jon Francis. FOUR MILES TO PINECONE.
Ages 10-14. 254
Myers, Walter Dean. HOOPS.
Ages 12 and up. 437
Myers, Walter Dean. IT AIN'T ALL FOR NOTHIN'.
Ages 11-13. 438
Myers, Walter Dean. THE YOUNG LANDLORDS.
Ages 11-14. 440
O'Dell, Scott. KATHLEEN, PLEASE COME HOME.
Ages 12 and up. 447
Strasser, Todd. ANGEL DUST BLUES.
Ages 14 and up. 576

Crippled
See: *Deformities; Handicaps; Limbs, abnormal or missing; Paraplegia; Quadriplegia; Wheelchair, dependence on*

Cruelty
See also: *Child abuse; Violence*
Fox, Paula. A PLACE APART.
Ages 12 and up. 188
Golding, William. LORD OF THE FLIES.
Ages 13 and up. 211

Cults
Veglahn, Nancy Crary. FELLOWSHIP OF THE SEVEN STARS.
Ages 12 and up. 590

Cultural/Ethnic Groups
See: *Specific groups (e.g. African-American; Puerto Rican-American)*

Curiosity
See also: *Creativity*
Wolde, Gunilla. BETSY AND THE VACUUM CLEANER.
Ages 3-6. 636

Custody
See: *Parental: custody*

D

Danger
See: *Risk, taking of*

Dating
See: *Boy-girl relationships: dating; Sex*

Day-Care Center, Going to
See also: *Nursery school*
Simon, Norma. I'M BUSY, TOO.
Ages 3-5. 540

Daydreaming
See also: *Fantasy formation; Magical thinking; Nightmares; Reality, escaping*
O'Hara, Mary, pseud. MY FRIEND FLICKA.
Ages 11 and up. 448
Shreve, Susan Richards. THE BAD DREAMS OF A GOOD GIRL.
Ages 8-10. 531

Daydreaming (cont.)
Viorst, Judith. I'LL FIX ANTHONY.
Ages 3-6. 593

Deafness
See also: *Education: special; Muteness*
Arthur, Catherine. MY SISTER'S SILENT WORLD.
Ages 5-9. 21
Hallman, Ruth. BREAKAWAY.
Ages 12 and up. 247
Keller, Helen Adams. THE STORY OF MY LIFE.
Ages 11 and up. 324
Levine, Edna S. LISA AND HER SOUNDLESS WORLD.
Ages 5-9. 358
Litchfield, Ada Bassett. A BUTTON IN HER EAR.
Ages 5-8. 374
Litchfield, Ada Bassett. WORDS IN OUR HANDS.
Ages 7-9. 376
Peterson, Jeanne Whitehouse. I HAVE A SISTER—MY SISTER IS DEAF.
Ages 4-7. 470
Rosen, Lillian D. JUST LIKE EVERYBODY ELSE.
Ages 11 and up. 508
Wolf, Bernard. ANNA'S SILENT WORLD.
Ages 5-9. 640
Zelonky, Joy. I CAN'T ALWAYS HEAR YOU.
Ages 7-10. 656

Death
See also: *Guilt, feelings of; Loss: feelings of; Mourning, stages of*
Maruki, Toshi. HIROSHIMA NO PIKA.
Ages 7 and up. 404

Attitude Toward
Arnothy, Christine. I AM FIFTEEN AND I DON'T WANT TO DIE.
Ages 12 and up. 16
Buck, Pearl Sydenstricker. THE BIG WAVE.
Ages 9-11. 71
Coerr, Eleanor. SADAKO AND THE THOUSAND PAPER CRANES.
Ages 11 and up. 130
Coutant, Helen. FIRST SNOW.
Ages 7-9. 147
Dixon, Paige, pseud. MAY I CROSS YOUR GOLDEN RIVER?
Ages 12 and up. 166
Donnelly, Elfie. SO LONG, GRANDPA.
Ages 9-11. 167
Harris, Audrey. WHY DID HE DIE?
Ages 4-7. 251
Hermes, Patricia. YOU SHOULDN'T HAVE TO SAY GOOD-BYE.
Ages 10-13. 270
Jacobs, Dee. LAURA'S GIFT.
Ages 10-13. 313
Krementz, Jill. HOW IT FEELS WHEN A PARENT DIES.
Ages 8 and up. 347
Lee, Virginia. THE MAGIC MOTH.
Ages 8-11. 355
Lund, Doris Herold. ERIC.
Ages 12 and up. 391
Mazer, Norma Fox. DEAR BILL, REMEMBER ME? AND OTHER STORIES.
Ages 12 and up. 415
Miles, Miska, pseud. ANNIE AND THE OLD ONE.
Ages 6-9. 429
Sallis, Susan Diana. ONLY LOVE.
Ages 12 and up. 518
Singer, Marilyn. IT CAN'T HURT FOREVER.
Ages 9-12. 543
Stein, Sara Bonnett. ABOUT DYING: AN OPEN FAMILY BOOK FOR PARENTS AND CHILDREN TOGETHER.
Ages 3-8. 563
Stevens, Margaret. WHEN GRANDPA DIED.
Ages 4-8. 572
Strasser, Todd. FRIENDS TILL THE END.
Ages 12 and up. 577
Stretton, Barbara. YOU NEVER LOSE.
Ages 12 and up. 578
Warburg, Sandol Stoddard. GROWING TIME.
Ages 7-9. 603

Funeral Issues
Brown, Margaret Wise. THE DEAD BIRD.
Ages 4-7. 70
Madler, Trudy. WHY DID GRANDMA DIE?
Ages 4-9. 397
Stevens, Margaret. WHEN GRANDPA DIED.
Ages 4-8. 572

Murder. *See also: Crime/Criminals; Violence*
Guy, Rosa Cuthbert. THE DISAPPEARANCE.
Ages 12 and up. 243
Hinton, Susan E. THE OUTSIDERS.
Ages 12 and up. 273
Pfeffer, Susan Beth. ABOUT DAVID.
Ages 13 and up. 474

of Father
Angell, Judie. RONNIE AND ROSEY.
Ages 11 and up. 14
Bawden, Nina Mary Kark. SQUIB.
Ages 10-13. 31
Blume, Judy Sussman. TIGER EYES.
Ages 11 and up. 47
Bradford, Richard. RED SKY AT MORNING.
Ages 13 and up. 57
Cleaver, Vera and Bill Cleaver. WHERE THE LILIES BLOOM.
Ages 11 and up. 126
Foley, June. IT'S NO CRUSH, I'M IN LOVE!
Ages 11-13. 185
Fox, Paula. A PLACE APART.
Ages 12 and up. 188
Greenberg, Jan. A SEASON IN-BETWEEN.
Ages 11-13. 219
Greenfield, Eloise. SISTER.
Ages 10-12. 235
Hunter, Mollie, pseud. A SOUND OF CHARIOTS.
Ages 12 and up. 304
Krementz, Jill. HOW IT FEELS WHEN A PARENT DIES.
Ages 8 and up. 347
Peck, Robert Newton. A DAY NO PIGS WOULD DIE.
Ages 12 and up. 463
Terris, Susan Dubinsky. NO SCARLET RIBBONS.
Ages 11-13. 582

Death (cont.)

of Fiancé/Fiancée
O'Dell, Scott. KATHLEEN, PLEASE COME HOME. Ages 12 and up. 447

of Friend
Cohen, Barbara Nash. THANK YOU, JACKIE ROBINSON. Ages 10-13. 132
Greene, Constance Clarke. DOUBLE-DARE O'TOOLE. Ages 9-11. 224
Greene, Constance Clarke. A GIRL CALLED AL. Ages 11 and up. 225
Hinton, Susan E. THE OUTSIDERS. Ages 12 and up. 273
Hunt, Irene. THE LOTTERY ROSE. Ages 11 and up. 300
Jones, Rebecca Castalldi. ANGIE AND ME. Ages 9-11. 317
Magorian, Michelle. GOOD NIGHT, MR. TOM. Ages 11 and up. 398
Paterson, Katherine Womeldorf. BRIDGE TO TERABITHIA. Ages 9-12. 455
Paulsen, Gary. THE FOXMAN. Ages 11-14. 458
Peck, Richard. CLOSE ENOUGH TO TOUCH. Ages 12 and up. 461
Pfeffer, Susan Beth. ABOUT DAVID. Ages 13 and up. 474
Slepian, Jan. LESTER'S TURN. Ages 11-14. 545
Smith, Doris Buchanan. A TASTE OF BLACKBERRIES. Ages 8-11. 551
White, Elwyn Brooks. CHARLOTTE'S WEB. Ages 8-12. 618
Zindel, Paul. THE PIGMAN. Ages 12 and up. 659

of Grandparent
Brandenberg, Aliki Liacouras. THE TWO OF THEM. Ages 3-7. 59
Coutant, Helen. FIRST SNOW. Ages 7-9. 147
De Paola, Thomas Anthony. NANA UPSTAIRS AND NANA DOWNSTAIRS. Ages 3-8. 157
Donnelly, Elfie. SO LONG, GRANDPA. Ages 9-11. 167
Fassler, Joan. MY GRANDPA DIED TODAY. Ages 4-8. 179
Madler, Trudy. WHY DID GRANDMA DIE? Ages 4-9. 397
Mohr, Nicholasa. FELITA. Ages 8-10. 432
Stein, Sara Bonnett. ABOUT DYING: AN OPEN FAMILY BOOK FOR PARENTS AND CHILDREN TOGETHER. Ages 3-8. 563
Stevens, Margaret. WHEN GRANDPA DIED. Ages 4-8. 572
Walker, Mary Alexander. YEAR OF THE CAFETERIA. Ages 12 and up. 601
Wilkinson, Brenda Scott. LUDELL AND WILLIE. Ages 12 and up. 622
Zolotow, Charlotte Shapiro. MY GRANDSON LEW. Ages 3-7. 667

of Great-grandparent
De Paola, Thomas Anthony. NANA UPSTAIRS AND NANA DOWNSTAIRS. Ages 3-8. 157

of Infant
Head, Ann. MR. AND MRS. BO JO JONES. Ages 13 and up. 262
Klein, Norma. CONFESSIONS OF AN ONLY CHILD. Ages 9-11. 336

of Mother
Bridgers, Sue Ellen. HOME BEFORE DARK. Ages 12 and up. 64
Giff, Patricia Reilly. THE GIFT OF THE PIRATE QUEEN. Ages 9-12. 201
Girion, Barbara. A TANGLE OF ROOTS. Ages 12-16. 208
Guy, Rosa Cuthbert. THE FRIENDS. Ages 12 and up. 244
Hermes, Patricia. YOU SHOULDN'T HAVE TO SAY GOOD-BYE. Ages 10-13. 270
Hunt, Irene. WILLIAM: A NOVEL. Ages 12 and up. 302
Krementz, Jill. HOW IT FEELS WHEN A PARENT DIES. Ages 8 and up. 347
Mann, Peggy. THERE ARE TWO KINDS OF TERRIBLE. Ages 9-12. 399
Oneal, Zibby. A FORMAL FEELING. Ages 12 and up. 450
Peck, Richard. FATHER FIGURE: A NOVEL. Ages 11 and up. 462
Radley, Gail. NOTHING STAYS THE SAME FOREVER. Ages 9-12. 488
Voigt, Cynthia. DICEY'S SONG. Ages 11 and up. 597

of Parents. *See also: Orphan*
Buck, Pearl Sydenstricker. THE BIG WAVE. Ages 9-11. 71
Fitzgerald, John Dennis. ME AND MY LITTLE BRAIN. Ages 9-12. 182

of Pet
Carrick, Carol. THE ACCIDENT. Ages 4-8. 102
Graeber, Charlotte Towner. MUSTARD. Ages 4-10. 213
Miles, Betty. THE TROUBLE WITH THIRTEEN. Ages 9-13. 427
Peck, Robert Newton. A DAY NO PIGS WOULD DIE. Ages 12 and up. 463
Rawlings, Marjorie Kinnan. THE YEARLING. Ages 12 and up. 491
Smith, Doris Buchanan. KICK A STONE HOME. Ages 11 and up. 549

Death (cont.)
Viorst, Judith. THE TENTH GOOD THING ABOUT BARNEY.
Ages 4-8. 596
Wallace, Bill. A DOG CALLED KITTY.
Ages 9-11. 602
Warburg, Sandol Stoddard. GROWING TIME.
Ages 7-9. 603

of Relative
Byars, Betsy Cromer. GOODBYE, CHICKEN LITTLE.
Ages 9-11. 90
Raskin, Ellen. FIGGS & PHANTOMS.
Ages 12 and up. 489

of Sibling
Bawden, Nina Mary Kark. SQUIB.
Ages 10-13. 31
Fitzgerald, John Dennis. ME AND MY LITTLE BRAIN.
Ages 9-12. 182
Greene, Constance Clarke. AL(EXANDRA) THE GREAT.
Ages 10-13. 222
Hermes, Patricia. NOBODY'S FAULT.
Ages 10-12. 268
Lee, Virginia. THE MAGIC MOTH.
Ages 8-11. 355
Little, Jean. HOME FROM FAR.
Ages 10-13. 378
Lowry, Lois. A SUMMER TO DIE.
Ages 10-14. 389
Mazer, Harry. THE ISLAND KEEPER.
Ages 10-14. 414
Mazer, Norma Fox. WHEN WE FIRST MET.
Ages 12 and up. 417
O'Dell, Scott. ISLAND OF THE BLUE DOLPHINS.
Ages 10 and up. 446
Pevsner, Stella. AND YOU GIVE ME A PAIN, ELAINE.
Ages 10-13. 471
Rodowsky, Colby F. WHAT ABOUT ME?
Ages 11-13. 507
Suicide. *See: Suicide*

Decision Making
See also: *Problem solving*
Beckman, Gunnel. MIA ALONE.
Ages 12 and up. 32
Blume, Judy Sussman. ARE YOU THERE GOD? IT'S ME, MARGARET.
Ages 10-13. 37
Butterworth, William Edmund. LEROY AND THE OLD MAN.
Ages 12 and up. 86
Carrick, Carol. THE FOUNDLING.
Ages 5-8. 103
Greene, Constance Clarke. AL(EXANDRA) THE GREAT.
Ages 10-13. 222
Gross, Alan. THE I DON'T WANT TO GO TO SCHOOL BOOK.
Ages 5-9. 239
Hall, Lynn. THE LEAVING.
Ages 12 and up. 246
Luger, Harriett Mandelay. LAUREN.
Ages 12 and up. 390
Myers, Walter Dean. IT AIN'T ALL FOR NOTHIN'.
Ages 11-13. 438
Pascal, Francine. MY FIRST LOVE & OTHER DISASTERS.
Ages 12 and up. 454
Pfeffer, Susan Beth. STARRING PETER AND LEIGH.
Ages 12-14. 477
Rodowsky, Colby F. H. MY NAME IS HENLEY.
Ages 10-13. 505
Slote, Alfred. TONY AND ME.
Ages 10-13. 547
Snyder, Anne. MY NAME IS DAVY—I'M AN ALCOHOLIC.
Ages 12 and up. 556
Waber, Bernard. IRA SLEEPS OVER.
Ages 6-8. 599

Deformities
See also: *Limbs, abnormal or missing*
Forbes, Esther. JOHNNY TREMAIN.
Ages 10 and up. 186
Gallico, Paul. THE SNOW GOOSE.
Ages 12 and up. 195
Hassler, Jon Francis. JEMMY.
Ages 11 and up. 255

Delinquency, Juvenile
See also: *Crime/Criminals; Detention home, living in; Gangs; Imprisonment; Rebellion; Stealing; Vandalism; Violence*
Ashley, Bernard. TERRY ON THE FENCE.
Ages 12 and up. 24
Bonham, Frank. DURANGO STREET.
Ages 11 and up. 50
Burch, Robert Joseph. QUEENIE PEAVY.
Ages 11-13. 77
Hinton, Susan E. THE OUTSIDERS.
Ages 12 and up. 273
Hinton, Susan E. THAT WAS THEN, THIS IS NOW.
Ages 12 and up. 275
Levoy, Myron. A SHADOW LIKE A LEOPARD.
Ages 12 and up. 359
Meyer, Carolyn. THE CENTER: FROM A TROUBLED PAST TO A NEW LIFE.
Ages 13 and up. 421
Murphy, Jim. DEATH RUN.
Ages 11 and up. 435
Myers, Walter Dean. WON'T KNOW TILL I GET THERE.
Ages 11-14. 439
Petersen, P. J. WOULD YOU SETTLE FOR IMPROBABLE?
Ages 11-13. 469

Dentist, Going to
Rockwell, Harlow. MY DENTIST.
Ages 4-7. 501
Watson, Jane Werner, Robert E. Switzer. MY FRIEND THE DENTIST.
Ages 3-6. 610

Dependability
See: *Responsibility: accepting*

Dependence/Independence

See also: *Autonomy*
Adler, Carole Schwerdtfeger. THE CAT THAT WAS LEFT BEHIND.
Ages 9-12. 2
Angell, Judie. RONNIE AND ROSEY.
Ages 11 and up. 14
Arrick, Fran. STEFFIE CAN'T COME OUT TO PLAY.
Ages 12 and up. 19
Bulla, Clyde Robert. SHOESHINE GIRL.
Ages 8-10. 74
Cleaver, Vera and Bill Cleaver. QUEEN OF HEARTS.
Ages 10-13. 124
Hutchins, Patricia. HAPPY BIRTHDAY, SAM.
Ages 5-7. 309
Jones, Rebecca Castalldi. ANGIE AND ME.
Ages 9-11. 317
Jones, Toeckey. GO WELL, STAY WELL.
Ages 12 and up. 319
Little, Lessie Jones and Eloise Greenfield. I CAN DO IT BY MYSELF.
Ages 5-7. 383
Mauser, Pat Rhoads. HOW I FOUND MYSELF AT THE FAIR.
Ages 7-9. 411
Mazer, Norma Fox. DEAR BILL, REMEMBER ME? AND OTHER STORIES.
Ages 12 and up. 415
O'Dell, Scott. KATHLEEN, PLEASE COME HOME.
Ages 12 and up. 447
Pascal, Francine. MY FIRST LOVE & OTHER DISASTERS.
Ages 12 and up. 454
Slepian, Jan. THE ALFRED SUMMER.
Ages 11-13. 544
Voigt, Cynthia. HOMECOMING.
Ages 11 and up. 598

Depression

See also: *Anger; Guilt, feelings of; Loneliness; Loss: feelings of; Mental illness*
Arrick, Fran. TUNNEL VISION.
Ages 12 and up. 20
Bridgers, Sue Ellen. NOTES FOR ANOTHER LIFE.
Ages 12 and up. 65
Guest, Judith. ORDINARY PEOPLE.
Ages 13 and up. 242
Hughes, Dean. SWITCHING TRACKS.
Ages 10-14. 296
Smith, Nancy Covert. THE FALLING-APART WINTER.
Ages 10-13. 554

Deprivation, Emotional

See also: *Parental: negligence; Security/Insecurity*
Byars, Betsy Cromer. THE CARTOONIST.
Ages 8-12. 88
Greene, Sheppard M. THE BOY WHO DRANK TOO MUCH.
Ages 12 and up. 230
Hinton, Susan E. RUMBLE FISH.
Ages 12 and up. 274
Holman, Felice. SLAKE'S LIMBO.
Ages 12 and up. 292
Hunt, Irene. THE LOTTERY ROSE.
Ages 11 and up. 300
Magorian, Michelle. GOOD NIGHT, MR. TOM.
Ages 11 and up. 398
Myers, Walter Dean. IT AIN'T ALL FOR NOTHIN'.
Ages 11-13. 438
Paterson, Katherine Womeldorf. THE GREAT GILLY HOPKINS.
Ages 10-13. 456
Smith, Doris Buchanan. TOUGH CHAUNCEY.
Ages 12 and up. 552
Van Leeuwen, Jean. SEEMS LIKE THIS ROAD GOES ON FOREVER.
Ages 12 and up. 589
Wortis, Avi. SOMETIMES I THINK I HEAR MY NAME.
Ages 10-13. 649

Desegregation

See: *Prejudice: ethnic/racial*

Desertion

See: *Abandonment*

Detention Home, Living in

See also: *Crime/Criminals; Delinquency, juvenile; Imprisonment*
Meyer, Carolyn. THE CENTER: FROM A TROUBLED PAST TO A NEW LIFE.
Ages 13 and up. 421

Determination

Bond, Nancy Barbara. THE VOYAGE BEGUN.
Ages 12 and up. 49
Brancato, Robin Fidler. WINNING.
Ages 12 and up. 58
Gardiner, John Reynolds. STONE FOX.
Ages 8-10. 197
Greenfield, Eloise and Alesia Revis. ALESIA.
Ages 10-14. 237
Hunt, Irene. WILLIAM: A NOVEL.
Ages 12 and up. 302
Knudson, R. Rozanne. RINEHART LIFTS.
Ages 10-12. 338
Knudson, R. Rozanne. ZANBOOMER.
Ages 10-13. 340
Lipsyte, Robert. ONE FAT SUMMER.
Ages 12-14. 373
Myers, Walter Dean. HOOPS.
Ages 12 and up. 437
Piper, Watty. THE LITTLE ENGINE THAT COULD.
Ages 3-7. 480
Sachs, Marilyn. A SUMMER'S LEASE.
Ages 11-14. 515
Slepian, Jan. LESTER'S TURN.
Ages 11-14. 545
Smith, Robert Kimmel. JELLY BELLY.
Ages 10-12. 555
Voigt, Cynthia. HOMECOMING.
Ages 11 and up. 598
Winthrop, Elizabeth. MARATHON MIRANDA.
Ages 9-11. 626

Education (cont.)
Levine, Edna S. LISA AND HER SOUNDLESS WORLD.
Ages 5-9. 358
Little, Jean. FROM ANNA.
Ages 9-11. 377
Melton, David. A BOY CALLED HOPELESS.
Ages 10 and up. 420

Value of
Cohen, Miriam. WHEN WILL I READ?
Ages 4-6. 137
Jones, Toeckey. GO WELL, STAY WELL.
Ages 12 and up. 319
Keller, Helen Adams. THE STORY OF MY LIFE.
Ages 11 and up. 324
Lipsyte, Robert. THE CONTENDER.
Ages 12 and up. 372
Strang, Celia. FOSTER MARY.
Ages 10-13. 575

Ego Ideal
See also: *Hope; Identification with others; Identity, search for; Values/Valuing*
Hamilton, Virginia. ZEELY.
Ages 10-12. 249
Sachs, Marilyn. THE TRUTH ABOUT MARY ROSE.
Ages 10-13. 516

Egocentrism
See also: *Empathy; Sharing/Not sharing*
Cleaver, Vera and Bill Cleaver. ME TOO.
Ages 9-11. 123
Moeri, Louise. FIRST THE EGG.
Ages 12 and up. 430
Sachs, Marilyn. A SUMMER'S LEASE.
Ages 11-14. 515

Embarrassment
See also: *Enuresis; Shame*
Lexau, Joan M. I SHOULD HAVE STAYED IN BED!
Ages 6-8. 362
Miles, Betty. JUST THE BEGINNING.
Ages 10-12. 424
Miles, Betty. LOOKING ON.
Ages 11-14. 425
Winthrop, Elizabeth. SLOPPY KISSES.
Ages 4-7. 628

Emotional Deprivation
See: *Deprivation, emotional*

Emotions
See also: *Self, attitude toward; Specific emotions (e.g. Anger; Jealousy)*

Accepting
Hill, Margaret. TURN THE PAGE, WENDY.
Ages 10-14. 272
Hogan, Paula Z. SOMETIMES I GET SO MAD.
Ages 5-8. 285
Oneal, Zibby. A FORMAL FEELING.
Ages 12 and up. 450
Simon, Norma. HOW DO I FEEL?
Ages 4-8. 538
Sobol, Harriet Langsam. MY BROTHER STEVEN IS RETARDED.
Ages 7-10. 557
Stanton, Elizabeth and Henry Stanton. SOMETIMES I LIKE TO CRY.
Ages 4-7. 562
Wolitzer, Hilma. TOBY LIVED HERE.
Ages 10-12. 645

Identifying
Grimes, Nikki. SOMETHING ON MY MIND.
Ages 5-9. 238
Oneal, Zibby. A FORMAL FEELING.
Ages 12 and up. 450
Wright, Betty Ren. I LIKE BEING ALONE.
Ages 6-9. 650

Empathy
See also: *Egocentrism; Identification with others*
Greenfield, Eloise. GRANDMAMA'S JOY.
Ages 4-8. 232
Knox-Wagner, Elaine. MY GRANDPA RETIRED TODAY.
Ages 4-7. 337
Leggett, Linda Rodgers and Linda Gambee THE ROSE-COLORED GLASSES: MELANIE ADJUSTS TO POOR VISION.
Ages 8-11. 356
Myers, Walter Dean. FAST SAM, COOL CLYDE, AND STUFF.
Ages 11-14. 436
Rodgers, Mary. FREAKY FRIDAY.
Ages 10-13. 504
Yep, Laurence Michael. KIND HEARTS AND GENTLE MONSTERS.
Ages 12 and up. 653

Encouragement
See also: *Courage, meaning of*
Simon, Norma. NOBODY'S PERFECT, NOT EVEN MY MOTHER.
Ages 4-8. 541
Stolz, Mary Slattery. THE BULLY OF BARKHAM STREET.
Ages 8-11. 573
Udry, Janice May. WHAT MARY JO SHARED.
Ages 5-8. 588
Wolf, Bernard. DON'T FEEL SORRY FOR PAUL.
Ages 8 and up. 641

Enuresis
See also: *Embarrassment; Shame*
Fassler, Joan. DON'T WORRY DEAR.
Ages 4-6. 177

Epilepsy
See also: *Brain injury*
Corcoran, Barbara. CHILD OF THE MORNING.
Ages 10 and up. 143
Girion, Barbara. A HANDFUL OF STARS.
Ages 12 and up. 207
Hermes, Patricia. WHAT IF THEY KNEW?
Ages 9-11. 269

Epilepsy (cont.)
Slepian, Jan. THE ALFRED SUMMER.
Ages 11-13. 544
Young, Helen. WHAT DIFFERENCE DOES IT MAKE, DANNY?
Ages 9-12. 654

Equal Rights
See: *Prejudice; Women's rights*

Equality
See: *Differences, human; Prejudice*

Escaping Reality
See: *Reality, escaping*

Eskimo
Houston, James A. FROZEN FIRE: A TALE OF COURAGE.
Ages 10-13. 295

Ethnic Differences
See: *Prejudice: ethnic/racial*

Etiquette
Hoban, Russell Conwell. DINNER AT ALBERTA'S.
Ages 5-7. 281
Konigsburg, Elaine Lobl. ALTOGETHER, ONE AT A TIME.
Ages 9-11. 342

Exceptional Children
See: *Education: special; Learning disabilities; Mental retardation; Talents*

Exile
See: *Ostracism*

Expectancy, Power of
See: *Expectations*

Expectations
See also: *Hope; Peer relationships: peer pressures*
Arrick, Fran. TUNNEL VISION.
Ages 12 and up. 20
Christopher, Matthew F. JOHNNY LONG LEGS.
Ages 9-11. 110
Greenberg, Jan. THE PIG-OUT BLUES.
Ages 12 and up. 218
Greene, Constance Clarke. YOUR OLD PAL, AL.
Ages 9-13. 229
Kerr, M. E., pseud. I'LL LOVE YOU WHEN YOU'RE MORE LIKE ME.
Ages 12 and up. 330
Okimoto, Jean Davies. NORMAN SCHNURMAN, AVERAGE PERSON.
Ages 10-12. 449
Platt, Kin. BROGG'S BRAIN.
Ages 12 and up. 482
Thomas, Jane Resh. THE COMEBACK DOG.
Ages 7-9. 584
Van Leeuwen, Jean. SEEMS LIKE THIS ROAD GOES ON FOREVER.
Ages 12 and up. 589
Wojciechowska, Maia Rodman. SHADOW OF A BULL.
Ages 11 and up. 631

Extended Family
See: *Family: extended*

F

Fairness
See: *Honesty/Dishonesty; Sharing/Not sharing*

Family
See also: *Age; Grandparent; Great-grandparent; Parent/Parents; Relatives; Sibling; Stepbrother/Stepsister; Stepparent*

Extended
Hunt, Irene. UP A ROAD SLOWLY.
Ages 12 and up. 301
MacLachlan, Patricia. CASSIE BINEGAR.
Ages 9-12. 393
Mazer, Norma Fox. DEAR BILL, REMEMBER ME? AND OTHER STORIES.
Ages 12 and up. 415
Simon, Norma. ALL KINDS OF FAMILIES.
Ages 5-8. 537
Thompson, Jean, pseud. DON'T FORGET MICHAEL.
Ages 7-9. 585
Wolkoff, Judie. HAPPILY EVER AFTER . . . ALMOST.
Ages 11-13. 646

Relationships. *See also: Sibling: relationships*
Angell, Judie. WHAT'S BEST FOR YOU.
Ages 11-14. 15
Asher, Sandra Fenichel. JUST LIKE JENNY.
Ages 10-12. 22
Barrett, John M. DANIEL DISCOVERS DANIEL.
Ages 7-9. 26
Blume, Judy Sussman. SUPERFUDGE.
Ages 8-10. 44
Byars, Betsy Cromer. GOODBYE, CHICKEN LITTLE.
Ages 9-11. 90
Cameron, Ann. THE STORIES JULIAN TELLS.
Ages 7-9. 99
Cleary, Beverly Bunn. RAMONA AND HER FATHER.
Ages 7-10. 116
Cleary, Beverly Bunn. RAMONA AND HER MOTHER.
Ages 7-10. 117
Cleary, Beverly Bunn. RAMONA QUIMBY, AGE 8.
Ages 8-10. 118
Cleary, Beverly Bunn. RAMONA THE BRAVE.
Ages 7-10. 119

Family (cont.)

Unity. *See also: Communication: parent-child*

Family (cont.)
Dixon, Paige, pseud. MAY I CROSS YOUR GOLDEN RIVER?
Ages 12 and up. 166
Girion, Barbara. A TANGLE OF ROOTS.
Ages 12-16. 208
Greenberg, Jan. A SEASON IN-BETWEEN.
Ages 11-13. 219
Hermes, Patricia. YOU SHOULDN'T HAVE TO SAY GOOD-BYE.
Ages 10-13. 270
Holland, Isabelle. DINAH AND THE GREEN FAT KINGDOM.
Ages 10-13. 288
Hunt, Irene. WILLIAM: A NOVEL.
Ages 12 and up. 302
Kingman, Lee. HEAD OVER WHEELS.
Ages 12 and up. 335
Lee, Harper. TO KILL A MOCKINGBIRD.
Ages 12 and up. 353
Lee, Virginia. THE MAGIC MOTH.
Ages 8-11. 355
Lexau, Joan M. STRIPED ICE CREAM.
Ages 8-11. 363
Little, Jean. LISTEN FOR THE SINGING.
Ages 10-14. 380
Lowry, Lois. A SUMMER TO DIE.
Ages 10-14. 389
Madler, Trudy. WHY DID GRANDMA DIE?
Ages 4-9. 397
Melton, David. A BOY CALLED HOPELESS.
Ages 10 and up. 420
Mohr, Nicholasa. FELITA.
Ages 8-10. 432
O'Hara, Mary, pseud. MY FRIEND FLICKA.
Ages 11 and up. 448
Rawlings, Marjorie Kinnan. THE YEARLING.
Ages 12 and up. 491
Reuter, Margaret. MY MOTHER IS BLIND.
Ages 5-8. 493
Rosen, Lillian D. JUST LIKE EVERYBODY ELSE.
Ages 11 and up. 508
Shyer, Marlene Fanta. MY BROTHER, THE THIEF.
Ages 10-13. 534
Simon, Norma. ALL KINDS OF FAMILIES.
Ages 5-8. 537
Sonneborn, Ruth A. FRIDAY NIGHT IS PAPA NIGHT.
Ages 5-8. 558
Strang, Celia. FOSTER MARY.
Ages 10-13. 575
Swartley, David Warren. MY FRIEND, MY BROTHER.
Ages 9-11. 580
Taylor, Mildred D. ROLL OF THUNDER, HEAR MY CRY.
Ages 10 and up. 581
Thompson, Jean, pseud. DON'T FORGET MICHAEL.
Ages 7-9. 585
Voigt, Cynthia. HOMECOMING.
Ages 11 and up. 598
Wilder, Laura Ingalls. BY THE SHORES OF SILVER LAKE.
Ages 8-11. 620

Fantasy Formation
See also: *Creativity; Daydreaming; Imagination; Magical thinking; Play*
Bawden, Nina Mary Kark. SQUIB.
Ages 10-13. 31
Sargent, Sarah. SECRET LIES.
Ages 11 and up. 519
Zolotow, Charlotte Shapiro. A FATHER LIKE THAT.
Ages 4-6. 661

Fat
See: *Weight control: overweight*

Father
See: *Communication: parent-child; Parent/Parents: single*

Fatso
See: *Name-calling; Weight control: overweight*

Fear
See also: *Anxiety; Courage, meaning of; Nightmares; Security/Insecurity*
Blume, Judy Sussman. OTHERWISE KNOWN AS SHEILA THE GREAT.
Ages 9-11. 43
Childress, Alice. RAINBOW JORDAN.
Ages 12 and up. 109
Fox, Paula. THE STONE-FACED BOY.
Ages 10-12. 190
Holman, Felice. SLAKE'S LIMBO.
Ages 12 and up. 292
Miles, Miska, pseud. AARON'S DOOR.
Ages 5-9. 428
Pfeffer, Susan Beth. WHAT DO YOU DO WHEN YOUR MOUTH WON'T OPEN?
Ages 10-13. 478
Sperry, Armstrong. CALL IT COURAGE.
Ages 9 and up. 559
Watson, Jane Werner, Robert E. Switzer. SOMETIMES I'M AFRAID.
Ages 2-5. 613
Wittels, Harriet and Joan Greisman. THINGS I HATE.
Ages 4-8. 629

of Animals
Little, Lessie Jones and Eloise Greenfield. I CAN DO IT BY MYSELF.
Ages 5-7. 383
Wallace, Bill. A DOG CALLED KITTY.
Ages 9-11. 602

of Darkness
Bonsall, Crosby Newell. WHO'S AFRAID OF THE DARK?
Ages 3-7. 54
Cleary, Beverly Bunn. RAMONA THE BRAVE.
Ages 7-10. 119
Crowe, Robert L. CLYDE MONSTER.
Ages 3-6. 148
Hoban, Russell Conwell. BEDTIME FOR FRANCES.
Ages 3-7. 279

Foster Home

See also: *Children's home, living in; Orphan; Parent/Parents: substitute*

Adler, Carole Schwerdtfeger. THE CAT THAT WAS LEFT BEHIND.
Ages 9-12. 2
Buck, Pearl Sydenstricker. THE BIG WAVE.
Ages 9-11. 71
Byars, Betsy Cromer. THE PINBALLS.
Ages 10-13. 93
Childress, Alice. RAINBOW JORDAN.
Ages 12 and up. 109
Guy, Rosa Cuthbert. THE DISAPPEARANCE.
Ages 12 and up. 243
Hansen, Joyce. THE GIFT-GIVER.
Ages 9-12. 250
Hill, Margaret. TURN THE PAGE, WENDY.
Ages 10-14. 272
Little, Jean. HOME FROM FAR.
Ages 10-13. 378
MacLachlan, Patricia. MAMA ONE, MAMA TWO.
Ages 4-7. 394
Myers, Walter Dean. WON'T KNOW TILL I GET THERE.
Ages 11-14. 439
Paterson, Katherine Womeldorf. THE GREAT GILLY HOPKINS.
Ages 10-13. 456
Strang, Celia. FOSTER MARY.
Ages 10-13. 575
Wolitzer, Hilma. TOBY LIVED HERE.
Ages 10-12. 645

Fractures

See also: *Doctor, going to; Hospital, going to*

of Arm
Wolff, Angelika. MOM! I BROKE MY ARM!
Ages 5-8. 642

Freckles

Blume, Judy Sussman. FRECKLE JUICE.
Ages 8-11. 39

Freedom, meaning of

Bennett, Jack. THE VOYAGE OF THE LUCKY DRAGON.
Ages 11 and up. 33
Gackenbach, Dick. DO YOU LOVE ME?
Ages 5-8. 194
Holmes, Efner Tudor. AMY'S GOOSE.
Ages 8-11. 293
Waterton, Betty Marie. A SALMON FOR SIMON.
Ages 4-7. 609

Friendship

See also: *Boy-girl relationships; Gangs: membership in; Identification with others: peers*

Mohr, Nicholasa. IN NUEVA YORK.
Ages 13 and up. 433
Zolotow, Charlotte Shapiro. THE WHITE MARBLE.
Ages 4-8. 675

Best friend
Angell, Judie. WHAT'S BEST FOR YOU.
Ages 11-14. 15
Asher, Sandra Fenichel. JUST LIKE JENNY.
Ages 10-12. 22
Brandenberg, Aliki Liacouras. WE ARE BEST FRIENDS.
Ages 3-6. 60
Burningham, John Mackintosh. THE FRIEND.
Ages 2-5. 81
Byars, Betsy Cromer. GOODBYE, CHICKEN LITTLE.
Ages 9-11. 90
Carrick, Carol. SOME FRIEND!
Ages 9-12. 104
Cohen, Miriam. BEST FRIENDS.
Ages 5-7. 134
Cuyler, Margery S. THE TROUBLE WITH SOAP.
Ages 10-13. 149
Danziger, Paula. THE DIVORCE EXPRESS.
Ages 11-14. 153
Due, Linnea A. HIGH AND OUTSIDE.
Ages 13 and up. 168
Foley, June. IT'S NO CRUSH, I'M IN LOVE!
Ages 11-13. 185
Giff, Patricia Reilly. FOURTH GRADE CELEBRITY.
Ages 8-10. 200
Girion, Barbara. A TANGLE OF ROOTS.
Ages 12-16. 208
Greenberg, Jan. THE ICEBERG AND ITS SHADOW.
Ages 10-12. 217
Greene, Constance Clarke. AL(EXANDRA) THE GREAT.
Ages 10-13. 222
Greene, Constance Clarke. I KNOW YOU, AL.
Ages 11 and up. 227
Greene, Constance Clarke. YOUR OLD PAL, AL.
Ages 9-13. 229
Greene, Sheppard M. THE BOY WHO DRANK TOO MUCH.
Ages 12 and up. 230
Guest, Elissa Haden. THE HANDSOME MAN.
Ages 12 and up. 241
Hautzig, Deborah. SECOND STAR TO THE RIGHT.
Ages 12 and up. 256
Hinton, Susan E. THAT WAS THEN, THIS IS NOW.
Ages 12 and up. 275
Knudson, R. Rozanne. RINEHART LIFTS.
Ages 10-12. 338
Marshall, James. GEORGE AND MARTHA RISE AND SHINE.
Ages 3-7. 403
Miles, Betty. THE TROUBLE WITH THIRTEEN.
Ages 9-13. 427
Mohr, Nicholasa. FELITA.
Ages 8-10. 432
Oppenheimer, Joan Letson. WORKING ON IT.
Ages 11-13. 452
Paterson, Katherine Womeldorf. BRIDGE TO TERABITHIA.
Ages 9-12. 455
Perl, Lila. HEY, REMEMBER FAT GLENDA?
Ages 9-12. 464
Pfeffer, Susan Beth. ABOUT DAVID.
Ages 13 and up. 474
Pfeffer, Susan Beth. KID POWER.
Ages 9-12. 476

G

Guilt, Feelings of

See also: *Accidents; Blame; Conscience; Crime/Criminals; Death; Depression; Justice/Injustice; Mourning, stages of; Self-esteem; Shame*

Arrick, Fran. CHERNOWITZ!
Ages 12 and up. 18
Arrick, Fran. TUNNEL VISION.
Ages 12 and up. 20
Bawden, Nina Mary Kark. SQUIB.
Ages 10-13. 31
Blume, Judy Sussman. TIGER EYES.
Ages 11 and up. 47
Byars, Betsy Cromer. GOODBYE, CHICKEN LITTLE.
Ages 9-11. 90
Garden, Nancy. ANNIE ON MY MIND.
Ages 13 and up. 196
Goff, Beth. WHERE IS DADDY? THE STORY OF A DIVORCE.
Ages 4-8. 209
Guest, Judith. ORDINARY PEOPLE.
Ages 13 and up. 242
Guy, Rosa Cuthbert. THE FRIENDS.
Ages 12 and up. 244
Hassler, Jon Francis. FOUR MILES TO PINECONE.
Ages 10-14. 254
Hautzig, Deborah. SECOND STAR TO THE RIGHT.
Ages 12 and up. 256
Hazen, Barbara Shook. EVEN IF I DID SOMETHING AWFUL.
Ages 3-6. 258
Hermes, Patricia. NOBODY'S FAULT.
Ages 10-12. 268
Hill, Margaret. TURN THE PAGE, WENDY.
Ages 10-14. 272
Hughes, Dean. SWITCHING TRACKS.
Ages 10-14. 296
Jordan, Hope Dahle. HAUNTED SUMMER.
Ages 11 and up. 320
Kingman, Lee. HEAD OVER WHEELS.
Ages 12 and up. 335
Liu, Aimee. SOLITAIRE.
Ages 13 and up. 384
MacLachlan, Patricia. CASSIE BINEGAR.
Ages 9-12. 393
Mazer, Norma Fox. WHEN WE FIRST MET.
Ages 12 and up. 417
McCaffrey, Mary. MY BROTHER ANGE.
Ages 8-11. 418
Meyer, Carolyn. THE CENTER: FROM A TROUBLED PAST TO A NEW LIFE.
Ages 13 and up. 421
Miklowitz, Gloria D. DID YOU HEAR WHAT HAPPENED TO ANDREA?
Ages 13 and up. 422
Murphy, Jim. DEATH RUN.
Ages 11 and up. 435
Myers, Walter Dean. IT AIN'T ALL FOR NOTHIN'.
Ages 11-13. 438
Oneal, Zibby. A FORMAL FEELING.
Ages 12 and up. 450
Pfeffer, Susan Beth. ABOUT DAVID.
Ages 13 and up. 474
Roberts, Willo Davis. DON'T HURT LAURIE!
Ages 10-14. 496
Rodowsky, Colby F. WHAT ABOUT ME?
Ages 11-13. 507
Schuchman, Joan. TWO PLACES TO SLEEP.
Ages 5-7. 521
Stretton, Barbara. YOU NEVER LOSE.
Ages 12 and up. 578
Van Leeuwen, Jean. SEEMS LIKE THIS ROAD GOES ON FOREVER.
Ages 12 and up. 589
Yep, Laurence Michael. KIND HEARTS AND GENTLE MONSTERS.
Ages 12 and up. 653
Zindel, Paul. THE PIGMAN.
Ages 12 and up. 659

H

Half Brother/Half Sister

See: *Sibling: half brother/half sister*

Handicaps

See also: *Education: special*

Jones, Ron. THE ACORN PEOPLE.
Ages 10 and up. 318
Stein, Sara Bonnett. ABOUT HANDICAPS: AN OPEN FAMILY BOOK FOR PARENTS AND CHILDREN TOGETHER.
Ages 4-8. 564

Amputee. *See: Amputee*

Asthma. *See: Asthma*

Blindness. *See: Blindness*

Braces on body/limbs. *See: Braces on body/limbs*

Brain injury. *See: Brain injury; Cerebral palsy; Epilepsy; Learning disabilities; Mental retardation*

Deafness. *See: Deafness*

Deformities. *See: Deformities*

Down syndrome. *See: Down syndrome*

Hemophilia. *See: Hemophilia*

Limbs, abnormal or missing. *See: Limbs, abnormal or missing*

Multiple

Greenfield, Eloise and Alesia Revis. ALESIA.
Ages 10-14. 237
Robinet, Harriette Gillem. RIDE THE RED CYCLE.
Ages 7-11. 497

Muteness. *See: Muteness*

Paraplegia. *See: Paraplegia*

Prejudice. *See: Prejudice: toward handicapped persons*

Prosthesis. *See: Prosthesis*

Quadriplegia. *See: Quadriplegia*

Speech problems. *See: Speech problems*

Visual impairment. *See: Visual impairment*

Wheelchair. *See: Wheelchair, dependence on*

Harassment
See also: *Bully; Practical jokes/pranks*
Arrick, Fran. CHERNOWITZ!
Ages 12 and up. 18
Garden, Nancy. ANNIE ON MY MIND.
Ages 13 and up. 196
Holland, Isabelle. DINAH AND THE GREEN FAT KINGDOM.
Ages 10-13. 288
Mohr, Nicholasa. FELITA.
Ages 8-10. 432

Hard of Hearing
See: *Deafness*

Hatred
See also: *Aggression; Anger, Hostility; Prejudice*
Arrick, Fran. CHERNOWITZ!
Ages 12 and up. 18
Hunt, Irene. THE LOTTERY ROSE.
Ages 11 and up. 300

Hearing Aid
See: *Deafness*

Heart Trouble
See: *Surgery: heart*

Heaven
See: *Religion*

Height
See also: *Appearance*

Short
Hutchins, Patricia. HAPPY BIRTHDAY, SAM.
Ages 5-7. 309

Tall
Christopher, Matthew F. JOHNNY LONG LEGS.
Ages 9-11. 110
Miles, Betty. LOOKING ON.
Ages 11-14. 425
Sachs, Marilyn. VERONICA GANZ.
Ages 10-12. 517

Hell
See: *Religion*

Helping
See also: *Cooperation*
Bond, Nancy Barbara. THE VOYAGE BEGUN.
Ages 12 and up. 49
Burton, Virginia Lee. KATY AND THE BIG SNOW.
Ages 3-6. 83
Clifford, Ethel Rosenberg. THE ROCKING CHAIR REBELLION.
Ages 11-13. 127
De Paola, Thomas Anthony. NOW ONE FOOT, NOW THE OTHER.
Ages 4-7. 158
Henriod, Lorraine. GRANDMA'S WHEELCHAIR.
Ages 3-7. 264
Melton, David. A BOY CALLED HOPELESS.
Ages 10 and up. 420
Rockwell, Anne F. and Harlow Rockwell. CAN I HELP?
Ages 3-6. 498
Winthrop, Elizabeth. MARATHON MIRANDA.
Ages 9-11. 626
Wolde, Gunilla. BETSY AND THE VACUUM CLEANER.
Ages 3-6. 636

Hemophilia
Pfeffer, Susan Beth. STARRING PETER AND LEIGH.
Ages 12-14. 477

Hitchhiking
Miklowitz, Gloria D. DID YOU HEAR WHAT HAPPENED TO ANDREA?
Ages 13 and up. 422

Homesickness
See also: *Separation anxiety; Separation from loved ones*
Brown, Marc Tolan. ARTHUR GOES TO CAMP.
Ages 5-8. 67

Homosexuality
See also: *Sex*

Female
Garden, Nancy. ANNIE ON MY MIND.
Ages 13 and up. 196
Levy, Elizabeth. COME OUT SMILING.
Ages 12 and up. 360
Mohr, Nicholasa. IN NUEVA YORK.
Ages 13 and up. 433

Male
Bargar, Gary W. WHAT HAPPENED TO MR. FORSTER?
Ages 10-13. 25
Holland, Isabelle. THE MAN WITHOUT A FACE.
Ages 13 and up. 290
Meyer, Carolyn. THE CENTER: FROM A TROUBLED PAST TO A NEW LIFE.
Ages 13 and up. 421
Mohr, Nicholasa. IN NUEVA YORK.
Ages 13 and up. 433

Honesty/Dishonesty
See also: *Conscience*
Angell, Judie. RONNIE AND ROSEY.
Ages 11 and up. 14
Blume, Judy Sussman. OTHERWISE KNOWN AS SHEILA THE GREAT.
Ages 9-11. 43
Childress, Alice. RAINBOW JORDAN.
Ages 12 and up. 109
Duvoisin, Roger Antoine. PETUNIA, I LOVE YOU.
Ages 3-7. 170

Honesty/Dishonesty (cont.)

Fitzgerald, John Dennis. THE GREAT BRAIN REFORMS.
Ages 10-13. 181
Levy, Elizabeth. LIZZIE LIES A LOT.
Ages 9-11. 361
Meyer, Carolyn. THE CENTER: FROM A TROUBLED PAST TO A NEW LIFE.
Ages 13 and up. 421
Myers, Walter Dean. IT AIN'T ALL FOR NOTHIN'.
Ages 11-13. 438
Ness, Evaline Michelow. SAM, BANGS, AND MOONSHINE.
Ages 4-8. 441
Rodowsky, Colby F. P.S. WRITE SOON.
Ages 10-12. 506
Sharmat, Marjorie Weinman. A BIG FAT ENORMOUS LIE.
Ages 3-7. 527
Shura, Mary Francis Craig. THE BARKLEY STREET SIX-PACK.
Ages 9-12. 533
Wartski, Maureen Crane. MY BROTHER IS SPECIAL.
Ages 10-12. 606
White, Elwyn Brooks. THE TRUMPET OF THE SWAN.
Ages 9-13. 619
Winthrop, Elizabeth. MIRANDA IN THE MIDDLE.
Ages 9-13. 627

Hope

See also: *Ego ideal; Expectations*
Blume, Judy Sussman. IT'S NOT THE END OF THE WORLD.
Ages 10-12. 41
Hamilton, Virginia. M. C. HIGGINS, THE GREAT.
Ages 12 and up. 248

Hospital, Going to

See also: *Accidents; Amputee; Cancer; Doctor, going to; Fractures; Illnesses; Leukemia; Separation anxiety; Separation from loved ones; Surgery*
Dacquino, Vincent T. KISS THE CANDY DAYS GOOD-BYE.
Ages 10-14. 150
Hautzig, Deborah. SECOND STAR TO THE RIGHT.
Ages 12 and up. 256
Hogan, Paula Z. and Kirk Hogan. THE HOSPITAL SCARES ME.
Ages 3-8. 287
Jones, Rebecca Castalldi. ANGIE AND ME.
Ages 9-11. 317
Marino, Barbara Pavis. ERIC NEEDS STITCHES.
Ages 4-10. 400
Rey, Margret Elisabeth Waldstein and Hans Augusto Rey. CURIOUS GEORGE GOES TO THE HOSPITAL.
Ages 4-9. 494
Singer, Marilyn. IT CAN'T HURT FOREVER.
Ages 9-12. 543
Stein, Sara Bonnett. A HOSPITAL STORY: AN OPEN FAMILY BOOK FOR PARENTS AND CHILDREN TOGETHER.
Ages 3-8. 566
Wolde, Gunilla. BETSY AND THE DOCTOR.
Ages 3-7. 635

Hostility

See also: *Aggression; Anger; Hatred; Prejudice; Trust/Distrust*
Arrick, Fran. CHERNOWITZ!
Ages 12 and up. 18
Paterson, Katherine Womeldorf. THE GREAT GILLY HOPKINS.
Ages 10-13. 456
Wartski, Maureen Crane. A LONG WAY FROM HOME.
Ages 11-13. 605
Zolotow, Charlotte Shapiro. THE QUARRELING BOOK.
Ages 4-7. 670

Human Differences

See: *Differences, human*

I

Ideals

See: *Ego ideal; Identification with others; Values/Valuing*

Identification with others

See also: *Ego ideal; Empathy; Imitation; Leader/Leadership; Values/Valuing*

Adults
Hall, Lynn. DANZA!
Ages 9-12. 245
Miles, Betty. LOOKING ON.
Ages 11-14. 425
Thomas, Ianthe. WILLIE BLOWS A MEAN HORN.
Ages 5-8. 583

Peers. *See also: Friendship*
Blume, Judy Sussman. FRECKLE JUICE.
Ages 8-11. 39
Hinton, Susan E. THE OUTSIDERS.
Ages 12 and up. 273
Pfeffer, Susan Beth. STARRING PETER AND LEIGH.
Ages 12-14. 477

Story characters
Foley, June. IT'S NO CRUSH, I'M IN LOVE!
Ages 11-13. 185

Identity, Search for

See also: *Adoption; Ego ideal*
Asher, Sandra Fenichel. JUST LIKE JENNY.
Ages 10-12. 22
Barrett, John M. DANIEL DISCOVERS DANIEL.
Ages 7-9. 26
Blume, Judy Sussman. THE ONE IN THE MIDDLE IS THE GREEN KANGAROO.
Ages 7-9. 42
Bridgers, Sue Ellen. HOME BEFORE DARK.
Ages 12 and up. 64

Identity, Search for (cont.)
Cleary, Beverly Bunn. RAMONA THE PEST.
Ages 8-10. 120
Delton, Judy. I NEVER WIN!
Ages 4-7. 161
Dyer, Thomas A. THE WHIPMAN IS WATCHING.
Ages 10-14. 172
Fitzgerald, John Dennis. ME AND MY LITTLE BRAIN.
Ages 9-12. 182
Foley, June. IT'S NO CRUSH, I'M IN LOVE!
Ages 11-13. 185
Forbes, Esther. JOHNNY TREMAIN.
Ages 10 and up. 186
Fox, Paula. PORTRAIT OF IVAN.
Ages 11 and up. 189
Greenfield, Eloise. SISTER.
Ages 10-12. 235
Hall, Lynn. THE LEAVING.
Ages 12 and up. 246
Hassler, Jon Francis. JEMMY.
Ages 11 and up. 255
Holland, Isabelle. THE MAN WITHOUT A FACE.
Ages 13 and up. 290
Kent, Deborah. BELONGING: A NOVEL.
Ages 11-14. 328
Kerr, M. E., pseud. I'LL LOVE YOU WHEN YOU'RE MORE LIKE ME.
Ages 12 and up. 330
Kingman, Lee. BREAK A LEG, BETSY MAYBE!
Ages 12 and up. 334
Le Guin, Ursula Kroeber. VERY FAR AWAY FROM ANYWHERE ELSE.
Ages 12 and up. 352
Lifton, Betty Jean. I'M STILL ME.
Ages 12 and up. 364
Little, Jean. FROM ANNA.
Ages 9-11. 377
Little, Jean. KATE.
Ages 10-14. 379
MacLachlan, Patricia. ARTHUR, FOR THE VERY FIRST TIME.
Ages 8-10. 392
Mazer, Harry. THE ISLAND KEEPER.
Ages 10-14. 414
Miles, Betty. LOOKING ON.
Ages 11-14. 425
Pfeffer, Susan Beth. STARRING PETER AND LEIGH.
Ages 12-14. 477
Raskin, Ellen. FIGGS & PHANTOMS.
Ages 12 and up. 489
Sachs, Marilyn. THE TRUTH ABOUT MARY ROSE.
Ages 10-13. 516
Sargent, Sarah. SECRET LIES.
Ages 11 and up. 519
Sharmat, Marjorie Weinman. I'M TERRIFIC.
Ages 4-7. 529
Smith, Doris Buchanan. KICK A STONE HOME.
Ages 11 and up. 549
Stein, Sara Bonnett. THE ADOPTED ONE: AN OPEN FAMILY BOOK FOR PARENTS AND CHILDREN TOGETHER.
Ages 4-8. 565
Van Leeuwen, Jean. SEEMS LIKE THIS ROAD GOES ON FOREVER.
Ages 12 and up. 589

Illnesses
See also: *Communicable diseases; Doctor, going to; Hospital, going to; Mental illness; Surgery*

Amyotrophic Lateral Sclerosis. *See: Amyotrophic Lateral Sclerosis*

Anorexia nervosa. *See: Anorexia nervosa*

Arthritis, juvenile rheumatoid. *See: Arthritis, juvenile rheumatoid*

Asthma. *See: Asthma*

Being ill
Brandenberg, Franz. I WISH I WAS SICK, TOO!
Ages 3-7. 61
MacLachlan, Patricia. THE SICK DAY.
Ages 4-7. 395
Rockwell, Anne F. and Harlow Rockwell. SICK IN BED.
Ages 3-6. 500

Cancer. *See: Cancer*

Cerebral palsy. *See: Cerebral palsy*

Diabetes. *See: Diabetes*

Epilepsy. *See: Epilepsy*

of Grandparent
De Paola, Thomas Anthony. NOW ONE FOOT, NOW THE OTHER.
Ages 4-7. 158
Gardiner, John Reynolds. STONE FOX.
Ages 8-10. 197

Hemophilia. *See: Hemophilia*

Leukemia. *See: Leukemia*

of Parent
Cleaver, Vera and Bill Cleaver. GROVER.
Ages 9-12. 122
Delton, Judy. IT HAPPENED ON THURSDAY.
Ages 5-8. 162
Greene, Constance Clarke. AL(EXANDRA) THE GREAT.
Ages 10-13. 222
Sachs, Marilyn. AMY AND LAURA.
Ages 9-12. 509

of Sibling
Wolde, Gunilla. BETSY AND THE CHICKEN POX.
Ages 3-7. 634

Terminal. *See also: Fear: of death*
Coerr, Eleanor. SADAKO AND THE THOUSAND PAPER CRANES.
Ages 11 and up. 130
Donnelly, Elfie. SO LONG, GRANDPA.
Ages 9-11. 167
Greenberg, Jan. A SEASON IN-BETWEEN.
Ages 11-13. 219
Hermes, Patricia. YOU SHOULDN'T HAVE TO SAY GOOD-BYE.
Ages 10-13. 270
Jones, Rebecca Castalldi. ANGIE AND ME.
Ages 9-11. 317
Lowry, Lois. A SUMMER TO DIE.
Ages 10-14. 389

Illnesses (cont.)
Mann, Peggy. THERE ARE TWO KINDS OF TERRIBLE.
Ages 9-12. 399
Mazer, Norma Fox. DEAR BILL, REMEMBER ME? AND OTHER STORIES.
Ages 12 and up. 415
Strasser, Todd. FRIENDS TILL THE END.
Ages 12 and up. 577
Stretton, Barbara. YOU NEVER LOSE.
Ages 12 and up. 578

Imaginary Friend
See also: *Fantasy formation; Imagination; Magical thinking; Play*
Greenfield, Eloise. ME AND NEESIE.
Ages 4-7. 233
Sharmat, Marjorie Weinman. GOODNIGHT, ANDREW; GOODNIGHT, CRAIG.
Ages 3-7. 528
Zolotow, Charlotte Shapiro. THE THREE FUNNY FRIENDS.
Ages 4-6. 672

Imagination
See also: *Creativity; Fantasy formation; Imaginary friend; Magical thinking; Play; Reality, escaping*
Adler, Carole Schwerdtfeger. THE SILVER COACH.
Ages 9-12. 4
Byars, Betsy Cromer. THE TV KID.
Ages 9-12. 94
Cameron, Ann. THE STORIES JULIAN TELLS.
Ages 7-9. 99
Cleary, Beverly Bunn. THE REAL HOLE.
Ages 3-6. 121
Conford, Ellen. THE REVENGE OF THE INCREDIBLE DR. RANCID AND HIS YOUTHFUL ASSISTANT, JEFFREY.
Ages 10-12. 142
Delton, Judy. MY MOTHER LOST HER JOB TODAY.
Ages 3-7. 164
Giff, Patricia Reilly. FOURTH GRADE CELEBRITY.
Ages 8-10. 200
Gross, Alan. THE I DON'T WANT TO GO TO SCHOOL BOOK.
Ages 5-9. 239
Hoban, Russell Conwell. BEDTIME FOR FRANCES.
Ages 3-7. 279
Holland, Isabelle. DINAH AND THE GREEN FAT KINGDOM.
Ages 10-13. 288
Lionni, Leo. FISH IS FISH.
Ages 4-8. 368
Ness, Evaline Michelow. SAM, BANGS, AND MOONSHINE.
Ages 4-8. 441
Paterson, Katherine Womeldorf. BRIDGE TO TERABITHIA.
Ages 9-12. 455
Viorst, Judith. MY MAMA SAYS THERE AREN'T ANY ZOMBIES, GHOSTS, VAMPIRES, CREATURES, DEMONS, MONSTERS, FIENDS, GOBLINS, OR THINGS.
Ages 4-7. 594
Zolotow, Charlotte Shapiro. IF YOU LISTEN.
Ages 5-7. 663

Imitation
See also: *Identification with others*
Blume, Judy Sussman. FRECKLE JUICE.
Ages 8-11. 39
Fitzgerald, John Dennis. ME AND MY LITTLE BRAIN.
Ages 9-12. 182
Freeman, Don. DANDELION.
Ages 3-8. 193
Hinton, Susan E. RUMBLE FISH.
Ages 12 and up. 274
Sachs, Marilyn. THE TRUTH ABOUT MARY ROSE.
Ages 10-13. 516

Immigrants
See also: *Prejudice: ethnic/racial; Refugees; Vietnam*
Little, Jean. FROM ANNA.
Ages 9-11. 377
Wartski, Maureen Crane. A LONG WAY FROM HOME.
Ages 11-13. 605

Impatience
See: *Patience/Impatience*

Imprisonment
See also: *Crime/Criminals; Delinquency, juvenile; Detention home, living in*
Burch, Robert Joseph. QUEENIE PEAVY.
Ages 11-13. 77
Shreve, Susan Richards. THE MASQUERADE.
Ages 12 and up. 532

Inconsistency
See: *Parental: inconsistency*

Independence
See: *Dependence/Independence*

Independent Thinking
See: *Autonomy*

Indian, American
See: *Native American*

Individuality
See: *Autonomy*

Individuation
See: *Autonomy; Dependence/Independence; Separation anxiety*

Infant
See: *Death: of infant; Sibling: new baby*

Jealousy (cont.)
Kerr, M. E., pseud. LOVE IS A MISSING PERSON.
Ages 12 and up. 332
Landis, James David. THE SISTERS IMPOSSIBLE.
Ages 9-11. 348
Paterson, Katherine Womeldorf. JACOB HAVE I LOVED.
Ages 12 and up. 457
Pfeffer, Susan Beth. WHAT DO YOU DO WHEN YOUR MOUTH WON'T OPEN?
Ages 10-13. 478
Rodowsky, Colby F. WHAT ABOUT ME?
Ages 11-13. 507
Wolde, Gunilla. BETSY AND THE CHICKEN POX.
Ages 3-7. 634

Jew/Jewish
See also: *Ghetto*
Arrick, Fran. CHERNOWITZ!
Ages 12 and up. 18
Frank, Anne. ANNE FRANK: THE DIARY OF A YOUNG GIRL.
Ages 11 and up. 191
Girion, Barbara. A TANGLE OF ROOTS.
Ages 12-16. 208
Kerr, Judith. WHEN HITLER STOLE PINK RABBIT.
Ages 10-12. 329
Konigsburg, Elaine Lobl. ABOUT THE B'NAI BAGELS.
Ages 10-13. 341
Little, Jean. KATE.
Ages 10-14. 379
Little, Jean. LOOK THROUGH MY WINDOW.
Ages 10-14. 381
Neville, Emily Cheney. BERRIES GOODMAN.
Ages 11 and up. 443
Reiss, Johanna. THE JOURNEY BACK.
Ages 10-14. 492
Sachs, Marilyn. PETER AND VERONICA.
Ages 10-12. 513

Job
See also: *Baby-sitting; Chores; Money: earning; Responsibility; Retirement; Work, attitude toward*
Bulla, Clyde Robert. SHOESHINE GIRL.
Ages 8-10. 74
Cleary, Beverly Bunn. HENRY AND THE PAPER ROUTE.
Ages 7-10. 113
Lipsyte, Robert. ONE FAT SUMMER.
Ages 12-14. 373
Lowry, Lois. ANASTASIA AT YOUR SERVICE.
Ages 9-12. 387
Pfeffer, Susan Beth. KID POWER.
Ages 9-12. 476

Judgment, Effect of Emotions on
O'Dell, Scott. KATHLEEN, PLEASE COME HOME.
Ages 12 and up. 447

Justice/Injustice
See also: *Blame; Guilt, feelings of; Prejudice*
Fitzgerald, John Dennis. THE GREAT BRAIN REFORMS.
Ages 10-13. 181
Garden, Nancy. ANNIE ON MY MIND.
Ages 13 and up. 196
Guy, Rosa Cuthbert. THE DISAPPEARANCE.
Ages 12 and up. 243
Hentoff, Nat. DOES THIS SCHOOL HAVE CAPITAL PUNISHMENT?
Ages 11 and up. 265
Knudson, R. Rozanne. ZANBANGER.
Ages 10-13. 339
Lee, Harper. TO KILL A MOCKINGBIRD.
Ages 12 and up. 353
Taylor, Mildred D. ROLL OF THUNDER, HEAR MY CRY.
Ages 10 and up. 581

Juvenile Delinquency
See: *Delinquency, juvenile*

Juvenile Detention
See: *Detention home, living in*

K

Killing
See: *Death: murder; Violence; War*

Kissing
See: *Boy-girl relationships; Sex*

L

Latchkey Child
See: *Parent/Parents: Mother working outside home; Parent/Parents: Single*

Laziness
See: *Chores; Daydreaming; Responsibility: avoiding; School: achievement/underachievement; Work, attitude toward*

Leader/Leadership
See also: *Identification with others; Responsibility: accepting*
Dygard, Thomas J. WINNING KICKER.
Ages 11-14. 173
Greene, Bette. GET ON OUT OF HERE, PHILIP HALL.
Ages 9-12. 220
Jeffries, Roderic. TRAPPED.
Ages 11-13. 315

Learning, Love of
See: *Education: Value of*

Loneliness (cont.)
Le Guin, Ursula Kroeber. VERY FAR AWAY FROM ANYWHERE ELSE.
Ages 12 and up. 352
Lee, Mildred Scudder. THE SKATING RINK.
Ages 10-13. 354
Miles, Miska, pseud. AARON'S DOOR.
Ages 5-9. 428
Mohr, Nicholasa. IN NUEVA YORK.
Ages 13 and up. 433
O'Dell, Scott. ISLAND OF THE BLUE DOLPHINS.
Ages 10 and up. 446
Perl, Lila. ME AND FAT GLENDA.
Ages 9-12. 465
Perrine, Mary. NANNABAH'S FRIEND.
Ages 7-10. 467
Rawlings, Marjorie Kinnan. THE YEARLING.
Ages 12 and up. 491
Roberts, Willo Davis. DON'T HURT LAURIE!
Ages 10-14. 496
Sargent, Sarah. SECRET LIES.
Ages 11 and up. 519
Snyder, Anne. MY NAME IS DAVY—I'M AN ALCOHOLIC.
Ages 12 and up. 556
Stolz, Mary Slattery. THE BULLY OF BARKHAM STREET.
Ages 8-11. 573
Zindel, Paul. THE PIGMAN.
Ages 12 and up. 659
Zolotow, Charlotte Shapiro. JANEY.
Ages 4-7. 665

Loss

Feelings of. *See also: Abandonment; Death; Depression; Mourning, stages of; Separation anxiety; Separation from loved ones*
Bridgers, Sue Ellen. NOTES FOR ANOTHER LIFE.
Ages 12 and up. 65
Graeber, Charlotte Towner. MUSTARD.
Ages 4-10. 213
Hermes, Patricia. YOU SHOULDN'T HAVE TO SAY GOOD-BYE.
Ages 10-13. 270
Knox-Wagner, Elaine. MY GRANDPA RETIRED TODAY.
Ages 4-7. 337
Lowry, Lois. ANASTASIA KRUPNIK.
Ages 9-11. 388
Miles, Betty. THE TROUBLE WITH THIRTEEN.
Ages 9-13. 427
Peck, Richard. CLOSE ENOUGH TO TOUCH.
Ages 12 and up. 461
Radley, Gail. NOTHING STAYS THE SAME FOREVER.
Ages 9-12. 488
Smith, Doris Buchanan. A TASTE OF BLACKBERRIES.
Ages 8-11. 551
Stolz, Mary Slattery. A DOG ON BARKHAM STREET.
Ages 8-11. 574
Wright, Betty Ren. MY NEW MOM AND ME.
Ages 8-10. 651
Zolotow, Charlotte Shapiro. THE NEW FRIEND.
Ages 3-7. 668

of Possessions
Hughes, Shirley. DAVID AND DOG.
Ages 4-7. 298

Lost, Being
Benson, Kathleen. JOSEPH ON THE SUBWAY TRAINS.
Ages 7-9. 34
Mauser, Pat Rhoads. HOW I FOUND MYSELF AT THE FAIR.
Ages 7-9. 411

Lou Gehrig's Disease

See: *Amyotrophic Lateral Sclerosis*

Love, Meaning of
Bates, Betty. PICKING UP THE PIECES.
Ages 10-13. 29
Borack, Barbara. GRANDPA.
Ages 3-6. 55
Brandenberg, Aliki Liacouras. THE TWO OF THEM.
Ages 3-7. 59
Bridgers, Sue Ellen. ALL TOGETHER NOW.
Ages 11 and up. 63
Childress, Alice. RAINBOW JORDAN.
Ages 12 and up. 109
Clifton, Lucille. EVERETT ANDERSON'S NINE MONTH LONG.
Ages 4-7. 128
Gallico, Paul. THE SNOW GOOSE.
Ages 12 and up. 195
Garden, Nancy. ANNIE ON MY MIND.
Ages 13 and up. 196
Guest, Elissa Haden. THE HANDSOME MAN.
Ages 12 and up. 241
Hallman, Ruth. BREAKAWAY.
Ages 12 and up. 247
Hautzig, Esther Rudomin. A GIFT FOR MAMA.
Ages 8-12. 257
Hazen, Barbara Shook. EVEN IF I DID SOMETHING AWFUL.
Ages 3-6. 258
Holland, Isabelle. THE MAN WITHOUT A FACE.
Ages 13 and up. 290
Holland, Isabelle. NOW IS NOT TOO LATE.
Ages 10-13. 291
Hunt, Irene. THE LOTTERY ROSE.
Ages 11 and up. 300
Hunt, Irene. UP A ROAD SLOWLY.
Ages 12 and up. 301
Irwin, Hadley, pseud. THE LILITH SUMMER.
Ages 9-13. 310
MacLachlan, Patricia. THE SICK DAY.
Ages 4-7. 395
Magorian, Michelle. GOOD NIGHT, MR. TOM.
Ages 11 and up. 398
Mazer, Norma Fox. DEAR BILL, REMEMBER ME? AND OTHER STORIES.
Ages 12 and up. 415
Mazer, Norma Fox. WHEN WE FIRST MET.
Ages 12 and up. 417
Melton, David. A BOY CALLED HOPELESS.
Ages 10 and up. 420
Miles, Betty. AROUND AND AROUND—LOVE.
Ages 3-8. 423

Love, Meaning of (cont.)
Mohr, Nicholasa. IN NUEVA YORK.
Ages 13 and up. 433
Paterson, Katherine Womeldorf. THE GREAT GILLY HOPKINS.
Ages 10-13. 456
Peck, Richard. CLOSE ENOUGH TO TOUCH.
Ages 12 and up. 461
Pevsner, Stella. AND YOU GIVE ME A PAIN, ELAINE.
Ages 10-13. 471
Power, Barbara. I WISH LAURA'S MOMMY WAS MY MOMMY.
Ages 4-7. 485
Raskin, Ellen. FIGGS & PHANTOMS.
Ages 12 and up. 489
Sallis, Susan Diana. ONLY LOVE.
Ages 12 and up. 518
Schlein, Miriam. THE WAY MOTHERS ARE.
Ages 3-6. 520
Slepian, Jan. LESTER'S TURN.
Ages 11-14. 545
Strang, Celia. FOSTER MARY.
Ages 10-13. 575
Voigt, Cynthia. DICEY'S SONG.
Ages 11 and up. 597
Wartski, Maureen Crane. A BOAT TO NOWHERE.
Ages 9-12. 604
Williams, Margery Bianco. THE VELVETEEN RABBIT: OR, HOW TOYS BECOME REAL.
Ages 5-10. 624
Wolff, Angelika. MOM! I NEED GLASSES!
Ages 10-13. 643
Wortis, Avi. SOMETIMES I THINK I HEAR MY NAME.
Ages 10-13. 649
Zindel, Paul. I LOVE MY MOTHER.
Ages 3-7. 658
Zindel, Paul. THE PIGMAN.
Ages 12 and up. 659

Loyalty
See also: *Sibling: loyalty*
Angell, Judie. IN SUMMERTIME IT'S TUFFY.
Ages 11-13. 13
Burton, Virginia Lee. MIKE MULLIGAN AND HIS STEAM SHOVEL.
Ages 4-8. 84
Carrick, Carol. SOME FRIEND!
Ages 9-12. 104
Hassler, Jon Francis. FOUR MILES TO PINECONE.
Ages 10-14. 254
Knudson, R. Rozanne. ZANBOOMER.
Ages 10-13. 340
Sachs, Marilyn. CLASS PICTURES.
Ages 10-13. 511
Viorst, Judith. ROSIE AND MICHAEL.
Ages 4-7. 595
White, Elwyn Brooks. CHARLOTTE'S WEB.
Ages 8-12. 618

Lying
See: *Honesty/Dishonesty; Values/Valuing*

M

Magical Thinking
See also: *Daydreaming; Fantasy formation; Imaginary friend; Imagination*
Goff, Beth. WHERE IS DADDY? THE STORY OF A DIVORCE.
Ages 4-8. 209

Mainstreaming
See: *School: mainstreaming*

Make-believe
See: *Fantasy formation; Imagination; Play*

Manipulation
Peer
Shura, Mary Francis Craig. THE BARKLEY STREET SIX-PACK.
Ages 9-12. 533

Manliness
See: *Gender role identity: male*

Manners
See: *Etiquette*

Marijuana
See also: *Drugs; Smoking*
Hentoff, Nat. DOES THIS SCHOOL HAVE CAPITAL PUNISHMENT?
Ages 11 and up. 265

Marriage
Interreligious. *See also: Prejudice: religious*
Blume, Judy Sussman. ARE YOU THERE GOD? IT'S ME, MARGARET.
Ages 10-13. 37
Little, Jean. KATE.
Ages 10-14. 379
Teenage
Head, Ann. MR. AND MRS. BO JO JONES.
Ages 13 and up. 262

Masculinity
See: *Gender role identity: male*

Masturbation
See also: *Sex*
Blume, Judy Sussman. DEENIE.
Ages 10-12. 38

Maturation
See also: *Puberty*
Adler, Carole Schwerdtfeger. THE SILVER COACH.
Ages 9-12. 4

Maturation (cont.)

Bargar, Gary W. WHAT HAPPENED TO MR. FORSTER?
Ages 10-13. 25
Bauer, Marion Dane. SHELTER FROM THE WIND.
Ages 10-13. 30
Blume, Judy Sussman. THEN AGAIN, MAYBE I WON'T.
Ages 12 and up. 46
Blume, Judy Sussman. TIGER EYES.
Ages 11 and up. 47
Bond, Nancy Barbara. THE VOYAGE BEGUN.
Ages 12 and up. 49
Bonham, Frank. DURANGO STREET.
Ages 11 and up. 50
Bradford, Richard. RED SKY AT MORNING.
Ages 13 and up. 57
Bridgers, Sue Ellen. ALL TOGETHER NOW.
Ages 11 and up. 63
Bridgers, Sue Ellen. HOME BEFORE DARK.
Ages 12 and up. 64
Brink, Carol Ryrie. CADDIE WOODLAWN: A FRONTIER STORY.
Ages 9-12. 66
Byars, Betsy Cromer. THE ANIMAL, THE VEGETABLE, AND JOHN D JONES.
Ages 10-12. 87
Calhoun, Mary Huiskamp. KATIE JOHN AND HEATHCLIFF.
Ages 9-11. 98
Colman, Hila Crayder. DIARY OF A FRANTIC KID SISTER.
Ages 10-13. 139
Danziger, Paula. THERE'S A BAT IN BUNK FIVE.
Ages 10-14. 155
Fitzhugh, Louise. HARRIET THE SPY.
Ages 10-12. 183
Fox, Paula. BLOWFISH LIVE IN THE SEA.
Ages 11 and up. 187
Frank, Anne. ANNE FRANK: THE DIARY OF A YOUNG GIRL.
Ages 11 and up. 191
Girion, Barbara. A HANDFUL OF STARS.
Ages 12 and up. 207
Girion, Barbara. A TANGLE OF ROOTS.
Ages 12-16. 208
Greenberg, Jan. A SEASON IN-BETWEEN.
Ages 11-13. 219
Greene, Constance Clarke. AL(EXANDRA) THE GREAT.
Ages 10-13. 222
Greene, Constance Clarke. I KNOW YOU, AL.
Ages 11 and up. 227
Hallman, Ruth. BREAKAWAY.
Ages 12 and up. 247
Hansen, Joyce. THE GIFT-GIVER.
Ages 9-12. 250
Harris, Robie H. I HATE KISSES.
Ages 2-5. 252
Hartling, Peter. OMA.
Ages 8-11. 253
Head, Ann. MR. AND MRS. BO JO JONES.
Ages 13 and up. 262
Herman, Charlotte. OUR SNOWMAN HAD OLIVE EYES.
Ages 9-11. 267
Hinton, Susan E. THAT WAS THEN, THIS IS NOW.
Ages 12 and up. 275
Holland, Isabelle. NOW IS NOT TOO LATE.
Ages 10-13. 291
Hunt, Irene. UP A ROAD SLOWLY.
Ages 12 and up. 301
Hunter, Mollie, pseud. A SOUND OF CHARIOTS.
Ages 12 and up. 304
Irwin, Hadley, pseud. MOON AND ME.
Ages 11-14. 311
Jacobs, Dee. LAURA'S GIFT.
Ages 10-13. 313
Jones, Rebecca Castalldi. ANGIE AND ME.
Ages 9-11. 317
Jones, Toeckey. GO WELL, STAY WELL.
Ages 12 and up. 319
Kent, Deborah. BELONGING: A NOVEL.
Ages 11-14. 328
Kerr, M. E., pseud. LOVE IS A MISSING PERSON.
Ages 12 and up. 332
Kingman, Lee. BREAK A LEG, BETSY MAYBE!
Ages 12 and up. 334
Konigsburg, Elaine Lobl. ABOUT THE B'NAI BAGELS.
Ages 10-13. 341
Konigsburg, Elaine Lobl. FROM THE MIXED-UP FILES OF MRS. BASIL E. FRANKWEILER.
Ages 9-12. 343
Konigsburg, Elaine Lobl. THROWING SHADOWS.
Ages 10-12. 344
Kraus, Robert. LEO THE LATE BLOOMER.
Ages 3-7. 345
Levoy, Myron. A SHADOW LIKE A LEOPARD.
Ages 12 and up. 359
Lionni, Leo. FISH IS FISH.
Ages 4-8. 368
Liu, Aimee. SOLITAIRE.
Ages 13 and up. 384
Lowry, Lois. ANASTASIA KRUPNIK.
Ages 9-11. 388
Matthews, Ellen. GETTING RID OF ROGER.
Ages 8-10. 409
Mazer, Norma Fox. UP IN SETH'S ROOM.
Ages 13 and up. 416
McCloskey, Robert. ONE MORNING IN MAINE.
Ages 5-8. 419
Miles, Betty. JUST THE BEGINNING.
Ages 10-12. 424
Miles, Betty. LOOKING ON.
Ages 11-14. 425
Miles, Betty. THE TROUBLE WITH THIRTEEN.
Ages 9-13. 427
Moeri, Louise. FIRST THE EGG.
Ages 12 and up. 430
Myers, Walter Dean. FAST SAM, COOL CLYDE, AND STUFF.
Ages 11-14. 436
Myers, Walter Dean. HOOPS.
Ages 12 and up. 437
Myers, Walter Dean. WON'T KNOW TILL I GET THERE.
Ages 11-14. 439
O'Connor, Jane. YOURS TILL NIAGARA FALLS, ABBY.
Ages 8-10. 445
O'Hara, Mary, pseud. MY FRIEND FLICKA.
Ages 11 and up. 448

Maturation (cont.)
Pascal, Francine. MY FIRST LOVE & OTHER DISASTERS.
Ages 12 and up. 454
Paterson, Katherine Womeldorf. JACOB HAVE I LOVED.
Ages 12 and up. 457
Paulsen, Gary. THE FOXMAN.
Ages 11-14. 458
Peck, Richard. FATHER FIGURE: A NOVEL.
Ages 11 and up. 462
Peck, Robert Newton. A DAY NO PIGS WOULD DIE.
Ages 12 and up. 463
Petersen, P. J. WOULD YOU SETTLE FOR IMPROBABLE?
Ages 11-13. 469
Pevsner, Stella. AND YOU GIVE ME A PAIN, ELAINE.
Ages 10-13. 471
Pevsner, Stella. A SMART KID LIKE YOU.
Ages 10-13. 473
Platt, Kin. BROGG'S BRAIN.
Ages 12 and up. 482
Radley, Gail. NOTHING STAYS THE SAME FOREVER.
Ages 9-12. 488
Reiss, Johanna. THE JOURNEY BACK.
Ages 10-14. 492
Sachs, Marilyn. CLASS PICTURES.
Ages 10-13. 511
Sachs, Marilyn. A SUMMER'S LEASE.
Ages 11-14. 515
Sargent, Sarah. SECRET LIES.
Ages 11 and up. 519
Seredy, Kate. THE GOOD MASTER.
Ages 9-12. 526
Smith, Doris Buchanan. KICK A STONE HOME.
Ages 11 and up. 549
Stretton, Barbara. YOU NEVER LOSE.
Ages 12 and up. 578
Walker, Mary Alexander. YEAR OF THE CAFETERIA.
Ages 12 and up. 601
Wartski, Maureen Crane. A BOAT TO NOWHERE.
Ages 9-12. 604
Wilkinson, Brenda Scott. LUDELL.
Ages 10-14. 621
Wojciechowska, Maia Rodman. SHADOW OF A BULL.
Ages 11 and up. 631
Wojciechowska, Maia Rodman. TUNED OUT.
Ages 12 and up. 632
Wolff, Angelika. MOM! I NEED GLASSES!
Ages 10-13. 643
Wortis, Avi. SOMETIMES I THINK I HEAR MY NAME.
Ages 10-13. 649

Mennonite
Swartley, David Warren. MY FRIEND, MY BROTHER.
Ages 9-11. 580

Menstruation
See also: *Puberty*
Blume, Judy Sussman. ARE YOU THERE GOD? IT'S ME, MARGARET.
Ages 10-13. 37
Fitzhugh, Louise. THE LONG SECRET.
Ages 9-12. 184
Greene, Constance Clarke. I KNOW YOU, AL.
Ages 11 and up. 227
Miles, Betty. THE TROUBLE WITH THIRTEEN.
Ages 9-13. 427

Mental Illness
See also: *Anorexia nervosa; Depression; Illnesses; Reality, escaping*

of Adolescent
Guest, Judith. ORDINARY PEOPLE.
Ages 13 and up. 242
Van Leeuwen, Jean. SEEMS LIKE THIS ROAD GOES ON FOREVER.
Ages 12 and up. 589

of Parent
Bridgers, Sue Ellen. NOTES FOR ANOTHER LIFE.
Ages 12 and up. 65
MacLachlan, Patricia. MAMA ONE, MAMA TWO.
Ages 4-7. 394
Moeri, Louise. THE GIRL WHO LIVED ON THE FERRIS WHEEL.
Ages 13 and up. 431
Riley, Jocelyn. ONLY MY MOUTH IS SMILING.
Ages 12-14. 495
Roberts, Willo Davis. DON'T HURT LAURIE!
Ages 10-14. 496
Sachs, Marilyn. THE BEARS' HOUSE.
Ages 9-12. 510
Scoppettone, Sandra. THE LATE GREAT ME.
Ages 12 and up. 524
Shreve, Susan Richards. THE MASQUERADE.
Ages 12 and up. 532
Smith, Nancy Covert. THE FALLING-APART WINTER.
Ages 10-13. 554
Wolitzer, Hilma. TOBY LIVED HERE.
Ages 10-12. 645
Yep, Laurence Michael. KIND HEARTS AND GENTLE MONSTERS.
Ages 12 and up. 653

Mental Retardation
See also: *Brain injury; Education: special; Learning disabilities*
Bridgers, Sue Ellen. ALL TOGETHER NOW.
Ages 11 and up. 63
Cleaver, Vera and Bill Cleaver. ME TOO.
Ages 9-11. 123
Fassler, Joan. ONE LITTLE GIRL.
Ages 5-8. 180
Hunt, Irene. THE LOTTERY ROSE.
Ages 11 and up. 300
Shyer, Marlene Fanta. WELCOME HOME, JELLYBEAN.
Ages 10-13. 535
Slepian, Jan. THE ALFRED SUMMER.
Ages 11-13. 544

Mental Retardation (cont.)
Slepian, Jan. LESTER'S TURN.
Ages 11-14. 545
Sobol, Harriet Langsam. MY BROTHER STEVEN IS RETARDED.
Ages 7-10. 557
Wartski, Maureen Crane. MY BROTHER IS SPECIAL.
Ages 10-12. 606
Wright, Betty Ren. MY SISTER IS DIFFERENT.
Ages 6-9. 652

Down syndrome. *See: Down syndrome*

Messiness
Bottner, Barbara. MESSY.
Ages 4-7. 56

Middle Child
See: *Sibling: middle*

Migrant Workers
Bridgers, Sue Ellen. HOME BEFORE DARK.
Ages 12 and up. 64
Strang, Celia. FOSTER MARY.
Ages 10-13. 575

Minding
See: *Discipline, meaning of*

Minority Groups
See: *Differences, human; Prejudice; Specific groups (e.g. African-American; Native American)*

Mistakes, Making
Lexau, Joan M. I SHOULD HAVE STAYED IN BED!
Ages 6-8. 362

Misunderstandings
See: *Communication: misunderstandings*

Money

Earning. *See also: Job*
Hoban, Lillian Aberman. ARTHUR'S FUNNY MONEY.
Ages 6-8. 276
Hurwitz, Johanna. SUPERDUPER TEDDY.
Ages 4-7. 307
Lowry, Lois. ANASTASIA AT YOUR SERVICE.
Ages 9-12. 387

Management
Cleary, Beverly Bunn. RAMONA QUIMBY, AGE 8.
Ages 8-10. 118

Moral Values
See: *Values/Valuing: moral/ethic*

Mother
See: *Communication: parent-child; Parent/Parents: mother working outside home; Parent/Parents: single*

Mourning, Stages of
See also: *Death; Guilt, feelings of; Loss: feelings of; Separation from loved ones*
Angell, Judie. RONNIE AND ROSEY.
Ages 11 and up. 14
Arrick, Fran. TUNNEL VISION.
Ages 12 and up. 20
Blume, Judy Sussman. TIGER EYES.
Ages 11 and up. 47
Buck, Pearl Sydenstricker. THE BIG WAVE.
Ages 9-11. 71
Byars, Betsy Cromer. GOODBYE, CHICKEN LITTLE.
Ages 9-11. 90
Cleaver, Vera and Bill Cleaver. GROVER.
Ages 9-12. 122
Fassler, Joan. MY GRANDPA DIED TODAY.
Ages 4-8. 179
Girion, Barbara. A TANGLE OF ROOTS.
Ages 12-16. 208
Greene, Constance Clarke. AL(EXANDRA) THE GREAT.
Ages 10-13. 222
Hunter, Mollie, pseud. A SOUND OF CHARIOTS.
Ages 12 and up. 304
Krementz, Jill. HOW IT FEELS WHEN A PARENT DIES.
Ages 8 and up. 347
Mann, Peggy. THERE ARE TWO KINDS OF TERRIBLE.
Ages 9-12. 399
Mazer, Norma Fox. WHEN WE FIRST MET.
Ages 12 and up. 417
Oneal, Zibby. A FORMAL FEELING.
Ages 12 and up. 450
Peck, Richard. CLOSE ENOUGH TO TOUCH.
Ages 12 and up. 461
Pfeffer, Susan Beth. ABOUT DAVID.
Ages 13 and up. 474
Raskin, Ellen. FIGGS & PHANTOMS.
Ages 12 and up. 489
Smith, Doris Buchanan. A TASTE OF BLACKBERRIES.
Ages 8-11. 551
Viorst, Judith. THE TENTH GOOD THING ABOUT BARNEY.
Ages 4-8. 596
Walker, Mary Alexander. YEAR OF THE CAFETERIA.
Ages 12 and up. 601

Moving
See also: *Change: new home; Separation from loved ones*
Brandenberg, Aliki Liacouras. WE ARE BEST FRIENDS.
Ages 3-6. 60
Conford, Ellen. ANYTHING FOR A FRIEND.
Ages 9-11. 140
Greenfield, Eloise. GRANDMAMA'S JOY.
Ages 4-8. 232
Hughes, Shirley. MOVING MOLLY.
Ages 3-5. 299
Hurwitz, Johanna. ALDO APPLESAUCE.
Ages 7-9. 305
Lowry, Lois. ANASTASIA AGAIN!
Ages 9-12. 386

Moving (cont.)
Miles, Betty. THE TROUBLE WITH THIRTEEN.
Ages 9-13. 427
Mohr, Nicholasa. FELITA.
Ages 8-10. 432
Schulman, Janet. THE BIG HELLO.
Ages 3-7. 522
Sharmat, Marjorie Weinman. MITCHELL IS MOVING.
Ages 5-8. 530
Smith, Janice Lee. THE MONSTER IN THE THIRD DRESSER DRAWER AND OTHER STORIES ABOUT ADAM JOSHUA.
Ages 5-8. 553
Tobias, Tobi. MOVING DAY.
Ages 3-6. 586
Wilder, Laura Ingalls. BY THE SHORES OF SILVER LAKE.
Ages 8-11. 620
Zelonky, Joy. MY BEST FRIEND MOVED AWAY.
Ages 6-9. 657
Zolotow, Charlotte Shapiro. JANEY.
Ages 4-7. 665

Murder
See: *Death: murder*

Muscular Dystrophy
See also: *Wheelchair, dependence on*
Jacobs, Dee. LAURA'S GIFT.
Ages 10-13. 313

Muteness
See also: *Deafness*
Caudill, Rebecca. A CERTAIN SMALL SHEPHERD.
Ages 8 and up. 105
Keller, Helen Adams. THE STORY OF MY LIFE.
Ages 11 and up. 324
White, Elwyn Brooks. THE TRUMPET OF THE SWAN.
Ages 9-13. 619

N

Name, Dissatisfaction with
Conford, Ellen. ANYTHING FOR A FRIEND.
Ages 9-11. 140
Grant, Eva. I HATE MY NAME.
Ages 5-8. 215
Hurwitz, Johanna. ALDO APPLESAUCE.
Ages 7-9. 305
Mosel, Arlene. TIKKI TIKKI TEMBO.
Ages 4-9. 434

Name-Calling
See also: *Aggression; Teasing*
Brown, Marc Tolan. ARTHUR'S EYES.
Ages 4-7. 68
Christopher, Matthew F. JOHNNY LONG LEGS.
Ages 9-11. 110
De Paola, Thomas Anthony. OLIVER BUTTON IS A SISSY.
Ages 4-7. 159
Lee, Mildred Scudder. THE SKATING RINK.
Ages 10-13. 354
Philips, Barbara. DON'T CALL ME FATSO.
Ages 5-9. 479
Stolz, Mary Slattery. THE BULLY OF BARKHAM STREET.
Ages 8-11. 573

Narcotic Habit
See: *Drugs*

Native American
Dyer, Thomas A. THE WHIPMAN IS WATCHING.
Ages 10-14. 172
Hassler, Jon Francis. JEMMY.
Ages 11 and up. 255
Miles, Miska, pseud. ANNIE AND THE OLD ONE.
Ages 6-9. 429
O'Dell, Scott. ISLAND OF THE BLUE DOLPHINS.
Ages 10 and up. 446
Perrine, Mary. NANNABAH'S FRIEND.
Ages 7-10. 467
Waterton, Betty Marie. A SALMON FOR SIMON.
Ages 4-7. 609

Nature

Appreciation of
Gallico, Paul. THE SNOW GOOSE.
Ages 12 and up. 195
George, Jean Craighead. MY SIDE OF THE MOUNTAIN.
Ages 11-14. 199
North, Sterling. RASCAL: A MEMOIR OF A BETTER ERA.
Ages 11 and up. 444
Rawlings, Marjorie Kinnan. THE YEARLING.
Ages 12 and up. 491
Zolotow, Charlotte Shapiro. ONE STEP, TWO . . . .
Ages 2-5. 669
Zolotow, Charlotte Shapiro. THE WHITE MARBLE.
Ages 4-8. 675

Living in harmony with
Bond, Nancy Barbara. THE VOYAGE BEGUN.
Ages 12 and up. 49
George, Jean Craighead. MY SIDE OF THE MOUNTAIN.
Ages 11-14. 199
Mazer, Harry. THE ISLAND KEEPER.
Ages 10-14. 414

Respect for
Byars, Betsy Cromer. THE HOUSE OF WINGS.
Ages 9-12. 91
Gackenbach, Dick. DO YOU LOVE ME?
Ages 5-8. 194
Holmes, Efner Tudor. AMY'S GOOSE.
Ages 8-11. 293
Paulsen, Gary. THE FOXMAN.
Ages 11-14. 458
Waterton, Betty Marie. A SALMON FOR SIMON.
Ages 4-7. 609

Naughty Child
See: *Discipline, meaning of*

Negative Attitude
See: *Inferiority, feelings of; Shame*

Neglect
See: *Chores; Job; Parental: negligence; Responsibility: neglecting*

Neglected Child
See: *Abandonment; Deprivation, emotional; Parental: negligence*

Negro
See: *African-American*

Neighbors/Neighborhood
See also: *Cooperation*
Mohr, Nicholasa. IN NUEVA YORK.
Ages 13 and up. 433
Myers, Walter Dean. THE YOUNG LANDLORDS.
Ages 11-14. 440
Shura, Mary Francis Craig. THE BARKLEY STREET SIX-PACK.
Ages 9-12. 533

Nervous Breakdown
See: *Mental illness*

Neurosis
See: *Mental illness*

New Baby
See: *Sibling: new baby*

New Home
See: *Change: new home; Moving*

Nightmares
See also: *Daydreaming; Fear*
Holland, Isabelle. NOW IS NOT TOO LATE.
Ages 10-13. 291
Hunter, Mollie, pseud. A SOUND OF CHARIOTS.
Ages 12 and up. 304
Kingman, Lee. HEAD OVER WHEELS.
Ages 12 and up. 335
Mayer, Mercer. THERE'S A NIGHTMARE IN MY CLOSET.
Ages 3-7. 413

Nursery School
See also: *Day-care center, going to*
Rockwell, Harlow. MY NURSERY SCHOOL.
Ages 3-5. 503
Wolde, Gunilla. BETSY'S FIRST DAY AT NURSERY SCHOOL.
Ages 2-5. 638

Nursing Home, Living in
Clifford, Ethel Rosenberg. THE ROCKING CHAIR REBELLION.
Ages 11-13. 127
Sallis, Susan Diana. ONLY LOVE.
Ages 12 and up. 518

O

Obedience/Disobedience
See: *Discipline, meaning of*

Obesity
See: *Weight control: overweight*

Old Age
See: *Age*

Oldest Child
See: *Sibling: oldest*

Only Child
Holmes, Efner Tudor. AMY'S GOOSE.
Ages 8-11. 293
Klein, Norma. CONFESSIONS OF AN ONLY CHILD.
Ages 9-11. 336

Operation
See: *Hospital, going to; Surgery*

Orphan
See also: *Adoption; Children's home, living in; Death: of parents; Foster home*
Cleaver, Vera and Bill Cleaver. TRIAL VALLEY.
Ages 12 and up. 125
Fitzgerald, John Dennis. ME AND MY LITTLE BRAIN.
Ages 9-12. 182
Forbes, Esther. JOHNNY TREMAIN.
Ages 10 and up. 186
Hartling, Peter. OMA.
Ages 8-11. 253
Hinton, Susan E. THAT WAS THEN, THIS IS NOW.
Ages 12 and up. 275
Holman, Felice. SLAKE'S LIMBO.
Ages 12 and up. 292
Kerr, M. E., pseud. LITTLE LITTLE.
Ages 11 and up. 331
Magorian, Michelle. GOOD NIGHT, MR. TOM.
Ages 11 and up. 398

Orphanage
See: *Children's home, living in*

Peer Relationships (cont.)
Butler, Beverly Kathleen. LIGHT A SINGLE CANDLE.
Ages 10 and up. 85
Byars, Betsy Cromer. THE ANIMAL, THE VEGETABLE, AND JOHN D JONES.
Ages 10-12. 87
Cleary, Beverly Bunn. HENRY AND THE PAPER ROUTE.
Ages 7-10. 113
Greene, Bette. GET ON OUT OF HERE, PHILIP HALL.
Ages 9-12. 220
Hassler, Jon Francis. FOUR MILES TO PINECONE.
Ages 10-14. 254
Kingman, Lee. BREAK A LEG, BETSY MAYBE!
Ages 12 and up. 334
Levy, Elizabeth. COME OUT SMILING.
Ages 12 and up. 360
Myers, Walter Dean. HOOPS.
Ages 12 and up. 437
Perl, Lila. ME AND FAT GLENDA.
Ages 9-12. 465
Platt, Kin. THE APE INSIDE ME.
Ages 12 and up. 481
Slepian, Jan. THE ALFRED SUMMER.
Ages 11-13. 544
Wartski, Maureen Crane. MY BROTHER IS SPECIAL.
Ages 10-12. 606

Avoiding others
Fitzhugh, Louise. HARRIET THE SPY.
Ages 10-12. 183
Guy, Rosa Cuthbert. THE FRIENDS.
Ages 12 and up. 244

Clubs. *See: Clubs*

Gangs. *See: Gangs*

Identification with peers. *See: Friendship; Identification with others: peers; Leader/Leadership*

Isolation. *See: Peer relationships: avoiding others*

Jealousy. *See: Jealousy: peer*

Manipulation. *See: Manipulation: peer*

Ostracism. *See: Ostracism*

Peer pressures. *See also: Expectations*
Bates, Betty. PICKING UP THE PIECES.
Ages 10-13. 29
Brown, Marc Tolan. ARTHUR'S EYES.
Ages 4-7. 68
Cuyler, Margery S. THE TROUBLE WITH SOAP.
Ages 10-13. 149
Danziger, Paula. CAN YOU SUE YOUR PARENTS FOR MALPRACTICE?
Ages 10-14. 151
Greenberg, Jan. THE ICEBERG AND ITS SHADOW.
Ages 10-12. 217
Hogan, Paula Z. I HATE BOYS I HATE GIRLS.
Ages 5-8. 283
Jeffries, Roderic. TRAPPED.
Ages 11-13. 315
Murphy, Jim. DEATH RUN.
Ages 11 and up. 435
Neufeld, John. EDGAR ALLAN.
Ages 10 and up. 442
O'Dell, Scott. KATHLEEN, PLEASE COME HOME.
Ages 12 and up. 447
Scoppettone, Sandra. THE LATE GREAT ME.
Ages 12 and up. 524
Shura, Mary Francis Craig. THE BARKLEY STREET SIX-PACK.
Ages 9-12. 533
Winthrop, Elizabeth. SLOPPY KISSES.
Ages 4-7. 628

Rejection. *See also: Ostracism; Rejection: peer*
Greene, Constance Clarke. THE UNMAKING OF RABBIT.
Ages 10-13. 228

Perception, Distortions of

See: *Communication: misunderstandings; Mental illness*

Perseverance
Fassler, Joan. HOWIE HELPS HIMSELF.
Ages 5-8. 178
Hoban, Lillian Aberman. ARTHUR'S FUNNY MONEY.
Ages 6-8. 276
Hogan, Paula Z. SOMETIMES I DON'T LIKE SCHOOL.
Ages 6-9. 284
Irwin, Hadley, pseud. MOON AND ME.
Ages 11-14. 311
Keller, Helen Adams. THE STORY OF MY LIFE.
Ages 11 and up. 324
Melton, David. A BOY CALLED HOPELESS.
Ages 10 and up. 420
Pfeffer, Susan Beth. WHAT DO YOU DO WHEN YOUR MOUTH WON'T OPEN?
Ages 10-13. 478
Robinet, Harriette Gillem. RIDE THE RED CYCLE.
Ages 7-11. 497
Simon, Norma. NOBODY'S PERFECT, NOT EVEN MY MOTHER.
Ages 4-8. 541
Watanabe, Shigeo. I CAN RIDE IT!
Ages 2-5. 608

Persistence

See: *Perseverance*

Personal Appearance

See: *Appearance*

Pets

See also: *Animals*
Hurwitz, Johanna. SUPERDUPER TEDDY.
Ages 4-7. 307
Lindgren, Barbro. SAM'S COOKIE.
Ages 2-5. 367

Death of. *See: Death: of pet*

Guide dog. *See also: Blindness*
Butler, Beverly Kathleen. LIGHT A SINGLE CANDLE.
Ages 10 and up. 85

Pets (cont.)

Love for
Carrick, Carol. THE FOUNDLING.
Ages 5-8. 103
Gackenbach, Dick. DO YOU LOVE ME?
Ages 5-8. 194
Gardiner, John Reynolds. STONE FOX.
Ages 8-10. 197
North, Sterling. RASCAL: A MEMOIR OF A BETTER ERA.
Ages 11 and up. 444
O'Hara, Mary, pseud. MY FRIEND FLICKA.
Ages 11 and up. 448
Peck, Robert Newton. A DAY NO PIGS WOULD DIE.
Ages 12 and up. 463
Rockwell, Anne F. and Harlow Rockwell. I LOVE MY PETS.
Ages 3-5. 499
Stolz, Mary Slattery. THE BULLY OF BARKHAM STREET.
Ages 8-11. 573
Stolz, Mary Slattery. A DOG ON BARKHAM STREET.
Ages 8-11. 574
Wallace, Bill. A DOG CALLED KITTY.
Ages 9-11. 602
Willoughby, Elaine Macmann. BORIS AND THE MONSTERS.
Ages 4-7. 625

Responsibility for
Barton, Byron. WHERE'S AL?
Ages 3-7. 27
Little, Jean. MINE FOR KEEPS.
Ages 10-13. 382
North, Sterling. RASCAL: A MEMOIR OF A BETTER ERA.
Ages 11 and up. 444
Rockwell, Anne F. and Harlow Rockwell. I LOVE MY PETS.
Ages 3-5. 499

Substitute for human relationship
Holland, Isabelle. DINAH AND THE GREEN FAT KINGDOM.
Ages 10-13. 288
North, Sterling. RASCAL: A MEMOIR OF A BETTER ERA.
Ages 11 and up. 444
Wright, Betty Ren. MY NEW MOM AND ME.
Ages 8-10. 651

Phobia

See: *Fear*

Physical Handicaps

See: *Handicaps*

Planning

See: *Careers: planning; Problem solving; Responsibility*

Play

See also: *Fantasy formation; Imaginary friend; Imagination; Peer relationships; Reality, escaping; Sharing/Not sharing*
Isadora, Rachel. MAX.
Ages 4-7. 312
Lindgren, Barbro. SAM'S CAR.
Ages 2-5. 366

Popularity

See: *Boy-girl relationships; Friendship; Peer relationships*

Poverty

See also: *Differences, human; Ghetto; Prejudice: social class*
Mathis, Sharon Bell. LISTEN FOR THE FIG TREE.
Ages 12 and up. 406
Mohr, Nicholasa. IN NUEVA YORK.
Ages 13 and up. 433
Wilkinson, Brenda Scott. LUDELL.
Ages 10-14. 621
Wilkinson, Brenda Scott. LUDELL AND WILLIE.
Ages 12 and up. 622

Power Struggle

See: *Parent/Parents: power struggle with*

Practical Jokes/Pranks

See also: *Harassment; Teasing*
Addy, Sharon. WE DIDN'T MEAN TO.
Ages 8-10. 1
Cleary, Beverly Bunn. OTIS SPOFFORD.
Ages 8-10. 115
Lowry, Lois. ANASTASIA AT YOUR SERVICE.
Ages 9-12. 387

Pregnancy

See also: *Abortion; Sex; Unwed mother*
Head, Ann. MR. AND MRS. BO JO JONES.
Ages 13 and up. 262
O'Dell, Scott. KATHLEEN, PLEASE COME HOME.
Ages 12 and up. 447

Prejudice

See also: *Differences, human; Hatred; Hostility; Justice/Injustice; Ostracism; Rejection*

Ethnic/Racial. *See also: Apartheid; Immigrants; Refugees*
Blume, Judy Sussman. IGGIE'S HOUSE.
Ages 10 and up. 40
Guy, Rosa Cuthbert. THE DISAPPEARANCE.
Ages 12 and up. 243
Hassler, Jon Francis. JEMMY.
Ages 11 and up. 255
Jones, Toeckey. GO WELL, STAY WELL.
Ages 12 and up. 319
Kerr, M. E., pseud. LOVE IS A MISSING PERSON.
Ages 12 and up. 332

Relatives (cont.)

Living in child's home
Giff, Patricia Reilly. THE GIFT OF THE PIRATE QUEEN.
Ages 9-12. 201
Little, Jean. LOOK THROUGH MY WINDOW.
Ages 10-14. 381
Mathis, Sharon Bell. THE HUNDRED PENNY BOX.
Ages 8-10. 405
Wright, Betty Ren. I LIKE BEING ALONE.
Ages 6-9. 650

Living in home of
Blume, Judy Sussman. TIGER EYES.
Ages 11 and up. 47
Bulla, Clyde Robert. SHOESHINE GIRL.
Ages 8-10. 74
Hunt, Irene. UP A ROAD SLOWLY.
Ages 12 and up. 301
MacLachlan, Patricia. ARTHUR, FOR THE VERY FIRST TIME.
Ages 8-10. 392
Paulsen, Gary. THE FOXMAN.
Ages 11-14. 458
Sargent, Sarah. SECRET LIES.
Ages 11 and up. 519
Seredy, Kate. THE GOOD MASTER.
Ages 9-12. 526
Voigt, Cynthia. HOMECOMING.
Ages 11 and up. 598
Wortis, Avi. SOMETIMES I THINK I HEAR MY NAME.
Ages 10-13. 649

Parents. *See: Parent/Parents; Parental*

Sibling. *See: Sibling*

Religion

See also: *Prejudice: religious*

Faith
Swartley, David Warren. MY FRIEND, MY BROTHER.
Ages 9-11. 580

Questioning
Van Leeuwen, Jean. SEEMS LIKE THIS ROAD GOES ON FOREVER.
Ages 12 and up. 589
Veglahn, Nancy Crary. FELLOWSHIP OF THE SEVEN STARS.
Ages 12 and up. 590

Religions

Buddhist. *See: Buddhist*

Choice of
Blume, Judy Sussman. ARE YOU THERE GOD? IT'S ME, MARGARET.
Ages 10-13. 37

Jewish. *See: Jew/Jewish*

Mennonite. *See: Mennonite*

Roman Catholic. *See: Roman Catholic*

Remarriage

See: *Parent/Parents: remarriage of; Stepparent*

Remorse

See: *Conscience; Guilt, feelings of; Values/Valuing*

Report Cards

See: *School: achievement/underachievement*

Reputation
Conford, Ellen. FELICIA THE CRITIC.
Ages 9-11. 141
Guy, Rosa Cuthbert. THE DISAPPEARANCE.
Ages 12 and up. 243
Stolz, Mary Slattery. THE BULLY OF BARKHAM STREET.
Ages 8-11. 573

Resourcefulness

See also: *Creativity; Problem solving*
Alexander, Martha G. MOVE OVER, TWERP.
Ages 5-8. 7
Bennett, Jack. THE VOYAGE OF THE LUCKY DRAGON.
Ages 11 and up. 33
Beskow, Elsa Maartman. PELLE'S NEW SUIT.
Ages 4-7. 35
Cleaver, Vera and Bill Cleaver. WHERE THE LILIES BLOOM.
Ages 11 and up. 126
Gardiner, John Reynolds. STONE FOX.
Ages 8-10. 197
George, Jean Craighead. MY SIDE OF THE MOUNTAIN.
Ages 11-14. 199
Giff, Patricia Reilly. FOURTH GRADE CELEBRITY.
Ages 8-10. 200
Hautzig, Esther Rudomin. A GIFT FOR MAMA.
Ages 8-12. 257
Hill, Elizabeth Starr. EVAN'S CORNER.
Ages 6-9. 271
Hoban, Lillian Aberman. ARTHUR'S FUNNY MONEY.
Ages 6-8. 276
Holman, Felice. SLAKE'S LIMBO.
Ages 12 and up. 292
Houston, James A. FROZEN FIRE: A TALE OF COURAGE.
Ages 10-13. 295
Hughes, Shirley. ALFIE GETS IN FIRST.
Ages 3-5. 297
Hutchins, Patricia. HAPPY BIRTHDAY, SAM.
Ages 5-7. 309
Irwin, Hadley, pseud. MOON AND ME.
Ages 11-14. 311
Kellogg, Steven. MUCH BIGGER THAN MARTIN.
Ages 4-7. 326
Mathis, Sharon Bell. SIDEWALK STORY.
Ages 8-10. 407
O'Dell, Scott. ISLAND OF THE BLUE DOLPHINS.
Ages 10 and up. 446
Perrine, Mary. NANNABAH'S FRIEND.
Ages 7-10. 467

Resourcefulness (cont.)
Pfeffer, Susan Beth. KID POWER.
Ages 9-12. 476
Sperry, Armstrong. CALL IT COURAGE.
Ages 9 and up. 559
Waterton, Betty Marie. A SALMON FOR SIMON.
Ages 4-7. 609

Respect
See: *Age: respect for; Grandparent: respect for; Parent/Parents: respect for/lack of respect for; Sibling: respect for*

Responsibility
See also: *Chores; Job; Work, attitude toward*

Accepting. *See also: Leader/Leadership*
Bradford, Richard. RED SKY AT MORNING.
Ages 13 and up. 57
Bulla, Clyde Robert. SHOESHINE GIRL.
Ages 8-10. 74
Burton, Virginia Lee. KATY AND THE BIG SNOW.
Ages 3-6. 83
Butterworth, William Edmund. LEROY AND THE OLD MAN.
Ages 12 and up. 86
Byars, Betsy Cromer. THE NIGHT SWIMMERS.
Ages 10-12. 92
Cleary, Beverly Bunn. HENRY AND THE CLUBHOUSE.
Ages 8-10. 112
Cleary, Beverly Bunn. HENRY AND THE PAPER ROUTE.
Ages 7-10. 113
Cleaver, Vera and Bill Cleaver. QUEEN OF HEARTS.
Ages 10-13. 124
Cleaver, Vera and Bill Cleaver. TRIAL VALLEY.
Ages 12 and up. 125
Cleaver, Vera and Bill Cleaver. WHERE THE LILIES BLOOM.
Ages 11 and up. 126
Clymer, Eleanor Lowenton. MY BROTHER STEVIE.
Ages 8-11. 129
Danziger, Paula. THERE'S A BAT IN BUNK FIVE.
Ages 10-14. 155
Gramatky, Hardie. LITTLE TOOT.
Ages 3-7. 214
Hall, Lynn. DANZA!
Ages 9-12. 245
Hansen, Joyce. THE GIFT-GIVER.
Ages 9-12. 250
Hunt, Irene. WILLIAM: A NOVEL.
Ages 12 and up. 302
Konigsburg, Elaine Lobl. ABOUT THE B'NAI BAGELS.
Ages 10-13. 341
Konigsburg, Elaine Lobl. THROWING SHADOWS.
Ages 10-12. 344
Lowry, Lois. ANASTASIA AT YOUR SERVICE.
Ages 9-12. 387
Miles, Betty. JUST THE BEGINNING.
Ages 10-12. 424
Miles, Betty. LOOKING ON.
Ages 11-14. 425
Moeri, Louise. FIRST THE EGG.
Ages 12 and up. 430
Myers, Walter Dean. THE YOUNG LANDLORDS.
Ages 11-14. 440
O'Hara, Mary, pseud. MY FRIEND FLICKA.
Ages 11 and up. 448
Pascal, Francine. MY FIRST LOVE & OTHER DISASTERS.
Ages 12 and up. 454
Peck, Richard. FATHER FIGURE: A NOVEL.
Ages 11 and up. 462
Perrine, Mary. NANNABAH'S FRIEND.
Ages 7-10. 467
Pfeffer, Susan Beth. KID POWER.
Ages 9-12. 476
Philips, Barbara. DON'T CALL ME FATSO.
Ages 5-9. 479
Rodgers, Mary. FREAKY FRIDAY.
Ages 10-13. 504
Sachs, Marilyn. THE BEARS' HOUSE.
Ages 9-12. 510
Shreve, Susan Richards. THE MASQUERADE.
Ages 12 and up. 532
Snyder, Anne. MY NAME IS DAVY—I'M AN ALCOHOLIC.
Ages 12 and up. 556
Stolz, Mary Slattery. A DOG ON BARKHAM STREET.
Ages 8-11. 574
Strang, Celia. FOSTER MARY.
Ages 10-13. 575
Thomas, Jane Resh. THE COMEBACK DOG.
Ages 7-9. 584
White, Elwyn Brooks. THE TRUMPET OF THE SWAN.
Ages 9-13. 619
Wilkinson, Brenda Scott. LUDELL AND WILLIE.
Ages 12 and up. 622

Avoiding
Giff, Patricia Reilly. THE GIRL WHO KNEW IT ALL.
Ages 8-10. 202
Jordan, Hope Dahle. HAUNTED SUMMER.
Ages 11 and up. 320
Polushkin, Maria. BUBBA AND BABBA.
Ages 3-8. 483
Snyder, Anne. MY NAME IS DAVY—I'M AN ALCOHOLIC.
Ages 12 and up. 556

Retardation
See: *Mental retardation*

Retirement
See also: *Age; Grandparent; Job*
Knox-Wagner, Elaine. MY GRANDPA RETIRED TODAY.
Ages 4-7. 337

Revenge
See also: *Aggression*
Arrick, Fran. CHERNOWITZ!
Ages 12 and up. 18
Ashley, Bernard. A KIND OF WILD JUSTICE.
Ages 12 and up. 23

School (cont.)
Garden, Nancy. ANNIE ON MY MIND.
Ages 13 and up. 196
Hentoff, Nat. THIS SCHOOL IS DRIVING ME CRAZY.
Ages 11-15. 266
Hobby, Janice Hale with Gabrielle Rubin STAYING BACK.
Ages 6-12. 282

Nursery. *See: Day-care center, going to; Nursery school*

Phobia. *See: Fear: of school; Separation anxiety*

Pupil-teacher Relationships
Allard, Harry. MISS NELSON IS MISSING!
Ages 5-8. 10
Ashley, Bernard. A KIND OF WILD JUSTICE.
Ages 12 and up. 23
Bargar, Gary W. WHAT HAPPENED TO MR. FORSTER?
Ages 10-13. 25
Cleary, Beverly Bunn. RAMONA AND HER MOTHER.
Ages 7-10. 117
Cleary, Beverly Bunn. RAMONA QUIMBY, AGE 8.
Ages 8-10. 118
Cleary, Beverly Bunn. RAMONA THE BRAVE.
Ages 7-10. 119
Cleary, Beverly Bunn. RAMONA THE PEST.
Ages 8-10. 120
Clymer, Eleanor Lowenton. MY BROTHER STEVIE.
Ages 8-11. 129
Cohen, Miriam. FIRST GRADE TAKES A TEST.
Ages 5-7. 135
Cohen, Miriam. NO GOOD IN ART.
Ages 5-7. 136
Foley, June. IT'S NO CRUSH, I'M IN LOVE!
Ages 11-13. 185
Girion, Barbara. A HANDFUL OF STARS.
Ages 12 and up. 207
Gross, Alan. WHAT IF THE TEACHER CALLS ON ME?
Ages 5-7. 240
Kent, Deborah. BELONGING: A NOVEL.
Ages 11-14. 328
Oppenheimer, Joan Letson. WORKING ON IT.
Ages 11-13. 452
Perl, Lila. HEY, REMEMBER FAT GLENDA?
Ages 9-12. 464
Petersen, P. J. WOULD YOU SETTLE FOR IMPROBABLE?
Ages 11-13. 469
Pevsner, Stella. A SMART KID LIKE YOU.
Ages 10-13. 473
Sachs, Marilyn. A SUMMER'S LEASE.
Ages 11-14. 515
Wilkinson, Brenda Scott. LUDELL.
Ages 10-14. 621
Young, Helen. WHAT DIFFERENCE DOES IT MAKE, DANNY?
Ages 9-12. 654

Report cards. *See: School: achievement/under-achievement*

Retention
Hobby, Janice Hale with Gabrielle Rubin STAYING BACK.
Ages 6-12. 282

Transfer
Blume, Judy Sussman. ARE YOU THERE GOD? IT'S ME, MARGARET.
Ages 10-13. 37
Bulla, Clyde Robert. LAST LOOK.
Ages 8-10. 73
DeClements, Barthe. NOTHING'S FAIR IN FIFTH GRADE.
Ages 8-11. 160
Delton, Judy. THE NEW GIRL AT SCHOOL.
Ages 4-7. 165
Hermes, Patricia. WHAT IF THEY KNEW?
Ages 9-11. 269
Hurwitz, Johanna. ALDO APPLESAUCE.
Ages 7-9. 305
Schultz, Gwendolyn. THE BLUE VALENTINE.
Ages 5-8. 523
Wartski, Maureen Crane. MY BROTHER IS SPECIAL.
Ages 10-12. 606
Wood, Phyllis Anderson. THIS TIME COUNT ME IN.
Ages 12 and up. 648

Truancy
Hill, Margaret. TURN THE PAGE, WENDY.
Ages 10-14. 272
Smith, Doris Buchanan. LAST WAS LLOYD.
Ages 8-11. 550

School Phobia

See: *Fear: of school; Separation anxiety*

Schools, Private

See also: *Separation anxiety*

Boys'
Hentoff, Nat. DOES THIS SCHOOL HAVE CAPITAL PUNISHMENT?
Ages 11 and up. 265
Hentoff, Nat. THIS SCHOOL IS DRIVING ME CRAZY.
Ages 11-15. 266

Girls'
Cuyler, Margery S. THE TROUBLE WITH SOAP.
Ages 10-13. 149

Secret Keeping
Hermes, Patricia. WHAT IF THEY KNEW?
Ages 9-11. 269
Pfeffer, Susan Beth. JUST BETWEEN US.
Ages 10-12. 475

Security Blanket

See: *Transitional objects: security blanket*

Security/Insecurity

See also: *Deprivation, emotional; Fear; Trust/Distrust*
Ashley, Bernard. A KIND OF WILD JUSTICE.
Ages 12 and up. 23

Self, Attitude Toward (cont.)
Conford, Ellen. THE REVENGE OF THE INCREDIBLE DR. RANCID AND HIS YOUTHFUL ASSISTANT, JEFFREY.
Ages 10-12. 142
Danziger, Paula. THE CAT ATE MY GYMSUIT.
Ages 11 and up. 152
Gilson, Jamie. DO BANANAS CHEW GUM?
Ages 9-11. 205
Greenberg, Jan. A SEASON IN-BETWEEN.
Ages 11-13. 219
Guy, Rosa Cuthbert. THE FRIENDS.
Ages 12 and up. 244
Hermes, Patricia. WHAT IF THEY KNEW?
Ages 9-11. 269
Kingman, Lee. HEAD OVER WHEELS.
Ages 12 and up. 335
Le Guin, Ursula Kroeber. VERY FAR AWAY FROM ANYWHERE ELSE.
Ages 12 and up. 352
Litchfield, Ada Bassett. WORDS IN OUR HANDS.
Ages 7-9. 376
Paterson, Katherine Womeldorf. JACOB HAVE I LOVED.
Ages 12 and up. 457
Payne, Sherry Neuwirth. A CONTEST.
Ages 8-10. 459
Philips, Barbara. DON'T CALL ME FATSO.
Ages 5-9. 479
Stanek, Muriel Novella. I WON'T GO WITHOUT A FATHER.
Ages 8-10. 560
Zelonky, Joy. I CAN'T ALWAYS HEAR YOU.
Ages 7-10. 656

Hatred. *See: Hatred*

Pity
Little, Jean. MINE FOR KEEPS.
Ages 10-13. 382
Stanek, Muriel Novella. I WON'T GO WITHOUT A FATHER.
Ages 8-10. 560

Pride/False pride. *See: Pride/False pride*

Respect
Carrick, Carol. SOME FRIEND!
Ages 9-12. 104
De Paola, Thomas Anthony. ANDY (THAT'S MY NAME).
Ages 3-5. 156
Lipsyte, Robert. THE CONTENDER.
Ages 12 and up. 372
Wilkinson, Brenda Scott. LUDELL.
Ages 10-14. 621

Shame. *See: Shame*

Success. *See: Success*

Self-Concept
See: *Self, attitude toward; Values/Valuing*

Self-Control
See: *Self-discipline*

Self-Discipline
See also: *Discipline, meaning of*
Giff, Patricia Reilly. THE GIRL WHO KNEW IT ALL.
Ages 8-10. 202
Hogan, Paula Z. SOMETIMES I GET SO MAD.
Ages 5-8. 285
Meyer, Carolyn. THE CENTER: FROM A TROUBLED PAST TO A NEW LIFE.
Ages 13 and up. 421
Platt, Kin. THE APE INSIDE ME.
Ages 12 and up. 481
Smith, Robert Kimmel. JELLY BELLY.
Ages 10-12. 555

Self-Esteem
See also: *Guilt, feelings of; Self, attitude toward*
Greenberg, Jan. THE PIG-OUT BLUES.
Ages 12 and up. 218
Pevsner, Stella. KEEP STOMPIN' TILL THE MUSIC STOPS.
Ages 9-12. 472
Shyer, Marlene Fanta. MY BROTHER, THE THIEF.
Ages 10-13. 534
Smith, Doris Buchanan. KELLY'S CREEK.
Ages 8-13. 548
Smith, Doris Buchanan. LAST WAS LLOYD.
Ages 8-11. 550
Smith, Doris Buchanan. TOUGH CHAUNCEY.
Ages 12 and up. 552
Terris, Susan Dubinsky. NO SCARLET RIBBONS.
Ages 11-13. 582

Self-Identity
See: *Ego ideal; Identity, search for*

Self-Image
See: *Self, attitude toward*

Self-Improvement
Forbes, Esther. JOHNNY TREMAIN.
Ages 10 and up. 186
Greene, Constance Clarke. A GIRL CALLED AL.
Ages 11 and up. 225
Holland, Isabelle. DINAH AND THE GREEN FAT KINGDOM.
Ages 10-13. 288
Hurwitz, Johanna. TOUGH-LUCK KAREN.
Ages 10-13. 308
Lipsyte, Robert. THE CONTENDER.
Ages 12 and up. 372
Meyer, Carolyn. THE CENTER: FROM A TROUBLED PAST TO A NEW LIFE.
Ages 13 and up. 421

Self-Reliance
See: *Dependence/Independence*

Self-Respect
See: *Self, attitude toward: respect*

Sibling (cont.)
Garrigue, Sheila. BETWEEN FRIENDS.
Ages 9-12. 198
Greenfield, Eloise. SHE COME BRINGING ME THAT LITTLE BABY GIRL.
Ages 3-7. 234
Hoban, Russell Conwell. A BABY SISTER FOR FRANCES.
Ages 3-7. 278
Jarrell, Mary. THE KNEE-BABY.
Ages 3-6. 314
Keats, Ezra Jack. PETER'S CHAIR.
Ages 3-7. 323
Klein, Norma. CONFESSIONS OF AN ONLY CHILD.
Ages 9-11. 336
Lindgren, Astrid. I WANT A BROTHER OR SISTER.
Ages 3-7. 365
Lowry, Lois. ANASTASIA KRUPNIK.
Ages 9-11. 388
MacLachlan, Patricia. ARTHUR, FOR THE VERY FIRST TIME.
Ages 8-10. 392
Smith, Janice Lee. THE MONSTER IN THE THIRD DRESSER DRAWER AND OTHER STORIES ABOUT ADAM JOSHUA.
Ages 5-8. 553
Stein, Sara Bonnett. THAT NEW BABY: AN OPEN FAMILY BOOK FOR PARENTS AND CHILDREN TOGETHER.
Ages 3-8. 569
Watson, Jane Werner, Robert E. Switzer. SOMETIMES I'M JEALOUS.
Ages 3-6. 614
Wolde, Gunilla. BETSY'S BABY BROTHER.
Ages 2-5. 637

Older. *See also: Baby-sitting*
Cleaver, Vera and Bill Cleaver. QUEEN OF HEARTS.
Ages 10-13. 124
Hoban, Lillian Aberman. ARTHUR'S PEN PAL.
Ages 4-7. 277
Hogan, Paula Z. SOMETIMES I GET SO MAD.
Ages 5-8. 285
Matthews, Ellen. GETTING RID OF ROGER.
Ages 8-10. 409
McCaffrey, Mary. MY BROTHER ANGE.
Ages 8-11. 418
Peck, Richard. FATHER FIGURE: A NOVEL.
Ages 11 and up. 462
Peterson, Jeanne Whitehouse. I HAVE A SISTER—MY SISTER IS DEAF.
Ages 4-7. 470

Oldest. *See also: Baby-sitting*
Blume, Judy Sussman. TALES OF A FOURTH GRADE NOTHING.
Ages 8-11. 45
Byars, Betsy Cromer. THE NIGHT SWIMMERS.
Ages 10-12. 92

Rejection. *See: Rejection: sibling*

Relationships. *See also: Family: relationships*
Arrick, Fran. TUNNEL VISION.
Ages 12 and up. 20
Blume, Judy Sussman. SUPERFUDGE.
Ages 8-10. 44
Bond, Felicia. POINSETTIA & HER FAMILY.
Ages 4-7. 48
Bridgers, Sue Ellen. NOTES FOR ANOTHER LIFE.
Ages 12 and up. 65
Cameron, Ann. THE STORIES JULIAN TELLS.
Ages 7-9. 99
Cleary, Beverly Bunn. RAMONA THE BRAVE.
Ages 7-10. 119
Dixon, Paige, pseud. MAY I CROSS YOUR GOLDEN RIVER?
Ages 12 and up. 166
Fitzgerald, John Dennis. THE GREAT BRAIN REFORMS.
Ages 10-13. 181
Greene, Constance Clarke. DOUBLE-DARE O'TOOLE.
Ages 9-11. 224
Greenfield, Eloise. SISTER.
Ages 10-12. 235
Greenfield, Eloise. TALK ABOUT A FAMILY.
Ages 8-10. 236
Hassler, Jon Francis. JEMMY.
Ages 11 and up. 255
Hazen, Barbara Shook. IF IT WEREN'T FOR BENJAMIN (I'D ALWAYS GET TO LICK THE ICING SPOON).
Ages 3-7. 259
Hoban, Lillian Aberman. ARTHUR'S FUNNY MONEY.
Ages 6-8. 276
Hoban, Russell Conwell. BEST FRIENDS FOR FRANCES.
Ages 4-7. 280
Hurwitz, Johanna. SUPERDUPER TEDDY.
Ages 4-7. 307
Keller, Holly. CROMWELL'S GLASSES.
Ages 3-6. 325
Lee, Mildred Scudder. THE SKATING RINK.
Ages 10-13. 354
Lowry, Lois. A SUMMER TO DIE.
Ages 10-14. 389
Paterson, Katherine Womeldorf. BRIDGE TO TERABITHIA.
Ages 9-12. 455
Pevsner, Stella. AND YOU GIVE ME A PAIN, ELAINE.
Ages 10-13. 471
Robinet, Harriette Gillem. RIDE THE RED CYCLE.
Ages 7-11. 497
Sachs, Marilyn. AMY AND LAURA.
Ages 9-12. 509
Shyer, Marlene Fanta. MY BROTHER, THE THIEF.
Ages 10-13. 534
Sobol, Harriet Langsam. MY BROTHER STEVEN IS RETARDED.
Ages 7-10. 557
Voigt, Cynthia. DICEY'S SONG.
Ages 11 and up. 597
Voigt, Cynthia. HOMECOMING.
Ages 11 and up. 598
Zolotow, Charlotte Shapiro. BIG SISTER AND LITTLE SISTER.
Ages 3-7. 660

Speech Problems

Stuttering

Fassler, Joan. DON'T WORRY DEAR.
Ages 4-6. 177

Lee, Mildred Scudder. THE SKATING RINK.
Ages 10-13. 354

Sports/Sportsmanship

See also: *Competition; Little League*

Addy, Sharon. WE DIDN'T MEAN TO.
Ages 8-10. 1

Christopher, Matthew F. JOHNNY LONG LEGS.
Ages 9-11. 110

Cohen, Barbara Nash. THANK YOU, JACKIE ROBINSON.
Ages 10-13. 132

Dygard, Thomas J. WINNING KICKER.
Ages 11-14. 173

Greene, Sheppard M. THE BOY WHO DRANK TOO MUCH.
Ages 12 and up. 230

Knudson, R. Rozanne. RINEHART LIFTS.
Ages 10-12. 338

Knudson, R. Rozanne. ZANBANGER.
Ages 10-13. 339

Knudson, R. Rozanne. ZANBOOMER.
Ages 10-13. 340

Myers, Walter Dean. HOOPS.
Ages 12 and up. 437

Platt, Kin. BROGG'S BRAIN.
Ages 12 and up. 482

Slote, Alfred. TONY AND ME.
Ages 10-13. 547

Stretton, Barbara. YOU NEVER LOSE.
Ages 12 and up. 578

Status

See: *Peer relationships; Prejudice: social class*

Stealing

See also: *Crime/Criminals; Delinquency, juvenile*

Adler, Carole Schwerdtfeger. IN OUR HOUSE SCOTT IS MY BROTHER.
Ages 10-13. 3

Ashley, Bernard. TERRY ON THE FENCE.
Ages 12 and up. 24

Childress, Alice. A HERO AIN'T NOTHIN' BUT A SANDWICH.
Ages 12 and up. 108

Mohr, Nicholasa. IN NUEVA YORK.
Ages 13 and up. 433

Shyer, Marlene Fanta. MY BROTHER, THE THIEF.
Ages 10-13. 534

Slepian, Jan. THE ALFRED SUMMER.
Ages 11-13. 544

Shoplifting

Slote, Alfred. TONY AND ME.
Ages 10-13. 547

Van Leeuwen, Jean. SEEMS LIKE THIS ROAD GOES ON FOREVER.
Ages 12 and up. 589

Stepbrother/Stepsister

See also: *Family; Parent/Parents: remarriage of*

Adler, Carole Schwerdtfeger. IN OUR HOUSE SCOTT IS MY BROTHER.
Ages 10-13. 3

Greene, Constance Clarke. I AND SPROGGY.
Ages 9-11. 226

Holland, Isabelle. NOW IS NOT TOO LATE.
Ages 10-13. 291

Oppenheimer, Joan Letson. GARDINE VS. HANOVER.
Ages 11-14. 451

Pfeffer, Susan Beth. STARRING PETER AND LEIGH.
Ages 12-14. 477

Roberts, Willo Davis. DON'T HURT LAURIE!
Ages 10-14. 496

Terris, Susan Dubinsky. NO SCARLET RIBBONS.
Ages 11-13. 582

Wolkoff, Judie. HAPPILY EVER AFTER . . . ALMOST.
Ages 11-13. 646

Stepparent

See also: *Family; Parent/Parents: remarriage of*

Father

Childress, Alice. A HERO AIN'T NOTHIN' BUT A SANDWICH.
Ages 12 and up. 108

Clifton, Lucille. EVERETT ANDERSON'S NINE MONTH LONG.
Ages 4-7. 128

Hunter, Evan. ME AND MR. STENNER.
Ages 10-13. 303

Roberts, Willo Davis. DON'T HURT LAURIE!
Ages 10-14. 496

Terris, Susan Dubinsky. NO SCARLET RIBBONS.
Ages 11-13. 582

Wolkoff, Judie. HAPPILY EVER AFTER . . . ALMOST.
Ages 11-13. 646

Mother

Adler, Carole Schwerdtfeger. IN OUR HOUSE SCOTT IS MY BROTHER.
Ages 10-13. 3

Bunting, Anne Evelyn. THE BIG RED BARN.
Ages 4-7. 76

Hunt, Irene. UP A ROAD SLOWLY.
Ages 12 and up. 301

Lee, Mildred Scudder. THE SKATING RINK.
Ages 10-13. 354

Pevsner, Stella. A SMART KID LIKE YOU.
Ages 10-13. 473

Reiss, Johanna. THE JOURNEY BACK.
Ages 10-14. 492

Vigna, Judith. SHE'S NOT MY REAL MOTHER.
Ages 4-8. 591

Wolff, Angelika. MOM! I NEED GLASSES!
Ages 10-13. 643

Wolkoff, Judie. HAPPILY EVER AFTER . . . ALMOST.
Ages 11-13. 646

Wright, Betty Ren. MY NEW MOM AND ME.
Ages 8-10. 651

Stepparent (cont.)
Zalben, Jane Breskin. MAYBE IT WILL RAIN TOMORROW.
Ages 12 and up. 655

Stereotype
See: *Prejudice*

Stitches
See: *Doctor, going to; Sutures*

Stuttering
See: *Speech problems: stuttering*

Substitute Parent
See: *Foster home; Parent/Parents: substitute*

Success
Blume, Judy Sussman. THE ONE IN THE MIDDLE IS THE GREEN KANGAROO.
Ages 7-9. 42
Brown, Marc Tolan. ARTHUR GOES TO CAMP.
Ages 5-8. 67
De Paola, Thomas Anthony. OLIVER BUTTON IS A SISSY.
Ages 4-7. 159
Delton, Judy. I NEVER WIN!
Ages 4-7. 161
Giff, Patricia Reilly. TODAY WAS A TERRIBLE DAY.
Ages 6-7. 203
Greene, Bette. GET ON OUT OF HERE, PHILIP HALL.
Ages 9-12. 220
Hallman, Ruth. BREAKAWAY.
Ages 12 and up. 247
Hobby, Janice Hale with Gabrielle Rubin. STAYING BACK.
Ages 6-12. 282
Hogan, Paula Z. SOMETIMES I DON'T LIKE SCHOOL.
Ages 6-9. 284
Hughes, Shirley. ALFIE GETS IN FIRST.
Ages 3-5. 297
Hurwitz, Johanna. TOUGH-LUCK KAREN.
Ages 10-13. 308
Melton, David. A BOY CALLED HOPELESS.
Ages 10 and up. 420
Pfeffer, Susan Beth. WHAT DO YOU DO WHEN YOUR MOUTH WON'T OPEN?
Ages 10-13. 478
Robinet, Harriette Gillem. RIDE THE RED CYCLE.
Ages 7-11. 497
Wartski, Maureen Crane. MY BROTHER IS SPECIAL.
Ages 10-12. 606
Watanabe, Shigeo. I CAN RIDE IT!
Ages 2-5. 608

Suicide
Arrick, Fran. TUNNEL VISION.
Ages 12 and up. 20
Pfeffer, Susan Beth. ABOUT DAVID.
Ages 13 and up. 474

Attempted
Bridgers, Sue Ellen. NOTES FOR ANOTHER LIFE.
Ages 12 and up. 65
Due, Linnea A. HIGH AND OUTSIDE.
Ages 13 and up. 168

Consideration of
Brancato, Robin Fidler. WINNING.
Ages 12 and up. 58

of Parent
Cleaver, Vera and Bill Cleaver. GROVER.
Ages 9-12. 122
Hughes, Dean. SWITCHING TRACKS.
Ages 10-14. 296
Krementz, Jill. HOW IT FEELS WHEN A PARENT DIES.
Ages 8 and up. 347
Peck, Richard. FATHER FIGURE: A NOVEL.
Ages 11 and up. 462
Zalben, Jane Breskin. MAYBE IT WILL RAIN TOMORROW.
Ages 12 and up. 655

Superego
See: *Conscience; Identification with others; Values/Valuing*

Superstition
Delton, Judy. IT HAPPENED ON THURSDAY.
Ages 5-8. 162

Surgery
See also: *Amputee; Cancer; Doctor, going to; Fear: of death; Hospital, going to; Illnesses; Sutures*
Hogan, Paula Z. and Kirk Hogan. THE HOSPITAL SCARES ME.
Ages 3-8. 287
Rey, Margret Elisabeth Waldstein and Han CURIOUS GEORGE GOES TO THE HOSPITAL.
Ages 4-9. 494

Heart
Singer, Marilyn. IT CAN'T HURT FOREVER.
Ages 9-12. 543

Tonsillectomy
Stein, Sara Bonnett. A HOSPITAL STORY: AN OPEN FAMILY BOOK FOR PARENTS AND CHILDREN TOGETHER.
Ages 3-8. 566

Sutures
See also: *Doctor, going to; Surgery*
Marino, Barbara Pavis. ERIC NEEDS STITCHES.
Ages 4-10. 400
Wolde, Gunilla. BETSY AND THE DOCTOR.
Ages 3-7. 635

Sympathy
See: *Empathy*

T

Talents

See also: *Education: special; Giftedness*
Asher, Sandra Fenichel. JUST LIKE JENNY.
Ages 10-12. 22
Corcoran, Barbara. CHILD OF THE MORNING.
Ages 10 and up. 143
Landis, James David. THE SISTERS IMPOSSIBLE.
Ages 9-11. 348
Sachs, Marilyn. A SUMMER'S LEASE.
Ages 11-14. 515

Artistic
Bulla, Clyde Robert. DANIEL'S DUCK.
Ages 5-8. 72
Cohen, Miriam. NO GOOD IN ART.
Ages 5-7. 136
Hassler, Jon Francis. JEMMY.
Ages 11 and up. 255
Kingman, Lee. BREAK A LEG, BETSY MAYBE!
Ages 12 and up. 334
Magorian, Michelle. GOOD NIGHT, MR. TOM.
Ages 11 and up. 398
Rodowsky, Colby F. WHAT ABOUT ME?
Ages 11-13. 507

Athletic
Hallman, Ruth. BREAKAWAY.
Ages 12 and up. 247
Myers, Walter Dean. HOOPS.
Ages 12 and up. 437
Platt, Kin. BROGG'S BRAIN.
Ages 12 and up. 482
Smith, Doris Buchanan. LAST WAS LLOYD.
Ages 8-11. 550

Musical
Bridgers, Sue Ellen. NOTES FOR ANOTHER LIFE.
Ages 12 and up. 65
Delton, Judy. I NEVER WIN!
Ages 4-7. 161
Thomas, Ianthe. WILLIE BLOWS A MEAN HORN.
Ages 5-8. 583
Voigt, Cynthia. DICEY'S SONG.
Ages 11 and up. 597

Tantrums

See also: *Anger*
Burnett, Frances Hodgson. THE SECRET GARDEN.
Ages 10 and up. 78
Cleary, Beverly Bunn. BEEZUS AND RAMONA.
Ages 8-10. 111

Tattletale

See: *Name-calling*

Teachers

See: *School: pupil-teacher relationships*

Teacher's Pet

See: *Name-calling*

Teasing

See also: *Aggression; Bully; Name-calling; Practical jokes/pranks*
Burch, Robert Joseph. QUEENIE PEAVY.
Ages 11-13. 77
De Paola, Thomas Anthony. OLIVER BUTTON IS A SISSY.
Ages 4-7. 159
Giff, Patricia Reilly. THE GIRL WHO KNEW IT ALL.
Ages 8-10. 202
Grant, Eva. I HATE MY NAME.
Ages 5-8. 215
Hogan, Paula Z. I HATE BOYS I HATE GIRLS.
Ages 5-8. 283
Hurwitz, Johanna. ALDO APPLESAUCE.
Ages 7-9. 305
Keller, Holly. CROMWELL'S GLASSES.
Ages 3-6. 325

Temper

See: *Aggression; Anger; Tantrums; Violence*

Temptation

See: *Conscience; Values/Valuing*

Theft

See: *Stealing*

Thinking Ahead

See: *Careers: planning; Responsibility: accepting*

Thrift

See: *Money: management*

Thumb Sucking

Ernst, Kathryn. DANNY AND HIS THUMB.
Ages 3-7. 174
Fassler, Joan. DON'T WORRY DEAR.
Ages 4-6. 177
Sachs, Marilyn. THE BEARS' HOUSE.
Ages 9-12. 510

Toilet Training

See: *Enuresis*

Tolerance

See: *Patience/Impatience; Prejudice*

Tomboy

See: *Gender role identity: female; Name-calling*

Tonsillectomy

See: *Hospital, going to; Surgery: tonsillectomy*

Tooth, Loss of

Bate, Lucy. LITTLE RABBIT'S LOOSE TOOTH.
Ages 4-6. 28

Tooth, Loss of (cont.)
Cameron, Ann. THE STORIES JULIAN TELLS.
Ages 7-9. 99
McCloskey, Robert. ONE MORNING IN MAINE.
Ages 5-8. 419
Smith, Janice Lee. THE MONSTER IN THE THIRD DRESSER DRAWER AND OTHER STORIES ABOUT ADAM JOSHUA.
Ages 5-8. 553

Toys
See: *Transitional objects: toys*

Transitional Objects
See also: *Animals*

Security Blanket
Burningham, John Mackintosh. THE BLANKET.
Ages 2-5. 80

Toys
Harris, Robie H. I HATE KISSES.
Ages 2-5. 252
Hughes, Shirley. DAVID AND DOG.
Ages 4-7. 298
Kantrowitz, Mildred. WILLY BEAR.
Ages 4-6. 322
Schulman, Janet. THE BIG HELLO.
Ages 3-7. 522
Tobias, Tobi. MOVING DAY.
Ages 3-6. 586
Waber, Bernard. IRA SLEEPS OVER.
Ages 6-8. 599

Truancy
See: *Delinquency, juvenile; School: truancy*

Trust/Distrust
See also: *Hostility; Security/Insecurity*
Ashley, Bernard. A KIND OF WILD JUSTICE.
Ages 12 and up. 23
Guy, Rosa Cuthbert. THE DISAPPEARANCE.
Ages 12 and up. 243
Hunt, Irene. THE LOTTERY ROSE.
Ages 11 and up. 300
Pfeffer, Susan Beth. JUST BETWEEN US.
Ages 10-12. 475
Viorst, Judith. MY MAMA SAYS THERE AREN'T ANY ZOMBIES, GHOSTS, VAMPIRES, CREATURES, DEMONS, MONSTERS, FIENDS, BOGLINS, OR THINGS.
Ages 4-7. 594

Trustworthiness
See: *Honesty/Dishonesty*

Truth
See: *Honesty/Dishonesty*

Twins

Fraternal
Cleary, Beverly Bunn. MITCH AND AMY.
Ages 9-11. 114
Cleary, Beverly Bunn. THE REAL HOLE.
Ages 3-6. 121
Cleaver, Vera and Bill Cleaver. ME TOO.
Ages 9-11. 123
Paterson, Katherine Womeldorf. JACOB HAVE I LOVED.
Ages 12 and up. 457

Identical
Jacobs, Dee. LAURA'S GIFT.
Ages 10-13. 313
Kingman, Lee. HEAD OVER WHEELS.
Ages 12 and up. 335
Simon, Norma. HOW DO I FEEL?
Ages 4-8. 538

U

Uncle
See: *Relatives*

Underweight
See: *Anorexia nervosa*

Unemployment
See: *Parent/Parents: unemployed*

Unfairness
See: *Justice/Injustice*

Untruthfulness
See: *Honesty/Dishonesty; Values/Valuing*

Unwanted Child
See: *Abandonment; Parental: rejection; Rejection: parental*

Unwed Mother
See also: *Pregnancy; Sex: premarital*
Beckman, Gunnel. MIA ALONE.
Ages 12 and up. 32
Luger, Harriett Mandelay. LAUREN.
Ages 12 and up. 390

V

Vaccuum Cleaner
See: *Fear: of vaccuum cleaner*

Values/Valuing
See also: *Conscience; Differences, human; Ego ideal; Identification with others*

W

War

See also: *Violence*
Arnothy, Christine. I AM FIFTEEN AND I DON'T WANT TO DIE.
Ages 12 and up. 16
Bennett, Jack. THE VOYAGE OF THE LUCKY DRAGON.
Ages 11 and up. 33
Frank, Anne. ANNE FRANK: THE DIARY OF A YOUNG GIRL.
Ages 11 and up. 191
Kherdian, David. THE ROAD FROM HOME: THE STORY OF AN ARMENIAN GIRL.
Ages 12 and up. 333
Little, Jean. LISTEN FOR THE SINGING.
Ages 10-14. 380
Magorian, Michelle. GOOD NIGHT, MR. TOM.
Ages 11 and up. 398
Maruki, Toshi. HIROSHIMA NO PIKA.
Ages 7 and up. 404
Reiss, Johanna. THE JOURNEY BACK.
Ages 10-14. 492

War Orphan

See: *Orphan*

Wealth/Wealthy

See also: *Differences, human*
Blume, Judy Sussman. THEN AGAIN, MAYBE I WON'T.
Ages 12 and up. 46
Strasser, Todd. ANGEL DUST BLUES.
Ages 14 and up. 576

Weight Control

See also: *Appearance*

Overweight
Cohen, Barbara Nash. THE INNKEEPER'S DAUGHTER.
Ages 11-14. 131
Danziger, Paula. THE CAT ATE MY GYMSUIT.
Ages 11 and up. 152
DeClements, Barthe. NOTHING'S FAIR IN FIFTH GRADE.
Ages 8-11. 160
Greenberg, Jan. THE PIG-OUT BLUES.
Ages 12 and up. 218
Greene, Constance Clarke. A GIRL CALLED AL.
Ages 11 and up. 225
Holland, Isabelle. DINAH AND THE GREEN FAT KINGDOM.
Ages 10-13. 288
Holland, Isabelle. HEADS YOU WIN, TAILS I LOSE.
Ages 12 and up. 289
Hurwitz, Johanna. THE LAW OF GRAVITY.
Ages 10-13. 306
Konigsburg, Elaine Lobl. ALTOGETHER, ONE AT A TIME.
Ages 9-11. 342
Lipsyte, Robert. ONE FAT SUMMER.
Ages 12-14. 373
Miles, Betty. LOOKING ON.
Ages 11-14. 425
Perl, Lila. HEY, REMEMBER FAT GLENDA?
Ages 9-12. 464
Perl, Lila. ME AND FAT GLENDA.
Ages 9-12. 465
Philips, Barbara. DON'T CALL ME FATSO.
Ages 5-9. 479
Smith, Doris Buchanan. LAST WAS LLOYD.
Ages 8-11. 550
Smith, Robert Kimmel. JELLY BELLY.
Ages 10-12. 555
Stolz, Mary Slattery. THE BULLY OF BARKHAM STREET.
Ages 8-11. 573

West Indian-American

Guy, Rosa Cuthbert. THE FRIENDS.
Ages 12 and up. 244

Wetting

See: *Enuresis*

Wheelchair, Dependence on

See also: *Amputee; Muscular dystrophy; Paraplegia; Prosthesis; Quadriplegia*
Burnett, Frances Hodgson. THE SECRET GARDEN.
Ages 10 and up. 78
Fassler, Joan. HOWIE HELPS HIMSELF.
Ages 5-8. 178
Greenfield, Eloise and Alesia Revis. ALESIA.
Ages 10-14. 237
Henriod, Lorraine. GRANDMA'S WHEELCHAIR.
Ages 3-7. 264
Jacobs, Dee. LAURA'S GIFT.
Ages 10-13. 313
Kingman, Lee. HEAD OVER WHEELS.
Ages 12 and up. 335
Lasker, Joe. NICK JOINS IN.
Ages 5-8. 350
Payne, Sherry Neuwirth. A CONTEST.
Ages 8-10. 459
Rabe, Berniece Louise. THE BALANCING GIRL.
Ages 5-7. 487
Robinet, Harriette Gillem. RIDE THE RED CYCLE.
Ages 7-11. 497
Sallis, Susan Diana. ONLY LOVE.
Ages 12 and up. 518

Withdrawal

See: *Reality, escaping*

Womanliness

See: *Gender role identity: female*

Women's Rights

See also: *Gender role identity: female; Prejudice: sexual*
Dygard, Thomas J. WINNING KICKER.
Ages 11-14. 173

Y

AUTHOR INDEX

To locate a book through the Author Index, find the author's name; titles are listed alphabetically under each author's name. Numbers refer to annotation numbers.

C

H

I

J

K

L

P

Q

R

S

Y

Z

TITLE INDEX

To locate a book through the Title Index, find the title of the book; Titles are listed alphabetically. Numbers refer to annotation numbers.

A

B

C

D

E

H

I

J

K

L

M

T

U

V

W

Y

Z

PUBLISHERS/PRODUCERS DIRECTORY

A

Abingdon Press
201 Eighth Avenue South
P.O. 801
Nashville TN 37202

Addison-Wesley Publishing Company, Inc.
Jacob Way
Reading MA 01867

American Printing House for the Blind
P.O. Box 6085
Louisville KY 40206-0084

Arte Publico Press
4800 Calhoun
Houston TX 77204

Atheneum Publishers
Subsidiary of Macmillan Publishing Company, Inc.
866 Third Avenue
New York NY 10022

Atlantic Monthly Press, The
See: Little, Brown & Company, Inc.

Avon Books
105 Madison Avenue
New York NY 10016

B

Ballantine Books, Inc.
Division of Random House Inc.
201 E. 50 Street
New York NY 10022

Bantam Books
Division of Bantam Doubleday Dell Publishing Group, Inc.
666 Fifth Avenue
New York NY 10103

Beacon Press
25 Beacon Street
Boston MA 02108

Berkley Publishing Group
See: Putnam Berkley Group, Inc.

Bobbs-Merrill
See: Macmillan Publishing Company, Inc.

Bradbury Press
Affiliate of Macmillan Publishing Company, Inc.
866 Third Avenue
New York NY 10022

Buccaneer Books
P.O. Box 168
Cutchogue NY 11935

C

Carolrhoda Books, Inc.
241 First Avenue North
Minneapolis MN 55401-3344

Children's Press
5440 North Cumberland Avenue
Chicago IL 60656

Clarion Books
52 Vanderbilt Avenue
New York NY 10017

Collier Books
See: Macmillan Publishing Company, Inc.

Coward-McCann
See: Putnam Berkley Group, Inc., The

Crowell (Thomas Y.) Company, Inc.
See: HarperCollins Publishers, Inc.

Crown Publishers, Inc.
See: Random House, Inc.

D

Delacorte Press
245 East 47 Street
New York NY 10017

Dell Publishing Company, Inc.
Division of Bantam Doubleday Dell Publishing Group, Inc.
666 Fifth Avenue
New York NY 10103

Deutsch (Andre)
See: Penguin USA

Dial Books for Young Readers
See: Penguin USA

Doubleday
Division of Bantam Doubleday Dell Publishing Group, Inc.
666 Fifth Avenue
New York NY 10103

Dutton Children's Books
See Penguin USA

F

Farrar, Straus & Giroux, Inc.
19 Union Square, West
New York NY 10003

Fawcett
1515 Broadway
New York NY 10036

Feminist Press at The City University of New York, The
311 E. 94 Street
New York NY 10128

Four Winds Press
See: Macmillan Publishing Company, Inc.

G

Garrard Publishing Company
29 Goldsborough Street
Easton MD 21601

Golden Press
850 Third Avenue
New York NY 10022

Greenwillow Books
See: Morrow (William) & Company, Inc.

Grosset & Dunlap, Inc.
See: Putnam Berkley Group, Inc.

H

Harcourt Brace Jovanovich, Inc.
1250 Sixth Avenue
San Diego CA 92101

HarperCollins Publishers, Inc.
10 East 53 Street
New York NY 10022-5299

Hastings House Publishers, Inc.
10 East 40 Street
New York NY 10016

Herald Press
Subsidiary of Mennonite Publishing House, Inc.
616 Walnut Avenue
Scottdale PA 15683-1999

Holiday House, Inc.
40 East 49th Street
New York NY 10017

Holt (Henry) and Company, Inc.
115 West 18th Street
New York NY 10011

Holt, Rinehart and Winston, Inc.
See: Harcourt Brace Jovanovich, Inc.

Houghton Mifflin Company
One Beacon Street
Boston MA 02108

Human Sciences Press
233 Spring Street
New York NY 10011

K

Knopf (Alfred A.), Inc.
Subsidiary of Random House, Inc.
201 East 50 Street
New York NY 10022

L

Landmark Editions, Inc.
Box 4469
Kansas City MO 64127

Lerner Publishing Company
241 First Avenue North
Minneapolis MN 55401

Lion Books
P.O. Box 92541
Rochester NY 14692

Lippincott (J. B.) Company
See: HarperCollins Publishers, Inc.

Little, Brown & Company, Inc.
Subsidiary of Time Warner, Inc.
34 Beacon Street
Boston MA 02108

Lothrop, Lee & Shepard Books
See: Morrow (William) & Company, Inc.

M

Macmillan Publishing Company, Inc.
866 Third Avenue
New York NY 10022

McElderry (Margaret K.) Books
Division of Macmillan Publishing Company, Inc.
866 Third Avenue
New York NY 10022

McGraw-Hill, Inc.
1221 Avenue of the Americas
New York NY 10020

Messner (Julian), Inc.
See: Simon & Schuster

Morrow (William) & Company, Inc.
105 Madison Avenue
New York NY 10016

N

New American Library
See: Penguin USA

O

Oriel Press
P.O. Box 12373
Portland OR 97212

Overlook Press
149 Wooster Street
New York NY 10012

P

Pantheon Books
Division of Random House, Inc.
201 East 50 Street
New York NY 10022

Penguin USA
375 Hudson Street
New York NY 10014-3657

Perspectives Press
P.O. Box 90318
Indianapolis IN 46290-0318

Phillips (S. G.), Inc.
305 West 86 Street
New York NY 10024

Philomel Books
See: Putnam Berkley Group, Inc., The

Pocket Books, Inc.
See: Simon & Schuster

Prentice-Hall, Inc.
Division of Simon & Schuster
Route 9W
Englewood Cliffs NJ 07632

Puffin Books
See: Penguin USA

Putnam Berkley Group, Inc., The
200 Madison Avenue
New York NY 10016

Putnam's (G. P.) Sons
See: Putnam Berkley Group, Inc., The

R

Raintree/Steck-Vaughan Publishers
310 West Wisconsin Avenue
Milwaukee WI 53203

Random House, Inc.
201 East 50 Street, 31st Floor
New York NY 10022

S

Salem House Publishers
462 Boston Street
Topsfield MA 01983

Scholastic, Inc.
730 Broadway
New York NY 10003

Scribner's (Charles) Sons
See: Macmillan Publishing Company, Inc.

Simon & Schuster, Inc.
1230 Avenue of the Americas
New York NY 10020

Peter Smith Publishing, Inc.
6 Lexington Avenue
Magnolia MA 01930

Spinsters Aunt Lute Book Co.
P.O. Box 410687
San Francisco CA 94141-0687

T

Tempo/Grosset
See: Putnam Berkley Group, Inc., The

Triad Publishing Company, Inc.
1110 NW Eighth Avenue
Gainesville FL 32601

V

Viking Penguin
See: Penguin USA

W

Walker & Co.
720 Fifth Avenue
New York NY 10019

Warne (Frederick) & Company, Inc.
See: Penguin USA

Westminster/John Knox Press, The
100 Witherspoon Street
Louisville KY 40202

Whitman (Albert) & Company
5747 Howard Street
Niles IL 60648